How to Lead Academic Departments Successfully

For my daughters Victoria and Elizabeth, you make me proud every day—
Adam
For Maja, who makes it all worthwhile—Alan
For Anette with thanks for inspirational support—Flemming
For Thomas, the best leader I know—Thyra

How to Lead Academic Departments Successfully

Edited by

Adam Lindgreen

Professor, Copenhagen Business School, Denmark and Extraordinary Professor, Gordon Institute of Business Science, University of Pretoria, South Africa

Alan Irwin

Professor, Copenhagen Business School, Denmark

Flemming Poulfelt

Professor Emeritus, Copenhagen Business School, Denmark

Thyra Uth Thomsen

Professor (WSR), Copenhagen Business School, Denmark

PUBLISHING

Cheltenham, UK • Northampton, MA, USA

Published by
Edward Elgar Publishing Limited
The Lypiatts
15 Lansdown Road
Cheltenham
Glos GL50 2JA
UK

Edward Elgar Publishing, Inc.
William Pratt House
9 Dewey Court
Northampton
Massachusetts 01060
USA

Paperback edition 2022

A catalogue record for this book
is available from the British Library

Library of Congress Control Number: 2021947842

This book is available electronically in the **Elgar**online
Business subject collection
http://dx.doi.org/10.4337/9781789907155

ISBN 978 1 78990 714 8 (cased)
ISBN 978 1 78990 715 5 (eBook)
ISBN 978 1 0353 0903 0 (paperback)

Printed and bound by CPI Group (UK) Ltd, Croydon, CR0 4YY

Contents

List of figures	viii
List of tables	ix
List of contributors	x
Introduction to How to Lead Academic Departments Successfully	xix

PART I   CHALLENGES OF BEING AN ACADEMIC LEADER

1	On the particular challenges of managing professionals *Flemming Poulfelt*	3
2	Relevant leadership: the dynamic equilibrium of managing and leading academic departments *Rickie A. Moore*	14
3	The role of academic leaders of a business school: an internal tensions perspective *Matthew J. Robson*	19

PART II   TRANSFORMATIONAL AND PERFORMANCE LEADERSHIP

4	The head of department as the key transformational leader *Asbjørn Busk J. and Søren Barlebo Rasmussen*	29
5	Leading with purpose: developing the first business school for public good *Martin Kitchener*	52
6	Leading academic departments *Rob Goffee and Gareth Jones*	68
7	Individual performance management: enabler or threat to academic performance? *Andreas Werr and Katja Einola*	79
8	Deploying systems thinking to create a 'triple-crown' business school *Michael C. Jackson OBE*	98

PART III   INCLUSIVITY, TEAM SPIRIT AND CAREER DEVELOPMENT

9   'Don't think you can be everyone's friend': dealing with conflict in an
         academic department   117
         Alan Irwin

10   Smells like team spirit: a user's guide for department heads   127
         Peter Kjær

11   'Now you see it': gender, inclusion and diversity   137
         Maja Horst

12   Leading faculty as teachers   147
         Hanne Andersen

13   Inclusive onboarding in academic departments   164
         Daniel J. Petzer, Nicola S. Kleyn and Michele Ruiters

PART IV   BUILDING, LEADING AND FUNDING RESEARCH GROUPS

14   Building research groups   182
         Adam Lindgreen, C. Anthony Di Benedetto, Roderick J. Brodie and Peter Naudé

15   Dilemmas in university management: the case of Copenhagen Business School   211
         Nanna Mik-Meyer

16   Pathways to external funding at departments: how to strengthen
         a change of culture by empowerment, supportive organizing and leadership?   226
         Enno Hofeldt

PART V   COLLABORATION WITH OTHER DISCIPLINES AND
          PRACTITIONERS

17   Collaborating with practitioners   246
         *C. Anthony Di Benedetto, Adam Lindgreen, Marianne Storgaard and
         Ann Højbjerg Clarke*

18   Leading academics in a public–private partnership: balancing value and
         performance-based leadership in times of (climate) change   263
         Morten W. Jeppesen

19   Undertaking cross-disciplinary research   275
         *Adam Lindgreen, C. Anthony Di Benedetto, Roderick J. Brodie and
         Michel van der Borgh*

PART VI   LEADERSHIP IN DIFFERENT CONTEXTS

20   Framing business schools as a socio-technical system: issues around
complexity and emergence   285
Denis Fischbacher-Smith

21   Business school leadership in an era of change and uncertainty:
complex structures, executive education and accreditation   302
Kai Peters

22   Academic leadership: the Danish case   313
Jacob Kjær Eskildsen and Børge Obel

PART VII   PERSONAL LEADERSHIP REFLECTIONS

23   Responsibilities of the department chair: lessons from the frontline   325
Thomas G. Cummings

24   How to lead an academic marketing department: some personal
observations and reflections   342
Gerrit van Bruggen

25   From head to dean: academic leadership   353
Peter Møllgaard

Index   370

Figures

2.1	Quinn's competing values framework	18
4.1	Science in society	30
4.2	Universities on the periphery of society during the classic phase (earlier)	32
4.3	Universities in the vortex of society during the excellence phase (today)	35
4.4	Universities mobilizing the societal transformation during the impact phase (future)	41
6.1	Combining skill and authenticity	77
8.1	HUBS as a viable system	107
8.2	The University of Hull as a viable system	109
8.3	A rich picture outlining the multiple pressures on staff in HUBS	111
8.4	A rich picture to help explore the strategic positioning of HUBS	112
19.1	Domains of knowledge and levels of theory	277
19.2	Interfaces for theorizing	277
20.1	Core questions around systems design	288
20.2	Elements of the design of socio-technical systems	290
20.3	Framing a business school as a system	295
25.1	Comparison of four CBS departments in 2016	365

Tables

4.1	Roadmap of the classic, excellence and impact phases	31
4.2	Changes in the role as the Head of Department	46
5.1	Criticisms of business schools by function	53
5.2	Purposeful innovations at Cardiff Business School	60
8.1	Constitutive rules for the critical systems practice (CSP) multi-methodology	104
12.1	Example of a CV format that parallels teaching and research achievements	149
12.2	Extract from the Pedagogical Competence Profile developed at the University of Copenhagen	151
12.3	Entry-level qualifications for different career levels at the University of Copenhagen	155
12.4	Definition of progressive levels of teaching achievements according to the Career Framework for University Teaching	156
13.1	Critical incidents leading to positive experiences of inclusion	171
13.2	Critical incidents leading to experiences of exclusion	173
13.3	A summary of reflections beyond the critical incidents	176
13.4	Actions of heads of departments in enabling inclusive faculty onboarding	177
14A.1	IMP research: selected books and journal articles and number of citations	207
14A.2	CMP research: journal articles and number of citations	208
16.1	Project Model Canvas	238
20.1	Elements of Checkland's CATWOE acronym	298
23A.1	Faculty feedback to chair	341

Contributors

EDITORS

Adam Lindgreen

Adam Lindgreen completed a Ph.D. in Marketing from Cranfield University (in 2000), with 18 months spent at the University of Auckland's Business School. Since 2016, Lindgreen has been Professor of Marketing at Copenhagen Business School, where he also heads the Department of Marketing. In addition, he is Extraordinary Professor in the University of Pretoria's Gordon Institute of Business Science. He serves as co-editor-in-chief for *Industrial Marketing Management*. Lindgreen's publications have appeared in *California Management Review*, *Journal of Business Ethics*, *Journal of the Academy of Marketing Science*, *Journal of Product Innovation Management*, *Journal of World Business*, and *Organization Studies*, among others. Furthermore, his 30+ books include *The Emergence and Rise of Relationship Marketing*, *A Stakeholder Approach to Corporate Social Responsibility* (with Kotler, Vanhamme, and Maon; 2012), *Memorable Customer Experiences* (with Vanhamme and Beverland; 2009), *Not All Claps and Cheers* (with Maon, Vanhamme, Angell, and Memery; 2018), *Public Value* (with Koenig-Lewis, Kitchener, Brewer, Moore, and Meynhardt; 2019), and *Sustainable Value Chain Management* (with Maon, Vanhamme, and Sen; 2013). Beyond these academic contributions to marketing, Lindgreen has discovered and excavated settlements from the Stone Age in Denmark, including the only major kitchen midden – Sparregård – in the south-east of Denmark; because of its importance, the kitchen midden was later excavated by the National Museum and then protected as a historical monument for future generations. He is also an avid genealogist, having traced his family back to 1390 and published widely, including eight books and numerous articles in scientific journals (*Personalhistorisk Tidsskrift*, *The Genealogist*, and *Slægt & Data*), related to methodological issues in genealogy, accounts of population development, and particular family lineages.

Alan Irwin

Alan Irwin is a professor in the Department of Organization at Copenhagen Business School. From 2015 to 2018, he was also the school's Vice-President of Entrepreneurship and Innovation. Between 2007 and 2014, he was Dean of Research and, for a period, served as the Acting President. His Ph.D. is from the University of Manchester, and he has held academic positions at Manchester, Brunel, and Liverpool. He is a Fellow of the Academy of Social Sciences and a foreign member of the Royal Danish Academy of Sciences and Letters. He is currently the principal investigator on a research project examining research and innovation policies in China, Denmark, and the United States. He has published in *Environment and Planning A*, *Minerva*, *Public Understanding of Science*, *Science, Technology, & Human Values*, *Research Policy*, *Social Studies of Science*, and *The Sociological Review*, among others.

Flemming Poulfelt

Flemming Poulfelt is Professor Emeritus at Copenhagen Business School and a former Vice Dean of Research Communication. He has served in university faculties across Europe, the USA, and Australia. Poulfelt has held various leadership positions, including head of department, study board director, and leader of a research center serving four universities with more than 60 researchers. He has published in *Business Ethics: A European Review*, *Human Relations*, *International Journal of Business Strategy*, *Scandinavian Journal of Management*, and *The Service Industries Journal* and more than 25 books on strategy, management, and management consulting. He has been a frequent conference speaker, has consulted widely, and serves on various corporate boards.

Thyra Uth Thomsen

Thyra Uth Thomsen is Professor (WSR) of Consumer Research in the Department of Marketing, Copenhagen Business School. From 2017 to 2020, she was deputy head of the department, with a special focus on the delivery and development of marketing education. Her research interests lie primarily in consumer transformations and consumption-related individual and societal well-being. In the past, her research has mainly been conducted within the domain of food consumption, particularly related to consumer vulnerabilities and resources. Moreover, she has a keen interest in the scholarship of teaching and learning. She has published in leading journals such as *Journal of Business Ethics*, *European Journal of Marketing*, *Psychology & Marketing*, *Management Learning*, and *Journal of Business Research*.

CONTRIBUTORS

Hanne Andersen

Hanne Andersen is Professor in Philosophy of Science and has served as head of the Department of Science Education at the University of Copenhagen and as head of the Department for Science Studies at Aarhus University. She works on the structure and development of 21st-century science, including the importance of interdisciplinarity, innovation, and digitalization, and her work has been published in journals such as *Philosophy of Science*, *Studies in History and Philosophy of Science*, *Synthese*, and *Erkenntnis*. She is a member of the European Academy of Sciences and corresponding member of l'Academié Internationale de Philosophie des Sciences.

Søren Barlebo Rasmussen

Søren Barlebo Rasmussen is Managing Partner for Mobilize Strategy Consulting, a Nordic strategy consulting firm specializing in strategy development in knowledge-intensive organizations. He holds a doctoral degree from Copenhagen Business School and has been an associate professor in research and innovation management, head of department, and dean at that school. He has published many books and articles on strategy and leadership in research-based organizations, such as universities, hospitals, professional service organizations, and pharmaceutical firms.

Roderick J. Brodie

Roderick J. Brodie is Professor of Marketing in the Department of Marketing at University of Auckland. His 120-plus journal articles have appeared in leading international journals including *Industrial Marketing Management*, *International Journal of Research in Marketing*, *Journal of Marketing*, *Journal of Marketing Research*, *Journal of Service Research*, and *Management Science*, among others. He is an associate editor for *Journal of Service Research* and former associate editor for *Marketing Theory*. He has served on the editorial boards of *Journal of Marketing*, *International Journal of Research in Marketing*, and other leading international journals. He was the first president of ANZMAC, and in 2004, he was made a founding fellow; in 2011, Brodie also was made a fellow of EMAC.

Asbjørn Busk J.

Asbjørn Busk J. is currently an administrative officer in the Rector's Office at Roskilde University. He is also a recurring guest lecturer on paradox management at Copenhagen Business School. Previously, he worked as a business developer for the Danish Court Administration and project assistant at Mobilize Strategy Consulting. He has also been a research assistant at the Royal Danish Academy – Architecture, Design, Conservation. He holds a Masters of Science in Social Sciences in Political Communication and Management from Copenhagen Business School.

Ann Højbjerg Clarke

Ann Højbjerg Clarke is Associate Professor of Marketing and former Head of the Department of Entrepreneurship & Relationship Management, University of Southern Denmark. She has published in *European Journal of Marketing*, *European Management Journal*, *Industrial Marketing Management*, and *Journal of Business-to-Business Marketing*. Her research interests center on firms' commercialization competences and management of innovation, including market segmentation, commercialization, stakeholder involvement, innovation in networks, and innovation ecosystems. In recent years, Højbjerg Clarke has focused more on public–private innovation. She has a strong record in fundraising, societal impact, and management of research projects, as well as broad management experience through her work on advisory boards and steering committees, including leading some boards.

Thomas G. Cummings

Thomas G. Cummings is Professor of Management and Organization at the Marshall School of Business, University of Southern California. He has contributed to knowledge about strategic change and high-performing organizations with more than 80 articles and 25 books, including the critically acclaimed *Self-Designing Organizations: Learning How to Create High Performance* (with Mohrman) and *Organization Development and Change*, 11th edition (with Worley). Cummings was President of the Western Academy of Management, Chair of the Organization Development and Change Division of the Academy of Management, and Founding Editor of the *Journal of Management Inquiry*, as well as the 61st President of the Academy of Management, the largest professional association of management scholars in the world. He is listed in American Men and Women of Science and Who's Who in America.

C. Anthony Di Benedetto

C. Anthony Di Benedetto is Professor of Marketing and Supply Chain Management and Senior Washburn Research Fellow at the Fox School of Business, Temple University. He has held visiting professorships at Bocconi University, Politecnico di Milano, Technische Universiteit Eindhoven, Kansai University, Yonsei University, WHU, St Petersburg State University, Edhec Business School, and IESEG School of Management. In 2010, Di Benedetto was named the Fulbright-Kathryn and Craig Hall Chair in Entrepreneurship and spent a semester at the Wirtschaftsuniversität Wien. Di Benedetto is co-editor-in-chief of *Industrial Marketing Management* and editor-in-chief of *Journal of International Consumer Marketing*. He served as editor of *Journal of Product Innovation Management* for nine years.

Katja Einola

Katja Einola is a postdoctoral researcher at Hanken School of Economics, Helsinki. Her 20-year international career outside academia focused on project management, marketing, and resource management, as well as consulting. Since acquiring her doctoral degree in 2017, she has published articles on leadership and teamwork in *Human Relations*, *Leadership Quarterly*, and *Organization Studies*, among others.

Jacob Kjær Eskildsen

Jacob K. Eskildsen is Professor and Head of Department at the Department of Management, Aarhus University. He is the author of several books and articles in Scandinavian and international journals, including *Strategic Management Journal* and *International Journal of Human Resource Management*.

Denis Fischbacher-Smith

Denis Fischbacher-Smith is Professor of Risk and Resilience at the University of Glasgow, where he is currently Deputy Head of the Business School. He has previously served as the director of two business schools at U.K. universities. He received his Ph.D. from the University of Manchester and his DLitt from the University of Glasgow. His work has been published in, among others, *Journal of Management Studies*, *Environment and Planning A & C*, *Public Administration*, *Public Management Review*, *Financial Accountability and Management*, *Public Money and Management*, *Management Learning*, and *Transactions of the Institute of British Geographers*.

Rob Goffee

Rob Goffee is Emeritus Professor of Organisational Behaviour at London Business School. He received his Ph.D. from the University of Kent. He served as Chair for the Organisational Behaviour Group, Deputy Dean and Governor, Director of the Innovation Exchange, and Faculty Director of Executive Education. Goffee has published 10 books and hundreds of articles in the areas of entrepreneurship, managerial careers, organization design, leadership, and corporate culture. His articles feature in *Harvard Business Review*, *Leader to Leader*, *European Business Forum*, *Business Strategy Review*, *Management Today*, *People Management* and *The Financial Times*. His books (with Jones) include *The Character of a Corporation*; *Why Should Anyone Be Led By You?*; *Clever—Leading your Smartest Most Creative People*; and *Why Should Anyone Work Here?*

Enno Hofeldt

Enno Hofeldt (M.Sc., Public Governance) has worked as Chief Research Advisor, Head of Secretariat, and deputy to the Head in the Department of International Business Communication at Copenhagen Business School and University of Copenhagen. His professional focus areas include strategic leadership, department management, research support, and project management. With his background in pedagogy and Folk Highschool Teaching, he approaches these topics from a perspective of change management, (inter-)cultural communication, and narrative leadership.

Maja Horst

Maja Horst is Professor of Responsible Technology at DTU, Technical University of Denmark. From 2011 to 2019, she was Head of Department of Media, Cognition and Communication at the Faculty of Humanities in University of Copenhagen. Previously she worked at Copenhagen Business School, where she obtained her Ph.D. in 2004. Her academic field is science and technology studies, and she has published in journals such as *Public Understanding of Science*, *Science Communication*, *Journal of Responsible Innovation*, *Science Technology & Human Values*, *Social Studies of Science*, and *Science as Culture*.

Michael C. Jackson OBE

Michael C. Jackson is Emeritus Professor at the University of Hull and MD of Systems Research Ltd. He graduated from Oxford University; gained an MA from Lancaster University and a Ph.D. from University of Hull; and has worked in civil services, academia, and as a consultant. Between 1999 and 2011, Jackson was Dean of Hull University Business School, leading it to triple-crown accreditation. He has been President of the International Federation for Systems Research and the International Society for the Systems Sciences. In 2011, he received an OBE for services to higher education and business. In 2017, he received the Beale Medal of the U.K. Operational Research Society. He has been central to the development of critical systems thinking.

Morten W. Jeppesen

Morten W. Jeppesen is Director of the Danish Hydrocarbon Research and Technology Centre at the Technical University of Denmark (DTU). He has an M.Sc. in Geology from Copenhagen University and an Executive MBA from DTU. Prior to joining DTU, he held various international and Danish senior leadership roles in Maersk Oil.

Gareth Jones

Gareth Jones was a visiting professor at IE Business School, Madrid. He held academic appointments at London Business School, INSEAD, and Henley. He received his MA and Ph.D. from the University of Kent. His business career included positions as Senior Vice President, Global Human Resources, at Polygram and Director of Human Resources and Internal Communications at the BBC. With Rob Goffee, he was a founding partner of Creative Management Associates, a consultancy focused on leadership, culture, and innovation. Dr. Gareth Jones passed away in 2021.

Martin Kitchener

Martin Kitchener (FCIPD, FLSW, FAcSS) is Professor of Management at Cardiff Business School. He is currently collaborating on a European Union Horizon 20/20 study of public service innovations, co-created with citizens, and he serves as Chair of the Chartered Association of Business Schools' Task Force on Business Schools for the Public Good.

Peter Kjær

Peter Kjær is Pro-rector at Roskilde University. His main areas of responsibility are research, innovation, and external collaboration. Kjær has a Ph.D. in Political Science from Stockholm University. His research has focused on institutional change in public and private organizations, including firms, business associations, and business media and healthcare organizations.

Nicola S. Kleyn

Nicola S. Kleyn is a former dean and Professor of Marketing at the University of Pretoria's Gordon Institute of Business Science, as well as Dean Designate: Executive Programmes at Erasmus University's Rotterdam School of Management. Along with her academic leadership, Kleyn is an active teacher in the area of corporate marketing and has published in *Journal of Business Ethics*, *European Journal of Marketing*, and *California Management Review*.

Nanna Mik-Meyer

Nanna Mik-Meyer is a professor at Copenhagen Business School, where she also serves as Vice Dean of Research. Mik-Meyer received her doctoral degree from the Department of Sociology, University of Copenhagen. Her main research focus is identity work in organizations. She has published several books, as well as in journals such as *Human Relations*; *Work, Employment, Society*; *Sociology of Health and Illness*; *Gender, Work and Organization*; and *British Journal of Sociology*.

Rickie A. Moore

Rickie A. Moore (Ph.D.) is Professor of Entrepreneurship and Business and Management Innovation at Emlyon Business School (France) and had led several pedagogical teams comprised of full-time and adjunct faculty. He has also served as Chair of the Management Consulting Division of the Academy of Management.

Peter Møllgaard

Peter Møllgaard is Dean and Professor of Industrial Organization at Maastricht University, School of Business and Economics. He is also chair of the Danish Council on Climate Change. Møllgaard received his doctoral degree from the European University Institute in Florence. He previously worked as Professor and Dean of Research at Copenhagen Business School and, before that, at the University of Aarhus. He has published in *Economic Journal, Economics Letters, Journal of Industrial Economics, Scandinavian Journal of Economics, Industry and Innovation*, and *Beta*, among others.

Peter Naudé

Peter Naudé graduated in Marketing from the University of Cape Town and then in operations research from the University of Sussex. After teaching at the Graduate School of Business in Cape Town, he went to Manchester Business School where, after completing his Ph.D., he joined the staff. Between 1999 and 2005, he was Professor of Marketing at the University of Bath's School of Management, before returning to Manchester Business School in 2006. Naudé was Deputy Director of Manchester Business School between 2006 and 2012, and he retired in 2017. He currently holds joint appointments at Manchester Metropolitan University Business School and with the Discipline of Marketing at the University of Sydney.

Børge Obel

Børge Obel is a professor in the Department of Management, Business and Social Sciences, Aarhus University (Denmark) and professor at EIASM (Brussels). He has held leadership positions in multiple academic institutions, including Dean for the Faculty of Social Sciences, Odense University, and Rector for the Aarhus School of Business. He holds a Ph.D. and a Dr. Oecon. from Aarhus University. His research interests pertain to strategy, management, and organizational design. Obel has published several books, including *Organizational Design: A Step-By-Step Approach* (with Burton and Håkonsson), as well as many academic papers in journals such as *Strategic Management Journal, Organization Science, ASQ,* and *Management Science.*

Kai Peters

Kai Peters is Pro-Vice-Chancellor of Business & Law and of International Development at Coventry University, as well as a member of the Coventry University Group Leadership Team. Previously, he was Chief Executive of Ashridge Business School and Dean of the Rotterdam School of Management, Erasmus University, where he obtained his MBA. His research interests focus on management development and leadership.

Daniel J. Petzer

Daniel J. Petzer is a professor at Henley Business School (South Africa). He holds a Ph.D. in Services Marketing and Consumer Behavior. He publishes in reputable international journals and is an associate editor of the *European Business Review.*

Matthew J. Robson

Matthew J. Robson is Professor of Marketing and International Management at Cardiff Business School, Cardiff University. He also earned his Ph.D. at Cardiff Business School. Robson's teaching and research interests focus on international, strategic, relationship, and retail marketing. He has published in many journals of international repute, including *British Journal of Management, International Marketing Review, Journal of International Marketing, Journal of Marketing, Journal of World Business, Management International Review,* and *Organization Science.* He currently serves as Associate Editor of *Journal of International Marketing.*

Michele Ruiters

Michele Ruiters is a senior lecturer at the University of Pretoria's Gordon Institute of Business Science, where she teaches courses on women and leadership, diversity, and inclusion. Ruiters received her Ph.D. from Rutgers, The State University of New Jersey. She has published in *Agenda and Development Southern Africa.*

Marianne Storgaard

Marianne Storgaard is an associate professor at the University of Southern Denmark. She originally graduated in Engineering and later was awarded her Ph.D. in Management from Aarhus School of Business. Her work has been published in journals such as *Advances in International Management, Global Strategy Journal, Multinational Business Review,* and *Organization Studies.* Her research and teaching interests include international management, change management, and critical management studies.

Gerrit van Bruggen

Gerrit van Bruggen is Professor of Marketing at Rotterdam School of Management, Erasmus University. He studies the way marketing strategy and decision making can exploit the opportunities offered by advances in information technology. He has published in premier academic research journals, in both marketing (i.e., *Marketing Science*, *Journal of Marketing*, and *Journal of Marketing Research*) and information systems (i.e., *Management Science*, *MIS Quarterly*, and *Information Systems Research*). He co-authored the book *Marketing Management Support Systems* (with Wierenga). He has been a visiting scholar at the Smeal College of Business Administration, Pennsylvania State University, and was an ISBM (Institute for the Study of Business Markets) Distinguished Visiting Scholar at the same university. Van Bruggen has taken on various administrative responsibilities (doctoral director, Department Head, Dean of Faculty, Vice Dean) and was President of the European Marketing Academy.

Michel van der Borgh

With a Ph.D. from Eindhoven University of Technology, Michel van der Borgh is Associate Professor of Marketing at the Department of Marketing, Copenhagen Business School. He serves as Associate Editor of the *European Journal of Marketing* and is part of the review board of *Industrial Marketing Management*. His research focuses on the management of front-line employees and covers topics such as new product selling, ambidexterity, solution sales, and servitization. He has published in several journals including the *British Journal of Management*, *Industrial Marketing Management*, *Journal of Service Research*, *Journal of the Academy of Marketing Science*, and *Journal of Product Innovation Management*.

Andreas Werr

Andreas Werr holds the Lars Erik Lundberg Chair in Business Administration, focused on Human Capital Management, at the Stockholm School of Economics (SSE), where he also heads the Department of Management and Organization. He received his doctoral degree from SSE, and his research has been published in *Governance*, *Industrial Marketing Management*, *Organization Studies*, *Personnel Review*, and *Sloan Management Review*.

Introduction to *How to Lead Academic Departments Successfully*

Ask any group of academic heads of departments about their current projects and their current challenges, and a surprisingly large range of responses will follow. In preparation for an executive teaching program aimed at university heads, two of this book's editors collected feedback on exactly this. From a group of 20 departmental leaders, we received a total of 30 different projects and challenges. What was particularly interesting was not just the number of separate responses but also their diversity.

We will not list all the responses. However, some sense of this diversity can be taken from just a few examples:

- Retention and recruitment;
- Research underperformance;
- Academic citizenship;
- Own research time;
- Educational reform and development;
- Institutional accreditation/quality assurance;
- Organizational change;
- Trust and collaboration.

The list went on, citing generational shifts, working with industry, scientific impact, and external funding. Of course, we did our best to cluster these topics, but it is difficult to squeeze together international collaboration, time management, and societal challenges, for example, under one heading.

The point – which these 20 department heads agreed with, once they saw the entire list – is that each challenge is recognizable, but together, they look formidable. This moment sowed the seed and inspiration for this collection. In a practical sense, we uncovered a key question: How can we use the experience of heads of department, and others with relevant expertise, to help current academic managers increase their own efficiency and effectiveness? For those who are new to (or just curious about) this crucial position, how can we help them understand more? And for experienced academic leaders, how can we provide new ideas and reflections – and even some inspiration? Projects and challenges are unlikely ever to go away completely, nor is that a relevant goal. But how can we, as academic leaders, improve our knowledge and practices so that we can deal with them successfully?

In subsequent discussions with participants in the executive course, some additional shared challenges emerged. Roughly, we can group them under four headings. First, *strategic chal-*

lenges confront every departmental leader. Typically, they are not either/or questions but related to how to tackle multiple issues at the same time. Thus, leaders must balance between:

- Research and teaching requirements;
- National and international requirements;
- Research quality and quantity;
- Senior and junior staff;
- Top-down and bottom-up management styles.

Academic leaders note they cannot focus on just one "bottom line" but instead must deal with multiple factors, in what can become a messy process that appears to lack clear prioritization.

Second, these difficulties lead into the next set of issues, pertaining to the *roles and responsibilities* of the department head. Across the range of inputs, we derived some key requirements related to this task. The head of department must ensure:

- The department's contribution to the overall university research strategy;
- The long-term development of the department's main research, educational, and dissemination activities;
- Good internal working relations, based on inclusion, team spirit, and career development;
- Efficient coordination among staff at different career stages and with different administrative and academic competences.

The general point here is that good leadership must be exercised across several groups, including research staff and teachers, administrative personnel, and external stakeholders.

Third, there are *leadership challenges* associated with being head of department. For many new leaders, these represent the toughest challenges of all. If one is promoted into this position, how does one then take over responsibility for one's colleagues? If one is hired from the outside, how does one gain authority among the local academic and administrative community? Why would anyone be led by you? Put simply, we can think of this as:

- Leading upward to deal with senior managers, including deans and presidents;
- Leading downward to work with the staff over whom one has formal responsibility;
- Leading out among external stakeholders and collaborators;
- Leading across by making connections with heads of department and other internal colleagues;
- Leading oneself by working constructively with one's own strengths and weaknesses.

Fourth, notably, the role of the department head *varies across contexts*. In some countries, for example, department heads are classed as administrative personnel, even if they must have academic qualifications in order to be appointed. In other settings, a rotating leadership tradition requires each professor to take a turn, sometimes for a relatively short period of time. Even within a country, different departments and universities vary substantially in their size, complexity, and organizational culture.

Each one of us also has our own motivation for the position. For some, this will be a (hopefully) rewarding experience for a fixed period. Others might be considering the position of department head as one stepping-stone on a career path leading to the role of dean, vice president or university president – and even beyond. In the following chapters, we try to take account of these different contextual and personal factors.

Even as we specify these four categories of challenges, we also acknowledge that the job is never static. Issues come and go. However, some questions – including those pertaining to diversity management, social inclusion, ethics, and integrity – have grown so much in importance that they are unlikely to fade. In this sense, we also are reminded that the university might seem like a world unto itself, but it both reflects and responds to broader societal developments and changes. One other example of this is the increasing use of indicators, both across different staffing levels and as applied to leaders themselves. There can be benefits here, but many university leaders experience performance measurement as adding to their work pressures.

We think we have made the basic point that academic leadership is not the easiest task. As the chapters of this book explore in considerable depth, the range and diversity of challenges can be daunting, especially to a new leader, but also to those who have been in the position for some time. The old cliché about herding cats comes to mind. As several contributors argue, an over-directive, top-down leadership style is unlikely to succeed in most academic settings.

At this point, current departmental leaders and those thinking of accepting the task might be tempted to stop reading. If the challenges are so great, why would anyone want to take on such a role? Why bother to read further in this book? We offer three arguments for doing so, all of which flow through the subsequent chapters.

First, departments (or schools, institutes) are the foundation on which universities are built. When asked about their work environment, most academics describe their "home" department, whereas the university seems more distant from their everyday professional life. Thus, the departmental setting is extremely important, and in turn, the department head is extremely important.

Our collective experience of working in and around university departments strongly indicates that the performance of a department head can make a huge difference, whether in shaping a positive, inspirational setting or (as can happen with remarkable speed) in sending a negative message of limited opportunities and restricted possibilities. Sometimes, the work of a departmental head is invisible and taken for granted. Nevertheless, the argument throughout the following chapters is that the potential of each department head to make a difference cannot be underestimated.

Second, as our previous discussion of projects and challenges reveals, serving as a head of department can be demanding. It provokes new personal and intellectual demands. However, it also offers a unique opportunity to see the academic world in a fresh light, viewing the university from the perspective of the whole, not just one's own point of view. The change in perspective can be startling, unsettling, and downright tiring. Yet it also can be a tremendous opportunity to develop new skills and learn new things (not least, about oneself).

Just as one example, a common experience is that one does not stand alone as a leader. Instead, successful heads of department operate within a network of colleagues, with different positions, competences, and attributes. For those used to working alone, or perhaps as part of a very small group of teachers and researchers, such teamwork can be surprising and difficult to embrace. It can also be a source of great satisfaction and consolation when (as inevitably happens) the best prepared plans begin to crumble.

Third, we can learn from experience. In general, the chapters that follow do not offer a how-to guide or quick fix. Instead, many contributors have taken this opportunity to make sense of their own experience and offer the kinds of advice that they likely would have appreciated when they were starting their own personal leadership journey.

The ensuing chapters are grouped by broad themes, in what we hope is a coherent fashion. But we encouraged the contributors to express themselves in their own way. This diversity of approaches ideally makes the book engaging but also illustrates the central point that no recipe or formula for success exists. There are general lessons to learn, but no two leaders will follow exactly the same blueprint.

The book title, *How to Lead Academic Departments Successfully*, suggests though that beyond the diverse challenges of leadership, we will also cover its successes. Just as there is no exclusive bottom line, success takes different forms. Leadership involves a choice of focus and key goals, which requires asking about what is most important in any specific setting and what can, at least relatively, be assigned less emphasis.

The following chapters present varied approaches to success, both personally and in organizational terms. Together, they provide a practical, and hopefully stimulating, guide to success as a practicing or aspiring departmental head. We also hope this book is instructive for readers who want to understand how this crucial role in academia operates. Our experience, as editors, is that each contributor has introduced important new dimensions of this role, thereby showing us how much we still have to learn about this fascinating, and we would say crucial, leadership position in some of our most important institutions.

PART I: CHALLENGES OF BEING AN ACADEMIC LEADER

As mentioned in the introduction, the challenges that confront academic leaders in practice are numerous, particularly considering the developments taking place in academia but also what is happening in the external environment that affects universities. When asked whether it is more difficult or complex to be an academic leader today, compared with 20 years ago, the answer is not simple though; rather, because the context of leadership is constantly evolving, the best response is that "it is different." Furthermore, because there is no recipe for how to be a leader, whether in academic settings or in the corporate world, leadership always must be situational and aligned with followers. Leadership is not a mechanical device but a way to encourage each person's professional and personal talent in orchestrating a group of different actors and personalities. In the first section, three contributions thus highlight key issues, challenges, and rewards of being an academic leader, together with good advice for how to demonstrate successful leadership.

For example, Poulfelt challenges the myth that academics do not want to be managed or led. Rather, they require a particular kind of management, which eliminates the possibility of applying out-of-the-box solutions. This discussion "On the Particular Challenges of Managing Professionals" presents eight leadership virtues for academic settings, based on leadership theory and informed by the author's observations gained from four decades of experience with academic leadership. These virtues should inform leaders' daily practice, to increase their management success rate.

As Moore argues, because no perfect method exists for how to prepare academic leaders to helm the department, they encounter perpetual surprises, discoveries, and work-in-progress.

In "Relevant Leadership: The Dynamic Equilibrium of Managing and Leading Academic Departments," the author proposes that department chairs are like frontline workers, required to assume multiple roles, responsibilities, and functions, and those functions often compete, collide, or contradict one another. To train and survive, while also learning how to do the job, effective leaders need to embrace the dynamic equilibria; this chapter offers some suggestions for how.

Similarly, Robson argues that a successful leader recognizes and heeds the tensions that arise across inevitable faultlines, at the business school and institutional level. Taking a dialectical view on "The Role of Academic Leaders of a Business School: An Internal Tensions Perspective," Robson identifies three specific faultlines in business schools: managerialism/optimization versus entrepreneurialism/creativity; the individual versus the collective; and research versus teaching. Some leaders seek to rock the proverbial boat by introducing extreme policies, but best practices allow conflicting values to coexist within a broader equilibrium, which helps ensure institutional stability and success. The chapter therefore offers some ideas for how leaders might find some balance at the three identified faultlines.

PART II: TRANSFORMATIONAL AND PERFORMANCE LEADERSHIP

Leadership is not static; it occurs in environments that are constantly developing, sometimes very turbulently. This situation imposes pressures on leaders to ensure the organizational unit, whether a research group, a department, or a university, copes with the complexity and changes productively. Such leadership often is referred to as transformational, a form of leadership that emphasizes the capability to make meaningful changes that set the course of the organization and secure engagement and acceptance among most employees. It sounds easy. In practice, it is very demanding, particularly because the transformational leadership agenda requires a focus on performance at all levels – university, faculties, departments, and individual researchers. But such an intense focus on performance also creates new leadership challenges, including the need to balance autonomy with control. Therefore, this second section offers five contributions pertaining to the leadership roles and tasks required to secure valuable transformations and productive performance, by providing observations from the field, new insights, and valuable advice.

To start this section, Busk J. and Barlebo Rasmussen ask, what will it mean to be the head of department in the future? They note historical trends that suggest the answer will reflect contemporary perceptions of science in future society. Whereas in the recent past, the head of department mainly served a collective of autonomous faculty members, and then became something like an overseer managing a research factory, today they regard "The Head of Department as the Key Transformational Leader." Recognizing that the relationship between science and society continually changes, they identify growing demands for research with societal impact, which in turn means that the university's organization, strategy, and management must shift to meet them. As a key transformational leader, the head of department can lead this transformation and take on practical, meaningful management roles.

Kitchener agrees with the notion that society demands new roles of the university, which must ensure that its pursuit of accreditation or revenue does not distract it from its primary, societal purpose. He thus recommends "Leading with Purpose: Developing the First Business

School for Public Good." With a personal account of efforts to achieve purposeful change at Cardiff Business School (United Kingdom), the author highlights the urgent need for business schools to undergo repurposing. In line with corporate purpose literature, three approaches can promote the development of purposeful organizations: a chief purpose officer, purpose statements, and multi-capital reporting. In describing the applications of these approaches, this chapter explains how Cardiff became the first business school to focus on enhancing the public good and thus offers insights for how other academic leaders might lead a similar repurposing.

Taking a broad view on "Leading Academic Departments," Goffee and Jones propose three fundamental axioms of leadership: it is contextual, relational, and non-hierarchical. But in academic work contexts, filled with "clever" academics, leadership must take unique forms to support their success. In particular, leaders must balance benevolent guardianship against discipline. In the effort to "be yourself, more, with skill," they also need to find ways to engage in authentic self-expression while also connecting successfully with others.

Continuing the focus on managing academics, Werr and Einola ask "Individual Performance Management: Enabler or Threat to Academic Performance?" To ensure the quality and quantity of academic output, universities often ask department heads to manage members' individual performance and conduct systematic performance reviews. But traditional performance management systems and appraisals do not match well with academic contexts. The middle managers have little power; the employees (academics) naturally exhibit multiple loyalties and demand freedom and autonomy. Noting emerging trends and research evidence about the consequences of performance management practices, this chapter offers several suggestions for adapting individual performance management methods to university settings.

Another option for adapting and applying external concepts to academic settings, as detailed in "Deploying Systems Thinking to Create a 'Triple-Crown' Business School," relies on critical systems thinking. Jackson provides an account of his experiences as the first dean of a UK business school that achieved remarkable progress between 1999 and 2011. Following from its foundation, when Jackson left in 2011, the school had hired 165 staff, attracted 3,500 students, and earned £28 million annually. With an excellent reputation for teaching, research, and reach, it had gained three key accreditations and a ranking among the top 1% of business schools worldwide. As Jackson describes it, systems thinking, and particularly critical systems thinking, was essential to bringing about this success.

PART III: INCLUSIVITY, TEAM SPIRIT AND CAREER DEVELOPMENT

Among the diverse, relevant topics that find their way onto the agenda of academic leaders, dealing with conflicts represents a particularly complex theme. It arises for leaders of research groups and departments and requires consideration of different factors, including professionalism, rationalities, and emotions. Limiting the amount of conflict and resolving those that arise in a constructive way can ensure engagement, energy, and a team spirit. A team spirit in turn can have tremendous impacts on achieving optimal outcomes. Even though most academic institutions claim they want to attract the best academic researchers and staff, achieving that goal also represents a critical challenge, especially when addressed in conjunction with diversity goals. Therefore, this section, with five contributions, offers case stories, examples, and recommendations for dealing with these issues in practice.

The title of the first chapter in this section offers a clear caution: "'Don't Think You Can Be Everyone's Friend': Dealing with Conflict in an Academic Department." The author contests conventional views of conflict as an inevitable characteristic of academia that demands a rational, planned approach. Rather, the complexities linked to conflict in practice give rise to three stories, related broadly to interpersonal conflict, departmental conflict, and institutional conflict. Irwin argues that conflicts often cannot be neatly classified or defined but may encompass various directions, sometimes over considerable time; with personal insights, this author offers some further perspectives and advice.

The next title is evocative too: in "Smells like Team Spirit: A User's Guide for Department Heads," Kjær proposes ways to leverage team spirit, defined as a sense of belonging among members of a department, using concrete examples from his experience as the head of a department in a Danish university. He lists several relevant tools, reflecting different dimensions of managerial practice, to help departmental members make sense of and connect to the collective entity, as well as some dilemmas and paradoxes that arise in this process.

Even if a leader's normative framework centers on fairness and equality, as is the case for the author of this article, achieving inclusion and diversity can be challenging. Horst details three factors in "'Now You See It': Gender, Inclusion and Diversity" that emerged from her efforts to do so: structural decoupling, which reflects disconnects between diversity and other required managerial activities; unconscious bias, pertaining to implicit expectations of others; and recruitment. Using this framework, Horst also details what should have done differently. Other leaders can take inspiration from this to inform and improve their diversity efforts.

In Andersen's chapter, "Leading Faculty as Teachers," the focus is on two elements of leading academic departments that must offer both teaching and research, even though these two projects evoke different valuations. First, leaders must lead faculty in their career progression as teachers. Second, they must help faculty manage their workload distributions when allocating teaching duties. As heads of departments, these leaders have unique mediating functions, between institutional and faculty perspectives on the importance of teaching.

Another critical factor for leading faculty members is ensuring their integration into their departments, to achieve "Inclusive Onboarding in Academic Departments." By exploring the lived experiences of new faculty members in an academic department in a business school environment, Petzer, Kleyn, and Ruiters seek to understand the perceptions that new faculty develop, in terms of feeling included and assimilated. The qualitative data, gathered from new, full-time faculty members of a South African business school, reveal critical incidents that produce positive inclusion experiences, but also some evidence of exclusion. These incidents in turn indicate which actions heads of departments should undertake to guarantee inclusive faculty onboarding.

PART IV: BUILDING, LEADING AND FUNDING RESEARCH GROUPS

Strong and distinct research profiles can enhance a university's standing and competitive appeal, but research is rarely performed in isolation. High-profile research groups are critical, but to establish them, universities need methods for attracting and retaining the best talents and scholars, as well as sufficient external funding for those groups. Such efforts inevitably involve dilemmas, as the three contributions in this section acknowledge. In addition to highlighting fundamental issues associated with building and leading research units, from research and practice perspectives, these chapters continue to offer leadership advice.

When it comes to "Building Research Groups," Lindgreen, Di Benedetto, Brodie, and Naudé propose that attracting the top research talent requires a successful research environment first, which promises academic researchers that they will be able to produce a sustainable research stream. In turn, this environment demands several antecedents, including a clear business school research strategy, leadership, governance, and policy. To illustrate the conditions that can support the long-term success of research programs, the authors elaborate on two active research institutions: the Industrial Marketing and Purchasing (IMP) Group and the Contemporary Marketing Practices (CMP) Group. These examples in turn reveal which environmental conditions are most conducive to sustainable business school research, as well as the gatekeeping role of journal editors.

The Bologna initiative aims to standardize higher education policies. Its implementation by universities in Denmark has been relatively substantial, such that they offer a leading example of the dilemmas that this legislation has created. Copenhagen Business School provides an illustration in "Dilemmas in University Management: The Case of Copenhagen Business School." Mik-Meyer draws on her experience as Vice Dean of Research to highlight the benefits and detriments of using key performance indicators of research quality.

Another international issue is external funding, which departments and universities increasingly must seek, such that this pursuit shapes their organizational discourses and research practices. Hofeldt argues that departments are like "shop floors," where organizational cultures of support and empowerment can be established. Hofeldt phrases the question in terms of "Pathways to External Funding at Departments: How to Strengthen a Change of Culture by Empowerment, Supportive Organizing, and Leadership?" By also analyzing barriers to change, erected by both researchers and department managers, the author derives an integral, concrete, three-level approach, spanning the personal, the organizational, and the managerial levels. He also proposes a new project design tool, the Project Model Canvas, which reveals both individual-level competencies and strategic support and leadership frameworks at the departmental and university levels.

PART V: COLLABORATION WITH OTHER DISCIPLINES AND PRACTITIONERS

The three contributions in this section address cross-disciplinarity and collaborations, as increasingly popular methods for dealing with complex problems that pertain to multiple disciplines. Furthermore, many universities actively work to expand their community ties to exploit the notable benefits that can accrue from involving external stakeholders, such as corporations, public sector organizations, or nonprofit actors in research projects. Yet these developments also put additional pressure on academic leaders to develop new interaction and collaboration modes; working with practitioners in particular often requires a different approach on both sides, as Di Benedetto, Lindgreen, Storgaard, and Højbjerg Clarke describe in "Collaborating with Practitioners." Their meta-perspective on collaborations between academics and businesspeople suggests ways to encourage them. In particular, they show that academics often take the university perspective, intuitively and implicitly, when talking about collaborative research. They consider why, how, and what questions. But an outside, business perspective on the same collaboration might focus more on innovations. Comparing these two perspectives reveals not just their differences but also the learning opportunities they create.

Taking a finer-grained view, Jeppesen reviews a collaboration involving oil and gas industry firms and the Danish Hydrocarbon Research and Technology Centre at the Technical University of Denmark. In so doing, he proposes a new model for cross-disciplinary collaborations, as a response to the challenges that arose during the first six years of the collaboration. That is, "Leading Academics in a Public–Private Partnership: Balancing Value and Performance-Based Leadership in Times of (Climate) Change" outlines how, to deal with the difficulties, they fundamentally rejected a classic academic organization and embraced a closely managed, open collaboration model, then adapted the research and innovation strategy to reflect industrial and societal needs as they shifted. To do so, the project participants relied on professional portfolio and project management approaches, as well as leaders that took care to balance value against performance.

Similarly, business-to-business research is inherently cross-disciplinary, because theories about business relationships, systems, and markets come from economics, psychology, sociology, and management disciplines. When "Undertaking Cross-Disciplinary Research," academic researchers therefore need to overcome functional silos, which likely create differences in the collaborators' incentives, culture, terminology, and jargon, as well as a risk of opportunistic or counterproductive behaviors. Lindgreen, Di Benedetto, Brodie, and van der Borgh therefore seek recommendations for how to undertake cross-disciplinary research that advances the business-to-business literature stream, namely, by elaborating on theorizing processes and actively breaking down cross-disciplinary boundaries.

PART VI: LEADERSHIP IN DIFFERENT CONTEXTS

Leadership is contextually bounded; it must be exercised in a way that reflects the needs and situations of each specific organization or group. This is not to say that leaders cannot learn from others' examples, but they still must be able to transcend and translate these insights into specific contextual and organizational actions, as a form of contextual intelligence. The contributions in this section similarly call for contextual leadership, such that the lessons they provide should be translated to reflect readers' own leadership environment.

For Fischbacher-Smith, the dominant context reflects a systems approach. Calling for "Framing Business Schools as a Socio-Technical System: Issues around Complexity and Emergence," this chapter frames each school as a socio-technical system that contains various elements, reflecting its design. A change to the designed state then can push the system toward a new state, as can alterations to the operating environment. In combination, such shifts might generate control fractures that require attention from leaders and managers. Another issue arises from competing views of core processes, such that various members of the system generate sometimes incompatible demands.

For Peters, the context with the greatest relevance is the internal institution and the range of activities it must undertake. For example, undergraduate and some masters programs are more like consumer markets, but executive education often entails a business-to-business transaction. In "Business School Leadership in an Era of Change and Uncertainty: Complex Structures, Executive Education and Accreditation," Peters notes the different paths to market, delivery modes, staffing approaches, and skill sets required by these programs. For example, many executive education providers confront severe financial limitations, prompting mergers, acquisitions, and restructuring. In the parent university, similar pressures are leading to centralization initiatives that challenge business schools' control over their own destinies. Such changes ultimately will require accreditation bodies to review their expectations about institutional autonomy to develop more realistic requirements.

Finally, for Eskildsen and Obel, Denmark provides a meaningful context. Whereas academic institutions had remained basically stable for hundreds of years, a 1970 law prompted a long-running wave of dramatic, significant changes. As they recount in "Academic Leadership: The Danish Case," the new rules created new governance structures, financing models, incentives, academic roles, and leadership conditions. With a historical view on their own academic leadership experience, they use a theoretical framework to describe these changes and their implications for academic leadership, from 1968 to 2020.

PART VII: PERSONAL LEADERSHIP REFLECTIONS

Finally, the three contributions in this section offer personal observations and reflections on being an academic leader. These authors take readers to the frontlines of the leadership battle and offer hearty food for thought for anyone involved in leadership, whether as a newly appointed head or someone with vast experience.

Cummings cites 21 years of experience as department chair to offer advice for performing this role, based on six "Responsibilities of the Department Chair: Lessons from the Frontline": (1) norming, (2) strategizing, (3) guiding, (4) complying, (5) developing, and (6) behaving. This list, along with concrete examples, provides a useful summary of topics worth considering by department chairs.

Van Bruggen's reflections and insights on "How to Lead an Academic Marketing Department: Some Personal Observations and Reflections" combine into what he calls a "big plea": keep things simple, let go of control, and cherish other people's power and creativity by giving them freedom to work on what they really care about. Accordingly, van Bruggen argues that an academic leader's main purpose is to challenge, encourage, trust, and facilitate, so even if incentives and extrinsic rewards are nice, helping followers find their intrinsic motivations and realize their potential is really the key.

Finally, Møllgaard describes the journey "From Head to Dean: Academic Leadership" by outlining its purpose. That is, the purpose of leadership is to prioritize the activities of those they lead, over their own. Such purpose (or rationale for action) is not just essential but also essential to communicate. But leaders also confront dual loyalties, to protect the department from senior management and to embrace senior management when sharing information with the department. With good training, a dean can meet seven prominent challenges: selecting the right department heads, delegating managerial tasks, coaching, facilitating dialogue about departmental performance, allocating resources across departments, managing boundaries between them, and co-creating a purpose.

CLOSING REMARKS

We extend a special thanks to Edward Elgar and its staff, who have been most helpful throughout this entire process. Equally, we warmly thank our contributors with whom we have worked closely. They have exhibited the desire to share their knowledge and experience with this book's readers – and a willingness to put forward their views for possible challenge by their peers. We hope that this compendium of chapters and themes stimulates and supports colleagues in their teaching, learning, and leadership development.

PART I

Challenges of being an academic leader

1. On the particular challenges of managing professionals

Flemming Poulfelt[1]

We need to allow intelligent people to have freedom to think, while also recognizing that education's social role requires organization and management. (An anonymous academic: professor and former associate dean, 2015)

INTRODUCTION

Management and leadership together make up an interesting discipline. Running or orchestrating an organization in a smart way, to make it innovative, productive, effective, and attractive, has always been on the agenda for businesses and in the public sector. Principles around how to manage and lead have been proposed in thousands of textbooks and articles. Some of these are quite specific, directed at particular industries or vertical sectors; some toward certain kinds of organization; and others are geared to the different levels of management (e.g. directors, middle managers). For the purposes of this chapter, we will focus on approaches to leading or managing professionals, with an emphasis on the academic world.

THE PARTICULAR CHALLENGE OF MANAGING PROFESSIONALS: REALITY OR MYTH?

It is accepted wisdom in leadership circles, and particularly in academia, that 'professionals' are impossible to manage, and/or that they don't like to be led. The rationale is that these are people who are likely to have sizeable egos; who consider themselves masters of their domain. They believe they know the right way to go about things, and what not to do – without being instructed or guided. In an article published some years ago, managing professionals was likened to 'herding cats' (McKenna & Riskin, 1995). As cats are thought to be highly independent, generally suiting themselves, the simile would appear perfect.

In an article appearing in *Harvard Business Review* (written by two London Business School professors) about the particular challenges of attempting to lead intelligent people, the authors note a characteristic resistance to suggestion, or to perceived interference. "If clever people have one defining characteristic, it is that they do not want to be led," the authors note. "This clearly creates a problem for you as a leader," they warn (Goffee & Jones, 2007). From the TV or theater actor who behaves like a prima donna, to the lawyer who is certain of the truth in court, to the university professor with their already confident assessment, it can be difficult to influence these individuals' perspective or to encourage them to entertain alternative thinking or ways of behaving. They can seem defiantly and belligerently set in their ways.

In addition, professionals often expect to be involved in and give an opinion on everything. I recall the case of a law firm where the consensus was that the partners 'always knew best' – even down to the right color for the office curtains.

With so much anecdotal evidence to draw on, could it be that there is something about professionals that makes them fundamentally more difficult to lead or manage, or is this a self-perpetuating myth?

As it turns out there is considerable evidence to support the view that professionals expect to be left to manage themselves and decide what is right (self-management). But it is possible too that some bias has crept in along the way, and that this perspective may have been exaggerated. With this in mind, it feels appropriate to dig a little deeper. For instance, there is also considerable anecdotal evidence – from both the corporate world and across the academic domain – to suggest that many professionals *do* actually want to be led. The determining factor seems to be *how*.

Professionals' willingness to be led appears closely linked to the type of management and leadership they are exposed to. If there is a chance this will be 'wrong,' 'bad,' 'weak,' or 'incompetent,' professionals are more likely to be resistant. Unfortunately, responsible management has too often been found to be lacking in many professional organizations, both private and public. Maister (1994) suggests that, typically, "professional service firms have been managed in one or two ways: badly or not at all." Having worked with professional organizations (including consulting firms, law firms, and engineering firms), I readily concur.

More recent studies and analyses show that well-educated people would often welcome more management – with the caveat that those providing it are suitably qualified. In the corporate world there is a saying that "people leave managers, not companies," which highlights the critical role played by good management; and conversely the *risk* of poor or absent management or leadership.

In the academic world in particular, McCormack, Propper and Smith (2014) support this view in the context of managing researchers. They note: "Our results ... point to the important aspects of good management in the use of incentives ... to motivate academics. This contrasts with the commonly-held view that these individuals are impervious to good (or bad) management."

The point being made is that successfully managing professionals requires leaders that are capable of setting the direction, orchestrating the people and the organization, and driving strong performance. And it turns out that this is less about micro-managing these highly skilled people, and more about giving them the direction, freedom, and support to excel.

Jetley (2016) writes: "Manage less. The more you manage professionals, the more they will resist. Let them sweat it out. If they need help, they will ask. If they are really overworked, they will tell you. If they need reassurance, they will seek it." Jetley goes on to use a judo metaphor, urging leaders to harness the strength of the professionals rather than trying to *fight* it. "If you do this well, they will make all the effort and you will bask in the glory of the results they achieve," he writes, adding the disclaimer, "But do not expect any gratitude from them. They will still think of you as the chief clerk."

It seems quite incredible that universities function as well as they do when so few researchers have formal competency in leadership and management. It could be argued that if the same were true in a private company, in most markets that business would struggle to develop the competitiveness needed to survive and prosper. While academics leaders tend to be passionate professionally, most are happy/lucky amateurs in management, having limited formal skills and no actual leadership training to draw on.

THE VIRTUES OF ACADEMIC LEADERSHIP?

There is no doubt that managing academics is a challenging proposition, given the typical characteristics of high professionalism; a passion for their work; self-reliance; assuredness of their worth; and a low boredom threshold. In addition, Goffee and Jones (2007) argue that these knowledgeable individuals "won't thank you." "Even when you're leading them well, clever people will be unwilling to recognize your leadership," they note, adding: "Remember, these creative individuals feel that they don't need to be led. Measure your success by your ability on the fringes of their radar."

Many academics would admit to being self-centered, considering 'What's in it for me?' if asked to participate in a specific project or to contribute to a task. An important element of academic leadership, then, is the ability to read and understand researchers and what drives them. Empathy and understanding are critical tools in managing these professionals.

Of course, most managers in universities are academics themselves and have been (and perhaps are still) active researchers. This is typically true of presidents, deans, heads of department, and study board directors. And sharing that background provides important insight into those they must now lead, as well as bringing credibility to the role. As Sveiby and Lloyd (1987) argue, "It is impossible to lead professionals without being professional yourself." Assumed within this view is the *primus inter pares* (first among equals) perspective: that a leader of professionals must earn their spurs. For Sveiby, a worthy leader "is all but a patriarch." This manifests as "a creator of the work environment and a tutor, who creates opportunities for his employees"; someone who "channels intellectual energy, maintains a clear sense of direction and is the guarantor of continuity and security in [the] organization."

Whether it is definitively the case that the leader of professional teams must be an old hand at the given discipline is up for debate, since effective leadership comes down to how an individual exercises their role. But of course, having proven research credentials can be helpful in winning over larger egos.

In their book *Aligning the Stars* (2002), Lorsch and Tierney argue that outstanding leaders in professional service organizations aren't necessarily "the smartest, nor the most successful, nor the most experienced in their firm." Rather, what characterizes these individuals is *"who they are as human beings,"* the authors note, adding that *character, judgement,* and *intuition* are common traits; that and their ability to exercise *influence* rather than control.

Set against this context, I will now share some of my own observations about what constitutes good leadership in an academic environment, based on my own studies and experiences. These are summarized below as a series of eight 'leadership virtues' I have identified.

Setting the Direction

One of the key tasks of a leader is to direct the future development of the organization. For, as the Cheshire Cat in Lewis Carroll's *Alice in Wonderland* points out, "If you don't know where you are going, any road will take you there." For obvious reasons, employees within an organization need to know where they are going, which means that someone – the leader – must define that destination. With the pace of change accelerating all the time, leaders must also be able to review and reconfirm the roadmap over time, to ensure that employees know how they can contribute to getting to the target end point and what their performance achievements should be along the way.

The long-term perspective or strategy is today well-anchored within most universities and departments. This is inevitable as universities must think ahead to set priorities and plan resources. The strategy will also inform stakeholders about how the institution will contribute to society going forward.

Defining the organization's path will usually involve defining (or redefining) the institution's purpose and vision, as well as the priorities around achieving these ambitions. Effective leaders will need to develop a clear vision of where they want to go; be able to describe this future in simple language; and provide meaningful guidance about how to move forward. In most academic environments this should not be a lone exercise; rather, it should serve as a way to engage and secure the commitment of researchers to a shared course.

"Nothing makes professionals more cynical than a manager who is weak, uncertain and lacking direction," writes the leadership author Jo Owen. "But once you have set the direction and goals, do not micro-manage," he warns. "Be firm on the goals, flexible on the route they use to get there … let their professional pride and paranoia motivate them to achieve the outcome" (Owen, 2009).

LEADING BY EXAMPLE?

It is often argued that strategies are too ambitious, too ambiguous, or too complex, and therefore difficult to communicate. In contrast, the strategy at a Scandinavian university some years ago was a good deal more focused. In addition to setting out a vision for the university, the strategy comprised three clear priorities for the institution. These were formulated in such a way that most researchers could readily recall them, and were able to map their work to these priorities. This in turn saw the strategy come alive and make sense for the majority of employees.

On the other hand, I have also experienced strategies that have been formulated primarily at the top of institutions, without being anchored in the wider organization. In such cases, the scope to use the university strategy as a relevant and valuable leadership vehicle will decrease; rather, strategy feels more like an ethereal aspiration to show off to those looking in from the outside.

Making Meaningful Decisions

Leadership involves making decisions. Good leaders understand and know how to balance reason with emotions, and how to make decisions meaningful. Making grounded decisions that make logical sense is important in academic environments. Without sound reasoning, it will be hard to win acceptance and commitment from researchers. Unfortunately, many academic leaders seem to confuse the right to make decisions (given their power) with making them legitimate and accepted.

LEADING BY EXAMPLE?

Structural changes within the academic world are always tough because, generally, (too) many researchers have a say on the proposed changes. No wonder so many major reorganizations (e.g. department mergers; a new faculty structure; or a major educational reform) are subject to critique and resistance. Yet the scenarios inviting the most critical behavior tend to be those that are the least meaningful to researchers. That is, the 'narrative' behind the changes is insufficient, inviting dissent. If the structural changes were more clearly framed, backed by a meaningful and well-articulated rationale, they might be more palatable.

Creating Continuous, Two-Way Communication

In the academic world, communication – whether written or oral – is a vital part of what goes on in both teaching and research. It is equally critical in management. To be effective and to sustain trusted relationships, managers must ensure ongoing communication with all employees, from researchers to administrative personnel. There is a strong argument, when hiring a manager, that good communications skills should be sought as a high priority – not only to build trust, but also to enable influence/persuasion, allow clear assignment of responsibility, and motivate and provide support to teams.

Miller (2012), for example, argues that managers will typically spend 75% of their time on communication with their teams and others within the organization. Few would argue with this. Yet, still, in academic environments complaints are rife about the quality and frequency of management communication. It may come too late; lack precision; and/or involve too much talking and not enough listening. Leaders' communication styles matter greatly. McKenna and Riskin (1995) urge leaders to "crank up the communication effort," noting that, "We routinely underestimate the amount of communication necessary to make our efforts successful." Winston Churchill, former and acknowledged British Prime Minister once said, "the difference between mere management and leadership is communication," indicating that communication skills are at the heart of effective leadership.

The importance of truly listening should not be underestimated, as this is how leaders will understand the context and the individual needs they are working with. My own observation over the years has been that while many leaders – including consultants and academic managers – make very good listeners, this tends to be primarily to themselves.

Securing Real Involvement

Involving people more integrally in activities that affect them has long been part of the leader's toolbox, on the basis that this is likely to motivate people, giving them a sense of ownership of the outcome. This accepted wisdom has been exercised in most university environments. Yet, 'involving' people can also lead to dysfunction if the gestures of inclusion prove to be little more than lip-service, and if expectations are not clarified in advance.

LEADING BY EXAMPLE?

A newly appointed president at a Scandinavian university launched a process for a new strategy. Various taskforces were formed, comprising 6–7 people (primarily researchers), to take on specific themes. Initially there was a lot of goodwill and engagement. The process was scheduled to last for 3–4 months, including a pit-stop with the top management and the taskforce chair. During the process a consultant (from one of the top consulting firms, working on a pro bono basis) was assigned to each group – even though the group could not readily see the benefit of this resource. At the end of the allotted period, the groups submitted their report to the president. A fortnight later all the groups were invited to a strategy seminar – at which, to the surprise of most people there, a new strategy for the university was unveiled! No discussion had ensued since the submission of reports and in fact very few from the groups attending were able to recognize their contribution in the presented material. A project originally intended to increase engagement ultimately had the opposite effect: a drop in morale and poor support for the eventual strategy.

The hard lesson is that if you are going to invite people to participate in a project, it is vital that the intentions are sincere and that the mandate and associated expectations are clear.

Inspiring, Recognizing and Supporting Best Performance

The ability to inspire is perceived to be among the most important leadership traits, as this infuses energy, passion, commitment, and connection to an organization's mission and vision. According to Garton (2017), "inspired employees are themselves far more productive and, in turn, inspire those around them to strive for greater heights." An inspiring leader believes in others and themselves. They have a personality which can create passion, optimism, and enthusiasm. They believe in the mantra: 'If you want to change the way of being, you have to change the way of doing.'

LEADING BY EXAMPLE?

The most inspiring leaders within universities, to my recollection, have always been those able to make speeches in a convincing, optimistic, and meaningful way with profound insights – typically spiced up using humor. At the same time these leaders were able to hold conversations face to face, creating energy, optimism and action.

In the academic world there is a tendency to underestimate the value of recognizing people for their achievements, whether these are big or small. Sometimes there seems to be an assumption that acknowledgment is not necessary; that being an academic itself is a gift and source of passion. I disagree. I believe that recognition is a very inexpensive way of incentivizing people and of motivating researchers.

LEADING BY EXAMPLE?

During my time as vice-dean of research communication, I used to write thank-you notes to those researchers who voluntarily offered their involvement at a national event with the focus on disseminating research. What surprised me was the number of notes I received in return, commenting how good it had felt to be recognized. My conclusion was that this kind of acknowledgment is shown too seldom.

Leaders can afford to be generous with their recognition. As McKenna and Riskin (1995) put it, "If you can't find something to recognize on a daily basis, you don't know how to look."

The importance of showing acknowledgment and appreciation cannot be understated. "Like world-class athletes, professionals have an almost insatiable need to know how they are doing: the more able they are, the keener their need," write DeLong, Gabarro and Lees (2007). They continue: "One highly-regarded mentor in a law firm reflected, 'For some of my best performers, I have to tell them how well they are doing on Monday, and again on Thursday. No amount of feedback is enough.'"

Certainly, management support is important to employees: and not just in words. Meaningful support in academia means enabling researchers to do – and to excel in – their job. When they fail to provide this, managers inadvertently signal a *lack* of support. Demonstrations of support can take other forms too. It might be caring for a post-graduate student who is struggling to finalize his/her Ph.D. project. It could be supporting a research application for funding, or the initiation of a new research project. A colleague of mine once introduced the concept of 'management by mothering' as part of her leadership role, emphasizing the value of nurturing people as they grow. After all, the most important resources universities possess are their people – so why wouldn't an institution and its leaders do everything it takes to help them flourish?

LEADING BY EXAMPLE?

A president at a Scandinavian university took the view that good research initiatives should always be supported – as long as they were exceptionally good. This mindset encouraged innovation among the institution's researchers, inspiring new research initiatives. If someone had a solid idea and a strong outline they could approach the president for a meeting, always with the assurance that they would not have to wait for weeks. If their ideas were deemed to be sound and well-articulated, the researchers received support, often a small amount of seed money too – with the expectation that the individual would seek additional funding externally. It was common for people to leave these meetings feeling engaged, keen, and optimistic that research money would be found.

Another way of demonstrating managerial support is to shield researchers from 'organizational rain': that is, from the burden of policies and procedures imposed by the administration – so that researchers are able to concentrate on their principal tasks of research, education, and the dissemination of findings and knowledge.

Creating Engagement

Leaders of today could be thought of as being in the human energy business. Extending the metaphor, it should be a priority for leaders to maximize the human 'wattage' they generate – and to ensure this is sustainable energy (that does not burn brightly, only to soon lose its spark). Put a different way, leaders need to be proactive and strategic in creating engagement and drive within the organization, bearing in mind that its most valuable resources are the people who work there.

Employee engagement is a subject Gallup has surveyed extensively over the years (Gallup, 2019). Its studies show that typically less than a third of all employees, worldwide, could be categorized as engaged. Gallup's findings also highlight the common drivers of engagement. One is that "people want purpose and meaning from their work ...; to be known for what they're good at." Academic environments have something of an advantage here, in that most researchers already attach meaning to their own work. However, they still need to feel part of an organization where engagement levels are high, and fuel everyday work.

LEADING BY EXAMPLE?

The question of what makes and keeps people engaged tends to be more involved than some leaders realize. Conversely, disengagement is achieved relatively easily. I have observed this first hand in research organizations where the role and behavior of the top manager has had a detrimental effect on researchers' morale. Even in universities where self-management and an inherent passion for people's own work are typically the norm, overall engagement levels can be damaged by poor decision-making – leading to disengagement, dissatisfaction, and discouragement.

Promoting True Collaboration

Analyses show that great leaders know the value of cooperation and how to collaborate effectively with colleagues and employees. Analyses also show that leaders who cooperate, share, and foster belonging will be more influential and successful over time. A willingness to cooperate includes sharing of information. Openness and transparency almost always pay off, although of course there will be some information that cannot be made public. When employees feel they are part of the network, and that they are 'seen' and appreciated, their sense of belonging and loyalty will be elevated.

Academics are used to cooperating as part of research projects and educational programs. However, their ability to foster a collaborative culture, and to truly engage people so that they feel they belong and want to give their all, may vary considerably.

LEADING BY EXAMPLE?

On his appointment, a department head announced that one of his ambitions and personal strengths was creating a cooperative environment, which he believed gave rise to strong results. Both the researchers and the administrative staff were enthusiastic, sensing the dawning of a new era for the department. Others were more skeptical, having heard some rumors about their new leader's personality. Things started well but soon the spirit of cooperation morphed into a culture of order and control. This discrepancy between the promised culture and the reality created anger and frustration among the staff. The head had also begun to show favoritism toward certain researchers; a small group became so upset by this that they decided to leave the department.

It is one thing to talk the talk about establishing a collaborative culture, but if leaders promise one thing and deliver another, they have only themselves to blame if staff stage a mutiny! Another important point is that being a 'cooperative leader' should include being willing to share the 'spotlight.' Some leaders struggle with highlighting the work and achievements of others ahead of their own. But a smart leader recognizes that their power and status is best demonstrated by the success of those around them.

LEADING BY EXAMPLE?

As has already been noted, researchers have a reputation for being self-centered, unwilling to put themselves out for the wider cause unless they perceive that there is something in it for them (including glory). Some leaders exhibit these qualities too, putting themselves before their team and failing to acknowledge and hold up those who deserve honor and recognition. This type of leadership typically fails in the long run: employees soon realize that where they are soon singled out and criticized for any mistakes, they are not being given credit for their achievements.

Executing According to the Plan

For reasons that are self-explanatory, managers have a duty to get things done and to execute the strategy and plans of the organization. In practice, this can be difficult as daily operations get in the way. Yet, the value of any plan is in the ability to realize its ambitions. Ensuring that the organization 'lives' its strategy is a real leadership challenge, and a continuous one – including efforts to support and follow up on the work, keeping everything on track. If there is a discrepancy between the actions and the perceived values of the stakeholders, execution can easily be shorted.

LEADING BY EXAMPLE?

When I was a newly appointed leader of a research center serving four universities, I experienced the potential sensitivities of failing to consider other stakeholders sufficiently. The center had just been launched and we needed to advertise six positions for Ph.D. scholarships. All of the universities were involved and had contributed toward the wording for the advert, which I asked the HR department to place in a newspaper before the summer vacation. The ad appeared, large and prominent, in the Sunday issue of the biggest newspaper in the country. I was pleased with a job well done. But then trouble started. The HR people had used the format for ads at *my* university, showing only our logo. Although it was not my intention to exclude the branding of the other stakeholder institutions, some (a few) people were upset. Was this a kind of power-play; an indication of an uncooperative mindset, the other universities wondered. I was able to turn the situation around, but it was a stark reminder of how even small omissions can ruffle feathers and undermine harmony.

ADDITIONAL REFLECTIONS

In the introduction to this chapter, we have considered whether there might be something intrinsic to professionals that makes them fundamentally more difficult to lead or manage. The ensuing discussion and supporting evidence suggests that, contrary to the view that academic professionals are especially difficult to manage, the challenge is more specifically that they require a particular kind of management to bring out their best.

Leading or managing academics requires a careful blend of reason and emotion/the ability to 'read' the environment – as well as mindfulness that researchers are human beings with their own ambitions, needs, and expectations. Handling the subtle personal variances in personalities and expectations requires discernment and thought: there are no out-of-the-box solutions.

The eight 'leadership virtues' I have distilled above are based on leadership theory supported by my own observations from more than four decades of experience (on both sides of the desk) of academic leadership practice.

In summary, these can be boiled down to three primary recommended leadership behaviors:

- Ensuring that giving meaning to and making logical sense of strategies, plans, and requests is a priority;
- Inspiring, energizing, engaging, and supporting all human resources so people feel and give their best; and
- Ensuring that decisions and decision-making take place in this context.

I'll end with some refreshing advice proposed in a recent book (*Leadership in Higher Education*, 2019) by Kouzes and Posner – both very experienced leadership authorities. "Decide to do something different that will make you an even better leader," they propose. "Then hop off the log and get into the water!" The point being that it is only through our action that we are able to improve, learn, and perform.

NOTE

1. Disclaimer: The title of the chapter refers to management rather than leadership, which is not intended to confuse the reader. Of course, 'management' and 'leadership' can have different connotations in business literature. 'Management' tends to be characterized as the 'hard (and dull) part' while 'leadership' is more 'soft (and creative)'. Some will argue that management is about administration, planning, organizing, performance, and control while leadership is about developing the vision, inspiring and engaging people, coaching, communication, and trust. As former President Dwight Eisenhower said, "Leadership is the art of getting someone else to do something you want done because he wants to do it."
    While the distinction is important, I would argue that a successful leader/manager will combine and balance the two sets of qualities. A 'boss' (perceived negatively) is likely to have placed too much emphasis on the management part, where a more liberal leader may not always achieve results in the most effective way, it could be argued. Both of these standpoints are open to debate. In this chapter, the use of the terms leader and manager are applied with an element of discretion.

REFERENCES

DeLong, T.J., Gabarro, J.J. & Lees, R.J. (2007). *When Professionals Have to Lead.* Harvard Business School Press.

Gallup (2019). http://www.gallup.com.

Garton, E. (2017). How to be an inspiring leader. *Harvard Business Review.* April 25.

Goffee, R. & Jones, G. (2007). Leading clever people. *Harvard Business Review.* March 2007.

Jetley, V. (2016). What's the main obstacle in managing professionals? https://www.bayt.com/.

Kouzes, J.M. & Posner, B.Z. (2019). *Leadership in Higher Education.* Berrett-Koehler Publishers.

Lorsch, J.W. & Tierney, T.J. (2002). *Aligning the Stars: How to Succeed when Professionals Drive Results.* Harvard Business School Press.

Maister, D. (1994). *Managing the Professional Service Firm.* The Free Press.

McCormack, J., Propper, C. & Smith, S. (2014). Herding cats? Management and university performance. *The Economic Journal.* August.

McKenna, P.J. & Riskin, G.A. (1995). *Herding Cats.* The Edge Group.

Miller, P. (2012). Leadership communication – the three levels. *Today's Manager*, Singapore Institute of Management. Issue February–March.

Owen, J. (2009). 5 ground rules for managing professionals. CBSNews.

Sveiby, K.-E. & Lloyd, T. (1987). Managing Knowhow: Add Value by Valuing Creativity. Bloomsbury.

2. Relevant leadership: the dynamic equilibrium of managing and leading academic departments

Rickie A. Moore

It has been widely accepted that one of the foremost of the multi-faceted/multi-dimensional missions of education institutions is to educate citizens and to disseminate knowledge that would prepare them for the future. Educational excellence, through its various manifestos, is thus a key objective of these institutions, as they pride themselves on the performance of their graduates. Over the years, there have been and continue to be extensive debates among stakeholders about the purpose, virtues and values of education. According to the Association to Advance Collegiate Schools of Business (AACSB), research in several academic disciplines has enhanced organizational success in a number of areas, and the knowledge produced has taken on new dimensions as newer inquiries test the management techniques to validate or invalidate their pertinence and effectiveness. As a loci and a motor of the university ecosystem, academic departments thus play a critical role in helping universities and institutions of higher education to fulfill their societal missions in providing educational excellence to their members and beneficiaries.

Among the many journeys of academic life, some academics are entrusted with the opportunity of leading an academic department and with a mandate to facilitate the mission of the department and institution. Whether by recruitment and selection, invitation, nomination or cooptation, the mandate of leading an academic department is one of the most challenging missions an academic can undertake, and the journey is very often kaleidoscopic in emotions and rich in experiences. A litany of questions and reflections shape the decision of identifying the leader. Who should be chosen, why and on what basis? What criteria or qualification? What role should the leader play? Would the person be able to lead the department effectively and get the best from the staff? Would the leader be able to navigate the competing pressures of the job? Academic departments are doubtless one of the most important units in a university, yet the process of preparing their leaders leaves much to be desired. While training can help with the preparation, there is so much that needs to be prepared and trained for, that many institutions either train the leaders *a minima* or not at all, before they assume their mandate, or may eventually resort to the basic minimum *a posteriori*. With no perfect method on how best to prepare academic leaders for the job at the helm of a department, the result is a perpetual journey of surprises, discovery and work-in-progress.

THE ACADEMIC DEPARTMENT AND ITS LEADER

Whether you agree with Lane (2018) who argued that "the academic department is often the unheralded powerhouse of a college or university," it is difficult to dispute his analogy that "academic departments are to universities what mitochondria are to cellular organisms. Each cell is full of these little entities called mitochondria, which collectively are responsible for regulating the metabolism of the cell through respiration and energy production. In the same way, academic departments serve as the regulators of an institution's metabolism – they ultimately determine whether an institution operates at peak performance or not."

Given the importance of the function of the department head and the role that she or he is expected to play, it is arguably essential that the most ideally suited individuals are awarded the job. With the scope of job descriptions ranging from the very general but vague, to the rarely very specific, in many instances being a department chair is a "tour of duty" mission. No one really wants the job, but someone has to sacrifice themselves and do it.

In their 2005 article, Wolverton et al. drew upon studies conducted by Jackson (1999) and Eley (1994) who indicated that "most individuals that become department chairs have neither prior leadership preparation nor a clear understanding of what the job entails … Academic departments reach into their faculty pools … to insert some unsuspecting target into this critical leadership position." The candidate may understand departmental idiosyncrasies and the cartography of the department and organization, but may not be inclined toward effective leadership of individual and collective talent and capabilities. While being knowledgeable of the institution and organizational history, culture and context can be an asset for leadership, failure to grasp the fundamentals of effective leadership can often lead to numerous roadblocks and even extensive conflict. When faced with competing and contradictory pressures, especially in resource-strapped organizations, the lack of effectiveness of the leader can quickly become a debilitating handicap especially when implementing change that may be imposed by top management or as requested from the faculty.

With the demanding role as the interface between the management of the institution and the department faculty, department chairs are thus "front line" workers that are required to assume a multiplicity of roles, responsibilities and functions while remembering that they are also faculty. Navigating between being good shepherds and administrators, department chairs are the "glue" and conduit of alignment and communication. How can they exercise their effectiveness? How can they be efficient in the discharge of their functions? How can they get the best from their staff?

IDENTITY AND LEGITIMACY: MANAGER OR LEADER?

Throughout history, Management Education in particular has been regarded as the bedrock for the creation of knowledge about organizations. One of the most existential debates in management theory is on management and leadership – whether a manager is a leader or vice versa. There is an abundance of literature that has extensively investigated and continues to explore these two concepts and their qualities. The manager, based on the historical precepts of management, is tasked with ensuring efficiency in a given system of production. The leader, on the other hand, is expected to coordinate the actions of the group toward achieving a common objective. While some argue that they are exclusionary roles and profiles, others argue in favor of the opposite. Is it possible to be both at the same time? When should one demonstrate more of the former as opposed to the latter, or vice versa? The essence here seems to be one of balance and appropriateness. When to allow freedom of initiative and when to exercise control? How to inspire and initiate and when to hold to account? When to conform to policy and when to take risk or to innovate? Championing a vision or strategy is very different from spearheading its implementation and appropriate skillsets are required for each phase. Persuasion is not execution.

Usually the first port of call in ensuring the department works smoothly, department heads are not necessarily academic leaders in their own right. One important notion is the distinction between a department leader or chair, who is typically a member of faculty, and an academic leader who is someone recognized by her/his peers and the wider academic community as being either a thought leader or experienced academic with significant experience in the field. With considerable decision-making power, department chairs are able to influence and can even define the composition, roles, expectations and appraisals of their faculty and staff. However, exercising such power without the requisite legitimacy serves to undermine the credibility and validity of the appointment. One of the most critical responsibilities of an academic chair is to lead by example. Yet too often, many chairs fail in this regard and ultimately impair the very essence of the leadership initiative. Being an exemplary leader often requires appropriate emotional intelligence, people skills and mastery of the art of negotiation, as exercising the role can often lead to organizational conflict – "being exemplary in the eyes of top management" may not necessarily align with being exemplary for the department. Very often, department leaders find themselves in a dilemma where they "talk the talk" but do not "walk the walk." Consequently, this dilemma destroys their credibility, legitimacy and leadership effectiveness.

At the locus of a dynamic equilibrium between being a manager or leader, and leading and managing individual faculty and a department as a unit, the department chair must also be trustworthy and show empathy toward the members. Department chairs must also implement and demonstrate an appropriate and effective approach to autonomy and control – what leeway should be afforded to whom and under what conditions, when exceptions can be tolerated and when should the rules apply, and so on. With significant ability to initiate and influence changes in the department, the exemplarity of the leader is put into question should there be a lack of or insufficient transparency in decision making, as the situation becomes quickly perceived as one of cloakroom and secretive deals and arrangements.

HOW CAN ONE REALLY TRAIN AND SURVIVE THE JOB OF HEADING AN ACADEMIC DEPARTMENT?

Given all that a department chair is required to learn and implement, it is perhaps a delusion to think that one will be appropriately trained and prepared to lead an academic department – too many centripetal and centrifugal forces at play. Alternatively, it may be more appropriate to explore how one can learn to do the job.

1. Accept that the challenge is a special assignment and commit to working hard to succeed. This would mean stepping out of your comfort zone, taking risks, being challenged and accepting criticism, while seeking to be the best. Thrust at the core of a myriad of centrifugal and centripetal pressures, the academic leader is often at the interface of competing

roles and responsibilities. As a member of the faculty corps, the department chair has to assume profiles that would otherwise be considered as irreconcilable. This situation leads to significant tensions where the leader has to navigate between control and autonomy while catering to individual development and collective progress.

2. Take time to discover and comprehend the scope of the "system" (the unit) and the ecosystem in which the unit is located. Get to know the members of the department, their motivations and aspirations, while understanding the rules and bureaucracy of the institution. In academia, the environment is extremely complex and there are often many "unwritten" rules.

3. At a minimum, identify and understand the various roles and profiles you may be required to assume. The academic chair is often caught in the "eye of the storm" where she/he is required to integrate and navigate the clashing needs of the institution, the unit, the individuals and her/his own. One of the more insightful approaches to identifying and understanding how to respond to the challenges of the storms while demonstrating appropriate leadership is Quinn's competing values framework (Figure 2.1). Drawing upon the categorization of several factors of organizational effectiveness (flexibility/autonomy and stability and control), and focus (individual (internal) and external (unit)), Quinn (1988) integrated several leadership behaviors and roles to create a competing value framework which provides useful insight in guiding the department chair's actions. For Quinn, effective managers are not only required to perform all of the eight roles listed, but they will often play multiple ones which compete and contradict, simultaneously, and this requires agility, dexterity and adaptability. Academic leaders are therefore encouraged to comprehend the similarities, differences and expectations that underlie each role in order to better balance and execute them while promoting a culture of excellence. However, such a combination is not necessarily simple, nor without consequences. Given the diversity of the roles and expectations, and assorted behaviors, it is quite normal for the department chair to be seen as having a "personality disorder" or multiple personalities, as department members try to comprehend and decode the chair's actions. It is also not unusual that the competency and capability of the chair can be called into question as department members seek clarity, coherence and consistency in the decision making. Such a dilemma can often undermine the leadership effectiveness of the chair. To offset the conundrum, department chairs who are transparent and empathetic in explaining their actions, are able to obtain the endorsement and support of the department, especially in times of adversity.

4. Develop a support network of mentors and opinion leaders on whom you can rely for inspiration and support. They would be able to share their past experiences and help you decode and formalize your ideas and initiatives.

5. Demonstrate empathy and admit doubt. Once members feel confident in your approach to their situation, you will be able to earn their trust. Should you have a doubt, one useful approach is to reach out to members and seek their input. Beyond the empathy and engagement, they will bring new ideas to the table and help shape the outcomes of the decision. There is no need to reinvent the wheel when one might already exist and you did not ask!

In short, running a department is like being an athlete in a decathlon. It is perhaps impossible, and almost a certainty, that you will encounter problems. Therefore, the incoming chair needs to be aware and sensitive to their biases. As the head of an academic department, one is entrusted with a multi-dimensional portfolio of responsibilities: pastoral, managerial, leadership, mentor, facilitator, negotiator, and so on. Executing these responsibilities is often a ballet of conflicting values, norms, and political, managerial and organizational pressures. Given the diversity of backgrounds, qualifications and experience, the challenge then becomes how to ensure everyone is treated fairly and equally for their work. Whether it be, for example, teaching schedules, administrative duties or budget allocation, keeping the playing field level and equal becomes a daunting exercise. The issue is therefore how to harmonize the functioning of the faculty and minimize managerial and leadership biases. Ultimately, serving as the academic chair is the inevitable writing of a chapter in the history of the department. History, like the department members, will be your judge!

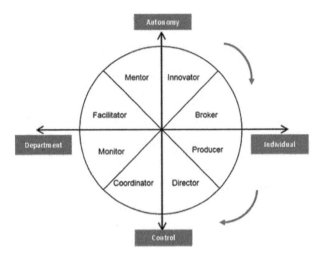

Figure 2.1   Quinn's competing values framework

REFERENCES

Eley (1994) "Management Training for the University Head of Department", *International Journal of Educational Management*, 8(2): 20–22.

Jackson, M.P. (1999) "The Role of the Head of Department in Managing Performance in UK Universities", *International Journal of Educational Management*, 13(3): 142–155.

Lane, J. (2018) Transforming Academic Leadership: It Starts with Department Chairs, *Higher Education Leadership Lens* (24 April), https://sunysail.org/2018/04/24/transforming-academic-leadership-it-starts-with-department-chairs/.

Quinn, R.E. (1988) *Beyond Rational Management: Mastering the Paradoxes and Competing Demands of High Performance*. San Francisco: Jossey-Bass

Wolverton, M, Ackerman & Holt, S. (2005) "Preparing for Leadership: What Academic Department Chairs Need to Know", *Journal of Higher Education Policy and Management* 27(2): 227–238

3. The role of academic leaders of a business school: an internal tensions perspective

Matthew J. Robson

But you must not change one thing, one pebble, one grain of sand, until you know what good and evil will follow on that act. The world is in balance, in Equilibrium. A wizard's power of Changing and Summoning can shake the balance of the world. It is dangerous, that power ... It must follow knowledge, and serve need. (Ursula K. Le Guin, *A Wizard of Earthsea*)

INTRODUCTION

The above quote sets out a guiding theme of Le Guin's book, namely Taoism, and its fundamental principle of living in harmony. The central character laments a foolish decision made during his youth to be a wizard that *acts* rather than a wizard content to simply *be*. I would argue that such a sentiment applies to academic leadership. Universities are not like businesses, despite the efforts of regulators and corporate sector-focused academic leaders to introduce market mechanisms. The sector tends toward continuity and stability rather than disruption and change.

An important university alumnus once said to me, "Mat, someone from the staff said something terrible to me. He said, 'Because that worked so well this year, we should do exactly the same thing next year'. This person doesn't get it. The University needs to be more dynamic." I realized as I was being told this that the person who had said that was probably me. Whether or not he knew this, what he had meant was that in his line of work – as a hugely successful entrepreneur operating in the fast-moving world of fintech and, before that, advertising – value creation needs to be dynamic, otherwise competition will catch up. But this is not the way academic processes work; these are resistant to direct competition and radical changes, often with good reason.

Leadership does not have to be about multifarious actions and the worst form of leader is one who acts without understanding the pattern of actions over time and the effects of extreme actions. Academic institutions are complex places. They have complicated and divergent goals, structures, staff, and stakeholders. The history of an academic institution is a history of its fault lines – between colliding agendas of different groups of staff and stakeholders and forms and levels of management. Indeed, there are often tensions between a business school and its university, with the latter being uncomfortably reliant on the scalability of the former's programs and resultant cash flows (Pitelis, 2019).

Academic leaders of schools and faculties, who act in extreme ways that fail to take into consideration the rich context of the academic grouping, do not tend to do well. A transitional type of Dean might say that, "I was recruited by the Vice Chancellor to do X, and I achieved X", but their actions can destroy the ethos and harmony of a school and damage its trajectory long after they themselves have left. Good academic leaders are adept at managing upwards to maintain good conditions for a school, but also at managing downwards to the faculty using contextual knowledge and subtle, nuanced, and well-judged approaches.

So how can an academic leader successfully *be*, in managing downwards? My own experiences as a leader – a Department Chair and faculty executive board member in the U.K. for several years – suggest the answer involves taking a *dialectical view* of academia. According to the dialectical view, the world is the unity of opposites. Within any entity, there are colliding events, forces, or values that compete against each other for primacy and control (Van de Ven, 1992). Opposing forces may well attempt to create an either/or position, but the reality is that the organization has an equilibrium orbit. Organization theorists assert that stability comes through striving for the *unity of opposites* (Das and Teng, 2000).

For a school's academic leader to successfully *be*, they must be sensitive to the dialectics of their own institution and not act in extreme ways that pull the organization out of its equilibrium orbit. A starting point in this is to fully understand major fault lines within the school and university. This chapter discusses three major ones that I have come across to date – ones that have occupied my time and thinking. These reflect the circumstances of business schools and the university sector in the U.K., but also apply in other countries. Of course, these and other fault lines exist to a greater or lesser extent in any given school and university, given the importance of context.

MANAGERIALISM/OPTIMIZATION AND ENTREPRENEURIALISM/CREATIVITY

Managerialism is about taking control and the measurement of actions and outcomes, establishing hierarchy and accountability within line management structures, and optimizing to achieve things by doing more with less (Sandgren, 2012). Entrepreneurialism, on the other hand, is about freeing up the staff to be the best they can be creatively. This implies carefully delimiting managerial control, decentralizing decisions, and instilling a culture of staff taking responsibility for their own creative work in the classroom and journals. In my experience, and from speaking to acquaintances at many business schools in many parts of the world, different institutions are at different places in terms of these two forces.

How can you tell which type of academic institution you are at? When a new staff member attends induction at their new school, if the Dean appears and focuses their talk on a list of gongs and trophies achieved on their watch, it is safe to say there is a more managerial style. Such an approach suggests there are top-down objectives and rules and your role is to fit into the agenda of maintaining these and, possibly, adding others. If the Dean instead talks more broadly about the culture of their school and how you might fit in as a learned academician, there is a more entrepreneurial style at play. In such a school, the staff do not expect to be closely managed – they are their own highly educated centers of activity.

Do academic institutions expect to be managing their staff, that is, encouraging performance improvements in line with management's goals? Line management in academic institutions does not always work well. In some countries, academic positions are temporary all the way through to full Chair-level staff. It stands to reason that staff on lengthy tenure tracks, fearing the axe, would be quite responsive to management. Such an incentive can easily be reinforced through a formal review process. Woe betide a staff member who loses their job and must relocate the family. But what happens to the winners, after their tenure has been won? An acquaintance who passed their tenure process was told by a colleague, "you've won the lottery." They asked why, and were told, "you've got decades until you retire, multiply your salary by that number, and that's what's coming to you."

Many academics move to the U.K. to escape such a model. However, line management has been stepped up in the U.K. too. An acquaintance of mine was telling me about their school's new traffic light, review system. They have two issues: (1) it was set by managers who would themselves struggle to secure green lights on the main metrics (e.g., top-tier publications); and (2) their institution did not provide anywhere near the right levels of support for staff to achieve green lights. However, since they were worried about their contract, they got on with it.

Still, most U.K. schools offer permanent jobs immediately following probation, and review processes are not really review processes. Schools favor an annual review with a small "r," so to speak, focusing much more on staff support and development. As a line manager, I was once obliged to attend a training program on "Supporting Performance Improvement." A key piece of advice – although one would not find this in the speaker's slide deck – was that once a staff member passes probation there is very little a manager can do to arrest poor performance with formal action. The advice seemed to be to grasp the nettle in probation to avoid a two-year process of informal and formal stages needed for a dismissal outcome.

Both approaches have downsides if taken too far. Extreme managerialism is not a good fit with the university sector, and business school academics – who research this type of thing and understand the downside – may be expected to react with cynicism. Stories of sharp managerial practices spread rapidly across the labor market. For instance, the Deputy Dean for Faculty micro-managing what staff in the faculty taught by going into their modules' virtual learning content. Business school staff at the receiving end of such practices, or close to others at the receiving end, would presumably be unsettled.

Extreme entrepreneurialism can result in staff setting their own objectives, and their doing so risks stripping away too much ambition. I recall once listening to a professor describe management's attempts to get them to publish in specific, high-quality journals as "deplorable." Their publishing strategy has since veered away from the quality game and the need to face-off against critical reviewers. If everyone does this, the school's research profile is bound to suffer. On the teaching side, an example of creativity going wrong is where a staff member revamps their module by ratcheting up the level of difficulty for students (e.g., multiple, hard to fathom assessments). The module becomes so labor-intensive for the students, they start to reduce the time they spend on doing other modules' work. If everyone does this, program-level satisfaction will reduce. In both these cases, top-down processes are needed to align individuals' decisions with the school's objectives.

Academic leaders need to blend elements of managerialism with entrepreneurialism, to avoid situations where they need to wade directly into an issue or otherwise; something that could be misconstrued by staff as overtly managerial or entrepreneurial. To this end, systems should contain both elements. For instance, if formal review processes are to be used, they should at least be paired with well-implemented mentoring and other support. On publishing strategy – have a mentoring strategy that encourages staff to work on research projects that interest them and to get their creative ideas in print, but also on projects that have the potential to target top journals (i.e., a one for you, one for us approach). On the teaching modules side, have a system of program review that favors teaching innovations in modules, but delves into what is happening across modules and corrects module elements that detract from students' program-level satisfaction. Further, if a leader is generally perceived as being managerial or entrepreneurial, assuming they are self-aware enough to spot this, they would benefit from putting together a leadership team that balances out this tendency.

The leader might also create designated areas of managerialism and entrepreneurship that effectively compensate each other – a managerial area might be the one the leader views as making the most difference to the performance of the group, while the entrepreneurial area might link strongly to the context of the school. A former line manager of mine used meetings to open up carefully selected issues for debate. They had the skill of being able to summarize the debate there and then. For one particular important decision, they would say, "this is not a democracy, so it is up to me to make the final decision," and then conclude with a well-justified decision. Although this has a managerial edge to it, staff had had their say and felt listened to.

THE INDIVIDUAL AND THE COLLECTIVE

An acquaintance of mine is prone to saying that "Institutions do not care about people; people care about people." They are implying that universities lack memory as key decision makers come and go. If your institution sees you as a row on a spreadsheet of accepted publications, research funding, teaching scores, and so on, you should take care of your own development and productivity and not go out of your way to contribute to the wider collective. Indeed, another acquaintance told me that they were asked by their Dean to develop a new center that established close links to an important practice community. They did so, even though this involved reskilling and a huge amount of travel. After the center was up and running, they overheard their Pro-Dean for Research saying, "X really needs to publish more." In response, this individual reduced time spent on the center and doubled down on what they deemed to be core business (i.e., quality publications and student satisfaction). One might argue that they became less important to the collective in doing so, as they had become an expert in the research engagement area. This example also seems to show an institution forgetting, in real time.

Theorists (e.g., Boulding, 1969) have identified two extreme caricatures of human nature in transactions with others, namely, the economic person and the heroic person. The former prioritizes the ethic of rational, cost-based calculation; they will be pretty quick to count costs and claim rewards in an exchange. The latter prioritizes nonrational, noncalculative aspects of any exchange system (Lado, Dant and Tekleab, 2008). In practice, these extreme positions rarely exist. Of course, this is shaped by national and work cultures – for instance, the Japanese traditionally are likely to eschew individual-level benefits (Slater and Robson, 2012). Still, a leader should understand where staff members fall on the continuum between the two positions, at any given time. An economic person will be in touch with the leader to count costs and claim rewards, when the time is right, in a businesslike manner. By contrast, the heroic person has a reputation that will likely precede them down the corridor. If you are their line manager, you are likely to receive benevolent emails from colleagues that they have helped when the going got tough.

The economic archetype is likely to be a good performer in specific ways – those that matter the most to their professional ambitions. One problem with them is that they may cause problems by being a little too sharp elbowed around colleagues or too distant. Either way, they are not the lubricant that keeps the university machine running when it stutters, and this will not be lost on others. Because the economic person is adept at managing upwards, the academic leader should try to devote their attentions disproportionately to the heroes to establish parity; checking in on the heroes and building links with them. I would argue that doing so is better for the collective, as these are your institutional loyalists and champions.

An academic grouping will inevitably contain economic and heroic types, and the academic leader will need to be adept at dealing with both kinds to maintain equilibrium. The economic person is not someone who wants to contribute more to a team relative to the costs incurred and benefits obtained. Still, their sensitivities and ambitions will need to be engaged with. Doing so is likely to boost the productivity of the team on specific goals as well as its reputation externally. But team spirit will be damaged if economic types become too self-interested and efficient (e.g., why respond quickly and constructively to colleagues' requests for support when someone else can do so?). The leader needs to draw them back from being too focused, by establishing and speaking to norms of collegiality and citizenship in the team; going to the trouble of defining explicitly what these are.

By contrast, the heroic person is someone that can give too much of themselves. And there is a risk that they might burn out and inadvertently move in a counting their costs direction; such as in the earlier anecdote. The academic leader's role is to help these individuals to not give too much of themselves by delimiting their duties and responsibilities. In my experience, this is especially important in ensuring that enthusiastic new starters feel that they have a soft landing. Taking work away from more established staff members who prefer to be overburdened requires careful explanation too.

Sometimes the academic leader needs to put the individual first. I recall an acquaintance being scathing about their Dean who had suggested publicly that staff should not take holidays, as these get in the way of work duties. This is such a poorly judged thing for a Dean to have said. By contrast, an acquaintance – and a true hero – once told me that when they were under huge pressure linked to a leadership role, they were advised by a senior staff member that while at work a person is effectively juggling four balls. These are health, family, spirit and work. While the first three are made of glass and will crack if dropped, the work ball is wooden and will bounce. This is great wisdom indeed. Of course, the collective stands to benefit if such individuals' spirit is put first.

My assumption here is that academic institutions contain both types of person and holding them in check – having individualists and collectivists – is the best for the team's enduring success and stability. There are institutions that overtly value one over the other, but I would argue that this is a temporal phenomenon that is unstable. For instance, the U.K.'s Research Excellence Framework encourages its institutions to buy-in CVs for the publications. Such a phenomenon encourages staff to jump ship before the census date to cut individualist deals (e.g., "I will come but do not give me any teaching for six months"). Institutions sometimes make a correction after the census date, which can come as a surprise to the new entrants that were promised great deals; seemingly, a case of faulty institutional memory.

RESEARCH AND TEACHING

Research and teaching are colliding forces within many business schools. Over the years, business and management schools have been scaled upwards and become revenue streams for their universities. In effect, this has created lop-sided staff–student ratios compared to other schools within a university (Pitelis, 2019). Usually, these other schools have not geared up to teaching large student numbers in the same way. The upshot is that academics in business schools are conscious that their students pay their own and (probably) others' salaries. While they might want to spend most of their work time on research-related activities, business school scholars are aware that research does not clean its own face. In terms of the way scholars understand their job responsibilities, there is a matrix structure and they serve two (or more) masters.

It is a truism that the short-term deadlines of teaching generally get in the way of the long-term deadlines of research. To be a good researcher you need to be researching every day, keeping your head in projects that require tunnel vision to complete. Taking your eye off research to complete an intensive series of lectures, tutorials and associated administration, comes at the detriment of research flow. Further, it takes experience and confidence to understand how to use teaching as a way to uncover and test new research ideas. On the other hand, research should help with teaching. Researchers are adept at explaining complicated phenomena in the simplest possible way, and this skill is a boon for the classroom. However, if knowledgeable researchers have the potential to be great teachers, this is easily hamstrung if they drill too much into conceptual/theoretical minutia or show a lack of effort. Students inherently know if a teacher does not want to be there.

Because of a raft of factors – the rise of accreditation, technological advances, moves toward casualization, large student numbers, and student fee increases – business schools have recruited large numbers of teaching-focused staff. The importance of pedagogy- and management practice-focused staff leading teaching innovations and boosting educational creativity across the board seems obvious. However, teaching-focused staff may feel less than mission central at research-intensive business schools, where half of the agenda focuses on research. Such a sentiment has not been helped by the research-focused staff. For instance, in some schools, research-focused staff are on teaching-only contracts, which are naturally of lower value to them. Further, among researchers, the Ph.D. is viewed as a key period of apprenticeship for academia, and teaching-focused staff usually do not come in with an equivalent qualification – or, at least, it is difficult for them to demonstrate that their professional experiences can offset the scholarly gravitas afforded by a doctorate.

Although there are inevitable tensions between research- and teaching-focused staff types, some individuals will feel them more than others. Indeed, there could be staff that are overly sensitive to signals that the academic leader is focusing on research resources and outcomes at the expense of teaching resources and outcomes, and vice versa. In these cases, the academic leader needs to ensure that (s)he is not providing them with evidence of bias and going too far in one direction. Individuals on the research and teaching sides may have a history of conflict. A leader cannot easily address baggage resulting from historical decisions and it would not be an efficient use of their time. Emphasis should be placed on ensuring current moderates do not take an either/or position on the research versus teaching dialectic.

There are several ways to foster commonality of staff with different foci. For instance, while conferences traditionally have been the preserve of research-focused staff, there are increasing opportunities to attend or organize major conferences with research- and teaching-related sessions, tracks, and communities. Further, modern public value stances on academic leadership call for formulating and managing a university's societal license to operate (Meynhardt, 2019). A more engaged form of research involves working closely with user communities to co-produce societal value from research outputs. Such an endeavor could be used to bring together research-focused staff with teaching-focused colleagues who may well be more accustomed to near-to-market work. This has real benefits for the researcher. Because numerous published academic papers go unnoticed, a more engaged scholar prioritizes being read and used over simply being published in a reputed journal (Marinetto, 2018).

Another shared agenda could involve expanding the academy. As the victims of their own successes, fast-expanding business schools require good staff in ever greater numbers. Yet, in some business enterprise fields, more staff are retiring than are coming through good doctoral programs. While research-focused staff can be relied upon to supervise the research work of doctoral students, the students also need to be taken under the wing of innovative educators who can mentor them in the classroom. Teaching-focused staff would seem best placed to fast-track the development of the next generation of teaching talent; early career staff who are confident in the modern classroom and fully understand how to forge synergies between research and teaching.

A final area of commonality is that the collision of research and teaching has been exacerbated by the level of administration associated with both activities. Indeed, administration has risen as a third major activity within business schools and on staff workloads. Here, activities to maintain multiple accreditations have not helped. Administrative duties have been taking time away from core efforts to publish in quality journals and deliver high student satisfaction. Because these tasks and achievements now need to be completed in a compacted timeframe, they are more likely to collide. Moreover, too often, intricate procedures introduced to administer research and teaching duties have not made it easier for staff to perform in the classroom and the journals. An acquaintance told me that their school was so worried about this form of bureaucracy they employed the services of a management consultancy to tackle it. The consultancy was quick to crack down on their meetings culture: staff are not obliged to attend meetings *unless* a decision needs making; meetings have strictly enforced time allocations per item and cannot go beyond a designated total amount of time; and the staff present must be 100 percent focused on the meeting's business (i.e., not multi-tasking and tapping on their laptops). The implication is that person hours are not wasted that could be devoted directly to research and teaching value creation.

DISCUSSION

The current chapter has taken the position that business schools have fault lines, that is, areas of tension between conflicting values, forces, and agendas. The areas of tension may be longstanding or more recent, they may be dormant or live, they may be pervasively felt or restricted in terms of who they affect. Irrespective, they are likely to be there in some form. The three fault lines featured above are pretty generic and have been selected for their applicability across institutions. Still, context is everything and institutions may have several other fault lines. For instance, business school staff may have siloed versus interdisciplinary work agendas. Some business school academics are of the view that their school, especially if it includes economics, is interdisciplinary enough. But a bona fide interdisciplinary approach would involve rolling out a suite of joint teaching programs and grand-challenge type research projects with other schools. A fault line I once heard an acquaintance mention involved two dominant nationalities dominating the faculty of a school, due to the location of the school near an international border. As such their school was a collaboration between different nationalities with different approaches to joint work (cf. Robson and Dunk, 1999). Clearly, this type of fault line is deeply contextual.

The chapter also assumes that there is a connection between the opposing forces, and that it is difficult for a leader – and counterproductive – to take their school outside of the equilibrium orbit. The forces hold each other in check and are mutually reinforcing; we are dealing with a dialectics rather than a dichotomous either/or type of situation (Collinson, 2014). The dialectics view would suggest that stability comes through striving for the unity of opposites. Of course, if a school's performance is poor, some instability may be desirable. But changes should still fall within an equilibrium orbit – heeding this *balance of the world*, as per the opening quotation. It is up to the academic leader whether they decide to act in a balanced way. Some do not; they achieve things, and they leave to take on the next leadership job. Presumably, the next incumbent is then tasked with resetting the equilibrium.

The leader needs to understand the ripples spreading from their actions. A key consideration here is that sometimes actions taken at one fault line affect other lines. For example, using a democratic mechanism to decide on a particular issue creatively in the group – balancing out contemporaneous managerial interventions – could open up the fault line of the individual versus the collective or research versus teaching, or still other fault lines. This point serves to reinforce the importance of context. To understand the bigger picture of relationships between fault lines, one must fully understand the context of the school and institution.

REFERENCES

Boulding, Kenneth E. (1969), "Economics as a moral science," *American Economic Review*, 59 (1), 1–12.

Collinson, David (2014), "Dichotomies, dialectics, and dilemmas: new directions for crucial leadership studies?," *Leadership*, 10 (1), 36–55.

Das, Tushar Kanti, and Bing-Sheng Teng (2000), "Instabilities of strategic alliances: an internal tensions perspective," *Organization Science*, 11 (1), 77–101.

Lado, Augustine A., Rajiv R. Dant, and Amanuel G. Tekleab (2008), "Trust-opportunism paradox, relationalism, and performance in interfirm relationships: evidence from the retail industry," *Strategic Management Journal*, 29 (4), 401–23.

Marinetto, Michael (2018), "Fast food research in the era of unplanned obsolescence," *Journal of Management Studies*, 55 (6), 1014–20.

Meynhardt, Timo (2019), "Public value: value creation in the eyes of society." In Adam Lindgreen, Nicole Koenig-Lewis, Martin Kitchener, John D. Brewer, Mark H. Moore, and Timo Meynhardt, eds., *Public Value: Deepening, Enriching, and Broadening the Theory and Practice*, London and New York: Routledge, 5–22.

Pitelis, Chris (2019), "A future for business education: why business as usual is bad business," *Global Focus* (June 5), https://globalfocusmagazine.com/a-future-for-business-education-why-business-as-usual-is-bad-business/.

Robson, Matthew J., and Mark A.J. Dunk (1999), "Case study: developing a pan-European co-marketing alliance: the case of BP-Mobil," *International Marketing Review*, 16 (3), 216–30.

Sandgren, Aljona (2012), "Managerialism and entrepreneurialism in universities: is there space for creativity?" In Lennart Wikander, Christina Gustafsson, and Ulla Riis, eds., *Enlightenment, Creativity and Education: Polities, Politics, Performances*, Rotterdam: Sense Publishers, 147–69.

Slater, Stephanie, and Matthew J. Robson (2012), "Social capital in Japanese–Western alliances: understanding cultural effects," *International Marketing Review*, 29 (1), 6–23.

Van de Ven, Andrew (1992), "Suggestions for studying strategy process: a research note," *Strategic Management Journal*, 13 (Summer), 169–91.

PART II

Transformational and performance leadership

4. The head of department as the key transformational leader

Asbjørn Busk J. and Søren Barlebo Rasmussen

INTRODUCTION

What will it mean to be the Head of Department at a university in the future? History tells us that the answer is closely linked to the contemporary perception of science in society. In the second part of the 20th century, the Head of Department was a *primus inter pares* serving a collective of autonomous faculty members. At the turn of the millennium, the Head of Department resembled an overseer managing a research factory. As the relationship between science and society is changing yet again, it is time for the Head of Department to take on a new key management role in the university.

The changing times revolve around societal *impact* of research (Belfiore, 2015; Benneworth & Jongbloed, 2010; Bornmann, 2013; Greenhalgh, Raftery, Hanney, & Glover, 2016; Matt, Gaunand, Joly, & Colinet, 2017; Pedersen, Grønvad, & Hvidtfeldt, 2020). The impact agenda has sparked a fierce debate. Advocates consider it a moral obligation for science to "pay back" to society by utilizing its research by improving the world and solving pressing societal problems. Critics accuse the impact agenda of instrumentalizing science making it subject to political and economic interests and ultimately compromising academic freedom (McCowan, 2018). However relevant this discussion is, in this chapter, we move beyond it. We consider the requirement of societal impact of research as a premise for universities and departments in the future, because many factors indicate that the impact agenda gains ground – whether we like it or not.

The overall aim of this chapter is to explore what it will mean to be the Head of Department in a future where the department is obliged to produce societal impact. In doing so, we look at the history of science in society. We identify three successive phases of science in society during the last 70 years: the *classic* phase, the *excellence* phase and the emerging *impact* phase.[1]

The three phases are distinguished in five dimensions: (1) The social contract between science and society, (2) science policy, (3) university's organizational configuration, (4) university strategy and (5) university management. The assumption guiding this chapter is that the role as the Head of Department has historically been, and will continue to be, constituted in the complex nexus of these five dimensions (Figure 4.1).

The progress of the chapter is straightforward: First, we examine the dimensions of the classic phase and the excellence phase through literature and own experiences. The primary case is the Danish university sector. Second, we attempt to capture and outline the dimensions of the emerging impact phase. Third and finally, we elaborate how the impact phase constitutes a new and important role for the Head of Department as the Key Transformational Leader. As a guide for the reader, we have provided an overview of the differences between the three phases (Table 4.1). We recommend revisiting this after the exploration of each phase.

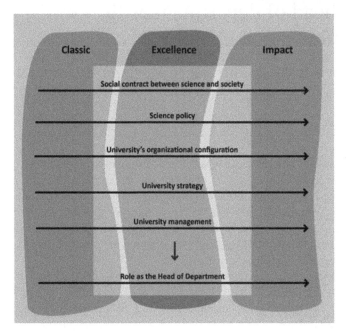

Figure 4.1   Science in society

THE CLASSIC PHASE

Vannevar Bush and the Arm's-length Principle

The classic phase began at the end of World War II. In 1945, President Roosevelt's scientific advisor, Vannevar Bush, made his recommendations on the relationship between science and society in the dawning peacetime. Bush recommended a social contract between science and society based on an exchange. Science should receive stable funding from the state while delivering original knowledge in return produced through basic research (Bush, 1945). Bush's recommendations became the ideal to follow in the years to come in the USA and other Western countries (Faye & Pedersen, 2012).

   In general, science policy of the classic phase followed the arm's-length principle. Politicians outlined overall priorities for research, while science itself was trusted to control the quality and efficiency of the research (Wenneberg, 2002). The feedback from science into society was typically thought of in line with the linear "push–pull" model. Science could "push" innovations into the market, or the market could "pull" innovations from science by expressing new needs (Tidd, 2006).

All in all, the classic phase separated science from the surrounding society to ensure an objective and independent production of knowledge (Wenneberg, 2002). The university was thereby constructed as an independent producer of knowledge on the periphery of society with economic stability and academic freedom (Figure 4.2).[2]

Table 4.1   *Roadmap of the classic, excellence and impact phases*

Phase dimensions	Classic phase	Excellence phase	Impact phase
Social contract between science and society	Society funds an independent science, which in return delivers long-term original knowledge	Society funds a supervised science, which is responsible for short-term competitive edge and economic growth	Society funds a supervised science, which is responsible for creating impact in the surrounding society
Science policy	Arm's-length principle	New Public Management reforms focusing on excellence, efficiency and relevance	Requirement of impact. Policy form still unknown
University's organizational configuration	Professional bureaucracy with autonomous operating core	Machine bureaucracy with less autonomy for operating core	Professional bureaucracy 2.0 with autonomous and transdisciplinary operating core engaging with surroundings through ecosystems
University strategy	Lacks ability to implement strategy ("strategic implementation defect")	Implements objective strategies through top-down managerial tools	Pursues impact ambition through strategic coordination of decentralized impact initiatives
University management	Non-hierarchical, informal management with democratically elected managers	Hierarchical, professional top-down management with appointed managers	Leadership mobilizing impact initiatives bottom-up through coordination and transforming culture
The Head of Department	*Primus inter pares* of a collective of autonomous faculty members	"Overseer" managing a research factory	"Key Transformational Leader" of societal and departmental transformations

The Classic University as the Professional Bureaucracy

To understand the organizational development of the university, we must first understand the organizational configuration of "the classic university." To do so, we draw on Henry Mintzberg's writings. In the last part of the classic phase, Henry Mintzberg identified and analyzed the university as the organizational configuration called the *professional bureaucracy* (Mintzberg, 1983, pp. 189–213). We will in the following use Mintzberg's (1983) description of the professional bureaucracy to understand the classic university.

First of all, the key organizational part of the professional bureaucracy is the *operating core* (Mintzberg, 1983, p. 189), which in the classic university was the faculty. Without the faculty's expert knowledge and skills, the classic university could not produce original knowledge for society through research and education. This dependency on the faculty resulted in a concentration of power among the faculty members, who enjoyed great autonomy and the right to make decentralized decisions concerning their research and teaching. The strong operating core of the professional bureaucracy leaves little room for another part of the organization that Mintzberg calls the *technostructure* (Mintzberg, 1983, p. 194). The technostructure consists of analysts standardizing the work of others through planning and regulations (Mintzberg, 1983, pp. 15–16). Thus, the operating core dominated the classic university, while the technostructure was small or non-existent.

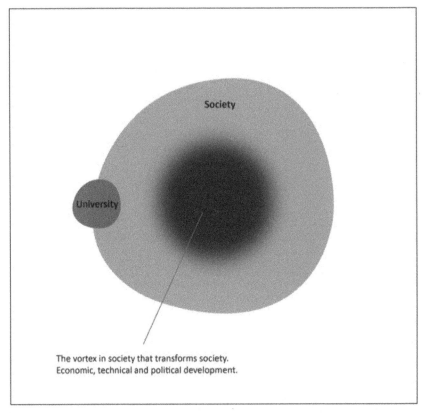

Society

University

The vortex in society that transforms society.
Economic, technical and political development.

Figure 4.2   Universities on the periphery of society during the classic phase (earlier)

Second, the professional bureaucracy has a certain way of coordinating work and making decisions. Instead of following rules and regulations from above, the autonomous members of the operating core make their decentralized decisions through what Mintzberg calls *standardization of skills* (Mintzberg, 1983, p. 190). In the classic university, standardization of skills happened when faculty members were indoctrinated into a scientific ethos and practice through training and participating in the scientific community. This ethos guided the faculty member in decisions – making rules and regulations unnecessary. A personal experience can serve as an example. One of the authors had a senior colleague who was a tremendous role model, and who demonstrated the importance of writing thorough research articles. When visiting his office, one would always find several ongoing writing projects on his desk. At project meetings, he would be swift and effective since he wanted to return to his office to continue the writing. Under his influence the author was socialized into writing articles in a disciplined and meticulous manner – without the need for rules, regulations or control.

Third, the professional bureaucracy emerges in *stable* yet *complex* environments (Mintzberg, 1983, p. 189). The expectations of society toward the classic university were stable: produce original knowledge and educate the students. At the same time, conducting research and teaching students is also a complex task, which required autonomy for the faculty.

Strategic Implementation Defect

Like all professional bureaucracies, the single biggest challenge for the classic university was its *strategic implementation defect* (our translation) – its inability to implement strategic change across the university as a whole (Barlebo Rasmussen, 2014, p. 64). By strategic change we mean, for instance, new research, teaching or funding strategies. The popular explanation for this defect is stubborn or incompetent faculty members. However, a better explanation can be found by looking at the inherited shortcomings of the classic university given its configuration as a professional bureaucracy. Let us in the following again draw on Mintzberg (1983).

First of all, strategic change requires loyalty toward the organization and top management. But in the classic university, the autonomous faculty members were more focused on their own personal strategies or the strategies of the greater scientific community. Second, with no local rules and regulation, the classic university had no infrastructure capable of coordinating and executing a local strategy for the university. Third, implementing strategic change often requires leadership as well as use and acceptance of hierarchical power, which leaders in the classic university did not have (elaborated below).

Primus Inter Pares

The classic university in Denmark was a collegial organization where leaders (Rector, Dean, Head of Department) were democratically elected by faculty and students (Christiansen, Harboe, Horst, Krogh, & Sarauw, 2013). Management had almost no formal power, and the Head of Department was a part-time position, which rotated among faculty members and included coordinative and administrative duties (J. G. Christensen, 2012).

The best way to summarize this role as the Head of Department might be as the *primus inter pares*. Formally, the Head of Department was almost equal to his colleagues, but informally his opinions carried weight. Thus, the Head of Department (and other well-respected faculty members) did indeed exercise management. But it was an informal and laissez-faire kind of management founded on professional reputation and socialization.

One of the authors experienced this rather contradictory management role, when doing a research interview with a Head of Department about his way of working with quality control at the department. The Head of Department would not explicitly accept being a "manager" of the department – mentioning it even sparked strong emotional reactions. In his own opinion, he was merely a colleague. However, when asked about his job, he calmly explained how he performed several managerial tasks across the department.

THE EXCELLENCE PHASE

Science and the Knowledge Society

The excellence phase gained strength in the 1990s when new mega trends such as globalization and the knowledge society dominated. The *knowledge society* is the perception that "... society and economy no longer primarily rely on industrial production, but on production of knowledge, innovation and education as foundation for economic growth and as basis for solving the challenges of society" (Faye & Pedersen, 2012, p. 11; our translation).

This caused a new political focus. In 2000, the EU set the goal of becoming the world's leading knowledge-based economy (European Parliament, 2000), which was followed by increased investment in research and development (European Commission, 2002). Danish politicians also caught sight of science. The infamous mantra "fra forskning til faktura" ("from research to invoice", our translation) dominated the 2000s, as the Danish government presented initiatives with the purpose of increasing industrial commercialization of research (Regeringen, 2003). In their globalization strategy, the Danish government emphasized the new role of the universities as being crucial for the "... competitiveness, growth and wealth ..." of the nation (Regeringen, 2006, p. 62; our translation).

Thus, the excellence phase changed the social contract between science and society. Science should no longer deliver independent long-term knowledge through basic science. Instead, science became responsible for delivering short-term competitive edge and economic growth through an increased focus on applied research (Faye & Pedersen, 2012).

New Means to a New End

The new social contract led to new science policies with the purpose of increasing quality (excellence) and relevance in public research and education. Quality and relevance were not new demands to science, but they were now characterized by the strong focus on utilization of research. An example is the aforementioned globalization strategy in which quality and relevance in public research were perceived as supporting high wealth and welfare for the society, for instance by supplying private companies with new knowledge. Likewise, university education was linked to supplying society with the needed highly educated labor force (Regeringen, 2006).

The policy instruments also changed. It was no longer an opportunity to leave science to itself, since the political system and society at large had lost its trust in science's ability to self-regulate (Frederiksen, Hansson, & Wenneberg, 2003). New instruments were needed. These were inspired by the concurrent wave of New Public Management, which promised to increase efficiency and accountability (which science had lost) in the public sector by applying instruments such as performance measurement, increased competition and private sector management tools (Hood, 1991).

Equipped with new means to a new end, the political level reformed the Danish university sector (elaborated below). The universities were no longer independent producers of knowledge situated at the periphery of society. Instead, they were becoming key knowledge producers – essential for the prosperity of the nation and therefore continuously held responsible for excellent, relevant and efficient research. In other words, universities were drawn right into the political and economic vortex of society (Figure 4.3).[3]

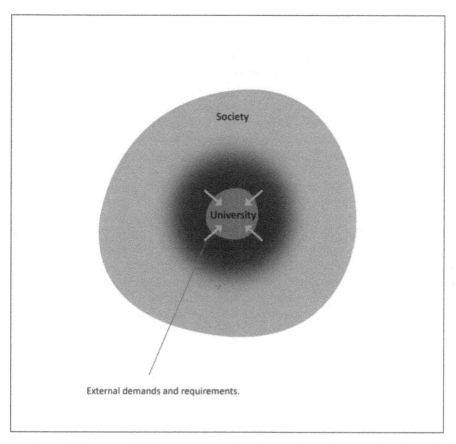

Figure 4.3   Universities in the vortex of society during the excellence phase (today)

From Professional Bureaucracy to Machine Bureaucracy

The reformations of the university sector transformed Danish universities. It started in 1999 with the so-called "forskerpatentloven" ("researcher-patent act", our translation) (Retsinformation, 1999). The act gave public research institutions permission to acquire the rights to an invention from the individual researcher. The institution could then commercialize the invention by licensing it or selling the patent to private companies or start-ups (Videnskabsministeriet, 2004). This is also known as "technology transfer" from university to business.

The university act of 2003 replaced the democratically elected managers with professional and appointed managers organized in a hierarchy from the new board of directors: Rector, Dean, down to the Head of Department (Retsinformation, 2003). The reform redistributed power in the university. The strong faculty members, who used to be aligned with (or even above) the management, were now under hierarchical managers, whom they could not get rid of through elections.

The next change was the implementation of globalization funds from 2006, which emphasized quality, relevance, and competition amongst the universities when allocating public research funds (Finansministeriet, 2006).

In 2007, the nationwide fusion of research institutions formed the establishment of eight Danish universities (Christiansen et al., 2013). To control these, on a Danish scale, very large organizations, more control, technostructure and top-down management were implemented. Summaries also show that across Danish universities the number of highly educated administrative personnel has increased since the early 2000s (Stage & Aagaard, 2020). According to one of the authors' memories, a tangible result of the university fusions was less visible Rectors. Before the fusions, the Rector was usually seen across the university at receptions, openings of conferences, seminars, and so on. After, the Rector became more occupied with meetings with the board and the ministry.

Finally, in 2010, measurement of research quality and results, through the use of the bibliometric research indicator, became influential for the allocation of basic funds for Danish universities (Dahler-Larsen, 2012). As Minister of Science, Helge Sander, stated: "Those universities who do it well shall be rewarded. And bad quality must have consequences" (Uddannelses- og Forskningsministeriet, 2009; our translation). In general, bibliometric evaluation pushed the research process from being an explorative creative process, toward an output and performance-oriented production controlled by external motivation structures. In accordance with the claim that external incentives can "crowd out" intrinsic motivation (Frey & Jegen, 2001; Georgellis, Iossa, & Tabvuma, 2011), the bibliometric system led to some faculty members losing their inner drive and passion for the research process. (For further elaboration on these and other consequences of the bibliometric research indicator, see Dahler-Larsen, 2012.)

In our perspective, the reforms of the 2000s tell a story of an organization that could not adapt to changing expectations from its environment on its own. The surrounding society required more accountability, efficiency, excellence and relevance from the universities. But being configured as professional bureaucracies, with the inherent strategic implementation defect and history of a stable environment, the universities were not geared toward meeting the changing requirements of society. Ultimately, the political system lost its patience and implemented the changes top-down by forcing hierarchy, performance measurement, competition and regulations into the university system. This transformed the classic university into an organization with strong traits of a *machine bureaucracy*, which is an organizational configuration characterized by regulation, formal hierarchy and a strong technostructure (Mintzberg, 1983, p. 163). In other words, the university became a "research and education factory."

In the machine bureaucracy, the faculty was stripped of the capabilities it had had as the operating core in the professional bureaucracy. The faculty lost the managerial power of the university, freedom over the research process and funding stability. Without these capabilities, the faculty members could not act out their professional identity as autonomous professionals. This led to strong personal feelings of hopelessness and frustration among many faculty members. Thus, the reforms of the 2000s came with massive collateral damage.

Today, many faculty members have fundamental mistrust toward top management and the political system. Our experience is that this is often expressed in the lunch break, when faculty members unite in criticism of management, society and the zeitgeist. Even though it is under-standable, in the long run, such lunch break bashing (and the deeper conflicts it represents) is hard on the motivation and spirit of the faculty.

Objective Strategy and Hierarchical Management

As a machine bureaucracy, the university developed new forms of strategy and management. In regard to strategy, the strategic implementation defect of the classic university was replaced with New Public Management's strategy approach. This is a corporate strategy method of setting, pursuing and measuring objective goals (Head & Alford, 2015). The strategic goals of the universities were specified in the development contract, which was a three-year agreement between the institution and the Minister of Research (Uddannelses- og Forskningsministeriet, 2020). Typically, the strategic goals were benchmarked through quantitative indicators. For instance, University of Copenhagen's first development contract from 2006 had goals such as: 632 new PhDs, 5% better student completion rate, 25% more revenue on postgraduate courses, 15 new English programs, 25% more registered inventions and 5% more media coverage (KU, 2006). In the subsequent three-year period, bibliometric measures on research production became goals as well (KU, 2007).

University management was also transformed in the excellence phase. As Hanne Foss Hansen et al. conclude in their study of management in Danish universities:

> This article has shown how coercive policy reforms in Denmark – and the reactions from various actors to them – effectively transformed collegial managerial roles into an empowered hierarchy of appointed line managers, who have very actively enacted their powerful roles within a new line management structure. (Hansen, Lind, & Stage, 2020, p. 455)

In other words, the laissez-faire management from the classic university was replaced with hierarchical management. For the Head of Department, this often meant turning away from the faculty and instead concentrating on reporting department performance upwards to the Dean with regard to publications, external funding, education evaluations, and so on, because, as the university act of 2003 stated, the Head of Department was responsible for securing the quality of research and education in the department (Retsinformation, 2003). One of the authors remembers how this played out: Each year, as the Head of Department, you were measured on the volume of your department's "publication-column" in a bar chart including all departments of the university. Ugh! Being the Head of Department with the most insignificant column was not funny. Gradually, the excellence phase transformed the Head of Department from being the *primus inter pares* into being more like an overseer managing the research and education factory.

THE IMPACT PHASE

A Growing Demand for Societal Impact

Currently, we are standing on the brink of a new phase of science in society. We call it the impact phase. In contrast to the two previous phases, the impact phase is still under develop-ment. Following our framework for science in society (see Figure 4.1), the top dimension of the impact phase (the social contract) seems to be the most developed, while the subordinate dimensions (science policy, university's organizational configuration, university strategy and university management) are still emerging. Naturally, the rest of this chapter will therefore also change perspective. We are no longer just learning from the past. Instead, we are using inspirational literature and our current experiences from practice to give our best predictions and solutions for the impact phase, which is still in the making.

In our view, the impact phase represents a new social contract between science and society. Science is now expected to produce and mobilize excellent and relevant knowledge that impacts and transforms society by solving pressing societal issues.

Major drivers appear to be the US, Australia, the European Union and the UK. Impact was one of three evaluation criteria (the two others had to do with excellence and implementation) for research proposals to Horizon 2020, the EU's latest research and innovation program (European Commission, 2017). Horizon Europe, the successor to Horizon 2020, will push the impact agenda even further. The program aims to solve global societal challenges by setting several societal missions achievable through research and innovation (European Commision, 2020). A similar view is found in the industrial strategy of Britain, which highlights more research and development as a way to address grand challenges of society (HM Government, 2017). In addition, the collective voices of 136 universities in the UK, Universities UK, named their strategic plan for 2018–23 "World-leading impact" (Universities UK, n.d.).

Some origins of the impact phase
Explaining the origin of the impact phase is naturally multifaceted. Its intellectual foundation seems to have developed in the 1990s, when the shift from the old *mode-1* to the new *mode-2* of knowledge production was conceptualized. In mode-2, knowledge is transdisciplinary instead of disciplinary and produced by multiple actors (also outside the university) with the intention of being applied in solving a particular problem (Gibbons et al., 1994).

Another important driver for the development of the impact phase was the experiences of the excellence phase. Toward the end of the excellence phase, Danish authorities concluded that the 2000s had seen a significant increase in knowledge exchange from university to society. However, the increase was driven by more collaborative research and innovation pro-jects between universities and companies, while the amount of technology transfers (licensing, patents selling) and start-ups had been modest (Styrelsen for Forskning og Innovation, 2014). An analysis from the independent Danish think tank DEA reached a similar conclusion:

> The analysis … concludes that the policies on the technology transfer initiative, to a great extent, have been based on unrealistic expectations of the direct economic value of university innovations, and that they have not sufficiently taken into account how universities and companies best enter into collaborations on development, transfer and utilization of research based knowledge and technology. (DEA, 2013, p. 4; our translation)

So, at the end of the excellence phase, the narrow focus on technology transfer (push–pull innovation) with the aim of direct economic commercialization was shelved. Instead, focus shifted to how universities could contribute to society through collaboration and acknowledg-ment of broader research impact.

Different kinds of impact

In order to pinpoint the concept of *impact*, it is useful to introduce the following distinctions from Pedersen (2017, pp. 4–6; our translations). The first distinction is between *academic impact*, which refers to the impact of research within the academic system, and *societal impact*, which refers to the societal impact of research in society. *Societal impact* can further be divided into *economic effects*, which refer to the economic return on investments in research for companies, regions or countries (e.g. Valero & Van Reenen, 2019), and *broader societal effects*, which refer to how research is absorbed and utilized in society, and how research has consequences for society and business in terms of changed opinions and practices.

One approach: measuring impact

One approach to impact is to focus on measuring it. This approach continues the performance measurement from the excellence phase. Today, the field of impact measurement has at least 14 specific methodologies at its disposal (Pedersen, 2017). One example is altmetric analysis of the broader societal impact of research on social media. Another example is assessment of the impact of a research project through impact case studies (Pedersen, 2017, pp. 27–8).

So far, measuring impact has proven difficult. As David Budtz Pedersen stresses: "A central observation in this report is that there are no simple shortcuts to effect measurements of research investments" (Pedersen, 2017, p. 3; our translation). Furthermore, when impact measurement is used prospectively (to evaluate the future impact of a given research project) the effect often seems to be speculations of potential impact. This leaves little attention to whether any real impact is actually created. This leads to another approach to impact, where the starting point is not to measure but rather to create impact.

A second approach: creating impact

The approach of creating impact is currently driven by universities such as Copenhagen Business School and The London School of Economics and Political Science, which set impact creation and societal transformation as a key strategic goal (CBS, 2020; LSE, 2020). For instance, the vision of Copenhagen Business School is to "… transform society with business by tackling challenges with curiosity, creative new ideas and collaborative engagement" (CBS, 2020, p. 3). Such statements reflect the idea that future legitimacy of universities also depends on their transformative impact on society.

The focus of the "creating impact" approach is the organizational actions required to create impact, rather than the administrative challenge of measuring it. Thus, not said, that "measuring impact" and "creating impact" are mutually exclusive. As impact is created, a need for measuring and documenting it will probably arise. But it will most likely be in that order: creating impact and then measuring it. Our hunch is that the approach of creating impact will dominate universities and their managers in the coming years.

One way of creating impact is commercialization in the private sector. Despite mixed experiences from the excellence phase, it is still a viable way for universities to create economic impact through technology transfer and entrepreneurial initiatives. In doing this, the lessons from the 2000s should be taken into account. Technology transfer and utilization of research inventions require a mature and binding partnership between the university and the company (DEA, 2013).

Another way is creating broader societal impact often through existing (private and public) organizations. This way is further split between two approaches. The first approach is creating impact inside the same organization that conducts the research (intra-organizational). For universities this means to utilize the research to make research-based education in the university. For university hospitals it is about adapting the research into clinical treatment of patients. The second approach is to create impact across organizations (inter-organizational). This approach acknowledges the university's responsibility for mobilizing research knowledge to impact practices in other organizations. The university can do this by entering and maintaining ecosystems with other organizations. We will elaborate further on ecosystems below.

The Risks of Impact Policies

In recent years, the question of evaluating research by its societal impact has gained significant political attention. While different countries have experimented with evaluation methods, the UK is a well-known example (McCowan, 2018). In 2014, impact was integrated as a criterion weighting 20% in the *Research Excellence Framework*, which is the UK's national assessment of research quality.[4] The information gathered was used by the funding bodies of England, Scotland, Wales and Northern Ireland to allocate research funds to higher education institutions (Pinar & Unlu, 2020; REF, 2014). The evaluation methodology was, for instance, impact case studies of concrete research projects. The Research Excellence Framework has succeeded in providing insights of the academic and societal impact of UK research, and it has resulted in a higher esteem of impact initiatives among researchers and institutions. However, the Research Excellence Framework has also been criticized for being too costly and for producing a "transfer-market" among UK universities, who recruited top scholars right before submission deadline to get a better evaluation score (Pedersen, 2017).

According to Tristan McCowan, the political impact agenda, as exemplified by the Research Excellence Framework and other initiatives, poses several serious challenges, which he sums up as "five perils" (McCowan, 2018). In short, they are (1) *The normative dimension*. The impact agenda risks pursuing a certain political or moral idea of the ideal society. (2) *Linear relationship*. The impact agenda risks simplifying the complex interrelations between science and society by using the one-way concept of "impact." (3) *Unpredictability and time lag*. The impact agenda risks seeking and prioritizing short-term impact from applied research at the expense of valuable and unpredictable long-term impact from basic research. (4) *Measurement*. The impact agenda tends to focus on trying to measure impact. But "… it is very hard to establish with certainty that a particular change in society is exclusively or even partly attributable to an action taken by a university" (McCowan, 2018, p. 290). (5) *Instrumentalization*. The impact agenda risks de-emphasizing the intrinsic value of research and education, which can lead to less autonomy and academic freedom.

In the coming years, impact policies will mature with regard to the definition of impact, the instruments used to achieve it, and – not least – how (or if) the risks of the impact agenda are mitigated. However, based on what we already know, the policies of the impact phase will most likely keep the university fixed in the vortex of society, but now with the additional expectation of mobilizing societal transformations (Figure 4.4).[5]

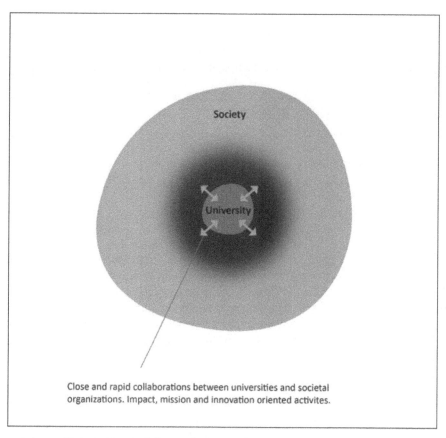

Close and rapid collaborations between universities and societal
organizations. Impact, mission and innovation oriented activites.

Figure 4.4　　*Universities mobilizing the societal transformation during the impact phase*
　　　　　　　(future)

The University as a Professional Bureaucracy 2.0

So far, we have seen how the shift from the classic phase to the excellence phase transformed
the classic university into a machine bureaucracy. Embarking on the impact phase, the university will most likely transform once more to accommodate the new expectations. In the
following section, we will attempt to outline a new organizational configuration for the university that we believe will enable it to produce societal impact as a core task. We name the new
organizational configuration of the university the *professional bureaucracy 2.0*. As the name
reveals, we are building on Mintzberg's (1983) legacy. The overall idea is to resurrect some
of the virtues and strengths of the professional bureaucracy, while compensating for its shortcomings in other ways than through the rules and procedures of the machine bureaucracy. Let
us start by outlining four key organizational capabilities of the professional bureaucracy 2.0.[6]

1.   The faculty must be brought into play
A key premise for the professional bureaucracy 2.0 is that research impact is created in the hands of, and depends on, the individual faculty member. Only they have the specialized knowledge and expertise to engage in a certain societal problem and create research impact. Therefore, the faculty must regain its lost autonomy and self-determination over the research process.

2.   Research must be transdisciplinary
Finding a cure for cancer or climate change does not necessarily respect the disciplinary and departmental boundaries of today's universities. The university must therefore be capable of conducting a transdisciplinary approach to research that transcends academic disciplines and integrates external non-academic stakeholders through common engagement in solving a societal issue (Hunt & Thornsbury, 2014).

3.   A new way of coordinating work
The professional bureaucracy 2.0 will use *strategic coordination* (our translation) to coordinate work (Barlebo Rasmussen, 2014, p. 128). Strategic coordination is the task of coordinating decentralized units' own initiatives with the overarching ambition of the university. Given the faculty's regained autonomy, strategic coordination should not be controlling. It is about formulating and maintaining an appealing overarching ambition that the faculty members voluntarily want to contribute to by aligning their own initiatives. Thus, strategic coordination is an ongoing management task of mediating and translating local strategic objectives (Barlebo Rasmussen, 2014).

4.   Engaging an ecosystem
In the professional bureaucracy 2.0, the university has to take responsibility for generating impact and innovation in surrounding organizations such as hospitals, schools, private companies, and so on. In other words, the university needs to open up. An approach to doing this is to design, facilitate and engage in *ecosystems* with external stakeholders (P. N. Andersen, 2020; Heaton, Siegel, & Teece, 2019; Markkula & Kune, 2015; Powell & Walsh, 2018). The ecosystem is an arena where academics and non-academic stakeholders can join forces in *co-creation* of knowledge, which is claimed to have a high potential for making societal impact (Greenhalgh, Jackson, Shaw, & Janamian, 2016). In other words, the ecosystem becomes an arena for creating value.

Strategizing the Creation of Impact

In the professional bureaucracy 2.0, university strategy will change to accommodate an evolving business model for the university. Let us explain. Strategy can be thought of as "… a means for reaching particular objectives" (Wit, 2017, p. 4). However, the question of which objectives the organization deems valuable might better be conceptualized by its *business model*. A business model "… describes the rationale of how an organization creates, delivers, and captures value" (Osterwalder & Pigneur, 2010, p. 14).

Up until today, many universities have, knowingly or unknowingly, been driven by the same business model of "climbing the ladder." Climbing the ladder refers to *The Carnegie*

Classification of Institutions of Higher Education, which was created in the USA in 1967. Originally, the purpose was to classify and stratify the US educational system to support plurality. However, as prestigious institutions were placed in the top category, the so-called "Carnegie ladder" was born. Since high ranking on the ladder meant more financing, institutions began to climb the ladder by imitating top institutions like Harvard. They did so by spending more money on research, adding programs and accepting more paying elite students (C. M. Christensen & Eyring, 2011). As a business model, the rationale of "climbing the ladder" is that the university exclusively generates value by producing world-leading excellent research and education – a remnant from the excellence phase.

In the impact phase, most universities cannot continue to rely solely on climbing the ladder. They will also need a business model where value is produced through creating societal impact, first because of uneven competition. A Danish medium-sized university has little chance of beating Harvard in research excellence due to a whole different financial scale and set-up – the Danish university needs another raison d'être. Second, the climbing-the-ladder model does not necessarily create value in ecosystems. Instead, value becomes more fluid since it depends on what is possible and desirable amongst the collaborating organizations. The impact phase therefore needs an approach to strategy that complies with a business model based on creating value in ecosystems. In the following, we outline four steps.

Step 1: A new collective impact ambition

The first step is to formulate a local *impact ambition* for the university that answers the question of "what kind of impact do we aspire to create?" It is important that this process involves all organizational layers of the university in an iterative top-down/bottom-up process. In addition, external stakeholders can also be involved in the process. By doing so, the external focus of step 4 (see below) will be incorporated from the outset. (For more on collective impact initiatives, see Kania & Kramer, 2011.)

Formulating an impact ambition initiates important reflections about what impact means for the university, and how the university stays relevant and legitimate to the surrounding society. It could begin by mapping the university's ongoing impact initiatives. Furthermore, the specific history and culture of the university, its existing positions of strength, external partnerships, current research profile and the needs of the surrounding region or nation should also be taken into account when making the impact ambition.

Step 2: Bottom-up impact initiatives

Following the new impact ambition, the next task is to start creating impact. It is now time for the faculty members to experiment with what impact means for them and how to make it. This will, and should be, a process of trial and error. The fuel for the faculty will be autonomy and professional back-and-forth with colleagues and the relevant leader.

Step 3: Strategic coordination of impact initiatives, teaching and basic research

When the faculty experiments with creating impact, it is time for management to use strategic coordination to coordinate two vital balances. First, the total portfolio of different impact initiatives should strike a balance that over time moves the university closer to achieving its impact ambition. Doing this requires continuous reporting on the progress of impact initiatives across the university, while still maintaining maximum autonomy for the faculty members.

A suitable tool for this is portfolio management (Bozeman & Rogers, 2001) based on quali-tative self-evaluation by the decentralized units. The second balance is between the portfolio of impact initiatives and the traditional operations of teaching students and conducting basic research. Impact initiatives and traditional operations should be seen as interdependent and not as opposites. To realize and maintain this in everyday life, approaches such as *organizational ambidexterity*, which addresses the challenge of exploring and exploiting simultaneously, can be useful (O'Reilly III & Tushman, 2013).

Step 4: Co-creating strategy
When the faculty members begin to initialize decentralized impact initiatives, they will form new connections and partnerships with external stakeholders. The ecosystem thus begins to develop. To realize the potential of the ecosystem, it is essential to formalize it by commit-ting to each other. This is done through mutual strategies, which transcends organizational boundaries. Typically, such strategies pinpoint how a faculty member or research group will collaborate with external stakeholders in addressing critical societal challenges over a longer period of time.

A close and binding relationship with external stakeholders naturally raises the question of academic freedom, which arguably has come under pressure in recent years (H. Andersen, 2019). *Politiken*, a major Danish newspaper, surveyed 1,200 researchers who had completed research-based reports and analyses for departments and government agencies – 92 of them had experienced that the authority edited their report before publication (*Politiken*, 2018). In such cases, the Head of Department must be on the side of science and the individual researcher to prevent suppression of basic academic freedom.

Managing the Creation of Impact

The professional bureaucracy 2.0 entails a new kind of university management that leans toward *leadership*.[7] In the following, we outline the most important aspects, as we see them.

1.   Seeing and coordinating the bigger picture
To see the bigger picture is to understand the plurality of different demands, needs and ration-ales in which the university is embedded. These different demands often result in struggles and tensions. For instance, when leading faculty members, tension between autonomy and control is always prevalent. On an organizational level, tensions emerge between departments, disci-plines and managerial layers – or between logics from the classic phase, excellence phase and the impact phase. And on the interorganizational level, the ecosystem is an arena for clashes between the different rationales of societal systems (e.g. science, politics, business and health care) (Luhmann, 2016). Without seeing the bigger picture, the manager is blind to the context in which impact is created.

In the professional bureaucracy 2.0, the manager will use strategic coordination in order to create coherence across the many demands. One way to do this is to conduct *both/and* leader-ship (Smith, Lewis, & Tushman, 2016), which rejects either/or choices of conflicting values, strategies and demands. Instead, pluralism and many truths are embraced.

2.   Less hierarchical top-down management

Due to the challenges of measuring impact, as mentioned above, it is difficult to control the creation of impact through hierarchical top-down management tools such as performance measurement. In fact, top-down management even risks being counter-productive when creating impact, because, as mentioned before, external motivation structures crowd out the faculty members' inner motivation. Therefore, management in the professional bureaucracy 2.0 needs to be less hierarchical and top-down than in the machine bureaucracy. Furthermore, the technostructure, which supports top-down management, will also shrink in size and importance. Instead, management will emphasize a bottom-up approach, where faculty is encouraged and supported in creating impact.

3.   Mobilize bottom-up

A new primary management task in the professional bureaucracy 2.0 will be to mobilize the faculty to experiment with impact initiatives. Mobilizing is quite the opposite of top-down management. Where the top-down approach manages at a distance, mobilization is about engaging with faculty members. It is about listening and understanding but also challenging their assumptions about impact of research. Such engagement requires a new focus on how articulation and everyday actions form sensemaking processes among the faculty members (Hammer & Høpner, 2019).

4.   A new "strategic" culture

In the classic phase, management was based on a "strategic" culture that pushed the university to "climb the ladder." In the professional bureaucracy 2.0, management will once again be based on a strong strategic culture and socialization. But now, the culture must influence the faculty to engage with the surrounding ecosystem and create impact. Thinking about and initializing impact initiatives should be the norm rather than the exception.

The Head of Department as the Key Transformational Leader

As we have demonstrated above, transforming the university into the impact phase requires change in its organizational configuration, strategy and management. Let us summarize. The university requires new organizational capabilities as the professional bureaucracy 2.0, including more autonomy for the faculty, transdisciplinary research, strategic coordination, and engagement in ecosystems. The university should also adopt a new approach to strategy based on a collective impact ambition geared toward creating value in ecosystems. Finally, the university must adopt a new form of management that sees the bigger picture, applies less top-down management, mobilizes faculty bottom-up, and which is not only tied to the manager but also works through a strategic culture. The common thread in these changes is the faculty members. Without their engagement, transformation into the impact phase will not succeed. Since their closest leader is the Head of Department, we find it natural to appoint the Head of Department as the *Key Transformational Leader* of the impact phase.

We have chosen the concept of "transformational" since it refers to the classic distinction between *transactional* and *transformational* leadership (Bass, 1990), which we find useful in summarizing the shift from the excellence phase to the impact phase. While the transactional leader manages through a "carrot and stick" approach, the transformational leader leads by working with a vision and a mission, gaining trust and engaging with the employees (Bass, 1990). Adopting this role as the Key Transformational Leader will be a fundamental change for the Head of Department in several dimensions (Table 4.2).

Table 4.2   Changes in the role as the Head of Department

The Head of Department	Classic phase	Excellence phase	Impact phase
Orientation	Downwards to the faculty	Upwards to own hierarchical leaders	Downwards to the faculty and outwards to ecosystem
Source of legitimacy	Democratically elected	Hierarchically appointed	Delivers on expectations of society
Type of management	Laissez-faire	Transactional management	Transformational leadership
Role in changes	None	Executing and implementing political reforms	Transforming departmental culture, mobilizing bottom-up impact initiatives and building ecosystems
Archetype	*Primus inter pares* of a collective of autonomous faculty members	"Overseer" managing a research factory	"Key Transformational Leader" of societal and departmental transformations

Seven key tasks for the Head of Department as the Key Transformational Leader

To begin a transformation into the professional bureaucracy 2.0 and the impact phase, we have concretized seven key tasks that the Head of Department can begin with in the new role as the Key Transformational Leader.

Task 1: Substantiate the "why"
The Head of Department should substantiate why the department is required to move into the impact phase. This could be done at a department seminar. Here, the emergence of the new social contract between science and society could be addressed. Furthermore, a prominent external stakeholder could also be invited to give a presentation on why it is important to activate the knowledge and research from the department – seen from the perspective of society.

Moreover, such a seminar must not fail to address the pressing question of why the individual academic should pursue impact when it does not further their international career. This question can be discussed in a productive manner by drawing on the distinction between *locals* and *cosmopolitans*, which represents different organizational identities (Gouldner, 1957). At the university, locals focus on contributing to the region and country – creating positive societal impact often sounds meaningful to them. On the other hand, cosmopolitans perceive science as an international system. They follow the international norms and rules of research publication, which rarely acknowledge societal impact. However, cosmopolitans should be made aware that societal impact provides legitimacy and funding for universities. Without this, the cosmopolitans cannot thrive.

Task 2: Working with culture

The Head of Department should lead a new culture in which impact is seen as an additional obligation for the faculty. This should definitely not be done by forcing the new culture through top-down instruments, or even worse, by handing out coffee mugs with printed cultural buzzwords on. A better approach would be to articulate the need for a new culture (the why) in a way that also respects the old culture. Moreover, the Head of Department should be the first to admit their own wrongdoings of the past on behalf of the management, if the needed reconciliation between faculty and management should be achieved. It is also important to stress that the future will not be more of the same. Instead, the faculty will regain structural autonomy if they also take responsibility for creating impact.

In practice, the new culture can be articulated when the opportunity arises: at seminars, job interviews, staff development interviews, in the cafeteria, and so on. Doing this will spark feelings and arguments, which can be handled by referring to the aforementioned "why" and by applying the aforementioned "both/and" approach: Creating impact will not mean the end of basic science, but we need to find a new balance between impact-oriented research and basic research – together.

Task 3: Developing new competences for the faculty

It is important that the faculty members feel they have the competences needed for creating impact. In practice, the Head of Department can join forces with other departments in the university (e.g. HR) to develop courses on research management for junior researchers. Relevant topics could be media training, project and innovation management, legal and funding support, and how to build internal and external partnerships. A case in point is the new UCPH Forward program at the University of Copenhagen (KU, 2020).

Task 4: Change management capabilities

The Head of Department must be capable of exercising change management. This entails two vital capabilities. The first capability is knowledge and understanding of change management as a management discipline (e.g. Kotter, 2020). This addresses questions such as: How do humans react to change? How to communicate change? How to plan for changes in phases? The other capability deals with the Head of Department's own personality and mind. Am I ready for change? Can I handle the strong cultural and emotional reactions followed by change? From where do I get my energy and my foundation – is it from other managers? My own boss? Developing these capabilities requires more than following a course – continuous everyday practice over a longer period of time is often needed.

Task 5: Ongoing strategic coordination

The Head of Department must adopt the new task of continuously coordinating the different impact initiatives to align with the overall impact ambition. This requires a finger firmly on the pulse to sense what is going on. To do this in practice, the Head of Department will have to reorder her priorities. More time should be spent with internal and external stakeholders, students, her own faculty, and other departments at the university. Less time should be spent on hierarchical management work. This requires streamlining or discontinuing the heavy reporting and control from the excellence phase. The Head of Department cannot do this alone – senior management must be involved in this change.

Task 6: Building infrastructure and portfolio management
Besides the informal coordination, the Head of Department also needs to build a portfolio management, which, more formally, is capable of mapping and managing the entire portfolio of impact initiatives. The portfolio management is used to pick and manage the pipeline of research projects, so more research is new, original, excellent, and at the same time has societal impact. It is vital that the portfolio management system allows for an open and objective debate amongst research leaders, and occasionally external stakeholders, about which projects should continue.

Task 7: Building the ecosystem
The ecosystem will not grow by itself. The Head of Department must take an active role in building it. This includes "… the entrepreneurial ability to identify emerging new fields and invest in research around them, build partnerships to create and maintain ecosystem infrastructure, and help to bring about an alignment of interests among stakeholders" (Heaton et al., 2019, p. 935). In practice, this implies spending more time with external stakeholders and mobilizing the department's research leaders, students and administration. It might even be necessary to establish a new position as vice Head of Department for impact, innovation and external relations.

   With these seven key tasks, we have tried to map some of the first steps on the Head of Department's road toward becoming the Key Transformational Leader of the emerging impact phase. Everyone can see that it will not be easy. In the impact phase, the Head of Department will be piggy in the middle – mediating the needs of society and the faculty. And while the Head of Department must take the initiative, it is up to senior management of the university to pave the way. This is done through clever transformational and adaptive strategic leadership (Uhl-Bien & Arena, 2017) – but that is another story.

NOTES

1.   This chronology is naturally a simplification. In many institutions, the three phases live side by side, resulting in cultural and structural mixes.
2.   A variation of Figure 4.2 is also used in Barlebo Rasmussen (2014, p. 121). The figure is reproduced in this chapter with permission from the publisher.
3.   A variation of Figure 4.3 is also used in Barlebo Rasmussen (2014, p. 121). The figure is reproduced in this chapter with permission from the publisher.
4.   The Research Excellence Framework defines impact in the following way: "'Impact' is any effect on, change or benefit to the economy, society, culture, public policy or services, health, the environment or quality of life, beyond academia" (REF, 2014, p. 6).
5.   A variation of Figure 4.4 is also used in Barlebo Rasmussen (2014, p. 121). The figure is reproduced in this chapter with permission from the publisher.
6.   See Barlebo Rasmussen (2014) for an elaboration on the professional bureaucracy 2.0.
7.   Dr. Ali Algahtani differentiates management and leadership in the following way: "Management skills are used to plan, build, and direct organizational systems to accomplish missions and goals, while leadership skills are used to focus on a potential change by establishing direction, aligning people, and motivating and inspiring" (Algahtani, 2014, p. 71).

REFERENCES

Algahtani, D. A. (2014). Are leadership and management different? A review. *Journal of Management Policies and Practices, 2*(3), 71–82.

Andersen, H. (2019). Problemer med forskningsfrihed. *Samfundsøkonomen, 2*, 59–70.

Andersen, P. N. (2020). Ecosystems are tools for transformative change. *Forskningspolitikk. Fagbladet for Forskning, Høyere Utdanning Og Innovasjon, 1*.

Barlebo Rasmussen, S. (2014). *Potentialeledelse: Om strategisk ledelse i fagprofessionelle organisationer* (2nd edition). Barlebo Forlag.

Bass, B. M. (1990). From transactional to transformational leadership: learning to share the vision. *Organizational Dynamics, 18*(3), 19–31.

Belfiore, E. (2015). 'Impact', 'value' and 'bad economics': making sense of the problem of value in the arts and humanities. *Arts and Humanities in Higher Education, 14*(1), 95–110.

Benneworth, P., & Jongbloed, B. W. (2010). Who matters to universities? A stakeholder perspective on humanities, arts and social sciences valorisation. *Higher Education, 59*, 567–88.

Bornmann, L. (2013). What is societal impact of research and how can it be assessed? A literature survey. *Journal of the American Society for Information Science and Technology, 64*(2), 217–33.

Bozeman, B., & Rogers, J. (2001). Strategic management of government-sponsored R&D portfolios. *Environment and Planning C: Government and Policy, 19*, 413–42.

Bush, V. (1945). *Science, the Endless Frontier*. Washington, DC.

CBS (2020). *CBS Strategy*. Copenhagen Business School.

Christensen, C. M., & Eyring, H. J. (2011). *The Innovative University: Changing the DNA of Higher Education from the Inside Out*. San Francisco, CA: Jossey-Bass.

Christensen, J. G. (2012). Magt og management på universiteterne. In J. Faye & D. B. Pedersen (eds.), *Hvordan styres videnssamfundet? Demokrati, ledelse og organisering* (1st edition). Frederiksberg C: Nyt fra Samfundsvidenskaberne, 237–262.

Christiansen, F. V., Harboe, T., Horst, S., Krogh, L., & Sarauw, L. L. (2013). Udviklingstendenser i universitetets rolle. In L. Rienecker, P. S. Jørgensen, J. Dolin, & G. H. Ingerslev (eds.), *Universitetspædagogik* (1st edition). Samfundslitteratur.

Dahler-Larsen, P. (2012). Betydningen af bibliometriske indikatorer. In J. Faye & D. B. Pedersen (eds.), *Hvordan styres videnssamfundet? Demokrati, ledelse og organisering* (1st edition). Frederiksberg C: Nyt fra Samfundsvidenskaberne, 337–357.

DEA (2013). *Fra Forskning til Faktura – hvad kan vi lære af ti års forsøg på at tjene penge på forskning?* København K.

European Commission (2002). *Presidency Conclusions Barcelona European Council 15 and 16 March 2002*.

European Commission (2017). Horizon 2020 – Work Programme 2018-2020 H. Evaluation rules. In *Extract from Part 19 – Commission Decision C(2017)7124*.

European Commission (2020). Missions in Horizon Europe. Retrieved October 17, 2020, from https://ec.europa.eu/info/horizon-europe-next-research-and-innovation-framework-programme/missions-horizon-europe_en.

European Parliament (2000). Lisbon European Council 23 and 24 March 2000 Presidency Conclusions. Retrieved October 17, 2020, from https://www.europarl.europa.eu/summits/lis1_en.htm.

Faye, J., & Pedersen, D. B. (2012). Videnssamfundets dilemmaer. In J. Faye & D. B. Pedersen (eds.), *Hvordan styres videnssamfundet? Demokrati, ledelse og organisering* (1st edition). Frederiksberg C: Nyt fra Samfundsvidenskaberne, 11–32.

Finansministeriet (2006). *Aftale om udmøntning af globaliseringspuljen. Opfølgning på velfærdsaftalen. Opfølgning på aftale om fremtidig indvandring*. København K.

Frederiksen, L. F., Hansson, F., & Wenneberg, S. B. (2003). The agora and the role of research evaluation. *Evaluation, 9*(2), 149–72.

Frey, B. S., & Jegen, R. (2001). Motivation crowding theory. *Journal of Economic Surveys, 15*(5), 589–611.

Georgellis, Y., Iossa, E., & Tabvuma, V. (2011). Crowding out intrinsic motivation in the public sector. *Journal of Public Administration Research and Theory, 21*(3), 473–93.

Gibbons, M., Limoges, C., Nowotny, H., Schwartzmann, S., Scott, P., & Trow, M. (1994). *The New Production of Knowledge: The Dynamics of Science and Research in Contemporary Societies*. London: Sage.

Gouldner, A. W. (1957). Cosmopolitans and locals: toward an analysis of latent social roles. I. *Administrative Science Quarterly*, *2*(3), 281–306.

Greenhalgh, T., Jackson, C., Shaw, S., & Janamian, T. (2016). Achieving research impact through co-creation in community-based health services: literature review and case study. *The Milbank Quarterly*, *94*(2), 392–429.

Greenhalgh, T., Raftery, J., Hanney, S., & Glover, M. (2016). Research impact: a narrative review. *BMC Medicine*, *14*(78). Accessed (18 September 20201): https://bmcmedicine.biomedcentral.com/track/pdf/10.1186/s12916-016-0620-8.pdf.

Hammer, S., & Høpner, J. (2019). *Meningsskabelse, organisering og ledelse: en introduktion til Weicks univers* (2nd edition). Samfundslitteratur.

Hansen, H. F., Lind, J. K., & Stage, A. K. (2020). Changing managerial roles in Danish universities. *Science and Public Policy*, *47*(4), 447–57.

Head, B. W., & Alford, J. (2015). Wicked problems: implications for public policy and management. *Administration & Society*, *47*(6), 711–39.

Heaton, S., Siegel, D. S., & Teece, D. J. (2019). Universities and innovation ecosystems: a dynamic capabilities perspective. *Industrial and Corporate Change*, *28*(4), 921–39.

HM Government (2017). *Industrial strategy: Building a Britain Fit for the Future*. Accessed (18 September 2021): https://www.gov.uk/government/publications/industrial-strategy-building-a-britain-fit-for-the-future.

Hood, C. (1991). A public management for all seasons? *Public Administration*, *69*(1), 3–19.

Hunt, F., & Thornsbury, S. (2014). Facilitating transdisciplinary research in an evolving approach to science. *Open Journal of Social Sciences*, *2*, 340–51.

Kania, J., & Kramer, M. (2011). Collective impact. *Stanford Social Innovation Review*, *Winter*. Accessed (18 September 2021): https://ssir.org/articles/entry/collective_impact.

Kotter (2020). 8-STEP PROCESS. Retrieved October 17, 2020, from https://www.kotterinc.com/8-steps-process-for-leading-change/.

KU (2006). *Københavns Universitets udviklingskontrakt 2006–2008*. København K.

KU (2007). *Københavns Universitets udviklingskontrakt 2008–2010*. København K.

KU (2020). UCPH forward. Retrieved October 25, 2020, from https://jobportal.ku.dk/ku-som-arbejdsplads/ucph-forward/.

LSE (2020). LSE 2030. Retrieved October 17, 2020, from http://www.lse.ac.uk/2030.

Luhmann, N. (2016). *Samfundets samfund* (1st edition). København: Hans Reitzels Forlag.

Markkula, M., & Kune, H. (2015). Making smart regions smarter: smart specialization and the role of universities in regional innovation ecosystems. *Technology Innovation Management Review*, *5*(10), 7–15.

Matt, M., Gaunand, A., Joly, P.-B., & Colinet, L. (2017). Opening the black box of impact – ideal-type impact pathways in a public agricultural research organization. *Research Policy*, *46*(1), 207–18.

McCowan, T. (2018). Five perils of the impact agenda in higher education. *London Review of Education*, *16*(2), 279–95.

Mintzberg, H. (1983). *Structure in Fives: Designing Effective Organizations*. Upper Saddle River, NJ: Prentice Hall.

O'Reilly III, C. A., & Tushman, M. L. (2013). Organizational ambidexterity: past, present, and future. *The Academy of Management Perspectives*, *27*(4), 324–38.

Osterwalder, A., & Pigneur, Y. (2010). *Business Model Generation: A Handbook for Visionaries, Game Changers, and Challengers*. Hoboken, NJ: John Wiley & Sons.

Pedersen, D. B. (2017). *IMPACT: Redskaber og metoder til måling af forskningens gennemslagskraft*. Odense: Det Frie Forskningsråd.

Pedersen, D. B., Grønvad, J. F., & Hvidtfeldt, R. (2020). Methods for mapping the impact of social sciences and humanities – a literature review. *Research Evaluation*, *29*(1), 4–21.

Pinar, M., & Unlu, E. (2020). Evaluating the potential effect of the increased importance of the impact component in the Research Excellence Framework of the UK. *British Educational Research Journal*, *46*(1), 140–60.

Politiken (2018). *Forskere svarer: vi er udsat for politisk pres*. Accessed (18 September 2021): https://politiken.dk/indland/politik/art6321797/Forskere-svarer-Vi-er-udsat-for-politisk-pres.

Powell, P., & Walsh, A. (2018). Mutualising the university: achieving community impact through an ecosystem. *International Review of Education, 64*, 563–83.

REF (2014). *Research Excellence Framework 2014: The results*. https://www.ref.ac.uk/2014/pubs/201401/.

Regeringen (2003). *Nye veje mellem forskning og erhverv – fra tanke til faktura*.

Regeringen (2006). *Fremgang, fornyelse og tryghed: strategi for Danmark i den globale økonomi – de vigtigste initiativer*.

Retsinformation (1999). Lov om opfindelser ved offentlige forskningsinstitutioner (LOV nr 347 af 02/06/1999). Retrieved August 9, 2020, from https://www.retsinformation.dk/eli/lta/1999/347.

Retsinformation (2003). Lov om universiteter (universitetsloven) (LOV nr 403 af 28/05/2003). Retrieved August 8, 2020, from https://www.retsinformation.dk/eli/lta/2003/403.

Smith, W. K., Lewis, M. W., & Tushman, M. L. (2016). "Both/and" leadership. *Harvard Business Review* (May). Accessed (18 September 2021): https://hbr.org/2016/05/both-and-leadership.

Stage, A. K., & Aagaard, K. (2020). Danske universiteter under forandring: konvergens og differentiering. *Forskningspolitikk. Fagbladet for Forskning, Høyere Utdanning Og Innovasjon, 1*.

Styrelsen for Forskning og Innovation (2014). *Vidensamarbejde under lup – evaluering af universiteternes erhvervssamarbejde og teknologioverførsel*. København K: Styrelsen for Forskning og Innovation.

Tidd, J. (2006). *A Review of Innovation Models*. Imperial College London.

Uddannelses- og Forskningsministeriet (2009). Universiteternes forskningsresultater belønnes. Retrieved October 17, 2020, from https://ufm.dk/forskning-og-innovation/statistik-og-analyser/den-bibliometriske-forskningsindikator/nyt/nyt-om-den-bibliometriske-indikator/universiteternes-forskningsresultater-belonnes2adc691f346c42a79662d32c44193e43.

Uddannelses- og Forskningsministeriet. (2020). Udviklingskontrakter 2006–2017. Retrieved April 13, 2020, from https://ufm.dk/uddannelse/videregaende-uddannelse/universiteter/styring-og-ansvar/udviklingskontrakter.

Uhl-Bien, M., & Arena, M. (2017). Complexity leadership: enabling people and organizations for adaptability. *Organizational Dynamics, 46*(1), 9–20.

Universities UK (n.d.). Strategic plan 2018–23: world-leading impact. Accessed (18 September 2021): https://www.universitiesuk.ac.uk/about/Documents/uuk-strategic-plan-18-23.pdf

Valero, A., & Van Reenen, J. (2019). The economic impact of universities: evidence from across the globe. *Economics of Education Review, 68*, 53–67.

Videnskabsministeriet (2004). *Evaluering af forskerpatentloven*. Accessed (18 September 2021): https://ufm.dk/publikationer/2004/evaluering-af-forskerpatentloven.

Wenneberg, S. B. (2002). Forskningsledelse som tillidsvækkende sammenkobling mellem samfund og videnskab. In F. Hansson & B. H. Jørgensen (eds.), *Forskningens dilemmaer: en debatbog om ledelse og evaluering af forskning* (1st edition, pp. 23–42). Frederiksberg C: Samfundslitteratur.

Wit, B. de (2017). *Strategy: An International Perspective* (6th edition). Andover: Cengage Learning EMEA.

5. Leading with purpose: developing the first business school for public good

Martin Kitchener

Purpose is as fundamental to an organization as it is to individuals. (Big Innovation Centre, 2016: 5)

INTRODUCTION

Although university business schools have been heralded as the success story of twentieth-century higher education (Thomas, 2017), they have also been criticized for sacrificing the pursuit of 'higher goals' (Khurana, 2007) to achieve outcomes such as student fee income, graduate salary premia, accreditations, and rankings (Parker, 2018). Similarly, corporations have been reproached for prioritizing profit over their purpose, or the reason for which they were created or exist (British Academy [BA], 2019). While some leading business school academics play a leading role within a nascent social movement that calls for corporations to (re)place purpose before profit (Hollensbe et al., 2014; Mayer, 2018), they have not yet issued a similar prescription to business schools.

In this chapter, I present an analytical autoethnographic (Anderson, 2006) account of my attempt, as department head (Dean), to lead a process of purposeful change at Cardiff Business School (CARBS) in the United Kingdom (UK). The chapter is presented in four main sections. It begins with my characterization of business schools as educational establishments in urgent need of repurposing. In the second section, I introduce the corporate purpose literature and synthesize from it three approaches suggested to support the development of purposeful organizations: the chief purpose officer role (CPO), purpose statements, and multi-capital reporting. In the third section, I describe the role these approaches played in the processes of organizational change at CARBS through which it became the first business school focused on enhancing public good. The chapter concludes with some reflections and lessons that may be useful for academic leaders wishing to develop purposeful university departments.

BUSINESS SCHOOLS: 'SUCCESSFUL' UNIVERSITY DEPARTMENTS IN NEED OF REPURPOSING

By 2017, the international field of business schools had swelled to nearly 13,000 in number, generating £400 billion in annual teaching revenues, and educating close to 20 per cent of all students in higher education (Parker, 2018). Despite these indicators of 'success', business schools have been accused of losing sight of their 'higher goals' such as the founding aim of some of the first North American business schools (e.g. Harvard and Wharton) to produce a responsible, reflexive and insightful management cadre (Khurana, 2007).

There is, of course, significant variation among the world's many business schools and especially between: (a) the majority that is university-based, and the minority of 'independents', and (b) a United States tradition, and a European variant that is more pluralistic and interdisciplinary (Kaplan, 2018). Despite this organizational heterogeneity, recent studies report convergence around an emphasis on the achievement of outcomes such as student fee income, graduate salary premia, accreditations and rankings (Arielli et al., 2016). This increasingly standard model of business school operation has attracted the set of criticisms that is summarized in Table 5.1.

Table 5.1   Criticisms of business schools by function

Function	Criticism	Indicative Sources
Teaching & Learning	Disciplinary-based and privileges the creation of (narrower) shareholder value over (broader) stakeholder value	Fotaki & Prasad (2015)
Research	Market-driven & conducted within a single discipline, e.g. economics or marketing	Ghoshal (2005), Bennis & O'Toole (2005)
Engagement	Focus on a narrow set of elite partners, e.g. large corporations & professional bodies	Khurana (2007)
Governance	Prioritization of outcomes	Arielli et al. (2016)
	Few attempts to develop the progressive management approaches that some schools teach, e.g. collaborative leadership	Archer & Cameron (2008), Parker (2018), Harley (2019)

Fuelled by the concerns summarized in Table 5.1, senior management academics from around the globe warn that business schools have "lost their way" (Bennis & O'Toole, 2005: 93) and face a "crisis of confidence" (Harley, 2019: 286). One leading British management scholar recently attracted significant media coverage for his suggestion that the condition of business schools is so acute that they should all be 'shut down' (Parker, 2018). Despite both the wide-ranging critiques of business schools, and their stated concern for organizational innovation, there has been very limited discussion of their purpose (Thomas & Starkey, 2019) and little fundamental change in their structures or operations (Thomas, 2017). For those business school leaders who realize that their schools are "lost", it is unclear in which direction they might "head" (Alajoutsijarvi et al., 2018: 219).

In the past, when organizational leaders found themselves in positions similar to those now faced by business school deans, many tried to rally their troops by pointing out that they all stood on a burning platform and needed to 'adapt or perish'. In contrast, a nascent corporate purpose reform movement argues that a more effective way to lead and motivate is not through fear, but by inculcating in colleagues a higher, clearer sense of their contribution to what the organization does, and why and how they do it; in other words, by giving them a sense of purpose (Harvard Business Review Analytic Services and EY [HBR/EY], 2015). The next section elaborates this concept of organizational purpose.

ORGANIZATIONAL PURPOSE

In the current political economy of structural weaknesses in capitalism, global challenges (such as sustainability), and reduced public trust in firms' behaviour, a reform movement argues that corporations should prioritize the pursuit of purpose over the achievement of outcomes such as profit (BA, 2018, 2019; BIC, 2016; EY Beacon Institute, 2016; Mayer, 2018). Although the academic wing of this movement has roots in the stakeholder (rather than shareholder) approach to strategic management (Freeman, 1984), it has more recently been led by accountants including Colin Mayer. His historical analyses of corporate governance (Mayer, 2013, 2018) report that following 4,000 years of operating purposeful and multi-faceted organizational models, many businesses transformed into a single-focused and self-interested entity following Friedman's (1970) doctrine that businesses exist *solely* to maximize shareholder value (profit). Mayer argues that as awareness of the damaging economic, social and environmental consequences of that entity has grown, the corporation should return to its original purpose of 'solving the problems of people and planet profitably'. In a similar vein, Alex Edmans (2020) contends that the purpose of corporations should be to create value for society – and by doing so, increase profits as a by-product.

In addition to this case for purpose to act as the "guiding star" directing corporate action (EY Beacon Institute, 2016: 11), reformers point to an increasing body of evidence demonstrating that 'purpose companies' deliver enhanced performance through mechanisms such as improved recruitment, retention and motivation of employees, less adversarial industrial relations, and greater resilience in the face of external shocks (BIC, 2016, 2017; Henderson & Van Den Steen, 2015; Hollensbe et al., 2014). Given this evidence, it is perhaps surprising that (a) corporate reformers acknowledge a current shortage of exemplar purposeful corporations, and (b) I can find no examples of purposeful change in higher education generally, or business schools more specifically. In the absence of cases of purposeful *organizations*, attention has rested on purposeful *activity* at 'pioneer' corporations including Unilever under Paul Polman (BIC, 2017), Handelsbanken (Rodriguez & Bharadwaj, 2017), Anglian Water (BA, 2019), and the John Lewis Partnership (Storey & Salaman, 2017).

(Re)Purposing Organizations

Building from the arguments and emerging evidence outlined above, much of the policy work of the corporate reform movement has concentrated on proposals for a new institutional framework comprising innovations in ownership models, corporate governance, tax, regulation and investment (BA, 2019). In addition to these institutional-level prescriptions, three approaches to developing purposeful organizations have been proposed that may be relevant for lost business schools.

First, for purposeful governance to be effective, organizations must be clear about their raison d'être (reason for being) and articulate it within a stakeholder-inclusive 'statement of purpose' that defines the positive contribution to society it will make (Eccles et al., 2020). This form of organizational statement of benefit 'for someone else' can be distinguished clearly from statements of corporate attributes such as (a) vision, typically an expression of what an organization wishes to be like at some point in the future, (b) mission, describing the 'road' to achieving the vision, and (c) values, describing a desired culture (Kenny, 2014). Earlier management scholarship holds that statements of organizational purpose should be distinctive and be sufficiently compelling and inspiring to convince stakeholders that their interests are served within the necessary trade-offs in which they have to make compromises and contributions towards the common cause (Freeman, 1984).

Second, building on established management research showing that leadership is crucial in all organizational change, the EY Beacon Institute's (2016: 14) review of the purpose literature surfaced a strong emphasis on *the* senior leader as "purpose champion". In an alternative approach, the contemporary business press reports the emergence of a specialized CPO role and suggests that it helps the development and leadership of purposeful organizations (Biderman-Gross, 2020). Common activities among early CPOs include efforts to inspire purposeful innovation from colleagues, and to report aligned activity upwards internally, and to external audiences (Izzo & Vanderwielen, 2018). Similarly, studies of attempts to introduce values/purpose-driven change in public service settings highlight the benefits of collaborative leadership approaches (Archer & Cameron, 2008) and the need for repeated 'hands-on' (Ayers, 2019) interactions between leaders and a wide variety of stakeholders, some of whom may not (initially or ever) share a belief in the desirability, or efficacy, of purposeful or values-based change (Moore, 1995).

Third, to help address the tendency for an implementation gap to emerge between espoused strategy (e.g. purpose statements) and enacted activity, management research has demonstrated the importance of the public reporting of purpose-related data, and signing up to voluntary codes such as the UN Global Compact (Nohria and Khurana, 2010). Similarly, the corporate reform movement recommends that organizational performance should be measured as 'progress towards purpose' (BA, 2019; EY Beacon Institute, 2016; HBR/EY, 2015). This involves extending beyond standard financial reporting approaches to include the production and usage of a broad range of capitals including human, intellectual, natural, social, material and financial (Mayer, 2018; Stroehle et al., 2018).

DEVELOPING A PURPOSEFUL BUSINESS SCHOOL

Having introduced the case for purposeful organizational change and outlined three approaches to help its implementation, I now explain their role in the following case study of change at CARBS. The research approach that I employed to produce the case is "analytic autoethnography" (Anderson, 2006: 378) which combines the following five key features: (1) 'complete member' researcher status, which is contrasted with ethnographers whose participation in the field is temporary and/or partial, (2) analytic reflexivity, (3) narrative visibility of the researcher, (4) theoretical analysis, and (5) discussion of case with informants and critical friends.

My engagement with the empirical world combined my role as 'complete member' (Head of School, leading a change process) with my scholarly interests in public services management. It was through these connections to social science theory that I have sought analytical reflexivity in order to develop understanding of purposeful leadership of academic departments. Of course, my participation rather than analysis dominated through the period of change that I report. It was then retrospectively complemented with the reflection and analysis reported in this chapter. That process of analytic autoethnography followed the approach outlined by Learmonth and Humphreys (2011: 114) in that my narrative was developed, initially from memory, and subsequently through retrospective analysis of data including meeting notes and internal documents. In addition, and reflecting Anderson's (2006) fourth feature of analytic autoethnography, I revised the case study iteratively through discussions with people who were part of the 'field', and participants at presentations I gave to various research seminars. Of course, those discussions did not produce a single shared narrative, and I report some of the divergences of view in the case below (e.g. Marinetto & Dallyn, 2017). While I am not claiming my view is 'the truth', I refer to reports and activities that are described on publicly available websites in order that readers can see more of what has been done. As is the case with all forms of autoethnography, I recognize that I am part of the representational processes in which I am engaging and part of the story I am telling (Atkinson et al., 2003).

Throughout the case reported here, my engagement with the empirical world combined my 'complete membership' role, as a Dean leading a change process, with my scholarly interest in public management (Kitchener, 2002; Kitchener et al., 2000). From the outset, my research background sensitized me to the political (Moore, 1995) and collaborative (Archer & Cameron, 2008) leadership work required for value-based change processes in public services. It later provided the basis of my initial analytical reflexivity directed towards the process reported here (Anderson, 2006). My attention was only later drawn to organizational purpose scholarship when I visited Said Business School at the University of Oxford for my, post-leadership, sabbatical for the academic year 2019–20.[1] Most importantly for this chapter, my engagement with Colin Mayer and his colleagues led me to start thinking of the CARBS change process in terms of organizational purpose.

The following account of my leadership of a purposeful academic change process summarizes a more detailed account with a different focus (Weberian modes of rationality) that was produced for a specialist business school readership (Kitchener & Delbridge, 2020). This report is presented in three parts. It begins with a brief introduction to the context of the case. I then explain how my adaptation of the CPO role involved me conceptualizing and articulating a purpose statement for a business school, from Brewer's (2013) work on the public value of social science. In the third part, I explain how my understanding of political (Moore, 1995) and collaborative leadership (Archer & Cameron, 2008) underpinned my approach to inspiring colleagues to develop purposeful innovations across the School's teaching research, governance and engagement activities.

Setting the Scene

In the summer of 2012, I was serving as CARBS' professor of public services management and the School's senior management team (SMT) lead for external relations. Our parent university (Cardiff) had just appointed a new Vice Chancellor (VC, akin to the president role at other universities). He quickly introduced a new corporate strategy to achieve the stated outcome of achieving a top 100 university world ranking (Cardiff University, 2012). Following a standard New Public Management (NPM) strategic playbook (Kitchener, 2002; Kitchener et al., 2000), this outcome was to be achieved through a combination of (a) enforcing managerial control over professional (academic) work through structural centralization, and (b) monitoring progress through key performance indicators (KPIs).

At Cardiff University, this managerialist agenda was prosecuted by merging all 27 academic schools (that had previously reported directly to the VC) into three colleges and subjecting them to a set of KPIs including income growth targets. In October 2012, I was appointed Dean of CARBS after the previous incumbent became head of the College to which the School had just been subjugated. I applied for the role because I was interested in introducing a values-based strategy (Moore, 1995) and collaborative leadership model (Archer & Cameron, 2008) in contrast to the outcomes-based strategic approaches that I had been researching. However, the first task assigned to me by the Head of College was to design a school strategy to 'support the University's strategy'. My initial response was to instigate a year-long review of the School via extensive informal discussions, staff workshops, committee meetings, reading the business school literature, and interactions with external stakeholders.

Three clear messages emerged from my review. First, the School had a distinctive combination of characteristics, including a broad social science base (including economics, critical management studies, and public services management), a strong commitment to social science's founding concern for social and human betterment, sustained research excellence (one of only two UK business schools ranked in the top ten of every UK government Research Excellence Framework [REF] assessment), and a strong record of growth (to *c.*300 staff, and 3,000 students in 2012). Second, and despite these characteristics, my review indicated that the School faced significant threats both (a) externally, from the reduction of state financial support for universities, increased competition for staff, students, and research funding, and the mounting criticism of business schools, and (b) internally, through threats to its finances and autonomy under the University's new structure and strategy. Third, the review surfaced a strong dislike in the School for what was perceived to be 'creeping managerialism' in the University, as exemplified by the recent introduction of structural centralization and KPIs.

The combination of my review findings and research background convinced me of the need to avoid replicating the University's outcomes-based strategy in the School, and instead investigate an alternative; which I then called collaborative and value-based, but now refer to as collaborative and purposeful. At the same time, however, the requirement for the School to report performance against KPIs made clear that I was not able to eschew the University's prioritization of outputs. By early 2013, I had become resigned to the idea that the *best I could do* in these circumstances was to try to find a strategic approach that allowed the accomplishment of the University's KPIs in a way that provided the autonomy and resources to support the School's pursuit of a purposeful change. The rest of this case report explains how, from this compromised position, I adopted a CPO role and worked collaboratively with colleagues to encourage the innovation of purposeful outcomes.

The CPO Role in Leading Purposeful Academic Change

After having engaged with the corporate purpose literature, I now see that by the late spring of 2013 while formally serving as the Business School's Dean, I had also informally adopted the role of CPO. It didn't start well though. My strategic review had failed to provide the inspiration for my development of a conception of the (then value, now purpose) of a business school that fit with CARBS' distinctive set of characteristics and aspirations. That spur came when a senior colleague and close friend (Professor Rick Delbridge) shared with me Brewer's (2013) thesis on the public value of social science.

Brewer's (2013) response to the challenges facing social science is a manifesto for a new public social science that is based upon consideration of the *value* of social scientific scholarship, post-disciplinary approaches to producing knowledge of relevance in addressing society's problems, and strong engagement with the public and policy spheres. Brewer's underpinning idea is that, just as when social science emerged out of moral philosophy in the eighteenth century, a new public social science is now *needed*. The specific need is for the nurturing of a moral sentiment towards each other, and to recognize we have a shared responsibility for the future of humankind through understanding, explaining, analysing and ameliorating grand challenges, with the hope of economic and social improvement. Whilst recognizing the need to also demonstrate the use and price values of social science (e.g. financial contribution to parent universities, and the wider economy), Brewer emphasizes its normative public value which arises from three features: (1) the distinctive *value* of its scholarship; (2) the potential of the post-disciplinary production of knowledge for use in addressing society's problems; and (3) wide engagement with civic society.

During discussions over the following months, Rick and I agreed that although Brewer does not discuss business schools, his advocacy of the public value of a social science – as normative and driven to promote economic and social improvement – could provide the basis for a conception of CARBS' purpose. More specifically, in developing what we came to refer to as the public value business school (PVBS), Brewer's work inspired us to conceive (a) the purpose of the business school to be the promotion of economic and social improvement (public good), and (b) its pursuit through research, teaching and governance that would become increasingly interdisciplinary, challenge-led, and designed to engage with all manner of publics.

Having interpreted Brewer's work as a call for social science organizations (in our case, a business school) to repurpose and deliver public good (Kitchener, 2019), I then worked collaboratively to translate Brewer's manifesto into (a) a statement of purpose for the PVBS, and (b) supporting 'directions of travel' for purposeful teaching, research, governance, and engagement activity. From late 2013 through 2014, my early iterations of a PVBS purpose statement and functional signposts were discussed and revised with close colleagues including the School's SMT (Cardiff Business School, 2013). These discussions were then broadened to include all the School's academic and professional services colleagues through a series of workshops. Over time, it emerged that for many colleagues the PVBS had two attractions: (a) it was intuitively appealing, 'who wouldn't want to try to enhance public good?', and (b) it signalled something very different to the University's reviled 'KPI strategy'.

As I had anticipated, when I further broadened discussions across the parent university and among external stakeholders, anxieties were raised concerning a 'potential' for negative impact on student revenue, and a threat of creating 'confusion with the University brand'. Through repeated 'hands-on' interactions (Ayers, 2019), I learned that some peoples' financial concerns could be allayed by emphasizing that the PVBS' commitment to social and economic improvement included growing financial contributions to the University. Similarly, I learned that anxiety about cross-branding could be allayed by stressing that the PVBS' prioritization of interdisciplinary scholarship required the School to work at the heart of the University and build collaboration across it.

By the summer of 2016, my many hands-on interactions had helped to secure support for the PVBS idea from my college head and feedback from consultations increasingly signalled that stakeholders felt that it fitted well with the School's character and aspirations. It was only after three years of collaborative conceptual and political leadership work (Moore, 1995), that I felt ready, in October 2016, to formally introduce the School's statement of purpose at a public event. Attendees were told that the purpose of our School was to:

> Promote economic and social improvement through interdisciplinary scholarship that addresses the grand challenges of our time, while operating a strong and progressive approach to our own governance.

In this, and subsequent presentations, I also introduced the supporting signposts outlined in Table 5.2 to encourage colleagues to develop purposeful outcomes in their practice. This combination of purpose statement and signposts quickly and widely became known as the 'School's strategy'. The next section describes my attempt to build on this foundation to work collaboratively to inspire innovative and purposeful outcomes from colleagues.

Delivering Purposeful Change Collaboratively

Having adopted a collaborative leadership approach (Archer & Cameron, 2008) to conceptualize and articulate CARBS' statement of purpose and signposts, I directed my attention towards encouraging colleagues to develop purposeful innovations across the four main practice areas of the School: governance, teaching, research, and engagement. Table 5.2 presents the signpost and summarizes the main innovations that emerged in each functional area. My outline of innovations in each area begins below with the School's new formal governance structures and systems which I hoped would help provide a supportive context for purposeful innovations to emerge organically across the School's three other functional areas of activity.

Purposeful school governance
One of the distinctive elements of the PVBS (and an extension of Brewer's thinking) is to deliver public good through a progressive approach to the governance of a university business school. At CARBS, this began with my commitment to collaborative leadership (Archer & Cameron, 2008) during the strategy-making process and continued during its implementation. My main aim was to try to get 'value from difference' through the involvement of a wide range of stakeholders.

Under the previous governance approach at CARBS and many other business schools, the combination of strong financial and academic performance and compliance with legal requirements would constitute satisfactory outcomes. However, Cardiff's PVBS statement of purpose has the desired effect of inspiring many equality and diversity initiatives (Table 5.2) and it provided the impetus for colleagues to lead the development of an innovative Shadow Management Board (SMB). This body scrutinizes the work of the SMT, conducts project work, and facilitates more diverse participation in the School's decision-making processes. In 2017, the initial SMB chair became the first board member to join the SMT, and she was then subsequently appointed Dean in 2018; the School's first female head. The School's commitment to enhancing public good through its governance has also inspired a range of academic and professional service colleagues to work together to introduce a series of other innovations in administrative areas including human resources and procurement (see Table 5.2 for examples).

Table 5.2   *Purposeful innovations at Cardiff Business School*

Function	Purpose Signposts	Innovations (Year of introduction)
Governance	Driven by statement of purpose to deliver public good. Strong and progressive governance e.g. collaborative leadership, participative decision making, progressive HR and sustainable procurement	*Statement of Purpose launch (2016) *Economic contribution £300M pa (2018) *Shadow Management Board (2017) *Senior Management Team 'rotating chair' (2018) *Inclusion of value-set in hiring (2018) *Staff return to work scheme (2018) *Annual Public Value Impact Report (2018) *Circular economy refurbishment programme (2019–20) https://blogs.cardiff.ac.uk/business-school/2020/02/27/our-circular-economy-makeover/
Teaching	Develops moral sensitivity towards, and the capacity for, economic & social improvement	*PVBS induction seminars & animated video (2018) *Student public value orientation experiment (2018) *Six new interdisciplinary/challenge-led masters programmes, e.g. sustainable supply chain management *Since 2018, all undergraduates offered work placement *Annual programme review process encourages public value content and student projects
Research	Interdisciplinary, challenge-led research that generates knowledge about society & that informs society & its constituents	*Led a major university investment in interdisciplinary, social science-led research that addresses societal challenges through a new bespoke facility, the social science park (ongoing from 2013) https://www.cardiff.ac.uk/social-science-research-park *New interdisciplinary groups in Corporate Governance, and Responsible Innovation Network (RIN); this is working with a charity in Eritrea to research and support women-run microbusinesses *Targeted school funding to support public value research projects including: (i) a team of economists working with colleagues from medicine, dentistry, and public policy to address alcohol-related crime through a 'Cardiff Model' that involves econometric analysis of the rate of violence-related injury and alcohol pricing, and (ii) sociologists and human relations specialists working with the UK's Living Wage Foundation to identify the benefits and challenges that are associated with applying an ethical wage standard

Function	Purpose Signposts	Innovations (Year of introduction)
Engagement	Broad range of partners including civil society, private, public & third (not-for-profit) sectors, directed towards social & economic improvement	*New Partnerships i. *50–50 by 2020* (http://5050by2020.org.uk/), a campaign to encourage organizations to increase women's representation in decision-making positions to 50 per cent by the year 2020 ii. Business in the Community (http://www.bitc.org.uk), a charity that enables businesses to work together to tackle key social issues iii. Enactus (http://enactus.org), a global community of student, academic, and business leaders "committed to using the power of entrepreneurial action to transform lives and shape a better, more sustainable world" iv. UNPRME (http://unprme.org), signatories adopt six principles of responsible management education developed under the coordination of the UN Global Compact and leading academic institutions v. Llamau (http://llamau.org.uk), a local homeless charity that is the focus of School fundraising vi. CABS Small Business Charter accreditation (one of only 36 business schools in the UK) *Public Value Entrepreneurs (2018) A diverse group of five entrepreneurs that helps develop links between researchers, students and small businesses, https://www.cardiff.ac.uk/business-school/people/entrepreneurs-in-residence. *Public value fellowships & engagement project funding (2018), https://www.cardiff.ac.uk/business-school/about-us/public-value/public-value-fellows. The first round of successful applications produced three projects building upon existing collaborative research with Disability Rights UK, Anti-Slavery International, Centre for African Entrepreneurship

Source: Kitchener and Delbridge, 2020.

In addition to the purposeful innovations in School governance, tensions continued to emanate from differences between purposeful PVBS aspirations and the outcomes-oriented strategy of our corporate parent. Through a combination of cost restraint, and the recruitment of an additional 550 students per annum, the School met both its PVBS goal of economic contribution, and the centrally imposed financial targets (Jones, 2018). However, this double 'achievement' was thought by many colleagues to have caused tensions including rising academic workloads, reduced diversity among the student population, and strains on professional services staff in student facing roles. Faculty, publicly and privately, questioned how compatible these conditions were with the PVBS. In response, I consistently iterated my belief that this was a cost of the autonomy and resources required to support 'our radical PVBS strategy' and the wide range of purposeful innovations that were emerging. Perhaps unsurprisingly, such tensions are reported to be standard within the CPO role in corporate settings (Biderman-Gross, 2020; Izzo & Vanderwielen, 2018).

Recognizing (some wisdom in) the managerial adage that 'what gets measured gets managed', the development of multi-capital indicators (Mayer, 2018; Stroehle et al., 2018) to capture and celebrate CARBS' enhancement of public good began when a professor of economics, with expertise in the measurement of social impact, volunteered to produce the School's first annual public impact report (Jones, 2018). This exercise is the first known attempt to measure and narrate a business school's public good against indicators of economic impact, sustainability and staff attitudes. Whilst demonstrating the School's strong economic contribution and colleagues' perception of progress towards purpose, the report also found that the largest contributor to the School's carbon footprint is the travel of international students who are, of course, its largest source of revenue. Once again, this surfaced the tension between the strategies of the School, and her corporate parent.

Purposeful teaching

As illustrated in Table 5.2, CARBS colleagues have made clear progress in delivering public good through innovative teaching and learning that develops moral sensitivities and capacities to promote public good through economic and social improvement. All new students participate in an assessment of their orientation towards public value (pro-social) values at induction. It is hoped that a second assessment in their final year (2020) will show that the public value orientation will have strengthened amongst students. In terms of curricula development, public value is now a key theme in the annual review of all programmes, encouraging multi-disciplinary and challenge-led content. Following Brewer (2013) a key aim is to help students develop a better understanding of the 'marginalized' who face challenges such as a lack of social protection, poor working practices, and wage stagnation. In one example of the public value teaching innovation in this regard, project work on the master's in business administration (MBA) Management Consulting module now focuses on local charities and non-governmental organizations.

Purposeful research

Following the launch of the PVBS in 2016, the School's Research Committee decided to re-direct its discretionary research budget to support interdisciplinary studies that address society's grand challenges. Of course, faculty are still encouraged to pursue their own research interests, and much public value research had been conducted in the School before this change process. However, as illustrated in Table 5.2, the prioritization of public value criteria in the allocation of research funding supports a growing portfolio of interdisciplinary research groups, public value research projects, and a stream of scholarship in public value (Lindgreen et al., 2019) including contributions from the Dean (Kitchener, 2019; Kitchener & Delbridge, 2020). As noted earlier, in keeping with the School's traditions in critical management and open debate, some colleagues have also been inspired to write questioning the potential for purposeful change in the political economy of higher education (Marinetto & Dallyn, 2017).

Purposeful engagement

In addition to maintaining conventional elite engagements (including hosting the Institute of Directors in Wales), CARBS increasingly promotes economic and social improvement through the diverse range of collaborations summarized in Table 5.2. While some of these are international in scope, (e.g. UNPRME), others are local including the School's partnership with Llamau, a Welsh homeless charity. Partners such as the School's new public value entrepreneurs are especially important to the purposeful change project because they help give credibility to an 'intrapreneurial' approach that challenges dominant assumptions and practices, and they provide examples and learning opportunities.

DISCUSSION AND CONCLUSIONS

This chapter began with the observation that corporations and business schools have both been criticized for placing the achievement of outcomes over the pursuit of purpose. It was then noted that while a few senior business school academics are prominent in a nascent reform movement that prescribes the repurposing of corporations, they have not yet directed their attention towards business schools. Reversing the normal direction of knowledge transfer between these two groups of organizations, this chapter drew inspiration from corporate reform literature to frame a process of purposeful change in a university business school.

In common with both the corporate reform movement (BA, 2019) and Brewer's (2013) new public social science, this chapter is not arguing that business schools (or any other university departments) should change purely in order to appease our critics, nor to appeal to our paymasters among students, universities, research councils and governments. Rather, the primary impetus for purposeful change is for university departments to operate in ways that better complement their essential worth and advance their prospects of making positive contributions to society.

Unlike many recent cases of strategic change in higher education and other public services, this chapter did not report a linear process model that followed the NPM principles of enhancing managerial control over professional work and monitoring their performance through KPIs (Fotaki & Prasad, 2015; Kitchener, 2002; Kitchener et al., 2000). In sharp contrast, my version of change leadership comprised four main features: a thorough strategic review, my adoption of a CPO role, a collaborative leadership approach, and the instigation of reporting against purpose. The change process began with a strategic review that was designed to ensure that the purpose statement and supporting functional signposts would reflect the School's distinctive tradition and aspirations. My search for conceptual inspiration in the 'home' literatures concerning business schools and management bore no fruit. It was only when a colleague directed me towards Brewer's (2013) thesis on the normative public value of social science that we began to conceive a purposeful business school as involving movement towards (a) teaching and learning that develops moral sentiments and capacities to promote economic and social improvement; (b) interdisciplinary research that addresses the grand challenges of our time; (c) extended engagement activity across a fuller range of external organizations and publics; and (d) a progressive model of governance.

On reflection, this conceptual form of purposeful leadership work (Moore, 1995) provided some of the most stimulating and enjoyable experiences of my tenure. While I firmly believe that it is a vital first step for purposeful change initiatives, I am fully aware that the resource luxury (particularly of time) that I was afforded may well not be available to other departmental heads in the current political economy of higher education.

The second key feature of my leadership approach was to adopt a role that I later learned was emerging in corporate settings and called CPO (Biderman-Gross, 2020). My early adoption of that role in a university business school began with me leading the conception and articulation of a statement of organization purpose and functional signposts that were designed to inspire colleagues to develop purposeful outcomes. It then continued with my attempts, through much hands-on interaction (Ayers, 2019), to encourage aligned innovation from colleagues, and to report purposeful activity upwards internally, and to external audiences.

Again, looking back, I thoroughly enjoyed these aspects of (the way that I constructed) my roles as Dean and CPO. The greatest challenges arose from the political work required to gain support for a change agenda that directed attention to the pursuit of purpose within a countervailing institutional environment that prioritizes the achievement of outcomes (Moore, 1995; Ayers, 2019). While the case presented here indicates that some success is possible for CPOs operating in these circumstances, it took considerable time, collaboration and resilience.

Third, from the outset, I adopted a collaborative leadership approach to try to get 'value from difference' through the involvement of a wide range of colleagues and partners (Archer & Cameron, 2008). Drawing from my public management research experience (Kitchener, 2002; Kitchener et al., 2000), I recognized that CARBS is, like many large multi-disciplinary professional work settings, a complex organization with many highly engaged experts on organizational matters. Against the current tide of managerialism in universities, it made sense to me to offer my knowledgeable colleagues opportunities to contribute at each stage of the purposeful change process including the conceptual work (e.g. during strategy workshops, and the edited book) and the more technical tasks such as curriculum development.

My leadership approach consciously took a relational and collaborative form that sought to orchestrate a purposeful university school, not so much through the heroic efforts of leaders employing bureaucratic power (à la NPM), but more by making an emotive connection with colleagues and partners to exert influence. The extent to which this was realized at CARBS is indicated through the strength and variety of 'bottom-up' innovations that emerged across teaching, research, engagement, and governance (Table 5.2). The collaborative approach also helped ensure that the process was able to interest and excite colleagues about the possibilities and benefits (both societally and closer to home) of embracing public value, without me needing to have answers to detailed questions about how to achieve this change. Rather, the whole point was for colleagues to engage in developing innovations which were both beneficial to the change and resulted in their autonomy and commitment.

While my collaborative approach to change leadership was clear to avoid the managerialist fixation on outcomes, it did recognize the necessity to report to purpose (Mayer, 2018; Stroehle et al., 2018). This spurred the development of the School's annual public impact report which assesses its contribution to public good against 'multi-capital' indicators of economy, sustainability and staff attitudes. While this is a very promising start, there is, of course, much to be done in both (a) extending this purposeful reporting approach, and (b) addressing the findings that it produces, such as the extent and nature of the School's carbon footprint. The amelioration of this and CARBS' other sustainability issues rest largely, of course, not on decisions made in the School, but in the corporate university boardroom.

As the CARBS case has shown, the development of a purpose statement, supporting signposts and aligned innovation is not enough to fully establish a purposeful business school within a countervailing institutional context. Instead, tensions continue to shadow the CARBS purpose project, as they would in most universities operating in political economies characterized by managerialism and reduced state funding. However, in contrast to Marinetto and Dallyn (2017), this chapter provides some hope that the only viable response to these challenges is *not* just for individual business school faculty to adopt 'tactics' to deliver public good through their own work, whilst complying minimally with conflicting institutional demands. Instead, it offers a set of constructive ideas on which to base purposeful business schools that may offer alternatives to the call for their wholesale closure (Parker, 2018).

It was argued earlier in this chapter that Friedman (1967) was instrumental in setting the outcome-oriented agenda that caused corporations and business schools to lose their way over the last half a century. He also opined that "only a crisis – actual or perceived – produces real change. When that crisis occurs, the actions that are taken depend on the ideas that are lying around" (quoted by Cannadine in BA, 2019: 13). As we (hopefully) begin to emerge from the coronavirus pandemic, I hope that this chapter might encourage some academic leaders, at the departmental and corporate levels, to develop purposeful academic entities that enhance public good.

NOTE

1.   I spent my sabbatical as a visiting scholar at Said Business School (Said) and Harris Manchester College (HMC) at the University of Oxford. I am very grateful for the generous hospitality and collegial support given to me by Sue Dopson, Colin Mayer and Peter Tufano at Said, and Jane Shaw at HMC.

REFERENCES

Alajoutsijarvi, K., K. Kettunen, and S. Sohlo (2018). 'Shaking the status quo: business accreditation and positional competition'. *Academy of Management Learning and Education*, 17(2): 203–25.

Anderson, L. (2006). 'Analytic autoethnography'. *Journal of Contemporary Ethnography*, 35(4): 373–95.

Archer, D., and A. Cameron (2008). *Collaborative Leadership: How to Succeed in an Interconnected World*. London: Butterworth Heinemann.

Arielli, S., L. Sagov, and E. Cohen-Shalem (2016). 'Values in business schools: the role of self-selection and socialisation.' *Academy of Management Learning & Education*, 15(3): 277–91.

Atkinson, P. A., A. Coffey, and S. Delamont (2003). *Key Themes in Qualitative Research: Continuities and Change*. Walnut Creek, CA: AltaMira Press.

Ayers, S. (2019). 'How can network leaders promote public value through soft metagovernance?'. *Public Administration*, 97: 279–95.

Bennis, W., and J. O'Toole (2005). 'How business schools lost their way'. *Harvard Business Review*, 83: 96–103.

BIC [Big Innovation Centre] (2016). *The Purposeful Company: Interim Report*. May. London: BIC.

BIC [Big Innovation Centre] (2017). *The Purposeful Company: Policy Report*. February. London: BIC.

Biderman-Gross, F. (2020). 'What's a Chief Purpose Officer and why should you hire one?'. *Forbes*, https://www.forbes.com/sites/forbesagencycouncil/2020/03/18/whats-a-chief-purpose-officer-and -why-should-you-hire-one/#79c948eea18e (accessed 18/5/20).

Brewer, J. D. (2013). *The Public Value of the Social Sciences*. London: Bloomsbury.

British Academy [BA] (2018). *Reforming Business for the 21st Century*. London: The British Academy.

British Academy [BA] (2019). *Principles for Purposeful Business: How to Deliver the Framework for the Future of the Corporation*. London: The British Academy.

Cardiff Business School (2013). 'Senior management team meeting notes, October'. Available from author on request.

Cardiff University (2012). '2012–2017: the way forward'. Cardiff: Cardiff University.

Eccles, R. G., L. Strine, and T. Youmans (2020). '3 ways to put your corporate purpose into action'. *Harvard Business Review*, 13 May, https://hbr.org/2020/05/3-ways-to-put-your-corporate-purpose -into-action (accessed 2/12/20).

Edmans, A. (2020). *Growing the Pie: Creating Profit for Investors and Value for Society*. Cambridge: Cambridge University Press.

EY Beacon Institute (2016). 'The state of the debate on purpose in business', https://www.ey.com/ Publication/vwLUAssets/ey-the-state-of-the-debate-on-purpose-in-business/$FILE/ey-the-state-of -the-debate-on-purpose-in-business.pdf (accessed 19/5/20).

Fotaki, M., and A. Prasad (2015). 'Questioning neoliberal capitalism and economic inequality in business schools'. *Academy of Management Learning & Education*, 14(4): 556–75.

Freeman, R. E. (1984). *Strategic Management: A Stakeholder Approach*. Cambridge: Cambridge University Press.

Friedman, M. (1970). 'The social responsibility of business is to increase its profits'. *The New York Times Magazine*, 13 September, p. SM12.

Ghoshal, S. (2005). 'Bad management theories are destroying good management practices'. *Academy of Management Learning and Education*, 4(1): 75–91.

Harley, B. (2019). 'Confronting the crisis of confidence in management studies: why senior scholars need to stop setting a bad example'. *Academy of Management Learning & Education*, 18(2): 286–97.

Harvard Business Review Analytic Services and EY [HBR/EY] (2015). *The Business Case for Purpose*, https://hbr.org/resources/pdfs/comm/ey/19392HBRReportEY.pdf (accessed 18/5/20).

Henderson, R., and E. Van Den Steen (2015). 'Why do firms have "purpose"? The firm's role as a carrier of identity and reputation'. *American Economic Review*, 105: 326–30.

Hollensbe, E., C. Wookey, L. Hickey, G. George, and V. Nichols (2014). 'Organizations with purpose'. *Academy of Management Journal*, 57(5): 1227–34.

Izzo, J., and J. Vanderwielen (2018). *The Purpose Revolution: How Leaders Create Engagement and Competitive Advantage in an Age of Social Good*. Oakland, CA: Berrett-Koehler.

Jones, C. (2018). *Cardiff Business School Public Value Report*. Cardiff: Cardiff Business School.

Kaplan, A. (2018). 'A school is a "building that has four walls … with tomorrow inside": toward the reinvention of the business school'. *Business Horizons*, 61: 599–608.

Kenny, G. (2014). 'Your company's purpose is not its vision, mission or values'. *Harvard Business Review*, 3 September, https://hbr.org/2014/09/your-companys-purpose-is-not-its-vision-mission-or -values (accessed 2/12/20).

Khurana, R. (2007). *From Higher Aims to Hired Hands: The Social Transformation of American Business Schools and the Unfulfilled Promise of Management as a Profession*. Princeton, NJ: Princeton University Press.

Kitchener, M. (2002). 'Mobilizing the logic of managerialism in professional fields: the case of academic health center mergers'. *Organization Studies*, 23(3): 391–420.

Kitchener, M. (2019). 'The public value of social science: from manifesto to organisational strategy'. In A. Lindgreen, N. Koenig-Lewis, M. Kitchener, J. D. Brewer, M. H. Moore, and T. Meynhardt (eds), *Public Value: Deepening, Enriching, and Broadening the Theory and Practice*, pp. 301–15. Abingdon: Routledge.

Kitchener, M., and R. Delbridge (2020). 'Lessons from creating a business school for public good: obliquity, waysetting and wayfinding in substantively rational action'. *Academy of Management Learning and Education*, 19(3), 307–322.

Kitchener, M., I. Kirkpatrick, and R. Whipp (2000). 'Supervising professional work under New Public Management: evidence from an invisible trade'. *British Journal of Management*, 11(3): 213–26.

Learmonth, M., and M. Humphreys (2011). 'Autoethnography and academic identity: glimpsing business school doppelgängers'. *Organization*, 19(1): 99–117.

Lindgreen, A., M. Kitchener, N. Koenig-Lewis, M. Moore, and T. Meynhardt (eds) (2019). *Public Value: Deepening, Enriching, and Broadening the Theory and Practice*. Basingstoke: Palgrave Macmillan.

Marinetto, M., and S. Dallyn (2017). 'The public value of academic research: a critique of John Brewer's public value social science'. Working paper, Cardiff Business School.

Mayer, C. (2013). *Firm Commitment: Why the Corporation is Failing Us and How to Restore Trust in It*. Oxford: Oxford University Press.

Mayer, C. (2018). *Prosperity: Better Business Makes the Greater Good*. Oxford: Oxford University Press.

Moore, M. H. (1995). *Creating Public Value: Strategic Management in Government*. Cambridge, MA: Harvard University Press.

Nohria, N., and R. Khurana (eds) (2010). *Handbook of Leadership Theory and Practice*. Cambridge, MA: Harvard Business Press.

Parker, M. (2018). *Shut Down the Business School: What's Wrong with Management Education*. London: Pluto.

Rodriguez, Vila O., and S. Bharadwaj (2017). 'Competing on social purpose'. *Harvard Business Review*, September–October. Accessed (26 April 2020): https://hbsp.harvard.edu/product/R1705G -PDF-ENG.

Storey J., and G. Salaman (2017). 'Employee ownership and the drive to do business responsibly: a study of the John Lewis Partnership'. *Oxford Review of Economic Policy*, 33(2): 339–54.

Stroehle, J. C., K. Soonawalla, and M. Metzner (2018). 'How to measure performance in a purposeful company'. *Journal of the British Academy*, 6(s1): 19–40.

Thomas, H. (2017). 'Rethinking and re-evaluating the purpose of the business school'. In D. Bradshaw (ed.), *Rethinking Business Education: Fit for the Future*, pp. 8–9. London: Chartered Association of Business Schools.

Thomas, H., and K. Starkey (2019). 'What should business schools be for?'. *Global Focus*, 30 October. Accessed (8 February 2020): https://www.globalfocusmagazine.com/what-should-business-schools -be-for/.

6. Leading academic departments

Rob Goffee and Gareth Jones

INTRODUCTION

Academic departments are full of clever people. Or, to be rather more precise, with lots of people who believe they are clever. But, as W. I. Thomas makes clear, "insofar as things are defined as real, they are real in their consequences." There are enormous challenges in leading clever people. It is, perhaps, one of the greatest challenges facing organisations today as we enter the age of the knowledge economy. It can be extraordinarily trying and often requires considerable personal sacrifice and a healthy humility on the part of the leader. Happily, it is also one of the most satisfying roles a leader can perform. It is about working with talented individuals, people who are capable of incredible achievements. We also believe passionately that those leaders who embrace the challenges and get them right have the opportunity to make an enormous contribution to their organisations and to the world at large. We face serious challenges – climate change, food shortages, poverty, health care, economic instability – and all these issues will require clever solutions. Well-led academic departments and universities have the capacity to make the world a better place for everybody.

Our observations are drawn from a larger data set relating to published research culminating in our book *Clever: Leading Your Smartest, Most Creative People* (Harvard Business Review Press, 2009). This research included academic departments. We also draw upon first-hand experience – over the past 40 years – of working in and leading academic departments in a variety of university settings in and beyond the UK.

Let's begin with some axioms about leadership. First, it is contextual. Leadership in a steel mill is different from leadership in a law firm. Leadership in the History Department will be different from leadership in Chemical Engineering. Context really matters. It follows from this that leaders must be good at reading context – collecting soft information which enables them to read the nuances of their situation. If those who aspire to leadership cannot do this, it is hard to see how they can exercise other leadership behaviours. The good news is that this capacity to read context can be learned. We often advise people moving into leadership roles in universities to keep a diary of their observations. Begin noticing what individuals' key motives are at work, where their greatest strengths lie, what allowable weaknesses they may have, and what fatal flaws they may possess. Over time, the leader will develop a rich picture of their people environment.

Second, leadership is relational. It is something achieved *with* people, not something done *to* people. So, fundamentally, leadership is a relationship between the leaders and the led. If it is a relationship it should be as much illuminated by sociological concepts as psychological ones. Too much of the traditional leadership research is excessively psychological. It follows from this relational aspect of leadership that a leader must stay close to their followers – those that they aspire to lead. In commercial organisations, most leaders are regularly exposed to 360-degree feedback, which can be a very effective way of staying in touch with followers' thoughts and feelings. However, this technique is rarely used in academic institutions.

Finally, leadership is non-hierarchical. Becoming the Head of Department does not automatically make you the leader. Being a leader is an ascribed not an achieved characteristic. It is given to you by others. Perhaps one of the persistent mistakes in classic leadership research has been to confuse hierarchy – which is a positional concept – and leadership which is concerned with praxis – it is enacted with others.

CHARACTERISTICS OF CLEVER PEOPLE

In order to lead clever people effectively it is essential to recognise some of the characteristics that they share. We introduce you to some of these in the following sections. Not all academics exhibit all of them, but many have several of these characteristics.

1.   Their Cleverness Is Central to Their Identity

Academics rarely become academics as some last-minute career choice. Rather, it is their passion, it is who they are, rooted deep in their being. It is almost as if they are their work. Listen to how people introduce themselves. Academics say that they are physicists, historians, economists and so on. They will rarely say "I work for the University of Michigan". They are defined by their passion, not their organisation. This passion can have some wonderfully positive effects, it inspires followership amongst colleagues and, perhaps especially, amongst research students. This can create a kind of intellectual hotspot. But it also means that they may become obsessive about their current project, often to the detriment of others – they find it hard to shut off or to keep to a schedule if it means not completing a task to their satisfaction.

The close association between what academics do and who they are also means that they often see themselves as not being dependent on others. The leader must therefore start by acknowledging their independence and difference. But, critically, the leader's job is to make them understand their interdependence. Really well-led academic departments have a real understanding of the overall strategy of the institution and recognise a symbiotic relationship between individual academics, research teams and the wider institutional context.

2.   Their Skills Are Not Easily Replicated, and They Know Their Worth

First-class academics have knowledge, skills and networks which are very hard to replicate. Some of these attributes are tacit. This begins to explain why knowledge management systems have had little impact in academic institutions. It follows from the non-replication characteristic that they increasingly know their worth. One striking development in universities in the last twenty years is the growth of a global market in talent. US, Canadian and, increasingly, Asian universities are prepared to recruit stars from around the world – sometimes trebling salaries and offering lavish research support. It becomes a crucial task for the leader to create a culture where people will resist these temptations; a culture in which people feel they can really do their best work. There is a kind of paradox here; they need to feel that they are left alone and, at the same time, that they are supported and valued.

3.   They Are Organisationally Savvy and Ask Difficult Questions

It is easy to assume that clever academics are organisational innocents, too focused on their own obsessions to play politics. The reality is starkly different. Academics will find the organisational context where their interests will be most generously funded. If the funding dries up, they have several options. They can move on to somewhere where resources are plentiful, exploiting their labour market clout; or they can engage in elaborate organisational politics to ensure that their pet projects are suitably indulged. This is a pattern we have witnessed repeatedly in academic and research-based organisations. A long way from organisational innocents, they are much closer to expert gamers. Academic leaders have frequently told us that they know they are dealing with very talented people who are prepared to argue with the hierarchy, persistently asking difficult questions.

4.   They Want to Be Connected to Academics Outside Their Organisation

Every academic Department Head will know the constant battle over the Conference Budget. Cynics may think that this is about academics just seeking exotic locations to visit. In our experience, it is much more about a deep-rooted drive to be connected with people pursuing research interests close to their own. There are several positive aspects to this. First, we know that creativity is crucially fostered by the cross-fertilisation of ideas. Effective academic conferences can prove wonderful places for questioning fundamental assumptions. Second, academics value recognition from peers with similar research interests much more than feedback from their own institution. Peer recognition validates their work. Finally, outside connections are a way of finding out where the next research hotspots will be, and where they can find access to research support and funding.

5.   They Don't Want to Be Leaders and They Don't Want to Be Led

This is perhaps the central and most infuriating aspect of academics. They will often do all they can to avoid taking leadership positions – becoming Departmental Head is often decided simply on a rotation basis. And yet, at the same time, they are resistant both to being managed and led. They want to be left alone to pursue their obsessions and, if that is Cornish piracy in the fifteenth century, then so be it. If there is little student demand for Cornish piracy electives, then that is absolutely not their problem. Think about the endless wrangling about teaching loads and research time. It's hard to think that this could go on in a commercial organisation. However, universities are increasingly exposed to commercial environments: they are big businesses.

Quite a lot follows for the leader from this characteristic. They must conceive of leadership as being very much to do with gently guiding people in the desired direction. Coaching and support will be more important than instructions. Leadership of academics rests upon building legitimacy and reputation much more than it does upon hierarchy.

6.   Not Great at Team Events

Clever professionals, such as doctors, lawyers and academics, can be found in a range of organisations – universities, business schools, law firms and hospitals. What they all have in common is that, as individuals, they identify more with their profession than with their organisation. Leading teams of such individuals, for example in an academic department, generates special challenges. Teams of professionals have a tendency to be wilfully naughty. It may sound slightly bizarre but, in our experience, there is no other way to describe it. Individuals who are highly professional and capable in many areas of their lives, can often behave rather like teenagers when they are put into teams. A well-renowned colleague of ours once astutely observed that, when groups of intelligent professorial colleagues were forced to sit together for meetings, it wouldn't be long before rather juvenile behaviour emerged. This took a variety of forms: the surreptitious passing of "humorous" notes, reading newspapers, giggling inappropriately, falling asleep – the list goes on. His advice was to keep team events short, sweet and focused, and to conduct more discursive interactions on a one to one basis. Another professor and department head complained that his senior colleagues acted like schoolchildren in their regular departmental meetings. Privately, they in turn told us that the department head behaved a little like a head teacher. A rather unproductive, negative feedback loop was produced. Academics may possess very high degrees of self-discipline but, at the same time, they often exhibit low levels of social skills.

7.   Feedback Avoidance

There are several reasons why academics tend to be resistant to feedback. In part, it is to be explained by their generally perceived high status which makes them highly sensitive to losing face. But there may be an even more fundamental reason. They see themselves as being the most competent judges of their own performance. Their research papers are always breakthrough, their teaching inspirational – it's just that the students can't see it – yet! And their administration is first class – it's just that the department's systems don't really fit with their way of doing things. Since their work is so tied up with their identity, negative feedback is especially painful, lest they come to the painful conclusion that they might not be quite as clever as they thought they were.

8.   They Won't Thank You

Earlier in this chapter, we alluded to academic leadership as requiring a large degree of humility. One very successful Dean told us that when you are leading well, academics may still be unwilling to recognise your leadership. You may have to measure your success by your ability to remain on the fringes of their radar. The Dean continued, "you know you are a success when you hear them say that you are not getting in the way too much!"

LEADING CLEVER PEOPLE

To lead in this context, successful department heads will require several of the traditional leadership virtues such as excellent communication skills and authenticity. As we pointed out in our introduction, good situation-sensing skills are a vital foundation for effective leadership.

You will not know what to do as a leader unless you properly understand where you are. A former Vice Chancellor of a world-class UK university told us that when he ran the university, he regularly took a late evening walk. As he strolled around the campus, he collected soft data. He bumped into people and started useful, unplanned conversations. He also noticed which departments had their lights on late at night and were still working. He discovered a correlation between activity levels and the quality of the outputs.

The relational nature of leadership also means that it is important to combine the ability to empathise and be close to colleagues with the necessity to create social distance (to appreciate the bigger picture and have a more objective view of how best to act). "Reluctant" department heads, for example, often struggle to create this type of non-hierarchical distance; they find it difficult to step out of the academic peer/equal role where necessary. The skill of leadership is to move between social closeness and distance in a way where relationships are sustained and performance enhanced. Finally, there is a need – always – to skilfully deploy personally distinctive qualities in a way that may engage others productively. Whilst the search for a universal set of personal "leadership attributes" has proved a hopeless quest, the need for aspiring leaders to know their personal qualities – and how they can be revealed to others in a way that energises them – remains fundamental.

But given the "clever" characteristics we have described above, the task of leading academics requires an approach that is, in many ways, unusual. It requires additional qualities.

In our research on academics and academic departments, we were constantly reminded that "things were different". The language used by more effective leaders was often all about "trust, guidance, support, listening, closeness, being valued, sharing values, parenting, helping, nurturing, creating the right atmosphere" and so on. Some might call these the soft skills of leadership. The emphasis is very much on identification rather than hierarchical distance; and creating an environment in which others can fulfil themselves and express their professional excellence.

Yet it would be a mistake to think of the most successful academic leaders simply as benevolent guardians. As one told us, "people need to know where the limits are – otherwise it's anarchy". A critical challenge, then, is to balance the need for empathy, affinity and humility, on the one hand, with discipline, on the other. The danger of over-indulged "ivory tower" academics is familiar; but equally the clumsy imposition of controls, measures and sanctions will likely dampen creativity and fun – so creating a workplace where the best academics do not want to be.

For academic department heads this often translates into combining a "light touch" with clear ground rules. Following this – and on the basis of our research – we have identified several "dos and don'ts" for this type of leadership.

1.   Explain and Persuade Rather Than Tell People What To Do

Academics value their autonomy and scope for self-expression. They rarely appreciate being told what to do – and tend to react badly if they are! Needing to be told undermines self-esteem – surely professors shouldn't need telling! So, this is leadership by listening and talking, by conversation not edict. Explaining and persuading requires that communication lines must always be open and two-way. If you tell people what's going on, they might reciprocate. A Vice Chancellor told us, "My experience of clever people is, they will live with anything, disaster, difficulty, providing they know what is going on. If they think back door deals are being done, you're done for."

Our experience is that whilst many academic heads may instinctively recoil from "telling" they also rarely have the time – or skills – required for regular conversations that typically form the foundations of effective feedback and coaching. In effect, they practise a kind of laissez-faire leadership that leaves colleagues to "sink or swim". The outcome is typically patchy: some *do* learn to swim – but the costs for those who don't can be high.

2. Use Expertise Rather Than Hierarchy

Heads of department have formal authority over those they lead. But academics tend to respond far better to expert rather than hierarchical power. Using hierarchy to justify decisions or behaviour is risky and likely to be self-defeating.

Of course, academics do not expect the department head's knowledge to equal their own unique or specialist knowledge. But they do expect them to demonstrate expertise in their own field. This may be a similar or related area of expertise or it can be completely distinct. Either way, this type of accredited (typically PhD) expertise lends the holder a legitimacy to communicate with – and influence – others in a way that is appreciated and respected.

3. Give Space and Resources but Don't Let Colleagues Burn Out

Academics typically perceive their own work to be important – and therefore should be well resourced. They can be prone to obsession – and, of course, from their obsessions huge value can be generated for academic institutions. This can mean labs, libraries, equipment, specialised facilities, support staff, dedicated sabbaticals and so on. Once resources are granted there is then a desire for minimal interference; for space to try things out and – literally – to push the frontiers of knowledge.

An additional benefit from providing appropriate space and resources is that it limits the need for academics to be distracted into Machiavellian politics in order to extract what they need from the system. Good heads get this balance right and so facilitate performance in inevitably political contexts.

With appropriate space and resources there is rarely a need to motivate. Conventional wisdom suggests that leadership involves lifting others through motivational visions – but academics are often scornful of such attempts. In our experience, big picture visions are often seen as vacuous and are the source of dark humour amongst academics. But an important leadership skill can be to ensure colleagues are not burnt out by their obsessions. Historically, sabbaticals have proved to be an effective mechanism for achieving this.

Of course, in the real world, resources are constrained, sabbaticals are limited – if not entirely abolished – and departments rationalised in ways that reduce discretionary time and space. Under these conditions academic environments can become very political. If so, a key leadership skill is to protect colleagues from the distractions of the "organisational rain". Although some academics may be organisationally savvy, they are not necessarily motivated to engage in extensive organisational politicking. Good department heads offer them protection – as far as they can – and ensure that their colleagues know this. In effect, they build up credit with grateful colleagues who, in turn, realise they must reciprocate favours.

4.   Tell Them What but Not How

While grand visions can be distracting, a sense of direction can constructively unify efforts. But going beyond *what* to *how* is risky because it deprives colleagues of the opportunity to work things out for themselves. So clearly establishing goals and objectives can be helpful – both for individuals and departments – but detailed instructions on accomplishment will be less appreciated, if not entirely ignored.

A department may aim, for example, for leadership in particular research domains, or for teaching excellence according to independent quality audits. If these objectives are established through skilful consultation and discussion, then they can be a mechanism for building commitment and departmental teamwork. But all of this can be undermined by clumsy imposition of guidelines and instructions that inappropriately bureaucratise processes and demotivate staff.

5.   Make Time for Questions – and Don't Pretend to Have All the Answers

Good leadership does not rest upon the pretence of perfection. Rather, it involves the judicious acknowledgement of certain shortcomings and weaknesses. But exposing ignorance to clever academic colleagues can feel like a risky manoeuvre.

Yet our evidence suggests effective department heads are candid and honest about the things they don't know, and are not afraid to ask "stupid" questions. Several of those we spoke with remarked that this approach could be particularly helpful during the early days of office since it not only helped them understand their contexts better, but also offered an exemplar to colleagues to also not be afraid of asking their own "silly" questions. Setting up situations in which questions can be asked and debates ignited is a neglected leadership skill. To facilitate it department heads need to show accessibility without allowing that to feel like interference to those who prize autonomy above almost everything else. As one research leader once shared with us: "Bad managers of clever people pull the flower out of the ground daily to ensure that the roots are healthy – checking and rechecking clever people is not appreciated – in the end the flowers die!"

6.   Give Recognition, But Not Too Often

What academics do in their work is central to their identity, so recognising their achievements is vital. Of course, much of this recognition comes from prestigious peers outside the department in other academic institutions of one kind or another. It is delivered in citations, professional awards, editorial board memberships and so on.

Some department heads may feel – mistakenly – that this excuses them from having to pay any more attention to this issue. But they are wrong. Small rituals of recognition can be powerful – for both individuals and teams. The celebratory drink at the end of the week to acknowledge a teaching award; the special display of a colleague's latest book; even the picture on the wall of departmental members – all can be powerful ways to communicate to colleagues that they are valued.

But overload at your peril. Good recognition comes from a legitimate source, is authentically delivered and is not so over-used that it loses value. Achieving the right balance requires good situation-sensing skills.

7. Talk Straight, Don't Bullshit

Our research on clever people taught us that they typically have a low threshold for tolerating corporate or organisational bullshit. We think this is particularly true of academics. Their typically uneasy relationship with organisations makes them supersensitive to perceived deceit, double dealing, or any other strategy that implies that they can be easily duped.

So, to flourish, academic leaders must be confident about their own expertise and abilities – and prepared to talk straight. If they are not – and pretend otherwise – their colleagues will sense it and undermine them.

But straight-talking carries risks. It can offend and upset, break relationships, create enemies with agendas, and demotivate. Heads who rotate from leadership positions back into the departmental membership can suffer long-term consequences of their (sometimes relatively brief) tenure in a leadership role. They may live to regret their honesty.

8. Create a Galaxy, Not Just a Star

The ability to attract and hold highly talented (and mobile) academic "stars" is a big challenge for any departmental head. It is typically contingent upon the ability to offer competitive market salaries, light teaching loads and generous research resources. Not all of this is in the gift of a departmental head.

But if a star is attracted, this can only ever be a beginning. The point of course is to create a galaxy – a peer group of like-minded individuals who thrive in each other's company and who are well led. Our guidelines above may be a way for departmental heads to help create that environment whatever the budget constraints.

9. Accept a "Fragmented" Culture and Don't Waste Time on Inappropriate Teambuilding

We have argued elsewhere that organisational cultures can be differentiated according to the strength of two different types of social relationship. First, *sociability*, a measure of friendliness amongst colleagues where people do things for one another because they want to – no strings attached; no deals implied. In effect, high sociability relationships are valued for their own sake. Second, *solidarity*, where relationships are based upon common tasks, mutual interests and clearly understood shared goals that benefit all parties – whether they personally like each other or not. In other words, solidarity is not contingent upon sociability (and vice versa).

We describe high sociability/low solidarity cultures as *networked*; high solidarity/low sociability cultures as *mercenary*; cultures high in both dimensions as *communal*; and those low in both as *fragmented*. We have also argued that these dimensions can be applied at various levels of analysis – from macro (societal or organisational cultures) to micro (occupational groups or teams).

The appropriate balance is driven by a wide set of contextual factors relating, for example, to type of work, market conditions, technology, socio-historical influences and so on.

In an academic context, it is possible that a highly focused, tight-knit research team, working together intensively for several years, may take on the *communal* form. Equally, professional associations of academics that extend far beyond individual university departments may be either predominantly *networked* or *mercenary* in their characteristics.

But we suspect that most academic departments are *fragmented* – and that this is not a bad thing! Fragmented cultures deliver the autonomy, focus upon individual excellence, and scope for creativity that underpins much of the very best academic work. But they can also produce selfishness, minimal knowledge sharing, intolerance of others, and anti-social behaviour. When we interviewed people at a top US business school, they told us that "I go to work to be alone". Their former Dean told us that leading at the school was "like herding cats – but I've got seventy world-class Professors".

So, the challenge, for most departmental leaders, most of the time, is not to attempt unachievable (and largely inappropriate) tightly knit *communal* teams. It is to sustain fragmented cultures that predominantly feature the positive rather than negative characteristics we describe above. This largely means establishing a set of simple, agreed, ground rules that guarantee (rather than constrain) the freedoms valued by academics – and then, policing them systematically.

CONCLUSIONS

In a previous book we advised leaders to "be yourself – more – with skill". It is a beguilingly simple message that involves more than is apparent at first glance. There are two variables: authenticity – the extent to which individuals both know and selectively show their true self; and skill – the extent to which individuals deploy themselves in situationally appropriate ways. These variables are represented in the simple matrix of Figure 6.1.

In box B, individuals combine skill and authenticity to produce effective leadership. The major challenge is to avoid complacency. Box A represents individuals with a strong sense of who they are and what they stand for, but who lack the skills to deploy these assets. They often fail to read contexts, to communicate well or to empathise with others. In box C there are individuals with good interpersonal skills but who lack a strong sense of self. Their colleagues may feel they are being manipulated by a "phoney". In box D, low levels of self-awareness and skill combine to produce the type of clumsy boss so successfully satirised in television's *The Office*.

In general, we suspect that box B is not highly populated. This is a limited but highly valued set. In the corporate world, sophisticated management training programmes have often produced the highly polished "players" that inhabit box C. The modern plea for "authentic" leadership has, in large part, been a plea for these individuals to take the risks necessary to show more of their "true selves".

But in the academic world, leadership development programmes are virtually non-existent. And we suspect that, even if they were available, they would be shunned. The problems lie more in boxes A and D.

In A are the larger than life academics (with matching large egos) who often have an under-developed interest in others – or how they might be best led. Some of these really could benefit from the interpersonal skills training programmes that – ironically – the best business schools around the world routinely provide.

In D the problems are greater – and, in some cases, possibly unresolvable. Intensive coaching that facilitates self-discovery – supported by experiential learning and skills training – may jolt some individuals up and out of this box.

In the corporate world, box D individuals are unlikely to be offered significant positions of authority. But in the academic world – where "amateur" academics rotate reluctantly in and out of departmental leadership positions, we fear they may remain a problem.

Academic departments deserve better than this. The challenge is to elevate academic leadership roles so that those who really care, and who want to do the job well, receive the guidance they deserve. We hope our guidelines above are a small contribution to the process.

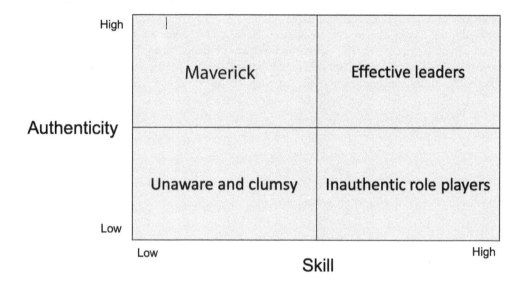

Figure 6.1   Combining skill and authenticity

ANNOTATED FURTHER READING LIST

We thought it would be helpful to suggest some further reading that academic leaders might find useful and relevant. Our own research can be most readily accessed in three pieces of work:

Rob Goffee and Gareth Jones, *Why Should Anyone Be Led by You?* (Boston: Harvard Business Review Press, 2019).

In this book we look at the skills required to be an authentic leader. It is based on twenty years of, mainly qualitative, research on leadership in a variety of contexts.

> Rob Goffee and Gareth Jones, *Clever: Leading Your Smartest, Most Creative People* (Boston: Harvard Business Review Press, 2009).

This book examines the peculiar changes of leading in the knowledge economy and is based on our Harvard Business Review article, "Leading Clever People" (Boston: Harvard Business Review, March 2007, https://hbr.org/2007/03/leading-clever-people).

> Rob Goffee and Gareth Jones, *The Character of a Corporation* (London: Profile Books, 2nd edn, 2003).

This is an extended treatment of the four cultures we reference above – with diagnostic toolkits for each culture and guidelines for change.

Finally, we would like to suggest Warren Bennis, *On Becoming a Leader* (New York: Perseus Book Group, 1989). This delightful book was produced by an academic who had spent most of his life studying leadership and then became Dean at a prestigious US business school. It is a wonderfully honest account of his experiences, successes and failures.

7. Individual performance management: enabler or threat to academic performance?

Andreas Werr and Katja Einola

INTRODUCTION

In recent decades, universities and institutions of higher education all over the world have been placed under greater scrutiny. Public and private stakeholders, both domestic and international, are increasingly interested in what universities actually deliver in terms of diplomas, research output, student satisfaction and impact on society. These developments are driving an increasing focus on both organizational and individual performance management. For someone not privy to academic traditions and culture, these changes seem rather reasonable. However, for individuals inside these institutions, where the ethos of academic freedom has for long implied being *left alone* for both legitimate and illegitimate reasons, this recent interest has been received with mixed feelings. While some in the community welcome increased transparency and applaud greater accountability (Gioia & Corley, 2002), others resent what is often referred to as unnecessary managerialism in the neo-liberal university that, as the critics say, increasingly resembles a private sector firm and has a corrosive effect on academic communities, work and freedom (Waring, 2013; Willmott, 1995).

Even though the work academics do is by its very nature open to scrutiny, it is hard to steer and control by means of traditional human resource management (HRM) and performance management practices (Einola & Werr, 2020). Research, ideally at least, lies at the heart of this work and forms the basis for teaching and outreach activities faculty members engage in. Different from almost any task professionals do for salary in other sectors, research is highly motivation-driven and triggered by interest individuals have in topics they have chosen themselves to be experts in, usually with very little top-down intervention. An academic's work is also nested in peer groups and dependent on a collective of other researchers not only at their home university, but also across more or less tight networks spanning other organizations and countries. It may also be sponsored by other institutions including private firms and public institutions, complicating the picture of control, affiliation and accountability further. Because of this complexity, processes that lead to quality output are impossible to standardize and capture into carefully documented routines controlled by a single manager in one organization. Even the meaning of "quality" is hard to define. While everyone in the community knows who the "top" performers and "star" groups are, no one quite knows how they got there – including these individuals themselves. There is no recipe for success.

In spite of these challenges, *some* kind of individual performance management – or at least monitoring – is needed to enact individual accountability and formal service assurance in an organization that entirely relies on its individual members' performance, intrinsic motivation and work ethics. This should be an important practice, especially to spot and act on budding problems before they become huge ones affecting many people. However, the management of performance is seldom high on the managerial – or employee – agenda at universities. The academic, more often than not, shuns away from any management initiatives to monitor and interfere with their performance, unless it is in their self-interest (Van den Brink, Fruytier, & Thunnissen, 2013; see also Chapter 1 by Poulfelt in this volume).

At the same time, academia as a profession builds on strong espoused principles of meritocracy; that knowledge and expertise are the only basis for recruitment, resource allocation and promotion (Scully, 1997). The underlying idea is that those admitted to and promoted in the exclusive world of academia are the most creative, expert, ambitious, well-networked, internationally minded, hard-working and highly motivated professionals who are willing and capable to cooperate with each other in a constructive way. Yet, sometimes meritocracy remains only a forgotten ideal, quality is not there and the "community" is no more than a collection of instrumentalist individuals pushing for their own agendas, personal needs, and defending their acquired benefits and career interests (Ekman Rising, Lindgren, & Packendorff, 2020). Instead of enacting meritocracies, some managers may create *mediocracies* by putting personal ties first and using their position to create inbred clans of like-minded individuals – without anyone interfering.

In this chapter, we focus on performance management as a formal practice of identifying, measuring and developing (through feedback) the performance of individuals (Aguinis, 2009), a practice that is becoming increasingly common in academic departments, often pushed by central HRM initiatives. These practices are expected to be implemented by department heads, further adding to the complexity university middle managers, responsible for both the collective outputs of their department and the performance of individuals employed to work there, encounter in their daily work. While we acknowledge that the academic middle manager has a broader set of tools to drive performance, including leadership practices (see, e.g. Chapter 1 by Poulfelt in this volume), formal performance management is becoming increasingly common and consequential, thus deserving closer scrutiny. We adopt a pragmatic point of view and approach the topic from the grassroots level where the academic manager enacting performance management needs to balance individual employees' situations, institutional goals and contextual constraints with their own multiple roles and special place in the organization.

In the following, we blend elements of a formal literature review, personal experiences and reflections. The first author's long experience in higher education and as a university middle manager has met the second author's observations as a newcomer in academia, mirrored against a background in organizational development and resource management in the private sector. Moreover, our text is influenced by numerous informal discussions with many other colleagues in higher education in different stages of their careers keen on exploring the question how (and if!) performance can (or should?) be managed in academia. This chapter is divided into five sections. *First*, we discuss some basic assumptions of individual performance management and how they fit in the academic context. *Second*, we conduct a short review of the ambitions and effects of performance management as discussed in contemporary literature. *Third*, we delve into recent performance management trends in academia and, *fourth*, some of their unintended consequences. *Fifth*, we propose a few ideas about better management of performance in academic settings.

PERFORMANCE MANAGEMENT IN ACADEMIA: AN UNEASY FIT

Aguinis (2009: 2) defines performance management as "a continuous process of identifying, measuring, and developing the performance of individuals and teams and aligning performance with the strategic goals of the organization". A key component of this process is more or less frequent but formalized managerial evaluations of employees. The purpose of these evaluations is two-fold: to help make decisions about awards (e.g. salaries, promotions) and sanctions (e.g. layoffs or terminations), and to provide feedback to employees in order to enable and support them to develop their skills and capabilities in line with the organization's goals (Murphy, 2020). These two purposes are, however, conflicting. While developing employees involves detailed developmental feedback and encouragement, evaluating for awards and sanctions means pitting people against each other, often focusing on their weaknesses. After all, not everyone is or can be a star performer. Performance management systems, thus, may serve some goals and work sometimes to some degree, but there are also critical voices claiming that they often or almost always fail to serve their purpose (Alvesson & Kärreman, 2007; Murphy, 2020).

Four key assumptions underlying individual performance management are problematic in the context of academia, thus making universities less than perfect ground for this practice. These assumptions are: (i) that managers have authority and control over valued resources that can be used to reward and punish individuals, (ii) that managers are interested in and capable of giving feedback and that faculty members are interested in receiving and acting on feedback, (iii) that managers have a strong enough mandate to act in their role, and (iv) that organizational performance is determined by the sum of individual performances in a way that can be assessed meaningfully and controlled by a formal performance management system.

Limited Managerial Control Over Valued Resources

Performance management relies on the idea that an individual's performance is influenced by differential rewards and, thus, that a manager has control over these rewards. In the academic context, however, faculty members (staff) seek a wide array of different resources and rewards other than salary increases and promotions under the control of their managers. These include peer recognition by other academics distributed across organizations and countries, favourable publishing decisions from editors and anonymous reviewers of scientific journals, positive student feedback, research funding from external institutions, leadership positions in professional organizations such as conference boards and journal editorial teams, side-jobs outside academia such as consulting assignments or giving public talks, collaboration and teaching opportunities in other universities, and so on. The relative appeal of rewards controlled by an academic manager (typically marginal changes to salary) is rather weak in comparison, especially for well-established professors and other senior faculty members. Even employment decisions and promotions are (at least ideally) not made by the manager alone, but collegially and typically also considering input from external evaluators.

Uncertain Impact of Feedback

The concept of performance management assumes that employees are open to receiving and appreciating managers' feedback on their performance, and that managers are in a position to give helpful feedback. Many academics act like entrepreneurs shaping their own research trajectories, careers, networks and work contexts, and gain resources from many different stakeholders. Hence, feedback from managers may be perceived as irrelevant or even inappropriate. The idea of "academic freedom" is strong among academics creating a natural resistance to performance management as illegitimate interference with this freedom (Van den Brink et al., 2013). For faculty members pursuing an academic career it may be much more relevant to receive feedback from research funders, peers and self-selected mentors than from department heads. Given that many academics view themselves as academic entrepreneurs rather than employees, they also show limited loyalty to their employers (Thunnissen, 2016), and, thus, view feedback from management as mostly irrelevant.

A Weak Management Mandate

The very idea of performance management presupposes that there are clear organizational goals and that middle managers engaged in performance management are committed and empowered to realize these goals. However, in academia, such goals are often multifaceted and contested (we will come back to this). Middle managers are typically appointed to the position from among their peers on a rotating basis, making their loyalty to any organizational goals as fragile as their subordinates' loyalty to the same goals. The motivation to forcefully manage the performance of one's colleagues who may not welcome these initiatives to begin with and who may in turn become *their* managers one day not too far in the future, is limited. A colleague of ours, freshly appointed to a managerial position, told us how his interviewers in the selection process for the position were more interested in getting guarantees that he was *not* going to make any changes than in his ideas about the improvements he thought were necessary, if chosen for the position. Another colleague had added the text *"Revenge has no expiry date"* to his email signature leaving us guessing whether this quote is an innocent attempt at humour, or a subtle threat to deter any potential over-eager managerial intentions of colleagues. In this context, the annual performance review, where much of the formal performance management work takes place in practice, easily becomes an awkward session between "managers" and "subordinates" who do not see themselves (or each other) as such, or simply an opportunity to chat about other things of concern or interest.

Difficulty in Defining Organizational Membership

Individual performance management, as defined by both theory and practice, presupposes an employment relationship which points out a manager responsible for the performance of his or her unit and for people working in it. Without a manager the very idea of performance *management* becomes void of meaning. A lot of both research and teaching in contemporary universities is, however, performed by staff on the periphery of the formal organization. These colleagues are academic entrepreneurs of a sort, working on temporary and often part-time arrangements, and they sometimes have contracts with multiple "clients" (e.g. different course or programme directors, institutions) rather than a single manager. There are also doctoral students and other researchers working on grants and stipends provided by institutions of different kinds other than the university they are affiliated with who work in a department but do not have a regular employment contract. Even though these organizational members are not employees in a formal sense, whose performance the academic manager is responsible for and has a mandate to manage, they contribute to the community and may produce a substantial amount of the teaching and research output central to the organization's performance.

Taken together, we can, thus, conclude that academia is a challenging context for individual performance management. In the following section we will review what we know about the use and effects of performance management more generally before we turn to performance management in academia more specifically.

THE AMBITIONS AND CHALLENGES OF PERFORMANCE MANAGEMENT

Although most modern organizations engage in performance management where individual workers are assessed in some way, the value of performance management systems has been increasingly debated. Both managers and employees are typically sceptical of their value. In a survey of employees' experiences of performance management, only three out of ten believed that their organization's performance management system helped them improve their performance (Aguinis, 2009). Research results on the effects of performance management share this scepticism. Murphy (2020: 15) concludes that "there is little if any evidence that these [performance management] systems have any real impact on the performance or effectiveness of employees" (see also Aguinis, Joo, & Gottfredson, 2011; DeNisi & Smith, 2014; DeNisi & Murphy, 2017; Pulakos, Hanson, Arad, & Moye, 2015).

Although much of the critique has been targeted at the enactment of performance management as annual performance reviews, there is evidence that other types of formal evaluation systems with an ambition to measure performance may be equally problematic. Murphy (2020), based on a review of research, presents a fundamental critique against performance evaluation which is a central feature in all individual performance management systems. This critique is linked to the fact that evaluations are built on subjective views on job performance and rely on "evaluative judgments about the performance and effectiveness of employees" (Murphy, 2020: 14). This critique is targeted at four areas: (i) that performance is normally distributed, (ii) that we can measure job performance in a reliable and valid way, (iii) that performance feedback is useful for individuals, and (iv) that evaluations provide important input to organizational decisions. All these assumptions are, however, problematic.

Performance is Not Normally Distributed

The assumption behind performance management systems is that performance is normally distributed and that by capturing this distribution, it can be affected. The purpose is to help low-performers to develop, and to reward high-performers – thus moving the performance curve of the organization to the right on a metaphorical continuum towards some elusive form of excellence. Studies, however, show that performance is not normally distributed. Rather, performance distribution may be more accurately depicted as a very small portion of star performers contributing disproportionately to the organization, whereas the large majority display good performance, but with, in comparison, low variability (Murphy, 2020). While it is usually easy to identify these star performers, performance management focuses on differentiating all employees. The meaningfulness of this differentiation may be questioned. What is the point of regularly and formally assessing all employees if the star performers are known and most other employees do not differ in meaningful ways in their effectiveness and job performance?

Performance is Difficult to Measure

Performance management is further based on the idea that performance can be accurately measured. Research, however, demonstrates that it is difficult to find reliable, objective measures of performance and avoid the trap of overly subjective and shallow assessments, for example giving disproportionate importance to what is easy to measure, to some recent or otherwise salient event, or to matters that have to do more with personal chemistry than with job output. This is especially true for the complex and multidimensional context of academia. Consequently, assessment to a large extent hinges on subjective judgements that have been shown not to be reliable. For instance, different individuals often rate the same person very differently. Studies have also shown low levels of validity in performance ratings. About two thirds of the variation in ratings has been found not to be related to differences in performance but to irrelevant factors such as rater biases. A lot of effort in research and practice have gone into changing this – but without any substantial improvements so far (Murphy, 2020).

Employees Do Not Find Performance Feedback Useful

Performance evaluations aim to provide feedback that will help people change their behaviours for the better. This has been shown to be true for individuals that are new to a job and in situations where feedback provides information that performers do not have access to themselves. Kluger and DeNisi's (1996) review of studies on feedback, however, shows that formal feedback leads to better performance only in about one third of studies, to worsened performance in one third and only to very limited effects in the last third of studies. Their review further indicates that feedback may have effects for some individuals under certain conditions. It has been shown, for instance, that some employees (typically high-performers) actively seek and act on feedback. However, low-performers, needing feedback the most, are typically not seeking it at all. Furthermore, there is some evidence that feedback systems have some effect while they are new, but that this effect diminishes as employees get used to the system and repeatedly get similar feedback. Also, for individuals to be willing to act on feedback they receive, it needs to be perceived as fair and valid, which, however, is seldom the case. Most people perceive their performance higher than it actually is, so if they get accurate feedback it is perceived as unduly low and easily dismissed as invalid and unfair (Murphy, 2020).

Performance Evaluations Don't Make a Difference to Organizational Decisions

Performance evaluations are typically motivated by the input they provide to important decisions, including salary increases, promotions and professional development. However, research has demonstrated the incompatibility of evaluations for salary and promotion purposes, on the one hand, and evaluations that are useful tools for individual development, on the other. For personal development needs a detailed, nuanced assessment is most valuable. If individuals, however, are seen in such a nuanced way, most will have both strengths and weaknesses and end up with rather similar overall ratings that, in turn, are of limited use for distributive purposes (e.g. salary, promotions, terminations). A lack of distribution among ratings is further produced by managerial considerations of how ratings may affect employee mood and motivation. Ratings in most organizations thus cluster around values of "above average" making them of limited value for distributive purposes. This use is further limited by the small variability in pay typically linked to performance evaluations. While performance-related pay increases are typically around 2–3%, research shows that in order to be perceived as meaningful they need to be at least 7% of annual pay. Although individual preferences may differ and some may appreciate even small increases for their symbolic value, anything below a certain baseline risks breeding cynicism, thus having the opposite of the desired effect (Murphy, 2020).

RECENT TRENDS IN PERFORMANCE MANAGEMENT IN ACADEMIA

Values and practices of autonomy, academic freedom and collegiality have long shielded academics against formal performance management practices at universities. While reviews of performance have existed before, these typically had a rather informal and developmental focus aimed at supporting faculty to increase the quality of their research and teaching. However, the adoption of New Public Management (NPM) ideology, the idea of which is to generate greater value for money and restore governability to an overextended public sector (Gruening, 2001), has gradually changed this. Current performance management systems, for both good and bad, have an increasingly evaluative, even judgemental focus, and aim at assessing performance as a basis for decisions related to the distribution of scarce resources such as research time and promotions (Ter Bogt & Scapens, 2012). For instance, if a faculty member has failed to publish in the preceding year, he or she may be "punished" by getting a heavier teaching load or more administrative duties for the following year, complicating further career progression and promotions that are to a large extent based on research outputs.

While performance management practices vary between universities and countries, there seem to be some general trends and characteristics that permeate most of these systems today.

Quantifying the Evaluation of Performance

Overall, the trend has been towards more formalized and quantified systems that formulate in some detail the performance standards to be attained (Aguinis, Cummings, Ramani, & Cummings, 2020). While these measures may be complemented by qualitative assessments, the relative weight of these is usually rather marginal. These performance standards are typically formulated in relation to the three basic tasks of academia – research, teaching, and engagement with society – although the last criterion is seldom specified (or assessed) in any detail (Helgesson & Sjögren, 2019).

The performance standard for research, on the other hand, is generally much more well-defined in terms of an expected number of publications, journal ranking lists and impact factors representing external, standardized quality measures adopted by most universities. This increasing reliance on performance metrics, where applied, has had some significant positive implications such as improved clarity and transparency, a potential reduction in bias in assessments and enablement of comparability between disciplines (Aguinis et al., 2020). Career progression of junior scholars in particular is typically linked to certain minimum levels of publication achievements. A recruit holding a tenure track position often knows exactly how many publications of what quality and in what time frame are expected to get the coveted tenure, stable employment contract. However, the further up the academic hierarchy a faculty member is situated, the less specific (and enforced) performance standards become. Senior professors' performance is often not defined and monitored in any formal way and institutions tend to let them act according to their own work-moral, ambition level and motivation.

As quantitative performance standards in research proliferate, an accentuated focus on "quality" is emerging when research universities focus specifically on a select list of "A journals" as the only ones that count in career and compensation decisions (Aguinis et al., 2020). Publishing in top journals is viewed a proxy for career success, an important measure for prestige in the community and a way for ambitious academics to benchmark themselves against each other. This narrowing down of research outlets that "count" has been argued to create a number of unintended consequences, including the increase of questionable research practices, the loss of relevance of research, reduced innovation and heterogeneity in research, shifting focus from internal to external motivation and the crowding out of all activities not directly related to publication (e.g. supporting PhD students, junior scholars and institution building) (Aguinis et al., 2020).

In teaching, performance is measured in terms of both teaching volume and quality, most often assessed through student evaluations. This practice is not without problems either. Relying on student evaluations as indicators of teaching quality has been subject to ample critique. The response rates may be too low to be indicators of anything, and the assumption that students are willing and able to assess their own learning in a reliable way stands on rather shaky ground (Berk, 2018). Students may simply mark down any lecturer who does not give them the grade they wanted, making student evaluations as the sole performance criterion in teaching a debatable practice. Research has also repeatedly shown discriminating effects of students' evaluations for minority groups, and to female lecturers (see, e.g. Basow, 2000; MacNell, Driscoll, & Hunt, 2015).

Sanctioning Underperformance

Failures to live up to performance standards may have different consequences in different institutions, departments and for different kinds of faculty. In their comparison of performance management practices in the accounting and finance departments of the University of Groningen and the Manchester Business School, Ter Bogt and Scapens (2012) found that performance assessments in Groningen had a direct impact on faculty's research time whereas in Manchester, they were more indirectly linked to promotion decisions. Other than that, performance standards are typically more clearly specified for more junior than for senior faculty, for whom the sanctions for not meeting performance standards are much less clear and rarely reinforced in practice, creating a situation of imbalance in terms of fair and equitable treatment of faculty members many universities have been slow to address.

An institutional culture that divides faculty into castes with unequal treatment, easily sinks the mood, corrodes the spirit of collegiality and creates feelings of frustration and anger, at least in countries where workplaces are otherwise more democratic and hierarchies flat. Junior colleagues may resent a system they perceive as unfair, in particular if the performance of some members of the senior staff is visibly poor and their workload trickles down in the organization while management looks the other way. In a highly competitive and performance-conscious work environment like academia, being tolerant of, or not sanctioning the underperformance of, some (or even one) of the most privileged community members is a much worse option than finding effective ways of dealing with the problem.

Paying More Attention to Productivity

A common motivation driving the proliferation of increasingly formal individual performance management systems is a desire to increase productivity in terms of more and higher quality output per faculty member. Although research on the effects of performance management systems in academia remains rather scarce, there are some recurring findings that point at both positive and negative effects. On the positive side, there is some research evidence that an increasing focus on measuring, following up and rewarding research publications leads to an increase in the number of these and to a lesser extent also to an increase in quality (as measured by impact factors and journal rankings) (Ter Bogt & Scapens, 2012). When the importance of publishing is openly discussed and publication targets are made explicit to faculty members, they also become more aware of these requirements and may start working harder towards these goals (Alajoutsijärvi, Kettunen, & Sohlo, 2018).

Some universities award publications in highly ranked journals with money and in some cases these bonuses can represent a substantial part of an academic's compensation and thus become an important motivational factor. Indeed, an investigation into the widespread use of cash publication bonuses in China has shown that these had a positive effect on research productivity (Quan, Chen, & Shu, 2017). However, paying cash to individuals for publications may also instigate instrumentalist behaviours by those who know how to "play the game". Having one's name in the author list of as many publications as possible while contributing little to each, or publishing for the sake of publishing, producing what Ashforth (2005: 400) calls *research as vanilla pudding*: "bland comfort food, with a lot of empty calories", can become a problem undermining the very purpose of conducting research (see also Aguinis et al., 2020).

Pitting Research Against Teaching

Even though research and teaching are often claimed to be of equal importance, research per-formance tends to be more or less implicitly prioritized in practice (Kallio & Kallio, 2014; Ter Bogt & Scapens, 2012). This clear hierarchy between teaching and research, both key activi-ties from an organizational performance point of view, influences both faculty behaviour and ranking of peers, and, at times, causes tension. Current performance management systems that more or less explicitly privilege research over teaching have been argued to lead to incentives to devote less effort to teaching innovation in order to protect research time (Cannizzo, 2018; Ter Bogt & Scapens, 2012). This shift in focus may become detrimental to higher *education* institutions, whose long-term legitimacy still hinges on their ability to educate students, even if it sometimes seems that what really matters (or counts) is the academic professionals' ability to produce publications in the most influential journals.

Research on the potential cannibalization of research on teaching is limited. Existing studies, however, find limited support for this. Cadez and colleagues' (2017) study of research and teaching performance of staff found no relationship between research productivity and teaching quality (as defined by student evaluations – itself a problematic measure as we discussed earlier). However, a positive relationship between research quality (as measured by publications in top journals) and teaching quality was found, supporting the idea that well-rounded "star performers" do and can exist in academia, indicating that there may not be a law-like contradiction between research and teaching after all.

UNINTENDED CONSEQUENCES OF PERFORMANCE MANAGEMENT IN ACADEMIA

Research evidence points at several unintended consequences of performance management in academia as it is conceptualized and practised today.

Pressure and Stress

Judgemental performance management systems contribute to a significant increase in stress levels experienced by faculty. As the purpose of course evaluations has shifted from course development to control, they are often made publicly available to both colleagues and students, which is perceived as stress inducing, especially by those with lower evaluations. In a similar vein, quantitative publication targets with material consequences if they are not met (e.g. less research time, no tenure) induce considerable stress among faculty (Ter Bogt & Scapens, 2012). Further, Cannizzo (2018) argues that it is the combination of the hierarchical management of academics' research performance with the desire to produce meaningful work that drives the expansion of a long hours culture in academia – easily leading to overwork and exhaustion. In a recent employee survey at one of the authors' departments, only 25% of the faculty agreed to the statement "I have enough time in normal working hours to do a good job". Further, 37% of UK academic staff reported having mental health issues (Else, 2017). With over one third of colleagues struggling, the whole community is affected, and problems may multiply. In a context where, at least for some (tenure track researchers, temporary employees, PhD students), a lot is at stake and demands are increasingly high, excessive stress and anxiety are hard to avoid.

A Vain Focus on Extrinsic Motivation

It is highly questionable to what extent managerial practices and the research environment actually influence research performance of individuals. Studies have shown that excellent scholars excel in both research and teaching *regardless* of the work environment and managerial practices of performance management that they are subject to (Cadez et al., 2017). Moreover, it has been demonstrated that high-performing individuals are primarily driven by intrinsic motivation, i.e. motivation deriving from performing the tasks of research or teaching itself, rather than any external incentives such as monetary or career rewards. Consequently, Edgar and Geare (2013) found that performance appraisal processes were viewed as the *least* effective managerial tool when it came to affecting research performance. Instead, academics valued their autonomy:

> [I]f I had one wish for, to make a better environment for research, I would wish to be left alone and given more time to get on with it. (Researcher quoted in Edgar & Geare, 2013: 784)

This indicates that extrinsic rewards may be ineffective as they are rather unrelated to the motivations of at least the most engaged and talented researchers. An extreme case in point is the Russian mathematician Grigori Perelman who has refused professorships in Berkeley, Princeton and Columbia and turned down the Fields medal and other sizeable cash rewards with the motivation "I'm not interested in money or fame; I don't want to be on display like an animal in a zoo" (Forrest, 2013: 98).

It has also been argued that extrinsic rewards are not only ineffective (Brown & Moshavi, 2002) but may even be harmful to the motivation of researchers as they may corrupt their intrinsic motivation. Such an effect was found by Kallio and Kallio (2014) who studied the effects of the introduction of performance-related pay in Finnish universities. They found that 41% of the researchers surveyed indicated that the quantitative evaluation regimes actually lowered their motivation, another 42% reported no effect on motivation and only 17% reported a positive effect. Quan and colleagues (2017), in relation to the prevalence of publication bonuses in China, further found a tendency that publishing in certain bonus-giving journals became the prime goal of researchers' activity, replacing an interest in knowledge production and advancement. In a similar vein, Cannizzo (2018) concludes:

> The pragmatic acceptance of evaluative mechanisms leads to a metaphysical emptying of the criteria of value for academic practice. In other words, the possibility of valuing academic conduct for its contribution to some private value, be that an idea of justice, truth, freedom and so on, becomes a secondary concern to the pragmatic functioning of the mechanism of evaluation. (Cannizzo, 2018: 88)

What has, however, been found to be effective in supporting researchers' motivation are transformational leadership practices, including charisma, intellectual stimulation and individualized attention, implying that these are more compatible with the professional ethos and desire for and expectation of autonomy (Brown & Moshavi, 2002; see also Chapter 1 by Poulfelt in this volume).

A Threat to Research Quality

Many academics believe that quantitative and judgemental performance management practices lead to a deterioration of research quality. A stronger focus on research productivity leads researchers to prioritize safer, short-term projects, where replications of previous research are pursued over more uncertain, creative projects (Kallio & Kallio, 2014; Ter Bogt & Scapens, 2012). The temptation to go for the low hanging fruits to "make it" to the FT50 list as often as possible simply becomes irresistible to many. Maximizing the amount of papers engaged in, while minimizing personal contribution to each, becomes a normal practice for many seasoned academics. Furthermore, opportunistic behaviours such as cutting up research findings in as many papers as possible and publishing similar findings to multiple audiences could be observed, all pushing towards a pursuit of marginal rather than more impactful contributions (Ter Bogt & Scapens, 2012). In the words of a senior professor:

> This also implies that, for example, people cannot spend six or ten years any more writing an important book. It is very difficult to do long-term research projects, because it takes too much time for the outputs to be produced. Many people also do not spend time on projects where it is very uncertain whether they can produce results that generally speaking will be publishable in international journals. Consequently, you see more replication of research projects that were successful elsewhere. (Quoted in Ter Bogt & Scapens, 2012: 477)

In the context of China, where publications are highly incentivized through cash bonuses that represent a large part of academics' remuneration, it has also been suggested that this may contribute to unethical research practices such as plagiarism, fabricated research, and ghost-written papers (Quan et al., 2017). There is no reason to believe that these ethical problems are limited to China. In fact, our ongoing research with early career scholars shows that such dubious characters as "free riders", "parasites" and even "thieves" of authorship are gaining terrain even in Europe (see also Aguinis et al., 2020).

When the focus on productivity is combined with a focus on a narrow number of top journals to publish in, creativity and novelty in research is further restricted by the agenda, format and kind of research that is currently prevailing in these (often North American) journals. This has been identified as a problem in, for instance, accounting research where European and North American traditions differ significantly (Ter Bogt & Scapens, 2012). This is, no doubt, also true for other management disciplines (Aguinis et al., 2020).

Crowding Out What Is Difficult to Quantify

Quantitative and evaluative performance management focusing on a limited range of activities and narrow measurements risks crowding out activities that are necessary for sustaining and developing academic institutions but are more difficult to "count", such as activities related to administration, community building and interaction with society. A considerable risk of free-riding is thus created as illustrated by the following:

> I have a colleague who neglects all the basic work tasks (doesn't come to meetings, ignores the development of the work community and mutual agreements, and teaches only some of the assigned courses) but is still highly recognized (also in terms of salary) in the department. This is because he publishes a huge number of articles and goes to various congresses, even though they have nothing to do with our discipline and its development. (Female lecturer, educational sciences, quoted in Kallio & Kallio, 2014: 584)

This type of environment is a fertile breeding ground for instrumentalists who see others as opportunities to advance their own career interests. Such a focus on individual achievements is problematic as we know from experience that research and teaching *as activities* require collective efforts, well-functioning communities, intellectual stimuli and effective peer-based support systems. If the community and, in particular, management applaud the type of character described in the quotation above as "stars", it easily comes with the consequence of those still "wasting their time" looking after the collective, giving collegial support to peers and walking the extra mile for students, becoming "laggards" in comparison. In many organizations, there is a clear mismatch between the tasks to be delivered and their measurement – and some rebalancing between individuals and the collectivity may be needed.

An Illusion of Objectivity

Ter Bogt and Scapens (2012) point at an interesting paradox of transparency in many contemporary, quantitatively focused and formalized performance management systems. Quantitative evaluative systems are perceived as both more transparent, but at the same time they are also considerably ambiguous (see also Helgesson & Sjögren, 2019). This is explained by the fact that subjectivity in judgements can never entirely be removed, which is also an important point in Murphy's (2020) more general critique of performance management systems discussed in the previous section. New performance management systems, however, move this subjectivity further away from those being evaluated, thus contributing to adding rather than reducing ambiguity:

> [A]ttempts to make performance measurement systems more objective can, in practice, create uncertainty as subjectivity is not removed, it is merely relocated at a greater distance from those who are the subjects of the performance measurement system. (Ter Bogt & Scapens, 2012: 484)

For instance, a promotion decision that previously was a subjective decision of individuals in a department, may in the name of transparency become an "objective" decision of a tenure review committee composed of representatives from different departments and institutions who rely on (subjective) letters of external experts and previous (subjective) publication decisions by editors making up the candidates publication list.

TOWARDS BETTER PERFORMANCE MANAGEMENT IN ACADEMIA

The above paints a somewhat depressing view of contemporary initiatives towards the formal management of performance in academic institutions. Although the increasingly popular quantitative and evaluative forms of performance management have been spreading quickly (along with the sprawling bureaucratization and managerialist manoeuvring most academics loath), their effectiveness beyond marginal increases in employee productivity seem to be limited. Also, these increases come with considerable costs, as we have discussed. However, we do not want to engage in unproductive nostalgia and what Ylijoki (2005) calls the collective yearning for the "good old days". Those days were not unproblematic either. The much-valued academic freedom needs to be accompanied by *academic responsibility* for institutions of higher education. To thrive and to preserve legitimacy they need to maintain the trust of their many stakeholders. Some control mechanisms and limits to individual freedom are needed. We need to forge a third way instead. We concur with Poulfelt (Chapter 1 in this volume) who argues that academic professionals are not impossible to manage by "nature", but that they require a particular kind of management to bring out their best. There are no ready-made solutions as each institution and academic professional is different.

In the following we will sketch out what effective performance management could look like in contemporary academia.

Recruit and Promote for Performance and Organizational Citizenship

As it is fair to assume that academics will be mainly intrinsically motivated, their performance is determined by their ability and opportunity to perform well and their willingness to put effort into their work (the latter will typically follow from the former). In their study on what drives research performance in academic departments, Edgar and Geare (2013) found that academics themselves found personal competence, motivation, time to do research and confidence to be the most important drivers of research performance. This implies that those with the right skills, attitudes and motivation will perform well regardless of the performance management systems, while those without these skills and motivations will struggle also with active performance management practices. In comparing the management practices of low- and high-performing academic departments, practices related to selection based on minimum requirements, a proven publication record and research skills were found to be significantly more prevalent in high-performing departments than in low-performing departments (Edgar & Geare, 2013).

However, a solid personal publication record is not enough. High-performing departments are populated by people with the right skills and motivation to contribute to the complex and multifaceted mission of academia, including being genuinely engaged and supportive of other members of the community and contributing to creating and sustaining a culture of collaboration. Making sure to feed the system with such individuals through a systematic and selective recruitment process is a key step towards high individual and organizational performance. Individuals should be promoted for both academic excellence and community building, and those engaging in excessive instrumentalism and ego-centrism should be held back by restricting their promotion to senior positions.

Establish Basic Performance Standards

Because performance management is aimed at aligning individual performance with organizational goals, academics need to understand these organizational goals and how they translate into a complex set of desired activities that make up a successful department and university. These broader goals and what attitudes and behaviours are expected of individuals so they can contribute to the community should also be included in tenure and promotion criteria and openly discussed in team meetings and during performance talks. Some basic individual performance standards identifying a *minimum* performance level over time may be one way of moving forward. By raising the bar for the organization, by making performance expectations explicit, and by finding suitable ways for acknowledging good performances, the academic middle manager can help improve the results of his or her department. In line with Aguinis et al. (2020), we argue that it is important that performance standards are inclusive, allowing for different publication strategies for different authors, topics and audiences, instead of a narrow focus on a few journals on the FT50 list, for instance, or to consider a broader set of quality indicators, such as impact of research on teaching or practice. In a similar way, teaching and citizenship standards could be defined (e.g. minimum teaching quantity and quality, minimum citizenship engagement related to one's area of expertise). Important, though, is that these standards are viewed as minimum levels rather than variables based on which performance will be differentially assessed and rewards distributed. This will enable the intrinsically motivated academic to find their best way to contribute to the organization and give the academic middle manager the means to identify underperformers to specifically target.

Leave the Good Performers Alone: Focus on Creating a Stimulating Environment

Most academics are motivated by the tasks related to research and teaching and thus perceive any activities (including formal performance management) a distraction potentially lowering their motivation and performance. This does not mean that they don't want to be part of a collective – nor that they do not appreciate a word of praise or a pat on the back from time to time. In their review of the literature, Edgar and Geare (2013) found that high research productivity is related to cooperative management, a sense of belonging to a department, active research seminars, methods training, mentorship and time to do research. However, it means that management intervention is focused on supporting knowledge creation rather than research productivity. This implies giving researchers autonomy. Besides recruitment and selection practices, giving academics "sufficient authority to fulfil research responsibilities" and "sufficient freedom to do research" were the management practices that most clearly distinguished the low-performing from the high-performing departments (Edgar & Geare, 2013). Given that most academics will remain motivated and thus productive if not managed actively, regular detailed evaluative performance reviews may thus create more harm than good. So, for those that live up to basic performance standards, the recommended strategy is to spare them the ritualistic performance evaluation and instead encourage and enable future performance.

Address Low-Performers: With Help from HR and Upper Management

We suggest that "active" performance management should focus on those colleagues who are clearly underperforming in relation to the established basic performance standards. For each role and core activity, a department should define explicit minimum performance expectations, as discussed above. A failure to reach these expectations should trigger a performance review aimed at identifying obstacles and supporting the individual to get back on track towards this standard. If this cannot be achieved, adjustments may be brought into play, such as a change of roles and tasks. However, an important challenge here is that in many research environments, academic managers have very limited tools (as well as incentives) to sanction underperforming colleagues. This is something upper management and HR should formally address and actively support the academic middle manager in dealing with low-performers. A work environment where the tasks of an underperforming colleague continuously fall on other colleagues and this underperformance is tolerated by management, is no more excusable in academia than in other workplaces. Stigma around "leaving academia" if motivation or ability is no longer there, needs to be lowered. It is not unusual for people in other fields and occupations to change jobs and occupations many times in their careers. Why should it be any different in academia?

Mentor New and/or Junior Faculty Members

Performance-related feedback should be focused where it is needed and where it makes a positive difference. One group that may be expected to benefit from such interventions are those either starting their careers or those new to the institution, especially if they are on tenure track contracts. It may take time to learn about the culture of a given academic institution, build social ties, and understand teaching standards and ways of working. This is not much different from onboarding processes in place in many other organizations. But they are often neglected in academic institutions. These employee groups, being in a relatively vulnerable and stressful position, will typically be more susceptible to performance management aimed at supporting them in reaching their targets. Active, coaching-oriented performance management should thus be put in place here – and be more frequent than the annual performance review.

Make Sure Extrinsic Motivators, If Used, Really "Count"

As discussed, academics are primarily motivated intrinsically and the use of extrinsic motivators, while having some positive impact on e.g. research productivity, has been shown to come with several unintended consequences and questionable side effects. Some examples of these include goal displacement (research is more about pushing out publications than knowledge development), reduced innovativeness (focusing on marginal but safe research contributions and pre-packaged and well-rehearsed teaching rather than risky novel projects), crowding out of non-measurable tasks, and increased perceived pressure and stress. The use of extrinsic motivators should thus be carefully (re-)considered.

A common use of extrinsic rewards in contemporary universities is performance-based pay where annual pay raises are linked to the department head's performance appraisals. The problem with these systems is, however, as pointed out by Murphy (2020), that pay rises are typically in the range of 1–3% and thus way too small to make a real difference to individuals. As individuals' pay is to a much larger extent determined by the salary and work contract they were able to negotiate when entering the organization, any subsequent performance-based annual salary rises are of marginal importance. While some may appreciate token rises for their symbolic value, many academics perceive performance assessments linked to salary increases as empty rituals, breeding cynicism among employees rather than something that drives motivation and performance.

This, however, does not mean that remuneration is not important in academia. Rather, it needs to be treated as the hygiene factor a lot of previous research has shown it to be (Herzberg, 1987). Better remuneration does not motivate employees, but too low remuneration demotivates and creates turnover intentions. This implies that universities, rather than focusing on marginal changes in individuals' salaries, need to monitor and adjust salaries in relation to developments among relevant peer organizations. In order to offer individuals a reasonable salary progression, more substantial increases may also be linked to career events – such as getting tenure or being promoted to professor.

Finally, if performance-based compensation is to be applied, it should be linked to objective criteria, such as publications in certain journals or teaching excellence. However, a word of caution is in order. Rewarding such excellence with money carries the risk of staff modifying behaviour in unwanted ways, such as neglecting other duties and adopting dubious research ethics (Quan et al., 2017) and should, thus, be used with care.

Support the Academic Middle Manager

While university top management tends to look at performance at the aggregate level – number of diplomas, research articles produced in a given year and national and international rankings – daily people management, housekeeping and good functioning of the department is the responsibility of the academic middle manager.

The position of these managers is in most cases part-time and temporary. From the outset, they may have very little formal managerial training and experience, possibility, power or even personal inclination to *lead* and make substantial changes. These managers, however, are in a key position to ensure the quality of teaching and research activities, equitable treatment of faculty, development work, and a myriad of other time- and energy-consuming tasks that are central to academic life. They need support and mentoring from upper management and the faculty HR manager to act effectively in their role. The effort needed to engage in managerial work needs to be formally acknowledged and enough time allocated so these individuals have an opportunity to enact their managerial roles with the professionalism and dedication needed. Ultimately, it is the responsibility of the middle manager to somehow sort out the complexities and paradoxes arising from the very nature of academic work itself so that the unit can meet the expectations of its increasingly demanding stakeholders. At the heart of the challenge is a work culture that has taken centuries to form and that has been subject to substantial changes in past decades.

CONCLUDING REFLECTIONS

Many academics feel that their highly valued academic freedom is increasingly threatened by managerial initiatives aimed at following up, measuring and assessing individual-level performance. Lingering behind these initiatives is a growing distrust towards the ability of the academic profession to take the responsibility that comes with the extensive freedom it has been granted for so long. In this chapter, we have acknowledged the need to ensure that the responsibility that comes with academic freedom is taken, but we have also argued that individual performance management, as one such mechanism to ensure this, may not have the desired effect. On the contrary, it risks reducing the quality of research, teaching and engagement with society, further threatening the legitimacy of academia and potentially fuelling calls for even tighter performance management.

Much has been written about the inevitability of a neo-liberal academia, the present-day managerialism in higher education, global competition in the sector – and the difficulty for local actors to resist these changes. In this chapter, however, we have argued that universities have some freedom at least to enact these global systems, including performance management, in different ways. In practice, much of this responsibility lies with the academic middle managers who are in a key position to help build thriving local communities of academic professionals that avoid many of the pitfalls of individual performance management identified in this chapter.

To conclude, we thus want to highlight the many often untapped possibilities academic middle managers have to contribute to healthy workplaces with faculty members delivering quality teaching and research and actively taking part in community building. Ideally, these managers can not only contribute to employee well-being and to the success of their organizations, but also ensure that the many stakeholders of academia do not lose their confidence in institutions of higher education. We hope that the thoughts provided in this chapter may inspire and empower academic middle managers to realize these possibilities.

ACKNOWLEDGEMENTS

We are grateful for comments on previous versions of this chapter by Mats Edenius, Johnny Lind, Sanne Frandsen and two anonymous reviewers. The chapter has also benefited from numerous discussions with colleagues in different roles and universities. Thank you all for these discussions.

REFERENCES

Aguinis, H. 2009. *Performance Management*. Upper Saddle River, NJ: Pearson/Prentice Hall.

Aguinis, H., Cummings, C., Ramani, R. S., & Cummings, T. G. 2020. "An A is an A": the new bottom line for valuing academic research. *Academy of Management Perspectives*, 34(1): 135–54.

Aguinis, H., Joo, H., & Gottfredson, R. K. 2011. Why we hate performance management—and why we should love it. *Business Horizons*, 54(6): 503–7.

Alajoutsijärvi, K., Kettunen, K., & Sohlo, S. 2018. Shaking the status quo: business accreditation and positional competition. *Academy of Management Learning & Education*, 17(2): 203–25.

Alvesson, M., & Kärreman, D. 2007. Unraveling HRM: identity, ceremony and control in a management consulting firm. *Organization Science*, 18(4): 711–23.

Ashforth, B. E. 2005. Becoming vanilla pudding: how we undermine our passion for research. *Journal of Management Inquiry*, 14(4): 400–403.

Basow, S. A. 2000. Best and worst professors: gender patterns in students' choices. *Sex Roles*, 43(5): 407–17.

Berk, R. A. 2018. Start spreading the news: use multiple sources of evidence to evaluate teaching. *The Journal of Faculty Development*, 32(1): 73–81.

Brown, F. W., & Moshavi, D. 2002. Herding academic cats: faculty reactions to transformational and contingent reward leadership by department chairs. *Journal of Leadership Studies*, 8(3): 79–93.

Cadez, S., Dimovski, V., & Zaman Groff, M. 2017. Research, teaching and performance evaluation in academia: the salience of quality. *Studies in Higher Education*, 42(8): 1455–73.

Cannizzo, F. 2018. Tactical evaluations: everyday neoliberalism in academia. *Journal of Sociology*, 54(1): 77–91.

DeNisi, A., & Murphy, K. R. 2017. Performance appraisal and performance management: 100 years of progress? *Journal of Applied Psychology*, 102(3): 421–33.

DeNisi, A., & Smith, C. E. 2014. Performance appraisal, performance management, and firm-level performance: a review, a proposed model, and new directions for future research. *Academy of Management Annals*, 8(1): 127–79.

Edgar, F., & Geare, A. 2013. Factors influencing university research performance. *Studies in Higher Education*, 38(5): 774–92.

Einola, K., & Werr, A. 2020. HRM i Akademin – byråkratiskt nonsense eller vägen till en bättre arbetsplats? [HRM in academia – bureaucratic nonsense or a path to a better working place?]. In M. Alvesson, & S. Sveningsson (eds), *Ledning och (sned-)styrning i högre utbildning*. Lund: Studentlitteratur.

Ekman Rising, M., Lindgren, M., & Packendorff, J. 2020. Omgiven av instrumentalister: har det akademiska medborgarskapet gått förlorat? [Surrounded by instrumentalists: has academic citizenship been lost?]. In M. Alvesson, & S. Sveningsson (eds), *Ledning och (sned-)styrning i högskolan*. Lund: Studentlitteratur.

Else, H. 2017. Academics 'face higher mental health risk' than other professions. *Times Higher Education*, 22 August 2017. https://www.timeshighereducation.com/news/academics-face-higher -mental-health-risk-than-other-professions.

Forrest, B. 2013. Shattered genius. In S. Mukherjee, & T. Folger (eds), *The Best American Science and Nature Writing*. New York: Houghton Mifflin Harcourt.

Gioia, D. A., & Corley, K. G. 2002. Being good versus looking good: business school rankings and the Circean transformation from substance to image. *Academy of Management Learning & Education*, 1(1): 107–20.

Gruening, G. 2001. Origin and theoretical basis of New Public Management. *International Public Management Journal*, 4(1): 1–25.

Helgesson, K. S., & Sjögren, E. 2019. No finish line: how formalization of academic assessment can undermine clarity and increase secrecy. *Gender, Work & Organization*, 26(4): 558–81.

Herzberg, F. 1987. One more time: how do you motivate employees? *Harvard Business Review*, 65(5). https://hbr.org/2003/01/one-more-time-how-do-you-motivate-employees.

Kallio, K.-M., & Kallio, T. J. 2014. Management-by-results and performance measurement in universities – implications for work motivation. *Studies in Higher Education*, 39(4): 574–89.

Kluger, A. N., & DeNisi, A. 1996. The effects of feedback interventions on performance: a historical review, a meta-analysis, and a preliminary feedback intervention theory. *Psychological Bulletin*, 119(2): 254–84.

MacNell, L., Driscoll, A., & Hunt, A. N. 2015. What's in a name: exposing gender bias in student ratings of teaching. *Innovative Higher Education*, 40(4): 291–303.

Murphy, K. R. 2020. Performance evaluation will not die, but it should. *Human Resource Management Journal*, 30(1): 13–31.

Pulakos, E. D., Hanson, R. M., Arad, S., & Moye, N. 2015. Performance management can be fixed: an on-the-job experiential learning approach for complex behavior change. *Industrial and Organizational Psychology*, 8(1): 51–76.

Quan, W., Chen, B., & Shu, F. 2017. Publish or impoverish: an investigation of the monetary reward system of science in China (1999–2016). *Aslib Journal of Information Management*, 69(5): 486–502.

Scully, M. A. 1997. Meritocracy. In R. E. Freeman, & P. H. Werhane (eds), *Dictionary of Business Ethics*. London: Blackwell.

Ter Bogt, H. J., & Scapens, R. W. 2012. Performance management in universities: effects of the transition to more quantitative measurement systems. *European Accounting Review*, 21(3): 451–97.

Thunnissen, M. 2016. Talent management: for what, how and how well? An empirical exploration of talent management in practice. *Employee Relations*, 38(1): 57–72.

Van den Brink, M., Fruytier, B., & Thunnissen, M. 2013. Talent management in academia: performance systems and HRM policies. *Human Resource Management Journal*, 23(2): 180–95.

Waring, M. 2013. All in this together? HRM and the individualisation of the academic worker. *Higher Education Policy*, 26(3): 397–419.

Willmott, H. 1995. Managing the academics: commodification and control in the development of university education in the UK. *Human Relations*, 48(9): 993–1027.

Ylijoki, O. H. 2005. Academic nostalgia: a narrative approach to academic work. *Human Relations*, 58(5): 555–76.

8. Deploying systems thinking to create a 'triple-crown' business school

Michael C. Jackson OBE

INTRODUCTION

This chapter describes the role that systems thinking, particularly 'critical systems thinking', played in building a successful UK business school between 1999 and 2011. When I took up a post at the University of Hull, in 1999, there was no business school in place – just some small departments pursuing a range of diverse interests. The University did not look favourably upon these departments and many of their activities. Their reputation outside the institution was poor. As presumptive dean of a new business school, it was my job to combine the departments, integrate them into a school, grow that school, and improve the reputation of business education at the University among local, national, and international stakeholders. By 2011, when I stood down as dean, those objectives had been achieved and Hull University Business School had gained 'triple-crown' accreditation from AACSB, AMBA and EQUIS.[1] In what follows, the situation 'before and after' is described; the systems thinking tools used to assist with the transformation are introduced; and an account is provided of how they were deployed in practice.

THE 'MESS' IN 1999

In 1999 I received an offer from the University of Hull to establish a new business school. I had left the University in 1994 largely because of a lack of progress in this regard. During those five years I was at the University of Humberside (also in Hull) which became the University of Lincolnshire and Humberside. I learned to be a dean and established a new Centre for Systems Research. But that university was intent on shifting everything to Lincoln. I had no wish to move out of Hull – why would you? As a result, the offer from the University of Hull was one that I could not refuse. I was dean of Hull University Business School (HUBS) for nearly 12 years.

There was a plan to establish a business school at the University and I was appointed to see it to fruition. The plan was a good one. On the ground, however, things were desperate. Two departments, Management Systems and Accounting and Finance, had agreed to join the new school but did not get on. The Department of Economics was reluctant to engage, and it took two years' work to get them into the new school. Further along the line, the University took on responsibility for a College of Higher Education in Scarborough and a small management group from that institution had to be integrated into HUBS. Taking all these units into account, the base staffing level was around 45, student numbers about 600 (not counting validated programmes), and turnover about £5 million per annum. At Hull there were small undergraduate programmes in Management Systems, Accounting, Business, and Economics. There was virtually nothing on-campus at postgraduate level. Most of the income came from Master of Business Administration degrees (MBAs) operated overseas through a variety of agents, in many different countries. Some perverse incentives for those responsible meant that there were over 30 different programmes, sometimes four or five in the same country. The MBAs in Hong Kong were featured, not in a favourable light, on a BBC *Dispatches* programme. There were further MBAs, validated by Hull, at private colleges and local higher education colleges throughout the UK. The MBAs had become the main business. There was no interest in the Hull departments in 'teaching quality', which was about to become a major issue in UK higher education. Research performance was poor and was being investigated. There were virtually no links with local, national, or international businesses. In 1999, when Hull University Business School was formed, it was part of a Faculty of Social Sciences and had no separate space of its own. The situation was a 'mess'.

THE SITUATION IN 2011

By 2011 everything had changed. HUBS had become an independent faculty and moved into new and refurbished buildings which were frequently described as 'world-class'. An academic leadership team, including the dean, deputy dean, and directors of teaching and learning, research, and external business, had oversight of the work of six subject groups (one in Scarborough) covering all the major business and management disciplines. HUBS had its own support units, under an administrative director, responsible for general administration, marketing, finance, human resources, recruitment, postgraduate admissions, alumni, business links, and IT. There were approximately 120 academic staff and a further 45 administrative staff. Student numbers had grown to over 3,500, including 900 at postgraduate level, and turnover was at £28 million per annum. HUBS had over 60% of the overseas students in the University. There were thriving full-time and part-time undergraduate programmes, offering the possibility of a year in industry or abroad, a range of extremely popular MSc programmes, and successful full-time and part-time, on-campus MBA programmes. The overseas MBAs had been rationalized to just four with two agents, one each for the Middle and Far East. There were a few validations, all at undergraduate level at local colleges. Efficiency was emphasized and the University received an annual contribution of around 45% of HUBS' income to cover overheads and make investments. Detailed attention was given to the programmes and to teaching quality. An early quality assurance assessment of the school gave a score of 23 out of 24. The MBAs, full- and part-time, home and overseas, were AMBA accredited. Research was encouraged and reorganized. The key research centre, the Centre for Systems Studies, prospered and a £9 million grant was obtained from Yorkshire Forward to establish a Logistics Institute. In the 2008 Research Assessment Exercise, HUBS came 16th among all business schools in the UK for 'research power' (number of staff entered multiplied by the average quality score given to each piece of work submitted). There was a large population of PhD students tied into the research activity. HUBS had massively increased its corporate connections with the help of a strong Advisory Board. There was significant executive, in-house and consultancy activity with local and national organizations. The success of HUBS led to EQUIS accreditation (from the major European accreditation body for business schools) and AACSB accreditation (from the US-based business school accrediting association). HUBS was the first business school in Yorkshire, and only the 13th in the UK, to gain 'triple-crown' (AACSB, AMBA, EQUIS) accreditation, putting it in the top 1% of business schools in the world. Five senior staff of HUBS went on to become business school deans at other universities.

My immediate boss, in the early days of the growth of HUBS, Deputy Vice-Chancellor Howell Lloyd, says:

> In 1999 the University of Hull set about consolidating its business-related programmes. Twelve years later, under Mike Jackson's leadership, those plans had resulted, beyond expectations, in a triple-crown accredited business school with some 3,500 students. The HUBS story is a remarkable one and in this chapter he describes some of the ways in which success was achieved. (Personal communication, 16/8/2018)

The Vice-Chancellor of the University, between 1999 and 2009, David Drewry, states:

> One of the most impressive developments in the University, during my time as VC, was the rapid growth and remarkable success of the business school. Working hand-in-hand with the University, and using systems thinking, HUBS formulated a vision of promoting 'responsible leadership for a complex world' and gained national and international recognition for what it achieved. (Personal communication, 18/8/2018)

PARTIAL DISCLAIMER

As dean, from 1999 to 2011, I played a part in bringing about a sea change in performance and was the person who received credit. I was elected a Companion of the Association of Business Schools and, in the Queen's New Year's Honours List of 2011, was awarded an OBE for 'services to higher education and business'.

Obviously, many other factors were instrumental in making the transformation in fortunes possible:

- It was a period in which business schools generally were booming and business subjects were popular with both home and overseas students.
- There was no business school at the University of Hull in 1999 and this made it possible to build one from scratch in a way that took advantage of the favourable environment.
- The City of Hull was crying out for a business school and there was strong local support.
- The leadership of the University was strong and far-sighted enough to encourage faculties to take responsibility for their own futures and not see their success as a threat to central control.
- HUBS was blessed with some extremely competent, imaginative, and hardworking staff who generated and led their own initiatives on behalf of the school.
- A significant proportion of the staff, as well as Pauline (my wife) and myself, were from Hull or the immediate vicinity. It was obvious to stakeholders that we were not putting the effort in simply to advance our careers and then move elsewhere.

In a later section, I hope to demonstrate that 'systems thinking', 'critical systems thinking' and 'critical systems practice' also played a significant role. First, I need to explain what I mean by those terms.

SYSTEMS THINKING, 'CRITICAL SYSTEMS THINKING' AND 'CRITICAL SYSTEMS PRACTICE'

Systems thinking, as an identifiable 'trans-discipline', established itself in the 1940s and 1950s based on the pioneering work of Ludwig von Bertalanffy in 'general system theory' and Norbert Wiener in 'cybernetics'. Its raison d'être was understanding systems of 'organized complexity' that could not be explained using the traditional methods of the physical sciences. The systems approach soon began to give rise to methodologies, such as systems engineering, socio-technical systems thinking and system dynamics, which sought to translate its findings into practice. Over time, a wide variety of such systems methodologies were developed, and it is this applied strand of systems thinking upon which we concentrate here. It is arguable that in the VUCA world (of volatility, uncertainty, complexity, and ambiguity), systems thinking is coming into its own. The 'wicked problems' confronted by decision-makers today transcend the boundaries of any one discipline and demand trans-disciplinary attention.

One of the newest developments in systems thinking is 'critical systems thinking' (CST). It represents a maturing of the trans-discipline in that it respects and seeks to build upon previous systems approaches. CST announced itself to the world with the publication of two books in 1991 – *Critical Systems Thinking: Directed Readings* (Flood & Jackson, eds) and *Creative Problem Solving: Total Systems Intervention* (Flood & Jackson). The latest rendition of CST is in my book *Critical Systems Thinking and the Management of Complexity* (Jackson, 2019). CST has been consistent, throughout its evolution, in its commitment to the three themes of 'critical awareness', 'pluralism' and 'improvement'.

Critical awareness, to summarize greatly, is about understanding what the various systems methodologies assume about the nature of complex problem situations and how these can be changed. This provides insight into their different strengths and weaknesses. In *Critical Systems Thinking and the Management of Complexity* (Jackson, 2019), I undertake a critique of the major established systems methodologies and divide them into six broad classes according to what aspects of complexity they give priority to in examining and seeking to improve problem situations. The six classes are:

- Systems approaches for 'technical complexity' ('hard' systems methodologies such as operational research, systems engineering and systems analysis) – concentrating on how to efficiently organize components and sub-systems to reach a pre-defined purpose.
- Systems approaches for 'process complexity' (the Vanguard Method or 'lean systems') – concentrating on putting together the necessary interdependent actions to achieve a purpose while eliminating 'waste' in the system.
- Systems approaches for 'structural complexity' (system dynamics) – concentrating on identifying the significant variables and interactions that influence system behaviour and modelling the interactions of positive and negative feedback loops and lags.
- Systems approaches for 'organizational and environmental complexity' (the viable system model, socio-technical systems thinking) – concentrating on making systems resilient, adaptive and anti-fragile so they can survive and thrive over time in the face of unpredictable internal disturbances and environmental turbulence.
- Systems approaches for 'people complexity' ('soft systems' approaches such as strategic assumption surfacing and testing, interactive planning, soft systems methodology) – concentrating on exploring different perspectives and world-views and ensuring that enough

agreement is obtained among stakeholders to enable them to come together to undertake beneficial action.
- Systems approaches for 'coercive complexity' (critical systems heuristics, team synteg-rity) – concentrating on achieving fairness by ensuring that those potentially disadvantaged by power have a say in decisions, if required by working on their behalf.

Critical awareness helps us to appreciate the theoretical orientations embedded in the different systems methodologies. Further, it suggests that all the various approaches have something to offer and all should be valued. They have complementary strengths and weaknesses. Understanding how the 'whole system' works is the privilege of God, but at least critical systems thinkers understand how particular systems methodologies fall short of being com-prehensive and can compensate by using them alongside others possessing different attributes.

It will come as no surprise, therefore, that the second commitment of CST is to 'pluralism' – using the different systems methodologies in combination in a way that maximizes the strengths and compensates for the weaknesses of each of them. This is necessary if we are to have any prospect of managing the multi-dimensional complexity of the VUCA world. In its pursuit of pluralism, CST regards it as an advantage that systems practice can now deploy systems methodologies that enact change according to the conclusions reached about the nature of social reality by a range of sociological paradigms. Its ability to do this is confirmed if we consider the social theories either implicitly or explicitly underpinning those method-ologies. To illustrate, hard systems approaches reflect the functionalist paradigm and exhibit a positivist orientation; system dynamics and the viable system model are similarly functional-ist but with a structuralist orientation; soft systems approaches are interpretivist/constructivist; and critical systems heuristics is emancipatory (Jackson, 2019). It is the paradigm embraced which influences the attention the methodologies give to different aspects of complexity. Of course, we then encounter another crucial issue – retaining coherence in a field of diverse per-spectives where different knowledge paradigms co-exist. We can rule out trying to resolve this by discovering 'the truth' about the nature of complex problem situations – this is unknowable. The 'critical systems practice' multi-methodology, which puts CST into action, proceeds differently, as we shall see below.

The third commitment of CST is to 'improvement'. But what criteria should be used to analyse progress and outcomes, and evaluate whether they constitute improvement? The argument is that they must be judged with respect to the primary concerns of the full range of systems methodologies. A reasonable starting point is to look at a 'critical systems practice' intervention to see whether it is increasing or has increased:

- Efficiency
- Efficacy
- Awareness of interrelationships
- Resilience/anti-fragility
- Effectiveness
- Empowerment
- Emancipation
- Sustainability.

A bar chart can be constructed, at the beginning of an intervention, showing the current state of the system according to the indicators used to measure the criteria. As the process of change proceeds, the bar chart will be updated with estimates of how things are going in terms of the different criteria. The extent and nature of the trade-offs between criteria should provoke constant discussion and possibly a rethinking about which systems methodologies to use. At the end, an assessment can be made of how the system appears to be performing in terms of all the criteria. The final chart will also suggest what needs attending to next – what other systems approach or approaches should be brought into play. Over a long-term 'critical systems practice' engagement, we will want to see improvement in relation to all the criteria.

We turn now to the 'critical systems practice' (CSP) multi-methodology – the practical face of CST. CSP is designed to help the user conduct an exploration of problem situations from a variety of viewpoints and then to employ the different systems methodologies in an informed manner in order to learn what works to bring about improvement in the real-world problem situation. It has four phases, beginning with *creativity*. This phase involves viewing the problem situation through the lenses provided by a number of 'systems perspectives'. Always essential are the 'technical', 'process', 'structural', 'organization/environment', 'people', 'coercive system' and 'ecological' perspectives. The aim is to reveal the range of issues that need addressing. CSP then proceeds to a *choice* phase. Although CST regards the nature of the 'multi-dimensional complexity' exhibited by 'messes' and 'wicked problems' as unknowable in advance, it argues that the knowledge of available systems approaches, yielded by critical awareness, provides the basis for an informed choice of systems methodology or methodologies to be made at the beginning of an intervention. Depending upon the type of issues surfaced during the creativity stage, a systems methodology, or often more than one, will be chosen to start the intervention. *Implementation* can then proceed according to the guidelines of the chosen methodology or methodologies. There is a need for flexibility because as the problem situation develops, and renewed iterations through the creativity and reflection stages demonstrate different issues are becoming dominant, appropriate changes in methodology need to be enacted. A *reflection* stage continually evaluates the success of action taken and seeks to derive learning about how to improve the whole CSP process. The complexity of 'wicked problems' ideally requires the use of all the systems approaches in combination. CSP provides a means of proceeding given that this is impossible in practice. It is a pragmatic response to the requirement imposed by multi-dimensional complexity to work with different knowledge paradigms and their linked systems methodologies.

Drawing upon the framework of 'constitutive rules' for methodologies, formulated by Checkland and Scholes (1990), it is possible to establish the principles that have to be respected in any intervention using the CSP multi-methodology. These are set out in Table 8.1. The 'rules' require more explanation than there is space for here (see Jackson, 2019 for a fuller account), but will still prove helpful in considering what was done in Hull University Business School in the next section.

Table 8.1   *Constitutive rules for the critical systems practice (CSP) multi-methodology*

1. The CSP multi-methodology is a structured way of thinking which understands and respects the uniqueness of a wide variety of systems approaches, and their underpinning sociological paradigms, and draws upon them to improve real-world problem situations.
2. CSP makes use of creativity-enhancing devices to discover and classify the main issues posed by a problem situation, ensuring minimally that it is examined through the lenses of seven 'systems perspectives' – 'technical', 'process', 'structural', 'organization/environment', 'people', 'coercive system' and 'ecological'.
3. CSP uses systems methodologies, which can be clearly related back to the different paradigms, as the basis for its intervention strategy – often employing the tactic of naming one methodology as primary and others as secondary, with the possibility of this relationship changing during the course of the intervention.
4. The methodologies used in CSP will themselves employ, in combination, methods, models, tools and techniques drawn from a variety of different sources, including 'decomposed' methodologies.
5. The choice of systems methodologies, and of the methods, models, tools and techniques used in a particular intervention, will rest upon an appreciation of their different strengths and weaknesses as revealed by 'critical awareness', learning from previous action research, and on the experience of the participants.
6. Since CSP, and the systems methodologies it employs, can be used in different ways in different situations, each use should exhibit conscious thought about how to adapt to the circumstances encountered.
7. Each use of CSP should yield research findings based on an understanding of relevant current knowledge as well as provide an evaluation of the outcomes derived from the concerns of the different methodologies and paradigms.

WHAT WAS DONE IN HULL UNIVERSITY BUSINESS SCHOOL USING CSP?

The emphasis here is on how CSP played a part in achieving the successful outcomes that emanated from the transformation of HUBS. It would not be useful to provide an historical narrative of events. First, because the intervention lasted nearly 12 years it would take a book to do so; second, because the use of CSP was episodic. Although it was always there in the background, it only broke the surface and became explicit if the situation seemed to demand it and the circumstances were propitious for that to happen. The solution I have adopted is to consider how aspects of CSP were used, both implicitly and explicitly, to address the six sources of complexity identified as being the focus of attention of the different systems methodologies – technical, process, structural, organizational and environmental, people, and coercive complexity. Again, I need to refer the reader to *Critical Systems Thinking and the Management of Complexity* (Jackson, 2019) for more detail on the systems methodologies and methods referred to in what follows.

Technical Complexity

The efficiency of HUBS meant that, over the last ten years of my time as dean, it was able to deliver a significant surplus to the University to cover its overheads and for further investment. Two initiatives contributed significantly to improving the 'technical' performance of HUBS and enabled it to deliver this surplus. The first was that the programmes were organized for maximum efficiency. At the undergraduate level, a common first year was introduced across all the degrees, and there was also sharing of modules in the second and third years. To take another example, a suite of Master of Science degrees was established, each in areas of strong market demand, and they shared a minimum of four common modules. The second initiative was the 'workload model'. The model allocated time for duties, such as teaching, research and administration, according to a precise formula. A simple linear programming model, from the 'operational research' stable, was employed in its construction. Each member of staff had a set number of hours (around 1,600) to fill and would negotiate their workload with their head of department before the beginning of each academic year. In terms of efficiency, the model had the benefit of ensuring that everyone fulfilled at least their minimum workload requirement and did so in a way that was beneficial to HUBS' ambitions. For example, if there was no evidence of research output from a member of staff then there were no more hours allocated to that person for research. The managing of 'technical complexity', through these two initiatives, produced an average return to the University, over those ten years, of 45% of annual turnover.

There was, of course, opposition to the initiatives from a few staff. The workload model will be taken as an example of how it was managed. There was no official workload model in the University at the time and so the HUBS model had, each year, to be agreed according to the democratic procedures of the business school. An extensive period of consultation was always involved and, as a result, I cannot remember a case when the model did not easily gain the consent of the School Board. The arguments for the model in terms of efficiency were overwhelming but they also had to be convincing from other perspectives. It was easy to make the case. From the 'people' perspective, the model did much to increase mutual understanding. The outcomes of the workload planning process were made available to all and this transparency meant every individual could see what HUBS was doing with its staff resources and how every individual was contributing. This also led, from the 'coercive system' perspective, to a belief that the model was 'fair'. Everybody could be seen to be doing the same amount of work even if it took different forms in the case of each person. If no formal model had existed, the workload would still have to be allocated. Left to happen by default the process was open to accusations of bias, favouritism and unfairness. The explicit HUBS model, and the way it was managed, removed the force of any such arguments. For individuals, the model created a greater sense of freedom. They were able, within the constraints of what HUBS required, to direct their efforts into activities they were good at and enjoyed, for example, postgraduate rather than undergraduate teaching. Further, the workload model set a notional limit to what they needed to do to fulfil their obligations to HUBS and the University. Beyond that, they were free to make a case that they were entitled to additional earnings from teaching on overseas programmes, from executive education, and from consultancy. This had, for some time, been a controversial issue for the University. The existence of the workload model, which contributed significantly to the 45% return, made it easy to argue that contractual duties were being more than fulfilled and that extra payment was necessary for overtime that, after all, served the University's own interests since it brought in additional revenue. From the 'organization/environment' perspective, the workload model contributed to HUBS' ability to develop and respond to shifts in its environment. It made it easy to demonstrate a shortfall in HUBS' capacity to deliver its ambitions with existing resources and so provided the basis for negotiations with the University about the need for additional staff in growth areas. As priorities changed because of external demands, for example as 'research excellence framework' (REF) deadlines approached, the model made it possible to shift staff time appropriately. I would not want to claim that the model did not have problems. A few used it to 'work to rule' but only the same people who would have done even less without the peer pressure to which the model gave rise. Over time it became bureaucratic and, by the time I stood down as dean, needed drastic simplification. Nevertheless, for many years it served HUBS well.

Process Complexity

HUBS managed a few of the 'processes' that were essential to success and depended on the University for providing others. The process of admitting postgraduate students was controlled in HUBS and was significant because the majority were from overseas and paid high fees. Using the Vanguard Method, explicitly, to check on this process revealed that it involved only three value steps from the point of view of the customer – receive and record application, check credentials, make an offer and include with that all the information the student might want to know. The turnaround time from receipt of the application to the offer going out became minimal and contributed to the success of the business school in attracting postgraduate overseas students – more than 70% of the total in the University. Other processes managed within HUBS came within the remit of an extremely competent school administrator and it was pleasing to hear reports of, for example, staff receiving the correct expenses and additional payments on time. Many key University processes, such as undergraduate admissions, also worked well. Frustration with others occasionally boiled over, however, and 'conceptual models' (a form of modelling associated with soft systems methodology) of 'a system to prevent HUBS making international links' and 'a system to prevent HUBS recruiting good staff' were built and compared to what the international office and human resources department were doing.

Structural Complexity

Familiarity with the basic tenets of system dynamics in the school made it easy to talk in terms of positive and negative feedback loops when examining structural complexity. HUBS, during my period as dean, operated in a positive cycle of growth. Success in attracting students, and in research and out-reach, brought in the money for recruitment of additional staff to strengthen existing activity and pursue growth in other areas. This was relatively easy to achieve and led, for example, to the establishment of new 'marketing and strategy' and 'organizational behaviour and human resource management' subject groups. At the same time, a close eye was kept on the possible unintended consequences of initiatives that might set in train negative influences. For example, it became apparent that the REF imperative to recruit staff capable of producing highly rated research could also lead to a decline in teaching quality. This would be reflected in poor results in the National Student Survey, lead to a fall in league table position, a decrease in applications and student numbers, a fall in income and, eventually, a fall in the ability to sustain high-level research. Another balancing loop had to be introduced to reinforce good quality teaching. It will be apparent that the CSP injunction, to look at how initiatives are progressing from a variety of perspectives, also encourages the search for crucial interdependencies. For example, the workload model not only brought greater efficiency, it also contributed to fairness.

Organizational and Environmental Complexity

The 'viable system model' (VSM) was constantly to the fore as HUBS sought to come to terms with 'organizational and environmental complexity'. In 1999, the business school was a 'green field site' and the VSM could be employed in the design mode. An important first step was to define the elements of System 1 of HUBS as undergraduate teaching, postgraduate teaching, research, and 'reach-out' (links with local colleges, executive education, consultancy activity, etc.). This is represented in Figure 8.1. Emphasizing these activities helped to focus minds on the business school as an entity rather than on the departments from which it was constructed. This was reinforced by appointing directors for each of the areas and distributing resources, through the directors, directly to these activities rather than to the departments. The departments were re-named 'subject groups' to further reinforce the message. The subject groups only appeared at recursion level two of the VSM, responsible for supplying resources to the main activities while taking responsibility for keeping up to date with their subject areas, staff development and workload planning. This worked extremely well for teaching and reach-out. For example, the degree programmes became suitably multi-disciplinary. Even students studying economics and accounting got a rounded management and business education to complement their specialist skills. It worked less well for research. Here the subject groups reasserted themselves and, apart from the Centre for Systems Studies, and later the Logistics Institute, no trans- or multi-disciplinary research groups took hold.

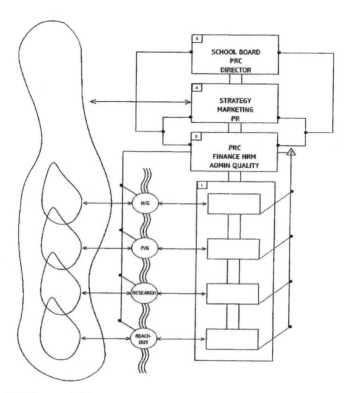

Figure 8.1   HUBS as a viable system

Towards the end of my time as dean, we tried again by abolishing all the existing research groups and starting things from scratch with significant encouragement to new multi-disciplinary centres. There were no REF deadlines looming and this attempt was inspired by complexity theory. Chaos could reign and, hopefully, new groups would self-organize and grow strong. It might have worked if I had stayed long enough to direct resources appropriately, but I was soon to stand down and, yet again, old disciplinary allegiances came to the fore.

Another advantage provided by the VSM, when used in the design mode, was that it helped HUBS to establish itself as the business school it wanted to be rather than the business school it appeared to be in its first year. We wanted to be strong in teaching at all levels, excellent at research, and to have good links with both local and national businesses. In 1999, there was some undergraduate teaching, a raft of overseas MBAs, the Centre for Systems Studies, and little else. It was decided that the structures of the business school, as modelled using the VSM, should reflect our ambitions, rather than the reality, and that appropriate management and other resources would be applied to all those areas corresponding to the ambitions even if, as was the case, they were currently realized only in the most rudimentary form. This worked well during an initial period of very rapid growth. Of course, we did not know exactly what kind of business school we wanted to be 12 years hence or what sort of business school the environment would permit, and so it was impossible to plan in detail. Fortunately, the VSM proved flexible enough to offer continuing guidance on what changes were needed – in primary units, levels of recursion, etc. – as HUBS and its environment continued to evolve. The VSM provided a way of thinking that encouraged anti-fragility as well as adaptation. It helped us to co-evolve with our environment and gradually discover what sort of business school was possible in Hull. The VSM was 'revealing' rather than 'enframing'. We learned our way to becoming a successful business school.

Thinking with the VSM in mind helped in other ways as well. It naturally focuses attention on the primary activities that the organization is directing to the market. This ensured that HUBS gave appropriate managerial attention, and the necessary support, to those aspects of its work that generated income. Students at the undergraduate and postgraduate levels brought in the most money. Excellent research and out-reach bring in some but, more importantly, contribute to improving reputation and gaining the external accreditations that lead to more applications from both home and overseas students. In the long term they make a significant, if less direct, difference to income. This is another example of understanding and following sets of linkages. The VSM assisted in discussions and negotiations between HUBS and the University. A recurrent issue that arises in universities with strong business schools is how to maintain some control over them, ensuring they operate for the benefit of the whole institution, while allowing them the freedom to flourish. At Hull, the VSM was used explicitly, during a senior management away day, to explain how the University could maintain overall cohesion while granting its parts significant autonomy. Figure 8.2 is the diagram that was used to start discussion on the relationship between the University of Hull and its faculties. It had an impact on thinking in the Vice-Chancellor's office. One aspect of the tension that often exists between universities and their business schools concerns the extent to which support services should be managed at the local level. Directors of support services usually make the case that centralization is good for the professional development of their staff. On the other hand, business schools face vastly different environments from other parts of universities and require specialist support staff with an awareness of the peculiarities of their markets. This is true when it comes to marketing, recruiting overseas students, engaging and winning contracts with external clients, career and professional development advice for students (especially MBAs), securing the best staff in a competitive market, and nurturing alumni. The argument is not easy to win for business schools in the face of opposition from other faculties and the directors of central functions. The VSM helped the HUBS leadership team frame the argument in terms of the business school's requirements as a viable system although, in this case, translated into the everyday language of why the business school needed devolved functions for its own success and so that it could contribute more to the finances and reputation of the University. HUBS won the argument and benefitted from its own administrative, marketing, finance, human resources, IT, recruitment, postgraduate admissions, alumni, and business engagement offices. It should be said that the VSM should also make managers of decentralized units acutely aware of their responsibilities to the whole. I am not sure how good I was, personally, at conveying this awareness.

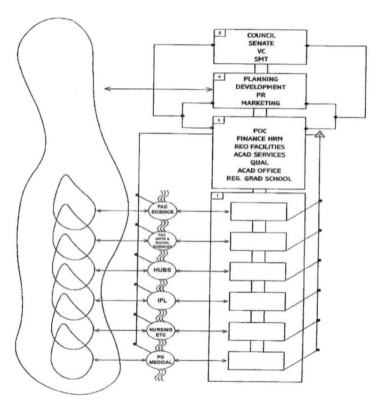

Figure 8.2   *The University of Hull as a viable system*

Socio-technical systems thinking complemented the VSM by stressing the importance of leadership at all levels, establishing autonomous work groups, and of senior managers acting in a 'boundary spanning' role to provide the stability within which other managers can operate to improve performance. All these matters were constantly on the agenda in HUBS.

People Complexity

Turning now to 'people complexity', HUBS arranged frequent meetings to discuss its overall mission, vision, and objectives and to develop strategic and operational plans. As a result, there was mutual understanding of what it was seeking to achieve and the means it was using to do so. The strap line 'responsible leadership for a complex world' emerged from a school open day, together with lots of ideas about the importance of 'connectedness' and the benefits that this could bring to our various activities. There were annual 'teaching conferences' and other, more social, events designed to bring the school together. When HUBS moved into its custom designed premises, a large and attractive space had to be retained as part of a protection order. It was an easy decision to turn this into a HUBS coffee expanse. Whereas it might be worrying, in other faculties, that staff were spending too long having coffee, in HUBS it was a concern if they were not spending enough. It was a forum for discussion and debate, and senior managers could always be located there at certain times of the day. It probably contributed more to encouraging an open, constructive and challenging culture in HUBS than anything else. Preparing students for responsible leaders in a complex world, and undertaking research and reach-out that contributed to responsible leadership, was at the pinnacle of HUBS' 'idealized design' (a key element in 'interactive planning'), but it needed translating into something much more concrete if it was to provide guidance on what exactly to do and gain staff commitment to change. In practice, it became the basis for plans which informed well-received bids for accreditation to the AACSB, AMBA and EQUIS. The demands of these bodies that HUBS meet their detailed requirements helped, in return, to mould the plans into specifications for action at a level of detail to which staff could respond. There were weekly, agenda-free meetings of senior managers to review progress. The achievement of each of the accreditations was a landmark to which people felt they had contributed and which they could celebrate together. The accreditations signified external recognition of everyone's efforts and the progress that was being made as a result.

Soft systems approaches were deployed, from time to time, to 'manage' people complexity. Aspects of Checkland's soft systems methodology were used explicitly to structure debate around issues that were causing unease in the business school. Figures 8.3 and 8.4 are 'rich pictures' which were drawn to start discussion, respectively about how to alleviate the 'multiple pressures on staff in HUBS' and 'to help explore the strategic positioning of HUBS'.

Our Rich Picture

Source: With thanks to Amanda Gregory.

Figure 8.3   A rich picture outlining the multiple pressures on staff in HUBS

More usually, 'soft systems methodology' was implicitly integrated into the everyday management practice of reviewing the current state of the 'mess', developing possible ways forward, informally discussing what to do, and agreeing to take action to implement changes deemed 'feasible and desirable'. Business schools have multiple stakeholders whose views they need to take into account if they are going to be successful – academic staff of different grades, administrative staff, students at all levels, the University, research funders, the local business community, other clients, accrediting bodies, etc. Although no formal 'strategic assumption surfacing and testing' exercises were carried out, we were aware of the importance of reviewing the assumptions we were making about the relevant stakeholders in taking strategic decisions. For example, we thought that a decision to withdraw from the validation of other institution's MBAs would please the MBA accrediting body, AMBA, but worry the University because it would lose income. Reviewing the assumptions made about stakeholders assisted in taking and justifying complex decisions. It helped HUBS to understand, based on 'critical systems heuristics', that the different stakeholders were using different 'boundary judgments' when considering what they wanted from the business school and assessing how it performed. We were keen to understand the relevance of these boundary judgments to future success and sought to learn about them using mechanisms such as staff–student meetings, regular meetings of an Advisory Board of local stakeholders, and regular contact with the accreditation bodies. In discussions with the University there were occasions when the boundary judgments of other stakeholders were employed in a 'polemical' manner to support HUBS' position. For example, the perspective provided by EQUIS could be relied upon to support arguments for greater autonomy. The membership of the Advisory Board contained many influential figures whose views the University would take account of.

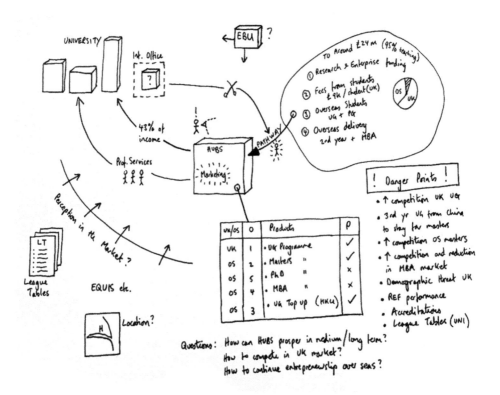

Source: With thanks to Giles Hindle.

Figure 8.4   A rich picture to help explore the strategic positioning of HUBS

Coercive Complexity

HUBS' attempts to manage 'coercive complexity' can be considered in terms of its embrace of 'discursive rationality' and some modest attempts at emancipatory practice. HUBS encouraged an ethos of treating with equal respect the contributions made by different categories and grades of staff. Arrogant professors were kept in check. No academic–administrative divide developed. Porters wanted to work in HUBS. The business school was an early signatory to the Principles for Responsible Management Education (PRME), maintained an active membership, and incorporated a commitment to global social responsibility in its teaching and research. For example, it was one of the first business schools to introduce an undergraduate module on sustainable business: 'Sustainable Business: Principles and Practice of Green Management'. HUBS collected data on female representation at senior levels in the school and performed well in this respect. The numbers of LGBT staff grew in a greater proportion than overall staff numbers and, as far as I am aware, there was no discrimination. There was one 'industrial tribunal' case involving HUBS while I was dean. This involved an alleged failure by the University to deal with racist behaviour by a couple of students. This case was dismissed and the HUBS investigation into the matter commended. The HUBS leadership group insisted that its coffee outlet be 'fair trade'. HUBS is based in a region of economic and social deprivation and responded to this in its actions. Links were made with local schools and specific information was provided to local students encouraging them to apply. Appropriate concessions were made. The growth of the business school provided direct employment opportunities and, through the numbers of additional students attracted, benefitted the city. The successful bid to Yorkshire Forward for £9 million, to establish a Logistics Institute, was conceived as the best possible way HUBS could support the regeneration of the regional economy. 'Community operational research' was encouraged as a means of making the management science and systems skills of staff available to the disadvantaged on a pro bono basis. In 2018, in recognition of its commitment to developing 'responsible leadership', the Chartered Association of Business Schools chose HUBS as a case study for a documentary seeking to demonstrate that some business schools do good in the world.

The intervention, I would argue, clearly illustrates good CSP – as we can see if we examine it in terms of the 'constitutive rules' (see Table 8.1).

1. The perspectives of the functionalist, interpretive, and radical change sociological paradigms were brought to bear, through the variety of systems approaches, to provide an understanding of the problem situation and to guide the intervention. It makes a difference. Anyone who does not believe this should read Martin Parker's account of two years as an employee in a business school run along strictly 'functionalist' lines. Parker writes:

> I arrived at EBS just after the appointment of a new Dean who was committed to a top-down change project which was to take the school in an even more hierarchical direction … . This involved telling a particular story about the past, and positioning anyone who defended it as conservative, fearful or disruptive. It also involved tight control over the means of communication, including shutting down the means by which collective disenchantment could be voiced and ensuring that there was a small senior management team of well-paid academics (most of them appointed by the Dean himself) who would not question the direction that the school was taking. (2014, p. 282)

2. The seven key 'systems perspectives' were all used, along with other creativity-enhancing devices, to review issues in HUBS as they arose.
3. A variety of systems methodologies, relating back to the different paradigms, was used throughout the intervention, e.g. hard systems thinking, the Vanguard Method, the viable system model, various soft systems approaches, critical systems heuristics. Different methodologies assumed the primary role at different times.
4. Methods were extracted from methodologies and used as appropriate to the situation. Rich pictures and conceptual models, used simply to encourage creative thinking and not as part of soft systems methodology, provide examples.
5. Academic and professional studies commenting on the capabilities of different systems methodologies and methods were always considered in deciding which to use.
6. Methodologies were employed sometimes explicitly, sometimes implicitly, as appropriate, and other adaptations made as necessary.
7. Learning about the strengths and weaknesses of the different systems methodologies took place and informed later stages of the intervention. The initiatives taken to change HUBS were constantly evaluated according to the concerns of the different paradigms and systems methodologies: What impact might they have or were they having on improving efficiency, efficacy, effectiveness, viability, anti-fragility, mutual understanding, commitment to purposes, empowerment, emancipation, sustainability? Could any possible unintended consequences be predicted or discerned?

CONCLUSION

Following my departure as dean, in 2011, the fortunes of HUBS declined. The University of Hull itself started to go down the rankings and this resulted in undergraduate recruitment becoming more difficult across the board. The market for MBA degrees shrank precipitously. Nevertheless, HUBS lost market share of both undergraduate and postgraduate students, home and overseas, to a much greater extent than can be attributed to these factors alone. Moreover, research power and external engagement also deteriorated. EQUIS accreditation was lost. My successors as deans failed to resist a centralizing current that took hold in the University. HUBS was reabsorbed into a faculty, including politics and law, and lost control of its own marketing, finance, human resources, recruitment, postgraduate admissions, alumni, business links, and IT functions. Staff morale plummeted and many key personnel abandoned ship. Perhaps I got out at the right time. On the other hand, perhaps a dean with a CST mind-set could have steadied the ship during those more difficult times. HUBS could then have gone forward to even greater success as it adjusted its vision, mission, structures, etc. to more effectively help meet the complex challenges of, for example, productivity, radical uncertainty, resilience, inequality, health, and climate change that plague organizations and societies today. My confidence in CST and CSP leads me to believe this optimistic scenario would indeed have been realized.

ACKNOWLEDGEMENT

This chapter draws on material already published in Chapter 21 of *Critical Systems Thinking and the Management of Complexity* (Jackson, 2019). I am grateful to John Wiley and Co. for permission to make use of this material.

NOTE

1. A 'triple-crown' business school is one that has been accredited by the three main accrediting bodies – Association to Advance Collegiate Schools of Business International (AACSB), Association of Masters of Business Administration (AMBA), and European Quality Improvement System (EQUIS).

REFERENCES

Checkland, Peter and Jim Scholes (1990), *Soft Systems Methodology in Action*. Chichester: Wiley.
Flood, Robert L. and Michael C. Jackson (1991), *Creative Problem Solving: Total Systems Intervention*. Chichester: Wiley.
Flood, Robert L. and Michael C. Jackson (eds) (1991), *Critical Systems Thinking: Directed Readings*. Chichester: Wiley.
Jackson, Michael C. (2019), *Critical Systems Thinking and the Management of Complexity*. Chichester: Wiley.
Parker, Martin (2014), 'University, Ltd: changing a business school', *Organization*, 21, 281–92.

PART III

Inclusivity, team spirit and career development

9. 'Don't think you can be everyone's friend': dealing with conflict in an academic department

Alan Irwin

INTRODUCTION

Look around for wise words about approaching conflict in academic environments and you will find no shortage. Very often, these take the form of sound practical advice about how the responsible academic manager should best deal with conflict situations. Find common ground. Establish a clear timeline and keep track of each step along the way. Operate in a transparent fashion. Set clear rules of conduct and be explicit about the possible outcomes. Get outside help when necessary. Be aware of the legal and institutional framework – and, specifically, get advice and support from HR professionals.

This advice can be helpful, partly because it provides some practical markers and sense of process when dealing with conflict, partly also because it reminds us that we are not the first to be in such a situation. We can apply Tolstoy's famous remark about families to the academic department: all happy departments are alike, each unhappy department is unhappy in its own way. But even amidst this difference one can find common patterns, common causes of conflict and common modes of response – and my basic rule of 'when in doubt, get advice' works pretty well in most situations.

But there are other ways of talking about conflict – and not all are based on the idea of defusing or trying to resolve conflict. I have certainly heard many war stories of conflicts won and lost – the fearless academic leader with a clear strategy who faced down resistance and succeeded against all the odds; the head who challenged the 'old guard' and brought new life to a notoriously difficult environment. There are stories, too, of leaders who were beaten by conflict – the academic head who lost support within her department and was eventually replaced; the head who was so frustrated by the lack of backing from senior university management that she decided not to keep fighting.

In my experience, academic staff are not often openly aggressive and our workplaces are generally rather polite and restrained. In a long career with several leadership positions, I have actually experienced what I would consider as direct conflict very rarely. This of course is also a reflection of my own management style – for good and for bad. I usually prefer not to personalize issues and, as this chapter will reveal, am generally reluctant to take conflict at face value. I would say that my typical approach to conflict is to ask not 'who is right and wrong?' but rather 'what on earth is going on?' However, it can also be a matter of choice for the academic manager whether to see conflict in every situation or else simply the ebb and flow of academic life. I have to say, too, that the capacity to laugh has helped me get by in some tricky situations.

But still conflict features a lot in the stories we tell about academic life. And when it does happen, it can absorb a large amount of energy, paralyze new initiatives and be tremendously damaging to external reputation. Then there is the aphorism attributed to various people, including Henry Kissinger: academic politics are so vicious because the stakes are so small.

I am not convinced that arguments between academics are more vicious than those that take place in many business organizations, political parties or voluntary associations (especially the last of these in my experience). And I am not sure that the stakes are necessarily smaller than one finds in other contexts. It is in the character of universities that academics should be passionate about their scholarly, educational and research commitments. It is better for a head of department to appreciate that – and if possible enjoy it – rather than trivialize it. Even so, the appearance of conflict can take even the most vigilant leader by surprise.

When, many years ago, I was first appointed as a head of department, I think that dealing with conflict was the aspect of the job I worried about the most. And it didn't help me much when a good colleague advised: 'don't think you can be everyone's friend'. Even after a couple of weeks in the job, I had already worked that out for myself. I don't think I often went looking for conflict. But as a head of department, you generally do not have the possibility of ignoring conflict when it comes around. And it may be that, whatever your intentions, you become the center of conflict yourself.

It is one thing to approach conflict among others; it is quite different when you are presented as part – even the cause – of that conflict. Blame, deserved or not, comes your way. Now the conflict is not taking place in some corner of your department; it is actually happening in and around you.

In what follows, I will start by presenting three fictional stories of conflict within academic life. My interest in these stories relates closely to my experience as a head of department in a UK university but also as a dean in three universities across two European countries.

Each story resonates with situations I have personally encountered. However, none of these stories should be read as referring to a real situation. They are all inventions, but inventions drawn from experience. It will also become clear that while I divide the stories into three categories – interpersonal conflict, departmental conflict, and institutional conflict – these separations can only be partial. In practice, conflicts do not respect even the most brilliant classification schemes. This fluidity may be what makes them so challenging, but also so very interesting.

THREE CONFLICTING STORIES

Interpersonal Conflict: When Colleagues Fall Out

How is a department head to react when members of one's department not only disagree with each other but create a situation where other colleagues can't help but get involved? In my experience, hiring decisions can be a particular point of tension and potential controversy. The need to make a zero sum choice can mean that disagreements which have been stepped around for some time suddenly come to the surface. I can certainly think of appointment decisions which have created waves for a very long time.

But hiring is not the only kind of choice that can produce conflict. It can also be a matter of who gets to teach which course, of a request for internal funding or the grading of student work. Sometimes, the issue itself seems miniscule compared to the long-term trouble it causes.

It is hard to be a department head and not experience situations of tension and disagreement between colleagues. But the question is whether such vicissitudes simply rise, fall and dissolve or else incubate, escalate and persist. In the case that follows, the decision over whether or not a PhD student should be allowed to proceed became the catalysis for a long-lasting departmental and personal split.

INTERPERSONAL CONFLICT

John Williams (1965/2012) has written one of the great novels set within an academic department (I hesitate to call it an academic novel since it is much more than that). At the core of *Stoner* is the man himself: a person of deep principles, an outsider from a hard farming background, a committed but undistinguished researcher. William Stoner is nevertheless dedicated to his job. And his job is to teach often-unresponsive university students in a manner that accords with his personal and academic values. He lives quietly – and rather unhappily – in a campus town. He does not seem to be the type who goes looking for trouble.

The interpersonal conflict surrounding Stoner can be described in different ways. But at its heart is a very simple and apparently innocuous disagreement over whether one PhD student should be allowed to progress – and specifically whether he should be permitted to pass a crucial oral examination. The PhD scholar in question has already failed with his assignment to one of Stoner's seminars. And now Stoner fails him again for his general academic performance. From Stoner's perspective, the PhD candidate in question is simply incompetent: he can't answer the most basic questions. And he is both lazy and untrustworthy. The PhD supervisor strongly disagrees. But Stoner won't compromise by giving a conditional pass. He does not consider that the PhD student should ever be permitted to teach in a college or university. As he puts it, it would simply be a disaster to let someone like him loose in a classroom.

In the end, Stoner loses out and the PhD student is allowed to continue. The aggrieved supervisor threatens to bring charges against Stoner. A departmental split has occurred which will last until Stoner's death. The two men do not speak to each other directly for the next 20 years. The situation is not helped by the deeply offended PhD supervisor becoming the new department head. He remains vindictive towards Stoner for the many years that follow (even if tenure means that it is hard to sack Stoner). Although it all started with one PhD student, a conflict was created which marked not only the lives of the two men in question but a whole academic department.

I suspect most readers of *Stoner* find this a rather depressing story. That is certainly how I reacted the first time I read it. Why couldn't the central character compromise? He seems willfully determined to create a situation where everything is stacked against him. The fact that he is no academic superstar and has no interest in becoming a department head himself hardly strengthened his standing in all this. Why couldn't he quietly admit defeat, protect his own self-interest and avoid a damaging departmental conflict? Stoner seems to have turned a minor academic disagreement over the competence of one PhD student (not even his own) into a pointless and self-defeating conflict. Doesn't this represent the academic world at its worst – vicious politics and small stakes indeed?

But there is also something heroic about Stoner – albeit in a stubborn, awkward and possibly annoying kind of way. Isn't it admirable that he sticks to his principles? He is intelligent enough to anticipate the consequences of his own action (even if he didn't see his new enemy becoming his departmental boss). But he acted anyway in accordance with what he believed to be true. Perhaps we need more people like that in our departments. We may get more conflict and it would hardly make life easier for academic heads, but isn't that better than empty consensus and managerialism? Perhaps the lesson from this story is less obvious than a 'conflict management' perspective would suggest?

We will return to this story later. But now let us move on to a very different tale of conflict – this time (at least on the surface) concerning the allocation of departmental resources.

Departmental Conflict: When Civil War Threatens

As already observed, hiring decisions can be a particular catalyst for conflict. This can relate not only to the specific individual being appointed (or otherwise) but also to the disciplinary or specialist field of the appointment. Does the wise head let new appointments follow undergraduate teaching demand or the requirement for cutting-edge research? Should one try to be 'democratic' by balancing new positions across the different sections and sub-fields? Or should one ignore sub-sections altogether and follow a larger departmental strategy? Weighing different appointment criteria can be a challenge that some heads are quite happy to 'pass up' to their dean in order to avoid internal conflict ('it wasn't me who decided that'). For others, this is a central aspect of departmental development and perhaps the most important means of shaping their department. That does not necessarily make any of this easy.

Sometimes staffing decisions are not just about whether Area A or Area B gets a new associate professorship. As with many other departmental conflicts, this can also be a question of the head's authority and legitimacy, of the trust which is placed in her and her capacity to act. All this can be particularly difficult when someone is new in the job.

DEPARTMENTAL CONFLICT

When the incoming head took office, she knew the task would not be easy. In fact, the previous head had found it difficult to balance the demands of the different departmental sub-groups and had left rather abruptly. There were three disciplinary groups within the department. One was in an area of high teaching demand: most of the department's income was generated here – and it was satisfactory in research performance. A second group was stronger in research terms – with a large external reputation in one specialized area. It did fine for teaching, but the research specialization and the area of teaching demand did not entirely match. A third group had an even higher research reputation, but students were not so easy to find. And, of course, the new head belonged to one of the groups herself (actually, the second). This had already prompted some remarks about her 'looking after her own'. The first group felt particularly aggrieved. Their research would also be excellent if they had more staff and therefore less teaching demands (the head was privately skeptical of this claim). There was already talk of that section breaking away to form its own department – which would certainly leave the other two groups very exposed.

The pressure built up over her first year as department head. The leader of the first group sent her a long email, detailing how his group had been unfairly treated over several years. Of course, he copied this around his group. The leader of the third group – who had been against her appointment – reminded her of how her predecessor had lost support by appearing to favor his own group. And the members of her own section expressed concern that, in trying to appear fair, her close colleagues might lose out. Worse than that, she might end up blocking the careers of some talented younger staff on short-term contracts.

The new head had read that transparency was crucial when dealing with difficult situations. She therefore worked out a budgetary model which would take full account of different sources of revenue, current salary costs across the groups and shared administrative charges. The outcome was that her own group was under-funded, the first group could do with a little more support and the third group was over-staffed.

The transparent budgetary model of which she was so proud did not have the desired effect. The meeting of professors where she presented it led to fury on all sides with threats of the protest being taken to the university's senior management. Talk of a split in the department became the main topic of academic conversation. She was particularly upset that some senior professors would not even listen to her explanation of the model. 'Smoke and mirrors!' was one comment. The future of the department lay in the balance.

It's hard not to imagine that some strong personalities are involved here and probably some interpersonal conflict too. But this story seems to be more about a structural conflict built into the fabric of a department. In this context, giving resource to one group also looks like taking resource away from the other two. It's hard to argue against transparency. However, this form of budgetary transparency had the effect of heightening tensions.

The accusation of 'smoke and mirrors' is clearly a direct challenge to the authority of the leader. But should the head ignore this or risk escalating matters even more? If she turns to the dean for direct support she might look weak in front of departmental colleagues. But any appeal to senior professors only leads to further lobbying and fresh challenges. Perhaps she should resign? Or perhaps the department should be broken up? However, she actually admires many of the people she is fighting with – and she is getting a lot of support from her administrative staff. The teaching evaluation went very well. If only these professors would not be so difficult.

Institutional Conflict: When Trouble Comes From Above

Once, when I was dean, I received a call from an upset neighbor, complaining about the noise the students were making on their way home from a bar. She suggested that I say something to them at our next morning assembly. I had to point out that with over 25,000 students on campus this might be a little difficult.

From the outside, the university can look like a single institution. But from the inside, one is very aware of the walls, particularly around departments. What takes place outside the department can seem, to many colleagues, like the uncharted territory on a medieval map. You know it's there, but for all practical purposes it's best to ignore it.

But sometimes decisions taken outside the department can have a huge influence. One classic case is the 'strategic restructuring exercise' when suddenly the continued existence of one's department is put under threat. And sometimes it can be the lack of support from the institution that puts a department head in a conflicting situation.

INSTITUTIONAL CONFLICT

The department was small but proud of its reputation. It had been a bold interdisciplinary initiative by the university and the postgraduate students who came were aware of being part of a very special community. Academic staff generally felt the same and the head knew that he had their support. The problem – apart from the small size of the department – was that bachelor students were hard to recruit. This meant scrambling every year to make up the undergraduate numbers. Many who came appreciated being part of an innovative and supportive environment, but some took the first opportunity to shift to a more 'mainstream' course. The head worried about this but all he could do was to keep trying.

And then two things happened in quick succession. First of all, a productive member of the department was turned down for promotion. The members of the faculty committee just didn't know how to evaluate such interdisciplinary scholarship – and sending the application to a different faculty only made matters worse. The *coup de grâce* came with the recruitment of one of the department's core lecturers to a neighboring university. The writing was on the wall. The dean sadly reported that such a small unit could not be prioritized for a replacement position at a time of financial constraint. The dean did, however, have an alternative suggestion. Close the undergraduate program and the department, keep the postgraduate activities and the research center, and disperse the current academic staff to other departments but allow them to keep their offices in what would become a Postgraduate and Research Center. All jobs would be protected.

Once news of the planned closure got out, student protests began, the trades unions offered their backing and angry letters started to arrive from colleagues in other universities. While the campaign built and a demonstration was organized outside the building, the head knew that this conflict presented him with a dilemma. Should he make himself a hero and confront his institution for its lack of support – or quietly negotiate the best arrangement for his administrative and academic staff? The failure by the university to offer special assistance was effectively killing his department. But he also had a personal responsibility to those who worked in it. No permanent solution to his department's problems seemed to be on offer. Perhaps, then, it would be better to lose this battle – even if it meant picking one's own defeat?

One could say in this case that the conflict was not deliberately caused by the institution. But the inability – or unwillingness – of the dean to protect the department in question certainly created a problem. The failure to grant a promotion followed by the refusal to create a replacement post demoralized the department in question, which already felt itself to be at the bottom of the pecking-order. Institutions can directly kill an activity. Or they can watch it fail. At this point, the institutional environment beyond the specific department becomes extremely important.

To be fair, the dean did come up with an alternative plan and he did work with the head in developing this. Together they found a way forward without too much conflict (despite the demonstration and some stormy meetings in the university). The question which lingers is whether the department head should have made this pragmatic settlement or else stoked up the conflict. What would Stoner have done in that situation?

If the head in the first case was an active participant in interpersonal conflict and the head in the second case was desperately trying to find consensus among growing conflict, the head in this third case decided that conflict could not deliver what was best for his departmental colleagues. Crucially, he had their support and they undoubtedly appreciated his honest, open and very practical evaluation of the situation. But they also looked to him for leadership and direction. He could not choose his victory, but he could choose his defeat – and perhaps that is a victory in itself.

LEARNING FROM CONFLICT

These are just three fictional stories which resonate with – and indirectly build upon – my own experience. There are no doubt others that deserve to be told. But for me each one suggests that, while following good practical advice about conflict management cannot do any harm, such an approach fails to recognize that conflict is generally bound up with the setting within which it occurs. Even in the 'interpersonal' case of Stoner, the context is crucial. Neither of the two main protagonists is going anywhere and the conflict is heightened by the fact that this all takes place in a closed community. Indeed, the intensity of the conflict (why get so worked up about one PhD student no matter how challenging?) can only be understood by paying attention to the pressures within that context.

Crucially, context includes one's own standing and room for maneuver. The head of department in the third story has collegial support of the kind that the head in the second story could only envy – even if the dean rejected his request for a replacement position. This gives him relative freedom of movement that an internally challenged head could not so easily possess. Whether that makes him a more effective head of department is, of course, a different matter.

There are other general points to be made about the three stories in all their difference. One obvious learning point is, as already suggested, that conflict does not fit into a single category but can flow around in surprising ways. That 'smoke and mirrors' challenge in the second story was presumably designed to provoke a personal response from the head – and probably did achieve that. Whilst the emphasis in the third story is on the extra-departmental level, such a situation will inevitably raise interpersonal and intra-departmental tensions. Who is pulling their weight in terms of teaching? Who has already made overtures to neighboring departments in order to safeguard their own position?

Meanwhile, one obvious question relating to the Stoner story is to ask where senior management was in all this. In fact, the dean was an old friend of William Stoner. However, perhaps ironically, he was so scared of causing a split in the department that he felt he had to support the incoming head. He could pressure the new head into dropping charges against Stoner, but he could not reverse the decision of a department head – at least not without firing him and thereby causing even more conflict. So, to some degree, the conflict was caused by the dean's wish to avoid conflict.

What, then, can we say about the role of the head of department in each case? At one level, they seem very different: an agent in the conflict – and perhaps the prime reason the conflict persisted; an ambassador for peace – even if the attempt at achieving consensus seemed to backfire; and a fair-minded negotiator – looking after his staff even while others wanted to turn this into a matter of academic principle. But the main point I want to emphasize here is that all three made a *choice*. And they made that choice knowing that, as the quotation in the chapter title suggests, they could not be everyone's friend. Whatever they did, there was going to be disagreement. Regardless of how many friends they would win or lose, they still needed to act. Let us look at that in terms of the three stories.

So far I have presented the new head in the first story (his name was Dr. Hollis Lomax) in a decidedly negative light. However, he was also a person of principle. With a PhD from Harvard, a steady publication record and a physical disability, one can guess that his life had contained challenges but also achievements – and finding a place in this inward-looking community must have been especially demanding. The dean was even a student buddy of the man who was trying to end the career of his talented PhD student! Lomax defended the PhD scholar in question but, beyond that, felt that Stoner had been extremely unfair. The student deserved sympathy and support – and he, too, had a disability. The only conclusion was that Stoner had let his prejudices overrule his academic judgment. How could anyone trust or respect a person like that? Lomax couldn't fire him and Stoner had general employment rights. But he could choose to control his negative influence by isolating him within the department.

The head in the second story seems to feel trapped. She wants to be fair and she would prefer to avoid conflict. If that gets out of control the whole department could fall apart – probably to the detriment of her own disciplinary group. But introducing a budgetary model is not the only way of being fair, and the professors were smart enough to see that any such model depends upon some key criteria and underlying assumptions. She clearly has strong views about the importance of research quality, the best response to student teaching demands and the claims being made by each group.

Whatever she does, she won't make everyone happy. But in the end it is her choice to opt for a model-based approach rather than to state her academic priorities more explicitly and directly. Conflict might not be avoided either way. However, in the end, it comes down to her own assessment, her own principles and how she chooses to move forward in a conflicted situation. There are a number of ways forward from here. Any intelligent choice has to take account of the context in which she is operating and the managerial discretion at her disposal. But she could do well to remember the words from Janis Joplin's old song: freedom is another word for nothin' left to lose.

Remembering that all three of my stories are fictions, one highly engaged reader was moved to ask me at this point: but what happened to this second department head in the end? Well, I like to think that she stood her ground. This conflict could not be resolved through a budget model or one meeting with senior staff. Possibly, it could not be solved at all. But a head can be resilient enough – and stubborn enough – to keep operating even through conflict. Sometimes the only approach to conflict is to acknowledge it and even own it, and then to move forward in the best manner. And when later the university in question came up with a radical plan to restructure the department in a manner that no one locally seemed to like, she found she had many internal supporters who had previously been her antagonists. In fact, the person who made the 'smoke and mirrors' comment might even have been heard on occasion wishing her a nice weekend.

But what about the head in the third case? He is a deeply principled individual. He has a loyal group of departmental colleagues – and possibly a group that appreciates that it is him taking on this role in a time of crisis rather than them (I often think of this as every head's secret weapon). He is extremely aware of making a choice in response to the dean's offer. However, he might not communicate that choice in the same way to everyone. And the choice with which he is presented is certainly not his preferred option.

Notice that his choice involves balancing what is best for individual colleagues against what might be best for this field of cross-disciplinary teaching and research. Of course, the dean's offer allows colleagues to keep an office even if their departmental home is elsewhere. But how long can that last before the same pressures of promotion, departures and new appointments lead to further contraction? In this case the main conflict might come from outside rather than inside the department (not least from unhappy undergraduate students who become the last in their line). However, the department head is not expecting champagne and chocolates whatever he does. Indeed, the outcome of all this could well be that a deeply principled head of department loses his job.

Three stories, three conflicts and three choices. All made in the knowledge that at least short-term disagreement was unavoidable, and that the head of department not only couldn't keep everyone happy, but shouldn't expect any thanks either. Of course, some conflicts can be contained more easily and some individuals seem to have a gift for causing conflict all by themselves. But dealing with even those simpler cases still involves choices – even if it is a choice not to act. Often it comes down to a best judgment about what is right and what is possible in a specific situation – about how we can live with our own choices, and of the stories we wish to tell about our actions when all is said and done.

I have not often encountered direct conflict in my career. But the conflicts I have met stay with me still.

FINAL REFLECTIONS

I started this chapter by displaying some skepticism about 'wise words' with regard to approaching conflict. Now at its end, I feel an irrepressible wish to offer some general advice of my own. Please forgive me for this. And use what follows, not as a final word, but as a stimulus to your own reflections and future actions.

- Try to understand, try to listen. But remember to act.
- Conflicts will mark your time as a leader and bring out much in yourself and in others that is otherwise buried. Do not expect chocolates and champagne. But do choose to learn.
- Especially in a conflict situation, treat people as you would wish to be treated yourself. Respect for others is also a way of respecting yourself.
- People will form their own views about your actions. These may or may not be fair. In the end, you must rely on your own judgment. Leadership is about making a choice and taking responsibility for that choice.
- Conflicts are usually part of a larger context. Be willing to examine that context rather than simply taking things at face value.

- You can't always pick your battles. Sometimes they pick you. But you can pick your response. Even in the middle of a conflict, there are always alternative paths.
- Conflict can take up a lot of energy and distract from other activities. Memories of it can fade slowly. Don't be afraid of it. You might even be able to make use of it, but handle it with care.
- Not all conflicts can be resolved in the short term. Sometimes, the only strategy is to acknowledge the issues and keep moving forward – step by step.

REFERENCE

Williams, John (1965/2012), *Stoner: A Novel*. London: Vintage Books.

10. Smells like team spirit: a user's guide for department heads

Peter Kjær

When you look up the term 'team spirit' in the online *Cambridge Dictionary*, there is a telling difference between two definitions.

The first, broad definition sees team spirit as "a feeling of belonging that the members of a group have towards others in the group", while the second, the *Business English* definition, sees it as "a way of thinking and acting that shows loyalty to your team and its members". The former conjures up an image of something elusive that emerges within a group of people; perhaps as they are busy doing other things. The latter definition makes team spirit a question of showing your loyalty to the team – in thought and action.

Anyone in a leadership position has to address these two definitions of team spirit. Leadership is to lead people and groups of people; to lead a group of people involves some notion of collectivity.

In today's academic institutions, there are strong tendencies towards individualization. However, unless one sees faculties, departments, centers or research units as random collections of individual performers, there is a need to consider the nature of collectives. In that consideration, the *Business English* definition sees the team as an entity defined by given goals and tasks and the allocation of individuals to those tasks. The broader definition, however, talks about 'the group' and does not presuppose shared goals or a given task structure. It just notes the feeling of belonging that one finds in a group of people.

In the following, I will describe how I worked with team spirit as a head of department. At the time, I did not talk about 'team spirit,' and I am sure most of my 'team members' would have resisted the term vehemently.

In retrospect, I clearly opted for the broader definition of team spirit. The narrow term may be relevant in research project management or in other specific projects for which one forms task forces, project groups, etc. to work on a particular task for a limited period. However, the idea of shared goals, given tasks, and loyalty is often problematic in a university setting characterized by academic freedom, extensive participation in outside networks, and deep reliance on external quality standards. To put it bluntly, a loyal researcher is not necessarily a good researcher. Perhaps more elegantly: a faculty member cannot be reduced to what was referred to as "an organization man" in a 1950s classic in organization theory (Whyte 1956).

Still, most faculty members are concerned with the group or team to which they somehow belong. People in academic departments are concerned with the everyday interaction with colleagues, with good and bad behavior, with the reputation of the department, and with the overall trajectory of the department as a research and teaching environment.

As a leader of a department, it is therefore important to attend to the spirit of the department. There are strong centrifugal tendencies in academic life (competition, rivalry, conflict, individualization, external commitments, etc.), so there is a need to continuously nurture the sense of belonging within the department.

A sense of belonging has both a spatial and a temporal dimension. The spatial dimension has to do with making sense of everyday events and situating the department within the university as an organization or the wider context of the university: vis-à-vis the university leadership, vis-à-vis other departments, or the world outside the university, etc. In the temporal dimension, it is important to have a shared history, while being somehow attuned to the present situation and having some joint notion of where the department is heading (or what sorry state it is removing itself from).

In the following, I describe concrete ways of working with team spirit as a head of department. The examples come from my six-year tenure as head of a university department. The department that I was leading was a social science department, established in the 1950s. When I took over, the department had about 25 faculty members (assistant, associate and full professors), and 20–25 Ph.D. students. Within a few years, there were about 35 faculty members. The department was in a process of generational transition and was hiring new faculty, especially at the senior level. At the same time, externally funded projects and extensive teaching obligations soon led to the recruitment of a new cohort of researchers at the postdoctoral level. My predecessor had embarked on a painful process of further internationalizing the department, most importantly in the field of research publications. When I took over, the department was just about to hire its first non-Scandinavian professor and its first non-Scandinavian Ph.D. student, and soon we spoke English at all meetings.

I am a big fan of lists, and an even bigger fan of user's guides. My discussion of leadership and team spirit will be a five-step user's guide. Although such guides are seldom as useful as one hopes for, they are invitations to think creatively and critically about a particular subject – and, hopefully, to make your own guide.

My Team Spirit User's Guide consists of leadership practices that address the spirit or 'morale' of the department as a group. The list is a post hoc construction. I did not have a plan, when I became head, nor did I ever formulate a coherent leadership strategy. The practices were simply some of the responses that came to feel meaningful in the face of particular challenges. They are also practices that I think resonate with the broad concept of team spirit that addresses questions of belonging, meaning and legitimacy, and of the nature of the 'we' of a group.

ITEM 1: ALL MEETINGS ARE CRITICAL

The first item in my guide concerns meetings.

As head of department, I spent an inordinate amount of time preparing for department meetings, writing presentations, designing PowerPoint slides, thinking about meeting formats, and so on. My obsession with meetings mirrored the culture of the department but was also inspired by my very first day as head of department.

Having found my desk in the corner office, organized my family photos and inspected the impressive agenda prepared for me by my predecessor, I was relieved to realize that it was time for lunch. I went to the department lunchroom and sat down with my meal next to my colleagues. Suddenly, the informal conversation died out. I looked up and realized that everybody was waiting for the new head to make his inaugural speech. The lunchbreak was also an information meeting, and I was the chair. I do not remember what I said or what the reaction was, but I remember the acute experience of this being a key leadership situation that I was not prepared for.

Ravn (2013) describes what he calls the "Folk Theory of Meetings," which is how most of us perceive meetings in our everyday lives. Key assumptions of the Folk Theory are that meetings are invariant aspects of office life, ruled by agendas, conducted through a set of formalized rituals but effectively owned by the leader, etc. Folk assumption #1 is perhaps the most important of them all: "Meetings will be meetings." Ravn observes that one finds curiously little research on meetings as an organizational phenomenon. We tend to carry on with our meetings, based on a commonly shared idea that is deeply fatalistic.

If anything, meetings are one of the sites where people have plenty of time to observe the group that they are part of: what are the patterns of engagement, who speaks, who responds, who says nothing, who is absent, what is the tone of comments, etc.? People also observe how the chairperson or the leader plays her or his part, going through the motions or overdosing on managerial enthusiasm.

Conducting meetings as head of department often becomes an administrative ritual where one becomes preoccupied with the logistics of the meeting: time, place, agenda, annexes – and, most importantly, coffee. We rarely consider the choreography of meetings or how people's anticipation may shape their participation.

More curiously, we often do not consider the outcomes of meetings. We naturally focus on opinions, decisions and conclusions, but rarely on what the meeting means to those who were there. Imagine talking about a concert, and only caring about the parking facilities, the concert starting on time, all songs being completed with no breakdown of the sound system, and beers and toilets being available during the intermission.

In my department, short biweekly information meetings held at lunchtime were probably some of the most important meetings of all, since this was where immediate news were shared, accomplishments were celebrated, newcomers were welcomed, and people's immediate responses to current events were aired. These meetings rarely lasted more than 20–30 minutes, but they were the key manifestations of 'the department' as a community. If these meetings were made meaningful, then perhaps other meetings could be too. So, more time went into the preparation of the information meetings, sharing positive stories or reflecting upon more problematic events, often laughing together or sometimes grieving together. There was never a formal agenda, no decisions, and no minutes taken.

There were many other and equally important meetings, to be sure: faculty meetings, department seminars, committee meetings, etc. Some meeting formats were reformed, and often we began to emphasize outcomes and adjust formats accordingly. One such process concerned an annual two-day research seminar, entitled the Winter Games. Here the ritual of paper presentation was reframed from being a matter of 'presenting your work and getting criticized for it' towards 'helping people improve and reorient a paper in order to publish it.' Commentator roles were redefined and specified, and oral feedback had to be followed by written comments and suggestions. The format change was a collective long-term effort that started years before I became the department head. It suggested that meetings were malleable and could be changed, so that, hopefully, a young scholar would now return from the seminar not only thinking that she survived the ordeal, but that it was worthwhile and that her colleagues were actually a group that she was proud to be part of.

ITEM 2: "WHAT THE DEAN IS REALLY SAYING …"

In today's university organizations, a head of department is a middle manager. In the Danish system, department heads are not elected but recruited in open competition. However, many are still homegrown.

The amount of discretion given to department heads varies across universities. The university that I worked at had a highly centralized managerial structure. Many important decisions were not mine to take, including key budget and recruitment decisions. That meant that my role was often that of implementing decisions taken by the senior management, i.e. adopting new quality procedures or using new formats when asking for the allocation of new faculty positions. That was the easy part.

The difficult part was that of communicating top management actions and decisions as I stood in front of the entire department at lunch meetings, faculty meetings or department seminars. From a leadership perspective, this was a critical task, not only because it was part of my job as a line manager to loyally communicate top-level decisions on matters big or small, but also because it was important for the department as a group.

People need to be informed about changes in their daily environment so that they can adjust expectations and behavior accordingly. That is the logic of line communication. Just as importantly, people need to be able to make sense collectively of the world that they inhabit in order for them to function as a group.

Faculty members are often skeptical of management, and especially the senior management of a university. Just as there are Folk Theories of meetings, there are also Folk Theories of leadership (Meindl et al. 1985). Some Folk Theories build on what has been termed 'the romance of leadership,' i.e. that the fate of an organization ultimately depends on its leader. According to that Folk Theory, both failures and successes can be attributed to the leader, while other factors, such as chance or context, are neglected.

In professional bureaucracies such as universities, Folk Theories are less heroic and will often see the role of leaders as that of working on the margins of the operative core of an organization, securing resources, mitigating conflicts, etc. Often, faculty members stress how the leadership of their university lacks basic insight into core tasks and how they 'work' in a remote, secluded space of official meetings, strategic plans and performance management.

The question was now, as head of department, which story to tell?

It can be very tempting to affirm the standard negative assumptions about leadership, and occasionally I did slip into the familiar 'another-crazy-edict-from-the-dean's-office' storyline.

Mostly, however, I sought to resist the temptation and focused on having a balanced debate with the people of the department on the merits, challenges and opportunities afforded by particular leadership decisions, not just because the dean was my immediate superior, but because I also thought it was the only responsible position, for two reasons.

The first is because the 'crazy-dean' line tended to reproduce a particular social dynamic in the department. Justifiable or not, management skepticism may also sustain local informal hierarchies that are challenged, directly or indirectly, by particular leadership decisions. There might, however, be other sub-groups (newcomers, international faculty, administrative staff, etc.) who welcome new initiatives from above, even when the initiatives seem out of place or even clumsy. People have the right to dislike leadership decisions, but they should also have an opportunity to support them.

The second is that it is not necessarily a good collective strategy for a group to build its interpretation of the environment on fatalism or cynicism. That could make it very difficult to mobilize constructive counter-moves in the complex arena of the university. If the 'we' of the group is always on a slippery slope towards disaster, and if 'they' are out to get you, then the odds against you may become so overwhelming that you might just as well return to your office and wait quietly for the next piece of bad news. It is important to remember that communication is not just a matter of relaying information; it is constitutive: how you communicate about the outside world both presumes and produces particular forms of belonging – and particular conditions for action.

As a local leader, the strategy of loyalty to top management is not risk-free. On one end of the spectrum, loyalty must not stand in the way of criticism. It is important to allow for critical voices and to use that criticism constructively when helping to qualify senior management decisions.

At the other end of the spectrum, loyalty is a bet on the accountability of senior management. In extreme cases, loyalty may simply not be a rational approach. One of my darkest moments as a department head occurred during a leadership crisis at the university. The leadership crisis involved negative media coverage, internal conflicts, and a lack of confidence in the top management group. After having attempted for several weeks to offer rationalizations of leadership decisions and statements, I came to the point where I could no longer offer a meaningful loyal account of what was transpiring. I could no longer make sense of things myself, and I could no longer offer coherent translations if people were to rely on me as a local leader. I could no longer 'stay real,' I felt.

That leads me to the next item on my list.

ITEM 3: STAYING REAL

The issue of 'staying real' not only emerged in a time of crisis, but seemed to be a pervasive aspect of being a head of department. Being a head of department is a Janus-faced position, where one has to balance what could be termed *managerial legitimacy* and *group legitimacy*.

Legitimacy is a conferred status; it involves a judgment by other actors. As a head of department, you are part of at least two conversations that confer legitimacy: that of management (the other heads, the deans, the president, etc.) and that of the people of the department. You have to balance legitimacy claims of both conversations.

There is a huge organization and management studies literature on the different sources of legitimacy, on processes of legitimation and on the dilemmas involved. An illustrative example of the dilemmas involved is what you call things: are we talking about 'personnel adjustment' or 'firing people'; are we facing 'problems' or just 'challenges,' etc.?

The problem with the two legitimacy conversations is that if you choose, you lose. If you only attend to the management conversation, you lose the confidence of the group that you are leading – and you may end up over-implementing problematic leadership decisions, regardless of local conditions. If you only attend to the departmental conversation, you lose the confidence of your management peers, and you may end up neglecting the concerns of the organization as a whole.

One solution is to engage in 'decoupling'. That entails paying lip service to e.g. management 'speak' but not enforcing it in any literal sense, letting it be known in your local network that as long as it appears that we follow orders, no one will care. Thus, if you are required by the senior management to set up departmental 'stakeholder boards,' you discuss the idea extensively, you define terms of reference for the board, you circulate lists of potential members, but you never get around to having any meetings (this is, naturally, a fictional example).

Another solution is organized collective 'sense-making' where you invite members of the department to interpret and construct new narratives that mediate between management solutions and what is workable and meaningful in an everyday context: what could be a relevant approach to international recruitment – or a pragmatic solution to strengthening stakeholder involvement?

A third solution is 'ambiguity.' Often one thinks of management as a question of creating accessible and transparent conditions for action and interpretation: these are our goals, these are the available actions, these are the rewards, etc. However, most people are able to live with significant ambiguity: 'this action may be right, but not always'; 'this goal is important – for now at least …'. Ambiguity calls for individual and collective judgment, for considering the situation, the people, the history, etc.

All three solutions are rational. Decoupling is sensible especially in organizations, such as universities, where the capacity for control is limited, but it is also a strategy that may seriously undermine leadership credibility. Sense-making has the capacity to both engage and adjudicate among conflicting concerns, but it is potentially very time-consuming as an organized activity, and it only works if there is room for local discretion or variation. Ambiguity allows for both individual and collective action but requires a certain preparedness for uncertainty and indeterminacy in the organization as a whole and within the department.

I came to use all three solutions, but I probably put particular emphasis on ambiguity. Here I used two particular vehicles: speeches and poetry.

As a head of department, you are expected to give speeches at formal and social events. Often this is ritualized practice, but a speech can also be a unique event that has the capacity to create its own interpretive space. A speech is, then, not just a series of statements; it is a unique performance that conjures up a shared space; a temporary community. In that space, things can be said and tied together that, for a moment, suspend pre-given rules, judgments and affiliations, and if, effective, you will laugh together, cry together, or reflect together. You can ridicule and praise the university's senior leadership at the same time; you can admit imperfections; you can describe the department as a 'band of brothers' on the eve of battle – and for a brief moment, it is okay. Most of my speeches failed to do just that, but occasionally they did not.

Poetry came up as an attention grabber. After some months in office, I begin sending out a weekly department newsletter with lists of recent publications, seminar dates, new grants, and all those other things that people put into management newsletters. I inserted a small quotation at the end of the newsletter – to add something unpredictable to each one. I mostly quoted songs that I liked.

Sam Cooke seemed to address questions of work ethics:

> Don't know much about history/Don't know much biology/Don't know much about a science book/ Don't know much about the French I took/But I do know that I love you/And I know that if you love me, too/What a wonderful world this would be. (*Wonderful World*, Keen Records, 1960)

Lou Reed, in a song about his relationship to Andy Warhol, seemed to be talking about the race to publish-or-perish in modern academia:

> He said, "How many songs did you write?"/I'd written zero, I lied and said, "Ten."/"You won't be young forever/You should have written fifteen"/It's work, the most important thing is work. (*Work*, Sigma Sound, 1990)

And Bob Dylan's words seemed to make sense during the leadership crisis:

> With a time-rusted compass blade/Aladdin and his lamp/Sits with Utopian hermit monks/Side saddle on the Golden Calf/And on their promises of paradise/You will not hear a laugh/Inside the Gates of Eden. (*Gates of Eden*, Warner Bros., 1965)

I honestly did not know what that all those lyrics really meant, but sharing them was part of 'staying real': keeping your senses awake and inviting people to use their best judgment. That sometimes worked.

ITEM 4: HISTORY LESSONS

The fourth item on the list concerns the role of history.

A group is not just an abstract sociological entity; a group is also a collection of people who are fellow travelers through time.

In a university department, history matters, both to the individual and to the group. To the individual faculty member, history is tangible in their curriculum vitae listing publications, grants, awards, courses taught, etc. People's offices are sometimes small intellectual museums with book collections, piles of papers and reports and various memorabilia. Researchers also record, in prefaces of books or in extended footnotes, their intellectual history in terms of supervisors, colleagues and students that have both been critical collaborators, sources of inspiration and friends. Departments and research groups also have histories that people recount at parties, receptions and in Festschrifts.

History is no trivial matter; historical events and experiences are often part of the broader narratives that define the 'we' of the department and the ways in which people connect to one another (Schultz & Hernes 2010).

Historical narratives often form particular genres that create particular affordances. When I became head, the department had a historical narrative that comprised three distinct phases. There were the crazy old days of the 1960s and 1970s, the golden age of scholarly and institutional leadership of the late 1980s and 1990s, and the present of the 2000s, which was often portrayed as the age of 'conformism.'

The problem with that narrative was that it privileged the senior members of the faculty and staff group (those who had 'been there'), and it devalued the present. Still, it gave the department a great advantage in that it *had* a history: we could be crazy and we could be great …

I spent quite some time on the 'management of history.' That entailed celebrating the glorious history of the department at anniversaries, retirement parties, and other formal occasions, and highlighting the contribution of the department to the development of the university and to our field of research. Thus, confronted with the intense pressure to conform to international academic standards in the first decade of the new millennium, it was important to remember that the department had actually been a frontrunner in developing European and transatlantic scholarly networks in the 1970s and 1980s. Could we revive that activism?

Attending to the history of the department also entailed a need to stress that the department did not belong to those who had created it – but to those who currently inhabited it. Senior faculty members did not have privileged access to the meaning of the department's past. The newcomers should have opportunities to interpret and reinterpret the history of the department: as part of an all-staff seminar, young faculty members interviewed old professors about the early formative years of the department and presented their (lengthy) findings in a short article circulated within the department. Some years later, we exhibited historical artifacts from the archives of department in a glass display case. Artifacts invite you to interpret them, so perhaps newcomers would ask, "What was the meaning of this wooden necklace to be carried by the head of department?"

In the film *Lawrence of Arabia* (Horizon/Columbia 1962), T. E. Lawrence states, "Nothing is written." I used the quote in my newsletter, hoping to suggest that the history of the department does not tell us what to do, but merely that something can be done.

ITEM 5: WASTE TIME!

My final item is the one practice that I probably over-emphasized as head of department, namely doing unnecessary things. By this, I mean the necessity of spending time as a leader on parties, excursions, jokes, designing t-shirts, art projects, dressing up, and so on.

Wasting time is both an exercise of freedom but also a kind of gift economy where you invite people to invest some of their time and energy in things that have few tangible returns, but rather reinforce a communal spirit by showing how one can create something unique together.

My department had a long-standing Friday Cake tradition. Any given Friday, according to a rigorous schedule managed by the department's administrative staff, somebody brought a cake (that would feed at least 20 people) to the lunchroom. If you tasted a cake, your name would invariably end up on the cake list. Importantly, 'bought cakes' were frowned upon; you were expected to bake your own. The highest form of praise was when somebody asked for the recipe of the cake you brought.

When the department celebrated its 60th anniversary, we came up with the idea of compiling a booklet of cake recipes. I wrote an introduction that was also a quick guide to the history and values of the cake-baking department. The illustrated booklet contained the 30 most popular recipes from a decade of cake baking. We then organized a large cake reception for all our friends at the other departments and across administrative levels – with 60 cakes (58 original cakes, and, alas, a couple of 'bought cakes'). Hundreds of people showed up and wasted time with us: the department that baked 60 cakes.

CODA: "LET US NOT TALK FALSELY NOW"

After five and a half years, my contract as Head of Department was up for renewal. I applied and had a job interview with an appointment committee chaired by the president of the university.

The committee reflected upon my leadership style and pointed to some of its weaknesses. I had struggled with certain types of decisions, and I was sometimes conflict averse.

I responded to some of the concrete issues, but I also recall saying to the committee something to the effect that, "This is who I am; this is what you get." It felt honest, and it did not dissuade the committee from reappointing me. However, it did suggest a pitfall in my approach to leadership.

To lead, for me, was to invest myself in the department – and in the university. To lead the department was to engage personally, emotionally, and professionally in strengthening the department as a group – as a 'we' – that felt compelling and attractive; thinking creatively about meetings, going to great lengths to communicate loyally, engaging in the art of ambiguity, working on storytelling, and spending time on seemingly useless activities. That was 'who I am.'

There was an irony to my leadership approach. It built on investing 'me' in the making of a 'we' – a 'we' that I was both part of and excluded from at the same time.

In a university department, professional relationships are often hard to distinguish from personal or private relationships. Colleagues are often engaged socially outside formal settings, and many are friends.

Many outside observers and newcomers had noted the visible sense of belonging and the strength of interpersonal ties within my department. Some referred to the department as a 'family,' which in this context is not a positive metaphor, but even critics acknowledged the team spirit of the department.

However, the intermeshing of professional and personal connections and even private relations can only work, I think, as long as one does not add power or authority to the mix. Once you have been granted the authority to make decisions in a group and for a group, you are not one of the gang.

If you, then, lead in a way that relies critically on you not just performing bureaucratic chores or exercising formal authority but engaging as a 'whole person' in the exemplary building of an attractive community, there is a risk of forgetting that a leader is a public persona. That persona can be personal, likable, authentic, etc., but it is not 'who I am.' You can never leave 'the corner office,' so to speak. If you do that, you are in trouble. Then people's criticism is a personal attack; your failure to help is a betrayal of friendship, etc.

One summer day in the year after having been reappointed, I left 'the corner office' for good, and moved to a senior management position at another university.

I had two profound emotional reactions to that move: on the one hand, there was a feeling of sorrow and loneliness – I sincerely missed my colleagues and, alas, friends, and I missed the feeling of being part of a 'gang,' a 'tribe' or a 'family.' On the other hand, there was a sense of relief as I moved into a much simpler role. As a member of a senior management team, I am never allowed to forget *what* I am.

I continue many of the practices outlined above. Leading an organization or any group of people will always involve the making of a 'we' – and although my User's Guide is neither authoritative nor exhaustive, this is what I do. It is not *who* I am.

REFERENCES

Meindl, J. R., S. B. Ehrlich and J. M. Dukerich (1985), "The romance of leadership," *Administrative Science Quarterly*, Vol. 30, No. 1, pp. 78–102.
Ravn, I. (2013), "A folk theory of meetings – and beyond," *European Business Review*, Vol. 25, No. 2, pp. 163–73.
Schultz, M. and T. Hernes (2010), "Powers of the past: evoking organizational memory in identity reconstruction," *The Academy of Management Annual Meeting Proceedings 2010* (Montreal).
Whyte, W. H. (1956), *The Organization Man*, New York: Simon & Schuster.

11. 'Now you see it': gender, inclusion and diversity

Maja Horst

In 2011, I took on a role as Head of Department in the area of Humanities in a Danish university. Before assuming this role, I had been an associate professor in a Danish Business School after having previously worked at other Danish universities. This reflects my interdisciplinary background in Science and Technology Studies. My management experience before 2011 primarily consisted of having been Director of a Doctoral School in Organization and Management Studies, but I also had academic knowledge in the field of research management. After eight years, I stepped down as Head in 2019 to become a full-time professor.

Before I became Head of Department, I had not really engaged explicitly with issues of gender, inclusion and diversity. This was not because I didn't experience such issues or consider them important. Rather, they seemed complicated and difficult to deal with – so I tended to dodge them. When I assumed a formal leadership role with responsibility for people's well-being, however, this habit became impossible to keep, as these issues were obviously part of my job. In what follows, I will try to describe how I tried to handle this challenge, what I think I have learned and how I would do things differently if I were to start all over again. But first, I will set the scene by explaining what I mean by 'dodging' the issues.

AVOIDING ISSUES OF DIVERSITY AND EQUALITY

The basis for my leadership roles has been a normative framework centred around the importance of fairness and equality. I believe it has been with me from childhood, but through interactions with others, I have come to realize that I am rather concerned with achieving justice. It is important to me that rewards are distributed fairly according to who deserves them. I do not feel comfortable if preferential treatment plays too big a part in my own achievements, just as I don't think it should do for other people. It is important for me that the playing field is level and that everybody has an equal chance of achieving what they want. This includes trying to help disadvantaged people so they can have the same opportunities as others. As I grew older, I also experienced that such efforts at levelling the playing field are not always very easy. The complexity of situations often means that helping in one way might create disadvantages in another. However, compared to many other walks of life, academia has always seemed to be a place where there was at least a good chance of achievement following effort in a fair way.

Indeed, academia is a meritocratic environment and during my formative years as a junior researcher, such meritocracy was what I mainly chose to notice. However, reflecting on what went on in those years, I did indeed also notice that meritocracy was not always the only guiding principle. Often people were praised according to the importance or innovativeness of their work – but some selected few seemed to be made disproportionally visible. When looking back, a couple of young men stand out as 'talents' of which the organization seemed to expect brilliance, even though this was not necessarily visible in their publication lists or grant acquisition. They just had an aura of academic expectation around them that set them apart.

Senior academics behaved in lots of different ways and particularly some of the older male professors were seen as 'characters'. Maybe the senior women did not have the same need for explicit performance, but it still seemed that the limits to their behavioural choices were much narrower. Also, the repercussions if they crossed boundaries were much more severe. However, differences in 'behaviour allowance' were not just about gender. Forms of cultural and academic capital seemed to be at least as important. The ease with which some people could expect to be listened to must have been formed a long time before they entered university and it was not the same for people who came from less academic upbringings.

There were instances of sexual harassment, but I did not consider that as something specific to academia. As a young woman I experienced it everywhere occasionally, so why should the university be different? Also, rather than noticing instances of inappropriate behaviour, I was much more preoccupied with the sense of finally fitting in. Having considered myself an outsider for much of my upbringing, it was life-giving to find myself in an environment where critical questions and intellectual challenge were the main game. So, when issues of gender and inequality came up in discussions, I could not find a way to participate in a comfortable way. It seemed that, as a young woman, I would have to present myself as a victim or as disadvantaged in some way to argue the case – and this was precisely how I did not want to position myself. I felt capable! Finally, I was good at something that was valuable. Why should I taint that by acting as if I needed extra help and could not do it on my own? On the other hand, I did not want to say that the issues were not important, so I ended up simply trying to avoid getting into it.

Looking back, I have a lot of respect for that young woman, but I can also see her blind spots. I missed how the structures often have influence – even when we ascribe things to our own achievements. I probably completely overlooked how much people actually helped me, because they had more awareness of structures than I had. Another point is that while I noticed class in the form of cultural capital, I had little sense of questions of ethnicity or other minority issues. To a large degree this reflects the overall structure of Danish society at the time. I hardly met anyone who was not white, apparently heterosexual and from a cultural Christian background, until I was out of my teenage years.

So my engagement with issues of diversity and inclusion does not stem from the fact that I have had an academic or a personal interest in these issues per se. Rather, I am concerned with fairness and justice. If anything, I had tried to avoid getting personally engaged in questions of gender and equality. The following account should be read in this light. I am not an expert. I see myself as someone who has – almost with slight resistance – had to realize that I had to engage with this issue when responsible for other people's work life, careers and well-being – and concerned with how to honour that obligation with fairness.

BEING HEAD OF DEPARTMENT

I became Head in a department consisting of four different sections, which had formerly been disciplinary departments in their own right. The position was a full-time management position with budgetary responsibility for approximately 10 million Euros, 50 permanent, full and associate professors, and 200 staff in total. The sections were quite different in size and gender composition. The two smallest sections had only one male permanent staff member whereas another section had no female permanent staff members. Overall, therefore, the gender distribution in the department was more balanced than in individual sections. But of the full professors, less than 20% were female. However, no one at leadership level ever problematized this as something I ought to do something about. This is where my story begins.

In what follows, I will focus on three themes that illuminate how I experienced the issues around gender, diversity and equality. I have called the first theme 'structural decoupling', because it concerns the disconnection between issues of diversity and all the other managerial activities that went on in the university. The second theme is 'unconscious bias', which is a concept pointing to the fact that we all have implicit and unacknowledged expectations (some would call them prejudices) about other people and that those expectations influence the way we assess, evaluate and react to things that happen in our daily lives (Easterly and Ricard 2011). The third theme is 'recruitment'.

Before I continue, I should say that my observations stem from a Danish context and, contrary to what many international colleagues expect, Danish academia is not at the forefront of gender equality. This is, for instance, visible in the 'She Figures' published by the European Union (2019), which demonstrates that Denmark is lying below the average on several indicators.

Structural Decoupling

Every year, I participated in a discussion in the faculty leadership team of the gender and diversity initiative at the university (focused primarily on gender – not wider diversity, despite the name). The effort consisted primarily of an action plan. Previously, the action plan had – controversially – included monetary benefits for departments who hired female full professors. This incentive had changed the overall composition towards more female professors. A closer look at the numbers, however, reveal that a disproportionly large number of new female professors had been hired as the time-limited 'professor with special responsibilities' compared to the new male professors, where a larger proportion was hired as permanent professors in the same period.

By the time I came to the university, this monetary scheme had run out and by then the university's diversity action plan mostly consisted of two rules: (i) that assessment committees should include both genders and (ii) that positions could only be filled if there were at least one applicant of each gender. As it turned out, it was relatively easy to comply with those rules. But they did not seem to have much impact. I have heard several people talk about how easy it was to make sure that 'some woman' would apply so that they could appoint the 'right' candidate. Furthermore, there are no reasons to believe that an assessment committee with female members is better at avoiding gender bias than an all-male one. In fact, women are often as structurally blind as men, and if not, they can find it extremely difficult to point to other people's biases precisely because they are women – just like I did not want to engage with the issue of diversity when I was younger.

The university's diversity plan also included some target numbers for future distribution of gender in staff composition. But it was very unclear how these targets should be reached. As time progressed, it was my experience that the actual distribution did not change despite the target numbers. At leadership level, it sometimes seemed to go the wrong way. However, it is hard to say, because there was no formal follow-up on these numbers other than an annual count. I therefore experienced this plan as completely decoupled from the rest of the managerial business at the university.

Each year we had a meeting to look at the action plan, and we complied with the rules about assessment committees, but other than that, the plan had no impact on how to be a Head of Department. No one ever made me responsible for, or even asked about, the staff composition in my department. No one ever problematized the distribution of tasks to various staff members, discussed whether our appointment interviews and decisions were planned to avoid bias, or asked about pay grades and the allocation of bonus allocations. Gender and other questions of diversity were simply not part of any discussion regarding the way I did my job. It was its own issue – firmly kept in a separate box to be taken out once a year, reviewed and then put back again.

So why do more than that? The answer is that as time went by, I came to notice the many ways in which one could question whether my department was organized and governed in a way that supported equality and fairness. There was the observable difference in terms of staff composition. Is it justifiable to have no permanently employed women (out of more than ten) teaching in a programme where a third to half of students are female? Is it acceptable that an educational line recruits less than 10% male students? Is it acceptable to have a gender pay gap of more than 10% in some positions? Is it acceptable that we recruit almost no non-white, culturally Christian students in most of our programmes?

My answers to these questions are negative, but that is based on more than a notion of gender equality. I generally believe that we could do better in both research and education at universities if we recruited in a more diverse way. First, the obvious argument. If we assume that talent is equally distributed in a population, then we need to recruit equally from the entire population. The second argument is harder to prove, but at least in my mind diversity breeds quality. I have seen several examples of how a uniform group can run out of innovative capacity and end up reproducing a limited perspective on the world. This is harmful to the research environment, the teaching programmes and the general work culture. One way of adding diversity to a group is to recruit in an inclusive way, but I would immediately like to add a word of caution. Successfully fostering innovativeness by diversity recruitment depends on the group's ability to collaborate. A diverse academic group which doesn't interact (and might not actually want to) is, in my eyes, usually not as innovative as a less diverse group with more collaboration. However, collaboration is something that also needs to be fostered and nurtured, but those questions are themes in other chapters in this book.

Unconscious Bias

Another way in which issues of diversity presented themselves in my daily life as Head was related to how people fulfil responsibilities and obligations vis-à-vis the way they ask for support and recognition. In short form, in order to treat your staff equally, you have to treat them differently. Some people ask for lots of support, whereas others fix everything themselves and do not expect pay rises, career advances and administrative support. Some people offer to take on tasks and you have to watch that they don't over-perform where less will be good enough. Others grumpily accept specific tasks when told to, but then do such a bad job of it that you really do not want to ask them again.

In my experience there are people of all kinds in these categories, but the traits of how people try to live up to expectations are not equally distributed across genders. Or maybe it just gets noticed more and frowned upon when women ask for lots of support compared to when men do. In general, such expectations of behaviour are one way in which I started to notice how we all have *unconscious biases* – and how important it is that we try to reflect in order to make such biases more *conscious* and explicit. In my experience, for instance, women have to do a lot more smiling and emotional labour than men if they don't want to be seen as hard or unapproachable. I don't mind smiling – in fact I like 'doing sociality'. But I also have 50 years of behaviour training, which means that I instinctively know how to let a sharp analysis of a budget be followed by smiles and self-ironic commentary.

It is relevant here to add a note about the way I use the term *unconscious bias*. It is not something men do to women; rather, it is something we all have – and do to each other – and of which we all have to try to become aware. Do we expect the young women to do the household work of academia, such as talking to depressed students or organizing coffee for the meeting? And do we penalize young men for doing the same by somehow thinking they are not up to the 'real job' of hard intellectual work? In general, there is a lot more to say about roles, expectations and diversity in academia than I have space for here.

Recruitment

A third type of experience was related to recruitment and career advice. Again, people are very different and behave in various ways regarding their future careers. Some people seem to think that it is their right to get a job at the university now that they want one. Or they talk about their achievements as second to none. Other people act much more as if they are visiting the premises, grateful that they have been let in for a while. It is my experience that young women are quicker to imagine themselves out of academia than young men. Maybe they give up too easily, but if you want to keep them in academia, you have to say it much more directly to the women than the men.

In general, recruitment is the area where unconscious bias and diversity issues became particularly visible to me. This is also because such decisions can have very long-term effects. Looking back at the processes of recruitment that I have been part of, I do not feel overly proud. Assessments of candidates' competences were not always related to the job advert's explicit description but rather to the assessment committee's general sense of 'what it takes to be qualified' as, for instance, an associate professor. This 'general sense' varied quite a lot between different committees and was often coloured by implicit biases for or against particular areas and modes of research.

According to the university rules, interview panels were relatively broadly composed, and it was important to let everybody on the panel ask at least one question. The downside of this inclusivity was that I generally experienced relatively large discrepancies in lines of questioning and that it was very hard to create a structured way of comparing the answers. I am sure we all tried to be as fair as possible, but I am not convinced we always managed that, particularly since no one on the panels received any training in how to avoid bias or even basic interview techniques – and there was no budget for consultants who might have helped.

At some point, I developed a strategy of trying to swap gender on candidates to see if it had any influence on my own opinion. I also used it as a reflection tool, if I felt deliberations of the committee were not fair. I am slightly ashamed to admit that on at least one occasion, it had a large influence on how I made a hiring decision. I was in doubt as to whether we should hire the woman or the man. The woman was better, but it would take a long time before she could join and I also needed someone to fill the post as fast as possible. When I swapped the gender in my head, there was no doubt that we should not compromise on competences only because we would have to wait longer. Unknowingly, I had been willing to hire a less competent man instead of the more competent woman – but not the other way around.

In terms of recruitment in specific areas where the gender balance was skewed, it was clear that all involved parties acknowledged that it would be good to recruit to change this balance. However, when it came to specific decisions it was much more difficult. Many people had no real awareness of the problem of unconscious bias and they seemed to quickly resort to standard arguments of meritocracy: we only appoint the best, and in this case the best is this person (of the over-represented gender, research area, methodology, ethnicity, etc.). In such a situation, it is almost impossible for a Head of Department to insist that the position should go to someone else. At least this was the case in my university where the word 'strategic' generally was seen to mean the same as 'un-academic'. Had I insisted, I would have risked hiring a person with a symbolic sign on their back saying: 'I am not a very good academic – I am only here because the leadership chose me for political reasons'. In some cases, however, it was possible to challenge the definition of 'the best'. But for this to work, there have to be staff members with high academic standing in the area who support the argument.

A related problem is the normative argumentation for increasing diversity. Both women and men seem to agree that the under-represented gender (or other minority) does not want to get a job or a promotion because of that characteristic: 'I don't want the job because I am a woman'. Neither did I, but I have come to think of this argument as extremely damaging. First of all, if there are structural biases in favour of, for instance, men, then it actually means that men are appointed because they are men. Then we might want to appoint women because they are women. Second, allowing this argument to flourish just means that it becomes even more difficult to change the situation, because you have to avoid talking about why it would be good to appoint a woman. If you say it anyway, people seem to think that you have now said she is not as good as the other candidates – she is appointed *because* of her gender and *despite* her academic track-record.

Finally in this section, I want to address the most common argument against any explicit diversity recruitment effort: should we not just be patient and let time sort out diversity issues? After all, there are a lot more women getting PhDs than previously. While I *do* believe that things change, I do not think this is the right attitude. First of all, it misses the point of the question of diversity and equality. It is not simply a question of getting more female professors, but a much more general question about how we assess competencies and distribute rewards fairly. It is about our unconscious biases and how we make ourselves better able to deal with them in order to treat everybody – not just women and men – in a just and fair way. Second, as a member of the Danish Council for Research and Innovation Policy, I was part of making a report identifying policy measures internationally which could increase gender equality in academia (DFIR 2015). This work made it rather clear that changes in diversity patterns do not come about by themselves. They need a conscious leadership effort and they need designated resources. In the next section, I will therefore reflect on what I would have done differently, if I were to start all over as a Head of Department.

WHAT WOULD I HAVE DONE DIFFERENTLY?

First, I wish I had been less scared and quicker to realize how important I believe issues of diversity and equality to be for good management. I should have been much more explicit and specific right from the start. However, my hesitation was related to the fact that to some degree the diversity issue is a zero-sum game, particularly when it is about recruitment.[1] There are only so many spots to be filled and if you choose a woman, you cannot choose a man. This underlying power dynamic can be unpleasant to deal with. I did not apply for a management position to exercise power, but because I liked things to be done right (as already explained, this is much to do with fairness, but efficient use of resources is also part of it), and I thought I could make a difference for the better. When I had to exercise power directly, I did it for the benefit of the collective organization, but it took me a while to realize how I could and should make a difference with regard to diversity.

Second, I would do much more to increase transparency on issues of diversity. I would have made our own departmental diversity index with a number of selected variables including gender, nationality and ethnicity. The index could provide statistical information across various factors such as staff members and students, pay averages, production numbers, distribution of academic household tasks and possibly more. I would then have a general discussion with the department about what we were looking at – are we happy with the picture or are there distributions that we would like to change? And if so, how do we do that? In my experience, it is much easier to generate a meaningful discussion – and potentially a cultural change – if one starts by making issues visible through transparency work.

Third, I would work specifically on the recruitment issue and make sure that all people involved in recruitment (which is most permanent staff) undergo training in unconscious bias. I would invest in consultants or help from the HR department to make a structured interview process (including using tests and other forms of controlled investigations of candidates) and look at the entire decision process in order to make it as fair and unbiased as possible. We all have gut feelings and sometimes they are important. But we need to be much more explicit about what our stomachs tell us and discuss whether it is relevant information. In other parts of society, people have devised a lot of techniques to make a better job of recruitment. Why don't we learn more directly from them?

Most importantly, however, I would make this into a joint learning space, with an expectation that it is constant work, which will never be completed. We do not get to the end of this. We all carry all sorts of prejudices and preferences with us – in many ways this is what lets us navigate the world. But it is precisely the great thing about working with other people that we can use each other's perspectives to become aware of our own blind spots. Diversity is an issue that allows us to help each other keep trying to be the best we can. to try to live up to the ideal of meritocracy, which we share in academia. All humans regularly say and do silly, stupid or hurtful things to each other. Rather than thinking we can completely stop doing this, we should develop a shared space where we help each other correct such missteps. Academia is a creative space and sometimes our creativity goes the wrong way. We should not aim to completely eradicate that, because that would probably make us into less good academics. But we should find a way of collectively dealing with it – as a shared responsibility – so that we take care of each other.

In line with this, I would also try to develop this shared space into a zone where we have to allow some discomfort, because we do not all agree on what is silly, stupid or hurtful. And this is probably the most difficult thing for me to argue. But let me try anyway. My university had a policy of zero tolerance of sexual harassment. It is hard not to agree with such a policy. Of course, we should not allow sexual (or other) harassment. It also makes sense that as leaders we were supposed to accept people's own feeling of having their boundaries crossed. If I feel sexually harassed, then the last thing someone else should do is to say that my feeling is not right. So we have to accept people's description of their own experiences and feelings.

However, in practice, the zero-tolerance policy meant that people thought that a feeling of being sexually harassed would then automatically lead to a sanction (zero tolerance). There are many reasons why this was not always possible and would not have been the right thing to do. Basically, we cannot sanction people without proof and without any agreement of what deserves a sanction. In practice, the zero-tolerance policy therefore appeared like a put-down for people who felt mistreated, and then did not get the form of justice they had imagined. And that in turn made a lot of other people shy away from getting involved in this. In general, I have heard many more private stories about harassment that were never taken forward, than I have seen actual cases being dealt with. So I do not believe zero tolerance is the best way to go. I would rather argue that all people have a right to have their experiences acknowledged and their feelings respected. Sometimes this means that we disagree about what is appropriate, and we have to live with that discomfort. Maybe we can even find ways of turning it into an exploratory space, where we use our discomfort to learn about ourselves and others in a creative way. Of course, a sexual harassment policy has to operate within the legal framework and cases should be handled according to that. But rather than focus an organizational policy on zero tolerance, I would like to focus it on enabling people's experiences to be heard and acknowledged.

ADVICE TO A NEW HEAD

So where does all this lead? In this last section, I will offer a few pieces of advice to a newly appointed Head. I am not an expert on these issues, so the advice I can give is based solely upon my own reflections on what I would have liked someone to tell me when I started.

The first piece of advice is to think carefully about how important the issue of diversity is to you. If you decide you wish to deal with it, it will probably take a lot of your resources, and there are no easy wins. There might be other more pressing concerns, or you might feel that this is not that important – if so, do not engage more than you have to. It is worse to do something half-heartedly which does not work than to do nothing – because bad policies will just create animosity towards other actions in this area. So if you are not sure, you might want to see if there are other people in your organization who want to take it on and then you can focus on supporting them. There is only so much a Head can do with her time, so make a conscious decision about how much time you will devote to this.

If the issue of diversity is something that matters to you and something you want to engage with, then address your hopes and fears directly. Consider how this is important to you. What constitutes a success and what are you afraid of? Prepare for how you will measure the first and how you will deal with the latter. Find at least one trusted colleague in your leadership team with whom you can discuss the issue and your efforts to address it. Issues of diversity usually become personal at some point or another. Whether you are a man or a woman, you will probably feel your own person drawn into this at some point. How should a white man address this issue without being patronizing? Isn't a female head just doing gender politics on behalf of the interests of her own gender? You need a safe space where you can share your thoughts and test various ideas, plans and reactions without having to watch what you say.

You are addressing a cultural issue and those things are extremely hard to tackle and take a long time. One of the ways in which you can persistently keep the issue on the agenda is by using transparency. Making the sore spots visible will slowly force the organization to deal with it and to accept the issue as relevant. I mentioned above how I would have created a local diversity index if I were to start all over again. This serves two purposes. The organization can be included in the development of such an index and the decisions on what parameters to include. Such work is already starting the discussion. And the transparency generated by regular discussion of the various distributions can be an occasion to discuss what you are doing about it – you and everybody else in the organization. For this to work, you have to make the numbers visible in all the various places you can. The annual review of the action plan that I experienced in my university did not work, because it was general and decoupled from other processes. You have to integrate it into all the other things you do.

Importantly, you should expect resistance. The rest of the organization might not back you up, so don't expect support from above. If you need support for a decision you want to make, and you think it might be controversial, check with your line manager that she is going to support you. It is possible to get this support in several ways and, as with other things, you need to consider how important this decision is for you compared to how difficult it is to get the support. In general, I advise against over-confrontational methods as they tend to backfire at some point – at least in the cultural context within which I have worked. Particularly with the diversity issue, it can be important to avoid confrontation as it quickly becomes a very emotional issue. In line with this, it is extremely important that you have allies who don't agree with everything you say – and that you listen to them. The more you learn about possible resistance beforehand, the easier it is to deal with it.

And lastly, avoid making diversity into an issue of right and wrong. As I described above, try to cultivate a sense of shared responsibility for the discomfort that is hard to avoid. It is going to be awkward sometimes and it is a lot easier if this awkwardness can be shared – or even laughed at. Don't expect to be able to solve or eradicate issues of diversity. See them instead as a possibility for learning. Accept that, while you will not always get it right, you can make a conscious effort to do better.

NOTE

1.   I would like to express gratitude to Member of Parliament and former Minister Sophie Carsten Nielsen, whose guidance allowed me to admit to myself that the diversity issue cannot avoid sometimes being awkward since it is also a power game. She is furthermore a person whom I know has used her influence to appoint me to an advisory role – not only, but also because I am a woman. I am proud of that support.

REFERENCES

DFIR. 2015. *Et internationalt perspektiv på køn- og ligestillingsudfordringer i forskningen.* Uddannelses-
     og Forskningsministeriet. Publication. https://ufm.dk/forskning-og-innovation/rad-og-udvalg/
     danmarks-forsknings-og-innovationspolitiske-rad/aktuelt/publikationer/publikationer-fra-danmarks
     -forsknings-og-innovationspolitiske-rad/et-internationalt-perspektiv-pa-kon-og-ligestillingsud
     fordringer-i-forskningen4fc6d92762d448ffbcd2f68d6498a055 (5 May 2020).
Easterly, Debra M. and Cynthia S. Ricard. 2011. 'Conscious Efforts to End Unconscious Bias: Why
     Women Leave Academic Research'. *Journal of Research Administration* 42(1): 61–73.
European Union, Publications Office of the European Union. 2019. *She Figures 2018.* http://op.europa
     .eu/en/publication-detail/-/publication/9540ffa1-4478-11e9-a8ed-01aa75ed71a1/language-en (5 May
     2020).

12. Leading faculty as teachers

Hanne Andersen

In an academic department, teaching and research together constitute the core activities. However, the balance between the two activities varies considerably between institutions. At research-intensive universities, teaching duties may constitute only a minor part of a faculty member's obligations, while at teaching-intensive universities faculty may be employed primarily to teach. How to lead and manage teaching will obviously differ substantially between such institutions.

Teaching and research tend to be valued differently by many faculty and in many institutions, and this also has important implications for how to lead and manage teaching. There are many reasons for the asymmetry between teaching and research, including historical traditions, changing institutional policies, faculty perceptions, and the degree of (mis)alignment between traditions, current policies and individual perceptions. This chapter will therefore open with a brief account of various perspectives on the asymmetry between teaching and research.[1]

From this vantage point, the chapter will cover two key areas in leading and managing teaching in academic departments for which the asymmetry between teaching and research plays a central role: first, how to lead faculty in their career progression as teachers, and second, how to manage workload distributions when allocating teaching duties. In closing, the chapter will reflect on the special role that heads of departments have as they mediate between institutional and faculty perspectives on the importance of teaching.

THE ASYMMETRY BETWEEN TEACHING AND RESEARCH IN ACADEMIA

It is a widespread myth that top researchers are also top teachers. However, meta-analyses of studies that investigate the linkage between teaching and research have concluded that teaching and research are essentially unrelated (Feldman 1987) or only very loosely coupled (Hattie and Marsh 1996).

Studies of the criteria used in tenure and promotion decisions show that research achievements tend to figure more prominently than teaching. For example, based on surveys and interviews among UK academics, Graham concluded in the UK report *The Career Framework for University Teaching* (2018) that for the vast majority of academics, teaching achievements appeared to make little difference to their career prospects. However, studies also indicate that at many institutions, priorities are gradually changing towards a higher emphasis on teaching (see e.g. Diamond and Adam 1998).

In recent years, many policy reports have argued that in order to improve the quality of teaching and learning, teaching achievement needs to be considered on a par with research achievement when hiring faculty or granting tenure (see e.g. McAleese et al. 2013). At the department level, these ongoing changes mean that department leadership often has the task to implement an institutional policy aimed at increasing the value of teaching, but also has to do this facing faculty that are not used to viewing their career progression as linked to teaching achievements. How to overcome this barrier and conduct performance reviews and tenure interviews in a way that values teaching on a par with research will be the first topic covered by this chapter. Policies aiming at a more equal focus on teaching and research also touch upon two additional aspects where teaching has traditionally differed from research, namely whether training is as necessary for becoming a teacher as it is for becoming a researcher, and whether teaching is an activity that can – or even should – be conducted in a scholarly manner that resembles research. These topics both relate to faculty careers, and they will be discussed in connection with performance reviews and tenure interviews.

Surveys of faculty workload at universities in Europe show that with respect to the proportion of work time spent on teaching and research, senior faculty devote a little less than one third of their time on teaching and a little more than one third on research, when averaged over total annual work time. However, although the time spent on teaching and research may not differ substantially, the same surveys also show that a majority of senior faculty express a stronger personal interest in research than in teaching (Teichler 2017). Hence, on average, there is a mismatch between interest and time allocation. This mismatch is often aggravated by the fact that, on average, faculty tend to work long hours. As a result, faculty may perceive their research time as that which remains after teaching and administrative requirements have been met (Houston, Meyer, and Paewai 2006), or as an activity that primarily takes place in their spare time (Lyons and Ingersoll 2010). This perception also affects how time allocations are described. Thus, time allocated to teaching is often described with negatively loaded terms such as teaching duty or teaching load, while time allocated to research is described neutrally as research time. Consequently, when heads of department allocate teaching tasks, they may be faced with faculty who aim at increasing the time they spend on research while decreasing the time they spend on teaching. How to manage workload distribution when allocating teaching tasks will be the second topic covered by this chapter.

TEACHING AND CAREER DEVELOPMENT

At most universities, teaching is an integral part of an academic career. However, as described in the first section of this chapter, teaching achievements have traditionally been perceived as less important for career progression than research. Nevertheless, today many institutions are aiming to change this. Consequently, heads of departments have an important leadership role in making it transparent which role teaching plays for academic careers locally at their institutions. In order to fulfill this role, a head of department must be able to articulate a clear policy for how teaching achievements are linked to career progression, and to address the development of teaching competences in annual performance reviews as well as in job interviews in a level of detail that is aligned with local policies for linking development and reward.

This section will first describe some tools for visualizing teaching achievements in the development of an academic career. Next, it will review different models for linking individual career progression not only to increasing teaching *experience*, but also to increasing teaching *competences*.

Articulating Teaching Competences

Typically, an academic career is described in an academic CV that lists education, employ-ment, publications, awards, grants and fellowships, conference presentations and invited talks, service to the profession, and teaching experience. This way of structuring the CV easily contributes to the perception of research achievements as more important for the career than teaching achievements.

At institutions emphasizing the equality of teaching and research, performance and career interviews may instead be based on a CV format that treats research and teaching achieve-ments in parallel, for example as shown in Table 12.1.

Table 12.1   Example of a CV format that parallels teaching and research achievements

Education	
Research education	Teacher education/structured staff training
Production and reception	
Publications, including description of author roles	Courses taught and students supervised, including description of teacher roles
Citations and other bibliometric indicators of impact or quality	Student evaluations, placement record, or other quantitative indicators of impact or quality
Experiences and responsibilities	
Description of the ability to attract research funding	Description of the ability to attract students, and of the ability to bring students to completion of their studies
Description of the development of responsibilities, e.g. from the role of contributor of subproject to individual projects to PI of collaborative endeavors	Description of the development of responsibilities, e.g. from teaching minor parts of courses organized by others, over independent sequences, to planning courses and program in which others participate
Trajectory and profile	
Description of how the scope of research interests has developed	Description of how the scope of teaching areas has developed
Description of important achievements/research highlights and how they relate to the overall research trajectory	Description of major teaching achievements, such as development of new courses or fundamental revision of existing courses, and how they relate to the overall teaching trajectory
Description of the wider implications of research results, including reflections on the audience(s) reached and the ability to address them	Description of the wider influence of teaching activities, including reflections on the audience(s) reached and the ability to address them
Service to the academic community	
Peer review	Peer supervision
Editor, program chair	Study boards, head of study, national boards
Assessment committees	National or international assessment of higher education programs or institutions
Research assessment of institution or field	
Wider role in developing the academic community	
Contributing to developing academia through activity in e.g. scholarly societies	Engagement in pedagogical development projects

While such a parallel CV structure ensures an equal focus on research and teaching achievements, it also remains focused on a quantitative description of teaching experiences. To include in the conversation how teaching competences may develop qualitatively in the course of a career, more is needed. For this purpose, many institutions have developed taxonomies or templates for detailed descriptions of teaching competences. An example is the Pedagogical Competence Profile developed at the University of Copenhagen (Table 12.2). This framework is divided into six themes:

- The areas of responsibility that teachers have had, ranging from teaching minor segments in courses organized by others, to independently planning long courses and cooperating with others in developing new courses or programs.
- Teachers' ability to establish and develop good teaching practices through continuous reflection on their teaching.
- Teachers' knowledge of teaching, learning and discipline-specific principles of teaching. Key areas of knowledge include knowledge of the students, knowledge of the study program and knowledge of university teaching.
- Teachers' engagement in knowledge sharing and peer collaboration, with the aims of developing as a teacher; developing the quality of teaching in the department; or contributing to knowledge sharing on a broader organizational, societal or international level.
- The formal pedagogical education that teachers have contributed to or participated in.
- Teachers' engagement in pedagogical development, which can be focused on subjects as well as programs. Pedagogical development projects usually take the form of practice-oriented activities and may include, for example, the introduction of new forms of teaching, supervision or evaluation. Engagement may range from participating to initiating or managing projects.

Within each theme, the Pedagogical Competence Profile provides a vocabulary for describing a detailed set of competences. Some of the competences develop in a quantitative way, others in a qualitative way. Similarly, individual faculty may develop their competences faster in some areas than in others (Kobayashi et al. 2017). Hence, the Pedagogical Competence Profile itself should be seen merely as a non-hierarchical taxonomy of competences, not as a hierarchical description of career levels.

Tools like the Pedagogical Competence Profile can be helpful for scaffolding performance reviews, tenure interviews and job interviews in a way that leads the conversation beyond a simple, quantitative focus on teaching *experience* to focus more on the qualitative development of teaching *competences* throughout a career.

Below is an example of how questions can be structured from an initial focus on "areas of responsibility" and "practice and reflection" over "knowledge sharing and peer collaboration" to "knowlege about teaching and learning" and "formal pedagogical training."

(1) **Areas of responsibility**
    (a) Which areas of responsibilities have you had as a teacher?
    (b) Which new areas of responsibility would you like to develop in the future?

Table 12.2   Extract from the Pedagogical Competence Profile developed at the University of Copenhagen

Areas of responsibility	Knowledge sharing and peer collaboration	Practice and reflection	Knowledge of teaching and learning	Formal pedagogical training	Engagement in pedagogical development
Organizes and teaches single classes	Using feedback from others to improve their own teaching	Focuses on the students' learning outcomes – both in class and in the students' work outside the room	How the students learn – both in general and in relation to the subject	Completed introductory course to the pedagogy of university teaching	Participating in pedagogical development projects
Organizes, teaches and evaluates series of classes	Taking active part in team teaching (planning, teaching and evaluating)	Acknowledges the students by seeking to understand their learning needs, conditions and challenges	The students' study and learning situation	Completed full program on teaching and learning in higher education	Initiating pedagogical development projects
Organizes, teaches and evaluates whole courses	Communicating and sharing knowledge with colleagues about teaching at program level	Sets out clear learning goals and organizes the teaching activities accordingly	The program's design, structure and content	Completed course on PhD supervision	Managing pedagogical development projects

Areas of responsibility	Knowledge sharing and peer collaboration	Practice and reflection	Knowledge of teaching and learning	Formal pedagogical training	Engagement in pedagogical development
Contributes to developing the quality of the study program	Providing pedagogical guidance and supervision to colleagues	Gives the students feedback on their learning study practices	The potential labor market for graduates of the program and the practical uses of the subject	Other completed courses on the pedagogy of university teaching and subject didactics	
Participates in faculty or inter-faculty program development and/or quality assurance	Taking part in dialogs on the societal function, challenges and developments of higher education	Designs exams to reflect the students' work with the learning objectives	The interaction between the academic disciplines of the program and its relations to other programs	Participation in and contributions to local workshops, courses and thematic days on university teaching and education	
	Contributing to developing university pedagogy and subject didactics nationally and internationally	Incorporates the study program's overall goals, structure and profile into the teaching and opens the subject to other academic perspectives	Different ways of strengthening the link between research and teaching	Participation in national and international meetings and conferences focusing on the pedagogy of university teaching and learning	
		Actively seeks to link research processes, values and results to activities in the classroom	Various forms of evaluation and teaching (including feedback, and online and blended learning)		
		Analyzes regularly own teaching, results achieved and students' feedback in order to change practices	Topics within university pedagogy and subject didactics		

Note: Knowledge of teaching and learning as well as practice and reflection are considered core competences.
Source: See https://employment.ku.dk/faculty/recruitment-process/job-application-portfolio/KUs_p_dagogiske_kompetenceprofil_31_10_UK.pdf.

These questions start from a quantitative description of teaching responsibilities as they are described in a traditional teaching CV that primarily lists taught courses. At the same time, they facilitate a shift in the dialog towards more qualitative topics, such as the scope of responsibilities. A special focus can be on how pedagogical competences need to develop as responsibilities broaden, from the individual course, over individual programs, to institution-wide responsibilities.

(2) **Practice and reflection**
 (a) Which aims do you have for your teaching? How do you work on facilitating student learning in your teaching?
 (b) What do you observe and reflect upon during your teaching? How do you use your observations and reflections later? Which other input do you draw upon in reflecting upon and developing your teaching? Exemplify from previous experiences.
 (c) How do you interact with students in developing your teaching? How do you use student evaluations in developing your teaching?
 (d) How do you engage in current institutional policies (e.g. increased feedback, use of digital tools, or focus on innovation and entrepreneurship)?

These questions may serve to facilitate a shift in focus away from a traditional teacher-centered view of teaching towards a student-centered view of teaching that is focused on what the students learn (see e.g. Kember and Kwan 2000; Trigwell, Prosser, and Waterhouse 1999). In addition, they serve to open a dialog on how to align teaching activities with institutional strategies or policies. A special focus can be on how teaching competences are lined to the quality of teaching.

(3) **Knowledge sharing and peer collaboration**
 (a) How do you go about it if something in your teaching does not function as planned?
 (b) How do you collaborate with colleagues in developing your own teaching, or how do you offer support to colleagues in developing their teaching?
 (c) How do you see the department increase its peer collaboration on teaching?

These questions may serve to facilitate a shift in focus away from a traditional perception of teaching as private, to a view of teaching as a collaborative activity. In addition, they serve to open a dialogue on the department as a community of teachers. A special focus can be on how the development of teaching competences can be linked to an increased influence among colleagues with respect to teaching.

In some institutional settings, it may also be an option to supplement individual performance reviews on the collaborative aspects of teaching with group conversations, for example with faculty collaborating on an individual course, faculty offering courses for the same population of students, or for faculty interested in similar pedagogical approaches.

(4) **Knowledge about teaching and learning, and formal pedagogical training**
 (a) How would you characterize your knowledge about teaching and learning? Exemplify from previous experiences how you draw on your knowledge about teaching and learning when developing your teaching.

(b)   Have you participated in or contributed to a formal teacher-training program in higher education? What was the most important insight you gained from your participation?

(c)   What would you like to learn more about in the future? What would you like to disseminate to colleagues?

This last set of questions opens a dialog on the usefulness of formal training. Traditionally, it has not been considered important for university teachers to acquire any substantial knowledge about pedagogy, such as, for example, students' learning processes, or how different teaching styles may affect students' learning outcomes. As a result, new university teachers have often modeled their teaching on the pedagogical approach they had themselves encountered as students. This has created a strong tradition for particular ways of teaching that can be difficult to change. At the same time, aiming for more iterative and evidence-based approaches to teaching, many institutions have developed policies for improving university teachers' pedagogical competences, for example through structured staff training.

While some faculty may embrace this development and welcome the opportunity to participate in formal pedagogical training, others may be strongly opposed to changing their teaching and may find that new policies directly or indirectly criticize their previous practices. Typical arguments from faculty opposed to structured staff training include that they are too busy to participate in faculty development; that it challenges their privacy, autonomy, or academic freedom; that they just need released time instead; that being a good teacher is an inborn quality; or that faculty development programs make little difference to teaching effectiveness (see e.g. Turner and Boice 1986; Sabagh and Saroyan 2014; Brownell and Tanner 2012; Pleschová et al. 2012). Conversations about how structured training may contribute to the development of teaching competences may therefore include such topics as studies showing that teachers' participation in pedagogical training does have an effect on students' learning (see e.g. Postareff, Lindblom-Ylänne, and Nevgi 2007), colleagues' experiences with the training offered locally, or central topics from the local courses and how they can contribute to developing teaching at the department generally.

Types of Career Progression

Academic career progression may be linked to increasing expectations regarding teaching in different ways, including

- Volume and range of experience
- Volume and range of responsibility
- Influence among peers
- Range and depth of teaching competences
- Quality of teaching.

Some institutions may expect progression along all dimensions, while other institutions may specify different career paths that focus on progression among specific dimensions. For example, the University of Copenhagen has defined entry-level qualification for different career levels in a way that assumes progression along all dimensions (Table 12.3).

In contrast, the Career Framework for University Teaching that has been adopted by a number of institutions globally, defines four levels of teaching achievement that can be linked to career progression in different ways. The four levels progress from an effective teacher who creates positive conditions for student learning and demonstrates effective teaching delivery that develops over time, to a national and international leader in teaching and learning who makes exceptional contributions to teaching and learning in higher education. In addition, it offers two parallel branches for progression: one focused on impact on the local educational environment, and one focused on pedagogical scholarship (Table 12.4).

Table 12.3   Entry-level qualifications for different career levels at the University of Copenhagen

Assistant professors	Associate professors	Full professors
Capable of providing research-based teaching within one or more fields	Capable of providing research-based teaching of high quality within one or more fields, and can contribute to developing, organizing and evaluating longer teaching sequences	Capable of providing research-based teaching of the highest quality within one or more fields, and can contribute to developing, organizing and evaluating longer sequences of teaching at all academic levels
Some teaching experience	Solid teaching experience, including experience with assessment and with course development that draws on knowledge about teaching and learning	Extensive teaching experience, including experience with assessment and experience with the assessment of PhD dissertations
Interested in supervising students at the bachelor and master level	Experience with supervision at the bachelor and master level	Experience with supervision at the bachelor and master level as well as at the PhD/postdoc level
	A teaching portfolio that documents teaching experiences and includes reflections on teaching competences	A teaching portfolio that documents teaching experiences and includes reflections on teaching competences
Interested in developing their competences as a teacher, for example by participating in an introductory staff training course	Ongoing development of teaching competences, for example by participating in more extensive staff training courses	Ongoing development of teaching competences, including not only their own practice, but also the practice of others
Interested in feedback from colleagues, students and others when developing their teaching	Interested in feedback from colleagues, students and others when developing their teaching, and in collaboration and knowledge sharing with colleagues about teaching	Interested in feedback from colleagues, students and others when developing their teaching, and in mentoring colleagues in developing their teaching

Frameworks such as these depict very different models for how teaching can be linked to faculty careers. Some institutions only expect faculty to meet the minimum threshold defined by the effective teacher, regardless of career level. Other institutions expect progression throughout a career, but may differ in whether they see this progression as linked to a broadening of experiences and responsibilities, or as linked to evidence-based approaches to teaching and contributions to the knowledge of teaching and learning.

Table 12.4   Definition of progressive levels of teaching achievements according to the Career Framework for University Teaching

Level	Description	Sphere of impact	Cumulative capabilities
1. Effective teacher	Takes a conscientious and reflective approach, creating positive conditions for student learning and demonstrating effective teaching delivery that develops over time	Their primary sphere of impact is the students they teach and tutor	**Attitudes**: Demonstrates a reflective and professional attitude that develops over time **Delivery**: Offers effective design, delivery and assessment of courses and materials
2. Skilled and collegial teacher	Takes an evidence-informed approach to their development as a teacher and provides mentorship to their peers to promote a collegial and collaborative educational environment across their school or discipline	Their sphere of impact encompasses their academic colleagues as well as students	**Skills**: Employs evidence-based teaching to support student learning and engagement **Collaboration**: Supports a collegial and collaborative learning environment
3a. Institutional leader in teaching and learning	Makes a significant contribution to enhancing the environment for inclusion and excellence in teaching and learning within and beyond their institution	Their sphere of impact encompasses the educational environment at their school/university	**Leadership**: Delivers lasting impact in teaching and learning across the institution
3b. Scholarly teacher	Makes a significant contribution to pedagogical knowledge by engaging with and contributing to scholarly research that, in turn, influences educational practice within and beyond their institution	Their sphere of impact encompasses educational knowledge at their institution and within the community in their pedagogical fields of interest	**Knowledge**: Contributes to pedagogical knowledge
4. National and international leader in teaching and learning	Makes exceptional contributions to teaching and learning in higher education through national and global influence and leadership in educational practice and/or in pedagogical research	Their sphere of impact encompasses the national/global education community	**Influence**: Exercises national and global influence in teaching and learning

Source: See https://www.teachingframework.com/.

And other institutions again may distinguish between research-oriented and teaching-oriented career trajectories, where faculty on the former track receive promotion primarily based on their research achievements, while faculty on the latter track may receive promotion based on the contributions to the collaborative educational environments at their institution.

Occasionally, special career options may be dedicated to scholarly inquiry into teaching and learning. Traditionally, being a scholar has largely been understood as being a researcher. However, over recent decades, it has become increasingly popular to argue that faculty need to embody multiple types of scholarship, including what is referred to as the scholarship of teaching (Boyer 1990; Boyer and Altbach 1997). On such a view, faculty not only develops teaching for the sake of their own classroom; instead, as scholars of teaching, they are expected to engage in teaching development as a meta-discipline that systematically investigates topics related to student learning and makes the results available to other scholars for critical scrutiny (Tight 2018). While some institutions may link such achievements to the ordinary reward structure, other institutions may dedicate special fellowships or teaching academies to the scholarship of teaching.

Given the wide variation between career models, the department leadership has an important role in making local policies for career progression visible and in aligning performance and promotion reviews with these policies. Further, another important task for the department leadership is to facilitate faculty members' development of their pedagogical competences when distributing teaching tasks. This will be covered in the next section.

TEACHING TASK ALLOCATION AND WORKLOAD DISTRIBUTION

At many departments, an important aspect of managing teaching is the allocation of multi-faceted teaching tasks. Some relate to academic questions about the future development of the discipline, specializations to be offered, the academic structuring of the curriculum, etc. These issues are closely related to the management of the educational program. Institutions differ on whether that responsibility lies at department level, and if so, with the head of department or, for example, with a separate head of studies; or whether such responsibilities lie at a higher level, for example a dean.

Other aspects of the allocation of teaching tasks relate to managing teachers as personnel. At many institutions, issues related to the management of faculty as personnel will be the responsibility of the head of department. This section will primarily focus on these aspects, in particular on how to develop models for the distribution of workloads.

At institutions that expect faculty to engage more or less equally in teaching and research, the relation between the two is decisive for the process of allocating teaching tasks. If teaching and research are not ascribed the same value in the academic reward structure, these inequalities will create incentives for faculty to prefer some tasks rather than others.

Hence, the different models for academic careers described in the section above provide different constraints for the allocation of teaching tasks. For example, if the local career structure specifies certain teaching experiences or pedagogical competences that faculty need to acquire in order to receive promotion, this provides incentives for faculty to engage in teaching activities that will help them acquire the needed experiences or competences. In contrast, if the local career structure only requires faculty to meet some minimum threshold with respect to teaching while promotion is dependent primarily on research achievements, this creates incentives for faculty to increase the amount of time they spend on research and limit the amount of time they spend on teaching. Further, since promotion and other forms of academic reward are often dependent on success in achieving research funding, this creates additional incentives directed at research rather than teaching.

Such asymmetries between the value of teaching and research, respectively, may create an incentive for faculty to aim at decreasing the amount of work dedicated to teaching in order to increase the time available for research.

At some institutions, the workload for teaching is understood as a fixed number of courses or contact hours, and there may even be a wide-ranging freedom for faculty to define the topic of their courses. In such settings, questions about how to distribute tasks and workloads may not seem relevant. At other institutions, teaching duties may, for example, be understood as a percentage of faculty members' total effort. Similarly, faculty may not themselves be in a position to define the topic of their courses, but are instead assigned to particular teaching tasks. In these settings, managers in charge of the allocation of teaching tasks will need a model for determining the workloads of individual faculty in a way that is transparent, and for distributing the workload among faculty.

In developing such a model, some of the key questions to consider are:

- Aim and scope of the model
  - What is the overarching goal in establishing a new (or modifying an existing) model for the distribution of workload (e.g. to ensure transparency and equity, to maximize faculty satisfaction, to reduce department labor costs)?
  - Should the model only include teaching and service/administration, or should it also include allocation of research time/tasks?
- Model parameters
  - What will be the relevant parameters of the model (e.g. faculty workload or department budget)?
  - Is it possible to quantify the relevant parameters to enable comparisons between faculty (e.g. workload quantified by contact hours or by estimated hours used, or department benefit quantified by income or by some measure of utility in achieving strategic goals)?
- Use of special incentives
  - Should the model enable individual faculty to optimize their personal workload, for example by reducing time for preparation by repeating courses or by selecting teaching formats that require little preparation?
  - Should the model enable department management to offer extra credit for tasks that are perceived as unattractive by faculty, but important for the department?
- Transparency, equity and fairness
  - How should conflicting interests among faculty be handled? Should interests be prioritized according to, for example, academic rank, length of employment, or previous performance?
  - How will the allocation of tasks and distribution of workload be related to annual performance reviews?
  - How should under- or over-performance be handled? Should it be possible to save up for a teaching-free semester later by teaching more than the standard load for a couple

of years? Vice versa, does under-performance in one year result in an increased load in the next year?

- Should individual distributions, preferences and/or performances be made public or remain private?

Answers to these questions depend on the local context. Although there is a growing literature internationally on work allocation models, especially from Australia and the UK, results from such studies cannot necessarily be translated to other settings with different legal constraints, workplace cultures, or academic career patterns. Nevertheless, results from interview studies that uncover types of satisfaction and dissatisfaction among faculty may serve to prepare managers for various types of reactions when introducing a new approach to the distribution of workloads. For example, faculty satisfaction and acceptance has been found to be linked to faculty involvement in the construction or revision of the model (Houston, Meyer, and Paewai 2006), and to the perception of the model as transparent or equitable (Burgess, Lewis, and Mobbs 2003). Similarly, faculty dissatisfaction has been found to be linked to models that are complex (Vardi 2009); favor one group of faculty over another (Burgess 1996); exclude particular tasks (Houston, Meyer, and Paewai 2006); or are not perceived as accurately reflecting the amount of time spent on tasks (Burgess 1996; Houston, Meyer, and Paewai 2006).

Some faculty may be skeptical of workload allocation models as such and perceive them as a divisive tool that makes people "nitpick over amounts" (Hornibrook 2012), as a management tool for controlling academic work, or as simply "more paperwork" (Boyd 2014). In contrast, other faculty may appreciate workload allocation models because they allow an opportunity to document their workload to the management, or are seen as a means of ensuring justice and transparency (Boyd 2014).

Box 12.1 briefly discusses some of the pros and cons of different workload distribution models.[2]

BOX 12.1 ALGORITHMIC MODELS FOR WORKLOAD ALLOCATION

Simple input model: Workload distribution is based on the number of contact hours for each faculty. This model is widespread internationally. It enables teaching duties to be listed in a simple way in contracts or job ads as the number of contact hours or the number of courses per year.

- Building on only one quantitative parameter, contact hours, the model is easy to understand and simple to use. However, that also means that it does not account for the different effort required for different activities or at different career levels, e.g. lectures/tutorials; new/repeat courses; new/experienced faculty. As a result, faculty who teach the same number of contact hours can have substantially different actual workloads, and this may be perceived as unfair.
- The model enables individual faculty to optimize their personal workloads, for example by reducing time for preparation by repeating courses, or by focusing on teaching formats that require less preparation. However, this also means that the model is diffi-

cult to use as a resource-optimization tool to improve the department's teaching budget. Further, some teaching formats that require less preparation may also be less efficient in facilitating students' learning. Hence, the model's inbuilt incentives for faculty may be aligned neither with the financial needs of the department, nor with the teaching needs of the students.

- The possibility for individual faculty to optimize their personal workloads may work as a strong incentive for all faculty to prefer particular activities that are perceived as "good bargains." Hence, the model may give rise to conflicting interests among faculty. Often, the model will need to be supplemented with guidelines for how such conflicts are to be resolved; for example, whether preference is granted to faculty of higher rank or longer employment history, or, from the opposite perspective, to faculty who have less teaching experience or are still working towards tenure.

Complex input model: Workload distribution is based on the number of actual work hours that each task is expected to take up.

- This model attempts to accommodate the differences in required effort between different types of activities, between differences in expertise, or between differences in experience.
- The model enables the department to optimize its teaching budget by focusing, for example, on teaching formats that are cost-efficient. Hence, in this model, resource-optimizing incentives work to the benefit of the department, rather than to the benefit of individual faculty. In addition, the model can easily be linked to department strategies, for example by allocating extra hours for specific focus areas, such as increased feedback to students, or similar.
- It can be very difficult to determine the time that a given task requires, and the time required may vary considerably from faculty to faculty. Hence, the specific time allocations easily trigger arguments. Further, the model can be perceived as cumbersome, time-consuming, controlling, or opaque.

Simple output model: Workload distribution is based on the number of equivalent full-time students that each faculty has taught, or full-time student years completed.

- Building on only one quantitative parameter, completed full-time student years, the model is easy to understand. Its use requires access to enrollment and/or completion numbers and is therefore less simple than a model based on contact hours.
- This type of model is primarily used at institutions where the local budget is directly dependent on student performance. In such settings, the model can provide a transparent link between teaching activities and a department's budget.
- The model does not account for the different effort required for different ways in which a full-time student year can be completed, e.g. the difference between teaching one large or multiple small courses. As a result, faculty who produce the same number of full-time student years can have substantially different actual workloads. On the one hand, this creates a strong incentive for engaging in large-scale introductory courses. On the other

hand, the model may present a substantial problem for small subfields that attract only few students.

In many departments, the distribution of teaching tasks is based on a workload distribution model similar to one of those briefly discussed above. However, faculty have many other interests invested in teaching than only the question of workload. Having the possibility of pursuing personal academic interests, being able to attract advanced students, or preference for particular teaching formats are all among the factors that influence faculty satisfaction with a given distribution of teaching tasks. Such individual preferences can be difficult to accommodate explicitly in an algorithmic workload distribution model and may instead require individual negotiation (Box 12.2). In this way, there will often be a trade-off between collective transparency and individual satisfaction.

Further, as institutions increasingly stress the importance for faculty of developing their teaching competences, such needs also have to be included in the local workload allocation model. Hence, in developing (or refining) a workload allocation model, the department leadership increasingly needs to include questions such as the following:

- How can the allocation of tasks and distribution of workloads facilitate the development of faculty members' teaching competences?
- Should the model enable individual faculty to negotiate personal workloads linked to the development of teaching competences?
- Should the model enable individual faculty to negotiate personal workloads in order to optimize other preferences, for example by accepting a higher number of contact hours in return for the opportunity to pursue special academic interests?

Again, such considerations related to individual careers can be difficult to accommodate in a purely algorithmic model and may instead require individual negotiation. Hence, in conclusion, the more value the institution ascribes to teaching and to the development of its teachers' teaching competences, the more detailed negotiation is required from department leadership when managing and distributing teaching at the department level.

BOX 12.2 WORKLOAD ALLOCATION BY INDIVIDUAL NEGOTIATION

Individual negotiation of teaching, research and service/administration tasks.
This approach allows an individual tailoring of the allocation of tasks to career level, individual preferences, or personal career aspirations. However, individual negotiations across all faculty in a department can be very time-consuming, and a solution that optimizes overall satisfaction across the department does not necessarily represent an optimal solution for each individual faculty. It can require strong leadership to avoid the loudest voices getting the better bargains, and it is easy to criticize the result as being inequitable.

LEADING TOWARDS SYMMETRY WHILE MANAGING ASYMMETRY

This chapter opened with a description of some widespread perceptions of asymmetry between teaching and research. On this basis, the chapter has discussed how the asymmetry between research and teaching constrains both career development and workload distribution in an academic department. It is now time to step back and reflect once more on the asymmetry between teaching and research, and on how it affects the role of the head of department.

As described earlier in this chapter, the relation between teaching and research is complicated. On the one hand, more and more institutions emphasize the equivalence of teaching and research in their policies for hiring and promotion. On the other hand, faculty do not necessarily recognize this equivalence in the actual hiring and promotion practices. In addition, universities' increasing dependence on external research funding contributes to maintaining a strong focus on the value of research achievements over teaching achievements. Often, it will be at the department level that these various expectations clash. It is at department level that conflicting expectations for whether time should be spent on teaching or on research creates tensions when computing and distributing workloads. And it is at department level that conflicting expectations for whether reward is granted on the basis of teaching achievements or research achievements creates tensions when conducting performance reviews or recommending promotions.

Hence, heads of departments may easily find themselves caught in a situation characteristic for mid-level managers in charge of implementing top-down decisions while facing bottom-up resistance. From that position, they are expected to be loyal both to their institution's policies aimed at increasing the value of teaching, and to their faculty who are faced with strong competition on research funding. Often, there will be no simple and easy solution to this potential tension, and transparency in policies and decisions will be of key importance.

NOTES

1. This chapter provides a brief introduction to the literature; for more substantial overviews, the reader is referred to e.g. Boyer and Altbach (1997), Teichler, Arimoto, and Cummings (2013), Shin et al. (2014), and Teichler (2017).
2. For more detailed discussions, see e.g. Burgess (1996), Barrett and Barrett (2007, 2008), Vardi (2009), or Robertson and Germov (2015).

REFERENCES

Barrett, Lucinda, and Peter Barrett. 2007. "Current practice in the allocation of academic workloads." *Higher Education Quarterly* 61 (4): 461–78.

Barrett, Lucinda, and Peter Barrett. 2008. *The Management of Academic Workloads: Full Report on Findings*. London: Leadership Foundation for Higher Education.

Boyd, Leanne. 2014. "Exploring the utility of workload models in academe: a pilot study." *Journal of Higher Education Policy and Management* 36 (3): 315–26.

Boyer, Ernest L. 1990. *Scholarship Reconsidered: Priorities of the Professoriate*. New York: Carnegie Foundation for the Advancement of Teaching.

Boyer, Ernest L., and Philip G. Altbach. 1997. *The International Academic Profession*. New York: Carnegie Foundation for the Advancement of Teaching.

Brownell, Sara E., and Kimberly D. Tanner. 2012. "Barriers to faculty pedagogical change: lack of training, time, incentives, and ... tensions with professional identity?" *CBE—Life Sciences Education* 11 (4): 339–46.

Burgess, T. F. 1996. "Planning the academic's workload: different approaches to allocating work to university academics." *Higher Education* 32 (1): 63–75.

Burgess, T. F., H. A. Lewis, and T. Mobbs. 2003. "Academic workload planning revisited." *Higher Education* 46 (2): 215–33.

Diamond, Robert M., and Bronwyn E. Adam. 1998. *Changing Priorities at Research Universities, 1991–1996.* [Based on Peter J. Gray, Robert C. Froh, and Robert M. Diamond, *The National Study of Research Universities on the Balance between Research and Undergraduate Teaching* (1992).] Princeton, NJ: Carnegie Foundation for the Advancement of Teaching.

Feldman, Ken. 1987. "Research productivity and scholarly accomplishment of college teachers as related to their instructional effectiveness: a review and exploration." *Research in Higher Education* 24: 227–98.

Graham, Ruth. 2018. "The career framework for university teaching: background and overview." Royal Academy of Engineering. https://www.raeng.org.uk/publications/reports/career-framework-for-university -teaching-backgroun.

Hattie, John, and Herbert W. Marsh. 1996. "The relationship between research and teaching: a meta-analysis." *Review of Educational Research* 66 (4): 507–42.

Hornibrook, Sue. 2012. "Policy implementation and academic workload planning in the managerial university: understanding unintended consequences." *Journal of Higher Education Policy and Management* 34 (1): 29–38.

Houston, Don, Luanna H. Meyer, and Shelley Paewai. 2006. "Academic staff workloads and job satisfaction: expectations and values in academe." *Journal of Higher Education Policy and Management* 28 (1): 17–30.

Kember, David, and Kam-Por Kwan. 2000. "Lecturers' approaches to teaching and their relationship to conceptions of good teaching." *Instructional Science* 28 (5): 469–90.

Kobayashi, S., J. Dolin, J, A. Søborg, and J. Turner. 2017. "Building academic staff teaching competencies: how pedagogic continuous professional development for academic staff can be organised and developed in research-intensive universities." In B. Stensaker, G. T. Bilbow, L. Breslow, and R. van der Vaart (eds.), *Strengthening Teaching and Learning in Research Universities*, 103–28. Cham: Palgrave Macmillan.

Lyons, Michael, and Louise Ingersoll. 2010. "Regulated autonomy or autonomous regulation? Collective bargaining and academic workloads in Australian universities." *Journal of Higher Education Policy and Management* 32 (2): 137–48.

McAleese, M., A. Blandh, V. Berger, C. Bode, J. Muehlfeit, T. Petrin, and L. Tsoukalis. 2013. *Report to the European Commission on Improving the Quality of Teaching and Learning in Europe's Higher Education Institutions.* Luxembourg: Publication Office of the European Union.

Pleschová, Gabriela, Eszter Simon, Kathleen M. Quinlan, Jennifer Murphy, and Torgny Roxa. 2012. "The professionalisation of academics as teachers in higher education." Strasbourg: European Science Foundation. http://archives.esf.org/fileadmin/Public_documents/Publications/professionalisation_academics.pdf.

Postareff, Liisa, Sari Lindblom-Ylänne, and Anne Nevgi. 2007. "The effect of pedagogical training on teaching in higher education." *Teaching and Teacher Education* 23 (5): 557–71.

Robertson, Michael, and John Germov. 2015. "Bringing the budget back into academic work allocation models: a management perspective." *Journal of Higher Education Policy and Management* 37 (5): 507–18.

Sabagh, Zaynab, and Alenoush Saroyan. 2014. "Professors' perceived barriers and incentives for teaching improvement." *International Education Research* 2 (3): 18–30.

Shin, Jung Cheol, Akira Arimoto, William K. Cummings, and Ulrich Teichler. 2014. *Teaching and Research in Contemporary Higher Education.* Vol. 9, *The Changing Academy – The Changing Academic Profession in International Comparative Perspective.* Berlin: Springer.

Teichler, Ulrich. 2017. "Teaching versus research: an endangered balance?" In Maria de Lourdes Machado-Taylor, Virgílio Meira Soares, and Ulrich Teichler (eds.), *Challenges and Options: The Academic Profession in Europe*, 11–28. Dordrecht: Springer.

Teichler, Ulrich, Akira Arimoto, and William K. Cummings. 2013. *The Changing Academic Profession.* New York and London: Springer.

Tight, Malcolm. 2018. "Tracking the scholarship of teaching and learning." *Policy Reviews in Higher Education* 2 (1): 61–78.

Trigwell, Keith, Michael Prosser, and Fiona Waterhouse. 1999. "Relations between teachers' approaches to teaching and students' approaches to learning." *Higher Education* 37 (1): 57–70.

Turner, Jim L., and Robert Boice. 1986. "Coping with resistance to faculty development." *To Improve the Academy* 5: 26–36.

Vardi, Iris. 2009. "The impacts of different types of workload allocation models on academic satisfaction and working life." *Higher Education* 57 (4): 499–508.

13. Inclusive onboarding in academic departments

Daniel J. Petzer, Nicola S. Kleyn and Michele Ruiters

INTRODUCTION

Carefully managing human capital is an important issue for any organization to consider (Cesário and Chambel 2019, p. 1465), and one of the vital roles played by heads of academic departments concerns the onboarding of new faculty members. When onboarding new employees, the objective is to ensure they adjust and swiftly contribute to attaining the organization's objectives (Graybill et al. 2013, p. 201). Baker and DiPiro (2019, p. 1233) profess that onboarding assists new employees in familiarizing themselves with the organization's values and mission, fosters the capacity to access the organization's resources, and supports new employees in determining their role in contributing to the organization's success and growth. Although onboarding is broadly considered a worthy practice, as it allows new employees to align with the organization's values and adapt to the norms of the organization, conventional onboarding methods are known to display shortcomings (Cable, Gino, and Staats 2013, pp. 23–4).

Fostering inclusion in academic departments involves the implementation of practices and strategies among diverse faculty members to encourage significant interaction between them (Tienda 2013, p. 467). Perceptions of inclusion are shaped throughout the faculty member's professional life cycle, but their lived experiences when entering an academic department are particularly important (Cheffen 2017, p. 83). We contend that the process of inclusion of faculty members in academic departments is imperative for the effective onboarding of new faculty members. Therefore, the purpose of this chapter is to explore the lived experiences of new faculty members in an academic department and, more specifically, a business school environment during onboarding, as well as to understand how these experiences shaped their views on the extent to which they felt included and assimilated into their new environment within a particular cultural context. We begin by exploring the background and literature on inclusion in higher education and onboarding. We also explain our methodology before reporting on results, discussing our findings and providing conclusions, limitations and directions for future research.

BACKGROUND AND LITERATURE REVIEW

Fostering Inclusion in Higher Education

As higher education institutions respond to the increasing pressure to hire and retain faculty members who represent the growing racially and culturally diverse profile of their students (Bhopal and Chapman 2019, p. 98), a critical task for academic leaders across institutional levels is to pursue strategies and create environments that foster diversity and inclusion.

An individual's social location is established where multiple identities like class, gender and race intersect (Spafford et al. 2006, p. 1), and although the navigation of the intersection of multiple identities is core to pursuing strategies of diversity and inclusion, there are important differences between the constructs (Tienda 2013, p. 468). Embracing diversity in the organizational context focuses on the employment and utilization of those with different identity groups in an organization (Roberson 2006, p. 214). In comparison, inclusion denotes the extent to "which individuals can access information and resources, are involved in work groups, and have the ability to influence decision-making processes" (Mor-Barak and Cherin 1998, p. 48). Inclusion begins to manifest in instances where diverse individuals participate in activities or tasks and can contribute fully to the task at hand (Walker et al. 2019, p. 3). Managing for inclusion involves pursuing practices and strategies that encourage meaningful academic and social interactions between those who have different views, traits and experiences (Tienda 2013, p. 467) within a particular cultural context.

The drivers that lead faculty members to view themselves as included or excluded in the academic environment are varied, interconnected and complex. Marginalization of faculty members, particularly those representative of minority groups, can occur as a result of university policies and their execution, institutional cultures and macro-level power relations (Bhopal and Chapman 2019, p. 99; Mohamed and Beagan 2019, p. 338). Exclusion may be experienced when faculty members (as individuals or part of minority groups) are assigned roles that are less valued than their counterparts and are less able to access decision-making opportunities (Bhopal and Chapman 2019, pp. 98–113). Excluded faculty members also report the pain of micro-level, everyday interactions like failing to introduce faculty members by their academic titles and calling them by their first names, conveying messages that they do not fully belong (Mohamed and Beagan 2019, p. 345). Interviews with racially minoritized academics in Canadian universities found that the level of inclusion depended on experiences with acceptance (through hiring, promotion and tenure), visibility (as it related to perceived power in formal and informal work interactions), support (shown through collegiality, encouragement, assistance, collaboration and resource allocation), and mentoring (Spafford et al. 2006, p. 1). Although faculty experiences across the faculty life cycle will shape perceptions of inclusion and exclusion, the lived experiences of faculty members during the early phases of their entry into a new department or faculty are particularly important (Cheffen 2017, p. 83).

Onboarding

The transition into a new community places pressure on newly appointed faculty members to navigate the challenges of preserving their individualism and autonomy while finding their place (Staniforth and Harland 2006, p. 185). In addition to the knowledge they need to acquire, new faculty members need to become social members of the institution. Organizational social-ization refers to the process of an organizational outsider who is unfamiliar with an organ-ization making the transition to becoming an insider, mastering the organization's norms, procedures and culture (Louis 1980, p. 226). Socialization over time depends on the new employee's behavior as well as organizational strategies and tactics to promote self-efficacy, role clarity and acceptance by insiders (Bauer and Erdogan 2012, p. 98).

Within the greater frame of the socialization processes, onboarding involves the practices an organization instigates to enable the acclimatization of an employee to the organization or a transfer to a new part or role within the organization concerned (Klein, Polin, and Sutton 2015, p. 263). It is also the process through which new employees are introduced to the vision, mission and organization values, aspects of their job and the expectations placed on them, as well as the institution's history, politics, people and culture (Graybill et al. 2013, p. 207). The term "induction" is used in a similar vein to refer to "professional practices designed to facilitate the entry of new recruits to an organisation and to equip them to operate effectively within it" (Trowler and Knight 1999, p. 178). Numerous scholars use the terms "onboard-ing" and "induction" interchangeably, without differentiating between the two constructs (Cooper-Thomas, Anderson, and Cash 2012, p. 42; Pandya 2017, p. 11; Trembath 2016, p. 123). Analysis of multiple definitions of the two constructs suggests that both terms refer to organizational processes designed to support new employees to assimilate into an organ-ization. In this chapter, we use the term "onboarding" to refer to employees' experiences of becoming acquainted with and integrated into their employer organization early in their tenure. Effective onboarding has been positively associated with work engagement and organizational commitment (Cesário and Chambel 2019, p. 1473).

Onboarding processes are multidimensional. A good onboarding process not only focuses on providing employees with technical information like appropriate policies (Graybill et al. 2013, p. 208), it also provides insight into an organization's values and culture (Cable, Gino, and Staats 2013, p. 23), and enables new faculty to engage in active dialogue in the social system they find themselves in (Staniforth and Harland 2006, p. 186). Ideally, faculty onboarding processes need to accommodate the needs of faculty members from various con-texts. New joiners from practice, for example, report that their initial experiences did not serve to engender confidence as faculty members (King, Roed, and Wilson 2018, p. 479).

Mentoring is an important aspect of onboarding programs that is widely used across many professions (Ehrich, Hansford, and Tennent 2004, p. 518), including higher education (Eisner 2015, p. 8). The implementation of any faculty mentoring program requires careful design and a diligent focus on execution. A study by Staniforth and Harland (2006, p. 190) reports examples of heads of departments who stressed that existing mentoring schemes are vital to onboarding. When their newly hired faculty members were asked about the role that mentoring had played in enabling their induction, most reported negative experiences. They had either not received mentoring, saw it as having an overly narrow focus on research, or felt that mentors alone were insufficient to build a sense of camaraderie (Staniforth and Harland 2006, p. 190).

Although human resource management is not always seen as an area that academic leaders prioritize in their own development (Marshall et al. 2000, p. 48), faculty onboarding is a man-agerial competency required from heads of departments (Potgieter, Coetzee, and Basson 2011, p. 81). In a higher education context, the role and experience of academic departmental leaders differ from their corporate counterparts in that the former context is likely to be less about direct management and more about promoting collegiality (Staniforth and Harland 2006, p. 187). Staniforth and Harland (2006, p. 194) found that "protecting new staff from excessive workloads and 'the university' to enable research development" was an important role played by heads of departments tasked with onboarding new faculty members.

As important as heads of departments are in the process of faculty induction, successful onboarding involves participation from other actors as well. In advancing a perspective of onboarding as a process of "welcoming", Cesário and Chambel (2019, p. 1472) suggest that organizations need to plan for welcomes in three dimensions – the organization, the management, and the co-workers. In higher education, other faculty members and support staff have been found to play a valuable role in assisting new faculty members (Staniforth and Harland 2006, p. 191). As Staniforth and Harland (2006, p. 195) state, "new staff should be the responsibility of everyone in their community."

The consideration of onboarding in organizations wanting to advance inclusion and diversity means that they should not only be paying attention to how outsiders – particularly those from minority groups – are welcomed, but also to understanding the role they can play as change-makers. While the onboarding benefits focus on efficacy and promoting functional outputs, adopting a narrow perspective on onboarding limits the important contribution that new employees can make in transforming the organizations they are joining (Graybill et al. 2013, p. 201). When the right circumstances are created, newcomers can stimulate change in operational procedures, structures and organizational culture (Bauer and Erdogan 2012, p. 105). However, for this to happen, newcomers need to not only absorb information about their new organization, but also need to be given opportunities and feel a level of comfort with being able to reflect their identity back to the organization. Newcomers also need to be proactive to make successful onboarding possible (Staniforth and Harland 2006, p. 194).

Cable, Gino, and Staats (2013, p. 23) note that one of the dangers inherent in traditional onboarding occurs when newcomers who are expected to internalize the organization's values may be expected to subordinate their own identities, leading to psychologically depleting processes. Cable, Gino, and Staats (2013, p. 24) advocate for an approach they term "personal identity socialization," which in addition to promoting organizational identity socialization, includes the encouragement of new employees to share distinct strengths and perspectives from the commencement of the onboarding journey.

Despite growing importance paid to attracting, developing and rewarding human capital, scholarly research into the construct of onboarding across corporate and higher education sectors is limited. When referencing the onboarding phase, Cesário and Chambel (2019, p. 1465) note that "no component of the human capital management has been more overlooked by companies than the process of welcoming newly recruited employees." Although research has been conducted from the perspective of heads of departments regarding their views of onboarding with some triangulation of inductee sentiments (Staniforth and Harland 2006, p. 188), reports in literature on the lived experiences of faculty members who have been recently inducted, and assessments of the effectiveness of faculty onboarding, are limited.

PURPOSE

The purpose of the study is to understand new faculty members' lived experiences of inclusion during their onboarding in an academic department, more specifically in a business school in a higher education institution.

METHOD

An exploratory research design was followed, and qualitative data was collected from full-time faculty members at a South African business school. Participants were purposively selected, as those taking part in the study had to be appointed as permanent faculty members during the two-year period preceding the study, which focused on the lived experiences of inclusion of the newly appointed faculty members during onboarding in the business school. The sample consisted of one male and five female participants between 35 and 60 years old. One participant was previously employed in industry, while five participants were previously employed at other higher education institutions. With respect to race, three participants are black, two are white and one self-identified as mixed race.

Flanagan's (1954) Critical Incident Technique, which has been used extensively in management and service quality literature (Edvardsson and Roos 2001, p. 251; Gremler 2004, p. 68), was utilized to uncover the lived experiences of inclusion during onboarding of the participants since their appointment at the business school. The participants were interviewed (Woolsey 1986, p. 248) by a researcher involved in this study with the objective of identifying and gaining insight into specific incidents that characterized their onboarding experiences. Each participant was required to relate incidents of inclusion during the interview, focusing on the participants' memorable experiences rather than their perceptions (Testa and Ehrhart 2005, p. 464).

An interview guide was designed to collect data from participants. The interview commenced with the collection of the participants' demographic data, including age, gender and a brief employment history. It was important that the interviewer clearly communicated the objective of the interview to the participants prior to delving into the relevant incidents of inclusion (Woolsey 1986, p. 247). Participants were then asked to respond to questions describing the incident in detail, the timing of the incident, the circumstances in which the incident occurred, and the verbal response from the other person or persons involved in the incident (Testa and Ehrhart 2005, p. 465).

The interviews were recorded and transcribed, and the incidents collected were sorted into meaningful categories (Testa and Ehrhart 2005, p. 464). Each incident was assessed against the following criteria to ensure validity (Bitner, Booms, and Tetreault 1990, pp. 71–84): (1) the incident involved interaction between the participant and a person who holds authority in the organization (for the purpose of this study, we also considered other employees in the business school who do not necessarily hold a position of authority but influence the core tasks of the participant); (2) the incident had a positive or negative impact on the participant; (3) a specific event was recounted; and (4) this account of the event was adequately detailed by the participant. The interview content was coded or themed using suitable umbrella categories that spoke to inclusion and inclusion through incidents within a business school context.

Furthermore, validity was confirmed by the context of the incident in so far as it related to an expected behavior within a higher education institution in bringing new staff on board. Validity of the incidents was assessed through relevance, content validity, concurrent validity and construct validity (Butterfield et al. 2005, p. 484).

Reliability was assessed through intra-observer reliability, inter-judge reliability, and inter-observer reliability (Butterfield et al. 2005, p. 484). The reliability of the information was confirmed by the number of comments that participants made about similar incidents of inclusion and exclusion. On inclusion through social incidents, such as the faculty tea, saturation was evident in all of the participants' comments.

Following the utilization of the Critical Incident Technique to elicit incidents that promoted or hindered participants' experiences of inclusion in their onboarding process, a content analysis was undertaken. The objective of content analysis is to achieve a brief and comprehensive account of a particular event that results in categories or concepts recounting the event (Elo and Kyngäs 2008, p. 108). The content analysis was undertaken, given the spillover from the critical incident to a protracted process that extends beyond the critical incident that is evident in the participant's "journey" as an employee over time. Thus, our analysis progressed from uncovering the characteristics of the critical incident (experiences of the participant in the moment) inductively through the development of codes from the data, to comprehending how these critical incidents developed over time by following a deductive approach and, in so doing, we applied the codes to the data (Elo and Kyngäs 2008, p. 107). Therefore, the analysis deductively uncovered insights that extend beyond participants' experienced recollections of specific critical incidents. Potter and Levine-Donnerstein (1999, pp. 270–71) identify validity through a two-stage process: developing a coding scheme, and assessing the coding by an agreed standard. In 1980, Krippendorf (cited in Potter and Levine-Donnerstein 1999, p. 270) referred to stability, reproducibility and accuracy as tests for reliability. Stability refers to a process that does not change over time, reproducibility is related to its ability to be reproduced in other contexts, while accuracy tests a function's ability to conform to what it is meant to achieve (Krippendorf 1980 cited in Potter and Levine-Donnerstein 1999, pp. 270–71), which in this case is inclusion.

FINDINGS

Reflections on Critical Incidents

The Critical Incident Technique provided a useful tool to prompt memories of incidents that had enabled or disabled perceptions of inclusion. Experiences that were recalled took place in formal and informal contexts, and typically occurred in the presence of others. Although asking participants to identify critical incidents prompted active memories, it also led to more general reflections on what they wished they had experienced more of or differently in their onboarding experiences. Table 13.1 provides a summary of critical incidents that fostered inclusion, describes participants' responses to these, and includes illustrative quotes. These incidents include informal engagement with peers on the first day, participation in a faculty training session, an invitation to attend and participate in an MBA orientation, inclusion as a team member in a new program design, having faculty observe teaching, informal peer assistance to navigate a formal occasion, deep engagement with a caring peer, informal social engagement with the faculty cohort, positive engagement with members of support staff, and an invitation to join a formal structure.

Table 13.2 provides a summary of critical incidents that led to exclusion, describes participants' responses to these and includes illustrative quotes. These incidents include unhelpful engagement with an allocated mentor, poor attendance from functional areas at an introductory meeting, poor administrative support, struggling to obtain opportunities to secure teaching opportunities, having uninvited faculty observe teaching and exclusionary experiences with peers.

Not all critical incidents were experienced as uniquely positive or negative. After a very positive reflection regarding a faculty member's inclusion in the development of a new program, a participant went on to observe:

> At the same time, without anyone saying anything, I felt excluded because I could feel that I had been forced onto people to have to bring me on board, and the experience of collaborating with colleagues was kind of sustained on that level of "we're just trying to make this work because we were told we need to make this work with you." If I submitted a course outline, we kind of did a whole surgery on mine in ways that we didn't do a surgery on other colleagues on the team. And so I felt that as an experience of exclusion, even though it started as an experience of inclusion.

Reflections Beyond Critical Incidents

Reflection on critical incidents also led some faculty to lament what was *not* experienced during their onboarding process. Three participants volunteered a need for more formalized support systems, with one stating:

> I think it would be great if there were just more deliberate and systematic support systems that are placed around incoming newly established, still establishing ourselves faculty. There's no kind of formal process of onboarding or incorporation into the organization. There's a lack of structure and process in terms of onboarding people.

When discussing the theme of inclusion, another participant questioned the absence of reference to the school's diversity and inclusion policy:

> It's a funny thing about diversity and inclusion and race, is that sometimes it's so subtle you can't touch and feel it. I think it's because [the school] for the longest time has relied on white lecturers and faculty members and staff that it has become okay that even the students expect to judge a non-white lecturer with a different level of scrutiny than they would do when they expect a white lecturer. So I say to you, what is the policy on diversity and inclusion amongst faculty at the institution? And what awareness has – have there been opportunities to communicate, or have a survey that talks about diversity and inclusion so that at least we can bring things that are maybe at the back of our minds to front of mind, and even the people that are sort of feeling a level of privilege can also when they tick they realize actually this might be true of me.

Table 13.1 Critical incidents leading to positive experiences of inclusion

Description of incident	Participant's experience	Illustrative quote
Informal engagement with peers on the first day	Felt inclusion from a peer from the beginning of the employment cycle	"I've always valued that on my very first day someone took their time out to share their experiences."
Participation in a faculty training session	Enjoyed being part of a peer-collective learning experience	"Faculty training sessions on teaching methodologies presented an interesting way of teaching. It was inclusive because it didn't feel like you are being trained how to teach, but it just served as a nice master class."
Invitation to attend and participate in an MBA orientation	Gained an insider view of the organization's lived teaching and learning ethos	"If one is exposed, one can learn a lot, one can grow very quickly, so the process of being new can be a challenge if the exposure is not there."
Inclusion as a team member in a new program design	Identified an opportunity to access established structures and groups within the faculty	"The MBA refresh came at an opportune time because it undid [academic fiefdoms], because people were then expected to teach in teams. And my experience with being in the leadership team of faculty was very much one of inclusion because it meant courses had to be opened up, and because I am a leadership scholar, I could then be considered without having to butt heads against a system of that belongs to so-and-so."
Having faculty observe teaching	Reduced a (perceived) hurdle of legitimacy in the eyes of peers	"A couple of faculty members watched me teach [on the MBA program] and that seems to have introduced another layer of inclusion, now that I'm kind of legitimized because I know how to teach. And so, people who were completely ignoring me before, suddenly I have this ability, I'm a person."
Informal peer assistance to navigate a formal occasion	Obtained insight into a seminal organizational ritual through an affirmative process	"I particularly remember how I did feel included just by other faculty who took time to explain to me this is what you do, this is why we have this academic procession, you need to put on a gown and this is what it means for the introduction of the program. So, it was certainly not structured or formal, but just feeling like there was a collegial welcoming and it didn't feel like I stood out as a brand-new faculty as I walked out in that procession."
Deep engagement with a caring peer	Felt valued as a member of a minority group	"One person I recall took most of her day out to find out where I am and shared her own personal experiences and starting out at the school. I think to find affinity as well with someone, because the school just doesn't look like a lot of people like me, so there aren't that many faculty of color, or women of color in particular."
Informal social engagement with the faculty cohort	Experienced acceptance and inclusion as a new joiner at a weekly faculty social engagement	"Tuesday staff sessions have been good platforms where you feel you are included because it has nothing to do with how long you've been in the organization. It gives you room to engage with colleagues who are there, share ideas, everybody is always open-minded there. These are one of the most inclusive platforms, in a way not intimidating but quite exciting. That's where relationships are built."

Description of incident	Participant's experience	Illustrative quote
Positive engagement with members of support staff	Appreciation for administration and coaching support staff who took the time to explain and upskill the new faculty member	"[I felt] included by the academic program managers and how they were very helpful in terms of starting from scratch to build up everything that you need in order to fit into this system, especially if you teach, so what is required. So, this was also by a custom program manager, they were also very inclusive, and it was nice – so I had a very nice encounter with the administrative people. I also found the coaches to be very inclusive, the coaches of the groups that I taught. So it was a bit bumpy last year with my first round of teaching, but the coaches met up with me and asked me how it went and since then I've built up a relationship with [one] and we are now at a point where we are writing a case."
Invitation to join a formal structure	The invitation created a sense of legitimacy	"Being invited to serve on school committees was the time when I felt most legitimate and included."

Table 13.2   Critical incidents leading to experiences of exclusion

Description of incident	Participant's experience	Illustrative quote
Unhelpful engagement with an allocated mentor	Encountered an inexperienced mentor who did not invest the time to provide useful support	"It wasn't productive at all, because she is busy and it was her first time mentoring someone; she was also learning in the process. We did not have an MOU, she introduced me to one of the program managers, but nothing came of it."
Poor attendance from functional areas at an introductory meeting	Inability to gain traction because formal introductions that should have been made never were	"Because most of the program managers were not there, I found they don't know me. I had to send e-mails again to introduce myself. We don't need to be spoon-fed but we do need some support."
Poor administrative support	Inability to access communication by being excluded from e-mail lists	"It took me probably three or four months to get on the mailing list. I think that organizationally we have to admit that 'induction' is something that we're not great at."
Struggling to obtain opportunities to secure teaching opportunities	Frustration with a system that favored an "in-group" of faculty with preferential access to teaching opportunities	"I need to get hours, but the difficult part of it is that the program manager says that [they've] already chosen the faculty to teach. So, for me as new faculty, I feel excluded. It's difficult because I can introduce myself but if there's nothing coming up …"
Having uninvited faculty observe teaching	Surprise and some resentment at unexpected appearances of peers during teaching	"I had a colleague sit in on my class, kind of invited themselves into it, and that hadn't been established as an agreed way of working that we all sit in each other's classes and – which is a very valuable thing under ordinary circumstances, and I'm always very open and welcoming of it. But I think under that circumstance, where it seemed it wasn't being done consistently, or at least had not been agreed as a way of working for us within the team, I didn't appreciate that."
Exclusionary experiences with peers	Feeling invisible/unseen by some (male) colleagues	"On a couple of occasions, I have been the only female colleague in a group and have felt almost like I wasn't there. Not by everybody but it happened on more than one occasion where somebody has greeted every single one of the colleagues around me and not greeted me. It was weird but I don't think it was intentional."

Whilst the participant above was focused on the role of the institution in fostering belonging, another was attuned to her journey in integrating personal identity with the external environment and referenced inclusion as follows:

> I think my working definition is kind of the scholarly definition around a place where both my uniqueness and sense of belonging are held in the organization and in my experiences there. And I think I've moved between feeling it or experiencing it as a place of inclusion when both my uniqueness and a strong sense of belongingness, you know, something like the academic procession I think has characteristics of that. But I do find it is also very much an inclusive culture in the sense of assimilation, and then expectation of assimilation, rather than holding the uniqueness that people bring.

One participant referenced the absence of role clarity in the early months of the new role:

> Role expectations were not clear because it was a new role. The role grew around me and the scope of the role grew around me, and because I was learning and investing it grew bigger and bigger. That's kind of the [school] way, we do to get done.

Another study participant discussed the absence of the opportunity to share vulnerability as well as pressures to drive inclusion:

> We have a culture of not gossiping and that's a really good thing and it's very honest, but it has a bad side to it. We also have a culture of silence and so you don't tell people how you are feeling, you don't tell people that you're having a problem, it's just not something that you volunteer. It does place the burden of responsibility of being helped on you as the person who is experiencing. So, it's like if I feel excluded, then it's my sole responsibility to figure out how do I get myself included. And a lot of that does rely on personality and then how you build relationships in the system. Whereas I do think there could be some things we do a little bit more systematically.

One participant's response showed exclusionary cumulative effects of not receiving a strong flow of structured information: "I have to go and find out who's teaching, when are they teaching, what subjects, where are they teaching. So the onus is all on you as faculty." In contrast, another recent joiner felt that the school's culture was sufficiently enabling and that additional formal processes were not necessary:

> I did feel like I belong to a community that is open-minded, that is engaging, that is willing to create room and space for new people with new ideas and new perspectives. It opened doors for me. It was better than any induction you can have.

Another participant commented on the transition in the experience of a faculty committee from being a stressed outsider to developing a sense of mastery and comfort:

> New committee members do not have an onboarding process, so you just have to kind of figure it out yourself and that's quite stressful. But then one day you just suddenly realize you know what you're doing and it's okay.

Table 13.3 provides a summary of elements participants perceived as lacking from the onboarding process.

The reflections of participants beyond the critical incidents also uncovered insightful feelings and sentiments regarding inclusion within the particular cultural context the school is located. A number of participants indicated that while feeling included occurred as a consequence of critical incidents, experiences over time built up a more generalized sentiment. When commenting on her lived experiences, one participant felt included, stating:

> There's an emotional inclusion that happens quite quickly. It is a kind of warm and welcoming personal space but there's a kind of practical, technical sort of legitimacy that actually takes longer to attain. It takes a while for you to be embedded in the actual operation of the organization.

Another respondent referenced the racial and cultural diversity in the faculty, but spoke about the difficulty of locating herself in the milieu:

> There are many white Afrikaans faculty members so there's a sort of kinship … lots of wonderful black faculty who I feel also have that kind of kinship. I don't feel like I'm part of being [black African], like that for me in my heart is who I am, but I don't feel like that's entirely recognized. Exclusion may be too strong a word, but I feel that.

The school's efforts over time to recruit and retain a more diverse group of faculty members were also discussed by a number of participants. One said that "There's pride now because we have a growing black faculty and I think it's amazing." While a different respondent stated:

> I have a full appreciation of how hard the work of building inclusive cultures and inclusive organizations is, and sometimes the starting point is just a recognition that it's something of value to aspire towards in organizational life. So I'm very appreciative that it's something we are being attentive to, particularly because we are inviting a lot of uniqueness into our academic program side.

One participant highlighted the nature of faculty socialization as evidence of the shift that had occurred in the school:

> I've also seen how those faculty teas have transformed from, I think, historically being a place and a cultural artifact of exclusion to being one of enormous inclusion. [They] have signaled a very fundamental shift and a lot more of an inviting and inclusive working culture.

Whilst acknowledging the school's changing focus on diversity, one participant noted that the treatment of faculty from minority groups still varied within the faculty peer group:

> Perhaps my own clashes with the culture are at the point of feeling that the pressure or the expectation is to assimilate and kind of – particularly, and I will say this, I find the older more traditional colleagues whose own training and their own scholarly development has been pretty traditional, I find are very resistant, and I feel the sense of expectation for assimilation a lot stronger from those colleagues than those of us who are doing it differently.

Table 13.3 also provides a summary of these reflections related to the feelings and sentiments regarding inclusion in the cultural context within which the school is located.

Table 13.3   A summary of reflections beyond the critical incidents

Elements missing from the onboarding process
Formalized support systems for new faculty
A visible diversity and inclusion policy
Role clarity during early months of the appointment
Opportunities to share vulnerability as new faculty
Strong flow of structured information
Onboarding processes for new committee members
Sentiments regarding inclusion in general
Inclusion occurs as a consequence of critical incidents, but experiences over time built up a more generalized sentiment
Although diversity is present, it could be difficult for faculty to locate themselves within the milieu
An appreciation of efforts of the school to build an inclusive culture is evident
The nature of faculty interaction serves as evidence of transformation within the school
The treatment of minorities within the school still varies

DISCUSSION

The participants' experiences indicated that in addition to the importance of onboarding, this phase of the employee life cycle makes an important contribution to a faculty member's impressions of the extent to which they experience their institution of higher education institute as being inclusive.

Whilst none of the faculty reported incidents of being assigned less valuable roles than their counterparts, they did recall struggles to access key decision-makers who assign faculty members to courses (Bhopal and Chapman 2019, p. 98). Despite acknowledging that the school's culture and climate were sensitive to transformation and diversity, individualized experiences of racial and gender bias were reported. At the same time, all the new faculty members reported incidents where individual peers had gone out of their way to make them feel welcome, included and accepted (Spafford et al. 2006, p. 1). These voluntary exchanges greatly enabled the faculty to accelerate their process of organizational socialization (Louis 1980, p. 226), and served to underscore the important role that a head of department plays in promoting collegiality across faculty (Staniforth and Harland 2006, p. 187).

The nature of critical incidents selected by participants spanned the dimensions of inclusion, accessing resources and information, affecting decision-making processes and involvement in work groups (Mor-Barak and Cherin 1998, p. 48) across the onboarding process. Whilst access to information through informal channels appears to have been readily available, limited dissemination of formal information was perceived as a barrier to effective onboarding by various participants. Invitations into work groups served not only to legitimize status for new joiners, but also provided valuable opportunities to acquire information and learn about the school's culture. Invitations to influence decisions through the mechanisms of a program design group in one case and a committee in another provided valuable opportunities for participants to be included in the deeper structures of the school. Although informal mentoring was appreciated, one faculty's negative experience of a formal mentoring process aligned with other reports in the literature (Staniforth and Harland 2006, p. 190), suggesting that faculty mentoring processes need to be thoughtfully designed and managed.

The role of academic leaders as actors and agents tasked with implementing the vision and values (Berdrow 2010, p. 500; Jones 2011, p. 279), which in this case included a strong focus on embracing diversity and creating an inclusive environment, was noted and appreciated by numerous participants. The observations about the lack of a formal orientation process and the flaws in the design of processes to ensure that new faculty receive the needed technical information and introductions to functional representatives suggest that additional attention should be paid to the managerial role that academic leaders must also play when designing and implementing onboarding processes (Graybill et al. 2013, p. 207).

CONCLUSION

This research sought to investigate the role that onboarding plays in new faculty's lived experiences of inclusion. The Critical Incident Technique was a useful tool to enable faculty members to access memories of experiences with their peers and other employees who enabled them to provide specific examples that led to more generalized perceptions of the extent to which they experienced the school as more or less inclusive.

The study's findings suggest that onboarding experiences play a vital role in shaping the extent to which faculty members experience a sense of inclusion and are able to reconcile their identities with the mission, vision and values of the institution and, in so doing, contribute to the organization and its own journey of change.

Although participants made limited direct references to the role that academic leaders played in enabling them to experience their new institutions as inclusive, analysis of the drivers of positive experiences suggests that there is much that academic leaders can do to foster inclusive onboarding. Our findings suggest that heads of departments have a role to play in the creation of formal and informal engagement opportunities for new faculty to engage with groups and individuals. The specific opportunities that were highlighted by participants are summarized in Table 13.4.

Table 13.4   Actions of heads of departments in enabling inclusive faculty onboarding

	Group	Individual
Formal	• Working with internal stakeholders to design effective processes for technical knowledge transfer • Involving new faculty members in committees, teams and student engagements • Providing well-organized orientation events • Enabling participation in general faculty training sessions	• Engaging regularly as head of department • Arranging and managing formal mentoring • Creating opportunities for peer observation and feedback on teaching (by agreement) • Organizing peer briefings for formal occasions • Facilitating meetings with functional representatives
Informal	• Arranging and encouraging attendance at regular faculty social events	• Promoting informal peer engagement and mentoring • Facilitating peer social engagements • Encouraging engagement with support staff

Academic leaders must guarantee that onboarding processes are designed to ensure new faculty members receive the technical information required to navigate their new role and context. Moreover, academic leaders are imperative in building collegial environments in which established faculty members are receptive and welcoming to newcomers. Academic leaders are also advised to do all they can to enable and encourage administrative staff to be accessible and supportive to new faculty.

When assigning mentors to new joiners, care needs to be taken to match mentors appropriately, to communicate the department's expectations of mentors and provide mentor development where required, and to regularly ensure that meaningful engagements are taking place. In addition to the ongoing management to promote diversity and inclusion across a department, academic leaders are advised to stay attuned to ensuring that new faculty members are able to access opportunities to make a meaningful contribution to their new workplaces. This is facilitated by not only ensuring that formal appointments are made, but also by creating appropriate informal socialization opportunities that enable new appointees to build relationships and learn about the institutional culture and practice.

The contextual setting of this research as a South African business school, coupled with the limited number of interviews with only permanently appointed faculty members, restrict the generalization of findings to all higher education contexts. Although nearly all faculty members, appointed over a two-year period prior to the study being undertaken, took part in the study, we were limited in the interviews we were able to conduct due to the small number of new permanent faculty members appointed every year. Whilst this research emphasized the lived experiences of new faculty, there is scope to also understand how faculty members with longer tenure experience their new counterparts. Besides deepening our understanding of the influences and outcomes of inclusive onboarding, exploring the extent to which clinical faculty with a practitioner experience enter the academy with different expectations relative to their counterparts who have joined from other higher education institutions creates fertile ground for future research.

REFERENCES

Baker, Bethany, and Joseph T. DiPiro (2019), "Evaluation of a Structured Onboarding Process and Tool for Faculty Members in a School of Pharmacy," *American Journal of Pharmaceutical Education*, 83 (6), 1233–8.

Bauer, Talya N., and Berrin Erdogan (2012), "Organizational Socialization Outcomes: Now and into the Future," in Connie R. Wanberg, ed., *The Oxford Handbook of Organizational Socialization*, Oxford: Oxford University Press, 97–112.

Berdrow, Iris (2010), "King among Kings: Understanding the Role and Responsibilities of the Department Chair in Higher Education," *Educational Management Administration & Leadership*, 38 (4), 499–514.

Bhopal, Kalwant, and Thandeka K. Chapman (2019), "International Minority Ethnic Academics at Predominantly White Institutions," *British Journal of Sociology of Education*, 40 (1), 98–113.

Bitner, Mary Jo, Bernard H. Booms, and Mary Stanfield Tetreault (1990), "The Service Encounter: Diagnosing Favorable and Unfavorable Incidents," *Journal of Marketing*, 54 (1), 71–84.

Butterfield, Lee D., William A. Borgen, Norman E. Amundson, and Asa-Sophia T. Maglio (2005), "Fifty Years of the Critical Incident Technique: 1954–2004 and Beyond," *Qualitative Research*, 5 (4), 475–97.

Cable, Daniel M., Francesca Gino, and Bradley R. Staats (2013), "Reinventing Employee Onboarding," *MIT Sloan Management Review*, 54 (3), 23–8.

Cesário, Francisco, and Maria José Chambel (2019), "On-Boarding New Employees: A Three-Component Perspective of Welcoming," *International Journal of Organizational Analysis*, 27 (5), 1465–79.

Cheffen, Jimmy E. (2017), "Onboarding and Staying: Experiences of Faculty of Color at a Midwestern Community College," doctoral dissertation, Graduate Faculty, Texas Tech University, Lubbock, Texas, United States of America.

Cooper-Thomas, Helena, Neil Anderson, and Melanie Cash (2012), "Investigating Organizational Socialization: A Fresh Look at Newcomer Adjustment Strategies", *Personnel Review*, 41 (1), 41–55.

Edvardsson, Bo, and Inger Roos (2001), "Critical Incident Techniques: Towards a Framework for Analysing the Criticality of Critical Incidents," *International Journal of Service Industry Management*, 12 (3), 251–68.

Ehrich, Lisa C., Brian Hansford, and Lee Tennent (2004), "Formal Mentoring Programs in Education and Other Professions: A Review of the Literature," *Educational Administration Quarterly*, 40 (4), 518–40.

Eisner, Susan (2015), "Onboarding the Faculty: A Model for Win–Win Mentoring," *American Journal of Business Education (AJBE)*, 8 (1), 7–22.

Elo, Satu, and Helvi Kyngäs (2008), "The Qualitative Content Analysis," *Journal of Advanced Nursing*, 62 (1), 107–15.

Flanagan, John C. (1954), "The Critical Incident Technique," *Psychological Bulletin*, 51 (4), 327–58.

Graybill, Jolie O., Maria Taesil Hudson Carpenter, Jerome Offord Jr, Mary Piorun, and Gary Shaffer (2013), "Employee Onboarding: Identification of Best Practices in ACRL Libraries," *Library Management*, 34 (3), 200–218.

Gremler, Dwayne D. (2004), "The Critical Incident Technique in Service Research," *Journal of Service Research*, 7 (1), 65–89.

Jones, D. Gareth (2011), "Academic Leadership and Departmental Headship in Turbulent Times," *Tertiary Education and Management*, 17 (4), 279–88.

King, Virginia, Jannie Roed, and Louise Wilson (2018), "It's Very Different Here: Practice-Based Academic Staff Induction and Retention," *Journal of Higher Education Policy and Management*, 40 (5), 470–84.

Klein, Howard J., Beth Polin, and Kyra Leigh Sutton (2015), "Specific Onboarding Practices for the Socialization of New Employees," *International Journal of Selection and Assessment*, 23 (3), 263–83.

Louis, Meryl Reis (1980), "Surprise and Sense Making: What Newcomers Experience in Entering Unfamiliar Organizational Settings," *Administrative Science Quarterly*, 25 (2), 226–51.

Marshall, Stephen J., Moya J. Adams, Alison Cameron, and Gavin Sullivan (2000), "Academics' Perceptions of Their Professional Development Needs Related to Leadership and Management: What Can We Learn?," *International Journal for Academic Development*, 5 (1), 42–53.

Mohamed, Tameera, and Brenda L. Beagan (2019), "'Strange Faces' in the Academy: Experiences of Racialized and Indigenous Faculty in Canadian Universities," *Race Ethnicity and Education*, 22 (3), 338–54.

Mor-Barak, Michal E., and David A. Cherin (1998), "A Tool to Expand Organizational Understanding of Workforce Diversity: Exploring a Measure of Inclusion–Exclusion," *Administration in Social Work*, 22 (1), 47–64.

Pandya, Saurabh (2017), "Early Success Experience as a Predictor of Fast-Track Career Growth," *Development and Learning in Organizations*, 31 (2), 10–12.

Potgieter, Ingrid, Melinda Coetzee, and Johan Basson (2011), "Management Competencies for the Development of Heads of Department in the Higher Education Context: A Literature Overview," *South African Journal of Labour Relations*, 35 (1), 81–103.

Potter, W. James, and Deborah Levine-Donnerstein (1999), "Rethinking Validity and Reliability in Content Analysis," *Journal of Applied Communication Research*, 27 (3), 258–84.

Roberson, Quinetta M. (2006), "Disentangling the Meanings of Diversity and Inclusion in Organizations," *Group & Organization Management*, 31 (2), 212–36.

Spafford, Marlee M., Vicki L. Nygaard, Fran Gregor, and Marcia A. Boyd (2006), "'Navigating the Different Spaces': Experiences of Inclusion and Isolation among Racially Minoritized Faculty in Canada," *Canadian Journal of Higher Education*, 36 (1), 1–27.

Staniforth, David, and Tony Harland (2006), "Contrasting Views of Induction: The Experiences of New Academic Staff and Their Heads of Department," *Active Learning in Higher Education*, 7 (2), 185–96.

Testa, Mark R., and Mark G. Ehrhart (2005), "Service Leader Interaction Behaviors: Comparing Employee and Manager Perspectives," *Group & Organization Management*, 30 (5), 456–86.

Tienda, Marta (2013), "Diversity ≠ Inclusion: Promoting Integration in Higher Education," *Educational Researcher*, 42 (9), 467–75.

Trembath, Jodie-Lee (2016), "The Professional Lives of Expatriate Academics: Construct Clarity and Implications for Expatriate Management in Higher Education," *Journal of Global Mobility*, 4 (2), 112–30.

Trowler, Paul, and Peter Knight (1999), "Organizational Socialization and Induction in Universities: Reconceptualizing Theory and Practice," *Higher Education*, 37 (2), 177–95.

Walker, Sarah S., Enrica N. Ruggs, Whitney B. Morgan, and Sandra W. DeGrassi (2019), "Diverse Perspectives on Inclusion: Exploring the Experiences of Individuals in Heterogeneous Groups," *Equality, Diversity and Inclusion*, 38 (1), 2–19.

Woolsey, Lorette K. (1986), "The Critical Incident Technique: An Innovative Qualitative Method of Research," *Canadian Journal of Counselling and Psychotherapy/Revue Canadienne de Counseling et de Psychothérapie*, 20 (4), 242–54.

PART IV

Building, leading and funding research groups

14. Building research groups

Adam Lindgreen, C. Anthony Di Benedetto, Roderick J. Brodie and Peter Naudé

1.   INTRODUCTION

For business researchers, establishing a solid research track record is a prerequisite to success. Business schools often have lofty publication expectations of their newly hired assistant professors before considering promotion and tenure. It is often in the best interest of the junior researcher to play it safe and pursue research in well-established research streams, at least until achieving tenure, when it may be possible to take more chances on more groundbreaking (and riskier) research. In fact, a promotion and tenure committee may be interested in seeing not just a number of publications in top journals, but two or three established research streams where the researcher has made contributions to the literature. Business schools also benefit greatly from the success of their top academics. More big research grants, and more A-level journal publications, leads to a solid research reputation, which in turn makes it easier to hire junior professors from top research institutions, attract top graduate and doctoral students to their programs, and offer chairs to big-name senior academics looking for a career change. It is in the interest of business school managers to know how to build an environment conducive to academic research at the highest level.

We examine the factors that have led to the establishment of a successful environment for business academic researchers. More particularly, we examine issues including business school research strategy, leadership, governance, and policy, and from this framework, we develop a set of conditions that are closely related to long-term success of academic research programs in business schools. We then present a brief history of two active research institutions, the Industrial Marketing and Purchasing (IMP) Group and the Contemporary Marketing Practices (CMP) Group, and discuss how each of these has implemented the conditions for success in their own particular settings. We conclude with general observations and implications for the environmental conditions most conducive to sustainable business school research, and briefly discuss the role of the journal editor as a gatekeeper in the process of supporting radically new research streams.

Throughout our discussion, we focus on the creation of the research stream as the desired outcome. Business school managers would like to invest efficiently, in terms of both their financial outlay and human resources. If a large investment is made, say, to funding a research center or institute, hiring faculty from top schools and recruiting the best junior researchers, the expectation would be to have a stream of research as an output from this investment. That is, the researchers would be able to conduct high-level research that results in sustainable research output in terms of published articles, additional outcomes that further the research stream in the pipeline, as well as other research planned and/or seeking funding approval.

Before continuing, we would like to make a distinction between a research stream and a school of thought. Consider, for example, the innovation literature (Di Benedetto, 2013) that emerged initially in a few articles and which has now grown and matured. In the early years, there was a narrow range of research streams: new product process, R&D–marketing interface, organizational issues, accelerated time to market, and a few others. Twenty years later, as the innovation discipline has matured, more academics have decided to be 'innovation scholars,' the research field becoming more multidisciplinary and multinational, construct measures more fully developed, and a wider range of methodologies being used. By this time, new research streams have emerged that were not even on the radar screen 20 years earlier: organizational learning, product architecture, mass customization, open innovation, entrepreneurial innovation, transformational leadership, information technology in innovation, and many other research streams. We define each of these as 'research streams' within the innovation 'school of thought.' Although scholars in a group are all innovation scholars, they have narrower and deeper research expertise. That is, research streams emerge through time, as scholars raise new questions for academic research. One could even subdivide this further if one considers that a research stream, which was originally, say, case-based or qualitative research, then attracted survey or experimental research, or vice versa.

The importance is that the scholars taking chances and doing research, which is not business-as-usual, need to be supported and recognized, and encouraged to make changes, and this can be provided by their own institution, as well as their chosen research organization. As an example, years ago, we saw the first few PhD graduates in innovation; earlier, a typical concentration would be a mainstream choice such as marketing or management. By the early 2000s, the first few assistant professors had been promoted and tenured based on an innovation publication record (many articles in *Industrial Marketing Management*, *Journal of Product Innovation Management*, and so on) rather than mainstream marketing or management. This was a significant turning point because it meant that one could pursue a career in innovation management per se. As such, it is probably a significant milestone in the recognition of innovation as a school of thought.

2.   STRATEGIES FOR RESEARCH SUCCESS

A goal of business school administration is to foster an environment of successful academic research. Especially in the case of the most research-intensive business schools, having a core of solid, productive researchers leads to recognition and ranking among the top business schools. This scholarly recognition attracts new PhD graduates eager to establish careers in a strong research environment, as well as mid-career academics looking for a chaired position. It also ensures the school is on the shortlist for the best students applying for PhD programs in business. But this is more easily said than done. What, indeed, is successful academic research? Those of us who do business research know that we intend to make contributions that will resonate with the practitioner community and aid their decision-making skills. Yet, we must also please the editors and reviewers in the academic community, and preferably place our research in the highest-rated journals in our field. It is easy for business school managers to establish quantitative goals for hiring, promotion and tenure, such as number of articles published in A-level journals. However, what can managers do to facilitate their faculty's achievement of their publication goals? In this section, we review issues such as business school research strategy and policy, leadership and governance issues, as well as choice of assessment metrics, which will aid in identifying the conditions most conducive to long-term research program success.

2.1   Strategy, Leadership and Policy

At research-intensive business schools, the aim of the research strategy should almost certainly be to conduct demonstrably impactful research that influences society; can be deployed usefully in developing education; and can be communicated to and used by practitioners. Fulfilling this aim starts with publishing research with a high impact on the research community, which generally means publishing in influential journals.

This ambitious goal demands great performance expectations of faculty members, in the form of high-quality world-class research. Faculty members must be committed to rigorous, theory-driven, empirical research and theory development – outcomes that are central goals for any reputable business school.

A business school's leadership can seek a governance structure that reflects and supports key areas including research and education. The governance structure also should support the recruitment, retention and expansion of faculty members, in line with support for personal development. Equally important is to set up research groups. Faculty members choose that (those) research group(s) that is (are) organized around themes they want to research and teach. Less important to a research group is the range of methodological approaches that researchers employ.

When developing its policies, a research group could be considering a range of initiatives, including the following:

- Which publication strategy should the research group follow? When the group wants to be proactive in both academia and society, the group will need to contribute to the ongoing debate about present and future societal challenges to which its research and education are relevant. Such dissemination often results in dialogue, interaction and reflection that can fertilize further research and identify new challenges. It also provides awareness, which can strengthen the position of the group in competition for research funding. We will discuss the issue of publications in more details in the following section 'Assessing for Success.'
- What will be the research group's funding strategy that will allow the group to undertake its research projects? To increase the number and quality of funding applications, the group could set up a funding committee to develop and leverage industry contacts. Colleagues who have been involved with research funding bodies could give feedback on outgoing funding applications. Another possibility is to form a writing club; this could involve peer reviews of funding applications, and it could, in the longer term, result in further collaboration between faculty members. This institution of brown-bag seminars and seminars with world-class researchers constitutes another avenue for discussing research ideas, detailing the funding landscape, and considering future developments, among others. For further ideas, such as building strategic alliances with key research centers, we refer to Lindgreen et al. (2019b).

- How will the research group contribute to the school's education? The group could contemplate offering research-based education; for example, when faculty members collaborate with students on research projects, those students become co-authors of conference papers or journal articles. Alternatively, the group could adopt a teaching-based approach, acknowledging that they discuss research-based issues with, say, executive students, and thus gain inspiration for their research through their teaching.
- Which services will the research group offer to the wider academic community? Such services should demonstrate impact on the research community. They could include reviewing for conferences and journals, participating in international networks, starting collaboration with international scholars, and arranging workshops, sessions or panels at conferences. It might also include being a journal editor, a member of influential journal advisory/editorial review boards, or at least being a reviewer for such journals.
- How will the research group interact with the wider society and, most importantly, deliver societal value? In the context of public life, value is an important measure on the contribution to business and social good of activities for which strict financial measures are inappropriate or fundamentally unsound. The group could demonstrate the ability to inform and engage broader audiences through media interviews or workshops with practitioners. For further ideas about possible actions pertaining to the multiple aspects surrounding public value, we refer to Lindgreen et al. (2019a).

2.2   Assessing for Success

Increasing academic success is assessed not only on the journals that work is published in, but also by the scholarly impact of the work. Journal rankings such as the Association of Business Schools' Academic Journal Guide (AJG; formerly ABS) and the Australian Business Deans Council's ranking (ABDC) are often employed. The AJG ranking, for example, is compiled by a scientific committee comprising 58 subject area experts spanning 22 research fields. Although the subject area experts do not act as representatives of their relevant learned societies in that research field, these experts do solicit advice from both learned societies and eminent scholars to judge the quality of a journal. Other important inputs include a journal's impact factor, submission and acceptance rates, age of journal, the journal's editor, reviewing process including the editorial review board, authors publishing in the journal, and the inclusion of the journal in other rankings, among others.

While the ranking of the journal is still an important indicator, other indicators of research quality are emerging that provide a broader view of innovation and academic contribution. Thus, there is a need for a meaningful portfolio of measures. Indeed, "one size does not fit all"; rather, what is needed is a dashboard of metrics coupled with qualitative judgment. The question then arises: which metrics should be used to judge research quality?

Citations increasingly provide an important measure of the research quality. Google Scholar, Scopus, and Web of Science are among the many software programs that retrieve and analyze academic citations. In addition to the number of publications and the number of citations, it is possible to include measures such as average citations per publication, Hirsch's h-index, Egghe's g-index, the hg-index (to retain the advantages of both h and g measures, as well as to minimize their disadvantages; cf. Soutar, Wilkinson, &Young, 2015), and the i10-index. The so-called Field-Weighted Citation Impact takes into account the differences in research behavior across different research disciplines, meaning that citations are compared with the average number of citations by all other similar publications (in the Scopus database). Another means of judging research quality is to set up effective benchmarking, that is, to identify a pertinent group of scholars or research groups that are committed to maintaining the very best research, for example, the Russell Group universities in the UK or the Group of Eight universities in Australia.

And yet, research is more than just publishing in influential journals. Research should have an impact that establishes the reputation of scholars or research groups among multiple stakeholder groups: scholars, the business community, and students, to name a few. PlumX Metrics, another software program, provides information about how scholars interact with articles, books, conference papers, and book chapters, among others. In addition to citations, categories include usage (e.g., clicks, downloads, views and library holdings), captures (e.g., bookmarks, favorites and reference managers), mentions (e.g., blogs, news articles, comments, reviews and Wikipedia links), and social media (e.g., likes, shares and tweets). Other measures include, for example, an article being included on doctoral seminar reading lists or best paper awards.

It also becomes important to assess the contribution that research makes to influence practice. To make this assessment, there needs to be an understanding of how research is used by both academics and practitioners. This requires paying explicit attention to the socialization of knowledge and the role academic research can play in these processes (Brodie & Peters, 2020; Nenonen et al., 2017). Therefore, faculty members also seek to publish in reputable practitioner-oriented journals (e.g., *Harvard Business Review*, *California Management Review*, and *MIT Sloan Management Review*, all on the FT50 (*Financial Times*) journal ranking) and to publish with well-respected publishers monographs and research anthologies that may contribute significantly to establish the reputation of scholars or research groups. This effort also is evidenced when popular media report on research findings and when government-sponsored research networks, in collaboration with scholars or research groups, communicate pertinent knowledge to industry and the wider public.

Methods for assessing research quality continue to be debated and developed. Aguinis et al. (2020) argue that the use of journal rankings comes "with negative effects on the field's research methods, knowledge generation, and social dynamics." For example, the San Francisco Declaration on Research Assessment (DORA) movement advocates, among other things, that research is evaluated on its scientific content rather than publication metrics of the journal in which that research was published. This could include some of the above measurements, for example, the research's influence on policy and practice. To illustrate, Cardiff Business School, a leading UK business school and one of only two business schools to be ranked in the top ten of the UK government's five research assessment exercises since 1992, now envisions itself as a school that improves social and economic conditions. The school's approach is interdisciplinary teaching and research that addresses grand challenges; also, the school has chosen to operate a progressive approach to its own governance (Kitchener, 2019a, 2019b).

3.   CONDITIONS FOR SUCCESS FOR A RESEARCH STREAM

Recently, Brodie and Juric (2018) reflected on the conditions that led to the successful development of a new research stream on customer engagement. Two seminal articles published in 2011 and 2013 initiated the research stream. The first article established the conceptual domain of customer engagement (Brodie et al., 2011a), and the second refined this conceptualization with empirical research (Brodie et al., 2013). As of July 2019, each article has had over 1,700 citations in Google Scholar. These two articles have led to a stream of other influential publications that have broadened the research stream (Breidbach & Brodie, 2017; Brodie et al., 2019; Storbacka et al., 2016). The first academic book on customer engagement (Brodie, Hollebeek, & Conduit, 2016) and three special issues of journals (*Journal of Marketing Management, Journal of Service Theory and Practice*, and *Journal of Strategic Marketing*), which involved contributions from over one hundred authors from North America, Europe, and Australasia, have played important roles in establishing this research stream. Building on this work, other special issues of journals, other articles, and book chapters are all contributing to what is now a substantial international stream of research. Scopus and Google Scholar have reported a steady increase in the number of articles using the concept of customer engagement and related concepts since 2011.

Drawing on the initial reflections by Brodie and Juric (2018) about the conditions that led to the development of the customer engagement research stream, we propose that there are five necessary initial conditions that determine the success of a research stream, and, additionally, five key conditions that build on these initial conditions and also impact the success of a research stream. The five initial conditions are:

1. *Research problems leading to research opportunities:* The first initial condition is to have the capability to identify an important research problem, which is of practical and academic interest that creates future research opportunities.
2. *Initiating research stream:* The second initial condition that builds on the first is to have the capability to initiate the research stream by bringing together talented groups of scholars to realize research opportunities. Key attributes include having scholars with creative curiosity, the ability to spot new opportunities, a passion to publish in the best journals, an ability to work cohesively as a team, and having complementary abilities.
3. *Clarity in expression:* The third initial condition is to have the capability to provide clarity in academic arguments that provide foundations for the emerging research stream. Academic scholarship requires an understanding of academic conventions, especially for written expression and theoretical framing. However, innovative new research streams are often challenging the status quo, meaning that careful consideration needs to be given as to why established academic conventions need to be challenged.
4. *Teamwork within a network of scholars:* The fourth initial condition is to have the capability to develop a network of talented scholars who continue to embrace research opportunities. The network starts with a core group that provides leadership to facilitate an international network and broaden the stream of research. Workshop forums and special sessions at conferences targeted at special issues of journals and books play an important role. Having well-known international scholars can play an important role in adding credibility to the emerging network. Central to the success of this formation and operations of teams is openness and honesty, as well as respect for the variety of skills, abilities and roles different researchers can provide. The network needs to build on mutual trust, and that can be enhanced by not only collaborating on research projects, but also socializing together.
5. *Platform to consolidate knowledge:* The fifth initial condition is that the network of scholars needs to produce research that consolidates the knowledge in the area. This provides

foundations for further innovative research. For example, in 2016, the customer engagement research stream produced the first academic book on customer engagement, which took stock of the development of the research area (Brodie, Hollebeek, & Conduit. 2016). The book comprises 16 review chapters, with contributions by 39 authors from Europe, North America, Australasia who have gone on to produce journal articles to further advance the research area.

The five key conditions that build on the initial conditions and impact the success of the research stream are:

1. *Role of theory and theorizing:* The first key condition is the need for fresh thinking about the role of theory and theorizing that leads to new approaches (Brodie & Peters, 2020). We suggest greater emphasis needs to be given to the process of theorizing rather than to the focus on theory. Being "stuck in the middle, neither being firmly based in real-world data, nor reaching a sufficient level of abstraction" should be avoided (Gummesson, 2004: 317).
2. *Sustaining leadership and innovation:* The second key condition is to put a process in place to sustain leadership and innovation. The group that provides the leadership to initiate the research stream needs to broaden as the research stream expands. With the research stream developing, the network needs to embrace distributed leadership that will provide empowerment to propagate new initiatives and to keep the momentum in the research stream. Eventually, when the network has achieved its research ambitions, it might embrace broader challenges in the field or, more drastically, reinvent itself by identifying a new important research problem and thus initiating a new research stream.
3. *Getting research accepted:* The third key condition is that scholars within the research stream have the persistence to get research accepted in high-quality journals. Innovative research that challenges conventional thinking can meet barriers in the review process because of 'similarity bias' of reviewers. Similarity bias occurs when research does not fit norms and practices that reviewers are familiar with. Editors have an important role in recognizing and supporting innovative research that challenges conventional thinking.
4. *Getting research recognized:* The fourth key condition is that the research stream needs to become visible and understood by other researchers. Workshops, forums and special sessions at conferences where leading scholars outside the research stream participate can play an important role in creating visibility and understanding for the research stream. In addition, online platforms such as Google Scholar, Mendeley, Academia, and publishers' platforms are playing an increasingly important role in creating recognition. Acceptance is more short term and micro (i.e., individual); in contrast, recognition is more long term and macro (i.e., collective). Individual authors get their manuscripts accepted for inclusion in high-quality journals. The research gets recognition when the research stream starts to head toward maturity with more manuscripts accepted for such journals and the authors begin to influence later scholars to pursue research in the stream.
5. *Tenacity and resilience:* The fifth key condition is for the researchers to have tenacity and resilience. Research that challenges conventional thinking can be expected to meet resistance, and it is tempting to give up. However, if the group of scholars believes strongly in what they want to achieve, there usually is a way to succeed. Innovative manuscripts take time to develop, and the review process based on rigorous critique can play an important role in improving manuscripts leading to clarity in expression. Researchers in a new

research stream that challenge conventional wisdom need the conviction to stick with the stream, even in the face of rejection by high-quality journals. It is easy just to give up and focus on writing something more conventionally accepted. That is, rather than making the radical contribution (which is risky, as reviewers or editors may not recognize the contribution), researchers can settle for making an incremental contribution, which still builds theory and is publishable, but at lower risk of rejection. A researcher with the required tenacity and resilience can overcome this rejection. Winston Churchill's famous speech at Harrow School in 1941 is of relevance here: "Never give in, never give in, never, never, never, never – in nothing, great or small, large or petty – never give in except to convictions of honour and good sense." Senior, tenured academics might find it easier to take chances later in their academic career and include a more radical research direction in their project portfolio. However, when senior, tenured academics have to deliver X number of articles in high-quality journals (this is, for example, the case in the UK where research assessments have been conducted since 1986), such academics will hesitate in pursuing radical research.

4.   REVIEW OF THE IMP AND CMP RESEARCH PROGRAMS

In this section, we first give a short history of the activities of the Industrial Marketing and Purchasing (IMP) Group and then of the Contemporary Marketing Practices (CMP) Group.

4.1   Industrial Marketing and Purchasing Group (IMP)

Coming together in 1976, researchers from five different countries formed the IMP Group (Turnbull, Ford, & Cunningham, 1996). The aim was to "make a comparative analysis of oper-ations, strategies and organization structures of companies involved in export marketing to, and international purchasing from France, Germany, Italy, Sweden, and the United Kingdom" (Cunningham, 1980: 322). The scale of the research project was enormous, based on 876 interviews, with the focus always on the interactions between the parties involved.

A basic starting point of the research project was the recognition of the interdependencies that exist in buyer–supplier relationships; something that the more traditional American approaches to understanding organizational buyer behavior had ignored (Robinson, Faris, & Wind, 1967; Sheth, 1973; Webster & Wind, 1972). The researchers' view, based on under-standing buyer–supplier relationships as an interaction approach, rejected the traditionally accepted '4Ps' approach. Instead, the researchers believed that "the great majority of business purchases do not exist as individual events and hence cannot be fully understood if each one is examined in isolation" (Turnbull, Ford, & Cunningham, 1996: 45). The researchers challenged the prevailing view of understanding organizational buying behavior on four different grounds (see Cunningham, 1980; Håkansson, 1982; Turnbull, Ford, & Cunningham, 1996).

The first was to challenge the prevailing view in which the industrial buyer behavior liter-ature concentrated on analyzing discrete purchasing decisions. Instead, based on some of the researchers' earlier work, their view was of the buyer–supplier interaction based on relation-ships, which often varied in length, complexity, and dynamism (Cunningham & White, 1973; Ford, 1978, 1980; Håkansson & Östberg, 1975). Such relationships were influenced not only by the different technological capabilities of the companies involved, but also by the roles of the different individuals involved in the buying and selling process, which was far more complex than 'a buyer' and 'a salesperson.'

A corollary of this was the second ground, which refuted the idea that business-to-business marketing involved the manipulation of the 'marketing mix' variables so often applied in more traditional business-to-consumer marketing. Rather than segmenting a market into different passive segments each of which then could be targeted by an optimally designed set of the 4Ps, the interaction approach demanded a more insightful understanding of what each party wanted from the relationship.

The third ground laid down challenged the adoption of the traditional view derived from the economic theory that saw markets as consisting of an atomistic structure with numerous buyers and sellers, with buyers moving freely between competing suppliers. Instead, the researchers' earlier work had identified the fact that business-to-business marketing was typified by a high degree of stability in buyer–supplier relationships, accentuating the importance of understanding the relationship management mechanisms utilized by both parties (Ford, 1978; Håkansson, Johanson, & Wootz, 1976).

The final ground of the early IMP researchers concerned the traditional separation in studying either the approaches adopted by industrial purchasing agents or industrial marketers. Instead, seeing them as opposite sides of the same coin, the researchers emphasized the similarity of the tasks, with both parties "involved in the search for suitable trading partners. Both parties recognize the costs of change and the benefits and risks involved in becoming dependent upon the other" (Cunningham, 1980: 323).

Having set out their grounds, the IMP Group proceeded with their program of research. Since we were not involved in this early process, it is not clear to us whether or how agreement was reached on the methodology to adopt. Cunningham (1980: 324) argues that, given the diverse theoretical backgrounds of the individuals involved, it was clear that "no single theoretical model could be imposed." Rather, he suggests that an incremental process of accommodating different ideas eventually resulted in the interaction model adopted. In order to understand buyer–seller interaction, it was argued that four sets of variables had to be studied simultaneously: the elements and processes of the interaction itself; characteristics of the individuals and organizations involved; the environment within which the interaction occurs; and the atmosphere affecting and affected by the interaction. This model "draws upon inter-organizational theory, the 'new institutional, economic theory' in addition to concepts such as risk reduction, power and dependence, interpersonal and distribution channel power, industrial buying behaviors and the internationalization process of the firm" (Cunningham, 1980: 324).

This original study, termed the 'IMP 1' study to distinguish it from subsequent rounds of additional data collected, focused exclusively on industrial products, ignoring services. As explained in both Cunningham (1980) and Håkansson (1982), a 'choice matrix' was developed that categorized suppliers' product technology into raw materials, parts and equipment; and distinguished between the customers' manufacturing technology as to whether it involved unit production, batch and mass production, or process manufacture.

An extraordinary amount of data was then collected. The 876 interviews were conducted with companies in France (260), Germany (161), Italy (117), Sweden (180) and the United Kingdom (158) (Cunningham, 1980: 330). Approximately half of these were marketing study interviews, and half were purchasing study interviews. Due to the complexity, and the strategic sensitivity of the relationships being studied, only personal interviews were used. Care was taken that only those with direct involvement in and experience of the relationship were interviewed. There were often multiple interviews in the same company, covering different customers or suppliers.

The objective at this early stage clearly was on theory building, not theory testing. As argued by Cunningham, "the development of a better theoretical understanding of the process of interaction between companies across different national and cultural barriers is a major academic objective. The research is not intended to test a model but rather to lead to the formulation of a model which integrates industrial marketing and organizational buying behavior" (1980: 337).

This early work of the IMP Group resulted in two books, which set much of the scene for the work that was to come: Turnbull and Cunningham (1981) and Håkansson (1982). Instrumental in encouraging the group was the Annual IMP Group Conference, held every year since 1984 (apart from 1987 in which no conference was held). This conference has been supplemented in some years with an additional 'IMP Asia' conference being held. The 'membership' of the IMP Group always has been seen as a very flexible concept: while there certainly is the core team of the original researchers, there are many others who remain connected to varying degrees. Membership of the group has always been free, and the IMP Group website currently shows a total of 403 people registered as members (http://www.impgroup.org). While this may be seen as evidence of success, it also has a natural disadvantage in that it is almost impossible to keep to the tight focus that categorized the IMP 1 study, with the conferences now increasingly general in scope, dealing with a number of topics or methodologies that some core members would see as peripheral distractions. This view is counter-balanced by others calling for more inclusion of different topics and methodologies (Cunningham, 2008). However, one developmental theme that has consistently stayed within IMP thinking is the extension of the area of study from relationships and interactions between buyer and suppliers to see such relationships as being embedded within a broader network (Håkansson & Snehota, 1989).

The annual conferences have resulted in a significant amount of published work: from some different sources (Henneberg et al., 2009; Wuehrer & Smejkal, 2013; see also the IMP Group's website), we calculate that over 4,000 papers have so far been presented at the annual IMP conferences. Since the conference held in Turku in 1998, a special issue of *Industrial Marketing Management* has been dedicated to highlighting the best papers from the conference. To date, there have been 19 such special issues of *Industrial Marketing Management*, and two special issues of the *Journal of Business and Industrial Marketing*. There have also been another 22 special issues of *Industrial Marketing Management* that have been edited by members of the IMP Group (for an excellent understanding of the co-creation activities that have taken place between *Industrial Marketing Management* and the IMP Group, see Möller & Halinen, 2018). Researchers from the IMP Group have contributed significantly to the academic debate over the years. Appendix 1 lists notable publications along with their number of Google citations as of November 2018.

4.2   Contemporary Marketing Practices Group (CMP)

In contrast to the IMP Group, the CMP Group operated on a far smaller scale involving a network of fewer than 30 scholars. The research in the fullest sense only lasted for not much more than a decade, but the timely nature of the research meant it had made an important con-tribution. Of note, the CMP research is still being cited. For example, in the last three years the *Journal of Marketing* article (Coviello et al., 2002) has averaged over 30 Google Scholar cita-tions per year. As with the IMP program, the CMP program was initiated by concern that the mainstream marketing management approach was failing to reflect the changes taking place. Since the 1980s, a fragmentation of mainstream marketing has occurred. Greater emphasis was now placed on marketing processes, relationships with customers, and relationships with other stakeholders including suppliers, channel intermediaries, and other market contacts. To reflect this change, the term 'relationship marketing' was coined back in 1983. Relationship marketing had gained support in the literature to the point where some researchers (e.g., Grönroos, 1990; Sheth, Gardner, & Garrett, 1988) suggested it as a 'new marketing paradigm.'

While the arguments for a paradigm shift in marketing were persuasive, there was a lack of research to understand the nature of the changes in marketing practices. This motivated a research group at the University of Auckland's Business School to establish an international investigation into marketing practices. The program's original objective was to profile mar-keting practices in a contemporary environment and to examine the relevance of relational marketing in different organizational, economic and cultural contexts. The research was initi-ated by seminal articles by Coviello, Brodie, and Munro (1997), which outlined the conceptual framework, and Brodie et al. (1997), which reported empirical research undertaken in New Zealand.

Over the next decade, the research from the CMP Group has grown to include a core group of researchers in New Zealand, the USA, the UK, and Argentina with a broader network of researchers in countries such as Canada, Finland, Holland, Germany, Ireland, Spain, Russia, Thailand, Malaysia, Ghana, Ivory Coast, China and Australia, who replicated and expanded the original research undertaken in New Zealand. The CMP research program resulted in over 50 published research articles (Brodie, Coviello, & Winklhofer, 2008). These included an article in the *Journal of Marketing* (Coviello et al., 2002). Appendix 2 lists the most highly cited articles.

Central to the CMP research program was the development of a typology of market and marketing practices. This was developed into the survey instrument that served as a basis for the research in the different countries. The CMP typology was informed by six general theoretical frameworks that relate to economic and social processes. These frameworks are services marketing, inter-organizational exchange relationships, channels, networks, strategic management, and the value chain and information technology within and between organiza-tions (Coviello, Brodie, & Munro, 1997). In parallel with its process of drawing on general theories, the typology also was informed by applied theory and empirical research about marketing practices. This included research undertaken with middle managers, who acted as participant observers for their organizations. In addition to responding to a structured ques-tionnaire, survey participants were required to reflect on the practices in their organizations. This provided qualitative assessments of the organization's marketing practices, changes to marketing practices in general, and any influences on these practices. When analyzing the results, researchers moved between statistical analysis of the quantitative data and the qual-itative analysis of individual responses and groups of cases. Thus, the mid-range theorizing process was characterized by abductive reasoning, where conceptual work is intertwined with empirical research (Brodie & Peters, 2020; Dubois & Gadde, 2002).

The CMP typology recognizes concepts associated with the market activity and concepts associated with management activities. The five concepts or dimensions relating to external or market activity are the purpose of exchange, nature of communication, type of contact, duration of exchange, and formality of exchange. The four concepts or dimensions relating to management activity are managerial intent, managerial focus, managerial investment, and managerial level of implementation. Having identified the dimensions that distinguish between market and managerial practices, the literature was then re-analyzed based on those dimensions to identify various ideal types of practice. For the initial classification scheme, four practices subsequently were identified (Coviello, Brodie, & Munro, 1997). The three most relevant practices to contemporary marketing are:

Transactional practice is the traditional managerial approach. It is defined as a practice using the '4P' transactional approach to attract customers in a broad market or specific market segment.
Traditional relationship practice is the relationship approach articulated since the 1980s and which has its roots in service marketing and business-to-business marketing. It is defined by the development of personal interactions between employees and individual customers.
Network practice is characterized by the development of relationships with customers and companies within the network and has its roots in the IMP Group (Axelsson & Easton, 1992).

With the emergence of e-business and the Internet in the 1990s, it became necessary to revise and expand the original CMP framework to include another generic type of practice. The framework now recognized the powerful influence that information and communication technologies were having in facilitating change in business and marketing. As with the development of the original CMP typology, an extensive content analysis was undertaken of the marketing, management and information systems literature to conceptualize the emerging practice. Consistent with the original typology, attention was given to the five market-related dimensions and the four management-related dimensions that distinguish this practice from other practices. This led to an additional practice (Coviello, Milley, & Marcolin, 2001; see also Lindgreen, Palmer, & Vanhamme, 2004).

Interactive practice is defined as "using interactive information and communication technologies to create and mediate dialogue between the firm and identified customers" (Brodie, Saren, & Pels, 2011b: 83).

Importantly, the mid-range theorizing process used by the CMP research program enabled the development of a comprehensive typology that could investigate multiple practices empirically. Rather than a simple either/or dichotomous classification of practices (transactions versus relationships), the typology assumes alternative types of practices within companies are not assumed to be mutually exclusive. Thus, empirical research can identify companies with different combinations of transactional, relational, network and interactive practices. Some companies may have practices with a stronger transactional emphasis, while others have practices with a strong relational emphasis, and yet other companies may have practices that are pluralistic. This broader view of markets and marketing means the typology can be used to investigate a comprehensive range of relevant empirical phenomena and then to classify these phenomena that are not mutually exclusive.

The survey phase of the CMP research led to generalizations about contemporary marketing practice, which challenged the view that a new paradigm for marketing was emerging based on relationships:

- While there is some support for consumer goods companies being more transactional, and business and service companies being more relational, there are many exceptions.
- Companies can be grouped equally into those whose marketing practices are predominantly transactional, relational or a transactional/relational hybrid. Each group includes all types of companies (consumer goods, consumer services, business-to-business goods and business-to-business services).
- Marketing practices tend to be pluralistic in that all types of practice are in evidence, and managerial practice has not shifted from transactional to relational approaches per se.
- Companies that adopt pluralistic practices tend to perform better.

In parallel to the survey-based investigations undertaken in the first phase of CMP research, some qualitative studies were also conducted. The qualitative research evidence concerned the influence of context on the implementation of relational marketing. It also offered insight into managers' perceived challenges and barriers to implementing relationship marketing. Other case study investigations were undertaken to understand specific sectoral influences. Examples include studies in wine (Beverland & Lindgreen, 2004; Lindgreen, 2001; Lindgreen, Antioco, & Beverland, 2003), the distribution of dairy products and online shopping (Lindgreen, 2008), and the automotive industry (Lindgreen, 2008). Such studies considered industry context more closely than did earlier CMP research, while others extended the early focus on marketing practices to encompass more specific topics such as innovation in marketing (Palmer & Brookes, 2002) and managerial perspectives specific to business-to-business marketing (Palmer, 2002). These extensions complemented the findings of other qualitative research and identified key trends impacting marketing practices (Brodie, Brookes, & Coviello, 2000; Brookes & Brodie, 2000; Lindgreen, 2001).

5.   REFLECTIONS ON CONDITIONS FOR SUCCESS

Earlier, in Section 3, we identified five necessary initial conditions that determine success of a research stream, and an additional five key conditions that build on the initial conditions and also contribute to success. At this point, we review and assess how both IMP and CMP Groups achieved the conditions and established successful research streams.

5.1   Initial Condition 1: Research Problems Leading to Research Opportunities

The first necessary initial condition is the capability to identify an important research problem that is of practical and academic interest that creates the research opportunities.

IMP: Given the remarkable success of the IMP Group in terms of both the number of articles published and the citations achieved, it is clear that a research problem with opportunities was indeed identified. It seems as if the source was a critical examination of the current theories to understand industrial marketing, which simply did not match with the reality that the early researchers saw around them. A number of these early articles clearly showed the importance of longer-term relationships rather than an approach of optimizing individual sales through systematic manipulation of the marketing mix variables (see, for example, Cunningham & White, 1973; Ford, 1978; Håkansson & Östberg, 1975). The identification of the research problem itself was laid down beautifully and emphatically in the four challenges identified above (see Cunningham, 1980; Håkansson, 1982; Turnbull, Ford, & Cunningham, 1996).

CMP: The CMP research program was initiated by practical problems that also were of academic interest. As discussed in the previous section, from the 1980s, relationship marketing gained support in the literature to the point where some researchers (e.g., Christopher, Payne, & Ballantyne, 1991; Grönroos, 1990; Sheth, Gardner, & Garrett, 1988) were suggesting it as a new marketing paradigm. While the arguments for a paradigm shift in marketing were persuasive, there was a lack of research to support the case. This led to the CMP program's objective to profile marketing practices in a contemporary environment, and to examine the relevance of relational marketing in different organizational, economic and cultural contexts. Of note is that the CMP research aligns with the research agenda by Day and Montgomery (1999) who in their *Journal of Marketing* article 'Charting new directions for marketing' identified 'How do firms relate to their markets?' as one of the four most important issues for academic research in the marketing discipline in the 21st century.

5.2   Initial Condition 2: Initiating Research Stream

The second initial condition is to be able to initiate the research stream by bringing together talented groups of scholars to realize research opportunities.

IMP: As discussed in detail in the previous section, the IMP Group was formed by researchers from five different countries coming together in 1976 (Turnbull, Ford, & Cunningham, 1996). The aim was to "make a comparative analysis of operations, strategies and organization structures of companies involved in export marketing to, and international purchasing from France, Germany, Italy, Sweden, and the United Kingdom" (Cunningham, 1980: 322).

CMP: The program was initiated by a group of researchers at the University of Auckland consisting of Nicole Coviello, Richard Brookes, Vicki Little, and Rod Brodie. The group's research was characterized by a creative curiosity, an ability to spot opportunities, a passion to publish in the best journals, and an ability to work cohesively as a team to take advantage of the different members' complementary abilities. As discussed, the two seminal articles by Coviello, Brodie, and Munro (1997) and Brodie et al. (1997) created international recognition and, subsequently, an international research group was formed.

5.3   Initial Condition 3: Clarity in Expression

The third initial condition is to be able to provide clarity in academic arguments that provide foundations for the emerging research stream.

IMP: One way in which the IMP Group supported its members in achieving this clarity was through the annual conference submission process. This helped authors to tighten their logic and clarity before ultimate submission to a journal after the conference. Full papers would be submitted some months before the conference itself took place. This meant that there was a period available in which the papers could be sent for review and then returned to the authors for improvement before being finally accepted. The papers were subsequently uploaded to the Group's website. It is therefore lamentable that external network pressures have forced a change in this practice: in spite of the conference never claiming copyright of the uploaded papers, several journal editors started rejecting submissions on the basis that the papers had already been published on the website. This has led to a change in procedures, whereby an extended paper is submitted and reviewed, but which is not made more widely available.

CMP: The seminal articles by Coviello, Brodie, and Munro (1997) and Brodie et al. (1997) provided the foundations for the emerging research stream. The subsequent sequence of articles by Coviello, Brodie and others led to the refinement of the core academic arguments that CMP was based on (see Appendix 2). This sequence of articles clarified the importance of the research, and this led to the *Journal of Marketing* article by Coviello et al. (2002) that established the CMP perspective within the mainstream literature of the marketing discipline. As with IMP, CMP ran some workshops and forums, and there was a sequence of conference papers that also led to clarity in expression. Peer review played an important role in this process, as did the rigorous reviews for the leading journals in which the research was published.

5.4   Initial Condition 4: Teamwork within a Network of Scholars

The fourth initial condition is to be able to develop a network of talented scholars who embrace research opportunities.

IMP: The IMP Group excelled in creating, maintaining and developing a network of scholars. Since its inception in 1976, the researchers involved managed to pull together a tightly knit and academically cohesive team that negotiated the way forward in terms of how to get a number of different academics from different countries and different theoretical backgrounds (Cunningham, 1980) to agree a common way forward to study business relationships in an international context. The argument is put forward that "it is also important to include leading scholars who add credibility." Interestingly, this was not the approach initially taken by the IMP Group. The (perhaps apocryphal) story goes that one of the early 'rules' of the group was 'no professors to be included,' based on the assumption that leading scholars had made it to the top by adopting the prevailing approach to studying marketing as the manipulation of the marketing mix variables, and that they would not be willing/able to contribute to a radical new interpretation of industrial marketing.

CMP: The publication of the conceptual article by Coviello, Brodie, and Munro (1997) and the empirical article by Brodie et al. (1997) generated interest from the UK and other European scholars who were attracted to the common sense practical aspects of the research. These scholars approached the University of Auckland group to join the research program. The network was enhanced by some PhD studies – they included Adam Lindgreen (Cranfield University, 2000), Roger Palmer (Cranfield University, 2001), Mairead Brady (Strathclyde University, 2001), and Vicki Little (University of Auckland, 2004). CMP research was presented at the International Colloquium on Relationship Marketing, initiated by David Ballantyne in the 1990s, and participants of this colloquium became part of the network. The network started to meet on an annual basis to discuss future directions for research. These meetings focused on openness and honesty, as well as respect for the variety of skills, abilities and roles of the members of the network.

5.5   Initial Condition 5: Platform to Consolidate Knowledge

The fifth initial condition is that the network of scholars needs to produce research that con-solidates the knowledge in the area that provides the platform for further innovative research.

IMP: The IMP Group has been extraordinarily proficient at providing a platform in a variety of ways. First, until the process was forced to change (as discussed above), the conference papers were always uploaded onto the website and made freely available, acting as a resource for all the researchers. Second, David Ford put considerable effort in to editing a number of books that sought to consolidate the existing best research (Ford, 1990, 1997, 2002). Third, there have been the special issues of *Industrial Marketing Management*, with 19 special issues being based on the best conference papers and a further 22 special issues based on other topics of particular interests. These special issues have acted to consolidate knowledge of both what was discussed in the particular year's conference and also to consolidate thinking of other topics of special interest. The final consolidation approach has been via other books. This has taken different forms. First, before the conference was allocated a special issue of *Industrial Marketing Management*, an attempt was made to consolidate knowledge from the conference by producing edited books based on selected papers (see, e.g., Naudé & Turnbull, 1998; Walter, Ritter, & Gemünden, 1997). Second, Ford and Håkansson have worked with a range of different IMP members over the years to produce a number of books on their latest thinking (see, e.g., Ford et al., 1998; Ford et al., 2002; Håkansson et al., 2009). The most recent attempt to consolidate the IMP Group's thinking can be found in Håkansson and Snehota (2017). This book was based on work done in 2015 and 2016, during workshops "at which researchers presented original research papers on three topics, namely (a) managerial, (b) policy and (c) research implications of the IMP research findings" (Håkansson and Snehota, 2017: x). These three themes were then integrated into a further workshop in 2016, which resulted in the book.

CMP: The most focused effort to consolidate knowledge about CMP was in the special issue of the *Journal of Business Research and Industrial Marketing* in 2008 that was edited by Brodie and Brady (2008). This special issue included seven articles that examined theoret-ical, empirical and educational issues. Brodie, Coviello, and Winklhofer (2008) provided the overview in their 'Contemporary Marketing Practices research program: a review of the first decade.' Other research that consolidated knowledge included books by Brookes and Palmer (2004), Lindgreen (2008) and over ten book chapters.

5.6   Key Condition 1: Role of Theory and Theorizing

The first key condition that builds on the initial conditions is to have fresh thinking about the role of theory and theorizing.

IMP: As mentioned above, a core objective of the original IMP 1 research project was indeed "the development of a better theoretical understanding of the process of interaction" (Cunningham, 1980: 337), based upon both a broad understanding of different academic fields and a keen understanding of the practicalities of practicing managers. In this way, IMP researchers have attempted to bridge the gap that can exist between general theory, on the one hand, and empirical observation, on the other.

The IMP Group has been fortunate to have at its core some extremely competent and original thinkers whose very starting point was to reconceptualize our understanding of how business-to-business markets function. This continual reconceptualizing and refining have continued, with notable contributions being made in terms of the ARA Model (Håkansson & Johanson, 1992) and also the expansion of the original thinking of the importance of interactions and relationships to include the study of the networks within which interactions and relationships are embedded (Håkansson & Snehota, 1989).

CMP: The CPM approach was informed simultaneously by theory and practice work with managers, attempting to work with managers to develop a mutual understanding of how to operationalize mid-range theories (Brodie, 2013) using abductive reasoning (Brodie & Peters, 2020). The abductive reasoning process led to research that theorized with managers (Nenonen et al., 2017). The theorizing approach led to multi-method research designs. The CMP Group initially used sequential designs with alternative methods being employed in stages, that is, using results from one stage to feed into the next stage in the sequence. The preferred CMP approach now, however, is to use a 'parallel design' where methods are carried out in parallel, with results feeding into each other simultaneously. For example, most CMP surveys are undertaken with middle managers, who act as participant observers for their organizations. In addition to responding to a structured questionnaire, middle managers are required to reflect on the practices in their organizations and, in so doing, provide qualitative assessments of their marketing practices, changes to marketing practice, and influences on these practices. When analyzing the results, CMP researchers move back and forth between the statistical analysis of the quantitative data and the qualitative analysis of individual responses and groups of cases.

5.7   Key Condition 2: Sustaining Leadership and Innovation

The second key condition that builds on the initial conditions is to have ways to sustain leadership and innovation to keep the momentum in the research stream.

IMP: Assessing the level of innovation attained is a multi-dimensional construct, and there are a number of areas in which the IMP Group has excelled. This includes the number of books published, the number of conference papers and journal articles published, the number of *Industrial Marketing Management* (and other) special issues published, and the number of citations (some of which are shown in Appendix 1), all of which point to a very high level of sustained innovation indeed. One aspect of innovation is the focus of that innovation: to what extent should it be encouraged to be kept narrow, or allowed to broaden? It is interesting that almost from the start of the IMP 1 research project, the level of innovation was kept extremely narrow and deep. Cunningham argues that in the original research project envisaged, the focus was to be on understanding "managers' perceptions of, and attitudes to, the buying and marketing behavior of their customer and suppliers," and also on "an analysis of how companies interact" (1980: 328). With the subsequent almost 40 years of work on developing our understanding of interactions, relationships and networks, a lot of extremely innovative work has emerged.

However, two areas identified by Cunningham largely have been ignored, the first of which is developing our understanding of the international dimension of how relationships are managed. As anyone attending the more recent IMP conferences will acknowledge, this international aspect is not a prominent theme. Second, a specific area of interest of the original work was to study 'the education, experience and cultural backgrounds of marketing and purchasing executives in the five countries'. To date, this examination of the composition of the different actor groups involved in the buying and selling process has largely been absent. The third area of potential innovation concerns the introduction of new research approaches and methodologies beyond the more traditional case study approach that has typified so much of the IMP Group's work. Over the years, this discussion has provided a natural tension between those researchers who want to maintain the traditional methodological focus, and those researchers who seek to introduce more methodological and analytical variance.

CMP: The founders of the CMP Group provided the hub for innovation with other members of the CMP Group. As discussed in the previous section, the CMP typology evolved to include IT-enabled interactivity. This ensured that CMP's conceptual foundations were redeveloped to remain contemporary. An important aspect of the CMP research that kept it contemporary was to apply action research with 'living case studies' where the executive students were treated as participant observers of the marketing practices in the organization they worked for (Little, Brookes, & Palmer, 2008). From the mid-2000s, some members started to undertake research within the broader service-dominant logic perspective (Vargo & Lusch, 2008) that was superseding the narrower relationship marketing perspective. As discussed by Brodie, Loebler, and Fehrer (2019), service-dominant logic is becoming a unifying paradigm, which hopes to provide the foundations for a general theory of the market and value co-creation. The CMP research, with its focus on the theory–practice interface to develop mid-range theory (Brodie, Saren, & Pels, 2011b), provided fresh thinking for empirically grounding service-dominant logic research (Brodie & Loebler, 2018; Lusch & Vargo, 2014; Vargo & Lusch, 2017). Hence, the innovation associated with the CMP research stream was subsumed into the broader service-dominant logic research stream.

5.8   Key Condition 3: Getting Research Accepted

The third key condition that builds on the initial conditions is that scholars within the research stream have the persistence to get research accepted in high-quality journals.

IMP: As noted above, the IMP Group has had considerable success in getting its work published via numerous conference papers, journal articles and a large number of books. It has a sustained record of getting its research accepted across a wide range of channels. Special thanks in reaching a wider audience must go to the previous editor of *Industrial Marketing Management*, Peter LaPlaca, who regularly attended the conferences and gave the IMP Group access to so many special issues over the years, covering both the conference papers and other, more focused issues (see the review by Möller & Halinen, 2018). This tradition has been continued by the journal's current editors-in-chief, Adam Lindgreen and Tony Di Benedetto. Three articles, in particular, deserve mention: Bengtsson and Kock (2000), Walter, Ritter, and Gemünden (2001), and Ritter, Wilkinson, and Johnston (2004) that are all among the top-ten most cited articles in the journal since 2000, with 1,995, 1,166 and 859 citations, respectively.

It is a moot point as to whether the IMP Group's introduction of the IMP Journal was a good idea or not. The journal was launched in February 2006, but ceased to exist as an independent journal in December 2014. As of 2018, the journal was combined with the *Journal of Business and Industrial Marketing*, in which it was given its own special subsection. On the one hand, for the IMP Group to have its own journal could be interpreted as being too internally focused, with there being a need to reach an audience wider than just the IMP Group itself if it was to continue to influence the broader marketing community. An equally valid interpretation of events is that it was done too hastily, and that the journal should have been given more time to be nurtured and grow (Purchase, 2018).

CMP: As with all new research streams that challenge conventional thinking, there are initial problems in getting the work accepted. For example, an article that outlined the CMP typology was rejected in 1996 from a special IMP issue of the *International Journal of Research in Marketing* on markets as networks. However, this rejection led to an improved version that had great clarity of expression that was accepted for the *Journal of Marketing Management* (Coviello, Brodie, & Munro, 1997). As discussed above, there was a sequence of CMP articles that refined the academic arguments about CMP which led to submission to the *Journal of Marketing* (Coviello et al., 2002). While this article eventually was accepted, there were some challenges that needed to be overcome. One of the most controversial demands was that the editor required that a sample of US companies be collected, even though the research had samples of companies from Scandinavia, New Zealand and Canada. A key factor for the *Journal of Marketing* article getting accepted, and also the other CMP work getting accepted, was very clear communication to the editors about the important contribution of the research. This was particularly important when resubmitting revisions to overcome the similarity bias of reviewers and editors.

5.9   Key Condition 4: Getting Research Recognized

The fourth key condition is that the research stream that builds on the initial conditions needs to become visible and understood by other researchers.

IMP: There is no doubt that the IMP Group has extremely high visibility. It has a well-attended conference each year, and it also has some additional workshops/seminars each year to which some people are invited. A good recent example is the book by Håkansson and Snehota (2017), which was the output of four such workshops. While these are all evidence of visibility and the research being understood by others, there is certainly incontrovertible evidence for its success in being cited. As shown in Appendix 1, some of the articles and books have received a very high number of citations indeed.

Given the Group's close cooperation with *Industrial Marketing Management* over the years, this journal is the one that is most aspired to by many within the IMP Group. This raises the issue not just of where the work is published, but also where it is cited, in that citations on their own are good, but citations in the top journals are better. The conclusion reached by Di Benedetto et al. is that "The citations patterns show very low citation rates for IMM in the top-tier marketing journals … indicating that IMM's share of knowledge imported by top marketing journals remains relatively small" (2018: 14). The journal citing most articles in *Industrial Marketing Management* is overwhelmingly *Industrial Marketing Management* itself. There is, however, clear evidence pointing to the increasing impact factor of *Industrial Marketing Management* over recent years, in spite of a "decreasing emphasis being placed on marketing strategy research in general (and consequently business-to-business/industrial marketing research" in the top journals (Di Benedetto et al., 2018: 15). The overall picture painted, therefore, is that the IMP Group's work, along with other articles in the business-to-business area, struggles to be cited in the top journals.

CMP: The two initial seminal articles and the *Journal of Marketing* article play pivotal roles in getting the CMP research recognized. This has led to high visibility and high citations for about 20 articles (see Appendix 2). The recognition for the CMP work is because of its unique contribution in bridging theory and practice in a way which provides practical implications. As discussed above, further recognition came from the books and book chapters.

5.10   Key Condition 5: Tenacity and Resilience

The fifth key condition, which draws on all of the other nine conditions, is for the researchers to have tenacity and resilience. Research that challenges conventional thinking can be expected to meet with resistance, and it is tempting to give up.

IMP: The importance of this condition in determining the success of the IMP Group's work does not seem particularly applicable. This is for two reasons. The first is that right in the beginning when launching the IMP 1 research study, a number of the researchers had already had their work published in the mainstream literature, and hence were both accepted by the academic community and knowledgeable about the process of getting published. Second, from an early stage, the group worked hard to support itself; as the Group expanded in numbers, so running the annual conference on a shoestring demanded hard work and commitment from the organizing committee each year, but it did build a wonderfully internal supportive network for older and newer members alike.

CMP: As discussed above, the importance of this condition in determining the success of the CMP Group's work was in getting the two initial CMP articles accepted and then getting the *Journal of Marketing* article accepted. In these cases, the researchers' tenacity and resilience played important roles in getting through the review processes. However, as with IMP, once the visibility and recognition were achieved, this condition did not play such an important role.

CONCLUSIONS

Business school managers would like to build, and maintain, their research portfolios; individual researchers working within a business-school framework would like to keep adding to their publication track record at leading journals. To accomplish these goals, managers need to consider how to invest effectively in research such that they can nurture sustainable research streams. We have identified five initial conditions, as well as five key conditions, which are most conducive to a sustainable and productive academic research environment. We have also presented detailed examples of these conditions in practice, in two successful research institutions, the IMP and CMP Groups. Our examination of the IMP Group presented evidence showing how this group has made significant research contributions. Similarly, the examination identifies unique aspects of the CMP research stream that led to its success for over a decade. We assess that the ten conditions are robust and identify the essence of what has led to the success of two research streams.

Of the ten conditions, 'sustaining leadership and innovation' requires further consideration. The IMP Group has grown considerably over time. This raises the issue as to the ideal size of a research group in order to sustain innovative research. If there are too few members, there may not be enough variance in ideas to sustain innovation. If there are too many members, innovation may become too diffuse and lack focus. Within the IMP Group, the rapid increase in the number of members has led naturally to this debate. The discussions center around whether the IMP research should stay focused, or whether it should welcome a fragmentation in focus and acceptance of a wider range of methodological approaches. In contrast, the CMP Group always was small, so the question did not arise. However, perhaps the CMP Group did not grow enough to sustain leadership in innovation.

Having its beginnings in the 1970s, the IMP Group has had a head start of almost 20 years over the CMP Group. As IMP became developed, the research published has increased, but the cohesiveness of its brand position has become less clear, as different topics and methodologies are adopted. In contrast, the main research thrust of the CMP Group only lasted a decade, where there was a singular focus based on the original research objective to profile marketing practices in a contemporary environment and to examine the relevance of relational marketing in different organizational, economic and cultural contexts. Rather than expand with a broader range of topics and methodologies, the CMP researchers migrated into other research streams, as the research had served its purpose. The pioneering CMP research that developed a typology of marketing practices based on mid-range theory using abductive reasoning is now playing a major role in service-dominant logic (Brodie & Loebler, 2018). Another research stream built upon the CMP research to develop an instrument to measure companies' use of purchasing practices and identified four configurations of practices ranging from transactional over interpersonal dyadic and interpersonal network to integrative relational configurations (Lindgreen et al., 2013).

As a final thought, one must also consider the substantial role of the journal editor(s) in supporting emerging research streams. An editor may on occasion see some promise in a radical new research study that has received reject reviews due to its being 'too different' or 'too challenging.' The editor may overrule the reviewers and make a major revision recommendation instead, thereby giving the author with the promising, but radical new research idea another chance to make a contribution. This editorial decision requires vision or insight on the part of the editor and is highly idiosyncratic. If the paper has been rejected from several A-list journals for being 'too different,' it might be a good idea for the author to try a good lower-level journal. The editor may be willing to take a rider on a paper if the editor is convinced of the promise in the research, and especially so if the editor is looking to boost the profile of the journal. After all, not all of the influential articles in marketing or other business disciplines were published in A-list journals. If anything, the highest-profile journals may sometimes be quite conservative in their selection decisions, depending on the editor at that given time.[1]

NOTE

1.   This chapter first appeared as an editorial in *Industrial Marketing Management* (see Lindgreen et al., 2020).

REFERENCES

Aguinis, H., Cummings, C., Ramani, R.S., & Cummings, T.G. (2020). "An A is an A": the new bottom-line for valuing academic research. *Academy of Management Perspectives*, 34(1), pp. 134–155.
Axelsson, B. & Easton, G. (eds.) (1992). *Industrial Networks: A New View of Reality*. London: Routledge.
Bengtsson, M. & Kock, S. (2000). 'Coopetition' in business networks: to cooperate and compete simultaneously. *Industrial Marketing Management*, 29(5), pp. 411–26.
Beverland, M.B. & Lindgreen, A. (2004). Relationship use and market dynamism: a model of relationship evolution. *Journal of Marketing Management*, 20(7/8), pp. 825–58.

Breidbach, C. & Brodie, R.J. (2017). Engagement platforms and value cocreation in the sharing economy: conceptual foundations and research directions. *Journal of Service Theory and Practice*, *27*(4), pp. 761–77.

Brodie, R.J. (2013). Future of theorizing in marketing: increasing contribution by bridging theory and practice. In Moutinho, L., Bigné, E., & Manrai, A. (eds.), *Companion to the Future of Marketing*. London: Routledge, pp. 88–104.

Brodie, R.J. & Brady, M. (2008). Introduction to the special issue on contemporary marketing practices. *Journal of Business and Industrial Marketing*, *23*(2), pp. 81–3.

Brodie, R.J., Brookes, R.W., & Coviello, N.E. (2000). Relationship marketing for consumer products. In Blois, K. (ed.), *Oxford Textbook on Marketing*. Oxford: Oxford University Press, pp. 517–33.

Brodie, R.J., Coviello, N.E., Brookes, R.W., & Little, V. (1997). Towards a paradigm shift in marketing? An examination of current marketing practices. *Journal of Marketing Management*, *13*(5), pp. 383–406.

Brodie, R.J., Coviello, N.E., & Winklhofer, H. (2008). Investigating contemporary marketing practices: a review of the first decade of the CMP research program. *Journal of Business and Industrial Marketing*, *23*(2), pp. 84–94.

Brodie, R.J., Fehrer, J.A., Jaakkola, E., & Conduit, J. (2019). Actor engagement in networks: defining the conceptual domain. *Journal of Service Research*, *22*(2), pp. 173–88.

Brodie, R.J., Hollebeek, L.D., & Conduit, J. (2016). *Customer Engagement: Contemporary Issues and Challenges*. London: Routledge.

Brodie, R.J., Hollebeek, L.D., Juric, B., & Ilic, A. (2011a). Customer engagement: conceptual domain, fundamental propositions, and implications for research. *Journal of Service Research*, *14*(3), pp. 252–71.

Brodie, R.J., Ilic, A., Juric, B., & Hollebeek, L.D. (2013). Consumer engagement in a virtual brand community: an exploratory analysis. *Journal of Business Research*, *66*(1), pp. 105–14.

Brodie, R.J. & Juric, B. (2018). Customer engagement: developing an innovative research that has scholarly impact. *Journal of Global Scholars of Marketing Science*, *28*(3), pp. 291–303.

Brodie, R.J. & Loebler, H. (2018). Advancing knowledge about service-dominant logic: the role of midrange theory. In Vargo, S.L. & Lusch, R.F. (eds.), *The SAGE Handbook on Service-Dominant Logic*. London: SAGE Publishing, pp. 564–79.

Brodie, R.J., Loebler, H., & Fehrer, J. (2019). Evolution of service-dominant logic: towards a paradigm and metatheory of the market and value cocreation? *Industrial Marketing Management*, *79*, pp. 3–12.

Brodie, R.J. & Peters, L. (2020). Increasing contribution in service research: fresh thinking about the process of theorizing. *Journal of Service Marketing*, Accessed (27 September 2021): https://www.researchgate.net/publication/341217934_New_directions_for_service_research_refreshing_the_process_of_theorizing_to_increase_contribution.

Brodie, R.J., Saren, M., & Pels, J. (2011b). Theorizing about marketing and the SD logic: exploring the bridging role of middle range theory. *Marketing Theory*, *11*(1), pp. 75–91.

Brookes, R.W. & Brodie, R.J. (2000). Introduction to marketing strategies. In Cravens, D., Merrilees, B., & Walker, R. (eds.), *Strategic Marketing*. New York: Irwin McGraw-Hill, pp. 1–20.

Brookes, R.W. & Palmer, R.A. (2004). *The New Global Marketing Reality*. Basingstoke: Palgrave Macmillan.

Christopher, M., Payne, A., & Ballantyne, D. (1991). *Relationship Marketing: Bringing Quality, Customer Service and Marketing Together*, London: Butterworth.

Coviello, N.E., Brodie, R.J., Danaher, P.J., & Johnston, W.J. (2002). How firms relate to their markets: an empirical examination of contemporary marketing practice. *Journal of Marketing*, *66*(3), pp. 33–46.

Coviello, N.E., Brodie, R.H., & Munro, H.J. (1997). Understanding contemporary marketing: development of a classification scheme. *Journal of Marketing Management*, *13*(6), pp. 501–22.

Coviello, N.E., Milley, R., & Marcolin, B. (2001). Understanding IT-enabled interactivity in contemporary marketing. *Journal of Interactive Marketing*, *15*(4), pp. 18–33.

Cunningham, M.T. (1980). International marketing and purchasing of industrial goods: features of a European research project. *European Journal of Marketing*, *14*(5/6), pp. 322–38.

Cunningham, M.T. (2008). Pictures at an exhibition of business markets: is there a case for competition? *The IMP Journal*, *2*(1), pp. 46–59.

Cunningham, M.T. & White, J.G. (1973). The behaviour of industrial buyers in their search for suppliers of machine tools. *Journal of Management Studies, 7*(3), pp. 189–202.

Day, G. & Montgomery, D. (1999). Charting new directions for marketing. *Journal of Marketing, 63*(special issue), pp. 3–13.

Di Benedetto, C.A. (2013). The emergence of the product innovation discipline and implications for future research. In Kahn, K.B. (ed.), *The PDMA Handbook of New Product Development*. Hoboken, NJ: John Wiley & Sons, pp. 416–26.

Di Benedetto, C.A., Sarin, S., Belkhouja, M., & Haon, C. (2018). Patterns of knowledge outflow from Industrial Marketing Management to major marketing and specialized journals (1999–2013): a citation analysis. *Industrial Marketing Management, 69*, pp. 13–17.

Dubois, A. & Gadde, L.E. (2002). Systematic combining: an abductive approach to case research. *Journal of Business Research, 55*(7), pp. 553–60.

Ford, D. (1980). The development of buyer–seller relationships in industrial markets. *European Journal of Marketing, 14*(5/6), pp. 339–53.

Ford, D. (ed.) (1990). *Understanding Business Markets: Interactions, Relationships and Networks*. London: Academic Press.

Ford, D. (1997). *Understanding Business Markets*, 2nd edn., London: Dryden Press.

Ford, D. (ed.) (2002). *Understanding Business Marketing and Purchasing*, 3rd edn., London: Thompson Learning.

Ford, D., Berthon, P., Brown, S., Gadde, L.-E., Håkansson, H., Naudé, P., Ritter, T., & Snehota, I. (2002). *The Business Marketing Course: Managing in Complex Networks*. Chichester: John Wiley and Sons.

Ford, D., Gadde, L.-E., Håkansson, H., Lundgren, A., Snehota, I., Turnbull, P., & Wilson, D. (1998). *Managing Business Relationships*. New York: John Wiley and Sons.

Ford, I.D. (1978). Stability factors in industrial marketing channels. *Industrial Marketing Management, 7*(6), pp. 410–22.

Grönroos, C. (1990). *Service Management and Marketing: Managing the Moments of Truth in Service Competition*. Lexington, MA: Lexington Books.

Gummesson, E. (2004). Qualitative research in marketing: road-map for a wilderness of complexity and unpredictability. *European Journal of Marketing, 39*(3), pp. 309–27.

Håkansson, H. (ed.) (1982). *International Marketing and Purchasing: An Interaction Approach*. Chichester: John Wiley and Sons.

Håkansson, H., Ford, D., Gadde, L.-E., Snehota, I., & Waluszewski, A. (2009). *Business in Networks*. Chichester: John Wiley and Sons.

Håkansson, H., Johanson, H., & Wootz, B. (1976). Influence tactics in buyer–seller processes. *Industrial Marketing Management, 4*(6), pp. 319–32.

Håkansson, H. & Johanson, J. (1992). A model of industrial networks. In Axelsson, B. & Easton, G. (eds.), *Industrial Networks: A New View of Reality*. London: Routledge, pp. 28–34 [reprinted in Ford, 2002].

Håkansson, H. & Snehota, I. (1989). No business is an island: the network concept of business strategy. *Scandinavian Journal of Management, 5*(3), pp. 187–200.

Håkansson, H. & Snehota, I. (eds.) (2017). *No Business is an Island: Making Sense of the Interactive Business World*. Bingley: Emerald Publishing.

Håkansson, H. & Östberg, C. (1975). Industrial marketing: an organizational problem? *Industrial Marketing Management, 4*(2/3), pp. 113–23.

Henneberg, S.C., Jiang, Z., Naudé, P., & Ormrod, R.P. (2009). The network researchers' network: a social network analysis of the IMP Group 1984–2006. *The IMP Journal, 3*(1), pp. 28–49.

Kitchener, M. (2019a). Cardiff Business School: the public value business school, https://www.cardiff.ac.uk/__data/assets/pdf_file/0008/572732/Cardiff-Business-School-Public-Value.pdf (accessed May 22, 2019).

Kitchener, M. (2019b). The public value of social science: from manifesto to organizational strategy. In Lindgreen, A., Koenig-Lewis, N., Kitchener, M., Brewer, J., Moore, M., & Meynhardt, T. (eds.), *Public Value: Deepening, Enriching, and Broadening the Theory and Practice*. London: Routledge, pp. 301–15.

Lindgreen, A. (2001). An exploration of contemporary marketing practices in the New Zealand wine sector: evidence from three cases. *International Journal of Wine Marketing, 13*(1), pp. 5–22.

Lindgreen, A. (2008). *Managing Market Relationships: Methodological and Empirical Insights.* Aldershot: Gower Publishing.

Lindgreen, A., Antioco, M.D.J., & Beverland, M.B. (2003). Contemporary marketing practice: a research agenda and preliminary findings. *International Journal of Customer Relationship Management, 6*(1), pp. 51–72.

Lindgreen, A., Di Benedetto, C.A., Brodie, R.J., and Naudé, P. (2020). How to build great research groups. *Industrial Marketing Management, 81*, pp. 1–13.

Lindgreen, A., Di Benedetto, C.A., Verdich, C., Vanhamme, J., Venkatraman, V., Pattinson, S., Clarke, A.H., & Khan, Z. (2019a). How to write really good research funding applications. *Industrial Marketing Management, 77*, pp. 232–9.

Lindgreen, A., Koenig-Lewis, N., Kitchener, M., Brewer, J.D., Moore, M., & Meynhardt, T. (2019b). *Public Value: Deepening, Enriching, and Broadening the Theory and Practice.* London: Routledge.

Lindgreen, A., Palmer, R., & Vanhamme, J. (2004). Contemporary marketing practice: theoretical propositions and practical implications. *Marketing Intelligence & Planning, 22*(6), pp. 673–92.

Lindgreen, A., Vanhamme, J., van Raaij, E.M., & Johnston, W.J. (2013). Go configure: the mix of purchasing practices to choose for your supply base. *California Management Review, 55*(2), pp. 72–96.

Little, V., Brookes, R., & Palmer, R. (2008). Research-informed teaching and teaching-informed research: the Contemporary Marketing Practices (CMP) living case study approach to understanding marketing practice. *Journal of Business and Industrial Marketing, 23*(2), pp. 124–34.

Lusch, R.F. & Vargo, S.L. (2014). *Service-Dominant Logic: Premises, Perspectives, Possibilities.* Cambridge: Cambridge University Press.

Möller, K. & Halinen, A. (2018). IMP thinking and IMM: co-creating value for business marketing. *Industrial Marketing Management, 69*, pp. 18–31.

Naudé, P. & Turnbull, P.W. (eds.) (1998). *Network Dynamics in International Marketing.* Oxford: Pergamon Press.

Nenonen, S., Brodie, R.J., Storbacka, K., & Peters, L.D. (2017). Theorizing with managers: how to achieve both academic rigor and practical relevance? *European Journal of Marketing, 51*(7/8), pp. 1130–52.

Palmer, R.A. (2002). Managerial understanding of contemporary industrial marketing issues. *Qualitative Market Research: An International Journal, 5*(2), pp. 135–43.

Palmer, R.A. & Brookes, R.W. (2002). Incremental innovation: a case study analysis. *Journal of Database Marketing, 10*(1), pp. 71–83.

Purchase, S. (2018). Personal communication.

Ritter, T., Wilkinson, I.F., & Johnston, W.J. (2004). Managing in complex business networks. *Industrial Marketing Management, 33*(3), pp. 175–83.

Robinson, P.J., Faris, C.W., & Wind, Y. (1967). *Industrial Buying and Creative Marketing.* Boston, MA: Allyn and Bacon.

Sheth, J. (1973). A model of industrial buyer behaviour. *Journal of Marketing, 37*(4), pp. 50–56.

Sheth, J.M., Gardner, D.M., & Garrett, D.E. (1988). *Marketing Theory: Evolution and Evaluation.* New York: John Wiley and Sons.

Soutar, G.N., Wilkinson, I., & Young, L. (2015). Research performance of marketing academics and departments: an international comparison. *Australasian Marketing Journal, 23*(2), pp. 155–61.

Storbacka, K., Brodie, R.J., Böhmann, T., Maglio, P.P., & Nenonen, S. (2016). Actor engagement in service ecosystems: directions for further research. *Journal of Business Research, 69*(8), pp. 3008–17.

Turnbull, P.W. & Cunningham, M.T. (1981). *International Marketing and Purchasing.* London: Macmillan.

Turnbull, P.W., Ford, D., & Cunningham, M.T. (1996). Interaction, relationships and networks in business markets: an evolving perspective. *Journal of Business and Industrial Marketing, 11*(3/4), pp. 44–62.

Vargo, S.L. & Lusch, R.F. (2008). Service-dominant logic: continuing the evolution. *Journal of the Academy of Marketing Science, 36*(1), pp. 1–10.

Vargo, S.L. & Lusch, R.F. (2017). Service-dominant logic 2025. *International Journal of Research in Marketing, 34*(1), pp. 46–67.

Walter, A., Ritter, T., & Gemünden, H.-G. (eds.) (1997). *Relationships and Networks in International Markets*. London: Pergamon Press.

Walter, A., Ritter, T., & Gemünden, H.-G. (2001). Value creation in buyer–seller relationships: theoretical considerations and empirical results from a supplier's perspective. *Industrial Marketing Management, 30*(4), pp. 365–77.

Webster, F.E. & Wind, Y. (1972). A general model for understanding organizational buying behaviour. *Journal of Marketing, 36*(2), pp. 12–19.

Wuehrer, G.A. & Smejkal, A.E. (2013). Diversity in homogeneity: a longitudinal bibliometric review of Industrial Marketing and Purchasing (IMP) Group Conferences from 1984 to 2012. *The IMP Journal, 7*(3), pp. 140–58.

APPENDIX 1: IMP RESEARCH

Table 14A.1   IMP research: selected books and journal articles and number of citations

Author(s), Title and Details	Number of citations
Anderson, J., Håkansson, H., & Johanson, J. (1994). Dyadic business relationships within a business network context. *Journal of Marketing, 58*(4), pp. 1–15.	3,078
Bengtsson, M. & Kock, S. (2000). 'Coopetition' in business networks: to cooperate and compete simultaneously. *Industrial Marketing Management, 29*(5), pp. 411–26.	1,995
Ford, D. (1980). The development of buyer–seller relationships in industrial markets. *European Journal of Marketing, 14*(5/6), pp. 339–53.	1,748
Ford, D. (ed.) (1990). *Understanding Business Markets: Interactions, Relationships and Networks*. London: Academic Press.	1,506
Ford, D., Gadde, L.-E., Håkansson, H., Lundgren, A., Snehota, I., Turnbull, P., & Wilson, D. (1998). *Managing Business Relationships*. New York: John Wiley and Sons.	2,298
Håkansson, H. (ed.) (1982). *International Marketing and Purchasing: An Interaction Approach*. Chichester: John Wiley and Sons.	4,164
Håkansson, H. (1987). *Industrial Technological Development: A Network Approach*. London: Croom Helm.	2,067
Håkansson, H. (1989). *Corporate Technological Behaviour: Co-operation and Networks*. London: Routledge.	1,301
Håkansson, H. & Ford, D. (2002). How should companies interact in business networks? *Journal of Business Research, 55*(2), pp. 133–9.	1,725
Håkansson, H. & Johanson, J. (1992). A model of industrial networks. In Axelsson, B. & Easton, G. (eds.). *Industrial Networks: A New View of Reality*. London: Routledge, pp. 28–34.	1,284
Håkansson, H. & Snehota, I. (1989). No business is an island: the network concept of business strategy. *Scandinavian Journal of Management, 5*(3), pp. 187–200.	2,130
Johanson, J. & Mattsson, L.-G. (1987). Interorganizational relations in industrial systems: a network approach compared with the transaction-cost approach. *International Studies of Management & Organization, 17*(1), pp. 34–48.	1,672
Johanson, J. & Mattsson, L.-G. (2015). Internationalisation in industrial systems: a network approach. In Forsgren, M., Holm, U., & Johanson, J. (eds) *Knowledge, Networks and Power*. London: Palgrave Macmillan, pp. 111–32.	2,824

Author(s), Title and Details	Number of citations
Snehota, I. & Håkansson, H. (1995). *Developing Relationships in Business Networks*. London: Routledge.	4,812
Walter, A., Ritter, T., & Gemünden, H.-G. (2001). Value creation in buyer–seller relationships: theoretical considerations and empirical results from a supplier's perspective. *Industrial Marketing Management*, *30*(4), pp. 365–77.	1,166
Wilson, D.T. (1995). An integrated model of buyer–seller relationships. *Journal of the Academy of Marketing Science*, *55*(2), pp. 133–9.	3,182

APPENDIX 2: CMP RESEARCH

Table 14A.2   CMP research: journal articles and number of citations

Author(s), Title and Details	Number of citations
Brady, M., Saren, M., & Tzokas, N. (2002). Integrating information technology into marketing. *Journal of Marketing Management*, *18*(5/6), pp. 555–78.	152
Brodie, R.J., Coviello, N.E., Brookes, R.W., & Little, V. (1997). Towards a paradigm shift in marketing? An examination of current marketing practices. *Journal of Marketing Management*, *13*(5), pp. 383–406.	544
Brodie, R.J., Winklhofer, H., Coviello, N.E., & Johnston, W.J. (2007). Is e-marketing coming of age? An examination of the penetration of e-marketing and firm performance. *Journal of Interactive Marketing*, *21*(1), pp. 2–21.	224
Brookes, R.W., Brodie, R.J., Coviello, N.E., & Palmer, R.A. (2004). How managers perceive the impacts of information technologies on contemporary practices: reinforcing enhancing or transforming? *Journal of Relationship Marketing Management*, *3*(4), pp. 7–26.	58
Coviello, N.E. & Brodie, R.J. (1998). From transaction to relationship marketing: an investigation of managerial perceptions and practices. *Journal of Strategic Marketing*, *6*(3), pp. 171–86.	339
Coviello, N.E. & Brodie, R.J. (2001). Contemporary marketing practices of consumer and business-to-business firms: how different are they? *Journal of Business and Industrial Marketing*, *16*(5), pp. 382–400.	188
Coviello, N.E., Brodie, R.J., Brookes, R.W., & Palmer, R.A. (2003). Assessing the role of e-marketing in contemporary marketing practice. *Journal of Marketing Management*, *9*(7), pp. 857–81.	58

Author(s), Title and Details	Number of citations
Coviello, N.E., Brodie, R.J., Danaher, P.J., & Johnston, W.J. (2002). How firms relate to their markets: an empirical examination of contemporary marketing practice. *Journal of Marketing, 66*(3), pp. 33–46.	660
Coviello, N.E., Brodie, R.J., & Munro, H.J. (1997). Understanding contemporary marketing: development of a classification scheme. *Journal of Marketing Management, 13*(6), pp. 501–22.	660
Coviello, N.E., Brodie, R.J., & Munro, H.J. (2000). An investigation of marketing practice by firm size. *Journal of Business Venturing, 15*(5/6), pp. 523–45.	343
Coviello, N.E., Milley, R., & Marcolin, B. (2001). Understanding IT-enabled interactivity in contemporary marketing. *Journal of Interactive Marketing, 15*(4), pp. 18–33.	245
Coviello, N.E., Winklhofer, H., & Hamilton, K. (2006). Marketing practices and performance of small service firms: an examination in the tourism accommodation sector. *Journal of Service Research, 9*(1), pp. 38–58.	123
Lindgreen, A., Davis, R., Brodie, R.J., & Buchanan-Oliver, M. (2000). Pluralism in contemporary marketing practices. *International Journal of Bank Marketing, 18*(6), pp. 294–308.	123
Lindgreen, A., Palmer, R., & Vanhamme, J. (2004). Contemporary marketing practice: theoretical propositions and practical implications. *Marketing Intelligence & Planning, 22*(6), pp. 673–92.	105
Lindgreen, A., Palmer, R., Vanhamme, J., & Wouters, J.P.M. (2006). A relationship-management assessment tool: questioning, identifying, and prioritizing critical aspects of customer relationships. *Industrial Marketing Management, 35*(1), pp. 57–71.	209
Lindgreen, A., Palmer, R., Wetzels, M., & Antioco, M. (2008). Do different marketing practices require different leadership styles? An exploratory study. *Journal of Business & Industrial Marketing, 24*(1), pp. 114–26.	53
Pels, J. (1999). Exchange relationships in consumer markets. *European Journal of Marketing, 33*(1/2), pp. 19–37.	172
Pels, J., Brodie, R.J., & Johnston, W.J. (2004). Benchmarking business-to-business practices in emerging and developed economies: Argentina compared to the USA and New Zealand. *Journal of Business and Industrial Marketing, 19*(6), pp. 386–96.	51

Author(s), Title and Details	Number of citations
Pels, J., Coviello, N.E., & Brodie, R.J. (2000). Integrating transactional and relational marketing exchange: a pluralistic perspective. *Journal of Marketing Theory and Practice, 8*(3), pp. 11–20.	98
Wagner, R. (2005). Contemporary marketing practices in Russia. *European Journal of Marketing, 39*(1/2), pp. 199–215.	71

15. Dilemmas in university management: the case of Copenhagen Business School

Nanna Mik-Meyer

The role of management in universities has become more complex over the last decades because of changes in legislation, the economy, student intake, the introduction of new performance indicators for research quality, relevance and output, and so on (de Boer and Goedegebuure 2009). According to Pulkkinen and colleagues (2019), Nordic universities are going through a 'rationalisation', with the 'introduction of a more formal structure in terms of a stronger emphasis on quality assurance, evaluation, accountability measures and incentive systems' (Pulkkinen et al. 2019, p. 4). The EU's modernisation agendas from 2006 and 2011 and the Bologna process of making the policies of higher education more similar have had strong effects on Nordic universities (Pulkkinen et al. 2019, p. 5). For instance, the role of university management and deanship has changed, giving deans 'substantial managerial powers' (de Boer, Enders and Leisyte 2007, p. 39). Today, the power of top management is linked to a more hierarchical organisational structure, in which deans and the central executive board have frequent meetings, predefining the main direction for the university, before engaging the remaining faculty. Although the Dutch study by de Boer and colleagues (2007) finds that while professors retain their traditional professional autonomy – including a significant voice in decision making regarding primary processes, and the deans do value their opinions – the new organisational structure of universities allocates formal power to senior management. Scholars argue that Denmark is an 'extreme case', as the reforms of the higher educational system have gone further than in most other European countries (Degn and Sørensen 2015, p. 931).

This chapter discusses three key issues. First, it discusses how a number of dilemmas of management relate to key conditional factors of Danish universities (e.g. law, management structure, economy, student intake). Second, it presents the strategy of the Copenhagen Business School (CBS) that aims to strengthen the quality of research by expanding the amount of external funding and implementing key performance indicators. Third, it examines the pros and cons of implementing key performance indicators to measure research quality. Throughout the chapter, I alternate between drawing on my insights from my position as the vice dean of research at the CBS and drawing from the academic work of my national and international colleagues on university management.

THE COMPLEXITY OF THE DANISH UNIVERSITY ENVIRONMENT

The Legal Framework

In the first section of the first paragraph of the Danish University Law, two key goals of universities are stated, namely, to conduct research and research-based teaching at the highest possible level and to secure freedom of research for its scholars:

> The University has the task of conducting research and providing research-based education up to the highest international level within its disciplines. ... The University has freedom of research. The university must protect the freedom of research of the university and the individual and the ethics of science. (Universitetsloven 2003, §§1–2)

This first part of the University Law reflects the perception of a classical university primarily striving for research excellence and freedom of research. I think it is fair to say that these aims are primary for most active scholars. However, the Danish University Law also establishes other key goals:

> The university shall cooperate with the surrounding community and contribute to the development of international collaboration. The results from the university's research and education must help promote growth, welfare and development in the surrounding community. As a central knowledge- and culture-bearing institution, the university must exchange knowledge and skills with the surrounding community and encourage its employees to participate in public debate. (Universitetsloven 2003, §2)

The classic university prioritisation of excellence and freedom of research is placed next to this new agenda emphasising the surrounding community, which stresses the promotion of the economic growth and welfare of Danish society.

First dilemma: How can a managerial structure support the two-sided objective of excellence, internationalisation and freedom of research (which implies a long time span and basic research) and of securing the economic growth and welfare of Danish society (which implies a short time span and applied research)?

Leadership Structure

As in other European countries, Danish universities have experienced significant changes in relation to the formal aspect of management. With the passing of the Danish University Law of 2003, the leadership structure of Danish universities was significantly altered. An important goal of the reform was to increase the research output of Danish universities by supporting the management system. The democratic setup, in which employees chose their leaders, was not optimal, due to factors such as very low turnout at elections and accusations of nepotism. The reform of 2003 shifted the leadership structure from an electoral system, where faculty members democratically elected their managers, to a recruitment system with open job postings, and so on. The reform also meant that the board of directors was composed of a majority of external partners, that is, those without personal experience working at a university. Consequently, Danish universities were transformed into self-governing institutions under the supervision of a board of directors (Ministry of Higher Education and Science 2003). In the new setup, the board of directors appoints the president of the university, who in turn hires the deans, who hire the vice deans and heads of departments, and so on (Ministry of Higher Education and Science 2003). The previous democratic election system, where faculty elected their managers, ended with this reform.

Second dilemma: How can the internal management system (president, deans and heads of departments) secure freedom of research and maintain the historically acclaimed autonomy of universities when a board of directors with a majority of outsiders sets the direction for the university's output?

The Economic Framework

In Denmark, universities are public, and the majority of their total funding stems from public funding (Universities Denmark 2018). The total share of the Danish GDP allocated to research nationally has been gradually decreasing since 2013, resulting in a decrease from 0.88% in 2009 to 0.75% in 2018. However, when including funding from the EU and the Danish National Research Foundation, the share of GDP allocated to public funding has remained at the set goal of 1% (Universities Denmark 2018). While public funding has remained stable, external private funding of Danish universities has seen an approximately threefold increase between 2007 and 2017 (Universities Denmark 2018). Approximately 30% of the total government funding of universities is allocated to research. Besides that, public funding of the universities is based on a number of performance criteria related to education and research.

For comparison, the first country to adopt a research performance-based funding system was the UK. The allocation of public funding in the UK is based on the Research Excellence Framework (REF), student fees, research grants, and so on. In the REF system, the concept of impact is based on an academic measurement of research performance as well as on the societal impact of the university, which includes the effects of research on the economy, public policy, civil society and culture. In the UK, measuring research performance is broken down into four profiles (world leading, internationally excellent, recognised internationally and recognised nationally). The UK model incentivises publications rated as world-leading or world-class research outlets (Jonkers and Zacharewicz 2016). In contrast, the Danish model has a strong emphasis on quantifiable output measures: number of students passing their exams (including PhD students), number of scientific articles and growth of external funding.

Third dilemma: When public, unrestricted funding has gone down and private (and public) strategic funding has gone up, the balance between securing freedom of research and basic research may tip towards the second goal of the University Law: to promote the growth and welfare of Danish society. This raises a key question: How can a managerial structure support the University Law's goals of freedom of research and excellence when the funding environment is gradually replaced by actors who have a strategic and applied approach to research that may challenge freedom of research and the goal of excellence?

Massification: From an Elite Institution to a Mass Institution

In line with developments in other European and Nordic countries, Danish universities have increased their student intake and developed into what some scholars term 'mass universities' (the process is called 'massification') (Barry, Chandler and Clark 2001; de Boer and Goedegebuure 2009; Kivinen, Hedman and Kaipainen 2007; Trow and Burrage 2010). The concept of 'mass university' or 'massification' emphasises that universities are going through a transformation from elitist universities to mass institutions with a large student intake. This change significantly affects the management of universities. This development is partly a response to the then government of 2007 launching 'the globalisation pool', that is, allocating DKK43 billion to increase public funding for research to 1% in 2010, and aiming to increase the number of students graduating with a higher education to 50% in 2015. In Denmark, between 2008 and 2018, there has been an increase in the intake of both bachelor's and master's degree students of 55% and 70%, respectively, although this tendency has been in spite of a significant decrease in the number of students in the humanities, especially on the bachelor's level (Universities Denmark 2018). It is costly for universities if students do not graduate within the five-year period of an MA.

Fourth dilemma: How can a perception of excellence and the goal of delivering the highest level of research and research-based education be sustained when a key performance indicator for Danish universities is primarily whether students graduate on time?

Summary

I have listed a number of conditional factors that affect the management of Danish universities. These conditions are evident in dilemmas in the everyday work life of managers and scientific staff. As the list demonstrates, a key challenge for research management at universities is to balance the goals of supporting research excellence, internationalisation and research freedom while at the same time securing the economic growth and welfare of Danish society. This key dilemma is visible in the University Law as well as in the model of management that uses a combination of an internal management system (president, deans and heads of departments) and an external board of directors whose goal is to set the direction for the university's output. The dilemma also shows itself in relation to the funding situation in Denmark, where unrestricted funding has gone down and private (and public) strategic funding has gone up, thereby potentially tipping the balance in favour of the economic growth and welfare of Danish society. Additionally, when a key performance indicator for Danish universities is whether students graduate on time, the goal of research excellence is at risk of being supressed unless management pushes back with tools that strengthen research excellence. However, as with any performance indicator of research excellence – e.g. ranking systems of journals, h-index, amount of prestigious funding – they often come with a cost of downplaying or setting aside other contextual factors of relevance for running a university. Consequently, the final part of the chapter includes a discussion of what research has termed 'the perverse effects' of quantifiable systems. However, I will first present the role of funding and key performance indicators for strengthening research excellence in Denmark and at the CBS.

THE ROLE OF EXTERNAL FUNDING

There is an increased focus on external funding in Nordic universities (Pinheiro et al. 2019). Similar to other Nordic countries, Danish public universities' financial situation is tight. However, private foundations are setting aside a larger and larger amount of money for supporting research that they determine is strategically relevant and likely to produce results that are applicable in practice. As research has documented long ago, funding from the industry – an important sector for the CBS – first and foremost leads to applied research (Gulbrandsen and Smeby 2005). A common reservation among scholars is whether the increased funding from industry will lead to more applied research at the expense of basic research. In recent years, funding from private foundations has amounted to 2% of GDP. In 2017, Danish universities received a total of DKK5.5 billion: 2.9 billion from national private foundations, 2.1 billion from international (primarily EU) foundations and 0.5 billion from private firms. Public funding amounted to 1% of GDP. In other words, private foundations play a significant role in the funding scheme in Denmark. Consequently, researchers are encouraged to apply for strategic funding even though they may prefer unrestricted funding for basic research without strategic elements. In Denmark, the increase in private funding is much larger than that of public funding. Additionally, funding from Horizon 2020 (soon to be Horizon Europe) to an individual Danish university is a success for the receiving university but simultaneously has a negative effect on the other national universities' basic funding. Each time a Danish university receives funds from the EU, the same amount is subtracted from the governmental basic funding divided among all universities. In summary, the development of the funding situation of Danish universities is that strategic funding is becoming more and more crucial and hence fitting the goal of the University Law of 2003.

One way to translate the 2003 emphasis on growth and welfare in the Danish University Law is that management should strengthen the ties between their universities and external stakeholders. The objective of management is to support the development of a more 'goal-oriented' organisation, strategically working on solving the problems of society (Pulkkinen et al. 2019, p. 12). The key issue here is the focus shift from basing decisions on funding and strategy on 'internal university dynamics' to basing key decisions of strategy and funding on the desires of external stakeholders (who have the majority vote on the board of directors) (Pulkkinen et al. 2019, p. 14). For instance, the current political and societal focus on a green, sustainable agenda has an effect on what topics politicians and other key actors in society – including public and private foundations – find relevant. From an economic point of view, it is evident that university management will find ways to encourage their researchers to get a share of the strategic funds set aside for (in this case) a sustainability agenda. However, seen from a researcher perspective, it is equally evident that strategic funding comes at a price if your research does not align with the current strategic interest of society and foundations. Strategic funding may challenge the perception of universities as institutions of autonomy that conduct basic research based on the researchers' free choice of scientific approach – at least in those situations where a particular agenda of politicians and foundations differs from the researcher's or department's research agenda.

The CBS Approach to Funding

At the time of writing, the strategy at the CBS is to encourage as many scholars as possible to apply for funding, if their heads of department agree that a particular funding instrument is a workable solution for them and the department. The CBS prioritises particular instruments, in relation to funding for both basic and strategic research. An incentive structure is put in place so that the scholars and their department receive bonuses when attracting funding.

However, writing an application takes time away from research. Similarly, leading a research project with many (international) partners may also take (too much) time away from research. For researchers, time is a scarce resource, which is why not all researchers wish to apply for funding at all times. For this reason, the head of department and the department's funding coordinator help researchers determine if a particular funding possibility is the right choice, considering their current career trajectory. Researchers without tenure are, for example, in a different position than tenured researchers. Similar to other universities in Denmark, the CBS has a research support unit that does all of the administrative work related to applications (e.g. budget, contract, filling out the administrative parts of the application). The goal is to outsource as much of the administrative work to this unit as possible, so that this part of the application effort does not hinder scholars from applying.

Additionally, the funding coordinator in each department, typically a senior scholar with experience in evaluating research proposals, helps with the content of the application. The goal is to raise the quality of the applications such that most applications are eventually funded and time is not wasted. At the CBS, there is also a system in place for sharing successful applications, tailored courses on do's and don'ts for applications and regular emails about funding possibilities focused on the needs of the 11 different departments. As an active researcher myself, it has been imperative to set up a helpful and beneficial administrative system – although this system and the accompanying routines may challenge certain administrative procedures for organising the work. If there are different views on how to organise the work, then I am inclined to favour researchers' point of view, since without their engagement, there will be no work to support, nor any external funding for the CBS.

In most cases, the researcher and university are thrilled when an application is successful. However, sometimes funding comes at a high price for both the scholar and the university. In those cases, it is usually because the researchers have to spend too much time during the funding period on reporting to the foundation, or too much time on coordination of activities and other kinds of administrative work. In the worst cases, a scholar's strong research CV can, after a 'successful' funding period, turn into a weaker research CV, due to not having had sufficient time to write and publish high-quality articles. In relation to the economy of the university, not all funding is equally good. Funding without overhead to cover (part of) the administrative costs accompanying a research project requires an expenditure by the university. Those projects have to fit perfectly with the research strategy of the department, as paying for administrative expenses is money that the university could have spent on research or education. In that sense, not all money is equally attractive for the university. While the global standards dictating the current transformation of universities has seen a slower pace at publicly funded universities, even public universities are to a lesser and lesser extent funded unconditionally by the government, which is also the case for the public universities in Denmark (Paradeise and Thoenig 2013, p. 214). For this reason, managers and faculty have to respond to this new funding landscape, which is why the CBS has strengthened its focus on funding.

IMPOSING GENERAL STANDARDS TO MEASURE RESEARCH EXCELLENCE

Although Danish universities have fewer years of experience with performance measurement systems that measure the quality and relevance of research compared to UK universities, the

CBS has worked with performance indicators for more than a decade. Parallel to other Danish universities, the CBS has developed performance indicators that form the basis for awarding bonuses, promotion and hiring. Since 2017, the CBS has worked with the REEAD model, an acronym for Research, Education, External funding, Academic citizenship and Dissemination. Similar to other international universities, the CBS places strong weight on a scholar's publication record (research), educational merits (education) and ability to attract funding (external funding) when awarding bonuses, hiring and promoting individual researchers, although the other criteria in REEAD count as well. The weighting of the individual criterion is continuously debated at the CBS, as there are different opinions on this issue and how transparent the key processes of promoting, hiring and awarding bonuses are in practice.

Nevertheless, the most revolutionary change concerning the measurement of scholars' research performance is the 2012 decision to measure their output against the journal list of the Academic Journal Guide (AJG, formerly ABS). Other ranking lists at the CBS are the University of Texas at Dallas (UTD) Top 100 Business School Research Rankings, the *Financial Times* Top 50 (FT50) and the Bibliometriske Forskningsindikator (BFI, the standard Danish bibliometric indicator). The AJG ranks a selection of journals from 4*, 4 (top) to 1 (bottom) – a total of five categories. The introduction of this performance indicator was a decision made by the then management of the CBS, a majority of the Academic Council (which includes representatives of the staff) and the board of directors. They agreed that this journal ranking system was a better instrument to measure the quality of publications than the official Danish (and Norwegian) BFI system, which includes all publication outlets and sorts journals into two categories: the top journals (20% of all journals within a field) and the bottom (the remaining 80%). This decision in 2012 to measure research performance against the AJG list led to quick changes in researchers' choice of journals. From 2012 to 2019, the increase of AJG-listed articles rose by approximately 80% (CBS 2012, 2018), and there was an increase of approximately 30% in top-level publications (AJG 4* and 4 articles) from 2015 to 2019 (CBS 2015, 2018). Additionally, as stated previously, the CBS increased its external (public and private) funding steadily, from a yearly intake of around DKK30–40 million at the beginning of the millennium to approximately DKK130 million in the last couple of years.

The strengthened emphasis on AJG-defined quality of research and a researcher's ability to attract external funding are two key parameters when deciding on promoting, hiring and awarding bonuses.

DISCUSSION

It is well known that management must take a university's history and culture into account (Borum and Hansen 2000). Some universities are old and large, with an 'ivory-tower' mentality; others are younger, and their raison d'être is to solve particular societal problems. Some are technical universities; others are business schools or IT universities, and so on. For instance, the CBS was originally a business college, and the transformation into a university meant major changes for the faculty. An international research agenda was introduced, the recruitment of researchers from abroad was intensified, adjustments were made to the educational programmes, and so on. Additionally, the CBS chose a broad translation of what counts as 'business', hiring scholars from very different disciplines, for instance, economics, finance, philosophy, law, political science and sociology. This multiplicity of disciplines has of course caused bumps in the road, but also created a culture of awareness that there is no one model that can fit all departments (or scholars) (Borum and Hansen 2000), as members of different disciplines have different perceptions of, for instance, research quality, research relevance and where to publish. Consequently, complex factors, such as a university's history and culture, cannot be reduced to one or two central dilemmas. However, the history and culture of an organisation, such as a university, are key areas to be attentive to, when (new) structures are put in place by management, if those structures are to have the intended effect.

Performance-based Measurement Systems

When introducing new performance indicators, the goal is to change behaviour. Often, the introduction of a new measurement system will lead to the intended results. However, as with any performance measurement indicator, there is a risk of unintended effects (Dahler-Larsen 2014). Accordingly, Butler (2007) argues for a 'balanced' approach when introducing quantifiable measurement tools. The goal of this balanced approach is for management to develop an awareness of how local contextual factors affect a new tool. This will allow management to take the unintended consequences of any performance instrument into account. For instance, if an incentive system is based on the sheer number of published articles, then researchers may end up changing their publication strategy and publish more articles in lower-ranking journals, with the effect of losing impact. In a highly cited Australian study, Butler (2003a, 2003b) found that a new performance-based funding system introduced by the Australian government led to a decrease in the research impact (number of citations) of Australian scholars, as they began to publish in lower-ranking journals. Similarly, a study of the effect of performance-based research funding in Norway found that it led to a large increase in publication output (Bloch and Schneider 2016) but had no effect on the Norwegian citation impact (Aagaard, Bloch and Schneider 2015). Although the Australian study's findings have been challenged by van den Besselaar and colleagues (2017), there is no doubt that incentive systems have unintended effects, if they are not continuously adjusted to the particular research environment in which they are introduced. As Dahler-Larsen (2014, p. 969) states: 'The idea that performance indicators in public management have unintended consequences is almost as old as performance measurement itself.'

Therefore, when management decides to implement the same quantifiable measurement tool in very different research environments and target different disciplines, they will see that the same performance indicator will have different effects – and this will be the rule rather than the exception (Aagaard, Bloch and Schneider 2015; Hammarfelt and De Rijcke 2015; Paradeise and Thoenig 2013). The next job for management is then to make sure that all effects – intended as well as unintended – harmonise with the problem that the management aimed at solving or the result that management wanted to achieve.

Researchers that critically investigate unintended (problematic) effects of performance indicators aimed at ranking journals often aim their critique towards the guidelines according to which journals are ranked. For instance, one study found that a strong focus on publishing in high-ranking journals can have unintended effects, given that these journals are centred around particular themes within the research field or the use of specific methodologies that may come at the expense of doing innovative research (Willmott 2011, p. 432). In extreme cases, a particular type of research may be abandoned in order to conform to the formal criteria of the high-ranking journal (de Rijcke et al. 2016, p. 163). According to Willmott's (2011) study, an unfortunate reinforcing effect may also occur: articles published in high-ranking journals will automatically be more likely to be cited, thus leading to more and more scholars wanting to publish in these journals, and, as a result, the effect is reinforced (Willmott 2011, p. 437). For instance, the AJG journal list may 'dominate and define the focus and trajectory of a field of research, with detrimental consequences for the development of scholarship' (Mingers and Willmott 2013). In this critical literature, a key point is that not all disciplines can be measured against the same indicators (Hammarfelt et al. 2016; Hammarfelt and De Rijcke 2015), which is why one set of performance indicators will most likely not produce the desired effect in all disciplinary milieus. In these milieus, the indicators may result in practices and production that neither management nor scholars want.

Although global standards, such as systems by which one can rank universities, journals and scholars, affect criteria for promoting and hiring, the local setting – the culture and history of the university and/or department – still matters (Aagaard 2015; Hammarfelt and De Rijcke 2015; Paradeise and Thoenig 2013). Paradeise and Thoenig's (2013) study shows that global standards have not led to a homogeneity of culture in universities and departments, although the same standards of quality (the AJG, for instance) may be used (Paradeise and Thoenig 2013, p. 215; Willmott 2011). There is, in other words, no straightforward connection between the ways global standards are transformed into local practices, as any performance measurement system allows for 'local solutions, also associated with intra-organizational dynamics and organizational characteristics' (Bleiklie, Enders and Lepori 2015, p. 892). Bleklie and colleagues (2015) suggest the concept of 'penetrated hierarchies' to emphasise that intra-organisational control systems (such as performance indicators) are dependent on various external factors. These external factors – for instance, a national funding system, nationally and historically based perceptions of research quality – outline the overall frame that is mediated by the actors in the specific organisational context. So, the control and meas-urement systems work differently in different countries and university environments (Auranen and Nieminen 2010, p. 831). For instance, a very competitive research environment that has a strong focus on research funding may not necessarily perform better than a less competitive funding environment (Auranen and Nieminen 2010, p. 831). Too much focus on funding may in fact be 'dysfunctional', as scholars may be competing with their colleagues for the same funds; thus the focus will result not in more funding but only in more time spent on securing research funding (Auranen and Nieminen 2010, p. 831). The same logic can be used if the tar-geted journals at the department or university level are too few, such that scholars end up com-peting with one another in an unproductive way that does not lead to higher-quality research.

The CBS Approach to Performance Measurement

There is no doubt that the incentive system set in place by management at the CBS affects the behaviour of researchers. Scholars are attentive to performance measurement systems (Ingwersen and Larsen 2014) such as journal lists, amount of funding (and from where), number of articles published and other factors that can easily be measured by their head of department (and colleagues). However, it would be wrong to argue that other criteria, such as academic citizenship, do not matter, or that researchers do not continue to publish books and in outlets outside, for instance, the AJG list, which is the list used at the CBS. This is what makes management complex. The REEAD model at the CBS can be perceived as an attempt to make management decisions concerning hiring and promoting more transparent. The goal of this model is to ensure that the criteria by which researchers are measured are transparent, so that scholars will not be taken by surprise if their career trajectory does not develop as they had anticipated. The goal of the REEAD model is to ensure a holistic focus on the researcher, that is, their accomplishments in research, education, external funding, academic citizenship and dissemination. Management is aware that a well-functioning managerial system must be able to award its scholars according to a number of criteria – including criteria that are not quantifiable. For instance, academic citizenship and dissemination criteria, such as if one is a good colleague, one takes one's share of departmental assignments (head of study programme, assessment work, etc.), one develops teaching skills, engages with the public and so forth.

When deciding on hiring and promoting at the CBS, all of the REEAD criteria are taken into consideration, even though research, education and funding have somewhat more weight than the others. Research is measured according to the AJG, but this instrument has to be supplemented by other information, so publishing with prestigious publishing houses counts as well. Similarly, there may be journals with a high impact that are not on the AJG list but are the best place to publish for a CBS scholar with expertise that falls outside of the AJG list. Education concerns an assessment of how the researcher profile fits the educational need of the CBS, as well as an assessment of the qualification of the researcher in the broader field of teaching. For instance, whether he or she is teaching on all levels, supervising master's and PhD students, developing new courses, engaging with electronic devices in teaching, receiving good evaluations from students, taking on demanding roles as a head of study programme and so forth. External funding concerns the amount of funding, as well as an assessment of the prestige associated with the foundations, for instance, European Research Council grants. External funding is also about team spirit and strengthening research environments. When senior researchers provide money for postdoctoral work to talented junior researchers, it is not only the principal investigator whose research profile will be strengthened but also the junior scholars involved in the project. Academic citizenship concerns the way in which researchers help colleagues in a more general sense. There are many assignments at a university that have to be done, and when deciding to promote and award bonuses, scholars' reputations do matter. In short, academic citizenship has to do with how one is evaluated as a colleague. Dissemination is also key in Danish universities today. As stated in the Danish University Law, universities must have a strong tie to key stakeholders, and their researchers must disseminate their research to the public. The taxpayers pay for the universities, so an important strategy for universities is to disseminate research in a way that makes it accessible to outsiders.

Scholars must score highly on most parameters and definitely have to do well in relation to research, education and external funding (a measurement that takes scholars' career trajectory into account). However, not all researchers perform excellently on all criteria. For instance, not all scholars may find the goal of disseminating their research to the surrounding community an easy (or important) task. These researchers might therefore be compelled to spend their scarce time on publishing in high-ranking journals instead. However, management communicates all criteria in the REEAD model to researchers, and the model is reflected in various documents related to hiring, promoting and the bonus system.

CONCLUSION

This chapter opened by presenting key conditionally based dilemmas that affect university management today. It is obvious that successful implementation of management decisions must consider these dilemmas in order to limit the unintended consequences of the decisions. I have emphasised discussions of the effects of key performance indicators, as organisational research on university management – as well as my own experience as a university scholar and vice dean of research – emphasises the importance of these tools in universities today. In the more critical literature on performance measurement, a central point is that it may lead to what Espeland and Sauder (2007) term 'reactivity', that is, that performance indicators affect researchers' strategies that underscore the perception of research quality embedded in the performance indicators.

However, another key challenge is that research quality cannot be defined in an unambiguous way, as different disciplines have different perceptions of what constitutes research quality. The 'rigour–relevance' debate in business and management research points to this challenge and discusses research quality as a matter of either academic rigour of method and approach, or as research that is relevant to particular stakeholders. Aside from the problem of making a clear distinction between academic rigour and stakeholder relevance, which in my mind do not have to be opposite and mutually exclusive categories, this 'rigour–relevance' debate has furthermore neglected that the two concepts are performed in particular contexts. What counts as rigour or relevance depends on the context and must consequently be investigated with this in mind (Irwin 2019).

Three key contexts for a business school such as the CBS are the academic context, the political context and the business context. The expertise of scholars, departments and universities is measured against international standards of excellence in research and research-based education. Danish universities are public and funded by the state, so certainly a political context is key for universities as well. The CBS produces candidates for the business sector (and to a lesser extent the public sector), which is why key stakeholders, especially from the business sector, represent the third context of relevance. In other words, the opinions of key actors from the international academic community, the political system and the business community are all legitimate contexts. It follows that management decisions must be based on all three contexts when deciding on which goals to strive for and which performance indicators to use to reach those goals.

However, in the critical debate about whether performance indicators are suitable in a university context, the participants frequently overlook that it is legitimate to ask a university to document how and why they are relevant to all three contexts: academically, politically and to the stakeholders that employ university graduates. Obviously, international academic standards – rigour if you like – are the base of a university. Without an aim of conducting research at the highest possible level and delivering research-based education to students, there is no university – either from an academic point of view or from a legal point of view. Key national stakeholders, such as politicians and the organisations hiring the candidates, must of course be heard so that the universities educate graduates with relevant competences (seen from a societal perspective) and conduct research that can help solve the challenges of today's society – large as well as smaller ones. As Irwin (2017) argues, it is legitimate for politicians to want to 'ensure accountability for public funding', to want tools that can help them 'manage universities at a distance', to want 'external quality standard[s]', and so on (Irwin 2017, p. 68).

However, the use of performance indicators should be qualified. The goal is to avoid them leading to 'greater disaggregation; enhanced competition ... a move towards more hands-on management; a concern for more explicit and measurable standards of performance; and attempts to control according to pre-set output measures' (Chandler, Barry and Clark 2002). If the use of performance indicators is not carried out in a qualified manner, ranking systems risk creating 'self-fulfilling prophecies', as Espeland and Sauder (2007) and Dahler-Larsen (2014) argue, because they are based on simplified information that does not reflect the complexity of the contexts that universities are based on. As discussed in this chapter, indicators 'constitute a reality that is put on stage so that it can be acted upon (Desrosières, 1998: 352)' (Dahler-Larsen 2014, p. 983). Performance indicators create a new reality. The goal of management is to continuously reflect on this new reality in order to check if it meets expectations and, if not, to adjust them accordingly.

When research quality is standardised and made quantifiable (in order to rank institutions and researchers), there is a risk of homogenisation in research that blocks novelty and intellectual diversity (Hicks 2012). This is, of course, not a managerial goal, although it may be the unintended consequence of management's approach if they are not continuously reflecting on the effects of the indicators. If international academic standards are dominating the political and business contexts, then the transfer of knowledge from university to society may suffer, because topics of relevance to the national context are not key to an international academic environment (see also the 'rigour–relevance' debate (Hicks 2012)). Hicks (2012, p. 259) refers to a study by Rafols and colleagues from 2011 that shows that a 'narrow and idiosyncratic view of excellence' ends up suppressing interdisciplinary research and hence perhaps a research agenda worth following from an applied point of view, and pertaining to the national stakeholders. However, it is important to reach a workable 'balance', as Butler (2007) argues, so that the historically acclaimed trust in universities is not substituted with an increased monitoring of scholars (Barry, Chandler and Clark 2001).

In summation, when going over the literature, two opposite positions appear: first, in favour of the old university (without performance indicators), and second, in favour of the new performance-based university. Since performance indicators are an integral part of all universities today – nationally and internationally – I will limit the discussion to the pros and cons of the current performance-based university.

The advantage of a performance-based university is that the criteria used for measuring the performance of researchers are transparent. Consequently, the power of management is reduced, and the power of scholars is increased. Visible performance indicators make it clear to all – including scholars – what it takes to be promoted or hired at a particular department and to be awarded a bonus. In relation to gender, research shows how 'the new managerialism' – quantifiable tools, and so on – may have a gendered bias such that female scholars' performance is evaluated lower than their male colleagues (Steinþórsdóttir et al. 2019). However, a key point in gender studies is that when a performance measurement system is transparent, then an opaque (male-dominated) culture is easier to combat. Performance indicators are one way of doing away with nepotism and the documented 'Huey, Dewey and Louie effect'. In addition to this, research has found that performance-based systems lead to more production in all areas.

There are also disadvantages to the quantifiable performance indicators used in today's universities. They cannot stand alone, as management decisions must be context sensitive. There are many ways of gaming the system, for instance, groups of researchers that are joint authors on all their individual publications, research groups that decide to cite each other whether it is relevant or not, research managers that demand to be co-author on all of their junior scholars' work, and so on. Moreover, as shown in the cited literature, performance indicators favour particular disciplines. For instance, in relation to the AJG performance indicator, this tool favours articles over books and monodisciplinary work over interdisciplinary work, as well as multi-author productions and publications in the English language when evaluating which journals are rated 4 or 4*. Despite the best intentions, performance indicators may also suppress research agendas that are based on a scientific approach that falls outside the more classical approaches of top journals.

The point is that university leadership is highly complex, and many management decisions have effects – especially if they are implemented through a quantifiable measurement system. Echoing de Boer and Goedegebuure (2009, p. 359), university management is indeed carried out in a 'complex environment'. Consequently, it is imperative to avoid viewing performance indicators as tools that do not have unintended and constitutive effects (Dahler-Larsen 2014), as this would wrongly imply that a university's culture was an objective, stable environment and that the particular departmental environments had no influence on how the indicators were picked up by staff and management. Indicators are also shaped by the pre-existing culture, as well as how they are framed (Dahler-Larsen 2014, pp. 982–3; Irwin 2017). Therefore, organisational members will pick up management decisions differently; some will be supportive and others will be unsupportive, and this response must be the point of departure for how to continually revisit and adjust decisions, so that they support the goal that they were intended for.

REFERENCES

Aagaard, Kaare. 2015. "How Incentives Trickle Down: Local Use of a National Bibliometric Indicator System." *Science and Public Policy* 42(5): 725–37.

Aagaard, Kaare, Carter Bloch, and Jesper W. Schneider. 2015. "Impacts of Performance-Based Research Funding Systems: The Case of the Norwegian Publication Indicator." *Research Evaluation* 24(2): 106–17.

Auranen, Otto and Mika Nieminen. 2010. "University Research Funding and Publication Performance: An International Comparison." *Research Policy* 39(6): 822–34.

Barry, Jim, John Chandler, and Heather Clark. 2001. "Between the Ivory Tower and the Academic Assembly Line." *Journal of Management Studies* 38(1): 88–101.

Bleiklie, Ivar, Jürgen Enders and Benedetto Lepori. 2015. "Organizations as Penetrated Hierarchies: Environmental Pressures and Control in Professional Organizations." *Organization Studies* 36(7): 873–96.

Bloch, Carter and Jesper W. Schneider. 2016. "Performance-Based Funding Models and Researcher Behavior: An Analysis of the Influence of the Norwegian Publication Indicator at the Individual Level." *Research Evaluation* 25(4): 371–82.

Borum, Finn and Hanne Foss Hansen. 2000. "The Local Construction and Enactment of Standards for Research Evaluation: The Case of the Copenhagen Business School." *Evaluation* 6(3): 281–99.

Butler, Linda. 2003a. "Academic Reactions." *Research Evaluation* 12(1): 39–46.

Butler, Linda. 2003b. "Explaining Australia's Increased Share of ISI Publications: The Effects of a Funding Formula Based on Publication Counts." *Research Policy* 32(1): 143–55.

Butler, Linda. 2007. "Assessing University Research: A Plea for a Balanced Approach." *Science and Public Policy* 34(8): 565–74.

CBS. 2012. *CBS Årsrapport 2012 [CBS Annual Report 2012]*. Frederiksberg.

CBS. 2015. *CBS Årsrapport 2015 [CBS Annual Report 2015]*. Frederiksberg.

CBS. 2018. *CBS Årsrapport 2018 [CBS Annual Report 2018]*. Frederiksberg.

Chandler, John, Jim Barry, and Heather Clark. 2002. "Stressing Academe: The Wear and Tear of the New Public Management." *Human Relations* 55(9): 1051–69.

Dahler-Larsen, Peter. 2014. "Constitutive Effects of Performance Indicators: Getting beyond Unintended Consequences." *Public Management Review* 16(7): 969–86.

de Boer, Harry and Leo Goedegebuure. 2009. "The Changing Nature of the Academic Deanship." *Leadership* 5(3): 347–64.

de Boer, Harry F., Jürgen Enders, and Liudvika Leisyte. 2007. "Public Sector Reform in Dutch Higher Education: The Organizational Transformation of the University." *Public Administration* 85(1): 27–46.

de Rijcke, Sarah, Paul F. Wouters, Alex D. Rushforth, Thomas P. Franssen, and Björn Hammarfelt. 2016. "Evaluation Practices and Effects of Indicator Use: A Literature Review." *Research Evaluation* 25(2): 161–9.

Degn, Lise and Mads P. Sørensen. 2015. "From Collegial Governance to Conduct of Conduct: Danish Universities Set Free in the Service of the State." *Higher Education* 69(6): 931–46.

Espeland, Wendy Nelson and Michael Sauder. 2007. "Rankings and Reactivity: How Public Measures Recreate Social Worlds." *American Journal of Sociology* 113(1): 1–40.

Gulbrandsen, Magnus and Jens Christian Smeby. 2005. "Industry Funding and University Professors' Research Performance." *Research Policy* 34(6): 932–50.

Hammarfelt, Björn and Sarah De Rijcke. 2015. "Accountability in Context: Effects of Research Evaluation Systems on Publication Practices, Disciplinary Norms, and Individual Working Routines in the Faculty of Arts at Uppsala University." *Research Evaluation* 24(1): 63–77.

Hammarfelt, Björn, Gustaf Nelhans, Pieta Eklund, and Fredrik Åström. 2016. "The Heterogeneous Landscape of Bibliometric Indicators: Evaluating Models for Allocating Resources at Swedish Universities." *Research Evaluation* 25(3): 292–305.

Hicks, Diana. 2012. "Performance-Based University Research Funding Systems." *Research Policy* 41(2): 251–61.

Ingwersen, Peter and Birger Larsen. 2014. "Influence of a Performance Indicator on Danish Research Production and Citation Impact 2000–12." *Scientometrics* 101(2): 1325–44.

Irwin, Alan. 2017. "If the Indicator Game Is the Answer, Then What Is the Question?" *Engaging Science, Technology, and Society* 3: 64–72.

Irwin, Alan. 2019. "Re-Making 'Quality' within the Social Sciences: The Debate over Rigour and Relevance in the Modern Business School." *Sociological Review* 67(1): 194–209.

Jonkers, Koen and Thomas Zacharewicz. 2016. *Research Performance-Based Funding Systems: A Comparative Assessment*. Luxembourg.

Kivinen, Osmo, Juha Hedman, and Pivi Kaipainen. 2007. "From Elite University to Mass Higher Education: Educational Expansion, Equality of Opportunity and Returns to University Education." *Acta Sociologica* 50(3): 231–47.

Mingers, John and Hugh Willmott. 2013. "Taylorizing Business School Research: On the 'One Best Way' Performative Effects of Journal Ranking Lists." *Human Relations* 66(8): 1051–73.

Ministry of Higher Education and Science. 2003. *Universitetsloven [University Law]*.

Paradeise, Catherine and Jean Claude Thoenig. 2013. "Academic Institutions in Search of Quality: Local Orders and Global Standards." *Organization Studies* 34(2): 189–218.

Pinheiro, Rómulo, Lars Geschwind, Hanne Foss Hansen, and Kirsi Pulkkinen. 2019. *Reforms, Organizational Change and Performance in Higher Education: A Comparative Account from the Nordic Countries*. Cham: Palgrave Macmillan.

Pulkkinen, Kirsi, Timo Aarrevaara, Laila Nordstrand Berg, Lars Geschwind, Hanne Foss Hansen, Helge Hernes, Jussi Kivistö, Jonas Krog Lind, Anu Lyytinen, Elias Pekkola, Rómulo Pinheiro, Björn Stensaker, and Johan Söderlind. 2019. "Does It Really Matter? Assessing the Performance Effects of Changes in Leadership and Management Structures in Nordic Higher Education." In R. Pinheiro, L. Geschwind, H. F. Hansen, and K. Pulkkinen (eds), *Reforms, Organizational Change and Performance in Higher Education*, pp. 3–36. Cham: Palgrave Macmillan.

Steinþórsdóttir, Finnborg S., Thomas Borsen Smidt, Gyða M. Pétursdóttir, Þorgerður Einarsdóttir, and Nicky Le Feuvre. 2019. "New Managerialism in the Academy: Gender Bias and Precarity." *Gender, Work and Organization* 26(2): 124–39.

Trow, M. and M. Burrage. 2010. *Twentieth-Century Higher Education: Elite to Mass to Universal.* Baltimore, MD: Johns Hopkins University Press.

Universitetsloven [The university act] (2003). Lov om universiteter (LOV nr 403 af 28/05/2003). Retrieved from https://www.retsinformation.dk/eli/lta/2003/403.

Universities Denmark. 2018. *Tal Om Danske Universiteter 2018 [Statistics on Danish Universities 2018].* Copenhagen.

van den Besselaar, Peter, Ulf Heyman, and Ulf Sandström. 2017. "Perverse Effects of Output-Based Research Funding? Butler's Australian Case Revisited." *Journal of Informetrics* 11(3): 905–18.

Willmott, Hugh. 2011. "Journal List Fetishism and the Perversion of Scholarship: Reactivity and the ABS List." *Organization* 18(4): 429–42.

16. Pathways to external funding at departments: how to strengthen a change of culture by empowerment, supportive organizing and leadership?

Enno Hofeldt

1. INTRODUCTION

External funding is in many ways playing a more and more important role for research at universities. It is increasingly shaping the discussions, the discourses, the 'way of working' and the management actions at university departments.

Departments are the 'shop floors' of universities, where novel academic knowledge, insight and new academic value are created and produced – to be disseminated and spread out to the academic world and society.

Departments are more and more dependent on external funding economically. And this dependency – and the need to tackle it – is a constant challenge for department managers, when confronted with the conflicting interests from their researchers on the one side, and the university top management and the strategic and political research funding agenda and landscape on the other.

I want to address this challenge from a two-fold position, first as an 'embedded administration manager' in research environments at departments.[1] Not being a researcher, or being a part of 'central administration' (which is the scapegoat for many researchers and research environments), I bring the perspective of an outsider to give a broader approach to the challenge.

My second position is one of intercultural and interdisciplinary bridge-builder between two different systems at universities – the culture of administration and organization striving to establish compliance and procedural order, and the culture of research and academia pursuing creativity and novel ideas. I have played many roles – as 'translator and moderator' between the often incompatible systems and as 'guide' for researchers through the vagaries of public administration, governance and compliance. Such roles demand compassion for 'the other' as well as personal engagement and interest in order to establish the necessary mutual trust and understanding.[2]

With these perspectives I want to address two key questions: what can departments as the shop floors of academic production do to strengthen and develop their capabilities to attract external funding? How can they bring empowerment of researchers to play together with supportive organizing and leadership in order to create strong environments capable of attracting external funding?

I have dual ambitions in this chapter. First, I want to develop and strengthen the inter-professional collaboration between research faculty and administrative staff on equal terms, advocating a greater integration of their respective professional competences to 'produce' innovative, creative, excellent and relevant research. And second, I want to promote a more holistic approach integrating bottom-up and top-down perspectives on external funding at departments.

2.   MY BACKGROUND

My career started in 'the bunker' of central HR administration at the University of Copenhagen (UCPH), advancing quickly into the role of internal consultant and organizational developer, ending as Head of Secretariat (HoS) at a newly founded department, merged from diverse disciplines and institutional backgrounds. Later, I moved on to a similar position at the Copenhagen Business School (CBS).[3]

I entered into an ever closer and integrated collaboration with my respective Heads of Department (HoDs), acting as de facto deputy and becoming more and more involved in the actual leadership and strategic management and development of the departments.

In the last couple of years, I have worked as Chief Research Advisor in the central Research Support Office (RSO) at CBS, supporting researchers and their departments to develop their ideas and strategies for research and external funding.

I am fully acquainted with the requirements of *compliance* to administrative rules and regulations, and to the organizational strategies from top management, as well as with the expectations of societal stakeholders and partners – knowing 'how to play the game' formally and informally.

I am experienced in the role of *co-leadership without formal authority* over engaged and creative professionals in situations where the professional stakes are high, and the organizational problems are sometimes 'wicked.'[4] I am also fully aware of the challenges and exigencies of *change management and communication* across organizational cultures and borders.

MY FIRST STEP TO BECOMING 'EMBEDDED'

I was preparing the bi-annual 'Welcome to the University' course for new staff and faculty – introducing the different elements of the university across faculties, disciplines and administrations.

Looking for interesting locations to show, I visited the Department of Biology. The HoD introduced me to the activities of the department, and then took me on a tour around the building. In the dark basement, we entered a room where some researchers were looking into a huge electron microscope. He introduced me:

"This is Enno Hofeldt from the University. He wants to see what researchers really are doing." I was invited to the microscope: "Have a look at this fantastic plankton; it has come right from the deepest depths of the Red Sea – that's the real world."

I left the basement a bit puzzled: we were all working at the same institution, but where is 'the real university' – in the 'bunker' of central administration, or here in a basement, looking at minuscule plankton from the Red Sea?

At the same time, however, I am – and will forever be – an 'intruder' with outside-in perspectives on academia and research environments. I was allowed to 'intrude' because I was considered a neutral and impartial outsider and non-competitor with regard to positions, funding or academic bonuses. Even in the position of HoS, I could maintain this role, while I played a more and more active role in the department's management and organizational framework for the research work at the department.

This chapter is based on my personal and professional experiences and reflections. As I have mainly worked in departments from or close to the social sciences and humanities (SSH) domains, it has always been quite easy for me – coming with Master's degrees in Public Administration and in Public Governance – to enter into the research domains of these departments. It would have been much more difficult if I had worked at departments of chemistry or nanoscience. Moreover, my work experience is confined to the Danish system, where universities are public institutions fully integrated into a strong professional culture of public service.

It has been a complex, challenging, but also highly rewarding position – requiring a great deal of *Fingerspitzgefühl* (intuition/flair) – and I feel deeply privileged and grateful to the researchers who have invited and taken me into the 'creative engine room of their research.' As so often, practical leadership is not (and never will be) an exact science but has to develop out of an explorative and mindful approach from any (newly appointed) manager's side, finding a fitting balance between the many sets of responsibilities attached to one's position.

3.   A CASE OF 'BARRIERS TO CHANGE'

I came to CBS some 13 years ago to take the position as HoS for two newly established departments. These departments faced some very tough challenges, which immediately became the defining priorities for the management team, of which I was an integral part as de facto 'deputy' to the two HoDs. The departments were in the humanities end of the wide spectrum of business university domains with a focus on business communication, languages, interculturality and computational linguistics. They had neither a long history, nor a rooted tradition for external funding, nor a competitive culture of international ranking and benchmarking.

At the same time, the departments in question faced an existential threat from changing trends in society, shifting political priorities, declining student enrollment and loss of recognition in the public perception. In short – they were not only facing the individual threat of 'publish or perish,' but they were also confronted with the real organizational threat of 'make yourself relevant and fundable – or perish.' The alternative was academic insignificance and the threat of being left without feasible economic and personnel resources and looming organizational closure.

SOME EXAMPLES OF THE QUESTIONS WE ASKED FACULTY TO CONSIDER, WHEN ELABORATING A NEW DIRECTION FOR THE DEPARTMENTS

How could your specific linguistic research help business and organizations to work in the cultural contexts of, say, France?

Where in an organization or business (at what level, in which function or position) could your findings on intercultural translations be most relevant and contributory?

What could be the job functions which students of your field could go for after graduating?

Many researchers perceived these questions as provoking, bordering on disrespect. However, they were often at a loss in terms of how to respond.

We – the management team – initiated a number of deliberate actions on different levels. We changed the narrative from an *inside-out perspective* (telling and retelling the importance of the field to the surrounding society) to an *outside-in perspective* (exploring how the research could contribute to the problems experienced in society). We invited stronger stakeholder involvement through advisory processes, bridge-building schemes and committed networks – with the department's full support. We allocated resources to qualified internal support. We tried to tell a story about 'what could be in it' for the researchers if they could frame their research as fundable. And we introduced a culture of dialogue and coaching processes of research ideas and projects, including formalized mentoring sessions, allocation of dedicated feedback and support resources.

However, it was to no avail in the end; the department was closed a couple of years ago – the external odds were too high and the internal barriers too strong.

WHY IS IT SO DIFFICULT TO UNDERSTAND 'THE OTHER'?

Coordinated management of meaning (CMM) and intercultural communication have developed a basic concept of the influencing and defining cognitive and mental layers involved when communicating – what we understand and perceive of our conversations:

* The cultural values
* The organizational perspective
* The professional values
* The individual 'life scripts'
* The relation and its history
* The episode and its context
* The content at the core.

Inspired by and collated from Pearce and Gudykunst (see endnote 6).

During the last couple of years as Chief Research Advisor in the central RSO, I have encountered corresponding barriers – though colored by their specific cultural and disciplinary contexts, when working with other researchers from across CBS. It showed me that it is a potential challenge faced by many researchers and many departments across academic fields.

I have drawn a number of lessons from this experience. First, as my immediate professional notion as an administration manager (to take a systematic and organizational approach to implementing change – 'how difficult can it be?') failed, I had to completely reconsider my 'toolbox of possible actions.' Substantial change in organizations for highly engaged and creative professionals requires a long-term change of mindset, culture and meaning, and I had to take my role as intercultural bridge-builder seriously.[5]

Second, such processes of change require mutual trust and understanding between researchers, management and administrative staff. Existing barriers to change have to be identified and addressed openly by engaging in meaningful and constructive dialogue with intercultural respect. To stimulate any change, you have to put yourself in the positions, perspectives and ambitions of your partners on 'the other side of the bridge' and co-develop a convincing narrative on 'what's in it for her or him?'[6]

Third, you have to provide the necessary support at the department in order to avoid and 'disarm' any notion from the researcher's side of 'being left alone to cope.'

And fourth, you have to develop a coordinated, holistic and strategic leadership practice at the department to support these processes of change.

In the following section, I will address some of the perceptions and reasons lying behind these barriers. In the final section, I will unfold some potential pathways for initiating, supporting and leading such necessary processes of change.

4.   WHAT LIES 'BEHIND' THESE BARRIERS TO CHANGE?

For many researchers – and here I once more have to stress the point that my experiences mainly stem from SSH – the concept of seeking external funding for their research, designing a project and actually writing an application, is still often shrouded in mystery and they may have many reservations about the process. Frequently they have had few – and often unsuccessful – experiences in this task. They do express uncertainties and doubts about their ideas, their chances, their competences, their approach and the societal and organizational contexts they are venturing into.

To be sure, there are generational differences – young researchers are now much more accustomed to the necessity of attracting external funding for their research. But especially they often express doubts and uncertainties based on an (often real) lack of experience and competences, while at the same time being overburdened by the many tasks, obligations and cultural pressure they face when starting out on a research career.

I will address some of the central barriers, which I as an outsider often hear 'between the lines,' when talking with researchers 'off guard.'

4.1   Why External Funding, and Why Bother About It?

External funding is increasingly crucial for universities and departments – and is increasingly framing and shaping their approach to organizing and doing research.

First of all, the proportion of unconditional government funding of university research in Denmark has fallen over the last 10–15 years. This is mostly due to a remarkable increase in research funding from private and other non-governmental sources. On the positive side, many more resources have become available. On the negative side, the research environments have increasingly 'to work for it' – it is no longer 'delivered unconditionally to their doorsteps,' a development that has resulted in profound changes in the 'rules of the game.'[7]

Research funding is now nearly exclusively allocated based on (more or less) strategic considerations,[8] be they explicit political priorities, particular priorities of independent corporate/private foundations, or following a very floating notion of 'current societal hot topics.'[9] Departments and individual researchers are now forced to develop more and more elaborate approaches and strategies to secure and increase a vital level of research funding for their research – and to be prepared, should any relevant call 'pop up.'

Second, policies for research funding from government sources are governed by an ever stronger focus on the relevance and societal impact of research. Research funding is seen as an 'investment' with specified goals and objectives to create 'value for the benefit of society.'[10] Even with regard to the basic public funding of research, the government is increasingly inspired by the 'good example' from the Research Excellence Framework (REF) concept in the UK, linking funding to the documented impact of research conducted at specific universities – a concept adopted by universities when distributing funds internally to research environments and departments.

Finally, the ability to attract external funding from competitive sources is increasingly integrated into performance assessment schemes and management priorities at universities – putting the 'responsibility to deliver' on the shoulders of the individual researcher and departments. From the perspective of department (and university) management, external funding is a potentially unlimited source of funding 'only waiting to be tapped.'

In short, the landscape of external funding has become a more important and discourse-setting dimension in the daily running of a department, with the ever-increasing number of funding sources each promoting their explicit (or tacit and sometimes even contradictory) interests in the research they want to fund. It has entailed a marked change in the conditions for research especially in the SSH domains, leading to frustrating discussions and existential tensions in the academic world. Who is to set the priorities for the research: the individual researcher under the banner of 'freedom of research,' or the funders, 'paying for the music and deciding the playlist'?

Even though many researchers see and (often reluctantly) accept these perspectives as 'prevailing conditions of the trade,' they still often do express a distance and even serious reservations towards these conditions.

4.2   What's In It for Me: Why the Effort?

Many researchers express frustrations – it is too much bother, it takes time from my research, where is the good idea, can it lead to an application? Many researchers even see the push for external funding as something imposed by politicians and university management – distancing themselves by only just complying to a minimum level, while declining the notion of seeking external funding motivated by a wish to enhance their own research.

SOME TYPICAL STORYLINES ABOUT EXTERNAL FUNDING

- It's something I have to do, HoD is checking up, I have to show something.
- We have this strategy at the university – but it is bollocks, they don't know what research really should be about.
- What's in it for me? I don't have time at all, I have to teach, I have to publish, I have to …
- The calls are never relevant for me, they are too strategic, too applied, too specific, too general – and they give no real scope for my research.
- I don't have the right network or the necessary experience or qualifications to have a chance.
- The administration is chasing me when I have projects. It takes too much time.
- Why do we have to make our research relevant? I do basic research …
- I have tried many times, but my research field does not seem to interest them.
- I do not receive the support I need, or the recognition from the department.

The list in the box can easily be extended – many people at universities know and express these storylines. They can seem anecdotal, but anecdotes often have a core of relevant truth behind them. Moreover, anecdotes do develop into narratives, condensing and transforming into organizational cultures – and are passed on to new recruits and younger generations.

I have increasingly seen it as my foremost task as research supporter to enter into a dialogue and demonstrate to researchers what could be 'in it for them' with regard to external funding, making the effort worthwhile.

4.3   The Burden of an Individualized Performance Culture

Over recent years, a more collaborative culture in the SSH domains has developed, formerly being characterized by a traditional role model of the 'lone rider' working in highly specific fields with her/his own methods, publishing (preferably) monographs. Many departments have established more or less formalized research groups, paper seminars and co-teaching concepts.

On the other hand, the increasing focus on performance assessment of the individual researcher, the rising practice of co-authored journal publications boosting the participants' individual h-factors,[11] the skewed valorization between articles and monographs in metrical assessment and the uneven valorization across disciplines have all affected and pushed the research culture and practice in a more individualistic direction. This is putting a high pressure on individual researchers – giving the 'call of publish or perish' an ominous tone. To new recruits to university administration (and non-researchers) I often use the metaphor of 'entrepreneurs in research' to describe the work situation of researchers.[12]

Is this individualistic performance culture the optimal way to develop ground-breaking and innovative research in an ever faster moving world with its ever more complex challenges? Under all circumstances, it puts a heavy burden on (especially the younger) researchers when establishing the base for their future career, and it raises a great challenge for responsible leadership at the department – how best to align these contradicting demands and perspectives?

4.4   External Funding Is Just a Lottery

Many researchers express great frustrations about the low success rates at many foundations and funders. In a way, many have 'given up in the lottery,' and many chances for leveraging innovative and creative ideas are lost.[13]

With success rates as low as 8% for rather prestigious starting grants from the Danish Research Foundation, for young tenured researchers establishing their career,[14] it is very difficult for them to make an 'entry' and develop a track record of external funding. Even senior researchers at CBS rarely have a long and continuous track record of successful external funding of their research. No wonder that voices proposing a change of the allocation system to a kind of (real) lottery have become stronger in recent years.[15]

When researchers ask: "What can we do to enhance our chances – which 'tricks' can we apply to be included on the shortlisted group?," it can be difficult and often impossible to give a satisfactory reply. Voices from funding institutions respond that they only go for 'pure quality and excellence of the idea and proposal.' However, I have misgivings about the decision processes at some funders, when having to prioritize too few funds between all too many qualified applications. Organizational decisions are never purely objective and neutral, but always subject to individual judgment and 'politicized discussions.'

My consoling explanation to researchers is (even though it is a little unsatisfactory) that they have to work on three lines – develop a 'selling and intriguing idea on a hot topic,' while at the same time design a sound academic project proposal – and then be prepared to try again and again. This poses an extra challenge for researchers – they are in general not familiar with 'presenting and selling their research' in communicative terms.

Finally, from a departmental perspective, this very uneven distribution of external funding gives a high degree of unpredictability and fluctuation of income streams over the years, making it a great challenge to develop strategic plans for sustainable 'income' from external funding to supplement the declining sources of regular institutional funding.

In short, external funding is not governed by a linear relation between 'effort and award,' but is a 'seriously messy affair' for the individual researcher as well as for the department management.

4.5   I Don't Have the Necessary Skills and Competences

I have met many researchers who were really challenged to their limits by the exigencies of applying for external funding. They gratefully welcomed the help I or my colleagues could give. They were engaged and absorbed by the creative process, but lacked the skills and competences to adopt their research visions to the often very explicit and complex concepts and procedures from the funders.

A STORY ABOUT 'A SOLUTION WITHOUT A PROBLEM'

Two senior researchers had received a number of rejections of project proposals. They could not understand the reasons for this, especially as their idea in all aspects was about a hot and very relevant societal topic.

After reading the rejected proposals, I had to tell them that they had presented their concept (which was their heart's blood) as a universal solution – while they had completely missed the point to relate this solution to a problem, a solution without a problem.

This is not meant disrespectfully. Researchers are experts and professionals at doing research. But they often do not know so much about the operational demands of designing and running a project of many millions of Danish kroner with 5–15 staff ranging from professors to PhDs and student assistants with a range of external partners from business or organizations. This does call for professional competences in organizational management and governance.[16]

Typically the lack of skills and competences is clustered around these topics:

- The design, structure and organization of the project;
- The involvement of internal and external partners with clear expectations and working arrangements;
- How to tell the story in an application – writing the narrative;
- Project governance, navigating between stakeholders, partners, participants and support staff;
- Project management, i.e., compliance with administrative rules and regulations;
- Communicating and negotiating with external partners, stakeholders and the public;
- Understanding 'how organizations work' – from internal politicizing and campaigning to 'playing the organizational game' of public institutions.

This situation is aggravated by the traditional silo-fication of universities along organizational and professional lines. Research faculty and administrative staff function and work in two distinct systems – the former oriented towards the content of research in an often international context, whilst the latter generally focus on procedures, correctness and administrative compliance in national terms. Researchers do not understand and often have difficulties accepting what they perceive as 'vagaries from administration' – while administrators 'despair' at researchers' lack of compliance and respect for rules and regulations. Such mutual perceptions stand in the way of developing a free-flowing collaboration and interchange of knowledge, practice and experience between the two groups.[17]

A COMPETENCE PROFILE FOR AN IDEAL RESEARCH SUPPORTER

- Full proficiency in administrative matters and in-depth experience from the funding landscape;
- Experience with coaching and supportive co-creative processes;
- A broad understanding of the strategic (research) landscape;
- A 'bridge-builder competence' enabling intercultural understanding;
- A talent for appreciative, constructive and empathetic communication.

The challenge for a university and its departments is how to provide this essential support; how to identify and develop the professional competences of the individual research supporters, and how – at the same time – to develop a strong, flexible, competent and strategic organizational set-up for making this support available. In my experience, universities and departments lose 'all too much gold on the ground' by not making this kind of support available to researchers in need.

5. NEW PATHWAYS TO EXTERNAL FUNDING: WHAT CAN DEPARTMENTS DO TO INSTIGATE CHANGE?

The central challenge for departments – the 'shop floors of academic value creation' – is how to address and overcome these barriers, and how to strengthen and develop strong capabilities to attract external funding.

My key notion is 'empowerment'[18] – how can department leadership best motivate, stimulate and support researchers and create a culture of collaboration and enthusiasm for external funding, whilst respecting the integrity of the individual researcher and their individual research ambitions?

New and sustained pathways to external funding can only be developed through a holistic bottom-up and top-down approach at the department. Many departments (and universities) put great effort into measurable and metric performance assessment systems as a basis for monetary bonus systems designed to incentivize researchers to engage more in external funding. However, appreciative systems purely based on 'metrics and money' must be supplemented with supportive 'soft measures' like providing opportunities to acquire the necessary skills and competences, providing qualified support and suitable tools to achieve these goals, and establishing supportive organizational cultures and recognizing engaging leadership practices.[19]

My approach to these challenges unfolds over three levels:

- On the **personal level**, focusing on *empowerment*;
- On the **organizational level**, focusing on *support structures and resources*;
- On the **management level,** focusing on *strategic and supportive leadership practices*.

These levels of approach can be taken up separately. However, in my experience, such complex and multidimensional challenges involving personal attitudes, organizational practices and management style, require matching, appropriate and multifaceted approaches. It is not enough to focus on just one or a few levels and instruments, when the overall challenge is a change of culture at the department.

5.1 Empowerment, Competences and Change of Culture

Departments cannot change the overall pressure for external funding. But they can actively engage in creating a supportive environment. On the personal level, a number of initiatives can be unfolded.

WHY APPLY FOR EXTERNAL FUNDING?

The benefits for the researcher(s) include:

- Enhancing one's CV and boosting one's career;
- Obtaining funds at one's own discretion;
- Profiling of the research field;
- Ready access to data 'from the real world' – benefitting research;
- Attracting junior researchers to boost the field and one's line of research;
- Establishing professional networks in and outside the university;
- Experience in project management;
- Freedom to do the desired research – with less interference from management;
- International networks and travel.

And some more collective benefits:

- Profiling of the research topic – a stepping stone for future funding;
- Attracting researchers to your group;
- Stepping stones leveraging access to potential organizational partners and collaborators.

What can be in it for me – and for us?

As external funding has become an 'unavoidable' part of being a researcher, it is important for departments to develop a positive narrative about it, exemplifying and demonstrating, 'what could be in it' for the individual researcher and the research environment.

Some focal topics include:

- Creating a spirit of collective engagement and ambition towards some high but still achievable goals, lifting the burden from the individual researcher's shoulder and giving it a collective drive;
- Creating a narrative of how to 'master the rules of the funding game' – how to (re-)gain power and ownership of one's research ambitions, plans and activities including applying for external funding – instead of working under an impression of 'always running after aims outside the actor's set-up';
- Creating a culture of mutual trust, supportive backing and recognition at the department to motivate and enthuse potential project makers to 'risk it.' As most first-time applicants for external funding fail, and even many senior researchers struggle, it is important to create a culture of trust and appreciation – you learn best from failures in appreciative collective settings;

Venturing into external funding demands high academic, personal and emotional investment from the researcher. The risks of failure are high – it is important to mitigate the risks to personal standing, to career development and to the ability to attract future collaborators and funding.

Oversights, skills and competences

It is very important that departments (and universities) provide both opportunities for researchers to acquire the necessary competences and skills, and the necessary qualified, competent and engaged support resources.

The initial step is a critical individual and/or collective appraisal of the research idea – is it a strong idea? Does it have the potential to create academic novelty? Will it create value and benefit for potential funders? In addition, is external funding the right instrument at this moment, or should the idea mature further over the coming years?

Second, it is important to acknowledge the *communicative character* of writing a project proposal. In very limited space you must convey the full picture of your envisioned research project, enabling the readers to fully understand and assess your proposal. Writing a proposal is a specific *genre* with its own rules and format.

Finally, it is very important to (begin to) develop a personal research strategy aligned with a concrete career perspective – a question also applicable and relevant to a collective perspective:

> *Where do I want to go with my research; what are the questions and problems I want to explore?*
> *What are my ambitions and aims and where can I find 'partners and backers'?*
> *Be explicit about your own core interests, and then try to frame and reframe your research ideas from an outward-in perspective – the funders only provide possibilities, but you set the agenda.*

And the answers can feed into a concrete research plan for the coming, say, three to five years with specific milestones like:

> *Preparing a proposition for X foundation next year, for Y foundation in two to three years, and aiming at a European Research Council application at the end of five years.*

These initial steps should be actively supported and integrated into a regular dialogue between the individual researchers (or group) and the Head of Department.

After these preparatory steps, the core skills and competences are:

- An overview of the funding landscape – what are the funding possibilities, what are the perspectives of the funders, what are the requirements?
- An awareness of the exigencies about research funding, i.e., how to frame and align one's research to the academic, strategic, political and societal priorities of the funders;
- An ability to 'tell the story' – how to create a convincing narrative;
- An ability to design and structure a project feasible and capable enough to explore and answer the problems one wants to address;
- Knowledge of project management, i.e., about the running of a project and the leadership of a team;
- Networking competences both inside university and academia as well as with societal actors;
- The ability to attract relevant and well-known researchers as well as junior partners like postdocs and PhDs;
- The broad aspect of 'organizational competences' – not exactly 'being an organizational expert,' but having a 'nose for hidden pitfalls' – and knowing who to engage and when in order to avoid them.

Based on my practical experience, I developed the *Project Model Canvas* as a conceptual framework for facilitating project development from idea phase through project design and organization to the final application (Table 16.1). This model unfolds over four logical steps and phases, and provides a hands-on toolkit to preparing a coherent research proposal.[20] The model can be applied on the personal level by individual researchers, and it can facilitate discussions in research groups.

Table 16.1   Project Model Canvas

PROJECT MODEL CANVAS		
The CONTEXT	**WHY and WHAT** The key perspectives	**The HOW**
The FUNDERS The *funding landscape: what are* the funding possibilities ? The priorities and strategies of the funders – what results do they want? Their "track record & practice" ?	The WHY The challenge – the problem Why important & relevant - and for who ? The state of the art – the academic context What's in it for you – motivation & ambition	Project DESIGN The structure & progression Methodology & data Project group & partners Core activities "Final event" & dissemination
The STAKEHOLDERS Relevant stakeholders for your project – from academia, business, organizations, civil sector etc. Legitimacy, support, partnerships.	**The PROJECT IDEA** **The core problem** **The research questions**	Project ORGANIZING Partners, participants and AB Detailed activity plan Timeline & project plan The budget Compliance to guidelines & rules
For WHO – the BENEFICIARIES Who will benefit from your results – and how – persons, sectors, organizations, societal segments, interest groups, academic fields ?	The WHAT The objectives – what do you want to achieve – the novelty and value created. Outcome & Impact – expected change in society – making a "better world".	The APPLICATION Who are the "readers" ? The narrative with convincing storyline & logic. The limits of space

Notes: A comprehensive approach to idea development and project design. The core idea is a spiraling process around the core PROJECT over multiple iterations. The process is logically structured over several phases, starting with the *WHY*, the *WHAT*, and the *FOR WHOM*, continuing to identify the *external contexts and funding sources*, coming to the *design and organizing* of the project, ending up in the 'last step' – telling the story and *writing the application*.

Other supplementary initiatives I can recommend to departments or RSOs include:

- Facilitated hands-on workshops for researchers to present and work with their ideas, while receiving input and constructive feedback from group members and a facilitator;
- Integrating the *Project Model Canvas* as a module into PhD programs or programs for assistant professors;
- Including this model in 'welcome packages' for foreign faculty, preparing them for the funding landscape and practices around external funding.

Networks, stakeholders and partners

Collaboration across domains, sectors and professions is becoming a more dominant element for research projects. Funders increasingly demand interdisciplinary approaches to solve complex societal problems, and they require more and more commitment and involvement of relevant societal actors and stakeholders.

THE 'NETWORK STAIRCASE'

As a researcher, you can develop your network strategically by thinking in terms of 'steps on a staircase' from small involvement to strong commitment:

- Start following up on your student's projects where they have established contacts to business or organizations;
- Invite these contacts as guest lecturers to your courses;
- See your graduates as ambassadors for your research;
- Promote the idea of PhD fellowships and industrial PhDs to your students and your network;
- Invite your contacts into your projects – first as contributors, then as advisory board members, as partners, or even as co-funders;
- Develop joint projects with them.

It is therefore very advisable to make a comprehensive stakeholder analysis for your research field broadly, and for your project proposal specifically. It can be immensely supportive and essential to have a clear overview: who are the stakeholders that could benefit or otherwise be affected and involved by your research?

Stakeholders can contribute by:

- Legitimizing and qualifying the problem and project concept;
- Showing relevance and interest;
- Participating with relevant perspectives, methods and concepts from other disciplines;
- Providing sources for data collection and fieldwork;
- Committed project partnership and co-responsibility.

Stakeholders can be manifold, and it is important not just to 'call in your friends.' My advice is to be ready to challenge yourself by inviting and involving diverse and even contradicting perspectives in order to sharpen and strengthen your research direction and your proposal.

Finding relevant project partners, contributors or advisory board members for specific projects just a few weeks before a deadline does normally not work. Establishing joint understanding, trust and alignment of expectations usually takes a much longer time. In addition, specific competences are required to act as 'scout and bridge-builder' between stakeholder and researcher to develop committed and lasting networks.

Many researchers, while having strong international academic networks, possess neither specific competences nor necessary time resources to engage in such a process. I therefore recommend that departments allocate dedicated resources to support researchers to develop their stakeholder-portfolios.

In addition, departments can strategically identify and engage relevant individual (and organizational) stakeholders as a broad form of *external advisory pool*, representing a multi-faceted 'outside-in' perspective to the department.

5.2   An Organizational Framework for Support

On the organizational level, all initiatives to strengthen and develop the capabilities at the department need qualified support structures. It is important to ensure the full integration of these structures and processes in the ordinary working and running of the department. With my experience of university practices, I recommend starting with these support functions at the department proper – the risk of losing momentum, when not having control and the full 'right to take action', is a well-known side-effect of many centralization processes.

I have four key proposals for departments (and universities):

- Appoint a *research coordinator* from faculty. The research coordinator could support and deputize for the HoD in all matters regarding research development and funding initiatives. He or she would be the vital link and coordinator between the researchers and supporting staff – i.e., the *project partner* – and would have the responsibility to initiate workshops and processes, ensuring the overall quality of research and funding activities.
- Appoint an *academic project partner*. A qualified and competent administrative person familiar with the funding landscape, proficient in project design and organizing, and – most important of all – proficient in giving feedback, supervision and coaching of researchers. In other words, a dedicated *project developer cum bridge-builder cum communicator cum mentor*, mastering the art of 'making things happen.' This project partner will follow researchers closely, becoming familiar with the research field, methods, potential topics and contexts, and network partners.
- In order to avoid the downsides of decentralization, the university should establish a centralized research support function, responsible for:
  - Specialized functions like coordination and support around EU programs and calls;
  - Constant coordination and upgrading of skills, competences and methods across all project partners from the departments;
  - Support to inter-department/interdisciplinary initiatives. This will build a sound base for constructive co-creation across the professional staff and research faculty, (hopefully) overcoming the 'silo-fication' I have so often experienced.
- Establish formalized, but flexible and adaptable *review and quality control processes* of research proposals.[21] Encouraging researchers to pitch their project idea and test their concept to an 'outsider' from another group, discipline, profession, or from the 'outside world,' can be a very strong and constructive way of providing qualitative feedback on potential relevance, value creation and project feasibility. Such initiatives need the creation of a culture of mutual trust, supportive backing and recognition, as mentioned above.

These initiatives can be supplemented with smaller, concrete actions like mentoring workshops for junior faculty (PhD and postdoc); paper presentation lunches; writing retreats; introductions for foreign faculty to the Danish and European funding landscape and practices;

or facilitated workshops directed at preparing proposals for specific sources like innovative or industrial research.[22]

It takes a long time before such new processes of co-creation become 'institutionalized' and an integral part of the department's daily practice and working. The managing of sustained cultural change in knowledge organizations is always an 'investment' in a long-term process. The fruits may only become visible over several years.

I can already hear some loud objections from departmental and university managers: "We do not have the resources to implement all these ideas, it's too expensive; the payback of the investment is too low." I would like to turn the question around – can departments (and universities) afford not to invest resources in strengthening their capabilities to attract external funding? Most of my proposed initiatives do not require many resources. Much can be gained by innovative rethinking, reframing and refocusing of roles, activities and practices at the department itself – and in intra-organizational collaboration at the university.

5.3   Create Supportive and Strategic Leadership Practices

Leadership practices are essential in order to leverage this great change of organization and culture within a department. Management of change is a long-term process, needs a clear strategic and visionary direction, and a 'daring, insisting and enduring' leadership effort from department management – first of all from the HoD, but necessarily also backed and actively supported by key persons from faculty at the department.

My most important recommendation to a newly appointed HoD, following my question from the outset – *what can departments do to develop their capabilities to attract external funding?* – is to take a step-by-step approach to initiating some of the most relevant small-scale changes mentioned above, constantly keeping the long-term perspective in mind, and slowly changing the discourse through constant dialogue, argument and open discussion. Too explicit top-down management will invariably lead to insecurity, distancing and outright resistance.

However, I also have a number of specific proposals:

- Establish multi-professional management structures with dual leadership from both academic and administrative backgrounds, organized in a committed leadership team;
- Develop accountable and fair practices for performance assessment and appreciative recognition, with criteria specific for the department and its field of research, to support the motivation, creativity and engagement from both faculty and staff in external funding – avoiding any drive for the 'easy way' of rigid metric and automatic models;
- Dedicate specific initiatives for recruitment, education and mentoring of talented and promising young researchers – and to retain them not necessarily physically, but as part of the knowledge network of the department;
- Develop the above-mentioned *external advisory pool* into a strong *network of relevant societal partners* closely collaborating with the leadership team, and supporting the research direction and strategy for the department. Their role should be to act as ambassadors for the research (and teaching) done at the department to the surrounding world, and act as a 'mirror from the outside world' asking the researchers how they can contribute to challenges 'in the real world.'

I can hear some further objections: "We have to focus on academic rigor and excellence in order to be able to attract world leading researchers and keep the high level of international recognition." Again I would like to turn the question around – can a department (and university) in the long run afford to prioritize 'the excellent few' and leave behind a broad group of well-qualified researchers and research fields deprived of attention and funding?

In my view, it is important to develop a broad, qualified base, from which many 'hotbeds' of innovative research groups with the potential of – one day – becoming (maybe world) leading environments may emerge. Therefore, it is important to support and nurse equally the broad base as the 'excellent few' at departments and universities.

6.   CONCLUSION

Embarking from the question of 'what can departments do?,' I have discussed many different aspects, approaches and 'knobs to turn.' There is no 'one size fits all,' there is no easy fix and there is no ready-made program to take down from the shelf.

And there are often many barriers – barriers based on multilayered personnel, cultural and organizational 'perceptions of reality' – if one is to open up to a long-term change of culture and practice.

Long-term results with external funding take many years to prepare. They demand a holistic and clear strategy and vision from department management, as well as engagement and backing from faculty and staff – and last but not least, from the university as well.

I hope that I have been able to provide insights and inspiration for new departmental managers, faculty and research support staff, navigating in the 'choppy waters' between professional and organizational silos. I particularly hope that I have been able to present the potential value of inter-professional collaboration and co-creation between faculty and support staff and between university and the surrounding society.[23]

7.   PERSONAL REMARKS

I am not a researcher, but I have always marveled at researchers since I first heard my brother-in-law, a physicist and postdoc in England in the 1960s, anxiously describing his wait for the shortest imaginable moment, when an iron block would make a (nearly unperceivable) hop at the instant when all its uncountable atoms would swing in the same direction. Well, I never did ask him about the societal relevance of the 'iron block hopping' – as I would have done today. However, he was engaged and driven by a quest for finding new knowledge.

Therefore, I often ask researchers: what is motivating and driving you, what is your dream and vision, what would you like to change with your research? In my view, research is not just about career, success and personal gain, but about 'something more profound and existential.' I always try to convey this enthusiasm and motivation – even when I hear researchers talking about everything being better in the old days and lamenting the stark conditions surrounding research and external funding.

In my relation to researchers, I'm very inspired by this ethical demand by the Danish philosopher K.E. Løgstrup:

> Trust is not of our own making; it is given. Our life is so constituted that it cannot be lived except as laying oneself open to another person and putting oneself into that person's hands either by showing

or claiming trust. By our very attitude to the other we help to shape that person's world. By our attitude to the other we help to determine the scope and hue of his or her world; we make it large or small, bright or drab, rich or dull, threatening or secure. We help to shape his or her world not by theories and views but by our very attitude towards him or her. Herein lies the unarticulated and anonymous demand that we take care of the life which trust has placed in our hands.[24]

I often feel myself as having a special responsibility for researchers who put their trust and 'heart's blood' into my hands, when I am trying to help and guide them and their dear ideas to places, where they (hopefully) can find funding and advance their careers. It has been a great privilege and I am very thankful for the trust they place in me.

NOTES

1. I use the term 'embedded' to indicate the need of '*being together on the business*', sharing the deliberations, experiences, successes and failures of the researchers.
2. Such fluctuating roles raise many ethical and existential questions on relations, leadership and management. Where do I belong professionally, how do I communicate, where is my loyalty? Personally, whenever in doubt, I side with the researchers.
3. CBS is a business university providing a broad portfolio of research domains and academic areas – supplementing the traditional business school fields with areas like psychology, communication, sociology, anthropology, philosophy and politics.
4. Encountering many academic prima donnas and fiefdoms at my departments, I was very inspired by Koppenjan and Klijn's perspective of networking in complex and fluctuating organizational set-ups around wicked problems – translated into a university's internal political landscape. See Helle Hein, Primadonnaledelse [*Management of Professional Prima Donnas* – my translation], 2013, https://www.saxo.com/dk/primadonnaledelse_helle-hedegaard-hein_epub_9788702122596, or Joop Koppenjan and Erik-Hans Klijn, 2004, *Managing Uncertainties in Networks*, London: Routledge, among many other publications on this topic.
5. I am inspired by leadership scholars like Steen Hildebrandt, Karl E. Weick, Flemming Poulfelt and Ole Fogh Kirkeby, who stipulate the necessity of understanding the organization and its people, focusing on meaning, relationships and dialogue.
6. Here I am drawing on inspiration from the concept of *Coordinated Management of Meaning CMM* developed by W. Barnett Pearce (see *Interpersonal Communication: Making Social Worlds* (Longman, 1994) and "The coordinated management of meaning (CMM)," in W. B. Gudykunst (ed.), *Theorizing about Intercultural Communication*, 35–54 (Sage, 2005)), and William B. Gudykunst's approach to Intercultural Communication (see "An anxiety/uncertainty management (AUM) theory of effective communication," in the same 2005 volume).
7. The Danish Think Tank (DEA) has produced a number of reports about research funding in Denmark, directing attention on some often overseen facts and effects; see, for example, "Universiteternes Økonomiske Råderum" ["The Economic 'Liberty of Action' of Universities" – my translation], 2019, DEA and CBS (only in Danish), https://dea.nu/i-farver/publikationer/universiteternes-okonomiske-raderum/.
8. Traditional research councils like Independent Research Fund (DK IRFD) and The National Research Foundation still have a very high focus on the academic aspects and quality of research as main criteria for allocation of funds. However, even IRFD has recently introduced thematic calls, the topics decided by the Finance Act in Parliament. And it had even a very specific call on research on COVID-19 in April 2020.
9. When the COVID-19 crisis struck, some four to five extraordinary calls were announced for research funding in specific COVID-19-related topics and challenges – mostly in health areas, but also with some focus on SSH implications.
10. The Innovation Fund Denmark (IFD) calls their contributions *investments* with the aim of developing unmet (societal) needs; see https://innovationsfonden.dk/en.
11. Following a long-standing practice in Health and Natural Sciences.

12. Researchers constantly have to design and redesign their field of 'research production'; they have to update and develop new 'products' in the form of new knowledge, insights and academic novelties. They even have to find 'investors and funders' to provide them with employment and funding for their projects – just like 'real' entrepreneurs do in the business sector.

13. Of course, much research is conducted without receiving any external funding, but applying for external funding provides the possibility of leveraging the potential impact of the research idea with more resources.

14. "Annual Report 2018 – Statistics," DFF Independent Research Fund Denmark, 2019, https://dff.dk/aktuelt/publikationer/annual-report-2018-statistics.

15. See, for example, David Adam, 2019, "Science Funders Gamble on Grant Lotteries," *Nature*, https://www.nature.com/articles/d41586-019-03572-7.

16. I am fully aware that things have changed since I organized the first course for newly elected HoDs at the University in 1997. Today there is a broad range of courses available from specific courses on university management to more broad scope master courses in public governance. And there are many focused courses preparing researcher leaders for the challenges of project responsibility. The IFD in Denmark even 'includes' an executive project management course for the PIs (principle investigator and responsible grant recipient) in their larger grants.

17. I have worked on both sides – and I know the perceptions and positions from staff and researchers alike. Even though Luhmann's autopoietic communicative systems usually apply on a society level, the conceptual framework and perspective can give a greater understanding of the challenges of university organization and how to navigate between these systems and silos (unpublished working paper by the author).

18. I understand 'empowerment' as all initiatives with the aim of enhancing and strengthening the capabilities of a person to navigate in a given context, including skills, competences, overview, agency and a feeling of 'being able to cope' with the challenges arising.

19. Flemming Poulfelt gives a very good and comprehensive description of such practices in his article "On the Particular Challenges of Managing Professionals"; see Chapter 1 in this book.

20. This model is until now unpublished. However, I apply it in my support and mentoring of researchers and research groups. A workshop series on this model: *PROJECT DESIGN for external funding – a hands-on workshop from concept over design to final proposal* is under preparation for CBS faculty and staff in October 2020.

21. Imposing obligatory processes on creative professionals in knowledge organizations, especially universities, can be very challenging. I come back to one of my *lessons learnt* above: *You have to argue, convince and empower researchers through constant dialogue, showing 'what could be in it for them' as well as for their academic field.*

22. The Innovation Fund Denmark (IFD), especially, has a very specific concept and approach for the projects they want to fund, with many requirements not familiar to many researchers.

23. I would be happy for any comments and feedback from readers. I can be contacted at eh.research@cbs.dk or ehofeldt@mail.dk.

24. K.E. Løgstrup, 1956, *The Ethical Demand*, Oxford: Oxford University Press (with slight linguistical adjustments).

PART V

Collaboration with other disciplines and practitioners

17. Collaborating with practitioners

C. Anthony Di Benedetto, Adam Lindgreen, Marianne Storgaard and Ann Højbjerg Clarke

---

1. INTRODUCTION

A recent editorial of *Industrial Marketing Management* (Lindgreen & Di Benedetto, 2018) noted that too often an article's managerial implications consist of "a simple rewording of the results section and little else" (p. 2). We offer insights to the explicit collaboration between academics and practitioners from the outset of a research undertaking. That is, research that is of interest to academics, but also clearly has meaning and importance to the practitioners involved. This is the 'rigor versus relevance' argument: rigorous articles that provide significant theoretical insight are influential and highly cited, but relevance means a real contribution to both academics and practitioners.

Inspired by Chesbrough's (2003) seminal work on open innovation, the principles of collaboration and the idea of working with many different partners and sources in order to innovate in a sustainable manner (Laursen & Salter, 2006) are prevalent in most organizations (Hernandez-Espallardo, Osorio-Tinoco, & Rodriguez-Orejuela, 2017). As no single organization is likely to possess all the resources needed to operate successfully and solve all the problems it faces (Pera, Occhiocupo, & Clarke, 2016), collaboration is used as a means to solve complex and diverse problems among individuals, teams, and organizations.

The basic aim of collaboration is to pursue goals collaboratively that otherwise would be difficult to pursue. Collaboration is described as situations where individuals or teams work together and share learning across disciplinary or organizational boundaries (Hibbert, Siedlok, & Beech, 2016; Huxham & Vangen, 2005). The idea is that while individuals lack adequate experience, context, and expertise to solve complex and diverse problems, collaboration offers greater epistemic authority, as collaboration allows the organization to solve problems that require capabilities based on inputs from multiple specialties (Beaver, 2004).

Although research historically has revolved around innovation (Desai, 2018), debate currently focuses on why and how academics should engage in university–business collaboration (Clauss & Kesting, 2017). Although university–business collaborations have increased markedly in relevance over the past decade, little remains known about them (Perkmann et al., 2013). For example, academics often intuitively and implicitly take an inside perspective (i.e., that of the university) when discussing 'collaborative research,' but this is just one side of the coin in university–business collaborations. The outside perspective (i.e., that of the business) is the other side of the coin in university–business collaborations, which then typically are termed 'collaborative innovation' (e.g., Hernandez-Espallardo, Osorio-Tinoco, &

Rodriguez-Orejuela, 2017; Lakemond et al., 2016; Najafi-Tavani et al., 2018). We contribute to the literature by identifying the similarities between, and the differences in, these two types of university–business collaborations. To this end, we draw on past literatures including that on academic–practitioner collaboration (Bartunek, 2007), collaborative theorizing (Nenonen et al., 2017), critical engagement (Bridgman, 2007), engaged scholarship (Van de Ven, 2007), and impact scholarship (Antonacopoulou, 2009).

The remaining parts of this chapter are organized as follows. In Section 2, we describe how universities and businesses often have very different motivations for, and expectations of, engaging in university–business collaborations. In Section 3, we outline typical challenges that each of the partners face when engaging in university–business collaborations. Finally, in section 4, we suggest how insights and advice given to practitioners about how to engage in university–business collaborations could serve as an inspiration for academics aspiring to engage really well in such collaborations. One place to start is for academics to recognize that practitioners are not a homogeneous group, and that it is important to develop competencies that permit ongoing learning and continuous improvement in collaboration skills.

2. MOTIVATIONS FOR, AND EXPECTATIONS OF, ENGAGING IN UNIVERSITY–BUSINESS COLLABORATIONS

2.1 Business Perspective

From a business perspective, collaboration, involving a wide range of external partners and sources, has long been an important part of business modus operandi. The meeting of people with different logics, mindsets, skills, and ideas spurs innovative thinking and allows room for radically new ideas (Beaver, 2004). Studies find that organizations generally benefit from collaborating with other organizations (e.g., Cruz-González, López-Sáez, & Navas-López, 2015; Feller et al., 2013) and from involving external partners including suppliers, customers, and competitors (e.g., Najafi-Tavani et al., 2018). For example, collaborative innovations have been shown to expand the knowledge base and the innovation capability of an organization (Alexiev, Volberda, & Van den Bosch, 2016; Heirati et al., 2016).

Collaborative innovation, however, is characterized by being complex and risky, and involving highly unpredictable outcomes. Therefore, collaborative innovation comes with many potential sources of conflict (e.g., De Araújo Burcharth, Knudsen, & Søndergaard, 2014). As a result, collaborative innovation efforts often are described as "troublesome arrangements" (Hibbert, Siedlok, & Beech, 2016: p. 26) and as "highly resource-consuming and often painful" processes (Huxham & Vangen, 2004: p. 200), with no clear criteria for a common approach. It is therefore not surprising that collaboration presents difficult problems that can lead to misunderstanding and ineffective learning (Hibbert, Siedlok, & Beech, 2016: p. 26). Recent studies describe how collaboration can be inhibited by cognitive barriers (Skippari, Laukkanen, & Salo, 2017), problematic power dynamics (Chicksand, 2015), and differences in relational norms (Zhou et al., 2015), among others.

Universities present particular important collaborative partners for businesses (Etzkowitz, 2010; Perkmann & Walsh, 2007; Winkelbach & Walter, 2015) because universities spur and enable both technical development and product and organizational development in businesses (Shaw & Allen, 2006). Universities promote real problem solving and continuous improvement (Pecas & Henriques, 2006) and act as co-producers of innovation (Muller & Doloreux, 2009). As research per se typically is not the goal of university–business collaborations when seen from a business perspective, businesses sometimes regard universities as advisors or consultants in innovation processes. This perspective underscores a traditional assumption that businesses mostly are interested in finding quick and efficient solutions to their immediate problems (Pasmore et al., 2008, p. 12) and in prescriptive knowledge immediately applicable in the organization.

Recent findings, however, that managerial interest in university–business collaborations is not limited to prescriptive knowledge, as managers equally are interested in using theoretical knowledge both conceptually and symbolically, challenge this traditional assumption (Åge, 2014). Following this perspective, businesses have ample reasons to engage with academic consultants rather than commercial or practice-based consultants. Academic consulting goes beyond the mapping stage (of benchmarking and comparative research); ideally, academic consulting challenges current practice and existing benchmarks (Docherty & Smith, 2007: p. 277). Furthermore, in contrast to commercial or practice-based consultants, businesses perceive academic consultants to be neutral. Rather than concerning themselves with the issue of 'repeat business,' academics are preoccupied with maintaining academic rigor while at the same time providing publicly accountable results (Docherty & Smith, 2007: p. 278). Businesses therefore know that they receive honest and direct advice from their university partners.

2.2   University Perspective

Most academics, basically, collaborate with practitioners in order to collect data that can give grounds for new academic knowledge. Academics ultimately are evaluated by their publication performance (Lindgreen et al., 2019). This is what grants academics legitimacy, and publishing in prestigious journals, therefore, is what typically drives academics. During past decades, academia has witnessed an increasing heterogeneity in research design. There is a tendency that academics within business and social science turn to more collaborative research design through which they engage with external partners (Antonacopoulou, 2010; Godin & Gingras, 2000; Pettigrew, 2003). Questions have been raised about the role that universities play in society and the relevance, or the societal impact, that universities have (Pettigrew & Starkey, 2016). This issue has been described as the 'rigor–relevance gap' (Hodgkinson & Rousseau, 2009) or the 'theory–practice gap' (Van de Ven, 2007).

University research typically is criticized for being too distant from practice to have real meaning for society. A one-sided focus on academic impact, therefore, can threaten the legitimacy of academics (Aguinis et al., 2014). As a result, academics are expected to be more innovative and collaborative (Darabi & Clark, 2012) in the way they do research. There is increasing acknowledgment that research within business and social science – in order to stay relevant – requires that academics transcend boundaries between communities and perspectives, and that academics form productive collaborations with practitioners (Antonacopoulou, 2010). Therefore, academics achieve knowledge generation through collaboration, as mutual engagement is a necessary stepping-stone to, and the most important enabler of, societal impact (Pera, Occhiocupo, & Clarke, 2016). Societal impact is increasingly an important motivation for academics to engage in university–business research collaborations. There are a wealth of studies debating research relevance, using different concepts such as 'applicability' (Barge, 2001), 'usefulness' (Learmonth, Lockett, & Dowd, 2012), 'impact' (Leahrey, Beckman, & Stanko, 2017; Smith, 2018), and 'relevance' (Vicari, 2013). Research projects are designed with specific regard for the nature and objectives of co-produced knowledge and the different ways that different audiences consume it (Nenonen et al., 2017).

Another widespread motivation for academics to engage in university–business research collaborations is based on economic considerations. Internationally, there has been a continuous decline in public funding of research activities, which has led many universities to search for new ways of generating income and to commercialize their skills and research (Darabi & Clark, 2012; Heckscher & Martin-Rios, 2013). This development has spurred an increasing motivation for universities to engage with businesses and to create stable relationships with them. Furthermore, due to rapid changes in general competition and speed of innovation, universities aim for stronger links with businesses (Plewa, Quester, & Baaken, 2005). Arguably, a paradigm shift is underway shifting the role of universities from primarily research and education towards also involving the role of "creating collaborative and innovative opportunities through engagement with industries" (Darabi & Clark, 2012: p. 478).

However, while establishing new funding streams is important for universities, few academics engage in collaboration with businesses only for financial gain. Academics assume, "or at least hope, that academia and practice are compatible" (Bartunek & Rynes, 2014: p. 1195). Walker (2010) questions the feasibility of close university–business collaborations, however, and points to problematic issues in the collaboration process such as who owns the right to define the problems to be researched: "who has the knowledge to state the questions, and whose language and forms of expression dominate. The question, therefore, is whether academics should engage only in weak versions of collaborations, that is, little more than conversations between academics and practitioners" (Walker, 2010: p. 206). Similarly, the scientific value of collaborative research sometimes has been questioned: while collaboration may be a sensible activity to undertake, it does not necessarily lead to improved research (Kieser and Leiner, 2009: p. 528). Academics should hold their cognitive and emotional distance to their research object(s) in order to fulfill their genuine function of generating knowledge characterized by critical reflections on current practices (Kieser & Leiner, 2009).

2.3   Discussion

Searching for answers to the question of how academics can engage really well with practitioners, a first relevant issue to address would be the differing motivations and expectations between universities and businesses for entering university–business collaborations. Businesses typically collaborate with their surroundings to challenge their own existing practices, to expand innovative thinking, and to use the knowledge to come up with new perspectives and ideas that could spur product, technical, and organizational development.

Universities, in contrast, tend not to search for challenging unexpected input, but rather to look for answers to problems they often have specified in advance. Publishing is a clear priority on academics' agenda, and too much improvisation and creative changes of direction in the collaboration process often is hard for academics to handle. Therefore, academics need to acknowledge this gap of motives and expectations, ensuring that the university–business collaboration is useful and relevant for both parties. This means that academics should have in-depth knowledge about why their practitioner partners choose to collaborate with them, and what these practitioners expect to gain from the collaboration. It is important to consider the needs for, and commitments to, the collaboration from both parties. The academic collaboration leader should thus be able to excel in management of expectations.

Practical relevance of university–business collaboration often is limited because much theory becomes "lost in translation" (Shapiro, Kirkman, & Courtney, 2007: p. 249) due to a lack of coherence between the problems investigated by academics and the actual problems that practitioners face. Academics sometimes assume that a theory is 'right,' and needs to be properly disseminated to practitioners, for the theory to gain relevance. It may, however, be better to assume that the theory itself can be improved through interaction with the practitioner community (Jarzabkowski, Mohrman, & Scherer, 2010: p. 1193). Traditionally, only academics have taken the role of defining research questions, but many practitioners are very well educated, some have obtained PhD degrees themselves, and therefore certainly are able to develop researchable research questions with meaningful theoretical contributions and managerial implications (Nenonen et al., 2017: p. 1136). For their part, academics increasingly are aware that they must engage in research that is useful to practitioners, as this will ensure trust between universities and businesses (Santini et al., 2016: p. 1841). The expectations from both parties about the outcomes of the collaboration, therefore, need to be managed in order to build trust within the relationship (Vangen & Huxham, 2003).

By continuously collaborating with practitioners within their research field, it becomes much easier for academics to engage and embed their research in ways that make it relevant for both parties. This has led scholars to call for increased contact and interaction between universities and businesses (Bartunek, 2007; Heckscher & Martin-Rios, 2013). The role of the academic leading a university–business collaboration thus calls for a certain professional outlook. The academic needs to be in touch with, and to join the conversation of, the practice field investigated. Through involvement in different collaborative research projects, academics build common ground and a bridging position in the business environment, which then can serve as building blocks and antecedents to the larger research projects (Spekkink & Boons, 2016).

As a final observation, through collaborations the involved parties get the opportunity to connect with previously unconnected partners and, along the way, trusting relationships between them may develop (Inkpen & Tsang, 2005). Academic research needs to return to pragmatism in the sense that not only should research produce relevant academic knowledge, but there is also a need for research to be socialized (Fendt, Kaminska-Labbe, & Sachs, 2008). Practitioners should be included in research processes as active, reflective, and empowered participants. Similarly, criticism that most discussions about including practitioners in research still revolves around an 'if' question, discussing whether or not it is possible to produce valuable research knowledge in collaboration with practitioners, it would be relevant to rather ask 'how' collaborative research can be managed in order to yield both theoretical and practical value (Nenonen et al., 2017).

3. CHALLENGES IN UNIVERSITY–BUSINESS COLLABORATONS

3.1 Business Perspective

Questions remain whether collaborating with universities actually is an advantage for businesses in terms of innovation performance (Du, Leten, & Vanhaverbeke, 2014). For example, practitioners are not likely to turn to academic journals and seek out research studies on management strategy or practice, when making business decisions (Rynes, Bartunek, & Daft, 2001). Practitioners experience that collaborations often turn out as unsuitable outputs that do not meet the needs of their businesses (Pertuzé et al., 2010; Marzo-Navarro, Pedraja-Iglesias, & Rivera-Torres, 2009). A literature review of university–business collaborations identifies that many businesses join collaborations with high expectations in terms of benefitting from these collaborations (Yassi et al., 2010). Yes, practitioners often are disappointed to find out that academics are most concerned about their own interests (obtaining data for publication purposes, obtaining research funding, or getting academic promotions), and not necessarily focusing on the practitioner's needs (Yassi et al., 2010). Practitioners thus find that the common university–business platform is often utilized for the sole purpose of serving the academic's interests.

From the outset of a business–university collaboration project, most businesses expect the collaboration to show feasibility and practical usefulness of the businesses' innovative ideas. A characteristic of universities, however, is that they work at a slower pace, and one that businesses may not be able to influence in the collaboration process (Lazzarotti et al., 2016). Businesses, therefore, sometimes find it almost painful to work with universities that focus on long-term academic endeavors (Darabi & Clark, 2012). Businesses find the bureaucratic system and the slow-motion culture of universities stifling of any kind of innovative progress (Darabi & Clark, 2012). Furthermore, "peculiar features" characterize academics and challenge practitioners (Lazzarotti et al., 2016: p. 144): Academics, for example, operate with more autonomy and freedom than practitioners do. For academics, the potential societal or monetary benefits of a collaborative outcome are less interesting than their own scientific publications and reputation. In general, studies identify how cultural differences between academia and business can result in differing attitudes and objectives of collaborations (Arvanitis, Kubli, & Woerter, 2008; Ylijoki, 2003). Additionally, the lack of trust between academics and practitioners can be a barrier to collaboration. Practitioners may fear outsiders and be unwilling to provide information to academics who may share it with competitors (Darabi & Clark, 2012: p. 487). While businesses traditionally have opposed the sharing of innovations by claiming exclusiveness in non-disclosure agreements (Lee, 2000), collaborations call for careful alignment of joint development agreements (Mehlman et al., 2010).

3.2 University Perspective

In academia, much debate is going on concerning what good research is and, ultimately, which approaches the academic society favors in terms of publishing. In focusing on how to theorize with managers, Nenonen et al. (2017) note that collaborative university–business research relies heavily on creative abductive approaches. Abduction may be defined as an approach where innovation and creativity play a role in the scientific method (Mingers, 2014: p. 53). Using an abductive approach, however, may cause problems for the academic in the reviewing process, because most journal reviewers are more comfortable with deductive and inductive reasoning (Nenonen et al., 2017). Proponents of collaborative approaches such as action research would argue that abductive action research provides results that practitioners may need, but academics may not value (Gustavsen, 2003: p. 93). Such collaborative research often is deemed of minor, less valuable importance than other scientific approaches. Consequently, despite its potential, action research is still very much underrepresented, especially in the A-level journals (Kieser & Leiner, 2012).

Collaborative research typically is somewhat more time-consuming than more classic approaches to research. For example, the effort of recruiting practitioners for collaboration is a lengthy process (Nenonen et al., 2017). Academics easily can end up in situations wondering whether engaging in a university–business collaboration is worth the effort. Successfully publishing academics may feel that there is not much to gain by collaborating with practitioners (Shapiro, Kirkman, & Courtney, 2007). Yet, few studies have sought to measure the effect of collaborative research and whether this assumption is true. The studies available suggest that researchers undertaking collaborative research do not necessarily compromise their other academic objectives by doing so (Godin & Gingras, 2000).

There also is the problem of objectivity. Collaborative, interventionist researchers do not simply observe and collect data, they also offer solutions to the organization's problems, and the fact that they are conducting their research within an organizational environment indeed alters that environment (Arnaboldi, 2013). Such an approach raises concerns about the quality of a study's theoretical contribution because researchers might be so absorbed in finding the optimal organizational solution that they do not sufficiently reflect on the theoretical implications of the findings (Arnaboldi, 2013).

Engaging in collaborative research and "socializing new knowledge" (Nenonen et al., 2017; p. 1146), comes with a cost because it challenges certain academic conventions. While the demands for more societal impact and relevance draw researchers towards more collaborative approaches, academics often are discouraged to follow such approaches because such efforts are often not adequately recognized by universities or included in their key metrics (Nenonen et al., 2017: p. 1146). Incentive systems currently dominating the universities result in scholarly work that may indeed be irrelevant, except to other academics (Bartunek & Rynes, 2014: p. 1187). The choice of whether and how to engage with businesses is often contingent on the particular management philosophy at the university. Local faculty attitudes are central in determining whether the university is willing to aim for impact beyond academia (Pettigrew & Starkey, 2016). If, from a faculty perspective, impact outside the realms of academia is of secondary concern, it could potentially widen the gap between academics' focus on publication and the expectation of outside stakeholders (Pettigrew & Starkey, 2016: p. 659).

Academics engaging in collaborative research also have to be aware of how their work could serve certain business interests and influence current business practices. Clearly, relevant academic knowledge can strongly upset the organizational power balance (Jarzabkowski, Mohrman, & Scherer, 2010: p. 1193). Academics must therefore reflect on who the recipient of academic insight should be: the powerful businesses and practitioners, or more marginalized decision makers who lack power (Jarzabkowski, Mohrman, & Scherer, 2010: p. 1193). Although there is a strong argument that research should stay relevant to the externally generated demands coming from the practitioner's world (Vicari, 2013: p. 173), this approach can result in ethical dilemmas. Yassi et al. (2010) suggest that while universities should engage in service learning and participatory action research, they should also protect the professional integrity of their faculty who are engaging in such research with their practitioner partners (p. 485). The ethical dilemmas that academics face when engaging in university–business collaborations can be considerable when participating businesses have invested significant amounts of money in the collaborative research. Indeed, Nenonen et al. (2017) hold that university–business collaborations may face scrutiny for ethical misconduct, especially in the case where private-sector research funding is a significant component in the university's faculty metrics and incentives (p. 1147).

3.3 Discussion

In essence, university–business collaboration represents a collision of logics and a clash of different perspectives and challenges. As very different actors, with very different agendas and dilemmas, participate equally to find answers to a shared problem, a great deal of epistemic reflexivity is called for from the academic collaboration leader, acknowledging that no one partner in the collaboration – not even the collaboration leader – has all the answers in advance. The involved partners collaborate to reach common reflection and cognition, not only in defining the research problem, but also throughout the research process. This means that the academic collaboration leader will need to approach the collaboration with an open mind and a willingness to learn. This is, however, a central challenge for many academics because this requires that they open the door to external constituencies and stakeholders and invite open discussion of their research purposes and objectives (Heckscher & Martin-Rios, 2013: pp. 137–8). Only a revolutionary change in mindset will enable academics to do this.

Collaboration fosters opportunities for co-poiesis, which Bouncken (2008) defines as "the joint birth of knowledge" (p. 43). Distinguishing between knowledge combination, learning, and co-poiesis, Clauss and Kesting (2017) regard co-poiesis as a two-way phenomenon that leads to a synergetic combination of knowledge, which provides benefit for all participants in the collaboration (p. 188). By combining different perspectives on problem solving in intense interaction, co-poiesis has considerable potential for joint innovative generation of new insights.

In a similar vein, Hibbert, Siedlok, and Beech (2016) distinguish between two modes of engagement, namely instrumental collaborative exchange and curiosity-driven dialogue. While a rather limited approach in which knowledge is borrowed from partners for the purpose of a particular project characterizes the former mode of engagement, the latter mode of engagement enables a process of self-change and learning through engaging with others. In a curiosity-driven dialogue, people are reflectively aware of how disciplinary specialization is a constraint for learning. Therefore, the curiosity-driven dialogue is based on an acceptance of less certainty about the issue being studied, the outcomes that might emerge, and the costs and benefits that may be accrued (Hibbert, Siedlok, & Beech, 2016: p. 38). Curiosity-driven dialogue opens the arena for new discussions and allows for deeper understanding of the knowledge and perspectives of others; there must exist a willingness to learn from those participants who may benefit from these discussions (Bartunek, 2007: p. 1328). Such relational attitude serves as an alternative to the more traditional linear attitude, in which the researchers some-times tend to bring not only the questions, but also the answers when interacting with practice.

Following this line of thought, collaboration leaders must carefully evaluate their own prac-tices and be aware of their own limitations and constraints. A single, specialized researcher will lack the required experience, context, or expertise to solve a sufficiently complex problem; collaboration allows the solution of complex problems, the solutions for which will not reside within the boundaries of any one academic specialty (Beaver, 2004: p. 403).

4.   DISCUSSION: HOW TO ENGAGE REALLY WELL IN UNIVERSITY–BUSINESS COLLABORATIONS

While most articles would end up suggesting a number of managerial implications, we con-sider here the implications that the preceding discussions might have for academics or, to be more specific, academic collaboration leaders engaging in university–business collaborations. In searching for answers to the question of how academics engage really well with practition-ers, we acknowledge that there are no simple or easy answers, or quick-fix solutions.

A wealth of studies have focused on systemic issues such as the need for the academic system to expand a culture of relating to, and collaborating with, businesses and to recognize and support those individuals who excel at developing relationships with the practitioner com-munity (Darabi & Clark, 2012: p. 490). It is important for the university system to learn from collaborating business partners, as these have shown an ability to engage with multiple stake-holders and to mobilize diverse knowledge sources in creating positive and practical results responding to complex problems (Heckscher & Martin-Rios, 2013). Although it would require tremendous changes in the university system to develop such collaborative capabilities, it is required in order to spur changes to current practice (Heckscher & Martin-Rios, 2013: p. 139). University faculties are central when it comes to setting a course of collaboration (Pettigrew & Starkey, 2016) and, therefore, there is widespread demand for the scientific community to rethink the metrics used to evaluate scholarship such that academics are encouraged to attempt interdisciplinary research (Leahrey, Beckman, & Stanko, 2017: p. 132). Also, at an individual level, there seem to be important issues that academics – with the ambition of engaging in collaboration with practitioners – could benefit from considering. In the following, we suggest three such issues: conversation with practitioners, collaborative competences, and constant learning.

4.1   Conversation with Practitioners

Most academics are busy with research, education, and funding applications. With a chronic lack of time, developing relationships with businesses risks becoming academics' lowest priority (Darabi & Clark, 2012). For some academics, relating to businesses is a rather exotic endeavor, which is much more challenging than the classical tasks of research, education, and funding applications. However, personal relationships and social networking are key require-ments in collaborative relationships, and in order to generate that academic collaboration leaders need to join the conversation of the field of practice that they want to engage in (Darabi & Clark, 2012).

To 'socialize research' (Fendt, Kaminska-Labbe, & Sachs, 2008), academics need to engage in a long-term relationship with practitioners. Successful collaboration typically is the culmination of a long-term relationship (Benneworth, 2001). Indeed, the real benefits of collaborations tend to arise in dealing with problems that arise during the collaboration process. That way, the collaboration impacts both the university and the business, possibly in unforeseeable ways, by affecting the social relationships that actually produce and use knowledge (Benneworth, 2001: p. 226). This implies that building long-term relations, and following an open-minded approach to the collaboration, are both important.

Academics, however, tend to be protective of their resources and traditions, having perhaps a perception that dealing with external parties such as practitioners can be unpleasant, time-consuming, and frustrating (Heckscher & Martin-Rios, 2013: p. 139). Recent studies speculate why collaborative approaches often are deprioritized. Power dynamics, a need for security, and egoistic individualism are some of the possible factors explaining why people avoid collaborations (Raelin, 2018). In a similar vein, decision makers in businesses tend to suppress their use of collaborative engagements with external stakeholders when their legitimacy is at risk, for example, when the business' actions are perceived to be controversial (Desai, 2018: p. 220). While these studies do not focus specifically on university–business collaborations, they might serve as inspiration here. For example, is the reason why academics refrain from university–business collaboration that they might find themselves challenged by lacking experience in leading such collaborations or that they experience little or no control of the collaborative research?

A collaboration leader needs to be appreciative that practitioners are far from being a homogeneous, uniform group of collaborative partners. Often, academics tend to treat practitioners as a kind of 'black-box group,' for example by using the term 'business' when referring to any non-university organization (Clauss & Kesting, 2017: p. 186). By regarding and treating all practitioners as one, academics risk overlooking the specificities of the very diverse group of practitioners from various sectors, businesses, and professional environments, and how they might represent very different approaches to, and aspirations for, the collaboration with universities. Maybe more sensitivity and reflexivity in discussing specifically how particular businesses can benefit from collaborating with universities would be of value.

Clauss and Kesting (2017) argue that most university–business collaborations are driven by academics who only are decision makers within the universities. Therefore, practitioners should know the particularities of working with academics and understand how they react. The question could be turned around: What should academics be aware of when collaborating with practitioners? A starting point would be to recognize that practitioners are not a homogeneous or uniform group of potential collaborative partners.

4.2   Collaborative Competences

Academics who hope to improve practitioner collaboration need to develop a skill set, which will serve them effectively. Collaborative research leaders often take on a role as the challenger, a role that involves "challenging, re-conceptualizing and generally thinking innovatively about practitioner agendas" (Pollitt, 2006: p. 261). The ability to challenge and question a business's taken-for-granted assumptions is a key competence that academics must have, but it requires both comprehensive professional knowledge and professional authority to engage in such a way. Universities that incentivize an intellectual environment in which assumptions are questioned and challenged obtain a unique competitive advantage and can substantially and positively influence the practitioner community (Paton, Chia, & Burt, 2014: p. 269).

Indeed, the role of academics should not be to offer immediate solutions of practical problems. Rather, academics must be prepared to open up the field of possible actions, shedding light on the situation itself, as well as on the problems to be solved (Jarzabkowski, Mohrman, & Scherer, 2010). An important element of this academic role is the capability to 'relevate' (Paton, Chia, & Burt, 2014), meaning to expand the range of issues under consideration, or to include issues previously thought irrelevant, into the decision process. Paton, Chia, and Burt (2014: p. 267) suggest that academics are, interestingly, in an ideal position to accomplish these changes, due to their ability to offer different and challenging viewpoints to practicing managers and decision makers. These authors note, however, that academics are more likely to contribute value to practitioners if they seek to challenge conventional wisdom and familiar decision-making mindsets, rather than simply focusing on decision makers' immediate concerns. It is the act of creating dissonance on the part of managers that leads to the consideration of new and previously ignored decision-making possibilities.

Taking part in and leading university–business collaborations call, however, for a careful awareness of a particular set of competences. Studies have stressed the importance of culture and competences among individual collaboration partners, as this determines the execution of the collaboration process (Del Giudice & Maggioni, 2014). While some academics might be naturals in leading collaborative processes, some would argue that "the pressures on universities around funding and near market commercial activities are such that many academics are being forced into such activities when they are perhaps not suited to the task" (Docherty & Smith, 2007: p. 275). Academics will need competences that stem from the fields of, for example, facilitation, consultancy, and project management, which are not part of classic academic training (p. 275).

For example, studies have shown that inter-organizational collaborations call for appropriate socio-psychological features and mindsets and a high propensity to interact and share knowledge (Jolink & Dankbaar, 2010; Lazzarotti et al., 2016). Bartunek (2007) points to the relational attitude of academics when arguing that "bringing one's whole self to an engagement with others, being genuinely interested in their experience, demonstrating trustworthiness, and seeking feedback from them represent crucial relational attitudes that create high-quality connections" (p. 1328).

In a similar vein, a genuine interest in the practitioner's life world is important. The concept of 'interactional expertise' is the competence that an academic can draw on when interacting with people whose practices and relationships the academic wants to study in a meaningful way (Collins, 2004). Interactional expertise involves the ability to understand and communicate about a domain that the academic does not practice. Academics that possess this interactional expertise have learned how to work with specialists, with their own particular knowledge and interests. That is, they encourage specialists to share this knowledge and discuss technical content and context. Thus, the academic not only accesses and becomes familiar with the specialist's knowledge, but develops a real appreciation for it (Langley et al., 2013: p. 6). Kieser and Leiner (2009) often are cited for their skepticism towards collaborative research yielding valuable academic output, but they address the value in academics facilitating collaboration where research is not the intended output. From that point of view, these authors point to the competences of being bilingual and bi-competent facilitators who are "able to speak the language of practice and science but also be able to transfer schemas between the two contexts" (p. 528).

4.3   Constant Personal Learning

To engage in fruitful collaborations with practitioners, academics must be willing to learn from their collaboration partners. There cannot be any collaborative research unless all partic-ipants share a fundamental interest in learning and in reflexively examining and questioning the shared work (Pasmore et al., 2008). In addition, academics should learn throughout the research process, through interaction with practice (Jarzabkowski, Mohrman, & Scherer, 2010). Theories are approximations of the real world, and new information results in better understanding, better theory, and ultimately, frameworks, which are more useful for appli-cation in practical settings. Therefore, every time an academic is involved in a practical application of an organizational theory, it is an opportunity to improve or modify the theory (Jarzabkowski, Mohrman, & Scherer, 2010: p. 1196).

While some studies on collaborative innovation highlight the concept of absorptive capacity when discussing "the ability of a firm to recognize the value of new, external information, assimilate it, and apply it to commercial ends" (Cohen & Levinthal, 1990: p. 128), these studies typically do so in evaluating the learning capacity of the practitioners (e.g., Najafi-Tavani et al., 2018; Wu, 2014). Following the idea that academics have to learn on equal terms as practi-tioners, it is relevant to discuss the concept of absorptive capacity on the academic side of the collaboration. As noted by Gioia (2013), academics often call for organizational change and may sometimes complain that practitioners are slow to change their organizations; however, academics themselves may not 'practice what they preach' in this regard.

Thus, instead of placing the locus of learning and change solely with the practitioners, as academics often do, the collaboration leaders might benefit from applying what has been called a practice orientation to research. According to this view, academics are seen as prac-titioners themselves, who collectively have accepted the implication that their own practice is incomplete and in a constant state of change (Antonacopoulou, 2010: p. 221). Antonacopoulou points to the potentials in practice-relevant scholarship, which focuses critically on the research practice itself and calls for research practitioners to engage in 're-search' and in "reflexive cri-tique about the ways in which they perform their research practices" (p. 220). This highlights the idea that academics engaging in university–business collaboration have to be open minded, ready to learn, and willing to change the course of direction of the collaboration if new relevant discoveries appear along the way. In the end, that is what university–business collaboration is all about.

Overall, we argue that we need to look for learning potential in the way academics engage with their surroundings, and we call for greater sensitivity and reflexivity in the way aca-demics collaborate with practitioners. Importantly, to improve collaboration, academics can themselves use some of the advice, which they dispense to management. The practitioner community is not homogeneous and time and effort must be taken to open the lines of com-munication and foster a collaborative environment. And despite the attractiveness of providing a 'quick fix' to an imminent decision-maker's problem, the greatest value (to academic and practitioner) occurs when the academic challenges conventional wisdom and traditional decision-making mindsets.[1]

NOTE

1. This chapter first appeared as an editorial in *Industrial Marketing Management* (Di Benedetto et al., 2019).

REFERENCES

Åge, L.-J. (2014). How and why managers use conceptual devices in business-to-business research. *Journal of Business & Industrial Marketing, 29*(7/8), pp. 633–41.

Aguinis, H., Shapiro, D.L., Antonacopoulou, E.P., & Cummings, T.G. (2014). Scholarly impact: a pluralist conceptualization. *Academy of Management Learning & Education, 13*(4), pp. 623–39.

Alexiev, S.A., Volberda, W.H., & Van den Bosch, A.J.F. (2016). Interorganizational collaboration and firm innovativeness: unpacking the role of the organizational environment. *Journal of Business Research, 69*(2), pp. 974–84.

Antonacopoulou, E.P. (2009). Impact and scholarship: unlearning and practising to co-create actionable knowledge. *Management Learning, 40*(4), pp. 421–30.

Antonacopoulou, E.P. (2010). Beyond co-production: practice-relevant scholarship as a foundation for delivering impact through powerful ideas. *Public Money & Management, 30*(4), pp. 219–26.

Arnaboldi, M. (2013). Consultant-researchers in public sector transformation: an evolving role. *Financial Accountability & Management, 29*(2), pp. 140–60.

Arvanitis, S., Kubli, U., & Woerter, M. (2008). University–industry knowledge and technology transfer in Switzerland: what university scientists think about co-operation with private enterprises. *Research Policy, 37*(10), pp. 1865–83.

Barge, J.K. (2001). Practical theory as mapping engaged reflection, and transformative practice. *Communication Theory, 11*(1), pp. 5–13.

Bartunek, J.M. (2007). Academic–practitioner collaboration need not require joint or relevant research: toward a relational scholarship of integration. *Academy of Management Journal, 50*(6), pp. 1323–33.

Bartunek, J.M. & Rynes, S.L. (2014). Academics and practitioners are alike and unlike: the paradoxes of academic–practitioner relationships. *Journal of Management, 40*(5), pp. 1181–201.

Beaver, D.D. (2004). Does collaborative research have greater epistemic authority? *Scientometrics, 60*(3), pp. 399–408.

Benneworth, P. (2001). Academic entrepreneurship and long-term business relationships: understanding 'commercialization' activities. *Enterprise and Innovation Management Studies, 2*(3), pp. 225–37.

Bouncken, R.B. (2008). Autopoiesis: the conception of joint learning. *European Journal of Management, 8*(4), pp. 40–46.

Bridgman, T. (2007). Reconstituting relevance: exploring possibilities for management educators' critical engagement with the public. *Management Learning, 38*(4), pp. 425–39.

Chesbrough, H. (2003). *Open Innovation: A New Imperative for Creating and Profiting from Technology.* Boston, MA: Harvard Business School Press.

Chicksand, D. (2015). Partnerships: the role that power plays in collaborative buyer–supplier exchanges. *Industrial Marketing Management, 48*(5), pp. 121–39.

Clauss, T. & Kesting, T. (2017). How businesses should govern knowledge-intensive collaborations with universities: an empirical investigation of university professors. *Industrial Marketing Management, 62*(3), pp. 185–98.

Cohen, W.M. & Levinthal, D.A. (1990). Absorptive capacity: a new perspective on learning and innovation. *Administrative Science Quarterly, 35*(1), pp. 128–152.

Collins, H. (2004). Interactional expertise as a third kind of knowledge. *Phenomenology and the Cognitive Sciences, 3*(2), pp. 125–43.

Cruz-González, J., López-Sáez, P., & Navas-López, J.E. (2015). Absorbing knowledge from supply-chain, industry and science: the distinct moderating role of formal liaison devices on new product development and novelty. *Industrial Marketing Management*, *47*(4), pp. 75–85.

Darabi, F. & Clark, M. (2012). Developing business school/SMEs collaboration: the role of trust. *International Journal of Entrepreneurial Behaviour & Research*, *18*(4), pp. 477–93.

De Araújo Burcharth, A.L., Knudsen, M.P., & Søndergaard, H.A. (2014). Neither invented nor shared here: the impact and management of attitudes for the adoption of open innovation practices. *Technovation*, *34*(3), pp. 149–61.

Del Giudice, M. & Maggioni, V. (2014). Managerial practices and operative directions of knowledge management within inter-firm networks: a global view. *Journal of Knowledge Management*, *18*(5), pp. 841–6.

Desai, V.M. (2018). Collaborative stakeholder engagement: an integration between theories of organizational legitimacy and learning. *Academy of Management Journal*, *61*(1), pp. 220–44.

Di Benedetto, C.A., Lindgreen, A., Storgaard, M., & Clarke, A.H. (2019). How to collaborate really well with practitioners. *Industrial Marketing Management*, *82*, pp. 1–8.

Docherty, I. & Smith, D. (2007). Practicing what we preach? Academic consultancy in a multi-disciplinary environment. *Public Money & Management*, *27*(4), pp. 273–80.

Du, J., Leten, B., & Vanhaverbeke, W. (2014). Managing open innovation projects with science-based and market-based partners. *Research Policy*, *43*(5), pp. 828–40.

Etzkowitz, H. (2010). *The Triple Helix: University–Industry–Government Innovation in Action*. London: Routledge.

Feller, J., Parhankangas, A., Smeds, R., & Jaatinen, M. (2013). How companies learn to collaborate: emergence of improved inter-organizational processes in R&D alliances. *Organization Studies*, *34*(3), pp. 313–43.

Fendt, J., Kaminska-Labbe, R., & Sachs, W. (2008). Producing and socializing relevant management knowledge: re-turn to pragmatism. *European Business Review*, *20*(6), pp. 471–91.

Gioia, D. (2013). Editor's choice introduction. *Journal of Management Inquiry*, *22*(1), pp. 2–3.

Godin, B. & Gingras, Y. (2000). Impact of collaborative research on academic science. *Science and Public Policy*, *27*(1), pp. 65–73.

Gustavsen, B. (2003). Action research and the problem of the single case. *Concepts & Transformation*, *8*(1), pp. 93–9.

Heckscher, C. & Martin-Rios, C. (2013). Looking back, moving forward: toward collaborative universities. *Journal of Management Inquiry*, *22*(1), pp. 136–9.

Heirati, N., O'Cass, A., Schoefer, K., & Siahtiri, V. (2016). Do professional service firms benefit from customer and supplier collaborations in competitive, turbulent environments? *Industrial Marketing Management*, *55*(4), pp. 50–58.

Hernandez-Espallardo, M., Osorio-Tinoco, F., & Rodriguez-Orejuela, A. (2017). Improving firm performance through inter-organizational collaborative innovations: the key mediating role of the employee's job-related attitudes. *Management Decision*, *56*(6), pp. 1167–82.

Hibbert, P., Siedlok, F., & Beech, N. (2016). The role of interpretation on learning practices in the context of collaboration. *Academy of Management Learning & Education*, *15*(1), pp. 26–44.

Hodgkinson, G.P. & Rousseau, D.M. (2009). Bridging the rigour–relevance gap in management research: it's already happening. *Journal of Management Studies*, *46*(3), pp. 534–46.

Huxham, C. & Vangen, S. (2004). Doing things collaboratively: realizing the advantages or succumbing to inertia? *Organizational Dynamics*, *22*(2), pp. 190–201.

Huxham, C. & Vangen, S. (2005). *Managing to Collaborate*. London: Routledge.

Inkpen, A.C. & Tsang, E.W. (2005). Social capital, networks, and knowledge transfer. *Academy of Management Review*, *30*(1), pp. 146–65.

Jarzabkowski, P., Mohrman, S.A., & Scherer, A.G. (2010). Organization studies as applied science: the generation and use of academic knowledge about organizations. Introduction to the special issue. *Organization Studies*, *31*(9/10), pp. 1189–207.

Jolink, M. & Dankbaar, B. (2010). Creating a climate for inter-organizational networking through people management. *International Journal of Human Resource Management*, *21*(9), pp. 1436–53.

Kieser, A. & Leiner, L. (2009). Why the rigour–relevance gap in management research is unbridgeable. *Journal of Management Studies*, *46*(3), pp. 516–33.

Kieser, A. & Leiner, L. (2012). Collaborate with practitioners: but beware of collaborative research. *Journal of Management Inquiry*, *21*(1), pp. 14–28.

Lakemond, N., Bengtsson, L., Laursen, K., & Tell, F. (2016). Match and manage: the use of knowledge matching and project management to integrate knowledge in collaborative inbound open innovation. *Industrial and Corporate Change*, *25*(2), pp. 333–52.

Langley, A., Smallman, C., Tsoukas, H., & Van de Ven, A. (2013). Process studies of change in organization and management: unveiling temporality, activity and flow. *Academy of Management Journal*, *56*(1), pp. 1–13.

Laursen, K. & Salter, A. (2006). Open for innovation: the role of openness in explaining innovation performance among UK manufacturing firms. *Strategic Management Journal*, *27*(2), pp. 131–50.

Lazzarotti, V., Manzini, R., Nosella, A., & Pellegrini, L. (2016). Collaborations with scientific partners: the mediating role of the social context in fostering innovation performance. *Creativity and Innovation Management*, *25*(1), pp. 142–56.

Leahrey, E., Beckman, C.M., & Stanko, T.L. (2017). Prominent but less productive: the impact of interdisciplinarity on scientists' research. *Administrative Science Quarterly*, *62*(1), pp. 105–39.

Learmonth, M., Lockett, A., & Dowd, K. (2012). Promoting scholarship that matters: the uselessness of useful research and the usefulness of useless research. *British Journal of Management*, *23*(1), pp. 35–44.

Lee, Y.S. (2000). The sustainability of university–industry research collaboration: an empirical assessment. *The Journal of Technology Transfer*, *25*(2), pp. 111–33.

Lindgreen, A. & Di Benedetto, C.A. (2018). Continuous improvement at *Industrial Marketing Management*: suggestions from the Editorial Review Board. *Industrial Marketing Management*, *71*, pp. 1–4.

Lindgreen, A., Di Benedetto, C.A., Brodie, R.J., & Naudé, P. (2019). How to build great research groups. *Industrial Marketing Management*, *81*, pp. 1–13.

Marzo-Navarro, M., Pedraja-Iglesias, M., & Rivera-Torres, P. (2009). The marketing approach in relationship between universities and firms. *Journal of Relationship Marketing*, *8*(2), pp. 127–47.

Mehlman, S.K., Saucedo, S.U., Taylor, R.P., Slowinski, G., Carreras, E., & Arena, C. (2010). Better practices for managing intellectual assets in collaborations. *Research Technology Management*, *53*(1), pp. 55–66.

Mingers, J. (2014). *System Thinking, Critical Realism and Philosophy: A Confluence of Ideas*. Abingdon: Routledge.

Muller, E. & Doloreux, D. (2009). What we should know about knowledge-intensive business services. *Technology in Society*, *31*(1), pp. 64–72.

Najafi-Tavani, S., Najafi-Tavani, Z., Naudé, P., Oghazi, P., & Zeynaloo, E. (2018). How collaborative innovation networks affect new product performance: product innovation capability, process innovation, and absorptive capacity. *Industrial Marketing Management*, *73*(6), pp. 193–205.

Nenonen, S., Brodie, R.J., Storbacka, K., & Peter, L.D. (2017). Theorizing with managers: how to achieve both academic rigor and practical relevance? *European Journal of Marketing*, *51*(7/8), pp. 1130–52.

Pasmore, W.A., Stymne, B., Shani, A.B., Mohrman, S.A., & Adler, N. (2008). The promise of collaborative management research. In Shani, A.B., Mohrman, S.A., Pasmore, W.A., Stymne, B., & Adler, N. (eds.), *Handbook of Collaborative Management Research* (pp. 7–31). Thousand Oaks, CA: Sage Publications.

Paton, S., Chia., R., & Burt, G. (2014). Relevance or 'relevate'? How university business schools can add value through reflexively learning from strategic partnerships with business. *Management Learning*, *45*(3), pp. 267–88.

Pecas, P. & Henriques, E. (2006). Best practices of collaboration between universities and industrial SMEs. *Benchmarking: An International Journal*, *13*(1/2), pp. 54–67.

Pera, N., Occhiocupo, N., & Clarke, J. (2016). Motives and resources for value co-creation in a multi-stakeholder ecosystem: a managerial perspective. *Journal of Business Research*, *69*(10), pp. 4033–41.

Perkmann, M., Tartari, V., McKelvey, M., Autio, E., Broström, A., D'Este, P., & Sobrero, M. (2013). Academic engagement and commercialisation: a review of the literature on university–industry relations. *Research Policy, 42*(2), pp. 423–42.

Perkmann, M. & Walsh, K. (2007). University–industry relationships and open innovation: towards a research agenda. *International Journal of Management Reviews, 9*(4), pp. 259–80.

Pertuzé, J.A., Calder, E.S., Greitzer, E.M., & Lucas, W.A. (2010). Best practices for industry–university collaboration. *MIT Sloan Management Review, 51*(4), pp. 83–90.

Pettigrew, A.M. (2003). Co-producing knowledge and the challenges of international collaborative research. In Pettigrew, A.M., Whittington, R., Melin, L., Sánchez-Runde, C., van den Bosch, F.A.J., Ruigrok, W., & Numagami, T. (eds.), *Innovative Forms of Organizing: International Perspectives* (pp. 352–374). Thousand Oaks, CA: Sage.

Pettigrew, A. & Starkey, K. (2016). The legitimacy and impact of business schools: key issues and research agenda. *Academy of Management Learning & Education, 15*(4), pp. 649–64.

Plewa, C., Quester, P., & Baaken, T. (2005). Relationship marketing and university–industry linkages: a conceptual framework. *Marketing Theory, 5*(4), pp. 433–56.

Pollitt, C. (2006). Academic advice to practitioners: what is its nature, place and value within academia? *Public Money and Management, 26*(4), pp. 257–64.

Raelin, J. (2018). What are you afraid of? Collective leadership and its learning implications. *Management Learning, 49*(1), pp. 59–66.

Rynes, S.L., Bartunek, J.M., & Daft, R.L. (2001). Across the great divide: knowledge creation and transfer between practitioners and academics. *Academy of Management Journal, 44*(2), pp. 340–55.

Santini, C., Marinelli, E., Boden, M., Cavicchi, A., & Haegeman, K. (2016). Reducing the distance between thinkers and doers in the entrepreneurial discovery process: an exploratory study. *Journal of Business Research, 69*(5), pp. 1840–44.

Shapiro, D.L., Kirkman, B.L., & Courtney, H.G. (2007). Perceived causes and solutions of the translation problem in management research. *Academy of Management Journal, 50*(2), pp. 249–66.

Shaw, S. & Allen, J.B. (2006). It basically is a fairly loose arrangement and it works out fine really. *Sport Management Review, 9*(3), pp. 203–28.

Skippari, M., Laukkanen, M., & Salo, J. (2017). Cognitive barriers to collaborative innovation generation in supply chain relationships. *Industrial Marketing Management, 62*(3), pp. 108–17.

Smith, S. (2018). In pursuit of rapid impact: research with a difference. *Journal of Organizational Studies & Innovation, 5*(1), pp. 1–7.

Spekkink, W.A.H. & Boons, A.A. (2016). The emergence of collaborations. *Journal of Public Administration Research & Theory, 26*(4), pp. 613–30.

Van de Ven, A.H. (2007). *Engaged Scholarship: A Guide for Organizational and Social Research.* New York: Oxford University Press.

Vangen, S. & Huxham, C. (2003). Nurturing collaborative relations: building trust in interorganizational collaboration. *The Journal of Applied Behavioral Science, 39*(1), pp. 5–31.

Vicari, S. (2013). Is the problem only ours? A question of relevance in management research. *European Management Review, 10*(4), pp. 173–81.

Walker, D. (2010). Debate: do academics know better or merely different? *Public Money & Management, 30*(4), pp. 204–6.

Winkelbach, A. & Walter, A. (2015). Complex technological knowledge and value creation in science-to-industry technology transfer projects: the moderating effect of absorptive capacity. *Industrial Marketing Management, 47*(4), pp. 98–108.

Wu, J. (2014). Cooperation with competitors and product innovation: moderating effects of technological capability and alliances with universities. *Industrial Marketing Management, 43*(2), pp. 199–209.

Yassi, A., Dharamsi, S., Spiegel, J., Rojas, A., Dean, E., & Woollard, R. (2010). The good, the bad, and the ugly of partnered research: revisiting the sequestration thesis and the role of universities in promoting social justice. *International Journal of Health Service, 40*(3), pp. 485–505.

Ylijoki, O.-H. (2003). Entangled in academic capitalism? A case-study on changing ideals and practices of university research. *Higher Education, 45*(3), pp. 307–35.

Zhou, Y., Zhang, X., Zhuang, G., & Zhou, N. (2015). Relational norms and collaborative activities: roles in reducing opportunism in marketing channels. *Industrial Marketing Management*, *46*(3), pp. 147–59.

18. Leading academics in a public–private partnership: balancing value and performance-based leadership in times of (climate) change

Morten W. Jeppesen

INTRODUCTION

> Help solve an urgent societal challenge by science and technology. Join the management team of the Danish Hydrocarbon Research and Technology Centre and help build and run a new innovative organization with substantial impact potential.

After working for more than 25 years for Maersk Oil on oil and gas industry projects in Denmark and internationally, it was time to move on; time to explore other ways of working and living; and time to help solve urgent and important challenges for Danish society through science and technology. The wording of the job advertisement above resonated well with my aspirations and in 2017, I switched from the private to the public sector as one of less than 1% of Danish leaders changing sector that year.[1]

I joined the leadership team of the Danish Hydrocarbon Research and Technology Centre (DHRTC), a major public–private partnership established at the Technical University of Denmark (DTU) in collaboration with Copenhagen, Aarhus and Aalborg Universities and the Geological Survey of Denmark and Greenland (GEUS). The centre was established in 2014 supported financially by the Danish Underground Consortium (DUC) with 1 billion DKK (approximately 130 million euros) over a 10-year period. In addition to funds, DUC agreed to provide the centre with open access to a large amount of industry data and to specialists within their organisations.

The objective of this unusually large-scale public–private partnership is to strengthen applied research and innovation within the Danish oil and gas sector, and to improve collaboration between academia and industry. It is anchored in the national strategy for the oil and gas sector. More specifically, the centre aims to develop innovative solutions to improve the way in which the Danish oil and gas resources can be produced in terms of safety, environmental impact, cost and recovery efficiency.

As a leader with an oil and gas industry background, I was inspired by the ambition to deliver research-based solutions with application potential at such a large scale and in a relatively short timeframe. Furthermore, to meet the needs of the centre's many academic and private stakeholders, a dynamic and innovative approach to management and leadership would be required.

Today, at the end of 2020, I look back at three years of successes and failures, some of which have been related to the challenges and opportunities of bridging between public and private stakeholders, and others related to the dramatic change of perspective on the national oil and gas resources during the past five years. All successes and failures have contributed valuable insights and new knowledge about the complexities of leading academics and managing conflict in a public–private partnership with a variety of stakeholders and widely different motivations and performance objectives. The experiences which I find to be most important are discussed in this chapter, together with some of my thoughts about their impact on the effectiveness and efficiency of DHRTC.

LEADERSHIP IN A LARGE PUBLIC–PRIVATE ENERGY PARTNERSHIP

The 2015 report on public–private leadership by the Danish think tank DEA, which is an initiative within the Danish Society for Education and Business, and the Network of Corporate Academics (NOCA)[2] provides a comprehensive overview of challenges and opportunities for leaders of public–private partnerships and public–private innovation collaborations. Most of the points made by DEA/NOCA bear resemblance to experiences with DHRTC. The leadership challenges I find most interesting are illustrated below by four examples.

Example 1: Different Languages

Lack of experience from more than one sector among leaders in a public–private partnership can make it difficult to overcome cultural barriers and cause conflict. Something as simple as misunderstanding language has the potential to completely derail collaboration, which illustrates the fragile nature of the partnership, particularly in the early phase of collaboration. Using the phrase 'failing fast' is an example. It is commonly used in a positive sense among private innovators and entrepreneurs as a way to test hypotheses quickly and move on. Surprisingly, it was found to have a very negative connotation among some researchers, who feared that 'failing fast' would be the end of their project funding and that their entire research career could be at risk. While the intention of their leaders with an industry background was to encourage an attitude of 'learning fast', the phrase caused temporary conflict and communication breakdown until the misunderstanding could be resolved.

Example 2: Different Collaboration Styles

Cross-disciplinary and cross-institutional collaboration has become a fundamental element in DHRTC's operating model as a way to stimulate radical innovation. When working with cross-disciplinary teams we have learned that one of the most significant risks to the collaboration is misalignment of individual, team and organisational objectives.

Alignment is relatively simple to achieve within the private sector, where a project's financial success is usually a shared goal between the organisation, the team and the individual.

Objectives of individuals, teams and institutions within academia are, in contrast, sometimes misaligned and even in conflict often as a result of competition and protection of interests.

In a few of our cross-disciplinary research projects, such misalignment of objectives has caused long-standing team conflicts, slowed down progress and led to poor research outcomes.

Example 3: Different Decision Criteria and Bottom Lines

Decision criteria and bottom lines can be widely different between the private and public sector partners. In industry, decisions are taken mostly on the basis of projects' bottom line impact together with an assessment of risks or chance of success and ease of implementation. In academia, decision criteria usually have more dimensions including research potential, relevance for education, public interest, and so on.

Public partnering between research institutions and a production company, like DUC, can therefore be challenging as decision criteria within production operations tend to depend on day-to-day operational needs, changes in companies' business strategy and organisational setup or other criteria that are changing with a frequency which is impossible for academic organisations to keep pace with. Since DHRTC was established in 2014, three of the four original industry partner companies and five of the six members of the steering committee have changed. Specialist industry focal points that are critical for the success of the research and innovation projects have changed even more frequently in connection with numerous company reorganisations.

Academic researchers are sometimes also motivated by the financial impact potential of their work, but usually their main interest is to produce academically acknowledged new insights contributing to science. To affect the academic bottom line, research topics have to match with the academic institutions' strategies, to have sufficient research potential to enable publication in reputable journals, to attract other researchers and students, and potential for gearing the project with additional funding, to mention a few important criteria.

Balancing these, sometimes deep differences in decision criteria are key to success of the public–private partnership and place a significant demand on the centre's project leaders' ability to influence, negotiate and compromise, usually without much formal authority.

Example 4: Academic Motivation, Public Opinion and Climate Change

To be of service to society is important for many public sector employees including academic researchers and is known as Public Service Motivation (PSM).[3] For the researchers engaged in the centre's activities this is no different, as they (we) contribute to solving an 'urgent societal challenge' by improving the way Danish oil and gas resources are produced efficiently and with minimum negative impact on the environment. While doing this, academics also develop new knowledge and educate new generations of talent, which are also important societal contributions. As long as this takes place in a relatively free setting, the academic researchers appear to be intrinsically motivated by this purpose to deliver high-quality results.

Since 2014, public opinion on oil and gas exploitation has changed as a result of the growing public realisation of the negative effects of fossil fuel combustion on the climate. In some cases, opposition against the oil and gas industries has also been directed towards academics and challenged their ethics and morals. Without judging whether this criticism is fair, which is not the purpose of this discussion, this negative attention from the surrounding society has challenged the PSM of some researchers and detracted others from working on oil- and gas-related projects. Adjusting DHRTC's strategic scope to include projects addressing the industry's environmental sustainability challenges has helped to improve motivation, particularly of some of the younger researchers.

LEADERSHIP CHALLENGES CHANGED DURING THE FIRST SIX YEARS OF OPERATION

Establishing a multi-disciplinary, multi-institutional, public–private partnership addressing a complex challenge through science and technology takes time. At the starting point in 2014, DHRTC only had a funding and collaboration agreement in place and an empty office at DTU. Today, six years later, the centre engages more than 250 researchers and specialists working on some 200 research and innovation projects; 65 employees work in the centre's core office at DTU.

Initially, the organisational structure of the centre was defined by a small number of scientific areas headed by scientific directors with top-level scientific accreditation. A significantly revised strategy with a new organisation was launched in 2015 and a new leadership structure was introduced, where key competences and practices from the industry sector became central for the leadership of the centre.

External evaluations of the centre were conducted in 2016 and 2018 to identify challenges and opportunities to improve DHRTC's operational setup and performance. The evaluations were performed by an international consultancy firm and were based on surveys and interviews with individual contributors and managers from the public and private partner organisations. They provided two snapshots in time and a comparison of the findings illustrates that organisational challenges and opportunities have changed over time as the partnership developed and the focus of the surrounding society changed.

Findings of the 2016 evaluation: The centre objective is clear, but its structure and collaboration model need to be improved to deliver results.

After approximately two years of operation and one year after the strategy re-definition and reorganisation, the overall objective of the centre was well defined and directly linked to industry needs. The strategy and objective were clearly owned by the management of the centre and by the industry partner. Unsurprisingly perhaps, this overall objective had not been sufficiently cascaded to project teams or communicated clearly to individual researchers who were not yet familiar with the new collaboration model.

A second important finding was that implementation of the centre's strategy was challenged by insufficiently defined support processes for portfolio and project management. Embryonic processes existed and were under development but had not yet been finalised, documented and applied to actual project management.

Third, cross-disciplinary collaboration was found to be an area with opportunity for improvement as DHRTC worked to challenge a traditional competitive and individualistic academic culture with a new collaborative model for applied research and innovation. It was observed that more communication of project objectives, business processes and the collaboration model was needed, particularly towards the academic researchers, to realise the full potential of what was assessed to be a world-class opportunity for public–private collaboration.

Findings of the 2018 evaluation: A well-structured centre, showing emerging results and improving collaboration but a new vision is needed.

Two years later, a second external evaluation took place. This evaluation was performed by the same organisation and used the same methodology and framework as in 2016 to allow comparison of the findings and to gauge progress.

By 2018, the centre had grown significantly and had established its new organisation with defined project and financial management processes, and a growing network of researchers was developing. The research and innovation projects showed positive signs of progress towards addressing the needs of the industry. The quality of collaboration and trust between the partners had improved, and a sense of community was emerging. Overall, all aspects had become better defined as DHRTC had moved into a phase of scaling and fine-tuning, whilst focusing on producing results.

Although research focus was one of the centre's strengths, some researchers expressed a need for deeper scientific research, which was slightly overlooked by the operating model. Projects were innovative, but their briefness compared to academic standards was a source of frustration for some senior researchers. Furthermore, engagement amongst specialists and researchers was modest, talent attraction was difficult and the industry partners' commitment had become unclear.

Researchers and specialists considered the centre's objective of significantly increasing oil and gas production from the North Sea to be less attractive than it had appeared at the outset of the centre's activities in 2014. As the mid-point of the 10-year funding period was approaching, a request for an update of the vision to address environmental sustainability challenges of the oil and gas industry and energy transition was emerging.

Encouraged by the progress of the partnership, the centre's leadership team decided to address the key findings of the survey: to deliver results, improve collaboration and adjust the strategic vision. However, as the partnership matured, it became clear that changes like these had to be managed in a manner which could bridge and balance different bottom lines, cultures and strategies of the public and private partners.

BALANCING PERFORMANCE AND VALUE-BASED LEADERSHIP

To realise the potential of a collaborative public–private partnership, such as DHRTC, the needs and expectations of the public as well as the private stakeholders must be considered by the centre's strategy. DTU as the public owner of the centre expects DHRTC to deliver excellent research, innovation and academic talent to contribute to Danish society. DUC, which is funding the centre as a private stakeholder, on the other hand expects the centre to deliver applicable new knowledge and technologies with potential to improve its business.

Therefore, not only is the nature of the expected results different but the approach to delivery also varies between the public and private stakeholders. Since the ownership of the centre resides in the public domain, the motivation and engagement of the academic researchers is a prerequisite for delivering results. Because their objectives largely align with the university's success criteria, a performance management approach with time-bound milestones and financial key performance indicators (KPIs), which is often used in the industry, is unlikely to be effective.

Consideration of both stakeholders' expectations requires a combination of performance management to deliver tangible results to the industry and a more value-based strategy to motivate and engage the academic researchers. Balancing the two leadership strategies in practice presents a number of strategic and operational leadership challenges and opportunities to be discussed next.

CHANGE MANAGEMENT IN PRACTICE

The DEA/NOCA study was based on desk studies and data gathered by interviewing leaders of public–private partnerships including DHRTC. It presents best practices and recommendations of ways to optimise the leadership of public–private partnerships. The actions recommended by DEA/NOCA relate in many ways to the elements of change management famously published by John Kotter in 1996,[4] initially as a series of change steps and later updated to reflect the more chaotic, fast-paced and non-linear reality of organisational change in practice.[5]

They both point at central elements of change leadership also in public–private partnerships: establishing a case for change, engaging leaders and a critical part of the organisation, communicating a compelling vision, capturing early successes and, eventually, institutionalising the change.

These elements have also been applied to implement the strategy and develop the DHRTC organisation. However, because the centre operates in a dynamic environment and the partnership has changed significantly since 2014, the actual organisational development has been less straightforward than proposed by the literature models. During the six years of operation, three significant changes of the internal and external environment have disrupted an otherwise steady development and called for change management and leadership action.

Internal and External Cases for Change

Collaboration between academia and the oil and gas industry was well established at DTU, but involved only a few disciplines and was usually based on existing relationships between researchers and industry specialists. The first case for change at DHRTC was related to an early realisation that multi- and cross-disciplinary collaboration was a prerequisite for developing radically new knowledge and innovative solutions to address industrial challenges.

It required that academic researchers had to adjust and combine research fields in collaboration with researchers from institutions and disciplines they were not used to working with. Industry specialists needed to openly share their challenges with the researchers and to welcome the external challenge of proven practices and conventional wisdom. To enable this at a large scale, deep-rooted cultural differences between the sectors had to be overcome.

Resistance to this change could jeopardise the development of new knowledge and innovative technology with application potential and a sense of urgency was required to deliver results within only ten years, which can pass rather quickly when research-based innovation is involved. Developing an entirely new collaboration model based on trust and openness in a short period was therefore needed and called for a radical change of the centre's organisational setup. This led to a major reorganisation in 2015, about one year after the centre's inauguration and one year before the first evaluation. The change introduced portfolio and project management with industry expertise, and other elements supporting an industrial system perspective in addition to a classic academic discipline perspective.

The second case for change was driven by a development in the external environment. From mid-2014, the oil price decreased from a historic high to a historic low level in a matter of months. This crisis led most companies within the sector to reduce the size of their organisations and adopt a cost conscious and short-term delivery focus. With this focus, the private partners became less open to potentially risky experiments with new technology and their interest in some of the early activities at the centre, which were initiated to develop new technology with potential to increase the recovery of oil and gas, reduced. In order to adapt to the new reality, the focus on research and innovation at DHRTC was gradually changed from being aimed at increasing oil and gas recovery to prioritising activities aimed at cost-efficiency improvements.

The third case for change was also related to development in the external environment. Climate gas emissions originating from the combustion of fossil fuels challenge the oil and gas industry globally and are also imposing pressure on the DHRTC partnership. On the one hand, the critical view on oil and gas challenges the motivation of some collaboration partners, especially students and researchers. On the other hand, it presents an opportunity for the centre to engage actively in energy transition. To meet this challenge and opportunity, the scope for the centre's research and innovation is again undergoing change to include activities aimed at reducing climate gas emissions from oil and gas production, and to support the energy transition with radically new knowledge and technologies.

The following sections discuss how strategic and operational leaders at DHRTC have addressed these three major cases for change.

Leading Change at the Strategic Level

The first case for change was initiated by a request from the industry partner to place more focus on research and innovation with application potential and on multi- and cross-disciplinary collaboration. The request was supported by the centre's board, which is composed of senior executives from industry and academia and holds the ultimate responsibility for the strategy. Meeting the request required a profound change to the operating model of the centre, which had been organised around a small group of academic research directors.

This change and the request for open collaboration were met with opposition from some of the researchers who felt that established academic work practices were being challenged and that they could be losing autonomy and decision authority. Despite the resistance, a change of the centre organisation was implemented and the composition of the leadership team was changed completely. A new team of leaders with an industrial background was established to manage and facilitate collaboration between researchers, and new project management processes were implemented. As indicated by some of the examples of collaboration challenges given previously, management of these changes was culturally complicated, very resource-intensive and time-consuming.

Today, the new operating model is fully implemented and institutionalised. It builds on principles for portfolio management in order to maximise the overall chance of success, in terms of application potential. The portfolio comprises more than 200 research and innovation projects organised in eight programmes to form more than 30 prototype solutions addressing specific, urgent and important industry challenges. A management system of selected business processes has been established to support a dynamic management of the portfolio, with quarterly prioritisation of projects and decisions. Semi-quantitative prioritisation and decision tools are used to maintain balance between the centre's three bottom lines: economic, environmental and academic.

After five years, it is observed that the change of operating model has improved the balance within the partnership and that a more equal business model addressing the needs for applicable solutions by the industry partner has been established.

The ongoing strategic adjustment of the centre's research and innovation portfolio from focusing on increased oil and gas production to supporting energy transition is taking place in full alignment with both partners' strategies. The universities have had climate and sustainability as important strategic themes for a while, and for the oil and gas industry climate and sustainability are becoming increasingly important drivers of their new business models. In this symmetric scenario, adjusting the centre's strategy is relatively straightforward compared to the first case for change. Working jointly towards a shared climate and sustainability strategy balances the partnership and reduces the sense of a customer–supplier relationship between the industry and academic partners.

All three strategic changes have involved elements of change management to adjust the business model, the organisation, or to build new organisational capabilities. In most cases, development of leaders or hiring of new leaders with different competencies is also necessary to support the change.

High-frequency, overlapping strategic changes and continuous change appear to be overlooked by the change management studies and models mentioned above, but can in reality lead to delay and failure. The time and effort to execute the element changes are usually considerable, and it can be expected that momentum, productivity and motivation will suffer during the process. When a strategy change process is implemented, a period of leadership hyper-care will usually also be required to ensure that the change is sustainable. The drain on leadership resources can therefore be considerable if change occurs too frequently or the change processes drag on. Based on the experience from DHRTC, it has been important to consider both the leadership and the remaining organisation's capacity for change before new change initiatives were taken. In cases where the case for change was not urgent or important enough, changes of strategy have had to be deferred until the ongoing process was completed and some of its benefits had been harvested.

Leading Change at the Operational Level

In the years following the 2015 reorganisation, DHRTC implemented a project organisation with a Programme Management Office (PMO) and programme leaders to manage and facilitate the research and innovation activities. The portfolio of activities involves tens of research and industry organisations and hundreds of people in several countries. While the magnitude and diversity of this network represents a grand opportunity for research and innovation, it also represents a mixture of norms, cultures, values and languages, not least because the DHRTC setup is very different from the normal academic system with Principal Investigators (PI) with full autonomy of the projects.

Operational leadership within this complex setup is a delicate balancing act to bring out the best of the partnership. It includes setting direction, facilitating collaboration, navigating between different and changing stakeholder needs, capturing results and more. To perform this role well, the operational leader and her organisation have little formal authority but are relying on a few simple business processes and a great deal of influencing and persuasion.

Setting Direction and Defining Project Purpose

Participation in research and innovation projects is the choice for individual researchers joining the project and is decided in competition with many other activities they could entertain. To ensure that they do not regret their choice, for example as a result of poor expectation management, it is important that the purpose of the project is defined jointly at the beginning. A well-defined and engaging project purpose is particularly important when the collaborators are driven by intrinsic motivation factors, which is the case for most of the academic researchers and industry specialists working on the centre's projects. To motivate collaborators to work with colleagues from other organisations they might not know, it is important to ensure that the project purpose is aligned and shared between all team members.

Due to the applied nature of the research and innovation, it is in principle relatively simple to define the purpose of a project at DHRTC. The industry challenges are well understood by the project leaders, who have an industry background, and the researchers can expect that there is an end-user pull for their results.

In reality, however, the definition of purpose is more complicated and usually a subject of negotiation to ensure that the industry challenge is defined widely enough that it also allows for scientific exploration. This negotiation can be difficult for the project leader but it is a key learning that this must not prevent the definition of project purpose at the beginning of the project. Without a clear, shared purpose from the beginning, there is a high risk that team motivation will suffer and the project may derail.

Facilitating Collaboration: Governance and Business Processes

Operations at DHRTC are governed at the highest level by the structure, rules and regulations of the agreement between DTU and DUC, which describes governing committees, their obligations and decision rights, intellectual property rights (IPRs), reporting requirements, confidentiality and so on. This overall agreement does not, however, describe the processes at the portfolio and project levels. They have been developed at the centre as discussed previously.

As the project portfolio developed in magnitude and complexity during the first years of operations, the need for a management system at the project level was realised. A fit for purpose management system was established in dialogue with the stakeholders and is available on the centre's website to provide transparency of the operation model.[6] The system was deliberately limited to include only the business processes required to manage the research portfolio and to fulfil obligations to stakeholders. This approach was taken as it was discovered that a system of comprehensive and elaborate processes, which is common within the oil and gas industry, would be viewed as overly bureaucratic and demotivating by the academic researchers, who are used to working with a higher degree of autonomy. The tailor-made management system was implemented at the time of the second evaluation and has since then supported the centre's operational leadership in mainly two ways:

1. The system has increased transparency within the project teams, by providing clear and consistent processes for project application, maturation, reporting, data management and so on, which has increased the level of trust between researchers and project managers.
2. It has also increased transparency towards the industry stakeholders by providing timely and relevant project information which has increased confidence in the centre's ability to produce useful results.

Facilitating Collaboration: Role Modelling

Research, innovation and cross-sector collaboration involves the risk of failure and conflict between collaborators, but when it succeeds it presents discoveries, shared success and fruitful relationships. In other words, the stakes are high and to manage this it is particularly important that operational leaders and project managers are able to facilitate collaboration profession-ally and with an appropriate balance between technical knowledge, determination, curiosity, passion and empathy.

Management and facilitation of these multi-year, multi-disciplinary, team-based collab-oration projects require a unique and rare combination of technical and personal leadership capabilities. Without technical capability, the leaders' legitimacy will soon be challenged by researchers and specialists. Without people leadership capabilities, the project team will encounter destructive conflict and can fall apart. Therefore, operational leaders should have both technical and leadership experience, preferably from both the private and the public sectors. However, as mentioned in the introduction, almost no Danish leaders have this combination.

The solution to this challenge has been to establish a group of experienced industry leaders and specialists with mixed technical and project management experience to lead DHRTC's project portfolio. Projects are typically managed by pairs of people, each with their strength and preference for the technical or people leadership aspects of their work. The benefit of this setup is that project leadership teams have proven collaboration skills, sufficient technical capabilities, as well as the maturity and robustness to manage teams and team conflict. The disadvantage is that, to be effective, they have to develop an academic network and a good understanding of the academic researcher's perspectives.

Capturing Results: Multiple Bottom Lines

The third important role of the operational leaders is to capture the results of the centre's activities. In practice, this involves identifying, describing and communicating the value of the research results in ways that are meaningful to the stakeholders. Only when results are captured is it possible to demonstrate the outcome of the activities to the private funding companies, the academic research institutions, the researchers and specialists involved, the employees of the centre and others.

Since the research and innovation activities have to result in solutions with application potential, their success are primarily described in one or more dimensions:

1. Economic impact potential.
2. Environmental impact potential.
3. Academic impact.

Economic impact potential originates from technologies or knowledge that can unlock oil and gas resources or improve cost efficiency; environmental impact potential will come from new ways to reduce discharges of harmful substances to the sea or climate gas emissions to the atmosphere. Academic impact is about deepening the understanding of how the universe and all its elements work down to the smallest parts. A proxy to this can be publications and citations of the research results, development of academic talent, attraction of funding and so on.

Communication of results and potentials as they emerge is operationally and strategically very important. Operationally, because it supports projects and project teams in making decisions to stop, redirect or continue their work. It also provides visibility of individual and team achievements, which is a prerequisite for recognition and reward of their accomplishments. Strategically, communication of the results is important for portfolio decisions, decisions regarding strategic changes such as those described earlier, for keeping senior stakeholders informed, and for promoting the centre to potential new partners.

DHRTC'S ROUTE TO SUCCESSFUL CROSS-SECTOR COLLABORATION LEADERSHIP

The examples and information given illustrate some of the pitfalls and challenges experienced during the first six years of operations at DHRTC. Some have been overcome relatively easily by familiarising project leaders with the two sectors and their different languages. Constructive interpersonal working relationships have usually been developed while familiarising as the result of the shared motivations of project leaders and their colleagues the academic researchers and industry specialists. With constructive professional relationships established, it has usually been possible to agree to engage in open dialogue regarding the projects.

Decision criteria tend to be different between industry and academia. Industry specialists mainly focus on the projects' financial and environmental bottom lines and are driven by timelines. The academic researchers have other 'bottom line' criteria related to the projects' potential to deliver on their academic KPIs including, for example, publications and financial gearing, which are driven by the quality of the research. When designing decision criteria for the complex research and innovation projects, the centre's project leaders have had to consider these different 'bottom lines' to create the necessary team alignment.

Other collaborative challenges have been much more complicated to manage. The preferred collaboration styles of the two sectors are quite different. Private sector innovation teams usually rely on discipline diversity. However, at DHRTC, considerable efforts have been required by the project leaders to inspire and facilitate cross-disciplinary and cross-institutional collaboration between academic researchers and institutions. These efforts are beginning to pay back now as examples are clearly demonstrating that new combinations of research disciplines can lead to radically new solutions to some of the most complex industry challenges. This suggests that although the value systems are clearly different in academia and industry, there are also tangible synergies in the collaboration when the areas and form of collaboration are carefully established.

At a strategic level, the flexible collaboration model of DHRTC has been a key to success. With the centre positioned at the interface between academia and industry, it has established a balanced business model bringing value to both academia and industry. Strategically, it has been achieved by stepwise adjustments of the research and innovation portfolio to match the evolving strategies of the private and public partners. Operationally, a balance between the sectors has been achieved by a management team, which has established a fit-for-purpose management system and adopted a cross-disciplinary collaboration style suitable for the teams of academic researchers and industry specialists.

ACKNOWLEDGEMENT

The author thanks Bo Cerup-Simonsen, CEO of the Maersk Mc-Kinney Moller Centre for Zero Carbon Shipping and director for DHRTC 2014–18 for contributing his experiences and for reviewing and providing valuable suggestions for improvements of the text.

NOTES

1. See https://www.djoef.dk/r-aa-dgivning/netv-ae-rkogkarriere/ledelse/artikler/2020/private-og-offentlige-ledere-kan-l-ae-re-af-hinanden-hvis-de-t-oe-r-skifte-sektor.aspx.
2. See https://www.datocms-assets.com/22590/1586180387-ledelsepaatvaersafoffentligogprivat0.pdf.
3. Jesper Rosenberg Hansen (2014), From public to private sector: motives and explanations for sector switching. *Public Management Review*, 16:4, 590–607.
4. John Kotter (1996), *Leading Change*. Boston, MA: Harvard Business School Press.
5. John Kotter (2012), Accelerate! *Harvard Business Review*, Nov. 2012, pp. 45–58.
6. See Danish Hydrocarbon Research and Technology Centre – Centre for Oil and Gas – DTU.

19. Undertaking cross-disciplinary research

Adam Lindgreen, C. Anthony Di Benedetto, Roderick J. Brodie and Michel van der Borgh

1. INTRODUCTION

As an applied social science, business-to-business research is inherently cross-disciplinary. This is because the general theories that provide insight into business relationships, systems, and markets have disciplinary foundations in the economics, psychology, sociology, and management disciplines. Commonly used general theories are, among others, Social Exchange Theory, Organizational Economics (Transaction Cost Economics, Agency Theory, and Plural Form Institutional Theory), Commitment-Trust Theory of Relationships, Structuration Theory, Actor-Network Theory, Corporate Social Responsibility, Stakeholder Theory and, more broadly, Systems Theory, Complexity Theory, and Evolutionary Psychology Theory. Different disciplines in business-to-business research make use of these general theories in varying degrees. For example, Transaction Cost Economics provides a framework for researchers seeking to explain and guide decision makers as to how to organize transactions, while Evolutionary Psychology Theory offers a framework for researchers trying to explain how consumers make their decisions.

Recently, Brodie and Peters (2020) proposed a theorizing process that explicitly considers the use of cross-disciplinary research. The theorizing process takes into account multiple theoretical pathways and recognizes how different general theoretic perspectives lead to the development of midrange theory and empirical research.

A major barrier that needs to be overcome when undertaking cross-disciplinary research comes from a parallel with organization structures, where there is a path from start-up to functional (silo) structure, to matrix structure, and to customer/project-based teams. Depending on the type of research challenge, the organization structure may relate to whether a multidisciplinary or monodisciplinary approach is necessary. Differences in incentives, culture, terminology and jargon, and so forth all can lead to opportunistic and counterproductive behavior.

The purpose of this chapter is to explore how to undertake cross-disciplinary research that advances knowledge and understanding in the domain of business-to-business research. To achieve this purpose, we first elaborate on the theorizing processes. Second, we examine how to break cross-disciplinary boundaries. Third, we provide practical guidelines for undertaking cross-disciplinary research.

2.   THEORIZING PROCESSES FOR CROSS-DISCIPLINARY RESEARCH

The theorizing process developed by Brodie and Peters (2020) provides guidelines for under-taking cross-disciplinary research by integrating general theoretic perspectives and contextual research to develop midrange theory. A distinction is made between the theoretical domain of knowledge and the empirical domain of knowledge; and, as depicted in Figure 19.1, midrange theory bridges these two domains. Fundamental to the domains of knowledge is the para-digmatic perspective. The paradigmatic perspective provides the outer ring for the recursive theorizing process between general theory, midrange theory, and applied research. A paradigm (e.g., positivism, pragmatism, or subjectivism) is the generally accepted perspective of a par-ticular discipline at a given time and provides philosophical consensus on how to understand reality and conduct research (Kuhn, 1962). While a theory explains something, a paradigm does not explain something, but exists before theory. We explore a paradigmatic perspective that is not based on a single discipline, but one that is cross-disciplinary.

Figure 19.1 distinguishes between three levels of theory, which we discuss next:

General theories: These theories are conceptions and perspectives utilizing theory that is framed at the highest conceptual level and provides a perspective or logic of explanation for a domain. The theories are broad in scope, integrative, and context-free, and thus do not directly lead to empirical investigation. The theories provide the foundations for understand-ing and explanation.

Midrange theories: Midrange theories are context-specific. Hence, these theories provide frameworks that can be used to undertake empirical observation and models to guide manage-rial practices. Most of the theories currently used in business-to-business research have these characteristics.

Applied theory: Applied theory is embedded in empirical research and context. While the focus of applied theory traditionally has been with empirical research, "theories-in-use" can play an important role (see, e.g., Beverland, 2004; Zeithaml et al., 2020). Theories-in-use recognize that practicing managers, customers, and other stakeholders in a service system use theory. Theories-in-use is context-specific and can be based on tacit mental models.

The theorizing process outlined in Figure 19.2 recognizes there are multiple pathways to develop midrange theory and hence undertake empirical research. An important distinction is made between the focal general theoretic perspective and other general theories. The market-ing discipline traditionally has been based on a dyadic buyer–seller perspective, and the focal general theoretic perspectives are based on general theories either from microeconomics or psychology. In contrast, within contemporary business-to-business research, a network per-spective is adopted where focal general theoretic perspectives inherently are cross-disciplinary and broadened, drawing on sociological and institutional foundations and the management dis-ciplines. For example, the focal general theoretic perspective provided by Service-dominant (S-D) logic is cross-disciplinary and is a synthesis of general theories including institutional theory, systems theory, complexity theory, complexity economics, and evolutionary theory (Vargo and Lusch, 2017). Specific examples where authors have interfaced other general theory with S-D logic to develop midrange theory include practice theory (Kjellberg and Helgesson, 2006), actor–network theory (Chandler and Vargo, 2011), and systems and eco-systems theory (Frow et al., 2014).

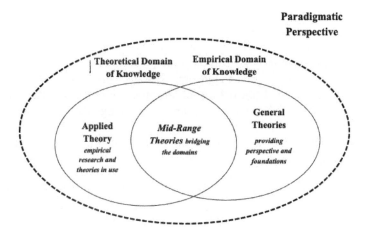

Figure 19.1   Domains of knowledge and levels of theory

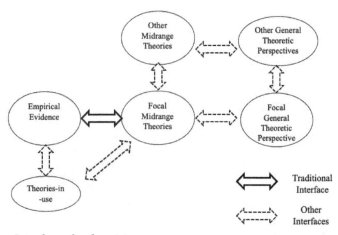

Figure 19.2   Interfaces for theorizing

As outlined in Figure 19.2, the focal general theoretic perspective can interface directly with midrange theory, but other general theoretic perspectives can also provide pathways that can lead to other midrange theories, which then leads to a focal midrange theory that can be used in business-to-business research. For example, when defining the conceptual domain for customer engagement, Brodie et al. (2011) adopted a focal general theoretic perspective from S-D logic, but also drew extensively on general and midrange theory from psychology, sociology, political science, and organizational behavior literatures to develop midrange theory. The theorizing process also drew on research, which can serve as an input for developing and refining a focal midrange theory. Applied theory drawing on theories-in-use provided valuable input to ensure the cross-disciplinary theorizing resonated with practice.

In summary, to undertake cross-disciplinary research, we suggest that there first needs to be a paradigm shift. Second, explicit attention needs to be given to the process of theorizing, rather than just focusing on theory as an outcome (Weick, 1995). Our approach meets the challenge by paying attention to both (1) theoretical frameworks and their cross-disciplinary foundations and (2) managerial practices to inform research processes. The recursive theorizing process leads to multiple pathways to develop midrange theory and hence undertake empirical research.

A somewhat different, but complementary perspective comes from design science research (Simon, 1969). Design science research is the standard paradigm in engineering disciplines such as mechanical engineering, chemical engineering, and information systems, but also common in medicine and law. By relying on a philosophy of pragmatism, design science researchers use any method, technique, and procedure to improve "the human condition by developing knowledge to solve field problems, i.e. problematic situations in reality" (Denyer, Tranfield, and Van Aken, 2008, p. 394). Being an applied social science, business-to-business marketing inherently can be typified as a design science.

Design science considers different types of design artifacts (Romme, 2016) including values (e.g., increase welfare of all stakeholders), concepts (e.g., customer engagement), models (e.g., SD-logic), design rules (e.g., to achieve Y do X), and instantiations (e.g., customer management system implemented in a company). The order in which these artifacts can be created are multitude. For instance, based on theories-in-use, practitioners can create instantiations, which then are studied by scholars to create midrange theories. In contrast, academics also can create design rules and instantiations from theoretical models. The creation and justification of all these artifact types belongs to the work domain of both academics and practitioners and can cross many disciplines.

Design science research centers on classes of problems, which refer to problems that share a set of commonalities and as such are considered generalizable across organizational settings (e.g., decision-making under uncertainty; allocation of marketing resources). Different framing of the problem (i.e., using a different theoretical lens or paradigm) may lead to different solution outcomes. As such, design science scholars acknowledge that there are no universal solutions to problems, but instead advance that multiple solution artifacts can co-exist within a class of problems. Operating in interdisciplinary research teams can be especially valuable, as it may help to identify the most promising research approaches and solutions.

3.   CROSS-DISCIPLINARY RESEARCH

3.1   Barriers to Breaking Cross-disciplinary Research

Although many university administrators may call for "interdisciplinary research," they often do not really know what to expect. It may be true that the biggest and most lucrative research topics may require a big-picture perspective, and the participation of researchers from several disciplines. This does not mean, however, that interdisciplinary research will necessarily come about organically. Next, we will discuss some barriers to breaking cross-disciplinary boundaries.

First, it is clear that a research team does not need to be made up of "interdisciplinary people" (however that is defined), but rather by experts in their own areas who have enough familiarity with the research problem, and understanding of the basics of each other's discipline so that they can communicate effectively. A business-to-business marketing strategy person does not have to be an expert in big-data analytics to coauthor a research grant proposal, or to work effectively on a research team (or vice versa). The construct "imported" from the other discipline should be well-defined, well-measured, and already well-published, making it easier to use in the new context. Some initial, intuitive, basic understanding of the concept by all involved in the research team would also help, but encyclopedic understanding is not required. This consideration has research team composition and even hiring implications. It would be better for the research team to be composed of these two (monodisciplinary) experts who have a good combination of skills and good communication abilities, rather than two interdisciplinary researchers who lack experience or expertise.

Incidentally, this same issue arises in industry as well. New-product teams are typically multidisciplinary in nature, with representation from marketing, R&D, engineering, design, manufacturing, and others all playing a part. In cases where a specific technical expertise is critical, say for example in the development of a new business-to-business product requiring state-of-the-art fluid dynamics, it would be better for the leading engineers on the new-product team to be experts on this topic. High levels of functional expertise are most valuable, and would be the expected contribution of these engineers (Ulrich and Eppinger, 2000, pp. 28–9). Their time away from the laboratory is better spent keeping up with the latest technological advances and going to top meetings in their field than learning about new-product launch strategy.

Another barrier to effective interdisciplinarity is that academic research usually is very monodisciplinary. An interdisciplinary research grant application might falter because the reviewers are likely to be monodisciplinary experts who may not understand the cross-disciplinary aspects, or who may fail to see the value of the joint research. Similarly, it is generally harder to get interdisciplinary research conducted, peer-reviewed, and published since the same reviewers will be gatekeepers in this process as well. Due to these factors, researchers under pressure from university administrators to conduct interdisciplinary research may fall back on opportunities in closely related fields (marketing can easily reach out to research partners in strategic management or organizational studies, for example), rather than stretching to riskier, but potentially lucrative partnerships with researchers in very different silos: engineering, mathematics, hard sciences, or medicine, for example.

University administration's efforts to support and reward interdisciplinary research may be misguided at times: interdisciplinary research should not be the end in and of itself! Forcing some vaguely defined interdisciplinary agenda on researchers can lead to wasted effort or, at best, research projects that are difficult to get funded or published for reasons stated above. A better approach would be to start with the research problem, identify to which problem class it belongs, and if the research problem is big or complicated enough to warrant interdisciplinary work, and if questions arise that require input across multiple disciplines, then the contacts are made and the joint research is initiated. Also, university administration should resist the temptation to reward interdisciplinary research for its own sake. It would be far more beneficial to create a research environment where researchers are doing quality work in their own disciplines, but rewarded for taking on the bigger interdisciplinary research challenges on occasion.

3.2   Suggestions for How to Undertake Cross-disciplinary Research

In this section, we provide some action-oriented guidelines that can serve as a starting point for breaking down the above identified silo barriers and fostering a research workplace environment that encourages and values cross-disciplinary work.

A great idea for researchers is to collaborate with colleagues from other departments inside their university or outside their university. For instance, researchers should try to join initiatives within their university that target big themes (e.g., sustainability, digitalization, or sharing economy). As an example, the Fox School at Temple has an Innovation and Entrepreneurship Institute (IEI), and faculty from all areas who are interested in innovation research (marketing, strategic management, entrepreneurship, and so on) can work jointly in this space. One of the goals of this institute is to collaborate with like-minded members of the business community, for example, by partnering with the Product Development & Management Association. Copenhagen Business School has conceptualized Business-in-Society platforms so that its researchers can engage in knowledge production based on "context-driven, problem-focused and interdisciplinary research that deals with complex societal and business problems." These platforms are funded for five years with regular evaluation of performance and success criteria after which research teams can apply for funding to set up new platforms. At this time, there are the following platforms: Diversity and Difference Platform, Inequality Platform, Digital Transformations Platform, and Maritime Platform.

Researchers should consider working with colleagues outside their domain, as this will increase the size of the audience coming across their research – and could open up entirely new research fields. A marketing department with strong interest in business-to-business and/or innovation may effectively collaborate with the engineering or medical schools. Try to profit from opportunities to present your work outside your area, as this leads to increased visibility, novel insights, and possibly future collaborative opportunities.

Researchers could connect with practitioners. Their requests for help are often interdisciplinary in nature and require input from other people. Important here is to have an open mind and be open to input from these other people. Ensure that you engage in research publishable in high-quality journals, though, at least eventually. Your business school may be pushing for closer ties with the business community, so these efforts may be seen as worthwhile service contributions at annual review time. A previous editorial recommended that universities provide incentives to foster an intellectual environment in which academics are encouraged to question assumptions and revisit their academic contributions, so that they can have greater relevance and offer more meaningful solutions to the business community (Di Benedetto et al., 2019).

Make sure you search for cross-disciplinary topics that have your personal interest, that is, what do you value? Think outside the box about who might be interested in cross-disciplinary work, or which department might provide insights for your research. As an example, your marketing department may have several researchers who are doing quantitative consumer research based on big-data analysis, or applying neuroscience techniques to understand consumer response to advertising. Could some of those concepts be equally applied in a business-to-business setting in a novel way?

Positioning cross-disciplinary research in monodisciplinary top journals is difficult. When targeting such journals, it is important to frame your own part of the research in terms of your own field. This will be a balancing act, as you do not want to lose your coauthors along the way. Be clear about your expectations and make sure that your collaborators understand what you want to get out of the research, and that your objective is indeed to collaborate – not to take over or usurp the coauthors' projects or ideas. This issue can possibly be addressed with a statement of research objectives that clearly positions the research in terms of what contribution it makes to the business-to-business literature stream.

Start with a clear and carefully constructed research question, which defines the precise problem class and knowledge gap. This will demonstrate the need for expertise from more than one scientific discipline, as the problem will require interdisciplinary collaboration to tackle properly. We mentioned earlier a possible collaboration with a research partner in neurosciences. One may identify a research gap, for example in managerial decision-making that could benefit from joint work with a neuroscience expert. It makes sense to hone this gap into a specific research problem that can pique interest among potential collaborators and can provide context and direction for the collaborative work.

Senior faculty in your department may have worked on cross-disciplinary projects in the past, and might have access to mentors in other departments. Reach out to these potential research partners. They may be able to identify possible collaborators for you, based on your research interests, and may know of available funding. A research partner from outside your department might even write an influential reference letter for an impending promotion of tenure decision. Look at your colleagues' university web pages, get to know their research agendas, and see what they are currently working on. If a cross-disciplinary institute exists, such as Temple's IEI or Copenhagen Business School's Business-in-Society platforms, it may be easy to reach out to researchers whose work is surprisingly close to yours, or who may want to work jointly with you in organizing outreach meetings or seminars with the business community.

Be sure there is a clear vision for the research. If two or more departments are involved, it may not be clear who is responsible for providing guidance. The right solution might be to establish a leadership team, which can call in other members to provide expertise to the team on an ad hoc basis. The leader, or leadership team, should set team objectives and timelines, and hold regular meetings, to ensure the project maintains momentum. It is also up to the leader(s) to make sure that all team members' voices are heard, including junior members and part-time members whose available time may be limited.

And here are a few additional thoughts for motivation:

- Visit networking events, for example, for funding opportunities that are cross-disciplinary in nature. Here, you often can connect with people from other domains and practitioners.
- Read topics outside of your main research area, not only scientific articles, but also books. Be inspired by people like Bill Gates and Warren Buffett who read a lot.
- Working with someone outside your discipline means that you will not need to know this literature in as much depth as otherwise. After some preliminary work to scope out mutual research interests, a good partner should be able to provide some direction regarding the most relevant articles and authors with which you should become familiar.

4.   CONCLUSIONS

Academic institutions know the value of cross-disciplinary research. The bigger, and more relevant, the problem is, the more likely it will require experts from many different research areas to provide their expertise to help solve the problem. We see cross-disciplinary teams, such as new-product teams hard at work in industry, with members contributing their own expertise to reach a common goal. But, as in industry collaboration, effective academic collaboration is not always easily achieved. Functional silo thinking may be difficult to overcome, and reward structures may be unproductive or may backfire if not well planned. Academic administrators should resist the temptation to push for cross-disciplinary research for its own sake, allowing cross-disciplinary bonds to form if deemed necessary for the research problem being undertaken.

We presented a theorizing process (Figure 19.1) that provides guidelines for cross-disciplinary research by focusing on midrange theory, integrating general theoretic perspectives and contextual research to develop midrange theory. Explicit attention needs to be given to the process of theorizing, not theory, as an outcome. The process we present is recursive in the sense that it considers both theoretical frameworks and their cross-disciplinary foundations, as well as managerial practices to inform these research processes. The process thus provides multiple possibilities for development of midrange theory. If it is decided that cross-disciplinary research is required to tackle a particularly challenging problem, researchers are incented to reach outside their comfort zone and work with collaborators from an unfamiliar part of the university, or from industry. We need to remind ourselves of the fact that all of us – designers and practitioners across different fields – are designers working collaboratively to solve a problem or address a challenge via the creation of artifacts.

With this process in mind, we proposed several practical steps that can be undertaken to facilitate effective cross-disciplinary research. These steps include: establish a clear vision for the research project, carefully construct a clear research question, work with senior colleagues who have access to mentors in different parts of the university, take advantage of institutes within your school that are problem-focused and are cross-disciplinary in nature, and develop a positioning strategy for your cross-disciplinary research that will interest the top academic journals.[1]

NOTE

1.   This chapter first appeared as an editorial in *Industrial Marketing Management* (Lindgreen et al., 2020).

REFERENCES

Beverland, M. (2004). Uncovering "theories-in-use": building luxury wine brands. *European Journal of Marketing*, *38*(3/4), 446–66.
Brodie, R.J., Hollebeek, L.D., Juric, B., & Ilic, A. (2011). Customer engagement: conceptual domain, fundamental propositions, and implications for research. *Journal of Service Research*, *14*(3), 252–71.
Brodie, R.J. & Peters, L. (2020). Increasing contribution in service research: fresh thinking about the process of theorizing. *Journal of Service Marketing*, *34*(3), 415–28.
Chandler, J.D. & Vargo, S.L. (2011). Contextualization and value-in-context: how context frames exchange. *Marketing Theory*, *11*(1), 35–49.

Denyer, D., Tranfield, D., & Van Aken, J.E. (2008). Developing design propositions through research synthesis. *Organization Studies*, *29*(3), 393–413.

Di Benedetto, C.A., Lindgreen, A., Storgaard, M., & Clarke, A.H. (2019). Editorial: how to collaborate really well with practitioners. *Industrial Marketing Management*, *82*, 1–8.

Frow, P., McColl-Kennedy, J.R., Hilton, T., Davidson, A., Payne, A., & Brozovic, D. (2014). Value propositions: a service ecosystems perspective. *Marketing Theory*, *14*(3), 327–51.

Kjellberg, H. & Helgesson, C.-F. (2006). Multiple versions of markets: multiplicity and performativity in market practice. *Industrial Marketing Management*, *35*(7), 839–55.

Kuhn, T.S. (1962). *The Structure of Scientific Revolutions*. Chicago, IL: University of Chicago Press.

Lindgreen, A., Di Benedetto, C.A., Brodie, R.J., & van der Borgh, M. (2020), Editorial: how to undertake great cross-disciplinary research. *Industrial Marketing Management*, *90*, https://doi.org/10.1016/j.indmarman.2020.03.025.

Romme, A.G.L. (2016). *The Quest for Professionalism: The Case of Management and Entrepreneurship*. Oxford: Oxford University Press.

Simon, H.A. (1969). *The Sciences of the Artificial*. Cambridge, MA: MIT Press.

Ulrich, K.T. & Eppinger, S.D. (2000). *Product Design and Development*, 2nd edition. New York: McGraw-Hill.

Vargo, S.L. & Lusch, R.F. (2017). Service-dominant logic 2025. *International Journal of Research in Marketing*, *34*(1), 46–67.

Weick, K.E. (1995). What theory is not, theorizing is. *Administrative Science Quarterly*, *40*, 385–90.

Zeithaml, V.A., Jaworski, B.J., Kohli, A.K., Tuli, K.R., Ulaga, W., & Zaltman, G. (2020). A theories-in-use approach to building marketing theory. *Journal of Marketing*, *84*(1), 32–51.

PART VI

Leadership in different contexts

20. Framing business schools as a socio-technical system: issues around complexity and emergence

Denis Fischbacher-Smith

> I don't know where I'm going, I don't know what I need
> But I'll get to where I'm gonna end up, And that's alright by me –
> Pete Townshend (*Let's see action (Nothing is Everything)*)

INTRODUCTION

I still remember the feeling when I was first appointed as a head of a business school and the nervousness that came with that responsibility. It was the stark realisation that colleagues would look to me to provide guidance around the school's strategic direction within a period of significant change that prompted that feeling of nervousness. Added to this was the fact that I had inherited a school that I had played no significant role in designing and a staff complement that I had not appointed. The often-expressed opinion by many academic colleagues that they could do a much better job of running the school than the incumbent also creates a perfect storm of challenges for any incoming head. Despite these challenges there was a requirement to try and help the school meet the demands of the university, even though the changes required would almost inevitably lead to some resistance.

In many respects Townshend's opening lyrics encapsulated that feeling of both nervousness and stoicism. It was clear at the outset that the school faced a range of competing task demands and that the latitude for making changes without meeting resistance from colleagues was limited. Even as someone who had trained to be a manager, the challenge of leading a business school in that context was daunting. Of course, there is an argument that those of us who have studied management should be in a better position to manage a university school or department than those who haven't. This in turn raises the question of why we expect staff within a business school to have a different perspective on being managed compared to colleagues in any other disciplinary area. In essence, whilst business schools are invariably different in terms of some of their external task demands, they are also similar to other academic departments in terms of the demands of balancing teaching and research and the reluctance of some colleagues to be managed.

The issues covered in the remainder of this chapter are not meant to be all encompassing, but reflect the experiences of the author in a series of managerial roles held over a 30-year period. These roles include being director/dean (on two occasions),[1] deputy dean, a head of section (the equivalent of departments – on two occasions), a research group leader (on three occasions), research director (on five occasions in four different institutions) and a programme leader. Anyone looking at that employment history might conclude that the author is probably in need of some form of therapeutic intervention for taking on those roles, especially in those institutions where the reward systems are invariably skewed towards research!

The aim of this chapter is to consider how we can frame and analyse the diverse and sometimes contradictory challenges facing any leader within a business school and, by extension, any other academic department or school. Whilst this discussion is contextualised within the author's experiential background, it is also analysed through the academic perspective of a systems approach. The starting point is a discussion of the nature of a business school, framing it as a socio-technical system. This is followed by a consideration of the design-based requirements that relate to the school's key performance elements. This is a longstanding issue within business schools that can be traced back to the work of Simon (1967) who advocated a design-based approach to managing the provision of business education. Simon highlighted many of the issues that are still relevant to the role of the dean, namely: the nature of the school in relation to other professionally focused schools within the university (not least, medicine, law, and engineering); the approach taken to management education and its impact on the learning and teaching process; and the role played by research in underpinning the school's professional mission. In an attempt to build on Simon's call for a design-based approach, the chapter draws on the work of Cherns (1976, 1987), Reason (1993a, 1993b, 1997), and Checkland (1989; Checkland & Scholes, 1990) in setting out a framework within which the design and management practices of the school can be contextualised.

The discussion is grounded in a systems perspective as a means of addressing the messy issues that can arise from competing goals and the structural limitations that are imposed on a business school as a function of the wider university structure. The discussion will explore the relationships between the actors, customers, and owners of the system that are highlighted within a soft systems approach, along with what Reason terms the "source types" of organisations (commitment, awareness, competence), and their impact on Cherns' notion of the "minimum critical specification" for the performance of the system. If we add to this the problem that many universities often see their business schools as a source of income, without fully considering what that means for the design and longer-term development of those schools, then the relationships between growth and design are brought into sharp focus.

THE BUSINESS SCHOOL AS A SOCIO-TECHNICAL SYSTEM

Business schools, like all other disciplines in a university, are required to meet the same teaching excellence and research quality requirements. However, business schools, like other professional schools, are also normally required to engage with practice, where the expectations relating to that research and teaching activity are focused on meeting the real-world requirements of practising managers and their organisations. Those managers who have professional qualifications may well have an expectation that those who teach them will also have similar standing within the professions and will not simply be textbook-only managers. The 'customers'[2] (that is, the beneficiaries in systems' terms) have a diverse set of requirements that the school has to try and meet.

Added to the issue of customer needs are the expectations of the business school that arise within the university itself. Business schools have grown in both number and size over the last 30 years, largely as a response to the market demand for courses across the range of sub-disciplines that constitute business education. There is often, therefore, an expectation that business schools will be an engine for growth in most institutions and in a way that allows other elements of the university to be cross-subsidised. It was this complex mosaic of task demands that was also a factor in my initial hesitation at taking on the role of head of school.

The nature of the business school has been debated extensively within the academy and the issue of its focus still remains an area of disagreement. Business schools are diverse in terms of the range of the goals that are often imposed upon them. This highlights a longstanding issue which relates to the design criteria that underpin the ethos and strategic direction that business schools take (Cheit, 1985; Glen, Suciu, & Baughn, 2014; Pfeffer & Fong, 2002; Starkey & Tempest, 2009). The fact that these issues are still being actively debated, points to the difficulties that have existed in terms of addressing them over the years. This is largely a function of the emergent and evolutionary nature of the underpinning task requirements generated for a business school by its parent institution, but also the differing perceptions that various stakeholders have of the nature of the activities that business schools provide. Many of the discussions around the purpose of business schools can be seen to have their origins in the design of the system at work and the movement of some schools away from their initial designed-for state (as a means of progressing practice-relevant business education) to a new emergent-state (that sees business schools as just another social science department).

Any change in the focus of a school obviously generates a challenge for those who have responsibility for managing them, especially as they will often have no mandate for the radical change that is required. Proposed changes may be resisted by colleagues, especially when they are perceived to impact adversely on established (but possibly outdated) working practices. In addition, the diversity in the academic subjects that constitute a business school often implies that obtaining agreement across those disciplines may be challenging.

This question of the purpose of a business school results in a series of debates about how it needs to be configured, who owns or has responsibility for that system, and what are its prerequisites and core characteristics. Figure 20.1 outlines some of the key questions that we need to ask of the system that we are seeking to change or develop. Fundamental to this discussion is the relationship between the core rationale for the school and its associated functions, along with the ways in which it delivers on its main goals. This is perhaps the most contentious of the areas of systems design. The linked question of who determines the systems' operating parameters is also a key area for debate, as many of the stakeholders within business education may not share the same sets of goals. This is partially evidenced by the standpoint and approach taken by some critical management scholars (see, for example, Parker, 2014).

It can be argued that the key challenges facing any dean of a business school are likely to centre around the linked issues of design and purpose, although it should be noted that the wider university context in which the school operates will clearly be an important factor in shaping those challenges. Some business schools are quite small, amounting to little more than a department, whereas others (such as Copenhagen Business School) are universities in their own right. This diversity within the ecosystem of business schools has the potential to generate local variation in provision and there has been considerable debate as to what form the business school should take as a consequence. This makes broad-based prescriptions impossible and, indeed, one might argue undesirable. Discussion here will, therefore, focus on a range of generic issues that could face any dean, almost irrespective of the overall orientation of the school's strategic direction. This is not meant, therefore, to be an attempt at prescription, but rather the provision of an analytical lens through which the challenges of managing a business school can be considered.

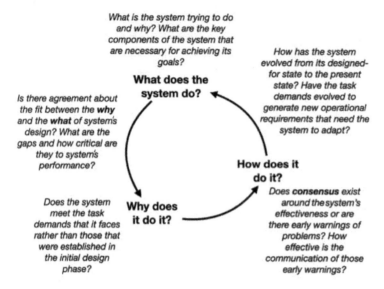

Source: Adapted from Checkland (1989), Checkland and Scholes (1990).

Figure 20.1   Core questions around systems design

SYSTEMS DESIGN: CHALLENGES AROUND THE CULTURE OF A BUSINESS SCHOOL

Many colleagues who take on the role of dean inherit a school that has evolved over a period of time and this may reflect a succession of historical factors that have generated customs and practices which can impact on the current performance of the business school. Contextualising the underlying factors that may impact on the design of a school as a socio-technical system is, therefore, a critical requirement for deans and directors and, in particular, the requirement to ensure that the school's managerial processes allow those elements of the system to match the task demands that the school faces.

In exploring the dynamics of systems design, Figure 20.2 takes the main elements of the Cherns framework that are relevant to the performance of business schools as a socio-technical system and integrates Reason's source types elements, along with the principal agents and associated worldviews that form part of Checkland's Soft Systems Methodology (SSM). The aim of any system's design is to ensure that the transformations (involving prerequisites, inputs and outputs) that take place within the system are carried out in an effective manner (Checkland, 1985b, 1989; Hollnagel, 2012). It is also important to remember that success and failure often emerge from the same root – what was a successful decision at one point in time may generate vulnerability as the environmental conditions change (Hollnagel, 2006, 2012).

For Cherns, the design of any socio-technical system requires the development of a consensus around the performance elements of the system and, we can argue, an understanding and commitment to those system goals amongst the various agents who are involved in its operation. By adopting Checkland's soft–systems approach, we can contextualise those agents in terms of those who own the system (that is, they have the power to shut the system down), those actors who operate the system (that is, they are directly involved in the transformation process), and the customers of the service or products that the system will provide (these can be both internal and external to the school). The principal argument is that any consensus around the performance criteria for a business school will need to satisfy the requirements generated by each of these groups if there is to be any agreement about the minimum design specification for performance and productivity.

Clearly, this is a process that would require a Solomon-like level of insight and understanding as well as an ability to constantly adjust the parameters of systems performance in order to meet the demands from each of the groups. In addition, it can be argued that each of these groups of agents will need to have a sufficient level of awareness around the task demands facing the school, the commitment needed in order to address those issues (as well as show insight into the nature of the problems that are generated), and the competence to be able to make decisions around systems design and performance (Reason, 1993a, 1993b, 1997). There is an argument which suggests that most business schools will struggle to achieve an effective consensus around performance criteria with each of those various stakeholders, and that many stakeholders may not themselves have the necessary insight and competence to recognise the managerial challenges that business schools face. This has the effect of generating a complex set of interactions between the main groups of agents, the awareness, commitment and competence that they have regarding the issues facing a business school, and the challenges around building a consensus around the main purpose of the school. This is shown in the top level of Figure 20.2 (expressed in terms of the system's cultural context). We can consider the main elements of this framework starting with developing consensus.

Developing Consensus

There is a question about whether it is possible (or even desirable) to generate consensus amongst the various agents involved in a business school, especially around the nature of the products and services that it seeks to provide. In those cases where it is not possible to achieve consensus, the school's leadership needs to clearly articulate its vision so that colleagues within the school can decide if it is a place that they wish to work in, or search for another academic department that is more compatible with their own position. Whilst such a stance may well sound managerialist, there is a requirement on those of us within the academy to reflect on our own position as academics and our decision to work in a school where we have significant differences or problems with that school's established strategic goals (see, for example, Parker, 2014). This is often a problem that faces those schools that see themselves as professionally focused, and especially those located in social science faculties. In some cases, there has even been debate as to whether a business school can be professionally focused, as business is not considered by some to be a profession (Miles, 2019).

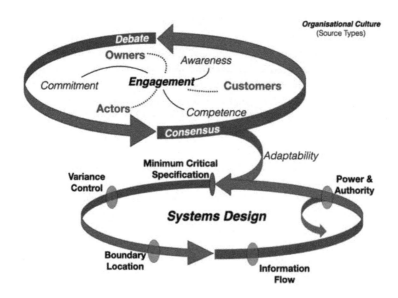

Source: Adapted from Cherns (1976, 1987) with additional material from Reason (1993a, 1993b) and Checkland (1989).

Figure 20.2   Elements of the design of socio-technical systems

Much of the discussion around systems design and the changing ethos of a school concerns the meaning of the need for change and the management of that meaning (Reynolds, 2020), which is a central element of the processes around systems design. It is the cultural dynamics that exist around awareness, commitment, and competence which are likely to effect the cultural change that is needed to move the organisation, in a purposeful way, from its current systems state to a new designed-for state. Organisational culture is, therefore, possibly the biggest challenge facing any dean as he/she shapes issues relating to recruitment, promotion, and staff development. Having managed an existing school and established a new one, it was the cultural change process in both examples that was invariably the most problematic, especially in terms of establishing the baseline specification for the school.

Minimum Critical Specification

In an ideal world, the performance requirements for the design of a school's strategic direction would be expected to meet what Cherns terms a "minimum critical specification". Achieving this would prove to be a challenging task, even if there was consensus amongst the principal agents around performance criteria, but it is almost impossible when the school has a fractured consensual landscape around the type of school that it should be. The school's ethos and its associated strategy becomes, therefore, a challenge for the management of meaning for each of the agents involved in the school as a system. For most academic units, the issues are often those of research performance (including grant income) and student satisfaction around learning and teaching. Professional schools could be seen to have additional requirements around accreditation and conformity with the professional standards of the various external bodies that provide a 'licence to practise' for graduates.

Combining the tasks of teaching, research, links to the professions, and income growth for the institution, puts an additional strain on academic staff which, in turn, often leads to the requirement for additional appointments. It is here that the origin of many longer-term problems can be found as a growth strategy can put the school on a treadmill that has to be sustained. That growth, unless carefully managed, can also shape the culture of the school if appointments are made which do not support the overarching ethos of the school. Any lack of clarity about what type of business school it should be will impact on the nature of the staffing complement and their expectations around performance across the range of task demands. Whilst the research and teaching requirements can be seen as the baseline for performance, it is often research that has a disproportionate impact on recruitment and promotion strategies. Some institutions have been so fixated on research league tables and the research assessment process that they have prioritised publications and grant income over other facets of the business school's portfolio, notably teaching and executive education.

This highlights a potential tension around the appointment of staff that can both publish in academic journals and also be relevant to the needs of practice. Given that most universities' promotion criteria are built around the requirements of research evaluations, this leads to what could be seen as a disproportionate focus on high-end academic journals that are often not accessible (or deemed relevant) by practitioners. As a consequence, these incentives have led, in some cases, to a relative neglect of the teaching and executive education aspects of the business school's portfolio. This puts a strain on the need to meet accreditation requirements relating to connections with practice. The result is the development of a staffing profile that can lead to a differentiated focus for some of the academic staff in terms of research, teaching, and engagement with practice.

For many business schools, the issue of triple accreditation is seen to be the Gold Standard in terms of external accreditation. This requires accreditation from the Association to Advance Collegiate Schools of Business (AACSB), the European Federation for Management Development (EFMD) EQUIS certification, and the Association of MBAs (AMBA). This so-called 'triple crown' is the benchmark for the leading business schools and there are around one hundred schools globally who hold this distinction. If triple accreditation is seen by the institution as the minimum specification for systems design for the school, the vast majority of business schools will not be able to achieve this standard. For those that do seek triple accreditation, there will often need to be a proportion of staff that are professionally qualified in the area of the external body for which accreditation is required.

The core question that often lies at the heart of consensus and the development of a minimum critical specification for performance is, quite simply, 'what kind of a business school do we want to be'? For a school that is seeking to be professionally focused, there will be a need for the provision of administrative support in the areas of external engagement, stakeholder communication (that goes beyond student groups), and liaison with professional and accrediting bodies. This will also require colleagues who are seen as credible within practice-based communities and who are willing and able to write for that wider audience (perhaps at the expense of more conventional academic outputs). The UK's impact agenda highlights the importance of research being seen to shape practice, but the introduction of impact require-ments has proven to be problematic in some business schools as many of the academic staff see engagement with the academy as their primary goal. The performance specification for the school will, therefore, have significant implications for its staffing profile as well as the client groups with which the school seeks to engage.

Dealing with Variance Control

Variance control is critical to determining the abilities of a school to deliver on its required task demands. For some schools, the COVID-19 pandemic has exposed a problem in the profile of academic staffing requirements, namely that of being able to engage in student-centred learn-ing that is delivered through an online environment. In the UK, where at the time of writing, large-scale face-to-face teaching on campus is not possible under the physical distancing rules, business schools have been forced to adapt and put their learning materials into an online format. Needless to say, most schools had not considered the provision of online capabilities to be a key aspect of the competency frameworks for appointing new staff prior to the pandemic. Schools are then likely to have found that the market is hardly replete with individuals with the required skill set and so schools have been forced to develop the capabilities of existing colleagues. This has shone a light on the staff development strategies of schools that goes beyond the narrow confines of research capability.

It is clear that the issue of learning and teaching has been neglected by many institutions, and especially during the period within which the research assessment process has been given a disproportionate amount of attention compared to the revenue that it generates. Each of us will have our own anecdotes about this imbalance. For example, one senior member of staff in a UK business school expressed consternation that a professorial colleague did not know how to write the learning outcomes for a course that they were teaching; whilst another member of staff kept asking what was meant by pedagogy. Similar confusion appears to reign over the meaning of blended learning, the importance and nature of student personas in shaping learning design, and the limitations of a lecturer-centric approach to teaching.

Many of us will have heard colleagues claim that students come to the school because of the reputation that it has for research (and, in some cases, their own research). Of course, it is rare that definitive evidence is articulated in support of this claim, and many undergrad-uate students choose a university first and foremost, rather than the business school itself. Postgraduate students often look to the accreditation status of the school when making their choices (whilst also considering the pricing of the various degrees). Whilst research does play a part in the reputation of any school, it is but one factor that shapes reputation and not the dominant one. The predominance of research is often a cultural legacy that a dean will have to address if they are to have a school that is professionally focused and seeks accreditation. This is also reflected in the methods by which business education and research is undertaken and the challenges associated with relevance and rigour within both of those core elements of the school's transformative processes. This can lead to tensions within the staffing complement of schools as those who take more social–science (and possibly critical) perspectives baulk at such a focus on practice. This tension is, of course, not new and has echoes in Simon's (1967) early exposition on business education.

Boundary Location

If we consider the nature of the designed-for systems state of the business school, its overarching strategy (and associated ethos) and the operating environment should determine the parameters around control for the input–transformation–output processes of the school. Clearly, this is a challenge given the difficulties in maintaining homeostasis within a turbulent task environment. The move to an online environment has served to shift the operating boundaries of many business schools and it has, in some cases, exposed the capability gap that can exist. Often the core tasks that are central to a school's learning and teaching activities generate many of the managerial challenges that we face – often due to the perception of conflicts with staff research priorities. Many of us will have experience of colleagues whose primary interest is with writing journal papers and who often relegate teaching to a secondary consideration. This is despite the fact that for many schools it is teaching income that cross-subsidises research activity. Managing disputes and expectations around the boundaries of those relationships becomes a challenge for managers. Additional challenges arise from the development of procedures and protocols around recruitment, the problems of sourcing 'talent' within a global market for business educators, and the tensions that these issues can create in terms of university human resource norms for recruitment and remuneration.

Information Flows

For any dean, the processes around feedback and information management are key to the effective fine-tuning of the performance of a business school. This includes market intelligence and the identification of emergent trends in terms of the needs of the client base (however defined). Key to this will be the structures that are used within the school to facilitate the enhancement of rigour and relevance associated with both teaching and learning, and the research that underpins that activity. One of the key roles within a school is, therefore, that of the chief information officer who can provide the dean and senior management team with effective information around financial, research, and teaching information. Gaining access to information and the extraction of effective meaning from available data has, in my experience, been one of the most challenging aspects of managing within universities.

From a managerial perspective, one area that has proved particularly challenging has involved obtaining effective information concerning admissions. At one institution, it was only on the day of admission that the actual number of students arriving could be confirmed. However, admissions policies vary by institution and the increased use of deposits in some universities has improved information flows. Similarly, real-time teaching assessments are inherently problematic and so issues typically only come to light when formal complaints are made by students or where the results of student satisfaction surveys are published. From a managerial perspective, both of these are challenging in terms of addressing performance perturbations in a real-time setting.

Information management also plays a critical role in the recruitment of staff. Given that the recruitment of staff is a key task requirement of the role of dean, there is a need to ensure that information about prospective candidates is collected prior to an appointment. There have been celebrated cases where the appointment of staff has proved to be problematic because information about their behaviour in previous institutions was not effectively captured prior to an offer of employment being made.

On one appointment panel, for example, it was found that an applicant had falsely claimed publications that he did not have. In another example, a background check identified that he did not have the qualifications that were being claimed. The individual had claimed to hold both an MBA and a PhD from two prestigious US universities. A check of those degree certificates raised some initial concerns which then had to be followed up with the institutions concerned, both of whom eventually confirmed that the individual was not an alumnus. This case highlights the issue of audit within any academic school and the challenges around identifying and acting upon early warnings of problematic behaviours. In this example, it was the individual's erratic behaviour, combined with the warning from a former colleague at their previous institution, which triggered the investigation. As a dean, the ability to secure timely and effective information is critical to the role and needs to be designed into the operation of the school.

THE BUSINESS SCHOOL AS A SYSTEM

Having set out the main elements of the Cherns framework, we can now focus on three issues that proved to be important within the author's experience of managing a business school. These relate to the management of variance within systems performance; the challenges of information flows; and the lack of an effective matching of the school's needs with the provision of services by the host university. Figure 20.3 illustrates the main elements associated with a business school and does so within the broader context of a systems framework. This is a generic model and the diversity in business schools will mean that the specific elements within such a systems approach will need to be modified for any particular school.

The core of the input–transformation–output process will normally be determined by the host institution. The question of the extent of that influence will, of course, vary. Some business schools are a faculty in their own right whilst others are part of a wider faculty structure and, therefore, have limited autonomy. Each business school will have its overarching ethos that will shape its strategy and associated transformations that occur. In the UK, there are several influences on this ethos that go beyond the host institution. These include, amongst others, the following:

- the Chartered Association of Business Schools (CABS),
- the British Academy of Management (BAM) and other professional groups that support academic specialisms within the business school portfolio,
- the various accreditation bodies (AACSB, EQUIS, AMBA along with a range of professional bodies that accredit programmes) and a range of other bodies that can be considered as connections with practice,
- the National Student Survey (NSS), the Teaching Excellence and Student Outcomes Framework (which is open to all UK institutions on a voluntary basis) and its equivalent in the devolved administrations (Scotland),[3]
- the Research Excellence Framework (REF) which is concerned with an assessment of the quality and impact associated with research.

Taken together, these elements illustrate the directions in which business schools can be pulled in terms of key influences. The school strategy (and, where appropriate, the university strategy) will determine the nature of the various inputs into the system and will require that certain prerequisites are in place to facilitate those transformations. It is here that the autonomy of a business school is important in ensuring that the prerequisites for any transformation processes are met.

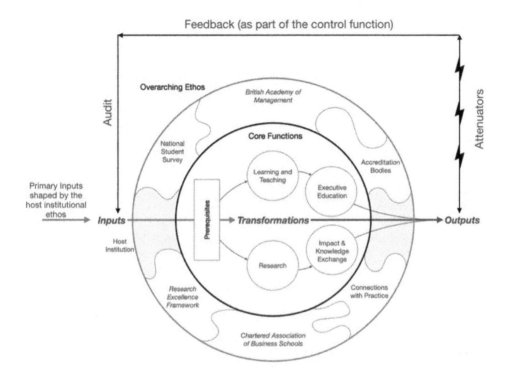

Figure 20.3   Framing a business school as a system

Figure 20.3 highlights four main activities that are generic to most business schools, namely learning and teaching, executive (and post-experience) education, research, and impact/knowledge exchange. Some of the elements here would include the following:

- funding for teaching (both formal government income and overseas fees),
- provision of qualified staff,
- students to be educated who meet the admissions standards (at all levels),
- the provision of a supportive teaching and learning environment (now including the capability for online provision). This will vary according to the groups being taught, as executive education programmes will require a different standard provision of learning environment compared to undergraduate teaching,

- service support around the main functional activities (mainly, but not exclusively, from within the school),
- research outputs as inputs into research-led teaching,
- research outputs as inputs into external validation and assessment processes,
- research funding (most research projects in business schools are typically unfunded). This would include Research Excellence Framework (REF) funding (which may be approximately 10%–20% of total income),
- service support provision from the university,
- the generation and maintenance of reputation and standing (as a proxy for quality).

The implication of the relative balance between funding streams suggests that research-related activities are generally institutionally funded (i.e. it is funded from within existing revenues which are largely from teaching).

In addition to the range of outputs from these processes, there are also feedback mechanisms that allow for the control of the system. The main challenge here is in terms of the granularity of the information that is available to managers (Beer, 1984, 1985; Boisot, 1995, 1998). There is also a need to ensure that the school is able to scan the current operating environment and to identify the potential future changes in that environment. A critical task here is the extraction of meaning from that information and its incorporation into the school's strategy (see, for example, Hidalgo, 2015; Omand, Bartlett, & Miller, 2012). Again, this intelligence function is a task that will inevitably fall to the senior leadership of the business school.

The issues identified by Cherns as key components in the design of a socio-technical system, and discussed above, have implications for the role of dean. We have set out some of the additional challenges that need to be considered when framing the school within a systems perspective. We can now reflect on the challenges around information flows by reference to some additional experiences arising from managing within a business school context.

REFLECTIONS ON THE PRAXIS OF BEING A DEAN

The aim of this section is to try and distil some of the main challenges and issues that face those of us who are charged with academic management and leadership. One of the main challenges that all university managers face is the need to try and ensure that their decisions are evidence-based and informed by an appropriate level of management theory. Of course, experience tells us that the process is not always successful, far from it. Inevitably, mistakes are made – both as acts of omission as well as commission. From my own experience, the majority of those problems were a function of the information flows that were available at the time of making decisions, along with the difficulties in auditing the validity of that information. We can consider this particular issue in more detail.

Information flows within universities are challenging for a number of reasons. Perhaps principal amongst them are the complexities that are generated as emergent conditions within a socio-technical system. The interactions between people and the associated technologies within such a system generate considerable potential for emergence and it is those emergent properties that provide the challenge for managers around information flows and weak signals of impending problems (Ansoff, 1975; Holland, 1998; Morowitz, 2002). Weak signal detection (Ansoff, 1975; Holopainen & Toivonen, 2012; Ilmola & Kuusi, 2006) is, perhaps, the single biggest challenge facing a dean. That is not to say that the dean is starved of information – far from it – the challenge arises from the verification of that information (Fischbacher-Smith & Fischbacher-Smith, 2014). Key to this is the triangulation of any weak signal information and the ability of the organisation to learn from rare events (Rerup, 2009; Smith & Elliott, 2007). University managers are dependent on colleagues for information around early warnings about potential problems and yet, in some cases, colleagues may for many reasons be reluctant to pass that information on. In other cases, the information is often codified in such a way that it is difficult for those in a managerial position to effectively make sense of the potential ambiguities that might exist within those communication signals (Brookfield & Smith, 2007; Fischbacher-Smith & Fischbacher-Smith, 2014). Whilst the management of weak signals is a generic problem, it is fair to say that it is particularly problematic for universities.

As an academic manager, I was always clear in my assumption that I was operating in an information deficit mode and yet senior university managers made the assumption that not only did I as the head of school have full access to the necessary information, but that the information available was clear and transparent. The following is an account of one conversation that took place with a vice-chancellor which illustrates the nature of those assumptions:

VC: Ah, Professor Smith, what is happening in the business school?
DFS: At the present point in time, I have absolutely no idea, vice-chancellor.
VC: (somewhat exasperatedly) But you are in charge, you should know!
DFS: Well, that is a reasonable assumption to make at a surface level. However, I currently have responsibility for 3500 students, some of whom are part-time, and we are operating on a 14-hour day. There are over 100 academic staff and some 25 administrative staff – many of whom are independent workers that we have to trust to do their jobs. The building has multiple points of access and egress and there is no mechanism for ID-based access. So, at any point in time, it means that I really don't have the full information needed to know what is going on.
VC: That's not really very good is it? As a manager you are in charge and so you should know what is going on.
DFS: That's a fair point, vice-chancellor. So let me ask you a question: what is happening across the university?
VC: What do you mean?
DFS: Well, you are also a manager and so by your logic you should know!

Now, let me be clear, that is potentially a career-limiting conversation. It is also as accurate an account as memory allows many years after the event. The conversation went on to discuss the challenges associated with the information flows that exist within a complex multi-layered organisation. That particular vice-chancellor was, at least, open to such a challenge and was willing to listen to the trials of managing at the sharp end. In that particular case it did not cause a schism between the two of us, but many of us will have worked for senior managers who would have taken exception to such a conversation. It highlights one of the most important elements of being an academic manager which was never to think that you are in control of a dynamic, multi-level complex system when you clearly are not!

The final point that I would like to emphasise relates to the ways in which the dean's role also requires the management of the expectations held by the various stakeholders who have some degree of involvement with the school. These expectations, or worldviews, sit at the core of identifying the components of a system as set out in Checkland's (1985a, 1989; Checkland & Scholes, 1990) SSM. They are also incorporated into the revision of the Cherns framework shown in Figure 20.2. In looking at the root definition of a system-based problem, Checkland argues that we should consider the CATWOE elements of that system in making our decisions

(Table 20.1). The various stakeholders invariably have different expectations and we only have to list the various groups to see how that might be challenging. Think about the needs of the groups shown in Table 20.1 and it is clear how the school can be pulled in different directions. Each of those groups will be either customers of the school and its activities, owners of the 'system' (and therefore able to shut it down or curtail or shape its activities) or be key to making the system work. Each of them will have their own worldviews about the school and its performance criteria. In addition, each will have slightly different expectations about the information that is given to them.

Table 20.1   Elements of Checkland's CATWOE acronym

CATWOE element	Description	Typical examples (not inclusive)
Customers	Those individuals who are beneficiaries of the system	Full-time students, part-time students, undergraduates, postgraduates (taught and research), alumni, local businesses, academic partners, other departments
Actors	Those individuals who are key to the operation of the system	Academic staff, professional service staff, students, funding bodies
Transformations	The transformations of inputs into outputs as required for the effective performance of the system	Production of graduates, relevant research outputs, impact, knowledge exchange
Worldviews	Described by Checkland as *Weltanschauung* which would be seen in terms of the core beliefs, values, and assumptions of those groups within the organisation. This can be seen to be critical in developing an agreed specification for systems performance	Various depending on the nature of the group. Each group is also likely to have a range of different worldviews within them
Owners	Those individuals or groups who can shut down or modify the system	Senior managers, professional bodies, research funders, government bodies and regulators
Environment	The wider context in which the system operates	Varies across space and time

One important lesson from my own praxis was to consider the implications of a CATWOE analysis for the management of the school. It is something that I have continued to use as a starting point for any academic department that I work in as a means of framing the problem space in which it operates. It also serves as a guide for considering my own interactions between the various agents involved in the system. Seeing the school or department within the wider context of a systems approach has been one of the most valuable lessons that I have learned and one that is essential to framing the parameters of systems performance.

CONCLUSIONS

This chapter has set out a framework within which the design challenges associated with business schools can be considered. It has adopted a systems approach and has highlighted some of the managerial challenges associated with the requirement to address the expectations of multiple stakeholders and the associated management of meaning within that context. Business schools are invariably managerially challenging because of the different environmental settings in which they operate – the academic, professional, accreditation, and practice-based contexts that are typified by those schools that seek to speak to a broad range of customer groups (students, executives, academics, and communities of practice). This doesn't necessarily make them unique as entities to manage – other professional schools will have the same range of issues – but compared to a more social science-oriented school, that does not seek accreditation, they are more challenging.

The use of systems frameworks has highlighted the important elements in the design of business schools and the problems that can be generated as a consequence of the dislocation between the school and the wider institution. Whilst universities are often content to see business schools as agents for growth, they struggle to provide those schools with established practices and processes that allow them to function effectively in that context. By framing the school within a systems perspective, it is argued that this allows the need to match the various components of the system with the next layer in the organisational structure. The transactions between the various levels of the organisation around information flows are often at the root cause of the, sometimes, dysfunctional relationships that can occur between a business school and its wider institution.

Business schools must also shoulder some of the blame for the mismatch between their needs – especially around accreditation – and the provision of central university services. The failure to require service level agreements between the school and central services is as much of a problem for the school as it is for the central administration. If business schools are to be seen as different to many other academic areas, especially within social science faculties, they need to ensure that they clearly articulate what those differences are and how, within the context of the university's funding model, they can be supported.

This does require that business schools practise what they preach and operate in line with the standards of management practices that are established within the professions. This will lead to shifts in the recruitment and staff development strategies of some schools, the academic and professional qualifications required of academic staff, and the relevance of the research carried out within the school.

If business schools wish to be treated differently from other areas in terms of access to resources, they may well have to change their orientation away from the conventional model of a social science-type of a department to one that can deliver across the demands of an accredited school. Be careful what you wish for as the task demands of that environment are exacting and, in some cases, unforgiving.

ACKNOWLEDGEMENTS

The author would like to thank Martin Reynolds, Moira Fischbacher-Smith, Kenneth Starkey, and Alan Irwin for comments on some of the arguments presented in this chapter. Needless to say, all acts of omission and commission remain those of the author as there is clearly no one else to blame!

NOTES

1. In the UK, the title is often Director or Head of School but I have used the internationally more common term of Dean within this chapter to describe the role of the head of the business school.

2. Within a learning and teaching context, the notion of a customer does not work well with many academic staff and its use here does not signify an approach towards the marketisation of education from a consumer perspective.
3. In Scotland, the Quality Enhancement Framework is an institutional review process carried out by QAA Scotland. Similar processes are in place in Wales and Northern Ireland.

REFERENCES

Ansoff, H. I. 1975. Managing strategic surprise by response to weak signals. *California Management Review*, 18(2): 21–33.

Beer, S. 1984. The viable system model: its provenance, development, methodology and pathology. *Journal of the Operational Research Society*, 35(1): 7–25.

Beer, S. 1985. *Diagnosing the System for Organisations*. Chichester: John Wiley & Sons.

Boisot, M. H. 1995. *Information Space: A Framework for Learning in Organizations, Institutions and Culture*. London: Thompson Business Press.

Boisot, M. H. 1998. *Knowledge Assets: Securing Competitive Advantage in the Information Economy*. Oxford: Oxford University Press.

Brookfield, D., & Smith, D. 2007. Managerial intervention and instability in healthcare organisations: the role of complexity in explaining the scope of effective management. *Risk Management: An International Journal*, 8(4): 268–93.

Checkland, P. 1985a. Achieving 'desirable and feasible' change: an application of Soft Systems Methodology. *The Journal of the Operational Research Society*, 36(9): 821–31.

Checkland, P. 1985b. From optimizing to learning: a development of systems thinking for the 1990s. *The Journal of the Operational Research Society*, 36(9): 757–67.

Checkland, P. 1989. Soft Systems Methodology. *Human Systems Management*, 8(4): 273–89.

Checkland, P. B., & Scholes, J. 1990. *Soft Systems Methodology in Action*. Chichester: Wiley.

Cheit, E. F. 1985. Business schools and their critics. *California Management Review*, 27(3): 43–62.

Cherns, A. 1976. The principles of sociotechnical design. *Human Relations*, 29(8): 783–92.

Cherns, A. 1987. Principles of sociotechnical design revisted. *Human Relations*, 40(3): 153–61.

Fischbacher-Smith, D., & Fischbacher-Smith, M. 2014. What lies beneath? The role of informal and hidden networks in the management of crises. *Financial Accountability & Management*, 30(3): 259–78.

Glen, R., Suciu, C., & Baughn, C. 2014. The need for design thinking in business schools. *Academy of Management Learning & Education*, 13(4): 653–67.

Hidalgo, C. 2015. *Why Information Grows: The Evolution of Order, from Atoms to Economics*. London: Penguin Books.

Holland, J. H. 1998. *Emergence: From Order to Chaos*. New York: Oxford University Press.

Hollnagel, E. 2006. Resilience: the challenge of the unstable. In E. Hollnagel, D. D. Woods, & N. Leveson (eds), *Resilience Engineering: Concepts and Precepts*: 9–17. Farnham: Ashgate.

Hollnagel, E. 2012. *FRAM: The Functional Resonance Analysis Method*. London: CRC Press.

Holopainen, M., & Toivonen, M. 2012. Weak signals: Ansoff today. *Futures*, 44(3): 198–205.

Ilmola, L., & Kuusi, O. 2006. Filters of weak signals hinder foresight: monitoring weak signals efficiently in corporate decision-making. *Futures*, 38(8): 908–24.

Miles, E. W. 2019. *The Purpose of the Business School. Alternative Views and Implications for the Future*. Cham: Springer Nature/Palgrave Pivot.

Morowitz, H. J. 2002. *The Emergence of Everything: How the World Became Complex*. New York: Oxford University Press.

Omand, D., Bartlett, J., & Miller, C. 2012. Introducing Social Media Intelligence (SOCMINT). *Intelligence and National Security*, 27(6): 801–23.

Parker, M. 2014. University, Ltd: changing a business school. *Organization*, 21(2): 281–92.

Pfeffer, J., & Fong, C. T. 2002. The end of business schools? Less success than meets the eye. *Academy of Management Learning & Education*, 1(1): 78–95.

Reason, J. T. 1993a. The identification of latent organizational failures in complex systems. In J. A. Wise, V. D. Hopkin, & P. Stager (eds), *Verification and Validation of Complex Systems: Human Factors Issues*, Vol. 110: 223–37. Berlin & Heidelberg: Springer.

Reason, J. T. 1993b. Managing the management risk: new approaches to organisational safety. In B. Wilpert, & T. Qvale (eds), *Reliability and Safety in Hazardous Work Systems: Approaches to Analysis and Design*: 7–22. Hove: Lawrence Erlbaum Associates.

Reason, J. T. 1997. *Managing the Risks of Organizational Accidents*. Aldershot: Ashgate.

Rerup, C. 2009. Attentional triangulation: learning from unexpected rare crises. *Organization Science*, 20(5): 876–93.

Reynolds, M. 2020. Personal communication.

Simon, H. A. 1967. The business school: a problem in organizational design. *Journal of Management Studies*, 4(1): 1–16.

Smith, D., & Elliott, D. 2007. Exploring the barriers to learning from crisis: organizational learning and crisis. *Management Learning*, 38(5): 519–38.

Starkey, K., & Tempest, S. 2009. The winter of our discontent: the design challenge for business schools. *Academy of Management Learning & Education*, 8(4): 576–86.

21. Business school leadership in an era of change and uncertainty: complex structures, executive education and accreditation

Kai Peters

In the business school landscape, context is everything. The ability to act depends entirely on the opportunities one has at hand as well as the constraints under which one works. While there are some business schools which originated and continue as stand-alone institutions and are largely masters of their own destiny, most business schools are parts of universities. Increasingly, universities, and as a consequence, business schools, have become more complex and complicated – with multiple activities, multiple locations and multiple audiences.

Many institutions now work across multiple sites bridging urban and suburban campuses; add to this feeder foundation year activities (where under-qualified students do a pre-university preparation year) and online education often delivered in conjunction with for-profit partners, international campuses, academic partnerships, and validation activities. For another layer of complexity, consider the different products and services ranging from 'business-to-consumer products' like undergraduate and postgraduate pre-experience degrees, through post-experience programmes, part-time programmes for working professionals ('business-to-business consumer (B2BC) products') right along to business-to-business executive education where corporate learning and development managers purchase education on behalf of their staff.

Lastly, scale these elements up to a global level. At last count, there are close to two hundred countries in the world. Many of these countries are involved in international student mobility either as exporters or importers of students. In some, direct student recruitment is possible. In most, educational agents intermediate between the university and the school.

One can thus view the managerial challenges of business schools as a three-dimensional Rubik's cube with one axis representing products, another locations, and a third markets. Defining the suitable strategies and structures for institutional success, alas, is neither simple nor as well developed as it ought to be in, it is my contention, most universities and business schools around the world.

This chapter has three goals. The first sets out to investigate what the present context means for increasingly complex business school internal management. The second focuses more specifically on the little discussed area of business schools: the business-to-business strand of services – executive education. The third is to reflect on what this increasing complexity means for business school associations and accreditation activities. Lastly, I'd like to add that the chapter seeks to capture insights gained over close to 30 years in business schools, 20 of which as a dean or pro-vice-chancellor. It is opinionated, and does not seek to reference every article, chapter and book ever written.

RECENT TRENDS

Many roads have led to these multi-campus, multi-activity institutions. In some cases, institutions were brought together through merger policies instigated by local, regional or national governments. In France particularly, funding that had previously been provided by a local Chamber of Commerce for business schools began to dry up leading to new constellations of multi-location institutions. In the above cases, the mergers were driven from above.

In other cases, mergers have occurred in more of a 'mergers and acquisitions' manner to achieve critical mass. Invariably there was the acquirer and the target. Taking place mostly in the private sector and often but not solely originating from US or UK for-profit educational groups, a 'buy and build' strategy has been pursued. In some cases, the portfolio of schools has become significant and invariably the range of institutions acquired has covered a wide range of subjects and degree levels.

Lastly, a number of individual institutions have expanded to the point where they have become small groups in and of themselves, having added suburban or urban campuses, international locations and online activities. My own institution has five sites in the UK, three internationally, extensive online provision, and a range of partnership arrangements.

MANAGEMENT CONSEQUENCES

In a short chapter, one can only conduct a whistle-stop tour of the strategic options open to a business school.[1] From my perspective, one needs to start with an assessment of the assets that a school has, a resource-based view of the firm, if you will. In which segments of the Rubik's cube is one already active? The questions are numerous, but a sensible approach is for the school to review existing programmes in the life-cycle of studies it is active in from 'the nursery to the nursing home' or perhaps more prosaically from pre-university feeder courses through to executive education. As noted earlier, there are basically three broad categories of programmes here. The first is the business-to-consumer (B2C) (and often business-to-consumers' parents) portfolio: undergraduate and pre-experience postgraduate programmes. In many countries, the student recruitment and admissions process for undergraduates is managed nationally through a clearing house function. Additional international students are largely recruited through agents. Pre-experience students are also largely within the remit of agents' networks while business schools also seek to retain as many of their own undergraduates as possible, or seek to attract them from competitor universities.

The second major segment is the postgraduate students who already have experience. They need to be enticed to leave their workplaces and clearly seek a return on investment for their studies. Recruiting these students into business schools is driven in large part by business school rankings which were popularised in 1987 in *Business Week* and now feature in numerous publications with the *Financial Times* being another key influencer.

Students studying on a part-time basis, whether in person, or through a largely distance educational basis, as well as participants on short open courses fall into the B2BC category.

They continue to be employed and wherever possible seek to convince their employers to foot the bill for their studies.

The last category is executive education, whether management development – the 'chronic' need for the development of managerial skills, or organisation development – the 'acute' need to change the organisation as quickly as possible. This broad category, more of which to follow, is a business-to-business activity more akin to a professional service firm than to a 'university' and it thus has a completely different set of drivers ranging from sales through to delivery and ongoing relationship management.

Each of these broad segments is differentially represented in the business school community. Some schools try and cover all segments, but most fall into a sub-set of the overall portfolio potential. This is largely determined by the institution's history and this, in turn, is a factor of the institution's location, teaching or research orientation, and financial resource base. Universities of Applied Science, often polytechnics in previous incarnations, have grown out from the undergraduate teaching end of the spectrum. Well-endowed research institutions then also place significant weight on postgraduate students including doctoral contingents and providers of post-experience and executive education tend overwhelmingly to be located in large urban, often national capital, regions. That is where the business community is based and where there is sufficient wealth to afford often very expensive executive education.

The first challenge for business schools is to optimise what they already have. It is not, as one sees all too often, to launch into another segment because it is seemingly more attractive and lucrative. Business schools can be compared to airplanes. Flying with an empty seat is bad business: everything in both 'industries' is about pricing and yield management, but all too many business schools have a profusion of courses with low student numbers that they do little about. Optimising the portfolio can mean the difference between scraping by and being financially well managed. Courses need to have some minimum number guidelines which are adhered to either by marketing them better, by consolidating similar programmes or by stopping them altogether.

The metric developed in the previously mentioned book (Peters, Smith and Thomas, 2018; see note 1) is to compare activities to calculate delivery income for faculty members on an income per day basis. While it is a terribly blunt instrument since it does not take costs, including preparation and grading, into account, it is quite illuminating. For example, 25 students in a typical UK undergraduate course pay 25 times approximately £10,000. They will get taught something in the range of 400 hours per annum – basically 50 eight-hour days. £250,000 divided by 50 days generates £5,000 per teaching day. Scaling-up to 50 students in the class, or 100, is financially even more attractive.

At the moment, certainly in the Anglosphere and the more developed world, the segment of the portfolio which is growing is the postgraduate pre-experience segment. In many countries, especially the non-UK European countries, the pre-Bologna Accord view of a combined Bachelors'/Masters' course has morphed into switching institutions between the Bachelors and Masters phases but staying loyal to the combination. This has also facilitated the expansion of provision and recruitment for UK and Irish institutions. Additionally, students are aware that their career prospects improve through Masters' study – both through the additional education and often because of greater resources, especially in terms of career services, offered to postgraduate Masters' students.

Challenging, on the other hand, is the Master of Business Administration (MBA) portfolio. Supply outstrips demand and a 'winner-takes-all' drift is clearly underway – certainly at the prestige end of the spectrum. The big-branded urban institutions are significantly outperforming more provincially located institutions, but even in the large cities, MBA volumes are not what they once were. I believe this is also due to the increasingly exorbitant tuition fees that have far outstripped inflation and seem unfair compared to tuition fees being charged for 'normal' Masters' programmes.

As with the undergraduate income-per-teaching-day calculations, tuition fees times participants provide a useful metric. Pre-experience programmes tend to charge in the £20,000 per annum range while MBA programmes start about there and continue up to £40,000 and more per annum. If an institution can recruit 70 students for an MBA class and charge them £40,000 each, the group value of £2.8 million will generate a per day income of £56,000. If, on the other hand, one recruits a motley crew of 12 students and only charges £20,000, then one is down to less than a healthy undergraduate group.

Having looked at optimising a business school's base case portfolio, it is time to turn to the second part of the resource-based view of the firm – to dynamic capabilities – the acquisition of new skills, abilities and product lines focusing on executive education.

EXECUTIVE EDUCATION

While many schools are already involved in some executive education activities, only a very few have engaged extensively in this domain. At a lighter level, existing faculty resources will be made available to teach 'working professionals'. This can be in credit-bearing programmes, but more often than not, executive education is non-credit bearing. In either case, it is more challenging than at first glance. Traditional faculty members are accustomed to being the expert in the room with a task of helping students to develop a knowledge base in an area hitherto unknown to them. In an executive education setting, the expectation is that the faculty member is there to facilitate the use of business school expertise to help develop appropriate strategies for the participants' own organisations.

In practice, the emphasis is very much on facilitation rather than on expertise. The expertise about the organisation, the markets, the customer base, the product lines, the management structures, etc. resides in the classroom participants and not with the faculty member. The faculty member is more akin to an orchestra director choosing the music and the tempo that the piece is played at. The faculty member, thus, is in a position to choose what to discuss and how to structure the conversation. After that, the conversation takes place in the room and the role of the faculty member is to gently steer the conversation in an appropriate direction. This involves managing the extroverts who enjoy hearing themselves talk as much as inviting the introverts into the discussion.

There are a number of other factors to consider in the executive education domain where there are significant differences to normal degree programme education. Executive education is compressed whereas degree programmes take place over a long period. Developing a curriculum for an intense 12-hour day, five-day programme is different from teaching a particular subject once a week for a 13-week-long term. Designing for this sort of an executive education intervention requires planning the appropriate mix of content and plenty of discussion and break-out opportunities. When it is a single company programme it requires understanding the hierarchies represented in the room and the relationships among participants – who is the boss, who cannot work together, is it an open environment, is there fear in the room? It requires planning accommodation, food and beverages, excursions and entertainment, and it sometimes requires picking up the pieces when an evening gets out of hand.

From a content perspective, a large proportion of projects encompass soft-skill subjects. Client organisations realise that there may well be some functional skills requirements like finance for non-financial managers or project management; the majority of organisational challenges involve leadership and team-work. A helpful guide is to define leadership as sense-making, on the one hand, and change management, on the other. Executive education thus seeks to help client organisations consider a range of possible strategic options. The executive education faculty member will work with the client to brainstorm ideas drawing not only on internal options but also by benchmarking competitors as well as adjacent industries where innovation has taken place.

On the change management side, three main concepts come up regularly: self-reflection, skills to manage a team, and skills to manage a whole organisation. Here, coaching skills, mentoring skills, change management capabilities, and dealing with ambiguity and uncertainty are all essential.

Because the rhythm of executive education is more project-based than a regular schedule, and because executive education activities can be delivered anywhere in the world (at least pre-COVID-19 they were), it is also a difficult activity to fit into the schedule of normally scheduled faculty members. If one is teaching every Tuesday morning at one's home business school, racing off across the planet to teach for a week creates timetabling problems for that institution.

For all of these reasons, the skill set required in the classroom, the need to attend to the group the whole time they are on a programme, and the scheduling and locational challenges, business schools that seek to significantly expand their executive education activities end up creating a parallel universe of faculty members who are more like professional service consultants than they are standard academics.

An interesting question arises for the schools. Where should these practical academics, 'pracademics' come from? Should the school make them or buy them? Most institutions will have a number of people who are suitable although that number tends to be quite small. As an aside, it is most entertaining to listen to business school deans laugh when they are asked about how many of their faculty are suitable to stand in front of a classroom of senior management from a large multinational. Many executive education faculty members thus come from outside of the traditional academy. They will often be mid-career professionals, often from management consultants and other professional service firms as well as from organisational psychology domains. These career switchers create a challenge for the business school in two ways. The first concerns a sufficiently broad grounding in theory which goes significantly beyond their own professional experience and the methodologies they have used previously as consultants or through popular business literature like airport management books. Mid-career Doctor of Business Administration (DBA) programmes rather than PhD programmes are an ideal approach as there is a desire to straddle academia and practice. What is also needed is a real effort to equip them with the facilitation skills that they will need to be able to engage successfully in the executive education setting. Surprisingly, there is very little literature about developing executive education teaching capacity. What there is, is summarised by UNICON, the university consortium for executive education in a short survey article from 2012 which lists the desire of participants to be engaged and have value;[2] lists a whole host of tools and approaches ranging from action learning through to drumming lessons; and concludes with a series of abilities that faculty members need including facilitation and coaching.

The second challenge is to define an appropriate workload and career path which needs to be something other than the traditional tenure-track publications-based academic standard. What is considered good? Is it teaching days, net promoter scores, tenders won? In business schools specialising in executive education there is not a single system but it is not uncommon to find teaching loads centred around a delivery expectation of 70 to 80 days a year. Invariably, this means creating a parallel system to the normal tenure-track promotional and management system where executive education faculty members are managed as a group apart. This generates tensions with the system at the core of the business school and often with the systems employed across the university campus.

In addition to the content side of executive education, a big challenge arises on the financial side. From a project perspective, it is impossible to realistically predict upcoming business in any real sense. At the semi-certain end, one knows what has been sold, but it is still not certain that it will actually happen. Clients pull out or send fewer groups than originally tendered for. This can obviously drive down income substantially. In other cases, winning the tender is not actually a guarantee for business but merely indicates a second stage whereby the executive education provider still has to market programmes within the client organisation. Further out, one can only look for calls for proposals and tendering opportunities but knowing whether one will win is impossible. This makes workload planning very difficult. If a faculty member is supposed to deliver the 70 or 80 days of executive education annually, but there are no clients for that individual, they are an expensive carrying cost. The second problem is the 'if you are a hammer, everything looks like a nail' problem whereby executive education faculty members stray into knowledge domains that they are unfamiliar with but where there is activity. Suddenly everyone wants to teach leadership whereas they are actually supposed to be teaching something completely different. My own view of financial viability has always been that the basis professional service firm calculation of a faculty member needing to bring in 3.5 times their fully loaded annual salary is appropriate. Given how difficult that is to realistically achieve, the business school solution is often to work with freelance faculty members because that is financially more prudent. This, however, then begs the question of whether the client is getting the 'business school experience' or some sort of second-tier diffusion brand staffed by freelancers or faculty members moonlighting from other business schools.

The actual process of selling also deserves some further attention. Whereas recruiting students in a B2C or B2BC channel involves reaching out to the potential attendees, selling executive education generally means interacting with the corporate learning departments of large organisations or occasionally with senior management directly. Developing the capacity for this business-to-business channel means having salespeople who understand learning and development, bid-writers who can respond to tenders, individuals who can sell at project pitches, customer relationship management (CRM) systems, and access to tendering databases.

Managing the response is also a challenge. Given that there is no specific science in designing an intervention, the same problem stated by the potential client can be tackled in a whole host of ways. An innovation challenge, for example, can be tackled with a curriculum proposal based on strategy, or innovation theory, or from an entrepreneurship perspective, or from all of the above. It really depends on who is writing the proposal and how that is organised within the business school – are there specific learning designers? Are executive education faculty members writing the proposals? Are they writing themselves into the proposals? Is that appropriate or not?

The business school will not be the only party responding to calls for proposals. They will be up against small specialist organisations sometimes involving faculty members who teach for them already. There will be head-hunters, consultants and other professional service firms in the picture. What has certainly been notable in the UK in the past few years is the arrival of large aggregator organisations – accounting firms, engineering companies and outsourcers primarily – who are bidding for and winning the really large contracts that have been out to tender on behalf of the public sector. Clearly there is a belief that while business schools may be subject area experts and thus appropriate sub-contractors, they are not organised well enough to manage the logistics for multi-million pound/euro/dollar projects. This leads to a question worth considering. How much executive education is good for a business school? Is more better? Or should a business school consider limiting executive education so that it is a balanced part of the overall business school portfolio? Answers on a postcard please. If pushed, my own personal opinion is that if executive education generates more than 25% of overall income, the risks become very significant indeed.

BUSINESS SCHOOL ACCREDITATIONS

Whether to attract more or more highly qualified students or to sell more executive education, business schools seek to build their brand through rankings. Being entitled to participate in not all, but certainly the *Financial Times* rankings, requires an accreditation from either the US-based AACSB or from EQUIS in Europe.

Of the estimated 12,000 business schools worldwide, at the time of writing this chapter (mid-2020) AACSB accredits 607 and EQUIS 142. Achieving accreditation is not a simple proposition. Members of the 'club' scrutinise candidates on the basis of a rule set developed by the members of the club. While it is not the role of this chapter to cover all of the details of the accreditation standards, there are expectations that business schools are sufficiently autonomous, sufficiently and academically staffed, research active and internationally present. There is also an indication that club members are to focus their collaborative efforts with other universities that are also club members. It's all a bit like the Freemasons really and clearly disadvantages business schools in emerging markets where structures are more polytechnic-like with faculty members expected primarily to teach rather than research and play the full academic game.

Candidate schools are of course permitted to apply through a self-assessment report which, if approved, lets the business school progress to the second phase whereby a mentor is forwarded by the accreditation body to further work issues through. If sufficient progress is made, a four-person visit involving accredited schools' deans will then be scheduled for a face-to-face review. This process can take a number of years and newly accredited schools are getting rarer over time.

INCREASING COMPLEXITY OF BUSINESS SCHOOL–UNIVERSITY RELATIONS

So far, the chapter has been describing what a business school with significant autonomy can do about its business model and product portfolio. There is, however, an additional spanner in the works which generally gets overlooked. A small deviation is thus in order – a deviation to what was pointed to in the introduction – to the level of the university. Here, many of the best laid plans of the business school often meet an untimely death because the university has the ultimate say over overall strategic direction. Universities, in our judgement, are on a centralisation drive at the moment and the business school community has not acknowledged this sufficiently.

There are two key effects of this reality that deserve attention. The first is definitely paramount for many university-based business schools. That is simply that business schools are often no longer, if they ever were, masters of their own destinies. Decision-making on scaling-up locations and activities largely happens beyond their control. New initiatives like branch campuses are almost always determined at a central university level, especially given that they often offer multiple subject area courses. Mergers and acquisitions are also centrally run. Over time, this leads to 'business school'-type activities in a variety of different forms, faculties and locations. The business school will no doubt have opinions and may well be consulted, but generally does not have the final say on the original initiatives or management later on.

Similarly, how support services are organised across the university is also not in the gift of the business school. There is presently a noticeable trend in many universities to centralise a whole host of services in the name of efficiency and of avoiding duplication or divergence. There is a marked increase in centralised marketing, student recruitment and admissions, of centralised student advisory services, and of careers planning services in addition to centralised legal, financial, IT and HR services. There clearly are benefits here, but, also downsides.

For both the university-based and multi-location stand-alone business schools, the increased complexity has also, of course, led to multiple challenges on the more prosaic educational delivery tasks like developing common educational goals among the various campuses; paying attention to the different groups of students and faculty members; ensuring that the curriculum is consistent; ensuring that standards of admissions and progression are consistent; ensuring that professional support services are consistent; and lastly ensuring that geographically separated staff members can meet each other and collaborate rather than compete. Sometimes these challenges have been met and group cohesion is successful; often and in other cases, the consequence is a group of largely autonomous entities related fundamentally in name only.

Higher education institutions increasingly ought to reflect on how corporations, professional service firms, or for that matter hotel groups or supermarkets, manage local responsiveness with overall cohesion. We live too much in a business school/university bubble. This is a theme I am investigating at the moment.

CONSEQUENCES FOR ACCREDITATION

While the business school accreditation bodies nobly seek to be aware of trends and developments in the 'sector', there is insufficient attention being paid to the role of the university and the expansion of institutions into complex groups. Increasingly, there is thus a need to expand the lens from a focus on the business school to a focus on the business school within its context, especially within the university. Presently, many accreditation guidelines assume business school autonomy and control which is simply not the case in many institutions. This can lead to ambiguity and disconnect between the 'rules' and the realities.

In touring the business school landscape extensively, one comes across myriad institutions where business subjects are taught in other locations and often in other faculties where faculty members are not 'academically qualified, research active and fully participating', whether this is in the range of the 15 or so regional university branch campuses here in London (or in Berlin, Paris, etc.), in regional campuses within country or in branch campuses internationally, in validation or franchise partnerships, online, or in Executive Master of Business Administration (EMBA) programmes and executive education. Teaching-only faculty, the extensive precariat of hourly paid lecturers, and visiting faculty, make up a large proportion of the workforce.

Validation and franchising arrangements, which exist in 84.7% of UK universities[3] and many Australian and Canadian universities, mean that parent university degrees are awarded to distant students who will not necessarily be as qualified or as 'academically qualified, research active, fully participating' well taught as 'headquarters' students are. These partnerships tend to generate modest incomes but can also be seen as a positive form of sharing expertise and thus worthy activities. It depends on one's lens.

In terms of the control of the marketing, student recruitment and management mechanisms, there are also issues where rules and realities diverge. Clearly ring-fencing the business school and suggesting it should control all of these means of production is laudable as the business school would almost always prefer this, but it is unrealistic in the context of university vice-chancellors and presidents who make the rules. Making sense of all of this and passing appropriate accreditation judgement is therefore a significant challenge, but one that must continuously be tackled.

It is hard to suggest a simple solution for the accrediting bodies for a number of reasons. The first is that the role of the university makes accreditation standards next to impossible to comply with – telling a university vice-chancellor that there should be no branch campuses; no trans-national education involving validation or franchising agreements; that there should be few if any teaching-only, non-PhD faculty members; that the business school should please control its own marketing, recruitment and admissions, and student and career services may be a wish, but it will not become a reality.

Second, it is clear to me that demographic changes, increased competition and societal disruptions like 9/11, SARS and now especially COVID-19 has led, and will continue to lead, to financial difficulties for some institutions. The quest for efficiencies, economies of scale, and internal university machinations will continue the trend towards increased size, complexity and ambiguity in those institutions that survive. By way of focus, since 1984 and just in the United States, the Department of Education's Federal Student Aid database notes that over 12,000 branch campuses and complete institutions have been closed for financial reasons. For anyone in business schools or any higher education institution for that matter, this ought to sharpen the mind.

CONCLUSION

Managing business schools has become notably more complex over the past few decades. As noted earlier, the portfolio of product/market combinations has expanded significantly. Business schools need to reflect on their own strengths in terms of products, locations and brand equity. Additionally, they need to sharpen pencils to really analyse where they are profitable or loss making. This is not to say that everything must make money, but somewhere in the mix, there must be enough resource to support the overall goals of the school.

Looking to executive education as a source of additional income is a possibility, but as noted in the section devoted to that domain above, it is more challenging than it appears at first glance. It has a whole range of special needs which effectively creates a separate business from the degree-based activities within the institution. It is unpredicatable, volatile and one of the first areas of spend that organisations cut when there are economic challenges on the horizon. The most sensible approach is to consider executive education as a potential source of income where the portfolio size is limited to an exposure that will not cause excessive damage to the business school in a downturn.

Not to be forgotten is the increasingly intrusive hand of the university. While business schools generally prefer to be left alone, this is not realistic and as such it is worth a grown-up discussion with their parent universities on what can be optimised where.

If we add some insights from professional service firms then we can, I suggest, look at these issues that exist especially at this interface between business schools and their parent universities more dispassionately. If we look at income versus cost control as well as centralisation versus decentralisation, we can draw some conclusions in those realms. For example, on the income generating side, overall brand cohesion and undergraduate recruitment in markets where there is a centralised governmental student application system make sense as centralised collective university or group endeavours. Specific 'product' marketing, especially at the postgraduate level, requires specific knowledge about the subject, local conditions, student recruitment markets, and the ecosystem of actors and employers in that field. This, I suggest, is best left to individual business schools and faculties.

How to organise executive education in a multi-faculty university is an interesting question. In many cases, it already exists and is based in the business school. In my present institution, where executive education was historically less developed, a pan-university unit has been established for business development and delivery management. This unit also draws on the appropriate internal or external faculty members from whichever subject area is required, thus healthcare, engineering and IT in addition to the business domains.

On the cost management side, professional services are generally best structured in a centralised manner for cohesion and fairness across the institution. I'd nevertheless posit that physical centralisation creates 'them and us' conflicts and that embedding professional services within business schools and faculties while drawing them together as a collective – however the hard and soft reporting lines are allocated – is preferable. Matrix management is clearly unavoidable here, but there are ways to make it work. In all cases, open and honest discussions rather than turf wars are necessary.

From an accreditation perspective, I would like to think that an open dialogue about these realities for business schools in the future should be ongoing and is well worthwhile. There will be no simple answers, but awareness and acknowledgement of these realities is paramount.

While there are a few business schools that are perfectly well rounded and have sufficient autonomy to fit the preconceived accreditation expectations from AACSB, AMBA, EQUIS and others, most business schools are parts of universities that ultimately make the rules. Others are doing their best in developing markets and thus making a significant contribution to their national environments. They also need to be recognised as being valuable, rather than being second-rate institutions.

Finally, we are clearly heading to an accelerated shake-up of the business school and educational landscape. The financial problems encountered over the past few decades are nothing compared to what we will be facing in the future. In the 2008–09 recession, executive education contracted by about 25% year-on-year. What the economic effects of the COVID-19 pandemic are is anyone's guess. Sound management is definitely called for.

NOTES

1. For a complete description of the business school product range, see Kai Peters, Richard R. Smith & Howard Thomas (2018), *Rethinking the Business Models of Business Schools: A Critical Review and Change Agenda for the Future*, Bingley: Emerald Publishing.
2. See https://www.uniconexed.org/wp-content/uploads/2017/01/Developing_Successful_Faculty _Research_Report_WELDON-01-2012-1.pdf (accessed 15 April 2020).
3. The scale of UK higher education transnational education 2016–17, Universities UK report, https:// www.universitiesuk.ac.uk/International/news/Pages/the-scale-of-higher-education-transnational -education-2016-17.aspx (accessed 9 August 2021).

22. Academic leadership: the Danish case

Jacob Kjær Eskildsen and Børge Obel

INTRODUCTION: WHAT CHARACTERIZES AN ACADEMIC INSTITUTION?

Academic leadership is determined by the particular conditions of the organization and the context in which it operates. Danish academic institutions and their conditions largely remained stable for several hundred years. The 1970 Government Act heralded a series of changes that is still ongoing. These changes have been much more significant and dramatic than previously witnessed by universities. The changes have created new governance structures, new financing models, new incentives, new academic roles and new academic leadership conditions.

The authors have been active in academic leadership since 1973.[1] We will describe the many changes and their effects on academic leadership from 1968 to 2020. We will use the contingency model for organizational design (Burton and Obel, 2004) as a framework to explain and understand the changes and their effect on academic leadership. Finally, we will give examples from our own leadership careers.

Academic institutions have always played a distinct role in society. The term "university" derives from Latin meaning "a whole", i.e. a number of individuals joined in a society or guild. At the time when universities started to emerge, the term became a denomination of organizations of students and professors modelled after the medieval guilds. The rights of students and professors were typically laid down in a charter issued by the nobility, a city or by the Church; the organizations were self-governing with the right to award degrees and to determine the qualification levels of the members of the organization (Rüegg, 1992).

The university as a formal institution has its roots in the Christian Church of Medieval Europe. For centuries, higher education in Europe took place under the auspices of the Catholic Church in the form of cathedral or monastic schools (*scholae monasticae*).

Through his Papal Decree of 1079 that ordered and regulated the establishment of cathedral schools, Pope Gregory VII in particular was instrumental in forming modern universities. These institutions later morphed into the first universities in Europe. Among these are the University of Bologna established in 1088, the University of Oxford (1096), the University of Salamanca (1134) and the University of Paris (*c.*1150) – all of these were established following a guild structure. This is also true for the University of Copenhagen, which is the oldest university in Denmark established in 1479 (University of Copenhagen, n.d.). All these universities were part of the universal Roman Catholic Church and operated as an academic republic with its own laws, courts and prison systems. Several of today's universities have preserved some of the old traits, such as operating their own police force.

The professorial members of these newly established scholarly organizations enjoyed special privileges and had done so for quite some time. Professors of literature and physicians were granted various kinds of immunity and privileges under Roman Civil Law dating back to between the first and fourth centuries (Kibre, 1961). The privileges were bestowed upon professors so that they could continue to devote themselves to teaching their profession (Kibre, 1961).

The most influential statement of scholarly principles is the *Privilegium Scholasticom* or *Authentica Habita* issued by emperor Frederick Barbarossa in 1158 (Kibre, 1961). It was intended to protect any scholar who travelled for the purpose of study. Over the centuries the interpretation of *Authentica Habita* granted scholars a widening area of privileges and protection against the actions of civil society (Kibre, 1961). What we today call academic freedom largely has its roots in the *Authentica Habita*.

These academic privileges have seen many adjustments over the years in both Denmark and elsewhere around the world. Since the inauguration of the University of Copenhagen in 1479, academic privileges in Denmark remained more or less stable for almost 300 years. The University of Copenhagen had an extensive degree of self-rule with a Senate (*Konsistorium*) as the supreme governing body. It operated as an autonomous organization that could not be held accountable by either royal officials or the general judiciary system. The professors of the organization elected their own leaders and thus operated according to its own rules, outside the boundaries of regular society. The university was also self-financing during this period, primarily through the ownership of a vast estate and other assets donated to the university by the royal family.

The next major shift in the academic community came in 1788 when the charter of the University of Copenhagen was changed. The new charter institutionalized much of the daily life of the university including how exams were to be conducted and regulated. Degree exams were implemented along with a system of external examiners; this structure continues until the present day. This was a way for society to exert some level of quality assurance of university education and was thus also a step towards limiting the autonomy of the academic community.

In principle, the university's financial independence lasted until around 1900. Since then the growth of university education and research and the subsequent increase in cost has led the government to assume more and more of the financing of the university sector along with an ever-increasing reliance on external funding of research activities. This also led to an increasing political desire for monitoring the functioning of the academic community, especially how public funds were spent and accounted for.

The 1968 student riots also left their mark on the academic community in Denmark. Students rebelled against the almost unlimited professorial power triggering a new government act in 1970 that covered not only the University of Copenhagen but also the universities in Aarhus, established in 1928, and Odense, established in 1966. This act decentralized power and through representation in elected bodies at various levels including the Senate, it empowered administrative staff as well as students regarding the operation of the organization. Furthermore, the act delegated responsibility for developing and maintaining the quality of educations to elected study boards where academic staff and students had equal representation. In many respects, the 1970 Government Act marked a fundamental break with past practices as in many ways it limited the autonomy of the academic institution and formally reined in the organizational power and influence of the professorial college.

In a subsequent revision of the act, the influence of the elected bodies was weakened resulting in an increase in power of the different layers of management in the organization. This marked the first step in dismantling the self-rule that had been the traditional form of governance in European universities since their founding. In Denmark, the management of academic institutions, however, was perceived as weak partly because academic management remained in the hands of elected officials.

This ended in 2003 when a new government act did away with the self-rule principle in Danish universities. Academic leaders were no longer elected by their peers but were hired into the management position. At the same time, the Senate was abolished and replaced by a board of directors where the majority of members are from outside the organization. The chair of the board is elected among the external members. The board of directors appoints the vice-chancellor but not necessarily from among the members of the professorial college.

Another academic privilege that has its roots in *Authentica Habita* is the freedom of the professors to pick their research topics. At the time, when the universities were self-governing and self-financing, this freedom was quite extensive. The principle of self-governance has since been abolished, and with university financing coming from external funding to an increasing degree, academic freedom is under pressure on an unprecedented scale.

As described above, in general university governance, structure and financing were unwavering. Since the major changes triggered by the student revolution in 1968, universities generally and Danish universities specifically have gone through a number of radical changes that have transformed the role of the university, the role of academics, and the role of academic leaders. In the next sections, we will look into these changes from the perspective of Danish universities.

THE ROLE OF ACADEMIC INSTITUTIONS IN SOCIETY: THE CHANGES IN DENMARK 1970

It has always been the role of a university to do research and offer higher education. However, the research and education activities are interconnected with the particular situation of the institution. At the beginning, the universities were tightly bound to the Church. Then the king and the nobility took over, and now they are tightly governed by the state and the political establishment.

The relationship between society and the universities has affected their governance and financial setup. It could be argued that the purpose of universities has changed from educating upcoming civil servants like lawyers, teachers and priests, to educating a much broader group that would work in the private sector also. Over that last one hundred years, Danish universities have changed from being "traditional universities" to becoming educational and research institutions serving a much broader part of society and being ruled by the political system through the power from funding and national regulation.

The tie to the political system became apparent with the changes in regulation and governance. The first step came in 1965 with the establishment of the Directorate of Higher Education under the Ministry of Education and with a decision to establish more universities. By this, the political system took over the overall governing of Danish universities.

Until the mid-1960s, the University of Copenhagen (1479) and the University of Aarhus (1928) were the only two universities in Denmark. A boost in the number of students in the early 1960s led to the founding of the University of Odense in 1964.

In 1970, the Danish parliament passed a governing act for the universities in Copenhagen, Aarhus and Odense. In 1973, this law was extended to almost all Danish institutions of higher education. Before 1970, the governing of the universities was independent, e.g. University of Copenhagen's Board of Government was founded on regulations from 1539, 1732 and 1788.

The 1970 Government Act covered the three universities that existed at the time regulating funding for research, teaching and administration. It also regulated the universities that were founded in the following years, i.e. Roskilde University in 1972 and Aalborg University in 1974. Also, certain schools of higher education like business schools and some technical colleges were called universities and regulated by the same government act.

The 1970 Government Act was a formalization of the modernization that took place in the wake of the 1968 youth uprising. It was pioneering – also internationally – for its decentralization and democratic university structure. In the pre-1970 era of professorial power, academic leaders were elected but only professors were eligible and had the right to vote. With the 1970 University Act, decision-making shifted to democratic, governing bodies at the university, faculty and department levels. The structure of these councils was unique in that faculty gained 50 per cent, administrative staff 25 per cent, and students 25 per cent of the power.

This law also introduced study boards, which were charged with responsibility for the educational programmes; these were also unique with a 50 per cent student/50 per cent faculty composition. Initially, the chair of a study board could be a student. In 1973, one of the authors as a student was elected chair of the study board for the newly established interdisciplinary programme in mathematical economics. The faculty came from the department of mathematics and the department of economics. As the two departments were at odds about resources and design of the curriculum, a student was chosen and had to negotiate a compromise between the two departments. Luckily, the chair had strong support from the administrative secretary of the study board. Nonetheless, the situation was tricky and somewhat awkward, also because the administrative secretary was married to his economics professor. The 1970 Government Act gave students a very strong position, particularly with respect to the design of educational programmes. This setup lasted only a few years before the regulation was changed so that the chair must be a faculty member.

After much criticism, the act underwent a major revision in the early 1990s, which resulted in a new University Act in 1993.[2] Much of the criticism had revolved around the weak senior academic leadership of the universities, so the new act reduced staff and student influence in the various bodies. From 1970 to 1992, the leadership of the universities was split into administrative leadership and academic leadership. The head of administration reported to the Ministry of Education and mainly had a controlling function. The academic rector had the overall responsibility for strategic activities related to academic issues, but very little could be done without the consent of the Ministry of Education. With the law amendment in 1993, the head of the university was the rector, and the head of administration reported to the rector. The democratic bodies continued to exist, but the university board and the faculty councils now had to include one external member, usually choosing an alumnus. The position of the rector and the deans was strengthened, but many of the political parties believed that the leadership of the universities remained too weak. In the case of conflicts between departments or faculty councils, it was difficult to sort them out, and some conflicts could drag on for years.

All academic leaders were elected among peers. From 1970 to 2003, leadership and decision-making involved a process where leaders had to make sure that a majority of members of the collegial bodies would support them. Based on recommendations from a review committee appointed by the faculty council, decisions about hiring academic faculty were made in the academic council. Therefore, the dean had to manoeuvre as a politician, both to be elected and to get his or her ideas approved. From 1993 to 2003, the dean's power was vested in negotiating the faculty budget and getting it endorsed by the university council. Here the dean had to join forces with some of the other deans to convince the rector. A major battle was how much of the budget should go towards administration and how much should go towards the academic faculties.

In 2003, a broad majority in parliament passed a new university act, one that in several ways marks a break with the past. An important part of the new act was the transformation of the universities into self-governing institutions, with a top management board composed of external members, administrative staff, faculty and students. The number of external members must exceed the total number of internal members, and the chair must be an external member. Further, students, administrative staff and faculty were only marginally involved in finding new external members of the board. An amendment of the act in 2018 laid down that the chair of the university board must be approved by the Ministry of Higher Education and Science.

Further, the act abolished internal self-government. This means that university leaders no longer were elected by and from the staff, but were appointed. The board of directors makes decisions on overall issues, approves the budget and hires the principal rector, who is responsible for day-to-day management. The rector hires the pro-rector, the university director and the deans of the individual faculties; the deans appoint the heads of department. This change put an end to professorial power.

One of the authors became the rector of a two-faculty university. He came from another university and, until he became rector, his relationship with his new university was very limited. One of the faculties of his new university had a financial budget that was significantly larger than that of the other faculty; this situation had created tension and made it difficult for the smaller faculty to develop its research activities in particular. The dean of the larger faculty and its faculty board had, so to speak, run the university. As a new rector with no old political ties, he restructured the university from a faculty structure to a matrix structure with a dean for education and a dean for research. Following an in-depth analysis of the problems and after being rector for 21 days, the new structure was presented to the university board of directors, who approved the change. Later that same day the change was announced to staff and faculty. In the old structure, it could have taken years to make such a change, and probably, in the democratic setup, the smaller faculty would never have been able to pull through a transformation like this. Now with the deans' new responsibilities, they were obliged to make all academic areas prosper, and there was no political majority to thwart changes. The new rector also reformed the budget discussion, with the rector now controlling the budget, and together with the new deans, he could set up new budget allocation routines.

In 2006, the liberal government signed an agreement with the Social Democrats, the Danish People's Party and the Social Liberals, entitled "Agreement on future prosperity and welfare and investment in the future".[3] One of the major goals of the agreement was to reduce student completion time by offering universities financial incentives. Among other things, this introduced a time limit on thesis writing and a reinforcement of the students following the study guide. In 2006, the parties mentioned above also signed a globalization agreement, with a focus on strengthening the quality of the educational programmes, among other things. The Danish Accreditation Institution was founded, its mission being to accredit first educational programmes and later institutions. Only accredited programmes and institutions would receive public funding. This established a new means of regulating university activities. The globalization agreement also increased funding for research significantly. The increased funding was allocated by creating a zero-sum competitive game situation for the universities where, based on performance criteria, they competed to attract funding and in particular new funding.

In 2006, Denmark had 12 universities. The government wanted the universities to serve the private sector to a greater extent as they had a philosophy of reducing the public sector. As a result, the government launched a university reform that reduced the number of universities from 12 to eight by merging special universities like engineering schools, business schools and the college of pharmacy with the traditional universities. Further, a number of applied national research institutes were integrated into the universities. Thus, the 2007 Government Act produced a university system mainly with broadly focused universities to serve society as a whole, primarily the private sector.

The rectors were members of the Danish Conference of Rectors and its activities were to influence the political system. Before 2007, the Conference of Rectors was the mouthpiece of the universities vis-à-vis the government. The 2003 act eroded solidarity among the universities slightly, and the 2007 act turned the eight Danish universities into fierce competitors. Until 2003, the rector was the visible head of the university. With an external chair of the university's board of directors, some of these chairs sought visibility in the academic political discussion. Consequently, they founded the Conference of University Chairs. This led to a significant change where the Conference of Rectors, which was embedded in the Ministry of Higher Education and Science, became independent and changed its name to Danish Universities. The university chairs and the university rectors now comprise Danish Universities.

From the 1970 University Act to the 2007 University Act, many minor adjustments have been made in various government regulations as well as many minor changes in the University Act. This includes the funding of the universities.

The 1970s saw fixed financing of education, administration and research based on the annual Finance Act. Changes in financing were due to negotiation with the government. Financing of education was based on a six-year moving average of student intake. This was a huge advantage for the old universities with slow growth and sometimes even a decline in numbers of students, while it was a struggle for new universities with an increase in number of students.

Slowly the system changed to being output-oriented, based on the number of students completing their education. Similarly, financing of research went from 50 per cent of faculty salary, with the Ministry of Education determining the number of positions, to freedom to hire but with a financing model based on output performance criteria. The effect of these changes was that uncertainty increased dramatically.

Parallel to this, university financing went from almost 100 per cent government financing to one third from education, one third from research financed by the government, and one third from research grants, including grants from private foundations and European Union financing.

The many transformations in regulation, governing and financing have had a significant effect on the perception of the academic role and academic leadership.

ACADEMIC LEADERSHIP 1970–2020

The period from 1970 to 2006 marked more transformations and more dramatic changes than in the previous more than 300 years. It changed the roles of the universities, the role of the students and the role of the employees, as well as the role of being a leader in a university.

Before 1970, the professors ran the universities with a number of "scientific helpers", focus being on the professors' scientific disciplines. The universities did not play any significant role in society, but quite a few professors were well known. The professors were formally the heads of their scientific discipline. This changed with the 1970 reform, which modified the roles of assistant and associate professors as well as that of the professors.

From 1970, the scientific discipline was still very much at the core, but the new universities in Odense, Aalborg and Roskilde each had a new approach to science and teaching. Focus shifted to problem solving for society, and the students had to take courses from different disciplines, and many old disciplines were challenged. The professor was still a figure with the highest scientific credentials, but the decision power of professors faded internally, and the importance of the occupation as a professor also weakened in society because the number of professors started to grow. One reason was the establishment of the new universities and later on the universities were allowed to appoint as many professors as they liked. Professors remained the only academic employees who were appointed civil servants by the queen. This meant that they could not go on strike, but more importantly, professors could not be fired. They kept some of their old privileges. All other employees were subject to the general rules as employees in the public sector, which gave a lot of protection, but you could be sacked, and some were fired for a number of reasons. For all academic employees, the freedom to do independent research continued.

The change in 1970 gave students, assistant and, in particular, associate professors a much stronger role in running the universities. It was still important to excel in your scientific discipline, but decisions on the design of teaching programmes, of departments and in which areas new jobs should be created, and who should be appointed, were now made by democratic, governing bodies. This meant that every student and employee had an additional role as decision-maker or member of a "political party". A sustainable political base was important to make sure that you could be elected, for instance, as a dean, and to make sure that you had a majority support in the councils. Consequently, you as an academic leader had to interact with disciplines outside your own.

The socio-political system became increasingly concerned that it was difficult to control the universities and that leadership was not consistent. Further, there were a number of budget overruns, where no one was responsible. In one case, the government had to take over and insert an external rector to run the university. Further, a number of "minor" adjustments ensued. For example, very early on, the option of having a student as the head of a study board was done away with.

Growing concern led to a change in 1993 where the deans and rector were afforded more power but at the same time, they assumed budget responsibility. As a result, the head of administration now reported to the rector. It was also decided that some of the democratic bodies should include external members. Without any discussion, it was decided that new full professors were no longer civil servants to be appointed by the queen, but public sector employees. This removed the last specific privilege that professors had compared to other employees. By 2020, there are very few professors left enjoying old privileges.

As described above, in 1993 the universities became independent organizations with a government contract. They had a board of directors with a majority of external members. Leaders were no longer elected from within but appointed. At the beginning, most of the appointed leaders came from within, but in 2020 probably more than half of the deans are from outside the university and most of the rectors are outsiders – often previous deans from other universities.

This has altered the role and the spirit of employees. Basically, all political groupings disappeared over night. You now must please your leader rather than find and establish a political majority. Since all employees are normal public sector employees, their role has transformed into being a "normal" employee with almost none of the old privileges left. As described above, a university's financial budget is dependent on short-term performance criteria, and focus is on meeting these criteria. Many universities directly or indirectly apply management by objectives; therefore, employees turn their attention to meeting their individual part of the objectives and do not focus on the overall operation of the university. Up to 2003, one of the roles of all professor categories was to be an important part of Danish democracy. As a professor, you could not easily be sacked by the university: it took an immensely complicated process involving the government and peers. So up to 2003, professors were a significant and sometimes vexing voice in the public debate.

The change in 2003 made defying your leader a bit risky, and the significance of professors' involvement in the public debate has dwindled to almost nothing, even more so because as a professor you belong to a university rather than to a discipline due to the fierce competition among the universities, as described above. The tension between loyalty to your organization and freedom of expression is intense.

The transformations that were launched in 1970 were significant from the point of view of employees, but they were also significant from the point of view of those assuming leadership.

Did the Changes in Governance and Leadership Make Sense?

The transformations that took place from 1970 to 2006 marked a significant change in the overall purpose of the universities – from being elite learning institutions to being a significant factor in the development of society. The political establishment developed the view that in a modern society, higher education and research are the foundation that enables a modern, globally oriented nation to prosper. This had a profound effect on the environment of the universities. It went from existing as a relatively stable environment with almost fixed budgets and a narrow focus on the scientific disciplines to much uncertainty and complex environments with variable and uncertain income as well as increased political pressure.

The radical impact on the environment came with the change in 2003 when the universities became independent institutions with an external board. To some extent, these boards took a "management approach" with new overall strategies to support growth and internationalization. In the period from 2003 to 2007, growth was primarily concentrated on expanding the number of students and, in particular, international students. It was an easy way to expand an institution, and except for at a few of the "old" universities, that was the path the universities took. With the change in 2006 that increased financial support for research, allocation mechanisms also became much more performance oriented. About five years later, the political system tightened public spending in general, which also hit the universities. This was implemented by means of cuts in research budgets and stricter performance criteria in the educational aspect.

In a stable and simple environment, leadership requirements differ significantly from those in an uncertain and complex environment (Burton and Obel, 2004). In a world of certainty, you must be efficient, control oriented and apply a centralized management style, while in an uncertain world you need leaders that delegate, inspire and take risks (Burton et al., 2020).

In the period from 1970 to 2003, university leaders were elected for a relatively short period – usually three years. However, you could be re-elected indefinitely. In this period, the universities saw two types of leaders. The first one saw the duty as a leader as an offer you had to make. Normally they would serve only three years – sometimes six years. At some departments, the department chair was organized by turns. Others saw leadership as a lifetime commitment and worked very hard to be re-elected. The leadership primarily had an internal focus and major strategies were related to scientific areas, and leadership tended to be reactive to political pressure.

This would work when the environment was stable. However, when political pressure was instituted through the change in 1993, including that universities must engage in society, this type of leadership failed to deliver what was required by the political system – despite the empowerment of the rector and the deans. In particular, the rector had a stronger position. First, all leaders including the managing director reported to him. Further, the allocation of financial resources went to the rector and not to the deans. Before 1993, funding to the universities was allotted in portions to each faculty, a portion for administration and finally a small portion for the rector. After 1993, the deans and the administrative director had to negotiate their budget with the rector every year. Of course, previous allocations from the old system played an important role in these discussions.

So in the period from 1970 to 1993, the leaders were politicians running democratic decision-making bodies. From 1993 to 2003, the leaders were forced to act more strategically in their leadership. At the same time, they had to manage democracy in each decision situation as well as priming the atmosphere for being elected or re-elected.

While the period 1970 to 1993 represented a time where leadership was aligned with the purpose and the environment, the period from 1993 to 2003 was not. Pressure from the environment was misaligned with the decision processes and particularly with the speed by which decisions were made. Ultimately, a decision could be reworked after the next election. This situation created the view that university leadership was too weak, leading to calls for a completely new setup.

From 2003, leadership changed to a structure with leaders that were appointed for a 3–6-year period with the option of a three-year extension. In some cases, the leaders salary increased by as much as 100 per cent. Before 2003, a leader received his usual salary with an increment for holding a leader position. The increment was in the range of 10 to 20 per cent of the usual salary. This meant that the salary paid depended on the leader's position. The idea was that in your current position you would occupy a function and be paid to fulfil that function. From 2003, the position as a leader became a job and you did not keep your previous position; however, you were entitled to return to a position equivalent to the one you had before becoming a leader. This meant that the leadership and strategy changed from a bottom-up process to a top-down one. Sometimes faculty and administrative staff were involved, but that would be at the discretion of the leader.

During these major changes, there were significant transition issues. Individuals lost power and prestige. Seemingly, no major issues appeared in 1970 because the professors constituted a minority, and in the new universities, individuals that were hired knew the name of the game. The transition issues going from elected leaders in a public university to appointed leaders in an independent university with an external primarily non-academic board of directors was much more apparent.

These issues became very visible in employee satisfaction evaluations. In the next section, some of these issues will be addressed.

LEADERSHIP AND EMPLOYEE MANAGEMENT: SOME REFLECTIONS

The after-effects of the changes of the last decades are still reverberating through universities. Many leaders are struggling with their role because they were brought up in the old academic system where a leader would represent the members of his/her guild in relation to senior management. This is in stark contrast to the expectations of the current leadership role where the individual leader is senior management's right-hand man.

This conflict of roles also creates cultural problems for the academic leader of today since the professorial college is still expecting the leader to be more of a representative of peers and will thus react strongly to any human resource-related steps towards individual members of the college. The likelihood of potential role-induced conflict is also strengthened by the fact that a majority of academic leaders in Denmark used to be a part of the professorial college that they are now leading, and most of them will resume their former role when they eventually step down from their management position. Academic leadership is still not a career path in its own right and the dilemma of sanctioning a professorial college that one is set to eventually join haunts the academic leadership role of most academic institutions, not only in Denmark.

There is, however, light at the end of the tunnel. More and more academic leaders have chosen leadership as a career path and are trying to develop their personal leadership style in a professional manner. This is also aided by a new generation of academics for whom the concept of professional academic leaders is a natural governance principle. Eventually, we can expect tensions between academics and academic leaders to diminish due to this generational shift.

Changes during the recent decades have also influenced the members of the professorial colleges and the concept of academic freedom. The protection that the tenure system gave professors is under pressure throughout the academic community. More and more academics are temporarily employed linked directly to external funding, and dismissal of members of a professorial college is not unheard of due to financial difficulties, poor performance or interpersonal strains. This affects professors' risk aversion, thus threatening the role that professors play as an important part of the democratic debate. This is very unfortunate considering the important role that universities play in today's society, and nothing indicates that this situation will be reversed. On the contrary, there is every indication that the concept of academic freedom will come under increased pressure in the coming years.

NOTES

1. The authors of this chapter have held leadership positions such as rector, dean, head of department, head of study board, and head of research centres in the Danish university system from 1973 until now. They have also been students and held positions as assistant, associate to full professor in the same period.
2. See https://universitetshistorie.ku.dk/overblik/1900-2000/styrelsesloven/.
3. See https://ufm.dk/uddannelse/videregaende-uddannelse/universiteter/om-universiteterne/reformer -pa-universitetsomradet-1/velfaerdsaftale.pdf.

REFERENCES

Burton, R. M., & Obel, B. (2004). *Strategic Organizational Diagnosis and Design: The Dynamics of Fit*, Dordrecht: Springer Science & Business Media.

Burton, R. M., Obel, B., & Håkonsson, D. D. (2020). *Organizational Design: A Step-By-Step Approach*, 4th edition, Cambridge: Cambridge University Press.

Kibre, P. (1961). *Scholarly Priviliges in the Middle Ages*, London: Medieval Academy of America.

Reformer på universitetsområdet (n.d.). https://ufm.dk/uddannelse-og-institutioner/videregaende -uddannelse/universiteter/om-universiteterne/reformer-pa-universitetsomradet-1 (accessed 9 August 2021).

Rüegg, W. (1992). Foreword: the university as a European institution. In H. de Ridder-Symoens and W. Rüegg, eds, *A History of the University in Europe, Vol. 1*, Cambridge: Cambridge University Press.

University of Copenhagen (n.d.). https://universitetshistorie.ku.dk/ (accessed 7 April 2020).

PART VII

Personal leadership reflections

23. Responsibilities of the department chair: lessons from the frontline

Thomas G. Cummings

I am writing to share 21 years of experience as department chair (Chair). My knowhow and "shoulds" about performing this role are based on what I learned chairing a department of management and organization in the business school of a private university in the United States from 1996 to 2017. My department has four staff and 39 faculty specializing in three broad areas of organizational behavior, organization theory, and strategic management. We comprise two kinds of full-time faculty: tenured/tenure-track (both research and teaching) and clinical (teaching). My department also includes an affiliated research center that does applied work in organization effectiveness. We teach undergraduate and graduate students, who total about 5,000 in the business school and 49,000 at the university. Our students are highly diverse, with about 25 percent international students and 20 percent underrepresented minority students. Various ranking services place the university and business school in the "top-tier," which conveys their strong emphasis on research and student selectivity. My longevity as Chair spanned seven 3-year terms, each with a formal assessment and recommendation for renewal. Department chairs are appointed by the dean with the advice of the faculty. In the administrative structure of the school, they report to the vice-dean of faculty and academic affairs. I served with three deans, five vice-deans, and several Chair colleagues from other departments.

The term "responsibility" captures my reflections on leading an academic department. It conveys how I experienced and performed the role of Chair. I felt responsible for leading the faculty in creating an academic community that performs at the highest levels of academic scholarship and education; a collegial community that values different ideas and methods, openness and sharing, and participation in managing the department. I felt personally accountable to my colleagues for doing everything that I could to help make this happen. My decisions and actions were not guided by a cohesive framework for how to lead an academic department. Rather, I relied on a few trusted management practices, such as active listening and participative decision making, and a good deal of learning by doing. In looking back on all this, my learned wisdom falls roughly into six broad topics that I call "responsibilities of the department chair": (1) norming, (2) strategizing, (3) guiding, (4) complying, (5) developing, and (6) behaving. They do not form a coherent conceptual model and are not listed in a pre-scribed order. Rather, they are best considered a checklist of things I feel are worth considering for those on a Chair's journey.

NORMING

Norms are the bedrock on which academic departments function. These shared expectations about how members should behave influence a variety of actions, such as attending meetings, performing relevant tasks, and collaborating with each other. Department norms appear over time through interactions among faculty. They are often implicit and shape behavior like an invisible hand. Norms are effective when they reinforce actions functional for the department, such as speaking up and listening to others; they are unproductive when they sustain dysfunctional behavior, such as secretly belittling a colleague's research or shirking menial yet necessary tasks. Openly discussing department norms can be awkward and uncomfortable, especially when they are ineffective. Thus, departments may tolerate or ignore dysfunctional behavior and the norms underlying it. And this can persist for years.

Yet, collegial norms beget collegial behavior, and the Chair is responsible for leading a process to make that happen. Faculty are more likely to respect norms they had a hand in making, particularly from taking part in a process of open discussion, active listening, and learning by doing. The Chair can facilitate a norming process that enables those behaviors. It might start with faculty discussing norms and agreeing on those they are willing to try behaving; then, they strive to behave consistent with those norms in their daily work lives; periodically, they meet to assess their behavior against the norms and plan for changes if necessary. This action-learning cycle continues, varying in formality, duration, and timing depending on faculty's interpersonal skill and normative behavior. When department norms are initially created or significantly altered, the norming process can be more formal, take longer, and involve quicker learning cycles. Later, when normative behavior is more established and effective, the process can be simplified and shortened, such as spending time at the end of faculty meetings to answer: How are we doing on our norms?

In my department, the norming process began early in my Chair tenure. It involved a half-day retreat where faculty discussed norms, considered several possibilities, and agreed on three norms essential to collegiality *and* faculty were willing to hold each other accountable for behaving:

- Speak up and engage
- Actively listen and appreciate others
- Be at school on Fridays to attend speaker series and department retreats and to "shoot the bull" (converse informally) with colleagues.

Going forward, we periodically took time at the end of department meetings to assess how well our behavior followed the norms and where we needed to improve. This process gradually revealed the need to develop our skills in active listening and giving and receiving feedback. We designed faculty development sessions to learn (and relearn) those interpersonal skills. Occasionally, I privately mentored faculty on their normative behavior. I explicitly discussed our collegial norms with all recruits when hiring faculty.

STRATEGIZING

Academic departments do teaching, research, and service, and department strategy guides how they go about performing those activities to achieve valued outcomes. Strategy involves a vision of what the department wants to accomplish with its teaching, research, and service. It includes values that direct how those activities should be performed and strategic objectives that need to be reached to enact the vision. Strategy guides decisions that touch on most activities that go on in the department and its relation to the outside. It directs how faculty are hired, assessed, and rewarded; how departmental funds are acquired and allocated; how courses and tasks are assigned; and how relations with the dean's office, academic programs, and other departments are managed. Academic departments vary in how well strategy steers their activities and outcomes. For a variety of reasons, decisions about teaching, research, and service may be more tactical than strategic. Departments may ignore their strategy or only pay lip service to it; they may not even have a strategy. Consequently, department decisions about resources, activities, and results may be piecemeal without a coherent direction; they may routinely replicate past choices that may not have been ideal or are no longer relevant. The department may muddle through, but risks wasting resources and performing suboptimally.

The Chair is responsible for the department performing strategically. This requires keeping its strategy up to date and applied to strategic choices; or if strategy is lacking or dormant, creating and revising department strategy. When a department's strategy is functional, the Chair can lead faculty in periodic check-ups to assess the strategy's continued relevance, make necessary changes, and reinforce its use in guiding decisions. This evaluation can vary in formality and timing depending on how well the strategy is applied and how stable are the forces affecting the department. An effective strategy in a stable situation may only need a short, informal assessment every few years; ineffective strategies in a changing environment may need more formal evaluation on a timelier basis.

When department strategy needs to be created anew or revised, the Chair can facilitate a strategizing process to make that happen. It can start with an assessment of what the department does well and needs to improve and what external forces are affecting its activities. This analysis also identifies the department's key stakeholders, such as students, business organizations, the wider scholarly profession, and the school and university, and assesses how well the department is serving their interests. Based on this broad assessment, members then share their vision for the department's future and explore how teaching, research, and service need to change to move in that direction. Department norms promoting open sharing and active listening support the quality of exchange and commitment needed to make the strategizing process realistic and the outcome worthwhile. Careful attention to the following basic elements of strategy can structure the process and meaningfully organize the results:

- Vision. A clear and compelling statement of the department's main purpose and what its teaching, research, and service should ideally be in five years or so.
- Values. The guiding principles of how department members should make decisions and behave.
- Strategic Objectives. Measurable teaching, research, and service outcomes the department needs to achieve to enact its vision.
- Action Steps. The concrete actions needed to reach strategic objectives.

My department initially created its strategy in 1992. An edited version of its most recent revision appears in Appendix I as an example of the basic strategy elements described above. During my time as Chair, we followed a basic strategizing process in assessing and updating the strategy about every five years. A task force of a cross-section of faculty led this process.

It first did a preliminary assessment of the strategy that faculty then discussed at a department meeting. Next, based on faculty feedback, the task force explored changes to the department's vision, values, and strategic objectives and drafted a revised strategy that faculty reviewed at another meeting. My department's vision and values were seriously discussed but not changed; revisions occurred in the strategic objectives. Last, the task force guided the faculty in laying out specific action steps for the coming year. My major roles during this strategizing process were to help the task force gather and analyze essential information and to facilitate faculty behaving department norms during the meetings.

GUIDING

Faculty are the core of academic departments, and their talent, motivation, and retention are vital to departments' performance and scholarly reputation. Decisions about hiring, rewarding, and promoting faculty are among the most important and consequential that departments make. Business schools and universities provide general procedures for these human resource decisions to ensure they are made consistently across academic units and follow relevant laws and regulations. These guidelines provide an overall structure for the decision process while affording departments considerable leeway in making specific judgments about who to hire, what performances to reward, and what academic record merits promotion and tenure. These choices can involve a good deal of subjective assessment. When decision criteria are unclear or differ among faculty, divergent opinions can be contentious and collective outcomes difficult to achieve.

The Chair is responsible for ensuring that clear procedures and shared criteria guide department decisions about faculty hiring, rewarding, and promoting. Procedures can be straightforward and follow university and school practices, such as timing of decisions, voting protocols, and format of reports. Decision criteria, on the other hand, are more prone to variation among faculty. Faculty may differ on what criteria should guide decisions on hiring, rewarding, and promoting; their assessments on criteria may vary. Indeed, variations in faculty judgments are a normal part of department decision making, and if openly expressed and constructively discussed, can improve the quality of decisions and faculty commitment to them. Department strategy can provide a shared perspective for addressing and resolving these differences. Strategic vision, values, and objectives represent faculty's collective views about the department's desired future and what it seeks to achieve in teaching, research, and service. They can serve as guideposts for assessing how well specific hiring, rewarding, and promoting choices serve those purposes. Faculty can address differences in criteria and evaluations in the context of what choices best serve the department's strategy and interests.

During my time as Chair, faculty hiring, rewarding, and promoting became more and more comprehensive and rigorous. Decisions increasingly rested on quantitative measures benchmarked with other departments in the school and comparative institutions. This standardization and calibration were a natural outgrowth of higher education becoming more managerially oriented, with performance and resource measures more objective and comparative. Competition for ranking status with other business schools also drove our benchmarking. My experience suggests this increased rigor can enhance the accuracy and fairness of human resource decisions.

Examples of my department's recruiting, rewarding, and promoting processes are described below.

Recruiting

We followed steps defining when, what, and how faculty recruiting activities needed to happen. They spanned about a year and included setting priorities, identifying, vetting, and interviewing candidates, and deciding on job offers. This process was driven by our strategic objectives aimed at strengthening the department's core competencies and sustaining a specific distribution of tenure-track faculty in organizational behavior, corporate strategy, and organization theory, 40, 40, and 20 percent, respectively. Subcommittees from those areas took the lead on recruiting with wider department discussion and approval at key decision points. Faculty participation and focus varied depending on whether we were recruiting tenure-track or clinical faculty; the former emphasized research, and the latter teaching. Throughout, we explicitly reminded ourselves that we are recruiting faculty for the department and not just a research area.

Rewarding

Our annual performance review of faculty informed merit pay allocations and developmental feedback. It closely followed school procedures for assessing faculty's teaching, research, and service performance. First, faculty performance in each of these areas was rated on a five-point scale based on relevant criteria, such as A-level journal articles for research, student evaluations for teaching, and committee assignments for service. Then, performance ratings were weighted by faculty's contractual workload profile, which consisted of how the nine-month workload was distributed across teaching, research, and service. For tenure-track faculty, the workload was weighted more towards research, and for clinical faculty more towards teaching. Finally, faculty were assigned an overall performance measure (five-point scale) based on their workload-weighted performance measure relative to the measures of other department faculty, either tenure-track or clinical. A department subcommittee and the Chair performed all these assessments separately from each other, then met to reach consensus and send the results to the vice-dean of faculty. Soon after, the Chairs of all departments in the school met and discussed their various performance assessments to assure conformity and fairness across the school. After any necessary revisions were made, each faculty member in my department received a detailed report of their performance review including a summary of the kinds of teaching, research, and service performances in each of the performance-rating levels in the department. I met personally with selected faculty members to go over their report and to discuss areas for development. Faculty also received a dean's report detailing how merit pay would be distributed across the different performance levels. Although this overall rewarding process may seem complicated and extreme, it took less than a month to complete each year, provided faculty with clear and fair measures of their performance, and tied performance directly to pay.

Promoting

My department adhered strictly to university and school procedures in managing faculty promotions and tenure. I will not elaborate them here as they followed standard university practices with evaluations from multiple levels of the university and from sources internal and external to it. A key criterion for successful promotion was how well the record of our candidates compared to the record of those faculty recently promoted at top-tier institutions. Consistent with my department's behavioral norms and strategic values, we also considered candidates' collegial behavior in promotion decisions. The promotion process for clinical faculty was conducted entirely within the school relying on internal evaluations of teaching and service performance.

COMPLYING

Today's modern universities face an enormous array of rules and regulations both from internal sources and external authorities. These policies and laws address innumerable activities and conditions related to research, education, employment, extracurricular pursuits, and the environment. They can affect everyone connected to the university and all that goes on there. They can involve straightforward issues, such as student records privacy and staff work hours, and far more complex matters, such as sexual harassment and race discrimination. Failure to follow these regulations can have legal, economic, and reputational consequences for universities; they can result in serious emotional and social problems for those people directly involved. Thus, universities tend to have extensive compliance structures staffed with experts who provide guidance, information, and training for attending to and following the rules. Academic departments can benefit from this support and the standard operating practices that go with it. It can help departments detect violations and promptly resolve them. Yet, departments may have problems using this assistance. Compliance directives are part of the administrative fabric of universities and can unwittingly recede into the background and receive little attention unless publicly violated. Departments may inadvertently neglect compliance matters when dealing with more persistent and immediate demands related to teaching, research, and service and to faculty hiring, awarding, and promoting. Departments may not receive correct or timely information that a violation has occurred; they may not know the correct response or may be slow to enact it. All of this can make compliance problems difficult to notice and address; it can result in negative unintended consequences for academic institutions and their members.

The Chair is responsible for the department complying with relevant rules and regulations and can help make compliance more visible and pertinent to faculty and staff. For example, department members can periodically discuss compliance issues at regular meetings or dedicated events. Compliance behaviors and outcomes can be part of the department's strategic objectives and action steps with attendant measures and assessments. The department can request staff experts to provide special training to help members learn how to address compliance issues prevalent in their teaching and research.

When becoming Chair in 1996, I was surprised and a bit overwhelmed by the sheer number and diversity of rules and regulations that governed university life; by my end date in 2017, that number and diversity had escalated enormously, as did the number of pages devoted to compliance in the university and school faculty handbooks. As Chair, I was in the official chain of command with both administrative and legal obligations for advising faculty on compliance issues, reporting violations, and staying involved in or keeping abreast of the proceedings. All of this followed strict confidential, procedural, and legal rules. Whenever I was doubtful about anything related to rule compliance, I immediately informed the vice-dean of faculty affairs and asked what to do. I always received prompt and clear directions, which came directly from the vice-dean or indirectly through higher-level administrators or staff experts. Over time, the university and school became progressively more effective in informing and educating faculty, staff, and students on compliance with rules and regulations. Recently, for example, the university requires all faculty and staff to complete an online training program in sexual harassment and discriminatory behavior every other year. The program is highly informative and useful, and I wish it had been in place in 1996.

DEVELOPING

Academic departments can engage in developmental activities to improve their capabilities and performance in teaching, research, and service. Development is particularly important in today's complex and rapidly changing education environment where departments can fail to keep pace with stakeholder needs and faculty expertise can quickly become outdated. Development of social relations among faculty can improve department decision making, information sharing, and collaborative activities. For example, team building, process consultation, and related group interventions can reduce coordination costs among faculty and enhance how well they function as a team. Similarly, attention to faculty development can enrich their social skills and expertise in research and teaching. Departments can reinforce faculty development through recognizing and rewarding their achievements. Regrettably, departments may neglect development activities in the face of heavy work demands and the busy professional lives of their members. Maintaining the status quo may seem easier than expending energy and resources to develop a higher level of department functioning. Sustaining existing faculty skills may seem more expedient than developing them further.

The Chair is responsible for developing the department. This includes helping it become better at serving stakeholders as well as assisting faculty to enhance their teaching and research expertise. The Chair can lead faculty in identifying developmental needs and creating opportunities for addressing them. This might include, for example, budgeting resources for faculty training, requesting university and school experts to instruct specific teaching or research skills, and leading department retreats to work on improving teamwork among faculty. The key to making development a useful part of department life is to ensure that it is integral to the department's strategic objectives and action plans. Then, it can regularly be measured and assessed along with other department goals and outcomes.

In addition to traditional university and academic workshops on teaching and research, my department's developmental activities centered around four half-day retreats each academic year. They included the following developmental activities, each assigned to a retreat.

State of the Department

This retreat occurred at the start of the school year and began with a review of the prior year's faculty achievements and awards, department committee activities, research publications, and course enrollments. Then, committee assignments and tasks for the coming year were presented. Finally, the greater part of the retreat involved a serious assessment of how well we reached last year's strategic objectives and planning for next year's objectives and action plans to achieve them. This assessment also included feedback from faculty on how well I was performing the Chair role. Shortly prior to this retreat, faculty anonymously filled out a questionnaire rating me on several performance measures. At the retreat, I summarized the results on an overhead, we discussed my performance, and I committed to specific improvements going forward. Appendix II is a copy of the Chair assessment questionnaire.

Teaching

We devoted this retreat to developing teaching knowledge and skills. Clinical faculty typically designed and led the learning activities with input from the rest of the faculty. The learning included panel presentations, experiential exercises, and small group discussions on a diversity of educational topics, classroom practices, and pedagogical expertise.

Research

We aimed this retreat at learning about faculty's research interests and gaining familiarity with different research methods and analytical techniques. Tenure-track faculty designed and led the developmental activities, which included poster sessions, exercises to explore connections among our research interests, and mini-workshops on quantitative and qualitative approaches to inquiry. Occasionally, we invited colleagues from other universities to present a session on a research method or analytical tool.

Department Development and Celebration

This retreat occurred at the end of the school year and was devoted to developing department teamwork and recognizing faculty's exceptional performance. We engaged in various assessment and team-building activities aimed at improving how we worked together, made decisions, and addressed emergent issues. We ended with a luncheon celebration where faculty received awards for exceptional teaching, research, and service.

BEHAVING

This last Chair responsibility is more personal than the others. It involves how a responsible Chair should behave in serving the needs of department members and relevant stakeholders. For me as Chair, these behaviors were more an aspiration than a reality; I learned their wisdom through considerable trial and error, to say the least. They include six behaviors described below.

Relate In All Directions

Chairing a department involves relating effectively with people in all directions, downward to staff, upward to deans, and sideways to department faculty, colleagues in other departments and universities, and other relevant stakeholders. The tendency is to relate with department staff and faculty and to deal with external relations when there is a pressing need such as a question from the dean or inquiry about a job opening from a faculty at another institution. This limited focus ignores the potentially valuable information, resources, and partnering opportunities the department might gain from external connections. It overlooks the personal networking and relationship-building that need to occur to gain access to them. For example, I often met informally with other department Chairs to share insights and explore how we might shape the dean's agenda for the school. My networking at professional meetings exchanged information with colleagues about opportunities for future faculty hiring and job placement for doctoral students.

Be Open and Direct, Yet Actively Listen

Chairs engage in frequent informal conversations without a task or outcome in mind; simply sharing stories and ideas among colleagues. These interactions require little attention to conversation formalities; indeed, a certain amount of discursive banter is expected. At other times, however, the Chair must be open, direct, and actively listen to others, such as mentoring a faculty, providing performance feedback, and discussing a complex issue at a department meeting. In these situations, it is essential to be forthright and clear and to listen emphatically, so communication is understood and trustworthy. Moreover, I learned that when faced with an emotional or conflictual exchange that matters, it is best to suspend judgment, try hard to understand where the other is coming from, and show you care. This often de-escalates the tension and opens a path for joint problem solving.

Admit Mistakes

Chairs make decisions and do things that can have unintended negative results. These may be as minor as ordering a main course for a department luncheon that few members find appetizing or as significant as changing the schedule or instructor for a popular course that subsequently has low enrollment due to the change. Chairs make mistakes that have adverse consequences for the department and its members. The key is to address and learn from them as quickly and effectively as possible. This involves openly admitting to the mistake, apologizing for the negative effects, making a correction if possible, or if not, simply moving on. In my case, colleagues were willing to forgive my mistakes, so long as I quickly owned up to them, apologized, and showed a willingness to learn from them.

Be Autocratic, On Occasion

A collegial culture favors participation in decision making where faculty make choices through consensus. Participation has benefits and costs, however, and the Chair needs to know when it is most applicable and when autocratic decision making is more practical. Faculty participation is essential when decisions are complex and can benefit from diverse inputs and when faculty involvement is needed to gain commitment to implement decisions. For example, these include decisions about hiring, rewarding, designing curriculum, and distributing department resources. For less demanding choices, such as committee assignments and course schedules, the costs of participation in faculty time and attention may outweigh the benefits, and the Chair should make the choice with limited, if any, faculty input. The key is to know which department decisions should be made participatively and which more autocratically. Early in my time as Chair, faculty and I divided department decisions into two categories, which then guided future decision making: Chair makes decision with limited faculty input or faculty participatively make consensus decision.

Protect Your Personal Time

Teaching, research, and service can take place around the clock and forces can affect the department and its members any time. The Chair is responsible for the department 24/7 and can become overwhelmed with the time demands of responding to all these matters. To safeguard time for rest, relaxation, and other private issues, the Chair needs to clarify this personal time with faculty, staff, and key stakeholders, and mutually agree with them what "emergencies" are okay to disrupt it. For reasons still a mystery to me, I did not set personal time boundaries and was available to address department issues most of the time. Fortunately, my home life was not unduly disturbed. I do not recommend this choice to Chairs, however, particularly in this digital age.

Have a Sense of Humor

Academic settings are serious-minded places where knowledge is created and taught. Faculty deeply invest in their craft and treat their research and teaching with utmost regard, as they should. At times, the workplace can seem intense and overbearing, creating excessive stress for faculty and staff. The Chair can help faculty cope with this strain by encouraging or providing a bit of humor. The knack, of course, is timing, appropriateness, and not making fun at someone's expense. For me, rather than prepared humor, I sought amusement or irony in the situation or circumstance at hand. When this worked, my colleagues and I laughed, and stress subsided. When my humor bombed, so to speak, I openly made fun of myself, which usually resulted in a few laughs or at least smirks.

THE RESPONSIBILITIES TOGETHER

For clarity of explanation, the six Chair responsibilities were described independently from each other and with equal significance. In situ, they are interdependent and vary in importance depending on changes in the department and its environment. The full intricacy of the Chair's responsibilities is beyond the scope of my recollections to describe here, but I will recall a notable change to provide a glimpse of this interdependence and complexity.

During my early tenure as Chair, the university and school underwent major strategic changes, with a new president and dean leading transformations in our intellectual culture, faculty and student selectivity, and research reputation. Among the major reforms were recruitment of renowned scholars and nationally recognized students; record-setting fund raising resulting in significant financial support for research and education; and much higher research standards for promotion and tenure and annual merit pay. These changes cascaded through all my Chair responsibilities at varying rates of speed and significance. To sustain and gain credibility, resources, and support from the university and school it was essential to significantly alter my department's research strategy including standards for faculty recruiting, rewards, and promotion. This involved a radical shift from primary attention to practical knowledge for organizations to more academic research aimed at the scholarly community. In turn, it required changing the department's faculty composition, which was weighted heavily to senior applied scholars, to more disciplinary researchers with an emphasis on economics, psychology, and sociology. At the time, only a few department faculty had this disciplinary focus. The department's criteria for recruiting faculty and rewarding and promoting them shifted increasingly to publication in top-tier scholarly journals.

All these changes started in my first year as Chair and involved gaining commitment and support from key senior faculty and rising mid-level researchers who supported the university and school's new strategic direction. Indeed, the department's most renowned faculty member chaired the committee that hired the new university president. Together these supportive faculty formed a loose but powerful coalition of change agents. They helped me lead the department through a series of meetings aimed at creating a new strategy and revising promotion, reward, and recruiting practices to be more in line with the school's research direction. Our collegial norms were invaluable in helping us work through differences and gain consensus on how to move forward. My learning the value of active listening was sorely tested yet rewarded. These initial changes occurred over a two-year period and then continued to unfold as the new strategy and practices took hold and guided department decisions and actions. Along with the university and school, the next two decades saw the department gain professional recognition for its research and scholarly performance. Its reputation for a collegial culture matched its academic success.

CONCLUSION

I have reflected on what I learned from being a department Chair and shared that experience with you. Although the Chair responsibilities described here seem generally applicable, they were learned in a particular period and place and need to be tailored to your situation. Moreover, my experience as Chair was highly personal and what I learned is intimately tied to my values, personality, and abilities and how they shaped my Chair behaviors, experience, and development. Being department Chair can be a deep personal experience and part of who you are as a person. I encourage you to learn and develop from the experience and to enjoy the journey.

APPENDIX I: DEPARTMENT STRATEGIC PLAN

BACKGROUND

The department plays a key leadership role in the School's research, teaching, and service. We are ranked near the top nationally in top-tier journal publications and our findings are often cited in the popular media for their practical relevance. Our faculty includes some of the best teachers at the School, who consistently win a good share of teaching awards. Our courses are renowned for providing knowledge and skills in leadership, negotiation, strategic thinking, management consulting, global management, and strategic human resource management. Our faculty members serve important leadership roles on School and University committees, on the editorial boards of top journals, and as officers in our professional associations.

The department has made a remarkable transition over the past decade. It had been well-known primarily for applied research and deep insights into problems of management practice. Reflecting changes in the University, the School, and the broader profession, recruiting gradually shifted to faculty with stronger ties to discipline-based research in such areas as psychology, sociology, and economics. Our applied tradition lives on in our shared commitment to "scholarship with consequence." Our scholarly work aims to inform not only our academic peers but also our non-academic stakeholders.

VISION

Our vision is to excel nationally and internationally as recognized by four important stake-holder groups:

- Scholars around the world who value path-breaking research relevant to management and organizations
- University students at all levels who expect excellent teaching and a curriculum that builds knowledge and skills that enrich their lives and advance their careers
- Leaders in business and other organizations who require useful knowledge and guidance that will improve their practice and organizations' performance
- School and University senior leaders who expect us to contribute to the school and society through our research, teaching, and service.

Our vision reflects the key themes of the University's and School's strategic plans:

- "Academic excellence": We envision a faculty that plays a prominent role in advancing scholarship. We therefore expect our faculty to publish in the most widely respected scholarly journals, serve on these journals' editorial boards, and play leadership roles in our scholarly professional associations. We also aim to build a world-class PhD program, albeit a small one, which attracts highly talented students and places them in top schools.
- "Scholarship with consequence": We envision a faculty whose scholarship addresses issues of importance not only to our academic peers but also to the other stakeholders we serve. We expect our research to have a significant impact on organizations' leaders and performance.

- "Global and local engagement": Through our research, teaching, and service, we aim to advance understanding and promote positive action within both the local and global contexts.
- "Accountability": We strive to hold each other accountable to the standards we have set and the values that guide us. We expect to be held accountable by our various stakeholders.

VALUES

In fulfilling our vision, we work closely together to develop a vibrant collegial culture that embodies the following values (in no special order):

- Mutual respect for different forms of inquiry, conceptual foundations, levels of analysis, and research topics
- Cooperation, openness, and trust in our relationships
- Accountable to the highest standards of research, teaching, and practice
- Transparency and fairness in department governance
- Care about people and their continued development
- Ethical behavior
- Hard work and having fun together while maintaining a reasonable balance between our work and non-work lives
- Meaningful contributions to professional, practitioner, and university communities.

PERFORMANCE METRICS

We will measure our progress and success through high achievement on the following metrics. The first three categories apply to both the department as a whole as well as to each of us as individuals; the last is a department-level metric:

Research

- Publication in high-quality research journals as well as favorably reviewed books for academics
- High citation impact of our publications
- Appointment as editors and editorial board members of top journals
- Publication in high-quality practitioner journals as well as favorably reviewed books for scholars/practitioners
- High media visibility in national and international outlets
- National and international awards for outstanding research.

Teaching

- Strong enrollment levels in all elective courses
- High teaching ratings in all courses
- High-quality course content and delivery as evaluated by department peers
- School and University awards for teaching excellence (including pedagogical innovations and use of technology).

Service

- Program participation at the Academy of Management and other leading professional organizations
- Appointment to officer positions in the Academy of Management and other leading professional organizations
- Serving on high-impact committees at the School and the University
- Consistent mentoring of doctoral students and faculty.

Placement and Promotion

- Placement of PhDs in top-25 and top-50 schools
- Promotion and tenure of faculty.

STRATEGIC GOALS FOR NEXT FIVE YEARS

Research-based Faculty

- Sustain proportions of tenure-track faculty of approximately 40, 20, and 40 percent in the organizational behavior, organization theory, and strategy areas, respectively.
- Strengthen our faculty having ties to disciplines such as economics, psychology, and sociology.
- Strengthen research connections between the department and our affiliated research center.
- Hire at least one senior person in each of the three areas.
- Recruit more women and minorities.
- Make success at the tenure hurdle the most common outcome.

Doctoral Program

- Place all our graduates well, and place at least 1/4th of them in business schools ranked in the top 25.
- Recruit at least two underrepresented minorities into our doctoral program.
- Leverage methods training at the University and other local universities to ensure that our graduates are well known for their methods expertise.
- Utilize disciplinary training at the University and other local universities to ensure that our graduates are renowned for their exceptional depth of knowledge in disciplines such as economics, psychology, or sociology.
- Ensure that graduating students have high-quality publications and a good pipeline of projects; the number of publications will likely vary with the student's research area.
- Ensure that all our graduating doctoral students are fully prepared for the job market through presentation rehearsals and mock interviews.

Teaching

- Assess more systematically our teaching performance and ways to encourage improvement among our faculty.
- Ensure that the faculty teams teaching our two required undergraduate courses meet regularly to plan the semester, review its progress, and mentor each other.
- Leverage our very best teachers to provide excellence to our required undergraduate and MBA courses and to attract students to our electives.
- Create at least one new elective with multiple sections in each of the undergraduate and MBA programs.

ACTION STEPS FOR THE COMING YEAR

Research

- Over the summer, we will formalize our recruiting process: how do we set priorities; *who* makes *what* decisions, *when*, and *how*; specify the role of each sub-group (OB, OT, Strategy) versus the department as a whole at each step.
- Over the summer, a committee of those who have headed our speaker series in the past 2–3 years will review the series and assess whether we have been bringing in the right kind of speakers, the right mix of OB, OT, Strategy, and the right mix of junior and senior people. This committee will also formulate recommendations to ensure that a broad range of our faculty participate in hosting guests and meeting them for breakfast and dinner.
- We will hire at least two junior faculty replacements.
- We will make at least one senior faculty job offer.
- Starting in 2012–13, we will conduct at least one "research fair" each year at which every research faculty member will discuss the main lines of current research. (Each faculty member should present at least once every three years.)
- Ensure that at least one research seminar every year is reserved for presentation of research being conducted at CEO and CTM.
- Explore "big data" research opportunities being built at USC (GIS, Census).

PhD Program

- Over the summer, the PhD committee will formalize the requirements of the PhD program in a document that will be discussed by the department faculty and our current PhD students, and, once approved, will be posted on the MOR website.
- Starting in May 2012, we will conduct at least one "research fair" each year at which every PhD student will discuss the main lines of research they have been engaged in.
- Starting in fall 2012, all graduating students will do at least one job talk rehearsal to the full department as well as mock job interviews.
- Over the summer, the PhD committee will formulate a recommendation to the Marshall PhD Committee concerning supplementary funding for PhD students to attend important research conferences.

Teaching

- Over the summer of 2012, a task force will formulate recommendations concerning the feasibility of institutionalizing a peer-review process for strengthening our teaching skills.
- Starting in 2012–13, we will conduct at least one "teaching fair" each year at which faculty will discuss their courses and pedagogies.

Department Culture

- In the next few months, Tom will lead a department task force to address making MOR more influential in the school including curriculum, governance, and strategic direction. The task force will draft concrete proposals for moving ahead and the faculty will meet to discuss them.
- Starting in May 2012, we will devote at least one MOR retreat each year to community building, especially how to maintain a culture of trust, mutual respect, and innovative inquiry so no one feels that their research, teaching, or views are disparaged; how to better integrate research faculty, clinical faculty, and doctoral students so we are a more cohesive culture with a shared identity; and how to have more fun and be playful with each other, so we do not become too serious and lose the ability to laugh at ourselves and to realize how trivial our differences and problems are in the bigger scheme of life.

APPENDIX II: FACULTY FEEDBACK TO CHAIR

Table 23A.1   Faculty feedback to chair

	Need to Improve	Doing OK	Doing Well
1. Articulate vision for department			
2. Lead culture change			
3. Strong advocate for Department			
4. Be tough & make hard decisions			
5. Develop junior faculty & doctoral students			
6. Be accessible			
7. Communicate clearly & frequently			
8. Be open to feedback & new ideas			
9. Be fair & equitable			
10. Keep confidential information private			
11. Set high performance standards			
12. Send clear signals for academic success			
13. Articulate & enforce behavioral norms			
14. Positive impression management in School			
15. Build community & facilitate collegiality			
16. Build strong relations with other departments and administrators			
17. Be strong role model			

24. How to lead an academic marketing department: some personal observations and reflections

Gerrit van Bruggen

INTRODUCTION

In this chapter, I will describe some personal reflections and insights, which I have gained over the years on how to (effectively) lead an academic marketing department. The editors of this book asked me a while ago to write a chapter on this. Although I certainly do not consider myself very knowledgeable in this domain, nor in the domain of leadership or organizational behavior, I have been part of a department for quite a while. Over the years, I was able to collect observations, and writing this chapter created an opportunity to reflect on what I have observed and experienced. My ideas result from a variety of roles, perspectives, and responsibilities, which I have gained over a little bit more than 30 years. In this period, I have been PhD student, faculty member, department head, (vice) dean for faculty, and faculty member again. Furthermore, I have been a member of many committees and boards within my own school and university, as well as outside it. All of this has clearly helped me in developing my ideas and perspectives. It is important to note upfront that these are clearly my own personal views and ideas, which are based on my personal experiences and observations. I am not sure whether there is one superior model for how a department should be structured and led. I guess that a lot will depend on the specific environmental and institutional context the department and its members are operating in.

What I will mostly do in this chapter is describe my experiences, trade-offs, and preferences based on what seems to have worked, and is working from my perspective. As you will read, I make a big plea for keeping things simple, letting go of control, and cherishing the power and creativity that is in most people, when given the freedom to work on the things they really care about. Incentives and extrinsic rewards work, but I think that benefitting from intrinsic motivations is superior. The main goal of academic leadership is to challenge, encourage, and facilitate people so that all the potential they have in them will be realized. Professionals should be trusted, and leadership should be able to do this. This is probably easier said than done and it will require substantial time and effort. Leadership will have to interact *with*, and work *for* their people, not direct them. At the end, it is about caring for and trusting your professionals. Only this will make the department do the best it can, and its leadership thus effective.

WHAT IS THE ROLE OF AN ACADEMIC MARKETING DEPARTMENT?

An academic marketing department comprises the group of people who collectively share the responsibility for generating and disseminating marketing knowledge in a business school or at a university. When we talk about knowledge generation, we often mean academic or scientific research on marketing topics. Clearly, this is the core and very important. However, knowledge generation is a broader concept, which can also refer to more applied research, developing case studies, and other types of inquiry. Different schools may value different types of knowledge generation. Marketing knowledge dissemination in a university and/or business school setting is primarily about teaching, but, increasingly also about other types of outreach to create so-called (societal) impact, engagement, or valorization. Dissemination can also take place through consulting, (social) media appearances, being part of (professional) organizations, speaking at practioners' conferences and so on. Knowledge generation and dissemination are the two fundamental, externally oriented, responsibilities of a department. With externally oriented I mean that these activities target a broad community not only within the department or school, but also and maybe mostly outside it.

Next to their tasks that deal with knowledge generation and knowledge dissemination, department members are also members of organizations or communities. They will also face responsibilities to make these organizations function effectively. A department needs a department head and a school needs committee members, directors, and (associate) deans. Furthermore, professional academic societies need to be managed, papers need reviewers, and journals need to be edited. So, an academic marketing department is a unit in a business school that is responsible for knowledge generation and dissemination in marketing and for supporting or performing administrative responsibilities that are needed to make their organizations work. The responsibilities are collective, and the department members have to contribute to these.

Within the department, the main task of its members is to contribute to the department's shared responsibilities. How this works out at the individual level can and will vary. Differences in focus can exist between department members, depending on individuals' interests, strengths, stage in their careers, etc. Ideally, individuals have a clear and limited set of responsibilities, and can focus on the things they are relatively strong at and intrinsically motivated for. The composition of the department should be so that things will add up at the department level, so that shared responsibilities are met, and the department performs as well as possible. Therefore, recruitment and people development are essential and key responsibilities for department leadership.

What I have found to be very important is to make sure that the set of shared responsibilities does not become too broad. Like every organization, departments need to focus as well. In my view, individuals in most cases do best if they can focus on a limited set of, preferably complementary, activities. Since, at the end of the day, individual faculty members have to do the work, it is important to constantly keep this in mind. Nowadays, many universities, schools, and departments are confronted with an ever-increasing demand for contributions. Even though it is important to be flexible and adapt to the situation, it is also important to realize that doing one thing will often result in the absence of another. Synergy effects are potentially, and in theory, great to strive for; however, in reality, they are also often impossible to achieve.

A lot of department strategy decision making is about making trade-offs, and, in most cases, it will not get any better than this. In my view, this also means that department leadership should look very carefully at what the departments' responsibilities are, and what are not. The same is true for school and university leadership. These kinds of organizations should be very protective of their people and not lead them into situations in which their performance will be structurally compromised. Leadership's main goal should be to facilitate their people to perform, not to exploit them as resources for achieving their personal goals. This is true for universities and schools, as well as departments.

WHAT IS AN EFFECTIVE DEPARTMENT?

The question now is, what do we mean by department effectiveness? A rather straightforward approach to defining effectiveness is by evaluating its research and teaching output and the extent to which it performs in making the larger organization work. This approach seems popular and well accepted. Evaluating research and teaching output is often done by looking at how the department does in ratings and rankings. The attractiveness of taking such an approach for assessing performance is that it is simple, straightforward, and that it thus seems widely accepted.

In my view, an important limitation of the above approach is that only things that can be measured and counted are considered. Also, even though counting and measuring suggests objectivity and transparency, many of the choices made in designing ranking and ratings frameworks are based on subjective inputs and sometimes arbitrary and political choices. Furthermore, it is often not very clear who is making the decisions and choices related to this. For me, it is questionable whether one should make the choices made by others, those who are designing the rankings, leading in how to operate as a department. Of course, if the reality is that funding bodies and student program choices are driven by these rating and ranking systems, they cannot be declared entirely irrelevant. However, this is different from a mechanistic approach in which the number of publications in, for example, the so-called *Financial Times* or University of Texas at Dallas lists and average student course evaluations determine how well you do as a department. Unfortunately, this is what seems to be increasingly the way people determine department or business school quality and performance. A key problem with such an approach is that the assessment of quality or performance of a department has been narrowed down to a uni-dimensional exercise of research productivity and popularity with students. Furthermore, it is not clear to me that things that may be important tomorrow are included in the ranking and rating systems of today. Real innovation and creativity may, therefore, not get the recognition they deserve and the resources they require.

For me, determining how well a department is doing should be based on a much broader assessment of quality, what is important, and how it will contribute, than just research productivity and student satisfaction. I strongly believe that a focus on intrinsic quality will always pay off in the end, also in terms of external reputation, and even rankings and ratings. Department leadership itself should decide on what is important and how things can be accomplished. Of course, departments operate in a wider environment and that environment cannot be declared fully irrelevant. However, the development of a strong and differentiating focus is a key responsibility for department leadership. This should be done with a clear "eye on the ball," a long-term focus, and without being distracted by what's fashionable in the institutional context. With "eye on the ball" I mean the realization that departments are there for knowledge generation and knowledge dissemination. Differentiation should take place through the nature and the quality of these activities. Therefore, for example, the kind of research that the department wants to host and do is extremely important. Departments themselves must make choices on which kind of problems they feel need to be studied, and whether these are important, fundamental, and relevant, and to whom? It should not be driven by ranking systems. In my view, differentiating and high-quality research will almost automatically lead to impactful publications in good journals. However, that is often the result of a long process, hard work, and perseverance without possibilities for shortcuts. Department leadership should realize this and facilitate it; therefore it also needs a long-term focus.

Most people seem to agree that we want faculty to work on important topics. However, in evaluating their work, oftentimes the number of publications is what counts at the end of the day. This most likely is because it is so easily measurable, and it seems less debatable. Not all (good) research will end up in top journals though. Does this make such research useless? My answer to that question would be a strong no. Research should be evaluated on its intrinsic merits. Of course, being published in a top journal will be a strong quality cue. However, journals also make errors in judging the value of research and may be biased towards certain types of research. By taking only productivity in top journals into account, innovation may be at stake and opportunities will be missed. The same reasoning will apply to the evaluation of teaching. When we only look at student satisfaction scores, innovation will be more difficult and opportunities for doing new things will be missed. Overall, doing new things means stepping away from the usual things. This will involve risks and possibilities of failure. Students may not immediately like things they are not used to. If such failure is not accepted, one cannot expect the returns of real innovation and differentiation.

So, an effective department in my view is one which successfully generates new and relevant knowledge and disseminates it successfully to the relevant audiences. These audiences are students, organizations, and/or society at large. Leadership of a department should facilitate this and should be able and have the confidence to evaluate and judge the intrinsic quality of the department's work. Metrics or benchmarks developed by outsiders can be informative but should not be leading.

Finally, an effective department is not only one that performs well. It is also one in which people enjoy working, feel they develop and grow, and in which they experience a high level of job satisfaction. It also is a place where people feel safe and where there is an open climate in which everyone can start discussions about whatever is on their mind. This does not mean that all people have to agree all the time – on the contrary. Different viewpoints and perspectives are actually very useful and productive. Narrow-mindedness should be avoided at all costs. However, relationships between people should be trusted and safe and such that people feel comfortable having different ideas. Colleagues do not need to be friends, but they should appreciate each other. Apart from the fact that the time we spend at work takes up a substantial part of our lives (so we had better enjoy it), such an environment will also be attractive for people to work in. Therefore, it will be easier to recruit and maintain talented people. Furthermore, such an environment will also facilitate the critical questioning of each other's work, which is an essential part of our work.

WHO SHOULD LEAD?

The next question is about the meaning of leadership or about who should lead the department. In many instances, an official department head will have the responsibility for the activities of the department and that is just fine. However, in a healthy and mature academic organization, I believe leadership is a collective thing. In professional organizations, as academic marketing departments are, there is a lot of knowledge and wisdom available and it would be a waste not to use this. Joint responsibilities and participative decision making will improve the quality of discussions and their outcomes. It will also create commitment and motivation to contribute to the department's activities and performance. This does not mean that all decisions and actions should be executed collectively but the major and strategic ones should. Of course, many of the daily tasks of the department's leadership involve more operational issues and these can be perfectly dealt with by one or a few people within the department. In many cases, some sort of delegation of responsibilities to several individuals will most likely work best.

Scientific work is about a critical exchange of substantive arguments to improve the quality of work. This quality will mostly benefit from the exchange of arguments. The same will also hold for determining the strategic course of a department. Different people will play different roles, but single-headed leadership and a hierarchical decision-making structure will be inferior to one where collective knowledge and capabilities are exploited. Participative decision making by all people involved will create commitment and a more inclusive organization. This in return will enhance job satisfaction and create an environment in which people will feel safe and be heard. Of course, one could argue that such an approach is less efficient than one in which decisions are being made by one or a small group of people. This may be true but decisions that do not resonate with the people who are involved will be much more difficult to execute (successfully). Furthermore, leadership by a single or a few persons will often mean that a few more senior people who are around for longer will make the decisions. This means that insights of new and younger people are not taken into account. In my view this means missed opportunities. New and young colleagues mean new perspectives and fresh insights. These will almost always improve the quality of decision making.

Despite my call for collective leadership and feeling responsible together, some coordination is needed. This will mean that at the end there will be an individual who is formally appointed as chair or head of department. As argued above, to me coordination is the main responsibility of such a person, not decision making. In that sense it is more about the coordination of the decision-making process. Many departments have a system in place in which regular rotation of heads/coordinators takes place. Some other departments have the same department head for a long period of time. Regular rotation is the preferred model for me. In general, fresh perspectives will be beneficial and each new person "in charge" can use his/her own strengths to improve things, while building on the good things that are already there. Rotation also prevents the development of information asymmetries where one or a few people know a lot about administrative things and most others only little or nothing. This will make the department vulnerable because of its dependence on these few individuals. It will also go at the cost of involvement and commitment of people. Finally, in many schools, being department head nowadays is a time- and energy-consuming responsibility and an individual's burnout should be avoided.

TASKS OF DEPARTMENT LEADERSHIP

The main responsibility of the department's leadership is making sure that department members can do their job well, and in such a way that the department meets its collective responsibilities. At the same time, individual members should feel that that they can do their job as well as possible to contribute to these responsibilities. Individual faculty will often also have their personal ambitions and goals and, ideally, individual and common goals are aligned. Department leadership plays a critical role in creating such alignment. This starts with developing a clear idea about the role of the department within the school and university. Only when school and department leadership agree and have a shared vision about the main responsibilities of the department, and how a department can contribute to the school's ambitions and goals, can people within the department operate in a stable environment.

As is the case with universities' and schools' leadership, it is important for departments as well that the vision about responsibilities is stable over time and does not change every time new individuals assume leadership positions. Of course, some change is necessary regularly, as is adaptation to new circumstances. However, stability and predictability are necessary for an academic environment and for faculty to do well. In general, the need for change should not be overestimated. Especially professional administrators seem to show such tendency regularly. Only by creating change are they able to make their mark on an organization and their own track record. Whether this really helps an organization is often questionable. Only organizations that are really failing may benefit from such leadership. For most others, more continuous and incremental improvement and adaptation is much better. It is also important that university, school, and department leadership remember that their primary reason for existence is knowledge generation and knowledge dissemination. The importance of these two activities can and should never be underestimated. There will always be reasons to get distracted from the core; however, good leadership stays focused and is not receptive to all kinds of fashionable seductions. Only by showing a long-term focus on, and commitment for, high-quality knowledge generation and knowledge dissemination, can a difference be made.

What I find really important is that one continuously keeps an eye on whether the majority of people employed by a university, school, and department are directly active in these positions or directly supporting the people who do so. When too many people do jobs for which this is not the case, the organization runs a real risk of loss of focus, and all the downsides and risks that come with that. Similarly, I think that, in general, it is really important that leadership is or recently has been active in knowledge generation and dissemination as well. Ideally, they are active professionals who temporarily and partially take up administrative responsibilities. In this way, leadership and faculty will speak the same language and stay aligned. Academic leadership will also stay credible for the organization. Preferably, administration should not be a career in and of itself. Of course, in certain situations, a fresh outside perspective may be useful. However, these are most likely exceptions. In most cases stability is preferable. The chances of realizing this with leadership, which knows the industry and the job, will be the highest.

When the responsibilities of the department are aligned with those of the school and university, it will then in turn be important that there is alignment between the responsibilities and goals of the individual faculty members within the department and the department itself. Most departments will find high-quality research and teaching the most important parts of their activities. This should be reflected in the core of their people, the faculty. In my view, it is essential that (most) faculty are involved in both knowledge generation and knowledge dissemination. Doing both will increase the quality of the two individual activities. Being active in research will keep faculty up to date on their domain and on the literature. This will be beneficial for their teaching. It will keep faculty intellectually sharp, on top of things, and creative. This is essential for the interaction with students and other audiences. In some sense, research activity provides a "license to operate" in the classroom. The other way around, research will benefit from lecturing. Classrooms and other external audiences will be critical settings for testing ideas and new research insights. They will also be fruitful places for idea generation, which will feed research agendas and make them more relevant.

Personally, I do not believe in a sharp division between knowledge generation and knowledge dissemination, and different faculty specializing in either of the two activities. Educators who are not research active can certainly be valuable but mostly for limited time periods only. In my experience they will have a hard time staying up to date as time passes, something that research activity almost automatically guarantees. Not staying up to date will result in a degradation of teaching quality. Similarly, only working on research without being active in the classroom or knowledge dissemination with other external audiences creates the risk of becoming irrelevant to broader audiences, which is problematic in applied fields such as business and marketing are. I think that it is critically important that departments recruit only individuals who are intrinsically motivated to be both research and teaching active. Only in very exceptional circumstances can people temporarily cut back on one of the two activities.

There seems to be a tendency to increasingly work with teaching-only faculty. Despite the fact that many seemingly credible arguments are made for employing such people, in most cases it is at the end mostly for budgetary reasons – allowing people to spend time on research costs money. However, in my view, research is essential for the quality and long-term viability of any academic organization. Without research, the organization will lose what distinguishes it and therefore its reason for existence – this risk should not be underestimated. When faculty do not share similar activities, there will also be nothing that unites them. This will lead to fragmented departments without a common purpose. For quality individual work, it is important to be able to share and exchange ideas and experiences with colleagues. For this, a critical mass of people with similar jobs is necessary. In departments with clearly separated job activities, exchanging ideas and experiences across the department will be much more challenging, if not impossible. The lack of a clear common and shared responsibility will easily create separate sections of people where most communication will take place within and not between sections. Making the exchange of ideas and communication between such sections happen will require substantial effort. In cases of people having similar job responsibilities and profiles, this will happen more naturally and automatically. Similar to my skepticism about teaching-only faculty, I also see no role for research-only faculty in academic marketing departments. Business schools and universities exist because of their commitment to educate people. People who do not want or cannot be part of this should not be part of departments but find a job at specialized research organizations or companies.

So, overall, I feel that all faculty should be active in sharing the joined responsibilities of knowledge generation, dissemination, and administrative service. However, this does not mean that every person does (exactly) the same and at all times. As long as most or all faculty feel that the allocation of duties and activities is fair and makes sense, and everyone feels that (s)he can spend sufficient time on the activities that are most valuable for her/him, things will be fine. In my view and experience it will be best for a department when more junior faculty have fewer and more focused responsibilities than their more experienced and senior colleagues. This means that junior colleagues get ample research time to make sure they have the opportunity to develop a research portfolio and realize journal publications. Whether we like it or not, the latter is essential for the development of an academic career. Ideally, their teaching is related to their research interests so that expertise is not a concern during first appearances in the classroom. In marketing departments, we often recruit not only people with a PhD in marketing, but we also regularly attract people from adjacent domains like psychology, statistics, economics and, more recently, computer science. Especially for faculty with such backgrounds, but most likely for all faculty, I think it is extremely useful to teach an introductory or core marketing course early in their career. One of the best ways of becoming familiar with the broader domain you are a faculty member in (i.e., marketing), is by teaching its basics.

As faculty become more senior and experienced, it becomes more reasonable to also expect them to participate in administrative services and in being actively part of the organization that is employing them. Some people will enjoy doing this; for others it will be something to avoid whenever possible. Ideally, responsibilities will be divided in such a way that the load for individuals is reasonable and that people perform the kind of task that exploits their relative strengths. In general, it is important that people are active in administrative jobs for fixed and limited terms to avoid wear out and stimulate opportunities for fresh perspectives.

Regarding course allocation, in many situations people will teach the same set of courses for a relatively long period of time. The benefit of this is that one can really become a specialist, develop a personal vision on the topic taught, and revise and improve the course based on experiences. A potential risk may be the development of a routine and doing things on automatic pilot. Most faculty themselves are probably able to realize how they are doing with respect to this. Teaching a completely new course every now and then will stimulate curiosity and learning new things again. Despite it taking a substantial time investment, it may, therefore, be a good thing for most faculty to teach a new course regularly.

Overall, it seems good for people to regularly renew themselves to learn, be creative, and stay energized. This is the case for administrative responsibilities and teaching, but for research as well. It is tempting for people to work on topics they have been working on for a long time, have been productive at, and have thus really invested in. There is nothing wrong with this and it will help the field to develop deep knowledge. However, there will also be faculty that need or want to change topics, approaches, etc., every now and then. Doing this will take time and happen at the cost of the productivity (temporarily). Still, when individual faculty want to do these things it should be encouraged and facilitated by department leadership. Again, such changes will stimulate creativity and innovation, key characteristics of leading research.

RECRUITING AND RETAINING

The most important asset of almost any organization is its people. For academic departments this is even more the case. The department will be as good as the people it is hosting. Recruiting the right people for a department is probably one of the most essential tasks of a department's leadership. In my experience, most people are who they are, and one should not overestimate the extent to which intrinsic qualities, motivations, and interests are malleable, and whether we should aspire to do this. So, recruiting deserves a lot of attention, and effort and the energy and time spent on that process is very much worth it.

The question now is what is meant by "the right people"? In my view, recruiting should always be focused on further strengthening the department. The goal is to find people who will add something to the department that is not already there. For example, knowledge about certain topics, a new set of methods skills, or a different approach to teaching. This will make the department stronger. Ideally, departments only recruit people that are potentially better than the people who are already there. This is sometimes seen as threatening for or by existing department members. However, everyone involved can benefit from new colleagues who can help them learn and improve themselves. Department members have a shared responsibility to make their department perform as well as possible. They should not be driven by self-interest when deciding about new recruits. A new colleague may be potentially interesting because (s)he may be willing to teach a course or do work that others are not too much interested in. However, if that person is not making the department better in any sense, but just makes life easier for the others, hiring will not be a good idea. At the same time, it is also important that new people share things in common with the people that are already there. Shared research values and a similar attitude to students and interacting with them will fit in more straightforwardly. Departments have to operate as a team and teamwork requires some commonalities. When an individual is too different from present faculty, hiring will not make much sense because complementary effects will be unlikely. What is also really important is to assess the likelihood of success of a new hire in the existing departmental context. Some people have potentially great intrinsic qualities; however, the situation and the conditions in the department may be such that it will be difficult to realize this potential. If this is the case, it will probably not be wise to hire such people. If people cannot perform according to their potential that is a waste and it will most likely lead to frustrations and dissatisfaction. Therefore, in recruiting, a department should be ambitious but realistic as well.

Recruiting is just the first step in talent management; helping people to realize their full potential is the crucial second one. This means facilitating people in doing the things they are good at and trying to challenge them regularly to do the kind of things that will help them develop and learn. To make people productive it is also important that the resources they need for their type of research are available. For example, if recruiting people who study consumer behavior using experimental approaches, the availability of a behavioral lab is most likely very important; recruiting such people will only make sense if such a facility is available. The same will be true for people doing quantitative modeling work and the availability of data sources and computing equipment.

It is thus essential to make sure that faculty can be productive and stay happy and motivated. However, some may decide to leave at some point in time. Many departments are internationally oriented nowadays and host faculty members from various countries – this brings a lot of benefits; through internationalization, the pool of talent to recruit from is much bigger. Furthermore, diverse backgrounds will create different perspectives, which will stimulate creativity and innovation. International faculty will in general be more mobile than local faculty. At some point in their career and life, they may decide to move on. There can be all kinds of reasons for this, both personal and professional. It is important to make sure that people never leave because of negative reasons. The goal should be to make sure that a faculty member's stay has been successful in terms of contribution, productivity, and development. When people leave, they should leave as ambassadors. This will be good for the department's reputation and also help future recruitment. Because of the increased mobility of faculty nowadays, recruitment has become an almost continuous process for many departments. This means extra work and it requires substantial effort by all faculty members. However, it also offers great opportunities for continuous renewal of the department and the opportunity to develop its position in the international research and faculty network.

SOME CONCLUDING REMARKS

Universities and business schools occupy an essential position in and responsibility for our societies, and their importance is hard to overestimate. Within these organizations, academic departments are core units, playing the role of the engine where the critical responsibilities of knowledge generation and knowledge dissemination are executed. To be able to play their important roles, these departments should be led well. Leading an academic marketing department is both a challenging and a rewarding job. Most department members are independent, smart, talented, nice, reasonable, and hardworking professionals. To make the department do well, the individuals that collectively form the department should be able to do as good as possible, and fully realize their potential – faculty are professionals, who should be given the trust, safety, and environment to do their job well.

In my view, the most important job of department leadership is to create the conditions in which people do the kind of things they are best at and facilitate them to do this as effectively as possible. Lately, many organizations, including academic ones, seem rather obsessed with controlling their people. There is a constant quest for accountability and for people to do well in metrics and benchmarks. Doing well in these metrics and benchmarks seems to have become the main goal in professional life for many administrators. I think this is really unfortunate because it will go along with a cost to the quality of work and harm the potentially great role and contribution to societies of our organizations. Metrics and measurement systems are often based on what was important in the past, but they do not necessarily provide guidance for what will make a difference in the future. Constantly minding people will also suppress creativity and innovation and is unnecessary and a waste of time and resources. I am convinced that most people really want to contribute and enjoy doing well. From what I have observed, the more you mind faculty with things that distract them from substance, the less happy, innovative, and creative they will become. An important reason for the increasing control-oriented culture lies most likely in an apparently intrinsic negative view of people and the conviction that they should be pushed to perform. Especially, when leadership is executed by professional managers without sufficient knowledge of and experience in faculty work, metrics and benchmarks are the only tools they have. I don't know where the need for control is coming from. However, it would be good to step back in many universities and business schools and realize that a huge number of resources are spent nowadays on monitoring the engine of the organization, which is departments and faculty. This is a waste of resources and creates large opportunity costs. More hands-off and "lazy" leadership if you will, is actually much better for creative organizations, as universities and business schools are. Leadership should trust professionals and enjoy working with them. Facilitating them to realize their full potential is just what needs to be done, and that will be enormously rewarding and beneficial for all people involved: the individual faculty member, the organization, society at large and for leadership itself!

25. From head to dean: academic leadership

Peter Møllgaard

To some, academic leadership is a contradiction in terms. Academics don't want to be led. It's like herding cats. And by the way, academics cannot lead.

All of this is wrong in my experience. Academics don't mind being led – but the way you do it matters greatly. And academics are typically not as individualistic as the cat herding expression suggests – most of them are very collegial. Finally, academics can learn how to lead – and end up enjoying it!

This chapter reflects my own journey from full professor to head of department to dean at two academic institutions: Copenhagen Business School (CBS) and Maastricht University School of Business and Economics (SBE). On this journey, I have continuously tried to learn from my mistakes and also to acquire the right set of skills and competences for the different roles. Throughout the chapter, I will draw both on my experience and relevant literature.

The two institutions differ, as does the role that I play(ed). First, in terms of student numbers, CBS is a stand-alone business university which by most comparisons is huge: it has around 20,000 students of which a fifth are foreign. It has a total staff of about 1,350 employees plus 775 part-time academic staff. The scope of CBS is wide, including philosophy, history, sociology, political science, and law, in addition to economics and the classical management disciplines. Education is relatively large scale, based on lectures of up to 600 students at a time and CBS has a number of cross-disciplinary programs combining classical disciplines with mathematics, law, or political science, to mention a few. Research combines excellence in various disciplines with transdisciplinary collaborative 'Business in Society' (BiS) platforms that allow CBS to address grand societal challenges, e.g. in inequality, digitalization, diversity and difference, and to engage with major societal stakeholders, e.g. in CBS maritime.

My role at CBS was dean of research, meaning I was responsible for twelve departments, all academic staff (675), PhD programs, BiS platforms and the quality of research, including academic integrity. The dean of education was responsible for all programs, the university director for shared central services: together with the president of CBS we constituted the senior management team. In that role, I had the pleasure of interacting with heads of department and dealing with the strategies and performance of their departments, often with an aim to facilitate collaboration across CBS.

SBE is one of six faculties at Maastricht University. Maastricht University has roughly 20,000 students and SBE has around 5,200, of which the majority (66%) are international. SBE has a total staff of 560, 400 of which are faculty. The scope is somewhat narrower than that of CBS, focusing mostly on economics and classical business disciplines, although in 2019 we widened the scope with a new department on Data Analytics and Digitalization as well as the inclusion of Maastricht Sustainability Institute and Maastricht Graduate School of Governance. Education is based on small-scale problem-based learning (PBL) with corresponding teaching facilities. Educational programs are also not quite as broad in scope, although recent additions such as a Bachelor of Business Engineering with the Faculty of Science and Engineering and a Minor of Sustainability add to the diversity. Since 2017, research has been organized in seven research themes aiming at ensuring cross-disciplinary collaboration within SBE. As of 2021, there will be a number of transdisciplinary spearheads aiming to solve a number of societal challenges within three focus areas: sustainable development, digitalization and globalization.

My role at SBE is dean, meaning that I hold overall accountability for SBE as well as primary responsibility for education and research. These overall management responsibilities for SBE have been mandated by the Executive Board of Maastricht University to whom I refer. The Executive Board consists of a President, a Rector Magnificus, and a Vice President, each with their own portfolio. The Executive Board and the six deans constitute the management team of Maastricht University. At SBE I am responsible for a similar number of departments as at CBS, but in addition I now have the responsibility for education and for administration. Thus in this role, I have the added pleasure of interacting with SBE's Education Institute that organizes bachelor and master programs and of engaging more directly with students.

Comparing the two positions at CBS and SBE, at SBE I have a full portfolio of responsibilities but for a smaller school (measured by the number of students) while at CBS my responsibility lay mostly with research. At SBE the group of stakeholders is different, since I refer to the Executive Board rather than being part of it. CBS is a stand-alone university, so university politics are different than at SBE which is one of six faculties. This also means that at SBE the control of shared central services (e.g. HR, finance, student services) is less direct than at CBS.

What difference did the different contexts make to my role? There are some clear differences that may be noted throughout the chapter but also some very clear similarities and my CBS experience certainly formed my leadership of SBE. But let me first take you back to where it all started.

WHY? ON PURPOSE IN ACADEMIC LEADERSHIP

Why would you want to assume academic leadership? My academic field is industrial organization, a branch of economics. Despite my background, clearly the motivation is not money: it is the possibility to make a difference, to contribute. In addition, it is the personal opportunity to grow and to learn. My personal leadership purpose is "to develop academic institutions to have impact on societies."

Two early experiences that shaped me in my teenage years and in my early twenties may help understand my personal leadership purpose (Craig and Snook, 2014) and my approach to leadership in general.

First, as a scout in my teens I joined a newly formed troop and quickly became leader of a patrol consisting of around seven scouts. This experience provided a very steep learning curve in terms of situational leadership: what is needed in the middle of the wilderness with a bunch of tired scouts is very different from what you need in the cozy warmth of the cabin in the weekly evening session. And since the troop was newly started there were ample opportunities to contribute to the development with the excellent team of inspiring troop leaders and other patrol leaders. Finally, the scouts offered my first, rather intensive, leadership courses with other patrol leaders from all over the country (Huiskes, 2019).

Second, during my economics studies I held a part-time job at the Danish Ministry of Finance. I got into a team that worked with the macroeconomic performance of the country. In the mid-1980s, the economy was overheating and the balance of payments went haywire. The team worked day and night to deliver advice on the macroeconomic policy that would best address the situation. We came up with a package that had a positive impact on society during the remainder of the 1980s. This experience showed me that the combination of analytical skills and practical knowledge of society can be used to address a societal challenge by providing knowledge-based advice to improve society.

In 2005 when I first got the possibility to formally assume academic leadership, I was working as a professor in the Department of Economics at CBS. The department was rather small and split between an ambitious group and a group that had not produced significant academic output for a number of years. The department was led by a representative of the latter group who essentially strived at maintaining the status quo.

It was clear to me (and to others) that the department had potential but also that this potential would not be released under the current leadership. The occasion to assume formal leadership came as a result of a change in the Danish Universities Act: all academic leaders from president (rector) to heads of department were to be appointed rather than elected. You could see that as a move away from a Humboldtian model of higher education towards a more Anglo-American model.

This move triggered a debate over what the consequences would be for the legitimacy of academic leaders: would academic leaders become undemocratic authoritarian dictators? My short reply is that experience shows that this concern is rarely relevant. As with other leadership, it is impossible to lead without followers and this is especially true in academia. The people you lead have normally no problem speaking their mind. In addition, the best of the academics you lead have outside options – they can get jobs elsewhere.

For these reasons, and because intrinsic motivation is a very strong driver in academia, as an academic leader you always have to listen carefully to the people in the organization and you always have to explain the reasons behind your suggestions; why you do what you do. In academia, purpose – understood as the rationale for action – is more important than anything else; communicating 'the why' clearly is key to success. If you fail to do this, you will have few followers. On the other hand, you cannot expect to get consensus for every initiative. This would stifle innovation and progress. But you need to get sufficient consent to move ahead. I will get back to the need to build consent in the section entitled "Co-creating the 'why'" below.

My first exhilarating experience with co-creating the 'why' came at a strategy workshop of the department about half a year into my term as head of department. I remember being nervous about the whole idea: would the department respond well to working with strategy, quite a novel thing to do in an academic organization more used to a Humboldtian approach (Foss and Møllgaard, 2020). Would they be constructive? Would they accept my leadership? Would they accept change? The answers to all these questions turned out to be positive and the strategy workshop marked a turning point in the history of the department.

Why? Yes, exactly. We had a reason to make it a success. At this point in time (2005), the department had just gone through an external peer review that pointed to six areas in which the department could improve:

1.   Strengthen the incentives for research.
2.   Improve the balance of burdens.
3.   Encourage innovative, research-based teaching.
4.   Increase the market share of economics in study programs.
5.   Expand the department.
6.   Get more PhD students.

We used the feedback of the peer reviewers to create a strengths, weaknesses, opportunities and threats (SWOT) analysis of the department and this in turn led to a new and more ambitious five-year vision for 2010. A key element in this was to get external funding to expand the research base and get resources to deliver strategic results in all the six areas.

In the ten years I headed CBS Department of Economics, it more than tripled in size. We attracted and retained international scholars of an increasingly high quality. We introduced incentives for research, both pecuniary (annual bonuses) and non-pecuniary (time for research). We introduced a differentiated research percentage, so that people with a good track record and convincing research plans would have more time for research, leaving other members to do relatively more education. We developed new educational programs and new courses. We increased our presence in educational program committees and other collegial bodies. We strengthened the quality control system regarding external funding in order to get fewer but better applications which ultimately led to improved rates of success – and to more PhD students. As a result of all of the above, the department had much more impact – academic and societal – than before.

In all these initiatives, I found it very useful to always be able to explain the purpose, 'the why.' Especially one initiative was controversial: the introduction of differentiated research percentages. Members of department who risked having their research time cut and their teaching time increased were not in favor and fairly vocal. I consulted more experienced leaders in this process and also listened to the concerns, so it was introduced gradually over two to three years allowing people time to both get used to the idea and in principle to improve the track record to avoid it. However, this was clearly a measure that did not reach consensus, but consent.

In this process, the department was increasingly seen as a success and we benefitted from this in 2009 when we started recruiting tenure-track assistant professors in the international job market for economists – in the midst of the financial crisis that started in 2008. Due to the crisis, American universities and business schools were not able to recruit as in previous years and the interest for CBS was for that reason unusually high. CBS senior management allowed us to recruit five assistant professors in this job market, rather than the two we had been allocated and this changed the reputation of CBS in this job market positively making a permanent change in CBS' ability to recruit internationally.

The above story mainly relates to learning on the job and from consulting peers. Apart from that, I have participated in a number of leadership programs over the past 15 years.

The first program started one year into my term as head of department. It was a four-module program to develop researchers into leadership roles and was organized by Universities

Denmark. Targeted at heads of department, the four modules were built on the classic text-book in organizational theory and behavior, *Reframing Organizations: Artistry, Choice, and Leadership* by Bolman and Deal (2003). Bolman and Deal suggest that a leader can look at their organization through four frames (lenses, perspectives):

1. The structural frame: the organization as a rational system (the organigram).
2. The human resource frame: the organization as a social system (the resources available).
3. The political frame: a scene on which power is exerted, conflicts play out and coalitions are made (the power structure).
4. The symbolic frame: the culture of the workplace (collegiality, coherence).

The ability to understand a challenge in a wider structural, resource-based, political and cultural context and to discover patterns, connections and relationships with past, present and future challenges is facilitated by this approach to leadership. To effectively lead academic departments, the head of department should be able to change perspective on dilemmas and use integrative thinking to find solutions.

To be an effective leader, it is important that you understand your own strengths and weaknesses, including what may trigger you to react counterproductively. Part of my first formal leadership training consisted of a psychological test. The Jungian Typology Index (JTI), is an alternative to the Myers–Briggs Type Index. Both tests are based on C.G. Jung's *Psychological Types* (1921).

In the first test I did, I was described as extravert, intuiting, feeling and perceptive. Translated into leadership style, this became an action-, process- and people-oriented innova-tive type. I base my judgments and decisions on values and possibilities. I received a 16-page psychological report that I later discussed with a trained business psychologist. What I found useful was not only to understand my strong sides, but also to reflect over the weak sides, which in terms of personal management were listed to be:

*   Starting new projects without first finishing projects already in progress.
*   Overlooking relevant details.
*   Working too hard in the attempt to do too much.
*   Procrastination.
*   Possible issues with prioritization and planning of own time.

I also got feedback on my own role in teams, and in general a solid feedback regarding points for development. All this was hugely important to me for effective personal leadership. This test, and later psychological and psychometric tests I have participated in, have helped me cover my weaker sides, either in terms of directing my own attention to them or by establishing leadership teams that are sufficiently diverse to compensate for them. I know, for example, that I need someone in my team who takes care of facts and details and reminds me to pay attention to these.

One of the most useful exercises we did during this leadership program was training for difficult conversations: to handle employees with performance problems or misconduct in the workplace is one of the most valuable skills to acquire as a head of department (or as a dean). The consistent handling of difficult situations is crucial for effective leadership in academia.

WHAT DOES THE HEAD BRING TO THE DEAN?

A middle manager needs to develop what I call a dual loyalty. This is especially important in academic organizations where 'the why' is so important. The dual loyalty means that a head of department is loyal to the department when she is together with senior management, and loyal to the senior management when she is with the department.

The head of department is the linking pin (Likert, 1967) between the department and the senior management. It is important for senior management to get an accurate picture of what goes on in each department and to get feedback from the department through the head, also when – perhaps especially when – this feedback is critical of senior management.

It is also important for the organization that the head of department explains the actions of the senior management to the department. For this to be possible, it is of course crucial that senior management is able to explain the reasons behind the actions, 'the why.' When the head of department does this, the department gets the best possible understanding of the direction of the school and while this may not lead to consensus (entirely too much to hope for), at least it may lead to consent – and increased satisfaction with the workplace.

Imagine a head of department who does not exhibit the dual loyalty. Essentially, this head of department is misrepresenting his department to the senior management, perhaps painting a rosy picture when it is not called for – or painting a bleaker picture than is actually the case. At the same time, he might misrepresent the reasoning behind the senior management's actions thus creating unnecessary unrest in the department. Essentially, this head of department is de-linking the department from the rest of the organization and causing dissatisfaction with the workplace. I have seen this lack of dual loyalty play out both at CBS and at SBE, leading to significant dissatisfaction in the relevant departments.

In a leadership program organized at CBS, I was introduced to the Leadership Pipeline. Over the last 20 years, the Leadership Pipeline (Charan, Drotter and Noel, 2001) has been one of the more influential approaches to leadership development and talent management. According to this approach, work values, time application and skills needed to lead differ according to where you are placed in the hierarchy. Based on these differences, it explains how you need to develop in a career moving from one level to the next; when you do 'a passage' from one level to the next.

In an academic setting, the Leadership Pipeline for heads of department and dean often goes through first getting a PhD (learning to do research) via an assistant professorship (learning to combine research with educational activity) through associate and full professorships. In these latter positions, in addition to research and education, you to an increasing extent add activities relating to external funding, to academic citizenship and leadership (for example, participating in assessment committees, refereeing, acting as coordinator for courses or program director for educational programs) and to dissemination or outreach activities.

At CBS, I developed a separate REEAD framework to align expectations and create transparency as to the roles of different academic positions and what is needed to get into these (Møllgaard, 2017). The acronym REEAD stands for Research, Education, External funding, Academic citizenship and leadership, and Dissemination and impact. I have further elaborated it at SBE (Møllgaard, 2020). This framework essentially describes the academic pipeline in which an academic grows from junior to senior, focusing on the *academic* content of the job.

The academic leadership pipeline is building on the academic pipeline but inspired by the original framework by Charan, Drotter and Noel (2001). When you become a head of department you make a transition from managing yourself to managing others. Your academic activities are of course important, but they are no longer the most important. The most important activities you do as a head of department have to do with the REEAD activities of those you lead. Probably the most important challenge of this transition is to accept this: if you accept formal academic leadership, your own academic activities are less important than the academic activities of those you lead. Failure to accept this inevitably leads to frustration both with your own academic progress and with your leadership.

In the words of the founders of the Leadership Pipeline:

> As you will discover, each passage requires that people acquire a new way of managing and leading and leave the old ways behind in the following three areas:
> * Skill requirements – the new capabilities required to execute new responsibilities
> * Time applications – new time frames that govern how one works
> * Work values – what people believe is important and so becomes the focus of their effort.
> The challenge for organizations is to make sure that people in leadership positions are assigned to the level appropriate to their skills, time applications, and values. Unfortunately, many managers often work at the wrong level: they're clinging to values appropriate to Passage One (managing others) even though they're working at Passage Two (managing managers), or they haven't acquired the skills or time application expertise appropriate to their current level. As a result, not only are they less effective (or ineffective) leaders but the people they manage are negatively affected as well. (Charan, Drotter and Noel, 2001, p. 20)

I have seen this happen also in academic environments. Some heads of department stick with their research, educational activities and outreach activities when they are appointed. They just add the academic leadership on top of a work day which is typically already long. However, as the Leadership Pipeline points out, if you are promoted from being a 'regular' academic to being head of department, Passage One, then you need a set of skills that is different from the one you used as an academic.

For this reason, your time application must change and so should your skill set. In addition, you should realize that you now operate in an official capacity and therefore need to understand administrative law and labor law. You sometimes act as an arbiter, sometimes as a mediator. Passage One is often difficult to accomplish. I strongly recommend leadership training supported by development initiatives within the organization to facilitate Passage One.

SEVEN KEY CHALLENGES FOR THE EFFECTIVE DEAN

Passage Two takes you from managing others to managing managers; from leading colleagues to leading leaders; from head of department to dean. In this new role, you should

1. select the right people for Passage One,
2. assign managerial tasks to heads of department,
3. coach them,
4. make use of benchmarks and indicators, partly to
5. allocate resources across departments,
6. manage the boundaries between departments, and finally
7. co-create the 'why' with the heads of department.

At this level, you are also expected to take a broad, long-term perspective, think about strategic issues and solve problems that cut across the entire organization. In addition, you will often be expected to contribute to the university in terms of entering management teams or chairing committees.

Finally, you are often expected to represent your school or faculty in a national or international context, liaising with other deans and for business schools: taking part in peer review accreditation teams. The typical challenge of Passage Two is that the leader must further divest individual tasks to only lead. In terms of changing work values, you need to learn to appreciate disciplines outside your own field and to get a holistic view of the school or faculty. In terms of skills needed, you need to be able to communicate clearly with much broader communities: students, administrative staff and the surrounding world.

The dean's seven tasks determine the content of the rest of the chapter.

1.   Choosing the Right Heads of Department

To have the right leaders is essential, and selecting and developing them is an ongoing activity. These positions are usually time limited and indeed should be.

When I signed on as dean of research at CBS, seven out of 15 positions as head of department expired. We – i.e. the dean's office supported by HR – decided to advertise these in one big process and to involve a recruiting company to assist us in:

- scouting for talent,
- approaching talent to ensure that we got a good pool of applications from internal and external candidates,
- short-listing the candidates together with department-specific selection committees,
- organizing the first interviews with typically five candidates,
- administering psychometric tests of two to three candidates that were selected for a second interview,
- debriefing the selection committees on the results of the psychometric tests, and
- organizing the second interviews that typically dealt with expected leadership behavior, taking the psychometric test as its starting point.

In drafting advertisements, we paid special attention to use a wording that would appeal equally to women and men, and equal opportunities were also important in scouting for talent and in the remaining processes.

In terms of experience and capabilities, we were looking for profiles that matched the following text which appeared in the advertisement:

CBS considers it important that a candidate for the position as Head of Department:
- is an acknowledged and respected scholar within his/her field in relation to the position's field;
- can present management results from a research and educational setting or from a similar company, focusing on research;
- displays credibility and impact in relation to the department's staff, students and other management, and generates involvement and collaboration when formulating and executing the department's and CBS's strategies;
- has a keen eye for identifying talents and is motivated to develop them;
- understands and sees the possibilities of creating academic and developmental synergies between related departments at CBS;

- is capable of contributing in the overall management discussion and development in CBS' management forums;
- contributes to the department's and CBS's academic/professional exposure internationally; and
- has a relevant professional and personal network, and the abilities to expand it in relation to the position's tasks.

We used this process to exchange views on academic leadership since we were recruiting half of the group of heads and since we involved continuing heads of department in the selection committees. The continuing heads of department were asked to chair the interviews, requiring them to represent CBS in a broad sense and allowing the dean to take a more listening role. After each interview, the committee would discuss each candidate and we asked the most junior, the student, to kick-start the discussion and then asked the members of the committee in order of increasing seniority.

This recruiting process led to a diverse team of heads of department with internal and external candidates with different profiles across gender, psychological profiles and leadership experience.

At SBE we have introduced open calls for all significant leadership positions. This also meets with resistance in some of the departments who favor the old ways in which the senior professors essentially took turns in leading the department, not necessarily because they wanted to lead but because it was thought of as service to the department. So in most cases there is a need to explain that there could be talent outside of SBE that would be as good as internal candidates and that it is a strength for the department if they have a department head that has actively decided to lead.

2. Assigning Managerial Tasks to Heads of Department

The overall managerial tasks of a head of department should be clear at the point of application and expectations should be managed during the application period. When we announced seven positions at CBS, a section of the job announcement read:

As head of department, your most significant tasks include ensuring:
- The department's contribution to the development and execution of CBS's overall strategy;
- Realizing the department's overall strategy within science, education and administration;
- The long-term development of the department's academic work field;
- An encouraging research environment and a comfortable working atmosphere;
- A well run department, including financial results, administration and collaboration with other CBS units;
- A highly qualified staff of researchers, lecturers and administrators, supported by focused recruiting and development of staff;
- Coherence between the department's research and education, as well as ensuring that the educational responsibilities are fulfilled in relation to CBS's course catalogue;
- Quality and coherence in the department's research, publication, education and knowledge dissemination, including follow-up on researcher and education evaluation;
- External financing of research activities and relevant projects at the department.

At SBE, we use a similar list. In addition to listing the tasks in a recent appointment letter, we added the board's expectations as to leadership development: we expect the head to participate in a management development trajectory; contribute to the development of REEAD, as well as diversity and inclusion; communicate clearly and openly in general; and in particular to communicate strategic issues and important developments to the department, to fellow department chairs, and to the board.

3.   Coaching Heads of Department and Other Leadership Development

As dean, one of my most important tasks has been to coach heads of department. At SBE, I have monthly bilateral meetings with each of them, and with other important leaders at the school/faculty. Very often this is about concrete issues that include tricky HR cases (for example, performance failure of senior full professor or harassment cases), recruiting or promoting talent, strategy development at the department, or crisis management relating both to external crises (e.g. COVID-19) or internally generated crises, such as, for example, academic misconduct.

At the time when I was about to take over as dean of research at CBS and be responsible for the heads of department, a role I came from, we engaged in leadership development facilitated by an external consultant. We divided the 15 heads of department into three teams of five. These teams were created to be as diverse as possible, taking gender, experience and field into account. The purpose of the teams was to allow for confidential sparring and exchange of practice across departments but they would also serve as taskforces for particular assignments from the senior management.

At the initiation of the three teams, the consultant helped us do a particular version of a 360-degree assessment of each leader: the leadership mirror. Each leader (*A* in the following) would choose four stakeholders, and the other four members of the team would each do a semi-structured interview with each of these stakeholders.

Typical stakeholders selected would be a member of the senior management, a colleague among the heads of department, and one or two members of the department, typically with different roles (academic and administrative), but some also found outside stakeholders. The interviews were carried out within a month, and after this, head *A* would report back to the team in a session that was facilitated by a business psychologist from the consultant. The team would then discuss how to interpret the image provided by the four mirrors and give further feedback to *A*.

As an example of the feedback given from a member of *A*'s department, *A*'s strengths were described as transparent, honest, loyal, engaged and accessible. *A*'s challenge was in her words too much loyalty to senior management: in terms of the dual loyalty described above, she found that he was to a large extent just a messenger for senior management. For this reason, the best *A* could do to improve his role as head of department was to co-create an understanding with senior management as to the negative effects of an externally driven performance culture in order to ensure a better work–life balance at the department. This would benefit both the department and CBS. In terms of a metaphor, she found that he was a bridge – connecting people and possibilities. He should become the best possible diplomat – someone like Henry Kissinger.

Another example of feedback came from a member of senior management to a different *A* with a completely different psychological profile: *A* was transparent and very clear about very high ambitions for his department. The major challenges were lack of empathy and not giving priority to leadership activities because he would rather engage in research. *A* could strengthen his role as head of his department by taking a coach that would facilitate more accountability with respect to leadership. To be of higher value to CBS, he could learn to recognize and reward applied research and collaboration with the business community.

In terms of developing the group of heads, I have found it important to have more or less informal meetings with the entire group. At SBE, we have monthly informal meetings, typically during lunch. There is no agenda and no minutes are taken. They serve a multitude of purposes: we can informally discuss an idea and provide early feedback; we share practices across departments, and I can better sense what is going on at SBE.

At CBS, after a year or so as dean of research, I started a series of quarterly workshops, entitled Practical Academic Leadership, or PAL. In these, one of the three leadership teams or I would choose an article on leadership or management, ideally short and to the point. We would all read this article and then discuss it in a plenary session, facilitated by the team that had selected the article. The idea was to discuss the practical implications of the idea in the article from the perspective of our own actual situation.

For the very first PAL session, I had selected a classic article from the management literature, Oncken and Wass' (1974) "Management time: who's got the monkey?" Essentially, the story is that managers often take over subordinates' problems ('monkeys'). That way they get overloaded, essentially working more and more and accomplishing less and less. In reality the manager becomes subordinate to the subordinate. Instead, what the leader should do – and that also applies to heads of department and deans – is to coach the subordinate to find a solution or at least to find the next step, but not take ownership of the 'monkey.'

I still (try to) practice this: when a head of department comes to me with a 'monkey,' we discuss it, but I want the department to take the 'monkey' out of my office when (s)he leaves. (S)he should have the next move, whether it be to make an appointment with the employee, set up a meeting with HR, or draft a letter.

But, of course, the discussion in the first PAL meeting went all over the place: did we share a world view developed in the USA in the 1970s? How are academic institutions different from private businesses and would that not affect the analysis? The article was about management, but were we not leaders more than managers? And was the problem not that the manager had not empowered the employees sufficiently in the first place (Covey, 1999)? The discussion demonstrated very well the blessings of leading people who are – in large or small part – experts in leadership!

This co-created on-the-job training of heads of department served its purpose. But since we had recruited new department heads quite extensively, we also felt a need for more formalized leadership training and so Alan Irwin and Flemming Poulfelt, both editors of this volume, co-created a leadership training program for heads of department together with CBS Executive. This program was in part inspired by the program that I had participated in a decade earlier but was, of course, modernized. It was a huge success in the sense that all department heads – also the very experienced ones – signed up for it, although some of the more experienced heads disputed the need for it.

4.   Using Benchmarks and Indicators in the Leadership Dialogue

Both at CBS and SBE there are formal meetings in which the state of the department is discussed along with future plans. At SBE, these meetings are called spring meetings and typically happen in the second quarter after the accounts of the previous year have been finalized. At these meetings, the management team of the department meets the board of SBE. The head of the department is asked to chair the meeting and asked to include the following items:

1. Looking back and looking ahead.
2. Contribution to the strategy of the faculty.
3. Financial affairs:
   a. Funding strategy of the department.
   b. Financial performance and reserve position.
4. HR:
   a. Strategic Personnel Plan of the department.
   b. Diversity and inclusion.
   c. Workload.
5. Sustainability.

These meetings give a possibility to give feedback to the head of department on the performance of the department. We use the meetings to give evidence and point towards issues that can be addressed. The purpose is to suggest directions for improvement. This should, of course, not only be done once a year but it is necessary to take stock in order to have a shared picture of the state of the department – and of the school.

At CBS, the similar meetings were supported by a huge data package that both the dean and the head of department could analyze before the meeting. However, because the data package was so rich, the discussion would often lack focus, because different data were used to support different points of view. For this reason, we developed the 'cobweb,' a simple benchmarking tool that used the data packages as input and then allowed us to compare the performance of the department along a number of dimensions, typically productivity measures for research, education and external funding.

The choice of data was subject to much discussion in the group of heads of department, since they typically argued for inclusion of indicators in which they would fare well and for the exclusion of indicators in which they would fare poorly. I very much emphasized that the benchmarking was not there to give all departments the same profile but to have a dialogue as to whether the profile was deliberate and if there were areas to develop, perhaps inspired by the experience in other departments.

In the end, we came up with indicators that would measure the quantity and quality of research, the quantity and quality of educational activities, the size and spending of external research grants, and the number of PhD students. Figure 25.1 gives an example. For each indicator, the activity was measured relative to the department's resources, viz. academic staff, typically measured in full-time equivalents (FTEs) for full, associate and assistant professors. However, for the PhD indicator, the level was measured against all tenured academic staff (full and associate professors). The quality of education was measured as the share of staff (in this case including part-time teaching staff) with an average course evaluation above 3.5 out of a maximum of 5.

Figure 25.1 benchmarks four departments against each other. In this comparison, 0 at the center of the cobweb marks the worst performance while 10 is best in class. Department 3 was doing very well in terms of external funding and quality of educational activities but was intermediate in other dimensions. Department 8 was doing very well in terms of the number of PhD students and also doing a lot of (well-evaluated) education but was again middle of the road when it came to other dimensions – and poorly when external funding was concerned. Department 13 was not doing well along any dimension – except perhaps in education where it is average. However, the self-perception in that department was that they were doing the bulk of the education at CBS and that this caused the low performance along the other indicators. Department 14 was top of the class when it came to research and also did some very well-evaluated teaching.

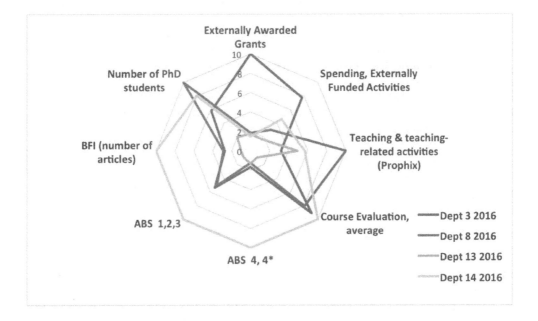

Figure 25.1   Comparison of four CBS departments in 2016

It may be interesting to note that my initiative met with resistance also within the senior management team, the argument against in short being that it would reduce management at CBS to key performance indicators (KPIs) and it essentially constituted Excel sheet management. My argument that it allowed for a dialogue with the head of department on an informed basis was not unanimously accepted.

5.   Allocating Resources Across Departments

At a university, a faculty or a business school, people are the most important resource – 75% of the budget of SBE is made up of salaries. In other words, when we are allocating resources across departments, we are basically talking about recruitment of new talent or retention of current talent. Since most universities abide by the notion of tenure, it is rare to lay off academic staff to adjust the size of a department, since this conflicts with tenure.

The allocation of these resources should be strategic. At CBS, we worked with centralized positions, so heads of department could request positions (new recruitment or promotion) in 'allocation rounds' once or twice a year.

Senior management (in this case in particular the Dean of Education and the Dean of Research) would assess the prioritized applications from all department heads and essentially determine the cut-off for each department based on the available budget and an overall view of CBS' strategy. In addition to these short-run decisions, we asked department heads to take a view at the longer run for the department and to both scout for and develop talent for the future – also with a view on diversity.

At SBE, positions are allocated to departments through a historic development and department heads feel they have the right to refill senior positions that become vacant. For this reason, it may be difficult to connect the resources of the school with its strategy. To address this, the board of SBE has asked the heads of department to develop strategic personnel plans (SPPs) for their departments to link their wish for resources with their own and SBE's strategies. The SPP answers questions such as: How are the demographics of the department expected to develop in the next five years? What type of employees does the department need during the next 3–5 years? How are the needs related to e.g. education? How should talent be developed to be able to take up new roles in the future? Who is expected to come up for promotion? Are there core people that need to be retained? The answers to these questions, of course, tie in with the academic pipeline and REEAD.

Starting a new department is a different approach to connecting strategy with resources. SBE perceived a need to recruit talent within the area of digitalization. Reacting to a reluctance of heads of existing departments to recruit specifically for this area, the board decided to obtain critical mass by establishing a new Department of Data Analytics and Digitalization (DAD) that came into existence on January 1, 2019.

A third approach to deploy resources across departments is through the establishment of cross-departmental initiatives. Inspired by a long CBS tradition of guided evolution (Foss and Møllgaard, 2020), at CBS we used a combination of a top-down call for letters of interest and bottom-up initiatives that ultimately led to three BiS platforms: a Digital Transformations Platform, a Diversity and Difference Platform, and an Inequality Platform. These platforms are cross-departmental and transdisciplinary by design and allow CBS to coordinate research across departments in response to societal challenges.

6.   Managing the Boundaries Between Departments

As mentioned above, one of the roles of a dean is to manage the boundaries between departments. In the words of Charan, Drotter and Noel (2001, p. 57):

> The manager of managers must be a silo buster. He must tear down the boundaries that impede the flow of work and information between different functions and other groups. … This means monitoring the flow of work between the … unit and others in the organization, asking questions, and recommending improvements. It also requires a more subtle form of boundary management: understanding and conveying functional strategies, business strategies and the corporate mission.

Both CBS and SBE are matrix organizations in which departments (row players) deliver services to education, research and life-long learning or postgraduate development activities (columns). At SBE, the column players are the Education Institute, carrying the responsibility of the bachelor and master programs, the graduate schools responsible for research master programs, PhD studies and other research activities, and UMIO, the executive branch that runs MBA programs, executive education and other postgraduate activities.

Navigating the matrix requires coordination both between row and column but also between rows, for example because a course or a program is delivered by multiple departments. Program directors or course coordinators are key to coordination, but they are also typically employed by one department. For these important leadership functions to work to the benefit of the entire faculty, it is important that they take a 'column' perspective, rather than a 'row' perspective, and it is sometimes difficult for heads of department to accept this, because departments take ownership of educational programs although the responsibility for those remain with the Education Institute.

7.   Co-creating the 'Why'

'Why?' This is invariably the first question you get as a dean or as a department head if you want to instill change in the organization. And for good reasons. First of all, why fix something that isn't broken? And many are ready to argue that the status quo ante is rather perfect. Second, even if there is a reason to change, why should we do it in the way suggested? There could be a number of other ways to change the organization that may be at least as good – probably better, if you think about it for a second.

For effective leadership and to instill change there is no way around co-creating the 'why' with the organization. It is hugely important to think in terms of processes that will allow people affected by the change to participate in decision making. They need to understand the need for change themselves and they need to investigate possible ways to achieve it. In a sense, it is easy for a dean to draft a strategy for the school over a weekend in a remote cabin. The problem with that is that he would be lucky if only one other person at the school would see it his way and so it would be a strategy on paper with no impact on the organization.

Strategy processes and other organizational development must be based on ideas and activities that originate in the organization. This does not mean that they cannot be provoked top-down from the dean (or from the department head), for example by explaining that the performance of the school (or the department) could be improved if we would use the resources differently.

In my experience, the group of department heads is central to this co-creation. Without their consent, understood as a certain level of acceptance or a sufficiently broad majority, little can be achieved in terms of positive impact on the organization. Consent is different from consensus where everyone agrees and it is different from compliance that may occur even if people disagree. In a sociocratic setting of dynamic governance (a very Dutch approach, see Endenburg, Lindenhovius and Bowden, 1998), consent means reaching an agreement after following a procedure to check that no unresolved objections remain.

Whether reaching consent in the sense of a certain level of acceptance or the purer sociocratic meaning, attention to processes is key. In my experience, it is wise to involve the group of heads of department at least three times: when identifying the challenge and brainstorming about its solution; when a concrete solution emerges; and when implementation starts. Other good processes involve a sub-group of department heads to work out a suggested solution.

CONCLUSION

My experience across two institutional and cultural contexts – as dean at CBS, a huge stand-alone university, and as dean of SBE, a faculty within the University of Maastricht – shows that many leadership challenges, dilemmas and solutions are the same.

Academics don't mind being led, but it matters greatly that you can explain why you are doing what you are doing. Most academics enjoy working in teams – both research and education are team sports nowadays – but they are also experts in their fields and so need no micromanagement. If they understand 'the why' behind decisions taken in their department or in the school, they are able to act wisely in most situations.

To ensure a good pipeline for the position as head of department, the head (and the dean) should ensure that a couple of employees try different roles as coordinators or managers in the department or in educational programs. However, it is also important to train heads of department in leadership programs, in part to make them understand that their role requires them to have different skills, to change their time application, and to value other peoples' research and educational activities over their own.

Selection of the right heads of department is one of the most important tasks of a dean. In addition, empowering and coaching them are important, and on top of that the dean must allocate resources strategically across departments and manage the boundaries between them. The group of heads of department is also crucial to get the organization to co-create the 'why' – the rationale behind the change needed – and the way forward. Consent to move forward is also important for the head of department that wants to instill change.

Academic leadership is not about herding cats. It has to do with who has got the monkey to some extent. It is about making time for gorillas and it is about dealing with old rogue elephants. That can be very demanding, but also very rewarding, when the performance of the organization – the department, the faculty, the school – improves. To develop academic institutions to have impact on societies – that has been my leadership purpose guiding me from head to dean.

ACKNOWLEDGMENTS

I thank Alan Irwin, Nikolaj Burmeister, and Anne Suhr of Copenhagen Business School as well as Nathalie Dirks, Andries de Grip, Marielle Heijltjes, Clemens Kool, Dominik Mahr, Pien Versteegh and Wilko Letterie from Maastricht University School of Business and Economics for comments that helped improve the chapter. The usual disclaimer applies.

REFERENCES

Bolman, Lee G. and Terrence E. Deal (2003), *Reframing Organizations: Artistry, Choice and Leadership*. San Francisco, CA: John Wiley & Sons.
Charan, Ram, Steve Drotter and Jim Noel (2001), *The Leadership Pipeline: How to Build the Leadership Powered Company*. San Francisco, CA: John Wiley & Sons.
Covey, Stephen R. (1999), "Making time for gorillas," in William Oncken, Jr. and Donald L. Wass, *Management Time: Who's Got the Monkey?*, Harvard Business Review Press, reprint 99609.
Craig, Nick and Scott Snook (2014), "From purpose to impact: figure out your passion and put it to work," *Harvard Business Review* 92(5): 105–11.

Endenburg, Gerard, Jasper Lindenhovius and Clive Bowden (1998), *Sociocracy: The Organization of Decision-Making: "No Objection" as the Principle of Sociocracy*. Delft: Eburon.

Foss, Nicolai J. and H. Peter Møllgaard (2020), "Strategy-making in a loosely coupled organization: the guided evolution of the Copenhagen Business School," DOI:10.18261/issn.1504-3134-2020-01-04.

Huiskes, Annelotte (2019), "From Viking to dean," interview: https://www.maastrichtuniversity.nl/news/viking-dean.

Jung, Carl G. (1921), *Psychologische Typen* [*Psychological Types*]. Zürich: Rascher Verlag.

Likert, Rensis (1967), *The Human Organization: Its Management and Value*. New York: McGraw-Hill.

Møllgaard, Peter (2017), "Pipelines in academia and leadership," https://www.cbs.dk/en/the-press/news/pipelines-in-academia-and-leadership (December 17).

Møllgaard, Peter (2020) "REEAD@SBE – general expectations for different position categories at SBE," *work in progress*, Maastricht University School of Business and Economics.

Oncken, Jr., William and Donald L. Wass (1974), "Management Time: Who's Got the Monkey?", *Harvard Business Review*, 340–62, https://weblogibc-co.com/wp-content/uploads/2018/07/HBRs-Must-Reads-Digital-Boxed-Harvard-Business-Review.pdf.

Index

Aalborg University 316, 319
Aarhus University 314, 316
abductive reasoning 192, 198, 202, 251–2
absorptive capacity 257
Academia 188
academia-industry collaboration *see*
    public-private partnership and Danish
    Hydrocarbon Research and Technology
    Centre (DHRTC)
academic citizenship and dissemination criteria
    220
academic consulting 248
academic departments *see* inclusive onboarding in
    academic departments (South Africa)
Academic Journal Guide (AJG) rankings 185,
    217, 219–20, 223
academic leadership in Danish academic
    institutions 313–23
    academic privileges 314–15
    administrative leadership 316
    characteristics of an academic institution
        313–15
    decentralization 316
    democratic university structure 316
    employee management 322–3
    external boards 320–21
    finance and funding 314, 315, 318–19, 321
    globalization agreement 318
    governance 315, 319
    leadership 1970-2020 319–22
    modernization 316
    regulation 319
    roles of institutions 315–19
    self-governing institutions with top
        management board 317
    socio-political system 317, 319, 321
    structure 315
    student revolution (1968) 314–15, 316
    study boards 316
academic marketing department: personal
    observations and reflections 342–52
    accountability 351
    collective leadership: joint responsibilities
        and participative decision making
        343–4, 346, 350–51
    commitment 347
    course allocation 349
    effectiveness of department 344–5
    focus 347
    knowledge generation and dissemination
        343, 345, 347–8, 351
    metrics or benchmarks 345, 351
    objectivity 344
    quality and performance assessment 344–5
    ratings and rankings 344
    recruitment and retention 349–51
    role of department 343–4
    rotation, regular 346
    stability and predictability 347
    tasks and responsibilities 347–9
    transparency 344
    trust 342
academic project partner 240
Academy of Management 338
accomplishments, recognition of 8–9
accountability 79, 131, 241, 248, 337, 351
accreditation
    business school leadership 308–312
    business school as socio-technical system
        291, 292, 299
    see also triple crown accreditation
action plans 140
action research 252
adaptability 17
administrative duties 25
administrative leadership 316
admissions 293
Aguinis, H. 81, 92, 186
Alghatani, Dr. A. 48
altmetric analysis 39
ambiguity 132, 306
analytical skills 355
Anderson, L. 56
annual review 21, 62, 145, 280
Antonacopoulou, E.P. 257
applicability 249
ARA Model 198
arm's length principle 30–31
Ashforth, B.E. 87
Asia 69

assessment committee 139–40
Association of MBAs (AMBA) accreditation 98,
    99–100, 110, 111, 291, 312
Association to Advance Collegiate Schools of
    Business (AACSB) accreditation 14, 98,
    100, 110, 291, 308, 312
audits 294
Australia 38, 159, 187, 188, 218, 310
    Business Deans Council (ABDC) ranking
    185
    Group of Eight universities 186
authenticity 71, 76
autocracy, leading by 333–4
autonomy and control 16–17, 33, 36, 42–5, 47,
    89, 93, 165, 295

balanced approach 218
Ballantyne, D. 196
Barbarossa, F. 314
Bartunek, J.M. 256
Beech, N. 253
belonging, sense of 10, 128, 135, 174
benchmarking 186, 345, 351, 363–5, 365*f*
Bengtsson, M. 199
best performance: inspiring, recognizing and
    supporting 8–9
bibliometric evaluation 36–7
Bibliometriske Forskningsindikator (BFI) 217
bigger picture, seeing and coordinating 44
Bleiklie, I. 219
Bolman, L.G. 357
Bologna process 211
both/and leadership 44, 47
bottom-up approach 30*t*, 43, 45, 46*t*, 64, 162,
    227, 235, 322, 366
Bouncken, R.B. 253
boundary judgments 111–12
boundary location 293
boundary management between departments
    366–7
Brady, M. 196, 197
Brewer, J.D. 56–9, 62–4
Brodie, R. 195, 197
Brookes, R.W. 195, 197
bureacracy/bureaucratization 25, 91
    see also machine bureaucracy
Burt, G. 256
Bush, V. 30–31
business context 221
business model 42–3
business school: internal tensions perspective
    19–26
    individual and the collective 22–3

managerialism/optimization and
    entrepreneurialism/creativity 20–22
research and teaching 24–5
business school leadership 302–312
    accreditation 308–312
    executive education 304–8
    increasing complexity in business
        school-university relations 309
    management consequences 303–5
    mergers and acquisitions 303, 309
    recent trends 303
business school as socio-technical system
    285–300
    accreditation 291, 292, 299
    CATWOE elements 297–8, 298*t*
    framing 295*f*
    systems design and cultural challenges
        288–94
        boundary location 293
        consensus development 289–90
        information flows 293–4, 296–7
        minimum critical specification 290–92
        variance control 292
business schools *see* business school:
    internal tensions perspective; business
    school leadership; business school as
    socio-technical system; Cardiff Business
    School (CARBS): public good and leading
    with purpose
Business in Society (BiS) platforms 280–81, 353,
    366
Butler, L. 218, 222
'buy and build' strategy 303

Cadez, S. 88
Canada 69, 165, 200, 310
Cannizzo, F. 88, 89
capability 17
Cardiff Business School (CARBS): public good
    and leading with purpose 52–6, 186
    criticisms by function 53*t*
    organizational purpose 54–5
        repurposing organizations 54–5
    purposeful business school development
        55–63
        collaborative change 59–63
        CPO role in leading change 57–9
        engagement 53*t*, 61*t*, 63–4
        governance 53*t*, 59–62, 60*t*
    innovations 60–61*t*
        research 53*t*, 60*t*, 62–3
        scene setting 56–7
        teaching 53*t*, 60*t*, 62

repurposing successful university
    departments 52–3
Research Committee 62
Career Framework for University Teaching 147,
    154, 156*t*
*Carnegie Classification of Institutions of Higher
    Education* 42–3
'Carnegie ladder' 42–3, 45
Carroll, L. 5
CATWOE elements 297–8, 298*t*
centralization 56–7, 108, 240
challenges of managing professionals 3–13
    virtues of academic leadership 5–12
        best performance: inspiring, recognizing
            and supporting 8–9
        communication, continuous and
            two-way 7
        engagement, creating 10
        executing according to plan 11–12
        meaningful decisions 6–7
        real involvement, securing 7–8
        setting the direction 5–6
        true collaboration, promoting 10–11
change of culture *see* external funding and change
    of culture at Copenhagen Business School
    (CBS)
change management 306
    capabilities 47, 306
    and communication 227
    see also under public-private partnership and
        Danish Hydrocarbon Research and
        Technology Centre (DHRTC)
Charan, R. 359, 366
Checkland, P. 103, 110–111, 286, 288–9, 297
Cherns, A. 286, 288–9, 290, 294, 296–7
Chesbrough, H. 246
Chia, R. 256
chief purpose officer (CPO) 52, 55–9, 62–4
China and cash publication bonuses 87, 89–90
choice matrix 190
choice phase 103
Churchill, W. 7, 189
citations 74, 149*t*, 185–7, 191–2, 194, 198–200,
    207–210*t*, 218, 273
class, culture, gender and race 165, 168, 175, 176
classic phase *see under* Head of Department as
    key transformational leader
classic university as professional bureaucracy
    31–3
Clauss, T. 253, 255
clever people *see under* leading academic
    departments
climate change and sustainability 265, 269–70
co-creation of strategy 44

co-leadership without formal authority 227
co-poiesis 253
coaching Heads of Department and other
    leadership development 362–3
coaching skills 306
coercive complexity 102, 103, 105, 112–14
collaboration 267
    promoting 10–11
    see also under public-private partnership
        and Danish Hydrocarbon Research
        and Technology Centre (DHRTC);
        university-business collaborations
collaborative leadership 55, 56, 57, 59, 63, 64
collaborative purposeful change 59–63
collective leadership: joint responsibilities and
    participative decision making 343–4, 346,
    350–51
collectivity 127
commercialization in private sector 39
commitment 166, 290, 347
communication skills 7, 71, 229
community operational research 113
community, sense of 267
competences 17, 235–40, 244, 290
    articulation of 149–50
    development for faculty 47
    lack of 233–5
competing values framework 17, 18*f*
competition 19, 34, 36, 43, 57, 95, 128, 130, 162,
    184, 222, 249, 265, 271, 310, 320, 328
complex input model 160*b*
compliance 227
conceptual models 106, 113–14
conflict in academic departments 117–26, 264–5
    common ground 117
    context 123–4
    departmental conflict 120–21, 124–5
    institutional conflict 121–3, 125
    interpersonal conflict 118–20, 123, 124
    intra-departmental conflict 123
    learning from conflict 123–5
    rules of conduct 117
    timelines 117
connectedness 110
consensus development 289–90
consent 355–6, 358, 367–8
constitutive rules 103, 104*t*, 113
Contemporary Marketing Practices (CMP) Group
    182, 189, 191–202, 208–210*t*
context 68, 123–4, 221, 302
continuity 19
control *see* autonomy and control
Cooke, S. 133
cooperation 10

see also collaboration
coordinated management of meaning (CMM) 229
Copenhagen Business School (CBS) 39, 287, 353–68
    benchmarks and performance indicators in leadership dialogue 363–5, 365*f*
    boundary management between departments 366–7
    choice of right Heads of Department 360–61
    co-creation of the 'why' 367
    coaching Heads of Department and other leadership development 362–3
    consent 367–8
    cross-departmental initiatives 366
    Department of Economics 355–6
    dual loyalty 358
    Executive 363
    external peer review 356
    five-year vision for 2010 356
    informal meetings 363
    key performance indicators (KPIs) 365
    Leadership Pipeline 358–9, 366
    managerial tasks assignment to Heads of Department 361–2
    Practical Academic Leadership (PAL) quarterly workshops 363
    problem-based learning (PBL) 354
    purpose in academic leadership 354–7
    REEAD framework 358–9, 361, 366
    resource allocation across departments 365–6
    skill requirements 359
    strategic personnel plans (SPPs) 366
    strategy workshop 355
    time applications 359
    work values 359
    see also dilemmas of university management at Copenhagen Business School (CBS); external funding and change of culture at Copenhagen Business School (CBS)
corporate governance 54
cost management 311
course allocation 349
COVID-19 pandemic 243, 292, 310, 312
Coviello, N.E. 192, 195–6, 197
creativity 103
critical awareness 101–2
critical incidents *see under* inclusive onboarding
critical systems heuristics 113

critical systems practice (CSP) *see under* systems thinking at University of Hull (HUBS) with triple-crown accreditation
critical systems thinking 98, 100, 101–4, 114
cross-departmental initiatives 366
cross-disciplinary research 275–82
    action-oriented guidelines 280–81
    applied theory 276
    barriers to breaking research 278–80
    domains of knowledge and levels of theory 277*f*
    focal general theoretic approach 276–8, 282
    general theories 276
    interfaces for theorizing 277*f*
    midrange theories 276–8, 282
    monodisciplinary approach 275, 279, 281
    multidisciplinary/interdisciplinary approach 275, 278–9, 281
    service-dominant (S-D) logic 276–7
    theories-in-use 276, 278
    theorizing processes 276–8
crowding out what is difficult to quantify 90–91
cultural factors 47, 235–40, 244, 251, 256, 264, 268, 289, 290, 340
    fragmented culture acceptance 75–6
    see also under business school as socio-technical system
Cunningham, M.T. 19, 191, 198
CV format paralleling teaching and researching achievements 149*t*, 150
cynicism 131

Dahler-Larsen, P. 218, 222
Dallyn, S. 65
Danish Hydrocarbon Research and Technology Centre (DHRTC) *see* public-private partnership and Danish Hydrocarbon Research and Technology Centre (DHRTC)
Day, G. 195
De Boer, H. 211, 223
Deal, T.E. 357
decentralization 240, 316
decoupling 132, 139–40
Delbridge, R. 57–8
DeLong, T.J. 9
DeNisi, A. 84
Denmark
    Aalborg University 316, 319
    Aarhus University 314, 316
    Accreditation Institution 318
    Conference of Rectors 318
    Conference of University Chairs 318

Danish Hydrocarbon Research and
　　Technology Centre *see* public-private
　　partnership and Danish Hydrocarbon
　　Research and Technology Centre
　　(DHRTC)
Directorate of Higher Education 315
Finance Act 243, 318
GDP 213, 215
Groningen University 86
Independent Research Fund (IRFD) 243
Innovation Fund (IFD) 243, 244
Maastricht University 353, 354, 358, 363
Ministry of Education 315, 316, 318
Ministry of Higher Education and Science
　　(now Danish Universities) 317, 318,
　　356–7
National Research Foundation 213, 233, 243
Odense University 314, 316, 319
researcher-patent 1999 35
Roskilde University 316, 319
socio-political system 317, 319, 321
Technical University (DTU) 263, 266, 267,
　　271
Think Tank (DEA) 38, 243, 264, 268
Underground Consortium (DUC) 263, 265,
　　271
Universities Act 355
University Act 1970 313–16, 318
University Act 1993 316
University Act 2003 35, 212, 214–15, 220,
　　315, 317, 318
University Act 2007 318
see also academic leadership in Danish
　　academic institutions; Head of
　　Department as key transformational
　　leader (Denmark); Copenhagen
　　Business School (CBS); University of
　　Copenhagen;
departmental diversity index 143, 145
design-based approach 286–7
Di Benedetto, T. 199
dialectical view of academia 20, 26
Digital Transformations Platform 280, 366
dilemmas of university management at
　　Copenhagen Business School (CBS)
　　211–23
　　Academic Journal Guide (AJG) rankings
　　　217, 219–20, 223
　　board of directors 213
　　complexity of Danish university environment
　　　212–14
　　　economic framework 213
　　　leadership structure 212–13
　　　legal structure 212

massification: from elite institution to
　　mass institution 213–14
　　external board of directors 214
　　funding/external funding 213–16, 219
　　general standards measurement of research
　　　excellence 216–17
　　performance-based measurement
　　　systems 218–19
　　internal management system 214
　　performance indicators 214, 216–17, 221–3
　　ranking journals 217, 218–19
　　REEAD model 217, 220
direction setting 5–6
directness 333
discipline 72
discouragement 10
discursive rationality 112
disengagement 10, 343
dissatisfaction 10
Diversity and Difference Platform 280, 366
diversity and gender inclusion 137–45, 165, 167,
　　175, 177–8
　　advice to a new Head of Department 144–5
　　assessment committee 139–40
　　avoiding issues of diversity and equality
　　　137–8
　　behaviour allowance 138
　　cultural and academic capital 138
　　departmental diversity index 143, 145
　　diversity plan and target numbers 139–50
　　equality 137–8
　　fairness 137–8
　　Head of Department 138–43
　　　structural decoupling 139–40
　　lessons learnt from hindsight 143–4
　　meritocracy 137, 142
　　nationality and ethnicity 143
　　recruitment 139, 141–3
　　sexual harassment 138, 144
　　unconscious bias 139, 140–41, 142, 143
doubt, admissions of 17
Drewry, D. 100
Drotter, S. 359, 366
dual leadership 241
dyadic buyer-seller perspective 276
Dylan, B. 133
dynamic equilibrium of managing and leading
　　academic departments 14–18
　　academic department and its leader 15
　　identity and legitimacy 15–16
　　training and surviving as Head of
　　　Department 16–18

economic considerations 249

economic effects 39
economic impact 273
economic person 22–3
ecosystem engagement 42, 45, 48
Edgar, F. 89, 92–3
Edmans, A. 54
effectiveness of department 344–5
Eisenhower, D. 13
Eley 15
emancipatory practice 112
emergent-state 287
empathy 5, 16, 17, 72
employees and non-usefulness of feedback 84
empowerment 235–40, 244
engagement 8, 17, 138, 149*t*, 241–2, 249, 253,
    267, 292
    business 109
    citizenship 92
    collaborative 39, 255–6
    collective 236
    common 42
    creating 10
    critical 247
    critical systems practice 103
    customer 186–8, 277–8
    deep 169, 171*t*
    ecosystem 42, 45, 48
    extended 64
    external 141, 291
    formal 177, 177*t*
    global and local 337
    Head of Department as key transformational
        leader 39, 42, 45
    informal 169, 171*t*, 177, 177*t*
    leading with purpose 53*t*, 55–6, 58–9, 61*t*,
        64
    meaningful 178
    mutual 248
    patterns of 129
    personal 226
    positive 170, 172*t*
    purposeful 53*t*, 61*t*, 63–4
    research 22
    societal 85, 95
    teachers 150, 151*t*, 152*t*, 156
    unhelpful 173*t*
    work 166
entrepreneurialism/creativity 20–22, 39
environmental sustainability challenges 62, 65,
    215, 265–7, 270, 273
epistemic reflexivity 253
equality 137–8
equity 158
Espeland, W.N. 221, 222

ethics and morals 255, 265
Europe 53, 90, 148, 187, 188, 196, 213, 313
European Federation for Management
    Development (EQUIS) accreditation 98,
    99, 110, 112, 114, 291, 308, 312
European Research Council grants 220
European Union 34, 38, 211, 215
evaluations
    external 266–7
    and non-difference to organizational
        decisions 84–5
    student 86
Evolutionary Psychology Theory 275
excellence 336
excellence phase *see under* Head of Department
        as key transformational leader
exclusion 165, 170, 173*t*, 175
executing according to plan 11–12
executive education 304–8
exemplarity 16
expertise, use of rather than hierarchy 73
explain and persuade 72–3
expression, clarity in 187, 195–6
external advisory pool 240, 241
external boards 320–21
external funding 37, 211, 213–14, 216–17, 220,
    314–15, 322, 356, 358, 364–5
external funding and change of culture at
        Copenhagen Business School (CBS)
        226–44
    barriers to change 228–35
        apathy in push for external funding
            231–2
        individualized performance culture,
            burden of 232
        lottery aspect 233
        reasons for external funding 230–31
        skills and competences, lack of 233–5
    new pathways for change 235–42
        empowerment, competences and change
            of culture (personal level)
            235–40
        networks, stakeholders and partners
            238–40
        organizational framework for support
            240–41
        oversights, skills and competences
            236–8
        positive narrative 236
        Project Model Canvas 238*t*
        strategic and supportive leadership
            practices (management level)
            235

support structures and resources
(organizational level) 235
supportive and strategic leadership
practices 241–2
EY Beacon Institute 55

faculty careers 147–62
symmetry, leading towards, whilst managing
asymmetry 161–2
teaching and career development 148–57
areas of responsibility 150, 153
articulation of teaching competences
149–50
Career Framework for University
Teaching 154, 156*t*
CV format paralleling teaching and
researching achievements 149*t*,
150
entry-level qualifications for different
career levels (University of
Copenhagen) 154, 155*t*
knowledge about teaching and learning
and formal pedagogical training
153–4
knowledge sharing and peer
collaboration 153
Pedagogical Competence Profile 150,
151–2*t*
practice and reflection 153
progressive levels of teaching
achievements 156*t*
types of career progression 154–7
teaching and research asymmetry 147–8
teaching task allocation and workload
distribution 157–61
aim and scope of model 158
algorithmic models for workload
allocation 159–60*b*
complex input model 160*b*
individual negotiation 161*b*
model parameters 158
simple input model 159–60*b*
simple output model 160*b*
special incentives 158
transparency, equity and fairness 158
'failing fast' 264
fairness 137–8, 158
fatalism 131
feedback, uncertain impact of 82
Fehrer, J. 199
Field-Weighted Citation Impact 185–6
finance and funding 9, 22, 70, 119, 303, 306–7,
339, 344, 354
building research groups 182–4

collaboration with practitioners 249, 251,
253–4, 256
Copenhagen Business School (CBS) 215,
218–19, 222
cross-disciplinary research 280–81
Denmark 314–16, 318–19, 321
framing business schools as socio-technical
systems 295–6, 298*t*, 299
Head of Department as key transformational
leader 30, 33, 36, 40, 46–7
individual performance management 81, 86
leading faculty as teachers 149*t*, 157, 162
leading with purpose in a business school
57, 60–61*t*, 63, 65
performance-based 213
public-private partnerships 264–7, 272–3
systems thinking in triple-crown business
school 99, 109, 114
see also external funding
Financial Times Top 50 (FT50) 217, 308, 344
Finland 89
flexibility/autonomy 17
focus 17, 347
Folk Theories of leadership 130
Folk Theory of Meetings 129–30
Ford, D. 197
Fox School (Temple) Innovation and
Entrepreneurship Institute (IEI) 280–81
fragmented culture acceptance 75–6
France 303
free-riding 90
Friedman, M. 54, 65
frustration 36
functional silos 282

Gabarro, J.H. 9
Garton, E. 8
Geare, A. 89, 92–3
Gemünden, H.-G. 199
gender inclusion *see* diversity and gender
inclusion
gendered bias 222
Gioia, D. 257
global standards, perverse effects of 216, 219
globalization agreement 318
globalization funds 36
globalization pool 214
globalization strategy 34
Goedegebuure, L. 223
Goffee, R. 5
Google Scholar 185, 187, 188, 192
governance 226, 228, 234, 271, 337, 340, 367
building research groups 182, 184, 186
Denmark 313, 315, 319, 320, 322

leading with purpose 53*t*, 54, 56, 58, 59–62, 60*t*, 64
Graham, R. 147
Groningen University 86
group legitimacy 131
Gudykunst, W.B. 243
guidance 6, 72, 77, 107, 110, 152*t*, 281, 285, 330, 336, 351
guidelines 74–5, 77–8, 103, 160, 218, 275–6, 280, 282, 304, 310, 328

Håkansson, H. 190–91, 197, 200
hands-on workshops 238
Hansen, H. F. 37
hard systems approaches 102, 113
Head of Department as key transformational leader (Denmark) 29–48
    classic phase 29, 30–33, 30*t*, 41, 44, 45, 46*t*
        arm's length principle 30–31
        classic university as professional bureaucracy 31–3
        primus inter pares 33
        strategic implementation defect 33
    excellence phase 29, 30*t*, 34–7, 38, 39, 43, 44, 46*t*
        new means to a new end 34–5
        objective strategy and hierarchical management 37
        professional bureaucracy and machine bureaucracy 35–7
        science and knowledge society 34
    impact phase 29–30, 30*t*, 37–48, 46*t*, 48
        bottom-up impact initiatives 43, 45
        change management capabilities 47
        changes in role as Head of Department 46*t*
        co-creation of strategy 44
        collective impact ambition 43
        different kinds of impact 39
        different types of impact 39
        ecosystem engagement 42, 48
        faculty must be brought into play 42
        hierarchical top-down management, reduction of 45
        impact creation 39–40
        impact creation, management of 44–5
        impact creation, strategizing 42–4
        impact initiatives, teaching and basic research 43
        impact measurement 39
        impact policies, risks of 40–41
        infrastructure and portfolio management, building 48
        initiatives 43

new competences development for faculty 47
        origins 38
        seeing and coordinating the bigger picture 44
        societal impact, growing demand for 37–40
        strategic coordination 42, 43, 47
        strategic culture, new 45
        substantiating the 'why' 46
        transdisciplinary research 42
        university as professional bureaucracy 2.0 41–2
        working with culture 47
    science policy 29, 30*t*
    university management 29, 30*t*
    university strategy 29, 30*t*
    university's organizational configuration 29, 30*t*
heroic person 22–3
Hibbert, P. 253
hierarchical management 36–7, 45
hierarchies, penetrated 219
Hildebrandt, S. 243
Hong Kong 99
hopelessness 36
Horizon 2020 (shortly Horizon Europe) 38, 215
'Huey, Dewey and Louie effect' 222
human capital 164, 167
human resource frame 357
human resource management (HRM) 79, 106, 166, 336
human resources 12, 59, 99, 106, 109, 114, 182
humility 72
Humphreys, M. 55

idealized design 110
identity 15–16
    personal identity
impact 248–9, 273
        phase *see under* Head of Department as key transformational leader (Denmark)
implementation 38, 103
improvement 101–2
incentive systems 218, 252
inclusive onboarding in academic departments (South Africa) 164–78
    acceptance 165
    acclimatization 166
    actions enabling 177*t*
    background and literature review 165–7
    class, culture, gender and race 165, 168, 175, 176
    diversity 165, 167, 175, 177–8

exclusion 165, 170, 173*t*, 175
findings 169–76
    critical incidents 168–70, 175–6
    critical incidents leading to experiences
        of exclusion 173*t*
    critical incidents leading to positive
        experiences of inclusion 171–2*t*
    reflections beyond critical incidents
        170, 174–5, 176*t*
    induction 166
    lived experiences 165, 167–8, 175
    marginalization 165
    mentoring 165, 166, 176–7, 178
    method 168–9
    organizational socialization 166, 175, 176,
        178
    purpose 168
    support 165
    visibility 165
income growth targets 57
individual and the collective 22–3
individual negotiation 161*b*
individual performance management 79–96
    ambitions and challenges 83–5
        employees and non-usefulness of
            feedback 84
        evaluations and non-difference to
            organizational decisions 84–5
        measurement difficulties 84
        uneven distribution of performance
            83–4
    feedback, uncertain impact of 82
    improved performance management 91–5
        basic performance standards 92–3
        extrinsic motivators 94
        low-performers, addressing with help
            from HR 93
        mentoring 93–4
        middle management, supporting 95
        recruitment and promotion for
            performance and organizational
            citizenship 92
        stimulating environment 93
    limited managerial control over valued
        resources 81
    management mandate, weak 82
    organizational membership, difficulty in
        defining 82–3
    recent trends 85–8
        evaluation quantification 85–6
        productivity, attentiveness to 87
        research pitted against teaching 87–8
        underperformance sanctioning 86–7
    unintended consequences 88–91

    crowding out what is difficult to
        quantify 90–91
    objectivity, illusion of 91
    pressure and stress 88
    research quality, threat to 89–90
individualism 165
individualized performance culture, burden of
    232
Industrial Marketing and Purchasing (IMP) Group
    182, 189–91, 194–202, 207–8*t*
Inequality Platform 280, 366
informal meetings 363
information flows 293–4, 296–7
infrastructure and portfolio management, building
    48
innovations 60–61*t*
input-transformation-output process 294
inside perspective 246
inspiring 8–9, 12
instrumentalization 40
inter-organizational impact 40
interaction model 190, 193
interactional expertise 256
interactive planning 110
intercultural communication 229
interdependence 69
internal stakeholders 47
internal tensions *see* business school: internal
    tensions perspective
internationalization 350
interpersonal ties 135
intra-organizational impact 40
involvement 7–9
Irwin, A. 221–2, 363

Jackson, M.P. 15
Japan 22
Jetley, V. 4
job interviews 148, 150
Johnston, W.J. 199
joint development agreements 251
Jones, G. 5
journal rankings 185, 186
Jung, C.G. 357
Jungian Typology Index (JTI) 357
Juric, B. 186–7
justice 138

Kallio, K.-M. 89
Kallio, T.J. 89
Kesting, T. 253, 255
key performance indicators (KPIs) 56–7, 58, 268,
    273, 286, 365
Kieser, A. 256

Kirkeby, O. F. 243
Kissinger, H. 118
Klijn, E.-H. 243
Kluger, A.N. 84
knowledge
    about teaching and learning and formal
        pedagogical training 153–4
    empirical domain 276
    generation and dissemination 343, 345,
        347–8, 351
    mode-2 of knowledge production 38
    platform to consolidate 187–8, 197
    sharing and peer collaboration 153
    theoretical domain of 276
Kock, S. 199
Koppenjan, J. 243
Kotter, J. 268
Kouzes, J.M. 12

Lane, J. 15
LaPlaca, P. 199
Lawrence, T.E. 134
Le Guin, U.K. 19
leadership team 281
leadership virtues 5, 12, 71
leading academic departments 68–77
    authenticity 76, 77f
    clever people, characteristics of 69–71
        cleverness central to identity 69
        connection to academics outwith their
            organization 70
        feedback avoidance 71
        no desire to be leaders but don't want to
            be led 70
        non-liking for team events 71
        organizationally savvy and asking
            difficult questions 70
        skills not easily replicated and
            knowledge of own worth 69–70
        thanklessness 71
    leading clever people 71–6
        expertise, use of rather than hierarchy
            73
        explain and persuade 72–3
        fragmented culture acceptance 75–6
        give recognition 74–5
        making time for questions, admitting to
            not knowing answers 74
        peer group of like-minded individuals
            rather than just a 'star' 75
        space and resources, giving but avoiding
            burn out 73
        straight-talking 75
        tell them what but not how 74

    skill 76, 77f
leading by example 16
leading with purpose *see* Cardiff Business School
    (CARBS): public good and leading with
    purpose
Learmonth, M. 55
Lees, R.J. 9
legitimacy 15–16, 131
Leiner, L. 256
Lindgreen, A. 196, 199
line management 20–21, 22–3
listening, active 333
Little, V. 195, 196
lived experiences 165, 167–8, 175
Lloyd, H. 100
Lloyd, T. 5
locals/cosmopolitans distinction 46
Loebler, H. 199
Løgstrup, K.E. 242–3
London School of Economics and Political
    Science 39
loyalty 10, 127, 131
    dual 358
Luhmann 244

Maastricht University
    Executive Board 354
    School of Business and Economics (SBE)
        353, 358, 363
    UMIO 367
McCormack, J. 4
McCowan, T. 40
machine bureaucracy 35–7, 41
McKenna, P.J. 7, 9
Maister, D. 4
management 38
    by mothering 9
    by objectives 320
    mandate, weak 82
managerial control over valued resources, limited
    81
managerial practices 278
managerial tasks assignment to Heads of
    Department 361–2
managerialism 20–22, 79, 91
    creeping 57
    new 222
managing academics *see* challenges of managing
    professionals
Manchester Business School 86
marginalization 165
Marinetto, M. 65
Maritime Platform 280

marketing *see* academic marketing department: personal observations and reflections
matrix management 311
Mayer, C. 54, 56
meaningful decisions 6–7
mediocracies 80
Mendeley 188
mentoring 17, 21–2, 93–4, 165–6, 176–8, 241
    skills 306
mergers and acquisitions 303, 309, 318
meritocracy 80, 137, 142
metrics 345, 351
middle management, supporting 95
Miller, P. 7
minimum critical specification 286, 290–91
Mintzberg, H. 31–3, 41
mission 54, 110, 166
mistakes, admission of 333
modernization 316
Montgomery, D. 195
motivation 342, 346, 349
    extrinsic 94
    intrinsic 88
multi-capital indicators 62
multi-professional management structures 241
Munro, H.J. 192, 195–6
Murphy, K.R. 83, 91, 94

National Student Survey 106
Nenonen, S. 251, 253
nepotism 212, 222
networks/networking 238–40, 243, 254
    events 281
    perspective 276
    practice 193
    staircase 239
New Public Management (NPM) 34, 37, 56, 85
New Zealand 192, 200
    University of Auckland Business School 192, 195, 196
Noel, J. 359, 366
non-disclosure agreements 251
non-hierarchical leadership 69
Nordic countries 200, 211, 213–14
    see also Denmark; Finland; Norway
normative dimension 40
norming 325, 326
North America 52, 90, 187, 188
    see also Canada; United States
Norway 218

objective strategy and hierarchical management 37
objectivity 252, 344

illusion of 91
obsessiveness 69
Odense University 314, 316, 319
on-the-job training 363
onboarding *see* inclusive onboarding in academic departments (South Africa)
Oncken, W. Jr. 363
openness 10, 268, 333
operating core 31–2
operational leadership 270–71
operational plans 110
opinion leaders 17
optimization 20–22
organizational ambidexterity 44
organizational commitment 166
organizational configuration 29, 30*t*, 31, 36, 38, 41, 45
organizational effectiveness 17
organizational and environmental complexity 101, 103, 105, 107–110
organizational framework for support 240–41
organizational purpose 54–5
'organizational rain' 9, 73
organizational skills 306
organizational socialization 166, 175, 176, 178
organizational strategies 166
organizational values 166
outside-in perspective 229, 246–7
oversights, skills and competences 236–8
Owen, J. 6

Palmer, R.A. 196–7
Paradeise, C. 219
paradigmatic perspective 276, 278
parallel design 198
Parker, M. 113
Paton, S. 256
Pearce, W.B. 243
Pedagogical Competence Profile 150, 151–2*t*
Pedersen, D.B. 39
peer group of like-minded individuals rather than just a 'star' 75
peer review 196
people complexity 101–2, 103, 105, 110–112
Perelman, G. 89
performance appraisal 89, 94
performance assessment 232, 235, 241, 344–5
performance criteria 290
performance indicators 214, 216–17, 221–3, 363–5, 365*f*
    see also key performance indicators (KPIs)
performance management 90, 91
    see also individual performance management
performance measurement 36, 39, 45

performance metrics 86, 337–8
performance reviews 148, 150, 329
performance and value-based leadership,
    balancing 267–8
performance-related feedback 93
performance-related pay 89, 94
personal identity 174
    socialization 167
personal observations and reflections *see*
    academic marketing department: personal
    observations and reflections
personal relationships 254
personal time, protection of 334
Peters, L. 275–6
placement and promotion 338
platforms 280–81, 366
Plum X Metrics 186
pluralism 101–2, 194
political context 221
political frame 357
political impacts 40
political leadership 56
political work 64
portfolio management 44, 269–70
portfolio of schools 303
Posner, B.Z. 4
Poufelt, F. 91, 243, 244, 363
practice orientation to research 257
pragmatism 278
predictability 347
pressure and stress 88
primus inter pares (first among equals)
    perspective 5, 33
Principal Investigators (PI) 270
Principles for Responsible Management
    Education (PRME) 112
privileges 314–15
problem-based learning (PBL) 354
process complexity 101, 103, 106
Product Development & Management
    Association 280
productivity, attentiveness to 87
Programme Management Office (PMO) 270
project management with industry expertise
    269–70
project partner 240
promoting 330
promotion 290, 338
    for performance and organizational
        citizenship 92
Propper, C. 4
psychological and psychometric tests 357

public good *see* Cardiff Business School
    (CARBS): public good and leading with
    purpose
public impact report 62, 65
public-private partnership and Danish
    Hydrocarbon Research and Technology
    Centre (DHRTC) 263–74
    change management in practice 268–73
        facilitating collaboration: governance
            and business processes 271–2
        facilitating collaboration: role modelling
            272
        internal and external cases for change
            68–9
        leading change at strategic level 269–70
        multiple bottom lines 272–3
        operational leadership 270–71
        setting direction and defining project
            purpose 271
    collaboration improvement 267
    cross-disciplinary and cross-constitutional
        collaboration 264, 266, 268–9, 272–3
    external evaluation 266–7
    leadership 264–6
        academic motivation, public opinion and
            climate change 265–6
        different collaboration styles 264–5
        different decision criteria and bottom
            lines 265
        different languages 264
    leadership challenges 266–7
    new vision, necessity for 267
    performance and value-based leadership,
        balancing 267–8
    re-definition and reorganization 266
    strategic vision adjustment 267
    structure and collaboration model
        improvement 266
    successful cross-sector collaboration
        leadership 273–4
Public Service Motivation (PSM) 265–6
public value business school (PVBS) 58–9, 62–3
publications 21–3, 37, 46, 133, 138, 149, 232,
    265, 291
    achievements 86
    building research groups 182–7, 201
    collaboration with practitioners 248, 251–2
    Copenhagen Business School (CBS) 213,
        217–18, 223
    and financial gearing 273
    individual performance management 85–92,
        94
    marketing departments 345, 349

responsibilities of department chair 332,
335–8
strategy 184
targets 87
Pulkkinen, K. 211
purpose
in academic leadership 354–7
statement 56, 63
see also purposeful business school
development *under* Cardiff Business
School (CARBS): public good and
leading with purpose
push-pull model 31, 38

quality assurance assessment 99, 344–5
quality of teaching 86, 88
Quan, W. 89
questions, making time for and admission to not
knowing answers 74
Quinn, R.E. 17

Rafols (in Hicks) 222
ranking 344
Academic Journal Guide (AJG) 185, 217,
219–20, 223
journals 217–19
Rasmussen, B. 48
Ravn, J. 129
reactivity 221
real involvement, securing 7–8
Reason, J.T. 286, 288
recognition, giving 74–5
recruitment 212, 241, 290, 293–4, 329, 349–51
diversity and gender inclusion 139, 141–3
for performance and organizational
citizenship 92
REEAD framework 217, 220, 358–9, 361, 366
Reed, L. 133
reflection stage 103
regulation 36, 319
relating in all directions 333
relational leadership 68–9, 72
relationship marketing 192
reporting against purpose 63
repurposing *see* business school for public good:
leading with purpose
research *see* cross-disciplinary research
research-based education 185
research coordinator 240
Research Excellence Framework (REF)(UK) 23,
40, 48, 57, 105–6, 213, 231
research groups 182–202, 207–210
abductive reasoning 192, 198, 202
clarity in expression 187, 195–6

conditions for success for research stream
186–9
Contemporary Marketing Practices (CMP)
Group 182, 189, 191–202, 208–210*t*
getting research accepted 188, 199–200
getting research recognized 188, 200–201
Industrial Marketing and Purchasing (IMP)
Group 182, 189–91, 194–202, 207–8*t*
initiating research stream 187, 195
platform to consolidate knowledge 187–8,
197
research problems leading to research
opportunities 187, 194–5
role of theory and theorizing 188, 197–8
strategies for research success 183–6
strategy, leadership and policy 184–5
success assessment 185–6
sustaining leadership and innovation 188,
198–9, 201
teamwork within a network of scholars 187,
196
tenacity and resilience 188–9, 201
research performance 290
research pitted against teaching 87–8
research productivity 88
research, purposeful 53*t*, 60*t*, 62–3
research quality assessment 186
research quality, threat to 89–90
research stream and school of thought distinction
183
research and teaching 24–5
research 'vanilla pudding' 87
resource allocation across departments 365–6
resource-based view of the firm 303
responsibilities 347–9
areas of 150, 153
shared 145
social 112
responsibilities of department chair 325–41
action steps for coming year 339–40
department culture 340
PhD program 339
research 339
teaching 340
behaving 325, 332–4
autocracy, on occasion 333–4
mistakes, admission of 333
openness, directness and active listening
333
personal time, protection of 334
relating in all directions 333
sense of humor 334
complying 325, 330–31
developing 325, 331–2

department development and celebration
332
research 332
state of the department 332
teaching 332
faculty feedback to chair 341*t*
guiding 325, 328–30
performance review 329
promoting 330
recruiting 329
rewarding 329
norming 325, 326
strategic goals for next five years 338–9
doctoral program 338
research-based faculty 338
teaching 339
strategizing 325, 326–8, 336–40
academic excellence 336
accountability 337
action steps 327
background 336
global and local engagement 337
performance metrics 337–8
placement and promotion 338
research 337
scholarship with consequence 336
service 338
strategic objectives 327
teaching 337
values 327, 337
vision 327, 336–7
responsible leadership 113
retention (of staff) 349–51
review and quality control processes 240
rewarding 329
rich picture 111*f*, 112*f*, 113
rigour-relevance debate 221–2, 246, 248, 293
Riskin, G.A. 7, 9
Ritter, T. 199
role clarity 174
role of department 343–4
role as Head of Department, changes in 46*t*
roles of institutions 315–19
romance of leadership 130
Roskilde University 316, 319
rotation (staff) 346
Russell Group universities (UK) 186

sabbaticals 73
San Francisco Declaration on Research
Assessment (DORA) 186
Sander, H. 36
Sauder, M. 221, 222
scaling and fine tuning 267

Scapens, R.W. 86, 91
Scholes, J. 103, 110–111
School of Business and Economics (SBE)
Department of Data Analytics and
Digitalization (DAD) 366
Education Institute 354, 366–7
science and knowledge society 34
Scopus 185–6, 187
self-centredness 11
self-determination 42
self-governing institutions with top management
board 317
self-management 4, 10
self-reflection 306
senior leader as purpose champion 55
sense of humor 334
sense-making 132, 306
service-dominant logic 199
sexual harassment 138, 144
Shadow Management Board (SMB) 59
Siedlok, F. 253
Simon, H.A. 286, 292
simple input model 159–60*b*
simple output model 160*b*
situation-sensing skills 71
situational leadership 354
skills
lack of 233–5
organizational 306
requirements 359
soft 72
standardization 32
Smith, C. 4
Snehota, I. 197, 200
sociability 75
social contract 29, 30*t*, 38
social responsibility 112
socializing research 255
societal impact 29, 37, 39–43, 41*f*, 46, 48, 213,
231, 248–9, 252, 343
socio-political system 317, 319, 321
socio-technical system 101, 110
see also business school as socio-technical
system
soft skills of leadership 72
soft systems approaches 101–2, 106, 110–111,
113, 286, 288–9, 297
solidarity 75
source types of organizations 286, 288
South Africa *see* inclusive onboarding at a South
African business school
space and resources, giving whilst avoiding burn
out 73
special incentives 158

stability and control 17, 19, 33, 347
staff development 290
stakeholders
    external 44, 46, 47
    involvement 229
statement of purpose 54–5, 58–9, 64, 65
statement of research objectives 281
stimulating environment 93
straight-talking 75
strategic coordination 42–3, 45, 47
strategic culture, new 45
strategic implementation defect 33
strategic leadership practices 241–2
strategic personnel plans (SPPs) 366
strategic plans 110
strategic review 63
strategic and supportive leadership practices
    (management level) 235
strategic vision adjustment 267
strategies for research success *see under* research
    groups
strategizing *see under* responsibilities of
    department chair
structural centralization 56–7
structural complexity 101, 103, 106
structural decoupling 139–40
structural frame 357
student evaluations 86
student satisfaction around learning and teaching
    290–91
study boards 316
success 182–8, 191, 194, 199–201
support services 309
supportive leadership practices 8–9, 12, 241–2
sustaining leadership and innovation 188, 198–9,
    201
Sveiby, K.-E. 5
symbolic frame 357
systems design 290
    see also under business school as
        socio-technical system
systems perspective 286
systems thinking at University of Hull (HUBS)
    with triple-crown accreditation 98–114
    AACSB accreditation 98, 100, 110
    AMBA accreditation 98, 99–100, 110, 111
    critical systems practice (CSP) 100,
        101–114, 104*t*
        coercive complexity 102, 103, 105,
            112–14
        conceptual models 106, 113–14
        critical awareness 102
        critical systems heuristics 102, 111, 113
        ecological perspectives 103

        hard systems approaches 102, 113
        organizational and environmental
            complexity 101, 103, 105,
            107–110
        people complexity 101–2, 103, 105,
            110–112
        process complexity 101, 103, 106
        rich picture 111*f*, 112*f*, 113
        socio-technical systems thinking 101,
            110
        soft systems approaches 101–2, 106,
            110–111, 113
        structural complexity 101, 103, 106
        systems dynamics 101, 102
        systems methodologies 113
        systems perspectives 103, 113
        technical complexity 101, 103, 104–6
        Vanguard Method or lean systems 101,
            106, 113
        viable system model (VSM) 101, 102,
            107–110, 108*f*, 109*f*, 113
    critical systems thinking 98, 100, 101–4,
        114
    EQUIS accreditation 98, 99, 110, 112, 114
    overseas MBAs 99
    quality assurance assessment 99
    Research Assessment Exercise (2008) 99
    situation in 1999 98–9
    situation in 2011 99–100
    systems thinking 100, 101–4

tasks 347–9
teaching achievements, progressive levels of 156*t*
teaching and career development *see under*
    faculty careers
teaching, purposeful 53*t*, 60*t*, 62
teaching and research 147–8
teaching task allocation and workload distribution
    see under faculty careers
teaching-based approach 185
team management skills 306
team spirit 127–36
    communication of top management actions
        and decisions 130–31
    criticality of meetings 128–30
    historical narratives 133–4
    personal and emotional engagement 135–6
    staying real 131–3
    wasting time as exercise of freedom 134
teamwork within a network of scholars 187, 196
technical complexity 101, 103, 104–6
Technical University of Denmark (DTU) 263,
    266, 267, 271
technology transfer 35, 38, 39

technostructure 32, 36, 45
tenacity and resilience 188–9, 201
tenure interviews 150
Ter Bogt, H.J. 86, 91
theoretical frameworks 278
theory building 191
theory and theorizing, role of 188, 197–8
theory-practice gap 248
Thoenig, J.C. 219
Thomas, W.I. 68
timelines 117, 273, 359
Tolstoy, L. 117
top-down approach 20–21, 79, 113, 162, 227, 235, 241, 322, 366–7
    Head of Department as key transformational leader 30*t*, 36, 43, 45, 47
Townshend, P. 285
Transaction Cost Economics 275
transactional leader 45
transdisciplinary research 42, 45
transformational leadership 30, 30*t*, 45–6, 46*t*, 48, 89
    see also Head of Department as key transformational leader (Denmark)
transparency 10, 17, 158, 222, 271–2, 344
    conflict 117, 121
    gender inclusion and diversity 143, 145
    individual performance management 79, 86, 91
triple crown accreditation 291
    Association of MBAs (AMBA) 98, 99–100, 110, 111, 291, 312
    Association to Advance Collegiate Schools of Business (AACSB) accreditation 14, 98, 100, 110, 291, 308, 312
    European Federation for Management Development (EQUIS) 98, 99, 110, 112, 114, 291, 308, 312
    see also systems thinking at University of Hull (HUBS) with triple-crown accreditation
trust 16, 17, 230, 236, 251, 267, 268, 342
tuition fees 305
Turnbull, P.W. 191
turnout 212

uncertainty 306
unconscious bias 139, 140–41, 142, 143
underperformance, sanctioning 86–7
unethical research practices 90
UNICON 306–7
United Kingdom 38, 159, 189, 196, 213, 216, 294, 299–300, 303, 304, 308, 310
    impact agenda 291–2

London School of Economics and Political Science 39
Manchester Business School 86
Russell Group universities 186
Universities UK - World-leading impact (2018-23) 38
see also Cardiff Business School (CARBS): public good and leading with purpose; systems thinking at University of Hull (HUBS) with triple-crown accreditation
United States 30, 38, 53, 69, 189, 200, 303, 363
    Department of Education Federal Student Aid 310
    University of Texas at Dallas (UTD) Top 100 Business School Research Rankings 217, 344
unity of opposites 20, 26
Universities Denmark 356–7
Universities UK - World-leading impact (2018-23) 38
University of Auckland Business School 192, 195, 196
university-business collaborations 246–58
    abductive approaches 251–2
    challenges 251–4
        business perspective 251
        university perspective 251–3
    instrumental collaborative exchange 253
    motivations and expectations 247–50
        business perspective 247–8
        university perspective 248–9
    successful engagement 254–8
        collaborative competences 255–7
        conversation with practitioners 254–5
        inter-organizational collaborations 256
        personal learning, constant 257–8
University of Copenhagen 37, 154, 313–14, 316
    entry-level qualifications for different careeer levels 154, 155*t*
    UCPH Forward program 47
University of Hull (HUBS) *see* systems thinking at University of Hull (HUBS) with triple-crown accreditation
university management 29, 30*t*
university as professional bureaucracy 2.0 35–7, 41–2, 44–6
university strategy 29, 30*t*
University of Texas at Dallas (UTD) Top 100 Business School Research Rankings 217, 344
unpredictability and time lag 40

validation and franchising arrangements 310

value from difference 59, 64
values and value systems 54, 57, 166, 273–4,
      278, 327, 337, 359
van den Besselaar, P. 218
Vanguard Method or lean systems 101, 106, 113
variance control 292
viable system model (VSM) 101, 102, 107–110,
      108*f*, 109*f*, 113
virtues of academic leadership *see under*
      challenges of managing professionals
vision 54, 110, 166, 327, 336–7
volume of teaching 86
von Bertalanffy, L. 101
VUCA (volatility, uncertainty, complexity and
      ambiguity) 101–2

Walker, D. 249

Walter, A. 199
Wass, D.L. 363
Web of Science 185
Weick, K.E. 243
welcome packages 238
'wicked problems' 103
Wiener, N. 101
Wilkinson, I.F. 199
Williams, J. 119
Willmott, H. 219
Winklhofer, H. 197
Wolverton, M. 15
workload allocation models 105, 159, 161
workload and career path 307

Yassi, A. 253
Ylijoki, O.H. 91